Macroeconomics

The Dryden Press
Hinsdale, Illinois
A Division of Holt, Rinehart and Winston, Inc.

Macroeconomics

John H. Makin
The University of Wisconsin at Milwaukee

MACROECONOMICS by John H. Makin

Copyright © 1975 by The Dryden Press,
a division of Holt, Rinehart and Winston, Inc.
All rights reserved
75 76 77 78 79 032 10 9 8 7 6 5 4 3 2 1
Printed in the United States of America
Library of Congress Catalog Number: 74-17799
ISBN: 0-03-012696-7

A Leogryph Book

Project director: **Karen H. Judd**
Design: **Caliber**
Line art: **Vantage Art**
Production manager: **Rodelinde Albrecht**

Contents

PART III Classical and Monetarist Macroeconomic Theory

Preface

This text is designed for use in a one-semester macroeconomics course at the college level. It assumes that the student has taken an introductory economics course but does not demand advanced mathmatics or statistics.

Macroeconomics is a field in ferment, both theoretically and in its application to problems of the economy. The economic environment of the 1970s has posed many new challenges—rapid inflation, peacetime wage and price controls, shortages of crucial resources, growth of multinational corporations, and an increasing ecological consciousness that questions traditional belief in the benefits of economic growth. A macroeconomic book for the seventies must respond to these challenges. In addition to covering the fundamentals of domestic unemployment and aggregate demand, therefore, this text, also focuses on the problems of current developments.

It is virtually impossible today to pick up a newspaper without finding a headline about economic problems. But the news media tend to concentrate on the political context and generally fail to relate a breaking story to larger principles of macro theory. This text makes that connection: the commentaries which accompany each chapter are designed to look at current economic developments in the context of the theory in the chapter, so that students can learn to apply the tools to the world around them. Subjects for commentary include such issues as tax credits, tax cuts, food prices, escalator clauses—viewing them not as political problems but as *economic* ones. These examples are especially current because the text has benefited from the publishing organization at Dryden, which has cut the lag between writing and the appearance of the book significantly.

Just as the economic environment has changed, so too has the academic environment. Required courses are disappearing, enrollments are declining, and students are more practically oriented. This means that competition among courses for students is greater than ever before. A good text cannot guarantee the success of a course, but a bad one can drive away students and make life difficult for those who do take the course. A superior text is especially important in a macroeconomics course. Macroeconomics can be extremely useful to students in such fields as history, political science, business—as well as to any educated person who wants to understand the forces that shape his or her world. As a professional economist specializing in international monetary problems but also teaching in the intimately related field of macroeconomics, I have often been struck by the difficulties that economists face in communicating the concepts of their discipline to interested nonspecialists. My impression has been that the "economic intuition" of most nonspecialists leads them to conclusions about economic questions that are roughly the reverse of the implications of economic reasoning. Dealing with these preconceptions and bridging the communications gap takes a special kind of book.

The first responsibility of any text is to convey concepts and facts clearly and without ambiguity. Students are often put off by economics textbooks because authors skip crucial steps in the reasoning or becloud explanations with unnecessary jargon. In this text, the manuscript has benefited from the attention of people whose business is clear communication, and their expertise has helped avoid the pitfalls that have made economics the "dismal science" for generations of students.

An aspect of readability for any text in this field is the handling of mathematical exposition of macro theory. Relying too heavily on the temptingly "neat" language of mathematics abstracts theory too far from reality; omitting the mathematical analysis altogether robs the student of the full grasp of the field. This text attempts to steer a course between these two obstacles. The initial explanation is presented verbally, often in terms of real-world examples without detailed mathematical reasoning. The neat mathematical exposition is provided in appendices to several chapters.

Because macroeconomic theory is developed over a number of chapters, students must be sure they have mastered one step or set of steps before proceeding to the next chapter. Using the end-of-chapter questions, the student can immediately review any concepts that present problems.

The four-part organization of chapters reflects the fact that macroeconomics is based on two strains of thought: classical monetary theory and Keynesian theory. In this text. Keynesian and monetarist theory are fully integrated in order to explore the problem of the coexistence of both employment and inflation in modern economics. After exploring the historical development of these two strains in Part I, the text offers an extensive explanation of each. The emphasis in Part II is therefore on aggregate demand and employment, considering the problems of changing price levels and the role of supply factors within the framework of the Keynesian model. The analysis of prices is extended in Part III, focusing on the monetarist model in order to explain fully the phenomena of inflation and changes in the rate of inflation. Policy implications are fully explored in each part, both on special chapters on fiscal and monetary policy and in the commentaries that accompany each chapter.

Part IV takes up the crucial long-term policy issues: the problem of the trade-off between the two evils of inflation and unemployment, the effects of international trade and exchange on domestic events, the alternative theories of policy approaches. It also includes a chapter on growth theory and policy in the seventies, and concludes with a look at a controversial American policy tool—wage and price controls. Each of these chapters combines a look at the historical background necessary to understanding the issues with an analysis of the theoretical implications that lend enduring significance to the facts. The balance thus achieved between alternative schools of economic theory and between theory and policy makes this a text for the seventies.

Acknowledgements

Any book represents the fruits of a relatively brief period of intense effort directed at bringing together material that has been acquired over a longer period of time. Over the long haul my primary debt is to my students, whose response to my presentation of earlier versions of this material has helped to refine and enlarge it over time. In the shorter run, I owe thanks, especially for the stimulating interchange in Chapter 20, to Timothy Dickinson, contributing editor at Harper's Magazine, and Marcella Arnow, writer and former business consultant. Considerable assistance concerning the level and treatment of material were provided by Ms. Arnow, Karen Reixach, and Barbara Quint, who also helped research the nontheoretical material. On the theoretical content, several people contributed helpful comments and suggestions, including Professor James Clarke of Villanova, Professor Alan Deardorff of the University of Michigan, Professor Jan Michal of SUNY at Binghamton, and Professor Don Nichols of the University of Wisconsin at Madison. Finally, special thanks go to my project editor, Karen Judd, who on many occasions had to convince me that what I had written was indeed not completely obvious.

Foundations of Modern Macroeconomic Theory

PART I

THE NATION'S trade balance showed a $171.3-million deficit in March, the first in nine months. Exports totaled $7.67-billion, and imports $7.84-billion . . . . Japan has agreed to lend the Soviet Union $1-billion to finance development of coal, gas and forestry resources in Siberia . . . . General Motors is negotiating a $100-million trade agreement with the Russians to supply earth-moving equipment in exchange for timber.

THE COMPOSITE INDEX of ʟ   Eᴄ
tors rose 1.7 per cent in Marᴄ
1967 base period . . . . The Bureᴀ
ported that productivity [output   worker-hour] in the
private sector fell 5.5 per cent in this year's first quarter

ian interests, has agreed to purchase up to 30 per cent of Signal Companies, which owns Mack Trucks, Inc., aᵒ Garret Companies . . . . Du Pont's French subsiᵈᵎ Société des Usines Chemiqᵘ to build a plant ʸ ʳ Mulhouᵗ of ᵃ componenᵗ

ᴺɢ.₁   Moᵗᵒₛ, quarterly net 41c vsᵃ Exᵃ   ₛₒ.15 vs. $2.27 . . . . Mobil Oil, $2.5ᵈ . . . . Texaco, $2.17 vs. 97c . . . . Amerada-Hess $1.33 vs. 99c . . . . Colgate Palmolive, 27c vs. 24c . . . Continental Oil, $2.19 vs. 94c . . . . Getty Oil, $3.93 vs $1.75 . . . . National Steel, $1.24 vs. $1.05 . . . . Philip Morris, $1.36 vs. $1.18 . . . . Rapid American, $3.14 vs. $2.3ᵈ . . . . Procter & Gamble, $1.17 vs. $1.06 . . . . Americaᵗ

Food Prices and Rate of Inflation Dip Just Slightly

A decrease in food costs in April has caused a temporary slowing of the nation's rate of inflation, as measured by the Consumer Price Index, and given a few signs for longer-range optimism.

The Labor Department reported last week that food prices declined by four-tenths of 1 per cent last month—the biggest monthly decrease in seven years—and that, largely as a consequence, the over-all rise in consumer prices was six-tenths of 1 per cent. That is only about half the increase in each of the preceding three months. In the New York Metropolitan region, the general price rise was even less—one-tenth of 1 per cent. There were other positive signs: gasoline prices, which have already risen 33 per cent, appeared to be leveling off, and there was a drop in commodity prices.

Herbert Stein, chairman of President ɴixon's Council of Economic Advisers, said the slowdown in the rate of inflation pointed to "a more durable change for the better," a reading consistent with Administration predictions earlier this year. But there was ɴo certainty that was the case. The drop in food prices stemmed mainly from short-term factors, primarily heavy sales of cattle and hogs prompted by recent high feed costs.

The over-all trend is still clearly upward and only the severity of the inflation is in doubt. Last week edᵗᵎ unlikely we'll get ᴇneral Electric ᵃˡʸ ₛⁱˢᵗⁱᶜᵃᵗᵉᵈ time soon. But there is ᵃᵐᵉʳⁱᶜᵃⁱ ᵗˢ. price spiral has beᵉ   ₒₗₛ ....

Other food priceᵗ   ₙₒₒₒ Soviet citizens, sumer feel too cₒᵗ   ₗy selected specialists and more rapidly and tₐ   tion indexes. Furthermore, ᵎutives from the mᵒ run down so low—and the outsiᵈ ₛ ᵗₒₑₛ world is so bleak—that exᵎmᵖᵗˢ   ᶠₒ   ₗₒₛₑₛ on year's harᵛ   ᵗᵉⁿᵗ   ₘₑₙₜ ₐₑ

Positive Growth Predicted For U.S. Economy by Ash

Budget Office Director Predicts 5% Drop in G.N.P. in First Part of Year

The United States economy took a dive during the first three months of the year, but should bounce back somewhat in the current quarter, according to Roy L. Ash, director of the Office of Management and Budget.

Although official Government figures will not be published until ₙ   ᵂᵉₑₖ. Mr. Ash said yesterₗ   ₜₕₑ Gross Naᵗⁱₒₙₐₗ   ₗᵤₑₑ than 5 peᵣ   ₜₕₑ rate during the ₗₐᵗ   the year. Inflation, he ₛᵤ₉ gested, was running at 10 per cent or more—up from an 8.8 per cent rate at the end of last year, as measured by the G.N.P. deflator.

Economists generally expected the economy to slide during the first quarter after growing at a slow 1.6 per cent rate in the end of 1973. But the size of the drop in real growth—deflated for price increases — is more than most analysts had anticipated.

Mr. Ash, who spoke at a luncheon of the board of directors of Reuters Ltd., said ₒₙ ₜₕᵤᵣₛₐₐᵧ ₜₕₐₜ ₜₕₑ

in first quarter growth indicates that most of the energy-induced slowdown is over and that the economy now will move into positive growth. Unemployment, which has hovered for three months just over 5 per cent will probably move some what higher Mr. Ash said—but he ruled out a return to anything like the 6.7 per cding or tax increases. Unrate of the early 1960s.

For the Administration, ₜₕₑ ing elections this fall, theₜₐ emphasizes that the f ᵏ rather hopeᵈ costly in terms of econo ᵣy low liⁱg industry. Financial marᵏ strain and could be hit sᵗ ᵗheir highest levPresident's ᵗᵉᵣs of declining output.

The possibility of skirting recession, however, generaᵗ little applause among priva institutions— inclundⁱ economists who learned yesteᵣ ₒᵤbles of Consolidated Ediₐ day of Mr. Ash's prediction ₐ Bank illustrated — could George Perry, of the Brookin ₛᵗ squeeze intensifies. There be getting to 6 per cent uneuation is extremely dangerₒ ployment by midyear. If yⁱⁿ could turn what had bₐ get there with a horrible fiⁱₙquarter and a flat scoₒump—into a bust. rather than two negative quₐₘᵃrd to hit the economy, or ters, does it make it betₜₛome support, affects fiscal Not in my book."

Chairman Burns wants ᵗᴴ a more restrictive program ₐxes to take some ₜ ₕₑ ₗₑₑ   ₘₑₐₛᵤᵣₑₛ ᵇᵣₑ ᵗᴴₑ   ₐₐₑₙₑᵧ assistance ᴴₑw Treasurys delegation was underₐgainst the other leading conᵗ to have received instruc-ₗg supremacy in the Administraⁱto go ahead with the pro-of the Office of Management andⁱ from Secretary of State holding out against cutting ᵗⁱnger, in Algeria. ₃₀₅ billion. Presumably the neⁱᵗᴴᵉ special ᵗ recession coordinator, Kenneth Rⁱ   ᵗₑₛₜ of Ash, or vice ᵛ   ₐₒumedine of plican Adminisᵗ   ⁱₛ unified ₜₕₑ name of the developⁱonal Democrats who want a taxₚⁱng countries. It was asith inflation still roaring and theᵉᵈ here that Mr. Kissinger ₅ per cent, the case for a tax cutₛₛᵉᵈ the American proposal or may not look as foolish sixg his talk yesterday with the black art of economic foreⁱᵈent Boumedine. tain as it is, it would certainlyᵈ by Algeria, the developⁱn from cutting taxes now, and tocountries have submitted e in unemployment proves to be ⁱown proposals to the As-ily over. If this present storm—ʸ, one being for emer-ₒrsens, the Administration andⁱ measures to help the

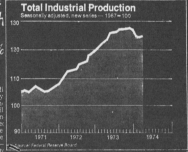

Total Industrial Production
Seasonally adjusted, new series—1967=100

130

120

110

100

90

1971   1972   1973   1974

Source: Federal Reserve Board

BURNS WARNS U.S. ON HIGH INFLATION

Present Tight-Money Policy ᵗo Be Maintained—Public Jobs Favored as Offset

Special to The New York Times

WASHINGTON, May 26—Dr. Arthur F. Burns, chairman of the Federal Reserve Board, said today that "the future of our country is in jeopardy" if the recent rate of inflation is not moderated.

cries most affected by economic problems—problems that have asserted have been d more by the high costs pay for general imports the industrialized coun-

Business Index Rises

450
440
430
420
410
400
390
380
370
360
350
340

Trend line
7 weeks moving
average

J F M A M J J A S O N D J F M A M J J A S O N D

ribbon-Cutting Ceremony management, drought in Afriᶜretary Dent went directly shortages of fertilizer and the ribbon-cutting cere-(changing diets, rising popularᵗ at the exhibit to the ards for much of the worldlin for his one-hour meet-countries such as the Sovietith Mr. Brezhnev in which supplies with purchases abroᵃssador Walter J. Stoessel fall). and other officials took part.

It is to the great plains ᵃ joint statement issued later up from Texas and into Sₐ   ₐ the 62-year-old Soviet looks for these supplies. Tⁱsized that the development region provides 60 per cent economic and commercial and most of the animal feed between our two countries

This dependence bolsterⁿ the basis of full equality politically as well as econⁿd mutual benefit without dis-been quick to capitalize orⁱrimination of any sort is an and world demand have ⁱₘportant element in the further $18-billion a year. It wasⁱⁿ improvement of Soviet-Ameri-transformed the Americaⁱ relations." from deficit to surplus. Bments about "full equality and for imported oil. ⁱmutual benefit without discrim-

A bountiful Americaⁱ inationⁱⁱ to emphasize Moscow's starvation in areas of keen interest in seeing Wash-Southeast Asia. Not onlⁱington end its system of high India for the last severaltariffs on imports from the Southeast Asia has fluctuⁱoviet Union.

A common problem is Despite Mr. Brezhnev's re-ₑₘₚₕₐₛⁱₛ ₒₙ ₜₕⁱₛ ₚₒⁱₙₜ

Preliminary Concepts

1

Most people who are over 40 today can remember the Great Depression of the 1930s. During the worst of that period, one-quarter of the labor force was unemployed. College graduates found no jobs waiting for them. Many people left the country in despair, and for the first time in U.S. history emigration actually exceeded immigration. The social disorder and economic hardship of that time have been documented by movies, novels, and social history. When economists and politicians determined to find the causes of this disaster and its long-run consequences, however, macroeconomic theory began to come into its own. As economic conditions have changed, that theory has been continually modified. The fact that few theoretical rules have proved invulnerable to real-world contradiction has not lessened the need for models which can provide the basis for effective control of the economy by enabling accurate analysis and prediction of its workings.

Macroeconomics and Microeconomics

Macroeconomics takes as its subject the measurement of economic aggregates and the search for systematic explanations of changes in these aggregates. National income and output, levels of employment, changes in the general price level, the capacity of the economy—these are some of the major concerns of macro theory. Micro theory, on the other hand, focuses on such areas as the composition of output, the distribution of income, and the allocation of resources. Microeconomics analyzes the behavior of the individual consumer, firm, or industry, using price theory as its tool, whereas macroeconomics studies the vast aggregates at play in the economy, using national income analysis and theory about the behavior of four markets—goods, money, labor, and bonds.

We know intuitively that what is true at the individual level may not be true at the aggregate level. One well-known example is the paradox of thrift. If one person puts away more than usual for a rainy day, he or she is considered prudent and thrifty. But if everybody saves more and spends less, then the level of aggregate demand falls, output falls, income drops, and the result may be that people end up with smaller total savings because of their lower income! The paradox of thrift does not really demonstrate the inconsistency of microeconomics with macroeconomics; it merely shows that aggregate behavior has its own rules.

In fact, the two branches take each other very much for granted. Microeconomics takes the total output and the general price level as given and measures the way in which resources shift between industries in response to changes in the price of individual goods or resources. Macroeconomics, on the other hand, takes total output and general price level as key variables and ignores the differential effects of economic conditions on a given industry. Macroeconomics is not simply a highly generalized form of microeconomic general-equilibrium analysis because its aims are quite different. General-equilibrium analysis on a micro level watches the shift of output and resources among industries or sectors; macroeconomic analysis watches the shift of total output, employment, and income levels.

Macroeconomic aggregates are not simply statistical constructs, although they are measured empirically. Purely statistical aggregates show the stable relationships of the past; they cannot explain why certain variables behave as they do or completely predict the effects of outside phenomena such as war or drought. Even economic phenomena, such as a strike or a change in tax rates, may send statisticians back to the drawing boards if the aggregate prediction of the impact of such events is based solely on past behavior. In order to formulate effective policy—for stabilization, growth, or a variety of specific goals—policymakers must know something about cause and effect and about how theoretical relationships hold up in practice.

Microeconomic theory contributes to this understanding. Let us take only two examples. First, the behavior of the components in any aggregate must be similar for the aggregate to be of any use. If one group of consumers in a sample responds to an increase in income by spending 90 percent of the increase while the majority responds by spending 70 percent, then an aggregate consumption function (which indicates the relationship between consumer spending and income) will not measure the "typical" response of either group's expenditure to a change in income. Second, if the income distribution also changes as income increases by putting a greater part of the increase in the pockets of the 90-percent "spenders," then the macroeconomic relationship between consumption and income might reflect the atypical responses of the spenders at higher levels of income. In this case, it is likely that differences in behavior would require disaggregation into two consumption functions. In more advanced macro theory the necessary amount of disaggregation is hotly debated, but at this level we shall employ a high level of aggregation, including in our model, for example, only one consumption function.

Once meaningful aggregates are developed and their relationships determined, the way is paved for prediction and control. Macroeconomic analysis is intimately involved in government policy determinations, if for no other reason than that the government is an important component of the total economy. Government spending, taxes, and the money supply are macroeconomic aggregates whose magnitude may be changed not only by the level of economic activity but also by direct policy decisions. Suppose, for example, there is widespread unemployment. Macroeconomic analysis can indicate the causes—the first step in correcting the problem. It can also predict the consequences of policy alternatives to stimulate greater output, employment, and income.

But suppose macroeconomic analysis indicates that unemployment could be cured by increasing government expenditures; the next question is what these expenditures should go for. Should we build more hospitals or more highways, for example? This is a question of values and priorities, and macro theory avoids it. Indeed, it also avoids the broader issue of whether the growth of the public sector implied by the choice of increased government spending will give society the balance of public and private goods it wants. When confronting questions of the allocation of resources and the distribution of output, policymakers must turn to micro theory to examine the costs and benefits of highways or hospitals, missiles or margarine. Microeconomics is concerned with the optimum use of society's resources; macroeconomics is concerned with the full use of resources, the growth of the economy, and its stability. More specifically, macroeconomic goals include full employment, capacity output, growth, price stability, and external balance.

Macroeconomic Goals

Macroeconomic goals must be capable of measurement. In order to direct policy toward reducing unemployment, for example, policymakers have to know how to measure unemployment—how to determine how much unem-

Commentary: What Price Meat?

In 1974 the United States economy was running a macroeconomic fever; the Consumer Price Index in the first quarter was rising at an annual rate of over 14 percent, and fiscal and monetary authorities both pledged tough anti-inflationary action.

In June of 1974, however, economic czar Kenneth Rush called a White House conference to discuss how to combat depressed livestock prices. Microeconomic conditions in this sector were creating hardships for cattle, hog, and chicken farmers and feeders. The index of prices received by farmers for meat animals had dropped 8 percent during the month ending May 15 and stood at 159 percent of the 1967 average. The index of prices paid by farmers for feed declined only 3 percent for that same period and stood at 173 percent of the 1967 average. From January to June the price of cattle dropped from over $50 per hundred pounds to $38 per hundred pounds. Because of this, cattlemen estimated losses at $100 to $200 a head, and industry losses were estimated at well over $1 billion.

The problem stemmed from disequilibrium between supply and demand that could be rectified in the short run only by falling prices. The previous year soaring meat prices had prompted an expansion of meat supplies. By January 1, 1974, a record 127.5 million cattle were in the pipeline, along with 61 million hogs. Farmers were holding large herds off the market in hopes of even higher prices. In February the bottom dropped out of the livestock market, and the rush was on to get the rest of the herds to market before prices fell even more. Panic selling drove prices sharply downward, and by May, 1.029 billion pounds of meat were in storage, an increase of 46 percent from the year before.

Meanwhile, consumption of meat remained stable. In Iowa—an important meat-producing state—nearly half the residents were substituting other sources of protein for meat in their own diets. Demand was further cut by Canada's refusal to accept beef containing DES, a fattening hormone that has been linked with cancer, and by Japan's protectionary ban on beef imports to bolster its own cattle industry. To complicate matters, the drop in wholesale meat prices was not showing up in the supermarket (a point hotly contested by food retailers). A survey by the Cattlemen's Association showed that retail prices of five cuts of beef averaged about the same as a month earlier, although the cattlemen were getting $5 less per hundred pounds. An Agriculture Department study indicated that in the year since April 1973, the spread between farm and retail prices had widened by 16 percent.[1] Not all of this was necessarily profit, since the costs of labor, transportation, and packaging had gone up, but the effect was to keep retail prices from falling and stimulating increased consumer demand.

The farmers felt their plight could be cured by higher prices. Secretary of Agriculture Earl Butz agreed: "Beef prices are simply going to have to go up if we're to maintain a viable cattle industry."[2] The federal government pressured retailers to offer weekend specials and other promotional campaigns to spur consumers to buy more meat. More significantly, the Agriculture Department planned to buy $100 million of beef for the federal school lunch program, and the Defense Department discussed increasing its meat purchases. Moreover, farmers pressed the government to restore meat import quotas abolished in 1973 to reduce meat prices at that time. Not only

1. William Robbins, "Cattlemen to Get Supermarket Aid," New York Times, June 18, 1974, pp. 1, 51.
2. Wall Street Journal, June 18, 1974, p. 8.

would this curtail the supplies of meat, thereby pushing up prices, but it would also ensure that domestic meat producers would sell more of their output. The government was reluctant to do so because foreign governments might retaliate with import quotas of their own that would create barriers for American agricultural and other exports. Some pressure was put on Australia for voluntary cutbacks on meat export to the United States, and Congress debated imposing official import quotas. Farmers also demanded their own version of the Lockheed loan, a credit plan that would guarantee government-backed or low-interest loans to them. Although the administration refused this aid, the chairman of the Federal Reserve Board, Arthur Burns, did urge banks not to cut off credit to hard-hit livestock producers in favor of the higher rates of return from investments in the money market. Congress was more receptive to the emergency loan program and began hearings in June 1974.

Here we see an apparent policy dilemma: the rescue of meat producers inevitably would raise prices, adding to inflation at a time when the government is trying to control it. Government spending was used to raise demands in this sector, selective monetary policy was also invoked, and the entire set of measures was designed to get those higher prices that Secretary Butz saw as crucial to maintaining the U.S. cattle industry. The two policies, while contradictory, are not mutually unattainable. Microeconomic policy is concerned primarily with the allocation of resources within the economy, and it can promote higher prices in one sector without a general increase in the consumer price level if macroeconomic policy is keeping a tight rein on the economy. Resources can be directed to one area, providing there are cutbacks in other areas. The result is the redistribution of income from the public to meat producers, in two ways. First, tax money from the public is given to meat producers for their surplus output; second, con-

sumers pay higher prices, with meat producers reaping the benefit. While anti-inflation macroeconomic policies can still be pursued, this boost to meat producers serves to jeopardize them, both by example and by definition.

Moreover, the farmer rescue program occurred at the same time that the Senate was hearing about the failure of the U.S. antihunger campaign because rising food prices had more than eaten up the increases in food stamp and welfare allotments. According to the report to the Senate Select Committee on Nutrition and Human Needs: "For those poor people who were participating in the food stamp program . . . their food expenses increased 22.6 percent more rapidly than did the size of their food stamp allotments."[3] In this case, two microeconomic policies are at odds; resources can not be directed to both the producers and the hungry at a time of overall restraint. While an anti-inflationary policy can be pursued at the same time as meat prices are encouraged to rise, feeding the hungry cannot.

3. "War on Hunger Lags, Report Shows," *Rochester Times-Union*, June 19, 1974, p. 2A.

ployment is voluntary, whether it is caused simply by too few jobs or by lack of information about existing jobs, and so on. Even operational goals achieve meaning only in terms of their mutual attainability and effectiveness.

Full Employment

The goal of full employment is mandated by law in the United States: the Employment Act of 1946 committed policymakers to promoting "maximum" employment. Certainly, unemployment and poverty go hand in hand, and studies have shown that prolonged unemployment results in individual symptoms that range from increased hostility to loss of sexual drive. But to the economist unemployment means a loss of output and income, fewer goods and services and less income with which to purchase them. This loss is both a present and a future one, since skills may deteriorate and career opportunities may be blocked by unemployment, reducing the output a worker can produce and limiting the income he or she will receive when back on the job.

Employment and unemployment are measured by the Bureau of Labor Statistics at the Department of Labor. Every month a scientifically selected group of about 47,000 households are surveyed to discover not how many work-hours are contributed to the economy but how many people are employed and unemployed. The distinction is an important one; it is the amount of labor (work-hours) supplied to the economy that determines the level of output rather than the number of people employed,[1] though the level of income may be more closely related to job figures. The Bureau counts as employed not only full-time workers, but those who are not at work because of vacation, sickness, a strike, and so forth; anyone who has worked at any time during the week for a public or private employer; anyone self-employed; and unpaid workers in a family firm who have worked 15 hours or more.

The unemployment rate is the ratio of people unemployed to people in the labor force (both employed and unemployed). To be counted as unemployed the individual must be a member of the civilian labor force, which means over 16 years of age (statistics for 14- and 15-year-olds are kept separately) and neither in an institution nor in the armed forces. Further, he or she must be out of a job and available for work during the survey week and must have been actively seeking work during the previous 4 weeks, except for temporary illness. Also included are those who are not working because they are (a) waiting to be called back to a job from which they have been laid off, or (b) waiting to report to a new job within 30 days.[2] Excluded from the labor force are students, housewives, and others not actively seeking work. The category of those not actively seeking work is a broad one, however, and

1. The Bureau of Labor Statistics does count number of work-hours weekly rather than the number of people who have jobs—but only for manufacturing.

2. Department of Labor, Bureau of Labor Statistics, *Employment and Earnings* 20 (May 1974), p. 1.

includes those who have become discouraged after repeated failure and have simply given up.

Moreover, the Bureau of Labor Statistics does not keep records of under-employment. Underemployed workers include part-time workers who wish to work full-time and/or workers whose current employment does not utilize their full skills—e.g., victims of racial or sexual discrimination. For example, in December 1970, the overall unemployment rate was 6.2 percent. The underemployment rate (unemployment plus those working part-time who wish to work full-time) was 7.8 percent—more than 25 percent higher. Some economists have estimated that the inclusion of victims of discrimination and discouraged workers, those who have simply stopped looking, could double the rate of unemployment.[3]

The national unemployment rate as it is presently calculated also obscures sectors of the population whose rate is much lower or higher. The rate for married men always runs below that of the nation, as does the rate for managers and administrators. On the other hand, the rate for women from 1963–1973 averaged about 1.5 times that of men. The rate for teenage males was over 4 times that of men over 20. For blacks the rate was twice that of whites.[4] Moreover, because the size of the labor force in relation to the total civilian population of employable age varies with economic conditions, the participation rate (which expresses that relationship) is higher when economic conditions are good. When unemployment is high, many people simply drop out of the labor force. They constitute "hidden" unemployment; in 1972, 765,000 people fell into this category, according to the Bureau of Labor Statistics.[5]

The census measure, whatever its imprecisions, provides the means by which to assess the economy's performance in relation to the full-employment goal. Full employment does not mean zero unemployment. As will be seen in Table 12.1, from 1953 to 1973 the unemployment rate ranged between 2.9 percent (in 1953) and 7.6 percent (in August 1958). By the measures of most policymakers, 3.3 percent is within the range of full-employment, but 6.8 is not. A rate of 4 percent is considered "full employment," and certain economists feel the figure should be higher under the economic conditions of the 1970s. Part of the residual unemployment is caused by people switching jobs. Somewhere around half of the unemployed are out of work five weeks or less, and many of these are simply in the process of getting a new job. Other reasons for residual unemployment are discussed in detail in Chapter 10.

Attaining full employment seems like an uncontroversial goal. Yet Treasury Secretary William Simon, in remarks before an international monetary

3. See, for example, Robert Lekatchman, *Inflation: The Permanent Problem of Boom and Bust* (New York: Vintage, 1973), p. 73.

4. *Social Indicators, 1973* (Washington, D.C.: Government Printing Office, 1974), Charts 4.2, 4.3, p. 113.

5. Ibid., Table 4.10, p. 140.

conference in 1974, said that in that year the United States might have to accept a higher rate of unemployment than the 5.2 percent then prevailing. "Our labor markets must not be too tight," he asserted.[6] Simon's position recognized the macroeconomic dilemma that full employment and low rates of inflation have been very difficult to achieve simultaneously, although the problem is generally transitional. Lower rates of unemployment seem almost always to be accompanied by some increase in inflation, whereas lower rates of inflation are accompanied by transitionally increased unemployment. With the rate of inflation hitting 10 percent in 1973–1974, Simon was apparently willing to deemphasize the goal of full employment in the interest of a transition to a lower rate of inflation.

Full-Employment Output

Another measure of economic performance is capacity, or full-employment output, the level of output the economy would produce if all but 4 percent of the work force were employed. The concept of potential Gross National Product (GNP) was devised by President Kennedy's Council of Economic Advisers (and abandoned by the Nixon administration in 1970), based on capacity utilization of about 92 percent. At lower capacity, businesses are less likely to buy new capital equipment; profits are lower, so they are also likely to cut back on research and development and not introduce new products.

Potential GNP increases with time. As the population grows, so does the labor force, creating a larger pool of potential "producers." As labor becomes more skilled and firms introduce more efficient management techniques and better equipment (or more capital per worker), the amount of output a worker can produce also rises. Together, these factors—larger labor supply, more and better capital equipment, and increased productivity—account for rising potential GNP. In a slump, actual GNP (or output) falls faster than employment. According to economist Arthur M. Okun, former chairman of the Council of Economic Advisers, "In the postwar period, on the average, each extra percentage point in the unemployment rate above 4 percent has been associated with about a 3 percent decrement in real GNP."[7] This greater reaction of output to increases in unemployment may be attributed to lower participation rates, reduction in hours worked, and more "on-the-job" underemployment as productivity falls.

The gap between actual GNP and potential GNP, shown in Figure 1.1, is the measure of lost output from less than full employment. During the late 1950s and early 1960s this gap never closed and grew as large as $50 billion. By 1966–1967 the highly stimulated economy was operating beyond full employment and actual GNP exceeded the potential; then in 1970 the gap returned and has persisted since that time.

6. "Less Buying, More Jobless," *Rochester Times-Union*, June 5, 1974, p. 10A.
7. Arthur M. Okun, *The Political Economy of Prosperity* (Washington, D.C.: The Brookings Institution, 1970), p. 135.

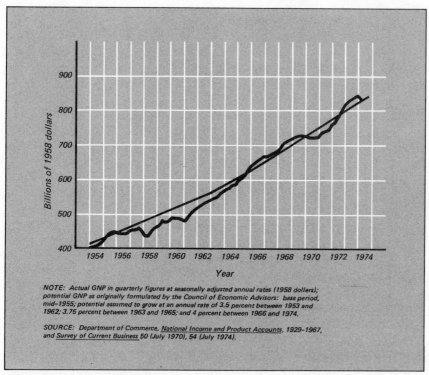

Figure 1.1 Actual and potential Gross National Product (billions of dollars)

Maximum Potential Growth

A third generally accepted goal of modern economies is maximum potential growth. With continuous full employment, the nation's capital stock will be likely to grow more rapidly; workers will not lose skills or drop out of the labor force entirely. To keep growth at this full-employment level, capacity must expand by about 4 percent a year, accompanied by sufficient expansion of demand to absorb the added output. The benefits of economic growth include not only the ability to gainfully employ more and more people but also the ability to furnish more and more income—income that can permit people to buy more of whatever goods they desire while the society devotes more to social welfare programs or to defense. Otherwise, people would have to give up some of one to get more of the other, an economic concept known as "opportunity cost." While growth makes more goods available to a society, it does not free its members from the need to make intelligent expenditure decisions which in turn will determine the composition of a rising level of output.

With a growing population, total income must increase just to maintain the same standard of living; any advances require economic growth to outstrip population growth. For an underdeveloped country, the difference between the two may be a matter of life and death to some of its citizens, since an improved standard of living may mean not starving. Today, however, growth is no longer so enthusiastically embraced as it was in the early 1960s when domestic and international poverty were being "discovered." Along with the expanding U.S. economy have come more pollution, faster depletion of nonrenewable resources, and technological unemployment, which some economists and politicians consider inherent in the nature of modern industrial expansion. Other economists contend that these problems are not inevitable, maintaining that it is only the manner in which our expanding capacity to produce has been utilized which has depleted such scarce resources as clean air and water. Economists and others are beginning to explore the economic and social consequences of a different use of the collective resources that are generally lumped together under the heading of "the environment" with an eye to what may have to be given up to obtain a more desirable environment.

Price Stability

Along with rapid growth, the importance of price stability as an economic goal has been recently reexamined. Conventional wisdom dictates that society must accept rising prices in return for lower unemployment. In the 1970s, however, unemployment has been over 4 percent most of the time and inflation has increased to over 10 percent. Most people consider inflation an economic evil because it hurts those on fixed incomes or those whose incomes do not rise automatically with the cost of living. The degree of price stability is measured by indices of consumer prices and wholesale prices. The wholesale price index dates back to 1890 and covers the prices of over 2,500 commodities at the time the manufacturer (or importer) sells the commodity or when a price is set for it on an exchange or centralized market; wholesale prices anticipate the rise in consumer prices. A more familiar measure is the consumer price index (CPI), designed to measure the changes in prices of goods and services bought by middle-income people who live in towns and cities (wage-earners and clerical, or about 55 percent of the total population). By 1977 this will be changed to include the wealthy, the poor, and the farm population, much to the dismay of those labor unions who feel this change will make it a less reliable guide for their cost-of-living escalator clauses.

The rising CPI has been the justification for many raises from social security to alimony payments. A 1 percent rise in the CPI currently results in about a $1 billion increase in such payments, which of course results in further inflationary pressure. Often criticized by economists and business people, the CPI to some extent overestimates increases in the cost of living. Changes in the market basket and the quality of goods are not fully accounted for because updating is so infrequent (about once every 10 years). If a good costs more because it is safer or more durable, consumers may actually be getting more for their money than before, and the price index should fall, not rise, for that commodity. Such problems with the CPI make some economists wary of relying too heavily on what is an internally biased index. We will look more closely at the performance of consumer and whole-sale prices in Chapter 12, when we examine the operation of fiscal and monetary policy.

External Balance

Price instability affects not only the domestic economy, but the nation's position in the international economic system. Higher prices make goods less competitive with those of other countries, so exports will fall and imports rise, creating a balance of payments problem. Combined with a large flow of capital abroad for investment in foreign business ventures and a large flow of transfer payments in the form of military and foreign aid, the balance of payments situation may reach a crisis point, as happened in the United States in 1971, when the administration devalued the dollar and instituted a program of wage and price controls to stabilize both the foreign and domestic sectors.

Although the foreign trade sector (the flows of goods and capital to and from foreign countries) is a very small percentage of the total economy (in 1973 exports were 7.9 percent of total GNP in current dollars), stability in this sector is closely tied to domestic stability. Even if external factors do not contribute directly to the domestic problem, they may interfere with their solution; in times of recession with a balance of payments deficit, for example, domestic needs demand expansion but international needs demand deflation and restraint. In addition, the United States must consider the implications of imbalance in its own foreign sector for smaller, more open economies. External balance is thus often considered a fifth economic goal. In the future the role of foreign countries in the economic stability of the United States may be even more direct; by cutting off energy supplies to the United States, the Arab oil embargo of 1973–1974 aggravated both unemployment and inflation. The nature of the foreign trade sector, its inter-action with the rest of the economy, and the ways in which a society can achieve balance of payments equilibrium will be explored in detail in Chapter 18.

Model Building

Success in achieving economic goals depends initially on the accuracy of the analysis. Once policymakers comprehend the broad implications of economic analysis, they must sell the ideas to the public and put them into practice. Macroeconomic models provide a device by which the aggregate behavior of the economy is analyzed in terms of the impact of economic policy measures upon variables such as employment, interest rates, income, prices, and balance of payments. A model is not a complete representation of reality; it is an abstraction of only those elements essential to predicting the behavior of those economic variables the model builders want to study. In a way, building a model is like creating a whole separate world which has an internal coherence all its own. If the builders err in its structure, it will produce answers logical within its own sphere but quite contradictory to what happens in the real world. Consequently, constant reference to reality must be made in order to test the model.

A macro model typically describes the aggregate behavior of consumers, investors, and holders of money. Models may be distinguished by their attention to or suppression of detail—the simplest model consists of but a single equation. More detailed models yield progressively more detailed information; the price of this information is the increased complexity of the model and the attendant difficulty of understanding and/or of testing it empirically. The "art" of model building is thus to get the maximum amount of information out of the simplest possible model.

Variables and Parameters

A few general principles of model building are necessary in order to understand existing models and construct new ones. First, one must decide how many economic **variables** will be determined by the model. All quantities subject to change in magnitude are called variables, and there must be as many equations as there are variables. Income, unemployment rates, interest rates, and prices are but a few of the variables of greatest interest to macroeconomists.

Second, it is important to distinguish between two types of variables: **endogenous** and **exogenous.** The prefix *endo-* comes from the Greek "within" or "at home," so endogenous variables are ones determined by the model. For example, the owner of a restaurant knows his income depends upon the seating capacity of the restaurant—income is an endogenous variable. But if a fire closes one room of the restaurant or the theatre next door closes or people develop a taste for fast-food places, his income may drop due to exogenous variables. The causes of changes in them are outside the model, but the effects on the model are quite marked. In macroeconomics the most important exogenous variables are fiscal and monetary policies, whose changes are usually determined outside a typical macro model, but whose effects can be anticipated from the model.

Relationships between variables are described by the term **function:** income is a function of seating capacity in the previous example. Income in this case is a **dependent** variable, whereas seating capacity is an **independent** variable. To say that something is a function of something else does not specify anything more than a relationship. Income could rise or fall with seating capacity; it would be a function of seating capacity in either case. **Parameters** define the manner in which the variables are related. For example, one parameter might be that an increase in seating capacity will bring an increase in income: that is, income is an increasing function of seating capacity. (In microeconomics the quantity supplied is an increasing function of price; in macroeconomics consumption is an increasing function of national income.) This relationship may be expressed as the **slope** of a line relating income and seating capacity; it measures the changes in the two variables. If the function is increasing, the slope

$$\left(\frac{\text{change in income}}{\text{change in seating}}\right)$$

is positive; if the function is decreasing, the slope is negative.

But as the restaurant expands, income may go up faster than the number of seats does. When we want to specify the degree of responsiveness of a change in one variable to a change in another, we will use a type of parameter called **elasticity.** The slope of one variable might be in thousands of dollars, the other in number of seats—which is rather like comparing apples and oranges. Elasticity enables us to put the apples and oranges in the same units by measuring the percentage change of each. The responsiveness of income to a change in the number of seats expressed in terms of elasticity would be

$$\frac{\text{percentage change in income}}{\text{percentage change in seats}} > 1$$

This means that a given percentage change in seats will call forth an even greater percentage change in income, so income is **elastic.** If the value were less than one, income would be **inelastic.**

The responsiveness of one variable to changes in another is an important feature of macroeconomic models. Major arguments in macroeconomic theory involve such issues as the responsiveness of the demand for money to changes in the interest rate, the responsiveness of consumption to changes in income and prices, and the responsiveness of investment expenditure to changes in the interest rate.

Stocks and Flows

A further distinction when studying economic models must be made between a **stock variable** and a **flow variable.** A stock variable is one which has no time dimension; it is simply a measurement of an amount at one point in time. The amount of money in a bank account is a stock variable; so is the net worth of a corporation, a piece of land, or a machine. In contrast, a flow variable makes sense only with reference to a unit of time. Five hundred dollars makes no sense as a salary unless we know that it is $500 per month, per week, or per year. And a finance company may charge an interest rate of 5 percent on a loan, but few people would be foolish enough to borrow without first ascertaining whether that 5 percent was a monthly, yearly, or semi-annual rate.

Look, for example, at a popular restaurant on a Friday night. Between the hours of 5 P.M. and midnight, the dining area is filled to capacity, and there is a waiting line of about 10 people. The number of patrons in the building, a stock measurement, is maintained at 250 all evening. Although the manager is delighted that every seat is filled all night, his satisfaction is not due solely to his assessment of this stock variable—for indeed, he would be quite upset if the same 250 people had settled into their seats at 5 o'clock and had not budged for seven hours. The manager is instead concerned with the turnover, a flow variable, which allows him to seat new customers at a rate of 150 per hour. This measurement does not mean that every hour exactly 150 seats are vacated to be filled by exactly 150 more diners; it is an average for the whole evening.

A stock variable changes only through a change in flows. The restaurant's population was maintained at 250 throughout the evening because of two flow variables: the rate of entry of the customer and the rate of departure. Had either one of these variables changed, it would have affected the average for the entire evening. A sudden slowdown in new customers, for example, would have meant empty tables (a decrease in stock) if patrons continued to leave at the same rate. And if service was so poor that customers took three hours to dine instead of just under two, the restaurant would remain filled to capacity, but the evening's customer total, another stock measure, derived from summing flows over time, would suffer.

The distinction between stocks and flows is important for even the simplest income determination model, which we will develop in Chapter 4. While saving (depositing $50 a month) is a flow, savings (the total balance as of the latest deposit, say $500) is a stock. Similarly, investment is a flow ($10,000 in January) while the cumulative total of investments is a stock ($50,000 as of January 30). A further distinction is necessary for those variables which do not fit either category. For example, price certainly needs to include no time period in order to be a meaningful measurement, but price can hardly be called a stock. It is actually a ratio describing the rate of exchange between a unit of money such as a dollar and unit of output, described as some good or collection of goods.

Equilibrium

In the example used previously, the restaurant could be said to have maintained a state of equilibrium during the evening hours when the crowd remained constant at 250. The term **equilibrium** holds the same meaning in economics as it does in any other science. It is a state of balance between opposing forces or actions—in this case, the equal influx and departure of guests. Likewise, **disequilibrium** in economics is the same as in any other science, a lack of balance. Equilibrium is not static and does not imply a lack of activity. Instead it is characterized by constant but repetitive processes. A measurement of the variables, however, will be the same at any one time as it is at any other.

Variables do not always automatically adjust to find a balance, but generally adjust over time. When the variables change too rapidly or erratically, equilibrium may not be achieved. In theory, however, the economy is continually moving toward a state of equilibrium, and even though this position may never be reached, the concept of equilibrium does help simplify the relationships between the variables. Long-term equilibrium requires that both flow variables and stock variables be constant. To use the example of the restaurant, the two flows of people entering and leaving were exactly the same, so that the stock of patrons seated also remained unchanged. Because stock and flows were both constant, the crowd maintained a state of equilibrium.

Another example of stock equilibrium is the macroeconomic notion of circular flow, in which household income and business production are in equal exchange, and any leakage of money into household saving is matched by a flow back into the system through business investment. This reflects the "stationary state" of classical economic theory, which assumed that saving would automatically equal investment, so that the economy would remain in equilibrium indefinitely. Such stock equilibrium never quite prevails in the whole economy because too many things change to permit a long-term balance. Flow equilibrium is more likely; flows remain constant but are not equal (except in the case of long-term equilibrium, where flow equilibrium is a necessary condition for stock equilibrium). Thus, flow equilibrium is short-term, because the constant inequality of flows will cause either stock build-up or shrinkage which will eventually force a change in flows. For example, if customers had been arriving at the restaurant at a constant rate of 153 per hour but had left at the rate of 150 per hour, the arrival and departure flows would be in equilibrium because they were maintained at a stable rate. But this flow equilibrium could not maintain itself indefinitely, for the waiting line would be growing at a rate of three people per hour and soon would begin to discourage new customers. The stock build-up would therefore eventually necessitate an adjustment in either the rate of people arriving or the rate of departures from the restaurant.

Statics and Dynamics

We have seen that the time dimension distinguishes flow variables from stock variables; similarly, the action of variables over time is what distinguishes **dynamic analysis** from **static analysis.** Static analysis examines the interaction of variables at one given period; a model depicting the equilibrium of supply and demand is an example of this type of analysis. It is a simple methodology which is most applicable to the study of the equilibrium positions where stock and flow variables are stable and there is no need to take into account the factor of time. Time can be introduced to some extent by comparing equilibrium positions, such as might be done if there were a shift in the supply curve. The model would not show how the adjustments were made to the new supply conditions, but they would inform us about the end result. This is known as **comparative statics analysis.** Most of the analysis in the book will be concerned with statics and comparative statics.

Since instability is so common in economic affairs, however, statics is not sufficient for advanced treatments of macroeconomics. Suppose that there is a lag between the time the supply contracts and the time the price begins to rise, requiring a parameter to describe how long the response takes. Dynamic analysis is necessary in order to incorporate time lags. Disequilibrium, movement, and change in economic models involve the interaction of variables not only in the present but in relation to past and future conditions. This form of inquiry is able to address itself to more complex questions about the process of change in the economy: How does the market shift? How long do changes in the market conditions take? What are the properties and causes of disequilibrium?

Qualitative and Quantitative Analysis

The first model we will construct, the income determination model, will largely ignore the dynamics of macro theory. The model will be primarily concerned with the direction of changes, not with their magnitude. Such analysis is qualitative rather than quantitative because it is concerned only with presenting the direction rather than the precise amount of changes in the endogenous variables of a model in response to changes in exogenous variables. Thus our model will not produce quantitative results that resemble the behavior of the real world.

This difference may be observed in the graphs as well as the text. Any relationship between two variables that is drawn as a straight line indicates that the relationship between changes in the variable on the vertical and horizontal axes remains constant at all levels. Look at Figure 1.2. Along line D_1 the relationship between a change in the price and a change in quantity demanded—a relationship described by the slope—is the same at P_2Q_2 and P_3Q_3, as can be seen from the equal triangles ABC measuring $\Delta Q/\Delta P$ at each of these points. If the demand schedule is drawn as a curve, such as curve D_2, the slope is altered by a movement along the demand schedule. Note that along curve D_2, the change in price measured by AB is identical at P_2Q_2 and P_3Q_3, while the induced change in quantity is higher, BJ greater than BF, at P_3Q_3. In short, the slope is not constant along a true curve such as D_1. In contrast to D_1, the responsiveness of quantity to price changes falls with the price level along curve D_3.

However, the fundamental feature of a demand curve, that a fall in price induces an increase in quantity demanded, is preserved by all demand schedules, curved or straight. They are qualitatively all the same. The distinction among them is quantitative, expressing *how much* of a change in quantity demanded will be induced by a change in price. (When lines are used, therefore, they will be expressing only qualitative features of the variables.)

Our concern, then, will be largely with qualitative, or what are sometimes

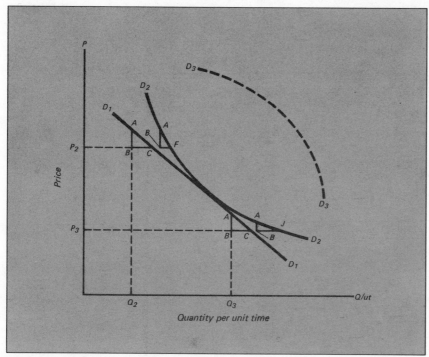

Figure 1.2 Qualitative and quantitative graphing

referred to as "first-order" effects. Quantitative questions regarding "how much," or "second-order" effects, will receive attention only where increased precision has an important bearing on the outcome of the analysis. This emphasis should give students a sense of the important structural and functional features of the national economy and some experience in seeing how the different views of these relationships affect policy prescriptions for the achievement of national economic goals.

Concluding Note

Macroeconomics measures and defines the relationships between economic aggregates. It takes the composition of output, the distribution of income, and the allocation of resources—the subjects of microeconomics—as given and explores variations in such aggregates as total output, income, interest rates, overall price, and employment levels. The knowledge of the performance of each variable enables formulation of policy to effect growth, stability, and the full use of resources. Microeconomics is used to investigate the optimum (or most efficient) use of the given level of resources.

Success in achieving macroeconomic goals depends ultimately upon the accuracy of analysis. Thus models are constructed to abstract the fundamental workings of the economy. But the usefulness of any model depends upon the precision of the observable data on which it is based. Thus we will start with a review of the national income accounts which provide most of the data for our first income determination model. First, however, it will be useful to quickly review the historical development of macroeconomic analysis.

Questions and Exercises

1. How can microeconomic analysis and macroeconomic analysis be used together? Show how varying family consumption patterns (varying marginal propensity to consume) respond to given increases in income level to yield varying increases in aggregate demand.

2. In what ways are macroeconomic goals quantitative? Are microeconomic variables always capable of measurement?

3. Is potential GNP a satisfactory measure of maximum potential economic growth? Explain in terms of static and dynamic analysis.

4. Are the macroeconomic goals of price stability, full employment, and rapid growth fully compatible?

5. Why should economic models be only approximations of reality? Do detailed models produce more accurate forecasts than those with fewer variables?

6. How would you go about building a simple income-determination model? Which endogenous and exogenous variables would you include? How would you derive your parameters?

7. Why is elasticity important in economic models? What relations would be relatively elastic in an income determination model?

8. How would you distinguish between a stock and a flow? Which of the basic macroeconomic variables are stocks and which are flows?

9. Why is full-employment GNP a dynamic rather than a static equilibrium? How do long-term and short-term equilibrium differ?

10. How can we introduce the time element into economic analysis? How is this useful?

HARROD, R. F. The Life of John Maynard Keynes. Augustu Kelley, 1969 (orig. pub. by Harcourt, Brace, 1951). (Reprints of Economic Classics) 68-30524. 17.50.

Still an indispensable source for the student of the career of greatest economist of modern times. Its value is not seriously di ished by the fact that — as an official biography — it is discreet or s on points in the subject's private life which have subsequently rece publicity. Later studies dealing with Keynes have tended to give thorough attention to the impact and significance of his econ thinking than is found in this volume. Harrod's treatment of debates among British economists during Keynes' most intellect productive years is enriched by the fact that he was himself an a participant in these exchanges.

Adam Smith on Pins

One man draws out the wire, another straightens it a third cuts it, a fourth points it, a fifth grinds it at the top for receiving the head; to make the head requires two or three distinct operations; to put their respective daily limits it on, is a peculiar business, to whiten the pins is another, it is even a trade by itself to put them into the paper; and the important business of mak ing a pin is, in this manner, divided into about eighteen distinct operations, which, in some manu- factories, are all performed by distinct though in others the sa **Money and Wealth:** perform two or three of them. **A Review Article** manufactory of this kind wher employed, and where some of them consequently performed two or three distinct operations But though they were very poor, and therefore but indifferently accommodated with the necessary machinery, they could, when they exerted them-

DROP IN GOLD HITS PRICE OF METALS

Silver, Platinum and Copper Slump—Grain Futures Up —Soybeans Show Drop

By H. J. MAIDENBERG

A sharp drop of 5 per cent n London gold bullion prices triggered heavy selling of in- ternational commodities yes- terday on both sides of the Atlantic.

Silver bullion, coins and platinum closed down here by along with copper and wo sugar, Cocoa dropped 2.6 cents a pound or the near de iveries and about 2 cents o he deferred month

Meantime, the go grain which factors staged at the in the closed with gains in all but the soybean pit. Wheat finished 6 to 9 cents bushel higher Corn was up to 3.25 cents, and oats up 2.5 to 4.25 cents Soy beans were off 4 cents in old-crop deliveries and changed in the forward p

CARLILE, William Warrand. The Evolution of Modern Money. Augustus M. Kelley, 1969 (orig. pub. by Macmillan, 1901). (Reprints of Economic Classics) 69-17029. 12.50.

This addition to the series still rates as required reading in money history for any serious student of that area of study. Though it several of the more significant respects been superseded by later on the subject, Carlile's book still contains valuable historica ments and interesting anecdotal material not available at all el for the student in evolution, quite speculations and *The Collected Writings of John Maynard Keynes* analysts al important cause the book is quite and historia raym once again owe a debt of gratitude to the pu reprinting this increasingly hard-to-find economic classic.

300 Monetary and Fiscal Theory and Institutions

310 MONETARY AND FINANCIAL THEORY AND INSTITUTIONS

Varieties of monetary experience. Edited by DAVID MEISELMAN. Economics Research Studies. London and Chicago: University of Chicago Press, 1970. Pp. 391. $13.75.

This collection of six papers could have been titled *Studies in the quantity theory of money* *revisited* except that the mission of popular- zation of what is now known as *monetarism* was successfully undertaken in the earlier vol- ume. These essays are rather workmanlike pa- pers (by 1970) established Chicago monetarist style. For the uninitiated, this empirical work (self-consciously called at Chicago) in which one seeks to est for param- ters of single macroecon the quan wever dea given a central role.

Aside from a tendency to follow the outline—which consists of problem, model, n- stitutional orientation, and empirical tests, followed by a data appendix—these studies have remarkably similar theoretical disposi- tions. Most importantly, the intellectual input— in terms of the actual models employed in the empirical tests—is based on a half dozen standard monetarist sources. John V. Deaver's study of Chile and Colin D. Campbell's study of Korea and Brazil use Friedman's and, espe- cially, Cagan's models from the earlier Chicago Collection Adolfo Cesar Diz study of Argen- tina uses Cagan of the *Studies* and, for a sup-

roduction and Produc industries, with the contrib and an introduction by the relationship, Cagan's form *minants and effects.* Georg study of Canada, leans on Ri per i nd on lat tzer, Che er two papers, Mich Japan and Morris Perlman's tfolio differences among 47 fit so neatly into the pattern, monetarist by the definition eran's model is not a simple o "open," while Perlman's is alm hoc, some interesting theoretical standing.

The studies are somewhat d with the earliest of them, that by pleted in 1961, and the latest sich, in 1967. Thus, expectations estimated by a simple exponent the models are usually single eq other equations are present, they as single equations, with the pa as if they are from the structure. production of this volume is u the contributors whose efforts, o anything in print at the time t finished, must now be judged p to specialists on the various coun

Deaver's paper is a direct ex gan's hyperinflation model. Caga the demand for real balances as the expected rate of inflation. model worked as well as it did l applied to cases of hyperinflatio case, the rate of inflation was income constra nent, improved odel substantially

The Diz project, of a later sents a direct improvement ove that it has both a supply and money. The behavior of the reser to dominate the movements i multiplier, in turn, these chang the result of bank responses to changes. The behavior of the po required reserves—not only doe ute significantly but may have s tered to offset *precious* changes serve ratio. Diz work on the money successfully adds anothe

King: On Political and Economic Power

Dr. Martin Luther King, Jr. in a recent major interview, stated his opinion that the tasks facing the civil rights movement today are to attack impressed with the argument. His Negro com munity are real political and economic power? He said

What we are faced with now I to mobilize our people into a so forged a genuine coalition to power up political economic

ommending to SCLC that we begin to train more field organizers so that we can really get out and organize these people and thereby move into the area of political action I think the Negro can his economic resources much more if resources are pooled and I intend to do much in this area as we can make economic

 o civil rights about the white backlash to say there is more because of w Lost an election they so California voted to repe house apted

Money Supply and Inflation

(Percent Change From Corresponding Quarter of Preceeding Year)

		U.S.	W. Germany	Japan	Switzer-land	Belgium	France	U.K.	Italy
MONEY	1973 I	8.2	12.7	26.6	—	14.4	—	10.3	18.6
SUPPLY	II	8.0	8.5	26.3	2.7	14.0	—	12.4	22.0
GROWTH	III	7.3	1.2	22.3	4.2	11.9*	7.5	7.7	18.0*
RATES	IV*	6.1†	0.0†	17.0	4.0	11.1	8.4	0.1	19.0
	1974 II*	6.0	3.5	15.0	4.0	11.0	13.5	10.0	16.0
	II*	5.9	6.5	15.0	5.0	12.0	8.6	8.0	15.0
	III*	6.2	8.5	16.0	5.5	13.0	12.1	6.0	14.5
	IV*	7.0	10.3	17.0	5.5	14.0	11.5	7.0	14.0
	1975 I*	7.1	10.8	17.0	5.0	13.5	11.6	7.0	14.0
	II*	7.1	9.5		5.0	13.5	12.1		
GROWTH IN	1973 I	4.1	6.6	7.1	—	6.3			
CONSUMER	II	5.5	7.4	10.5	8.2	7.2			
PRICES	III	6.9	6.9	12.8	8.3	6.7*			
	IV*	8.4†	7.3†	17.8	11.9	6.9			
	1974 I*	9.0	8.0	19.0	12.0	8.5			
	II*	8.6	8.8	18.0	11.0	9.0			
	III*	7.9	8.8	16.0	9.0	9.5			
	IV*	6.9	9.0	11.5	7.5	10.5			
	1975 I*	6.2	8.8	9.0	6.5	11.5			
	II*	5.8	8.5	—		6.5	12.0		
GROWTH IN	1973 I	8.6	5.3	9.3	—	8.1			
WHOLESALE	II	13	6.3	11.4	10.2	10.4			
PRICES	III	16	7.2	17.3	11.3	12.4*			

Was Keynes a "Keynesian"? *A Review Article*

Foundations of Macroeconomics

2

Macroeconomic theory today might be compared to an old city such as London, Jerusalem, or Boston; first built on a small scale, added to, partly torn down, rebuilt upon old foundations, it appears at any one time as an unfinished but functioning whole—despite half-finished structures, holes in the ground, and obsolete transportation systems.

The foundations of modern economic theory were extensively developed by Adam Smith (1723–1790) and added to by a succession of economists to make the "classical city," most fully described in the famous textbook of Alfred Marshall (1842–1924), *Principles of Economics*, published in 1890.[1] Parts of the city had never been built up, and much of it was destroyed by world events, particularly the Depression (1929–1934). The architect of the rebuilding was Marshall's most illustrious pupil, John Maynard Keynes (1883–1946); much, however, was rebuilt by others, notably the American Alvin Hansen,

---

1. Alfred Marshall, *Principles of Economics* (1890: 9th ed. annotated by C. W. Guillebard, London: Macmillan, 1961).

not always to Keynes' original specifications. In recent years, neoclassicists have discovered that some of the classical city is perfectly usable once certain repairs have been made.

Macroeconomic theory is derived from two strands of thought: classical monetary theory and the macroeconomics of John Maynard Keynes. The core of classical macroeconomics as monetary theory is really a theory of determination of the price level. The macroeconomics of Keynes focuses on the problem of maintaining full employment of the labor force. Extensions of both theories deal with the other two major macroeconomic problems—balance of payments equilibrium and growth.

Classical Monetary Theory

Based primarily on the teachings of British economists of the eighteenth, nineteenth, and early twentieth centuries,[2] classical monetary theory was concerned primarily with the relationship of the money supply to the price level. It sought to determine the effect of increases or decreases in the supply of money in an economy (brought about by actions of the monetary authority or balance of payments disequilibrium) upon prices. Both full employment and adequate purchasing power were thought by classical theorists to be assured by Say's Law, a concept central to classical economics.

Say's "law of markets" held that supply (or output) creates its own demand; the money spent to purchase productive resources would end up in the hands of consumers, who would spend in purchasing goods and services exactly the amount that it cost to produce them. Say's Law also held that each individual act of saving *necessarily* causes the resources not consumed to be used for the purpose of increasing investment, by an amount equal to the amount saved. This doctrine was explained by Alfred Marshall:

> The whole of a man's income is expended in the purchase of services and of commodities. It is indeed commonly said that a man spends some portion of his income and saves another. But it is a familiar economic axiom that a man pur-

2. In the words of John Maynard Keynes, "The 'classical economists' was a name invented by Marx to cover Ricardo and James Mill and their predecessors, that is to say for the founders of the theory which culminated in the Ricardian economics. I have become accustomed, perhaps perpetrating a solecism, to include in 'the classical school' the *followers* of Ricardo, those, that is to say, who adopted and perfected the theory of the Ricardian economics, including (for example) J. S. Mill, Marshall, Edgeworth and Prof. Pigou." (*The General Theory of Employment, Interest and Money* [London: Macmillan, 1961], p. 3). The main works of the chief members of the classical school are Adam Smith, *The Wealth of Nations* (1776; reprint ed., New York: Modern Library, 1937); David Ricardo (1772–1823), *Principles of Political Economy and Taxation*, 3rd ed. (1821; reprint ed. with an introduction by Michael Fogarty, London: J. M. Dent, 1965). The principal works of the followers of Ricardo include John Stuart Mill (1806–1873), *Principles of Political Economy* (1848; reprint ed., London: Longmans, 1909); W. Stanley Jevons (1835–1882), *The Theory of Political Economy* (1871; reprint ed., New York: Kelley and Millman, 1957), and *Investigations in Currency and Finance* (1884; reprint ed., New York: Augustus M. Kelley, 1964); Alfred Marshall, *Principles of Economics* and *Money, Credit and Commerce* (1922; reprint ed., New York: Augustus M. Kelley, 1960).

chases labour and commodities with that portion of his income which he saves just as much as he does with that he is said to spend. He is said to spend when he seeks to obtain present enjoyment from the services and the commodities which he purchases. He is said to save when he causes the labour and the commodities which he purchases to be devoted to the production of wealth from which he expects to derive the means of enjoyments in the future.[3]

The classical system perceived two mechanisms through which such an equilibrium at full employment would automatically come about. One was the interest rate, which ensured that savings equal investment, and the other was flexible wage rates, which ensured that there was always full employment at this equilibrium level of production. Classical theory held that all unemployment was voluntary or frictional—the latter created by a constantly changing "basket" of demanded goods to which employment patterns could not always adjust immediately. Involuntary unemployment was impossible; a laborer had only to reduce his wage demands, and automatic mechanisms would ensure that he would become employed.

The classical theory of interest rates held that when savings exceeded investment at a given interest rate, savers would be obliged to lend for less. This caused the interest rate to fall and persuaded investors to increase expenditure, so that investment would soon rise until it equaled savings. Classical economists, emphasizing the role of money as a medium of exchange over its role as a store of value, assumed that no one would wish to hold idle money balances. Therefore, all savings would be made available as loans in order to earn interest (such loans include stocks and bonds, savings accounts, and any other such instruments issued by either firms or financial intermediaries to ultimate lenders).

This classical belief was really the result of extending an analysis of a barter economy by analogy to a money economy. Say and the rest of the classical economists believed that money was essentially a means of exchange, a way of facilitating the exchange of goods and services. Although money freed production from the "double coincidence of wants" necessary to the barter system, it did not change the notion of transactions in the economy. Not until some years later did economics begin to recognize that the existence of money changed the underlying dynamics of an economy.

The classical city had been built largely by British economists, and therefore it was the British economy that served as a real-world check on the theory. In October 1929, the American "crash" began to affect Britain severely as American money was no longer available for loans, for the purchase of British goods, for other services—shipping, insurance—which Britain had used to help offset its imports of food and raw materials. Unemployment rose to 2.5 million, 20 percent of the labor force, by December 1930. Prices of imports fell, while prices of exports remained the same,

3. Alfred Marshall, *The Pure Theory of Domestic Values* (1879; reprint ed., London: London School of Economics and Political Science, 1949), p. 34, as quoted in Keynes, *General Theory*, p. 19.

Commentary: Back to Barter?

Barter was almost certainly the earliest form of economic exchange. It took place when one person had a good he didn't want as much as he wanted a good someone else had. In economic terminology, the owner of an excess supply of eggs who has an excess demand for cabbages would find someone—a neighboring farmer—in the opposite situation and trade eggs for cabbages. The result of such a trade would be equilibrium in the supply of and demand for both commodities in both households. (Note that the trade would occur *only* if the two households could agree on the relative trade value of the commodities involved; if one household thinks one egg is worth two cabbages and the other it is worth only one cabbage, there can be no trade.)

The invention of money provided what one might think of as an intervening good which could be bartered for anything for which there was a demand and a supply. Then, buyer and seller merely had to agree on the price of one commodity in terms of the currency involved. Eventually, a market would develop and an equilibrium price (expressed in money terms) was established at which the supply and demand of each commodity were equal.

Economists have nearly always argued that a barter economy is inherently less efficient than a money economy because trade can arise only when there is a "double coincidence of wants," to use the terminology of W. S. Jevons, a nineteenth-century British economist who was concerned with this problem. In his words, "the first difficulty of barter is to find two persons whose disposable possessions mutually suit each other's wants. There may be many people wanting and possessed of those things wanted; but to allow an act of barter, there must be a double coincidence which will rarely happen."[1]

Yet barter is still widespread; markets, for various reasons, do not always function freely. Barter characterizes trade among persons having little access to money, because their goods and services cannot be sold for currency on the open market. Aside from children (bubble-gum cards are usually traded, not bought or sold), such persons include prisoners and poor farmers and peasants who subsist almost exclusively on what they are able to grow. The complex economic life in Soviet prison camps described by Aleksandr Solzhenitsyn in *One Day in the Life of Ivan Denisovich* is an example. This internal economy is based on barter, particularly of food from outside for services of those in authority (the prison doctor, the gang boss, etc.) and for tobacco and clothing.

Barter among American farmers has nearly died out, but it was certainly commonplace until World War II, probably most commonplace during periods of tight money and/or depression. In *To Kill a Mockingbird* a lawyer is paid for dealing with an entailment with a "sack of hickory nuts . . . a crate of smilax and holly . . . and a crockersack full of turnip greens." These are all goods for which no market (in terms of money) existed in Depression-era Alabama, where Harper Lee's novel is set. One might consider whether the sharecropping system of the rural South could be

1. W. S. Jevons, *Money and the Mechanism of Exchange* (London: D. Appleton, 1875), p. 3.

considered a form of barter, since the tenants "paid" for their rent, seeds, store-bought food and other necessities with a portion of their cotton crop. (One also might argue that since the landlord invariably sold the cotton in the marketplace, this was not a true barter system because the "double coincidence of wants" was not present; rather, the landlord-treated the tenant's payment in cotton as a kind of pseudo-currency, to be held until he could exchange it for legal tender.)

In economies and among persons where economic exchange is almost always conducted with money, barter may reappear when the market economy is not functioning properly. When the currency has been debased or is mistrusted—during excessive inflation, for example—people may set up their own markets, trading commodities (including such substitutes for currency as gold, silver, and jewels) for other commodities *outside* the markets where prices have been established in terms of the mistrusted currency.

Barter in developed economies arises when an equilibrium in the supply and demand for a commodity cannot occur because of price controls. The diagram illustrates that when the price of commodity Q is fixed at P_0, demand will exceed supply by the amount Q_e. If the supply curve cannot be shifted to the right, shortages will arise which may lead to a "black market" in which purchasers illegally pay the equilibrium price, P_e. On the other hand, if shortages exist in many markets and for many commodities, including raw materials and intermediate products required for the production of final goods, producers having an excess supply of certain goods may have little use for cash. They may then attempt to barter these goods for those goods for which they have an excess demand.

This situation arose in the United States in 1973 and 1974 during the energy crisis, when some price controls were in effect. It is not possible to increase the supply of most petroleum-based products in the short run except

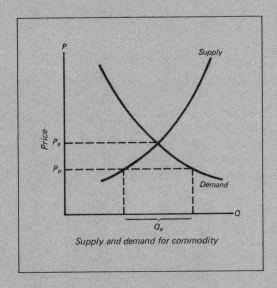

Supply and demand for commodity

through imports because of the long lead time required to build refineries, but imports could not be increased significantly because of the Arab oil embargo. The result was widespread shortages in many kinds of petroleum-based products, not only fuels, but also intermediate products required for an enormous variety of final goods, including drugs, paints, fabrics, automobiles, and many others.

Many corporations therefore turned to barter, trading goods they needed less for goods they needed more, or as a means to pay a price above the "ceiling" level for some commodity in short supply. One chemical company bartered a solvent, diethylene glycol, of which it had nearly all it needed for enough benzene to renew production in its plant manufacturing paint dyes. Bartering commodities for fuel also became widespread; for example, steel-manufacturing companies offered oil companies steel tubes required for their oil drilling in return for the heavy fuel they needed to operate their plants.[2]

2. *Wall Street Journal*, February 2, 1974, p. 1.

A slightly different type of bartering arises when future prices and supplies of a commodity are uncertain and the purchaser wishes to "tie up" future production of a good. This is particularly important in international trade, in situations in which the purchaser's currency is of uncertain value and/or simply not desired by the supplier. Such a situation has arisen between Western oil-consuming nations (and Japan) and the oil-producing countries, particularly those in the Middle East. As of March 1974, the Japanese had agreed to supply Iraq, Iran, and Algeria with industrial plants (including a 500,000 bbl per day refinery) in return for guaranteed supplies of crude oil.[3] Similar contracts were entered into by the British, the French, and the West Germans. More generally, the European Common Market has offered long-term economic and technical cooperation to the Arab world, recognizing the obligation to trade in something other than inflated currency.[4] But twentieth-century economists generally have been content with mathematical demonstrations of barter's inferiority to money as a medium of economic exchange,[5] and the study of barter as an important real-world phenomenon of imperfect market economies thus far has been left to journalists, anthropologists, and novelists.

5. More recent literature on the economics of barter include: Ross M. Starr, "The Structure of Exchange in Barter and Monetary Economies," *Quarterly Journal of Economics* 86 (May 1972): 290–302; J. Niehans, "Money and Barter in General Equilibrium with Transaction Costs," *American Economic Review* 61 (December 1971): 773–783.

3. *Business Week*, March 2, 1974, pp. 54–55.
4. *New York Times*, March 5, 1974.

thus improving Britain's trade balance. At the same time, in the face of extensive unemployment, real wages rose, as prices fell. The wholesale price index (1929 = 100) fell to 87.5 in 1930, and then to 76.8 in 1931.[4]

Obviously, the British economy was not behaving "properly"; wages did not fall the way they should have, and involuntary unemployment was to be found everywhere. Similar experiences were to be found in the United States and Western European nations. A large part of the classical city had come crashing down on the heads of those most determined to defend it, including government officials in the United States and Britain.[5]

Keynesian Theory

The architect of the rebuilding was John Maynard Keynes, an English intellectual who was as much at home in the City of London, where he made a fortune as a speculator, as in the halls of Cambridge University, his academic home for his entire career.[6] Keynes' occupations were surprisingly varied. He taught at Cambridge and worked as an advisor to the Treasury Office; he was the major shareholder and Chairman of the Board of *The Nation*, a highly respected literary and political magazine; he was involved in Liberal Party politics. His friends included famous artists and writers, such as Duncan Grant, Clive Bell, Lytton Strachey, and Virginia Woolf. His wife was a Russian dancer with Diaghilev's ballet troupe, and he founded a ballet company so that she could dance in England. Although Keynes enjoyed a successful career within the establishment, he was anything but a conformist. As a young man, he had a reputation for scandalous behavior; it was rumored he had once made love to Virginia Woolf's sister on the drawing room floor during a party, although most of his friends discredited the rumor since he was believed to love only young men. Keynes supplies a welcome bit of human interest in a profession whose members, rightly or wrongly, are mostly noted for their earnestness as they go about their business in the "dismal science."

Keynes had begun to consider the problems of aggregate demand after he was appointed the financial representative of the Treasury to the Paris Peace Conference ending World War I. Horrified by the prospective effects of the Treaty of Versailles, Keynes resigned the "scene of nightmare" and produced an impassioned book, *The Economic Consequences of the Peace*, in which he showed just how unrealistic and damaging to the economies of all Western European nations the treaty, with its demands for enormous reparations from Germany, would be.[7]

4. A. J. P. Taylor, *English History, 1914–1945* (New York: Oxford University Press, 1965), p. 284. Real wages refers to money wages divided by the price level.
5. See Robert Lekachman, *The Age of Keynes* (New York: Random House, 1966), Ch. 5, for a discussion of the behavior of the American economic establishment during the Depression (1929–1934).
6. See Sir Roy Harrod, *The Life of John Maynard Keynes* (New York: Macmillan, 1951).
7. Keynes, *The Economic Consequences of the Peace* (London: Macmillan, 1920).

Keynes' continuing involvement in public affairs was to play a significant role in the development of his economic theory, with its emphasis on the causative factors involved in the determination of the *level* of employment, as opposed to the distribution of that amount of employment (and other factors of production) used to produce a particular level of output.

Keynes began his demolition of part of the classical city with an analysis of the principles of classical theory that led to the theory that freely fluctuating wage rates would lead to equilibrium at full-employment levels. The argument is complex and often hard to follow, but the essence is that involuntary unemployment can occur because the classical theory of what Keynes calls "the marginal disutility of labor" in relation to the utility of the real wage (the money wage adjusted for the level of prices) associated with a given level of employment is wrong.

The classical economists argued that for any given worker, increasing work increased "disutility"; additional work becomes less "pleasurable" because it is harder and because the goods obtained for the additional wages have less utility, or are needed less urgently, than those purchased with previously earned money. Therefore, the quantity of labor supplied was seen by the classical economists to depend on the real wage of labor; as the real wage rose, so would the available supply of labor. The quantity of labor demanded by firms also was seen to depend on the real wage, falling with an increase in the real wage. Thus, if labor supply exceeded labor demand, the resultant unemployment would disappear with a reduction in the real wage which would reduce the quantity of labor supplied by workers and increase the quantity of labor demanded by firms until labor demand was equal to labor supply.

Keynes argued that, although firms' demand for labor depended on the real wage, labor supply depended on the money wage; he believed workers thought in terms of the money value of their wages rather than in terms of their real value, or purchasing power. Keynes went on to say that if the demand for output fell, thus reducing prices and raising the real wage, firms' demand for labor would fall too; but, at a given money wage, the supply of labor would remain unaffected. Thus, an excess supply of labor or involuntary unemployment would result. With workers unwilling to accept a lower money wage, the only way to reduce the real wage and thereby to restore full employment would be to increase aggregate demand. The resulting increase in the price level would lower the real wage, thus raising the demand for labor resources to a full-employment level.[8] That increase in aggregate demand, Keynes argued, might not be forthcoming in time to rescue a significant part of the labor force from unemployment. Therefore, an increase in aggregate demand induced by government spending or under some conditions by an increase in the money supply may be called for. The rationale for this procedure is developed fully in Chapters 10 and 11.

The problem was to explain why such a shortage of aggregate demand was

8. Keynes, *General Theory*, Ch. 2; see also Alvin Hansen, *A Guide to Keynes* (New York: McGraw-Hill, 1953), Ch. 1.

not automatically eliminated as the classical economists and Say's Law claimed; in other words, Keynes had to develop a new theory of aggregate demand. The essence of Keynes' discovery lay in the fact that in a modern economy savings and investment were carried out by two different sets of people: on the one hand, individuals and some businesses saving for a variety of motives; and, on the other hand, businesses intent on increasing their ability to produce output and thus, ultimately, their profits.

Because the motives for saving and investing differed, the possibility existed that total *income* (output or supply) would not necessarily equal aggregate demand, or the total *expenditure* made by that group of consumers (whose saving depended on income) and investors (whose investment depended on interest rates and expectations). If the reduction in demand due to savings (leakage) did not equal the increase in demand due to investment (injection), aggregate demand would be inadequate to purchase total output. If, given a shortage of aggregate demand, the price level fell, as we have seen, the result, according to Keynes, would be lowered demand for labor. Since the supply of labor would be unaffected by the change in the price level, the result would be involuntary unemployment.

Keynes thus sought to develop a theory which would explain the twin components of aggregate demand—consumption and investment; he further sought to explain savings and to explain the mechanisms which might serve to make savings and investment equal. From this theory would flow a set of hypotheses about public policy intended to bring aggregate demand to the level required to ensure purchase of the total output produced by a fully employed labor force—the level known as a full-employment equilibrium. Keynes developed the rudiments of the "consumption function"; in his words, "Men are disposed, as a rule and on the average, to increase their consumption as their income increases but not by as much as the increase in their income."[9] Since what was not consumed was saved, Keynes had effectively developed a simple theory of aggregate changes in savings; he assumed that individuals saved widely varying amounts of their incomes for widely varying reasons, at any given point in time, although changes in aggregate income were the chief causes of changes in aggregate savings. Keynes' view of investment was also complex; he saw investment as essentially a function of expectations, particularly expectations of the rate of profit which a firm anticipated would be generated by the investment.

Keynes was always concerned with the role of money in the analysis of both investment and savings. His refutation of Say's Law depended on the view that purchasing power could leak into idle money balances under some conditions, thereby breaking the link between income earned in the process of producing goods and services (supply) and the necessary spending of the income on current output (demand). In fact, Keynes was a well-established monetary economist by the time he wrote his best-known work, *The General Theory of Employment, Interest and Money*; his earliest publication had

9. Keynes, *General Theory*, p. 96.

been *Indian Currency and Finance,* and his two-volume *Treatise on Money* had been published in 1930. There is a great deal of innovative monetary theory in the *General Theory,* although until recent years this aspect of Keynes' thought was much less well known than his analysis of "real," as opposed to "money," variables. The classical theorists had largely overlooked the significance of the fact that money also served as a "temporary abode of purchasing power enabling the act of purchase to be separated from the act of sale," to use the illuminating phrase of economist Milton Friedman.[10] Keynes perceived that it was possible for savings to exceed investment, with the difference simply being held onto by savers as money balances. The money balances could serve as a store of value, representing as such an alternative to investment in capital equipment or claims on capital equipment (bonds).

The concept of money as a store of value was one of Keynes' most important contributions to monetary theory; in fact, his analysis of the demand for money was essential to this refutation of the classical theory of aggregate demand and his analysis of general equilibrium independent of the *level* of employment.

In identifying the role of money as a store of value, Keynes saw the possibility that all goods produced by a fully employed labor force may not be sold. Some income could flow into money balances and be held there as a store of value if alternative assets were particularly unattractive. This might occur if, for example, the rate of return on investment were too low to overcome the "liquidity preference" implicit in holding money. This possibility amounted to a violation of Say's Law, insofar as supply no longer necessarily created its own demand.

The liquidity preference approach simply refers to the desire on the part of investors to hold onto money. Keynes defined liquidity as "immediate command over goods in general," and money as the medium of exchange is obviously the most liquid of holdings. Keynes argued that individuals hold money not only for daily transactions, but also for speculation.

It is the speculative **motive** which suggests the basis for absolute liquidity preference or a "liquidity trap." According to Keynes, if the interest rate gets low enough, it eventually reaches a level where everyone expects it to rise. In anticipation of such a rise and the resultant increased profitability of investing in bonds, all savers hold as much cash as they are able to lay their hands on. The increased liquidity of savers in such a liquidity trap would not induce them to purchase more bonds and thereby lower interest rates and increase investment. So if investment were inadequate to keep expenditure at a full-employment level at the liquidity trap interest rate, the economy would not automatically move toward a full-employment level of expenditure. Consequently, Keynes reached the conclusion that in situa-

---

10. Milton Friedman and Anna J. Schwartz, *A Monetary History of the United States: 1867–1960* (New York: National Bureau of Economic Research, 1963), p. 650.

tions of absolute liquidity preference, government intervention to increase total expenditure was needed to restore equilibrium and full employment.

As we have noted, however, Keynes was working at a time when unemployment was the foremost concern, and inflation was not a problem. The need for altering government expenditures as a means to maintain full employment is the aspect of Keynes' thought that is generally emphasized over his contribution to the theory of money. During the first decade after World War II, with the high unemployment levels of the 1930s fresh in the minds of new macroeconomic policymakers, the "Keynesian" approach to macroeconomics, as opposed to the macroeconomics of Keynes, was dominant. Keynesian macroeconomics focuses on the problem of unemployment but does so with no attention to the monetary sector, whereas macroeconomics as developed by Keynes himself devotes considerable attention to the monetary sector.

The Keynesian approach dominated the early postwar era for two reasons. First, it provided a theoretical framework which dealt specifically with the forces determining the level of employment. This was welcomed by policymakers seeking an adequate means to achieve the pressing goal of full employment of the labor force. Second, as explained previously, classical theory, with which policymakers had been operating for the past two centuries, viewed full employment as automatically assured by means of the flexibility of wages. This view appeared particularly irrelevant in the face of high levels of unemployment and was therefore sometimes interpreted by Keynesians to demonstrate the irrelevance of monetary theory per se. In fact, classical monetary macroeconomic theory, with its heavy emphasis on determination of the price level and the view that money mattered little or not at all in affecting "real" economic magnitudes like employment or output, may well have seemed of little significance at a time when the greatest concern was not to repeat the disastrous unemployment level of the 1930s. A return to emphasis on monetary theory awaited the reemergence of inflation as a serious problem and theorists able to integrate monetary analysis into a postclassical world.

Modern Monetary Theory

Classical monetary theory in contemporary form is generally associated with the "monetarist" school of thought which, along with its principal spokesman, Milton Friedman, has become increasingly influential in the 1960s and 1970s with the reemergence of widespread concern over inflation. The "modern quantity theory," as Friedman's approach is frequently called, is discussed in Chapter 13. This approach draws upon classical theory for its focus on the link between the quantity of money and the price level, and upon the monetary theory of Keynes for its emphasis on money defined as a store of value.

Friedman's description of money as a "temporary abode of purchasing power enabling the act of purchase to be separated from the act of sale" is useful in understanding the monetarist viewpoint, as well as in clarifying the monetary contribution made by Keynes. Basically, the monetarist views the quantity of money demanded in an economy as a stable and predictable magnitude, linked to income by a stable and predictable concept of velocity. Velocity is defined as the ratio of the flow of income to the stock of money balances demanded, or the number of times money changes hands in a given period. In effect, Friedman has taken the equation of exchange first put forward by Irving Fisher and updated it to a theory of the demand for money. This transformation involves a transition from the medium-of-exchange emphasis of the Fisher equation to the store-of-value emphasis of Keynes, a change of emphasis Friedman himself pointed to in his often misunderstood statement: "We're all Keynesians now."

The primary implication of the modern quantity theory from the standpoint of macroeconomic policy is that, in the long run, the rate of change of the price level (or inflation, as it is usually called) will be equal to the rate of growth of the money supply less the rate of growth of output for any given economy. This conclusion is reflected in Friedman's "monetary rule" that the money supply ought to grow steadily at about the same rate as the economy grows, roughly 4 percent a year, if inflation is to be avoided. This prescription is in opposition to the discretionary control of the money supply that the U.S. Federal Reserve is empowered to exercise. Although this rule has not been followed by the Federal Reserve, it has to some extent influenced their policy actions since the late 1960s.

While the focus of Keynes' macroeconomics on the problem of unemployment differs from that of classical macroeconomics and the modern quantity on the price level and inflation, as we have seen, both Keynes' theory and the modern quantity theory involve a similar theoretical view of money. The primary difference lies in the exclusive concentration of the modern quantity theory on the monetary section of the economy, as opposed to Keynes' focus on both the monetary sector and the income-expenditure relationship. As such, the latter may be viewed as a general-equilibrium approach to macroeconomics, while the modern quantity theory represents a partial-equilibrium approach.

The modern quantity theory has not been the only postwar response to the theory of macroeconomics which Keynes developed. As we shall see in Chapter 15, a group which we shall call the general-equilibrium monetary theorists objected to the separation by the classical economists of the monetary sector from the rest of the economy. They also disagreed as to the emphasis placed by many Keynesian economists on the exclusive substitutability between money and bonds, with no attention given to the substitutability between money and commodities. This group of theorists, the foremost of their number being Don Patinkin, places heavy emphasis on the "real-balance effect," or the impact of the level of stocks of money balances on the demand for commodities as well as the demand for bonds. This effect was first pointed out by A. C. Pigou and is often called the Pigou effect. The general-equilibrium monetary theorists argue that the real-balance effect is necessary for there to be a determinate price level in the classical system. Moreover, the failure of Keynes to take adequate account of the real-balance effect leads, under certain conditions, to invalid claims that changes in the money supply can affect something other than the price level, such as interest rates and income. In short, the general-equilibrium monetary theorists argue that the classical separation of the monetary section from the rest of the economy led to correct conclusions regarding the impact on prices of changes in the money supply, but for the wrong reasons, while the integration by Keynes of the monetary sector with the rest of the economy led to incorrect conclusions regarding the ultimate impact on the interest rate and income of changes in the money supply. Of course, a full comprehension of these points will require an understanding of the macroeconomics of Keynes and of the monetarists. The sections that follow, therefore, will explore both these theoretical approaches, followed by a substantive investigation of the analysis by the general-equilibrium monetary theorists.

Questions and Exercises

1. Why did the Keynesian approach to macroeconomics become dominant during the decade following World War II? Why was full employment considered the most important policy goal at that time?
2. Was monetary policy irrelevant, as maintained by the Keynesians, in the years following World War II?
3. Why did the classical economists assume that full employment was automatically assured? How did Say's Law explain the occurrence of depressions?
4. How did Keynes and the classical economists differ on the equation of savings and investment?
5. Which function of money did the classical economists stress? Why did Keynes stress a different function?
6. How would you distinguish Keynesian economics and Keynes' economics?
7. Keynes posed the likelihood of less than full-employment equilibrium. How was this state made possible by money's store-of-value function?
8. How did the public's liquidity preference lead to a "liquidity trap"? Why was the speculative motive for holding money so strong at low rates of interest?
9. What accounted for the reemergence of classical monetary theory? How does it differ from its earlier formulation?
10. What is the basis for Friedman's monetary rule? How closely has this rule been followed by the Federal Reserve in recent years?

Keynesian Macroeconomic Theory

PART II

this period of double-digit inflation, administration economists are setting out to make the government's statistics more extensive, more accurate, more up-to-date and more useful. They hope the revised readings will better pinpoint the causes of economic trouble.

Upgraded Analytical Methods

Among other things, the economists are upgrading the calculation... of prices Americans ... ever... thing... have to ... now they ... expandi... surveys of ... are paid ... also revisi... measures ... U.S. bu... sell and to ... they sell it ... ey spend for re... inery, and how loud th... umming.

Innocent ... ugh these changes sound, some see dangers in them. Labor-union chiefs are boiling at plans to revise the consumer price index, which is used to help determine the size of wage demands and cost-of-living pay raises for millions of workers. Because a broadened survey would include prices paid by many Americans besides the urban wage-earners now focused on, labor leaders fear it will understate living-cost increases for union members.

Julius Shiskin, commissioner of the Bureau of Labor Statistics, acknowledges that some wage changes could result. "And even one or two cents an hour could represent a lot of money," he says. But he argues that the revised index will provide a truer picture of price movements.

In any case, the revisions will affect everyday decisions of industry and government. "It's crucial to policymaking that if the economy ... ahead by 4% our numbers are ... a 2% or 6% ... high-ranking ...

Timeliness ... racy. Some ... the White Ho... month-long ... controls had up-to-date statistics been available. Mr. Carlson recalls that President Nixon imposed his August 1971 price freeze partly on the basis of two-month-old price data that indicated inflation was accelerating. But when the figures for July and August were published, after the freeze action, they showed price rises had been slowing down.

Other administration officials say the sudden changeover in January 1973 to a less restrictive economic-controls system from the tougher Phase 2 might not have been made if government price statistics had revealed earlier the inflationary surge that erupted that month.

Even now, economists say figures may ... economic decision... ation, Congress and indu... if the readings are taken at face value. The main reason is simply that the indicators are not adjusted to allow for today's raging inflation.

Thus the government's 12 leading economic indicators, which often foreshadow broad movements in the economy, have zipped ahead at a 7% annual pace since last

Confusion over the energy crisis and the course of the economy in 1974 has ignited a movement to reform the government's data gathering procedures. The aim is to compel business generally—not just oil companies—to give Washington more timely and extensive information on prices inventories and

slipped substantially.

And corporate profit reports show a jump of about 20% from a year ago, but inflation-bloated inventories plus slow depreciation of those stocks suggest that profits are overstated substantially.

Without better figures to work with ... cials find it extra hard ... prognostications ... ration forecasts have ... Early last ... acted ... retail food p... uring the ye... ... n 20% ... White House ... serted that the cost of ... be mounting at a 2.5% rate at ... year-end; the actual rate then was a staggering 9%.

White House aides have been told by a special consultant that they don't know what's going on in the U.S. economy. "The whole federal establishment is ill-prepared in terms of data, models, analytical procedures and patterns of interagency communication for the tasks of forecasting and policy formation," asserts Karl A. Fox, economics professor at Iowa State University, in a little-publicized study conducted for Mr. Nixon's economic advisers.

Mr. Fox reports he found "no evidence that any U.S. agency did an adequate job of forecasting economic development during 1972-73." Indeed, the economist says, "couldn't find one agency that had an adequate model of the world economy.

Astounding Lack of Data

Those critical conclusions echo complaints voiced in recent months by administration wage-price controllers as they gradually decontrolled the U.S. economy. "We were astounded at the lack of data that could be used to make economic decisions," ... Do... ... associate director ... ... nd ... ... n ... ... ir ... ... statistics don't reveal all the ... know; the reasons for statistical changes and geographical breakdowns of national totals are often lacking. "There's no question we get lots of numbers from the government, but they're often not very useful in helping corporations make key planning decisions," says Michael Levy, an economist with the influential Conference Board, the New York-based business research group.

Spurred by the criticisms, administration economists last September began examining the government's statistical operations. Headed by Gary L. Seevers, member of the President's economic advisers ... ... ing to revamp a number of economic barometers and to initiate some new surveys. Among the changes are:

—A major revision of the Labor Department's consumer price index, aiming to extend it to prices paid by 80% of the population from the present 55%. Prices will be

ministration officials is that much of the information the government gets is almost useless. Says Cost of Living Council Director John T. Dunlop: "Most government statistics are great for professors to analyze after the fact but are of little value in making operating decisions. Business learned long ago that it needed a continuous flow of information to make decisions, and government needs the same capability."

Three proposals for reforming statis-

vices are purchased frequently enough to warrant inclusion in the consumer index.

—Develop... wage i... ...ie... ...rs. —Imp... index ... ... new measure of petroleum ... prices and to extend coverage to several new industries.

Consumer Spending Patterns

—Initiation of a new survey on consumer spending patterns to replace decade-old data. In a companion project, the Census Bureau will improve its measurement of personal income of Americans, making a larger sampling of welfare and Social Security recipients.

—Start-up of an annual survey of production capacity at U.S. factories, helping the Federal Reserve Board to compile its monthly figures on industrial production.

—Revision of the quarterly report on gross national product, which measures the country's output of goods and services, to expand coverage to some industries not now surveyed, as well as to nonprofit organizations and to more service firms.

"There's no doubt that the government ... credibility with businessmen ... ... "Mr. Seevers ... ... cisms.

But the best efforts ... won't necessarily quiet the critics. You could spend another $10 billion a year on gathering data and some people would still say that wasn't enough," says George Hagedorn, vice president of the National Association of Manufacturers.

FINAL SALES rose $43 billion

INVENTORY INVESTMENT declined $2½ billion

REAL OUTPUT grew about 8 percent

icit GNP deflator was 6 percent, a disturbingly high figure, compared with ... percent in the fourth quarter. Part ... that acceleration was caused by a January increase in Federal pay schedules; such increases enter the national accounts as straight increases in the price of government product. The implicit price deflator for private product, which was unaffected by the pay raise, increased at a rate of 5.5 percent in the first quarter compared with 2.8 percent in the fourth, with much of the acceleration caused by sharply rising food prices.

The major GNP components generally registered first quarter advances that were sizable but not out of line with recent trends or with widely held expectations. The exceptions were consumption spending, which increased very steeply not only in current prices but also in real terms, and inventory accumulation, which is estimated to have declined from the fourth quarter to the first. Business fixed investment, ... ial investment, and government ... ... quite solidly.

Higher ... both pay raises ... at growth—accounted for some $5 billion of the $7½ billion increase in combined Federal, State, and local government purchases. The Federal pay raise in January was responsible for about $2 billion of the advance in compensation.

Employment grew substantially in the first quarter, as measured both by the household survey of the civilian population and by the survey of nonfarm establishments. The first quarter gains in the employment aggregates reflected continuation of the strong growth that has marked the past year (table 1). However, growth of the civilian labor force has slowed, at least partly because the reduction of the armed forces is over; that reduction augmented the natural growth of the civilian population and thus of the civilian labor force.

Because the growth of employment in the first quarter was faster than the growth of the labor force, the unemployment rate dropped measurably—from 5.3 percent in the fourth quarter to 5.0 percent in the first. The rate had

Table 1.—Growth of Labor Force and Employment

[Percent change from previous quarter, seasonally adjusted at annual rate]

	Civilian labor force	Civilian employment		Nonagricultural payroll employ-
		Total	Nonagric.	ment

National Income Accounts

3

Today we are accustomed to knowing the level of economic activity. The newspapers report the rise in prices or employment or current output; policymakers rely on GNP, price level, and output estimates to forecast tax receipts, to assess expected levels of unemployment, to predict rates of inflation, and to monitor overall performance of the economy. It is hard to imagine that before World War I, no such comprehensive measurements were available; economics in general paid attention to laws of supply and demand and other aspects of microeconomic theory, reasoning that the national economy would then take care of itself. While government was not expected to do many of the things asked of it today, it *was* asked to fight wars, and when war came, the ignorance of national economic power complicated the task of mobilization. During World War I, a rudimentary analytical account of the nation's productive power was begun. The full development of the national income accounts, however, occurred during the late 1930s and World War II, as national challenges and the development of Keynesian macroeconomic theory reinforced the need for information on the level of income and expenditures.

The statistical difficulties in measuring the income of a nation are numerous. The official statistics are now maintained and refined by the Department of Commerce, using data from many different sources. The National Bureau of Economic Research continues to develop an alternative accounts system that is more inclusive. We will focus primarily on the official approach.

The basis for the national accounts is the fundamental identity between expenditures and income. The final value of any unit of output may be viewed in two ways, as its market price or as the sum of factor prices of its components. The market price times quantity sold represents total value of expenditure on consumption, investment, and government activities; the sum of payments to factors represents costs to businesses and income to each factor of production (land, labor, capital, technological expertise) from the productive activity. The identity of the two is one of the foundations of microeconomic theory, as price and cost (income to the factors) are equated at the margin.

Measures of Aggregate Income

When examining economic activity in a macroeconomic system, however, the equation of expenditure and income takes some adjustment. The sum of the market prices of all final goods and services produced in a given period totals Gross National Product (GNP). The sum of the income to all factors in the same period is National Income. The two are not identical because certain nonfactor costs are reflected in the market price, and hence in GNP. When these nonfactor costs are added to national income, the total equals GNP.

Ultimately, the most basic measurement of national income is the amount which can be consumed over some time period without impoverishing a nation, to paraphrase one of the great macroeconomists, J. R. Hicks.[1] This means that as a measure of current output of the nation, GNP overstates sustainable consumption inasmuch as current GNP includes not only new capital goods which will yield future consumption goods but also new capital goods to replace those worn out in production. Deducting the costs of these replacements reveals whether the economy has greater productive capacity, the same as, or less than before. When this deduction for depreciation is made, the result is Net National Product, or NNP. Subtracting indirect business taxes (such as property and excise taxes) from NNP gives a measure of national income, or NI, the total returns to each factor employed

---

1. J. R. Hicks, *Value and Capital* (Oxford, England: Oxford University Press, 1965), p. 172.

in current production. Whereas indirect business taxes are a cost of production, and thus are included in GNP and NNP, they do not accrue to any of the factors of production, and thus are excluded from NI.

National income must further be distinguished from personal income, or PI, the total income owing to but not necessarily received by persons in their capacities as factors of production and as citizens. To obtain personal income, we begin by subtracting those items which do not represent income of persons—total corporate profits and social security payments. Moreover, we must add income owing to persons which has not been earned in the person's capacity as a factor of production—primarily transfer payments, net interest, and net dividends. Personal income is roughly analogous to gross earnings on a weekly payslip. Take-home pay is closer to disposable income, or DI, because both show what is left to spend or save. DI excludes not only federal, state, and local income taxes, but also property taxes and all other personal taxes. Table 3.1 shows how disposable income is derived from the more inclusive measures of aggregate income.

Table 3.1 Aggregate Income Measures, 1972 (billions of dollars)

Disposable income may be thought of in another way—as one of the three flows from NNP. These flows are to business (in the form of retained earnings), to government (in the form of taxes minus transfers), and to households (in the form of DI).

The GNP Account

Gross National Product may be defined as the market value of all final goods and services produced in a country during a given period—a deceptively simple definition that contains a number of crucial concepts. "Market value" eliminates noneconomic things; "produced in a given period" eliminates such things as transfer payments or capital gains, which do not result from current production; "final goods and services" eliminates

Table 3.2   National Income and Product Account, 1972 (billions of dollars)

1.	Compensation of employees	707.1	18.	Personal consumption expenditures	726.5
2.	Wages and salaries	627.3	19.	Durable goods	117.4
3.	Supplements to wages and salaries	79.7	20.	Nondurable goods	299.9
4.	Proprietors' income	74.2	21.	Services	309.2
5.	Rental income of persons	24.1	22.	Gross private domestic investment	178.3
6.	Corporate profits and inventory valuation adjustment	91.1	23.	Business fixed investment	172.3
7.	Profits before tax	98.0	24.	Nonresidential structures	41.7
8.	Profit tax liability	42.7	25.	Producers' durable equipment	76.5
9.	Dividends	26.0			
10.	Undistributed profits	29.3	26.	Residential structures	54.0
11.	Inventory valuation adjustment	−6.9	27.	Changes in business inventories	6.0
12.	Net interest	45.2	28.	Net exports of goods and services	−4.6
13.	NATIONAL INCOME	941.8	29.	Exports	73.5
14.	Business transfer payments	4.6	30.	Imports	78.1
15.	Indirect business taxes	107.8	31.	Government purchases of goods and services	255.0
16.	Capital consumption allowances	102.4	32.	Federal	104.4
17.	Statistical discrepancy	−1.5	33.	National defense	74.4
			34.	Other	30.1
			35.	State and local	150.5
	CHARGES AGAINST GROSS NATIONAL PRODUCT	1155.2		GROSS NATIONAL PRODUCT	1155.2

SOURCE: U.S. Department of Commerce, *Survey of Current Business* 53 (July 1973), Table A.
Note: Total may not equal sum of items due to rounding and omission of minor items.

intermediate goods, goods purchased and resold, whether they are processed further or not. What remains after these exclusions is a flow of expenditures and receipts from current production. GNP therefore expresses production in two ways that result in an identical figure: the value of output and the total cost of producing that output.

Table 3.2, a GNP account for the United States, details the expenditures and receipts for 1972. The right-hand side shows the value of all goods and services produced in the United States in 1972 allocated to the type of demand. The left-hand side reflects the costs of producing the output. Compensation of employees, proprietor's income, rental income of persons, corporate profits, and net interest constitute income received by the factors of production used in the output for 1972. However, the final selling prices of the purchases are higher than this sum because of certain nonfactor costs, notably indirect business taxes and the depreciation (or in official terminology, capital consumption allowances) for the replacement of productive capacity.

Expenditures for GNP

One problem in counting these expenditures for output is that not everything has a price. Nonprofit groups such as private schools and universities, hospitals, churches, foundations, clubs, and the like pay out salaries, which are entered on the left-hand side of the account and demand an equivalent flow of output on the right-hand, or expenditures, side. The same is true of government, although taxes might be considered the charges for output. However, taxes seldom balance with expenditures, and the problem of how to treat deficits or surpluses arises. Therefore, nonprofit output is measured by wage and salary costs both on the income and expenditures side.

The four major categories of expenditures (purchases) which together constituted the Gross National Product of the United States in 1972 totaled $1,155,200,000,000, or nearly $1.2 trillion. The first of these categories, personal consumption, totaled $726.5 billion in 1972. Personal consumption is divided into purchases of durable goods ($117.4 billion), nondurable goods ($299.9 billion), and services ($309.2 billion). The most important component of services is housing ($105.5 billion). This figure is an attempt by statisticians to measure the value of services provided by the nation's stock of housing, not only that portion which is rented but also that portion which is owner-occupied. This latter figure is said to be the amount that would accrue to the owner if he rented the house, and is balanced on the left-hand side of the GNP account by the entry "Rental income of persons."

Gross private domestic investment (GPDI), the second major category on the right-hand side, totaled $178.3 billion in 1972. Gross investment includes all capital goods purchased, both those which make a net addition to the nation's stock of capital goods, and those which replace worn-out capital goods. The balancing item on the left-hand side of the account for the latter is capital consumption allowances, or depreciation. This figure ($102.4 billion) represents the cost of replacing worn-out capital goods, and when subtracted from GPDI yields net investment.

Gross private domestic investment does not include government purchases of capital goods. Thus, the cost of an airplane purchased by a private airline is a contribution to GPDI; an identical airplane purchased by the federal government is simply regarded as a component of government purchases of goods and services. This difference reflects the fact that the goods and services in GNP are categorized according to their *purchaser* rather than their *purpose*.

The first two components of GPDI, nonresidential structures ($41.7 billion) and producers' durable equipment ($76.5 billion), are often lumped together as business fixed investment. The other two components of gross private domestic investment are residential structures ($54.0 billion) and change in business inventory ($6.0 billion).

Nonresidential structures is the gross value of all construction undertaken by the business sector in order to enable that sector to produce other goods and services. It includes corporate headquarters, factories, warehouses, and so on. Producers' durable equipment includes every conceivable kind of good used to produce other goods and services, from tractors and mining machinery to electrical transmission apparatus and office furniture.

Residential construction is the gross value of additions to the housing stock. These investments in owner-occupied housing are considered in exactly the same fashion as are investment in nonresidential structures by the business sector. When a family purchases a new home, the Department of Commerce assumes that it is making an investment from which it will receive a flow of services which can be included as additions to the services component of personal consumption. The family is, in effect, treated as though it were purchasing services from itself. As noted earlier, these services totaled $105.5 billion in 1972, although it must be emphasized that this is the total value of services received from the *entire* housing stock, not merely that portion which is owner-occupied.

The question which arises at this point is why only housing should be treated in this fashion; surely there are many other goods and services which are really investments made by individuals from which they receive a flow of services. This is particularly true of goods which individuals must purchase and own in order to earn a livelihood. However, it is hard to determine where to draw the line between consumption and investment goods purchased by individuals. At one extreme, nearly every item purchased, including food and clothing, could be said to contribute to a person's ability to work. One might attempt to differentiate between the two types of goods by asking whether the individual purchases the good or service to improve his ability to produce (investment) or simply to consume or maintain his ability to produce (consumption plus depreciation). In this case, a large proportion of transportation services purchased by individuals ought to be regarded as part of GPDI, rather than personal consumption expenditures. However, an attempt to differentiate transportation services according to purpose is an example of the data-collection difficulties which would confront the Department of Commerce if it attempted to include other goods and services purchased by individuals as part of GPDI, rather than personal consumption. Therefore, the treatment of housing as an investment is unique.

The final component of GPDI is changes in business inventories, which include changes in the accumulations of finished goods, goods in process, and raw materials on hand. If business is booming inventories may be down from the year before; inventory investment would therefore be negative. If the levels of inventory do not change, there will be no effect on GNP—unless prices change. If business is slack, firms will be accumulating inventories which, as a stock of goods for future consumption, represent investment, even though the investment may be involuntary.

The third major component of the expenditures side of the GNP account is a net figure. Goods produced abroad and imported into the United States are consumed and appear on the right, or product, side of the GNP account. However, they do not generate equivalent costs of production and contributions to corporate profits on the left-hand side of the GNP account statement. On the other hand, goods which are exported appear on the left, or income, side of the account as part of production costs and profits, but not on the right-hand side, since they are consumed abroad. Thus, in order to balance the account, a figure for the value of goods and services exported must appear on the right-hand side of the account to balance the costs of production of exports. In addition, a figure for goods and services imported must appear on the left-hand side of the account to balance goods and services imported and consumed. In order to simplify, the balancing figure for imports is moved to the right-hand side of the statement, where it becomes negative and is subtracted from the balancing figure for exports, leaving us with the figure for net exports of goods and services. The effect of subtracting imports from exports on the expenditure side of the account is simply to obtain an expression of the net demand on domestic resources. Exports minus imports represents *net* expenditure by foreigners on domestically produced goods.

The final component of the right-hand side of the GNP account, government purchases of goods and services, totaled $255.0 billion in 1972. Despite the rapid growth of the federal government, its purchases of $104.4 billion were well below those of state and local governments ($150.5 billion). As noted above, these purchases include goods which would be regarded as part of GPDI if they were purchased by private corporations.

The expenditure items of the right-hand side of the national income account may be summarized in a simple equation:

$$E = C + I + G + (X - M) \qquad\qquad (3.1)$$

where:

$\quad$ E = total expenditure

$\quad$ C = consumption

$\quad$ I = total investment

$\quad$ G = total government expenditure

(X − M) = net expenditure by foreigners on domestically produced goods or exports minus imports

Considerable attention will be devoted in subsequent chapters to analyzing the determinants of each form of private expenditure, with particular attention given to consumption and investment. It will become evident that consumption represents expenditure on current goods and services while investment represents expenditure on the ability to produce goods and services in the future. Government expenditure will appear as consumption and investment by the public sector. Part of federal government expenditure is used specifically for the purpose of stabilizing the economy, in a manner that will be described in Chapters 4 and 5.

Income

The left side of the national income account may be broken down into the components of national income—returns to labor (compensation of employees), returns to land (rental income of persons), returns to entrepreneurs (profits and proprietors' income), and returns to capital (net interest), plus the balancing nonfactor costs—indirect business taxes, business transfers, and depreciation.

However, since income from the perspective of the disburser is a cost, this account may be examined in another way—as a gigantic cost total for the businesses in the economy, plus the costs of productive activity in the other sectors. The key items in the nonbusiness sector are proprietors' income and rental income of persons. The business sector includes the remaining items.

It will be useful to digress at this point to look more carefully at the meaning of business costs. For an individual firm, costs include purchases of capital and intermediate goods from other firms, labor costs, rent, and the difference between interest received and interest paid. Were national income statisticians to sum up all these costs, the total would be far higher than actual GNP because a large portion of costs are incurred in intermediate activities rather than final production. Buying transistors and plastic to make a radio is a cost to the firm, but their contribution to the final product, the radio, is reflected in its selling price. To count the price of transistors and plastic, plus the final radio in the national accounts would, in effect, be counting the materials twice. Therefore, these intermediate transactions are removed by eliminating purchases of noncapital goods and services from other firms, and rent and interest transactions within the business sector.

The same result may be obtained using an incremental approach instead of an aggregate one. Intermediate product is eliminated if we consider only the value each firm adds at each stage of production. Suppose the transistors and plastic are sold for $10.00, the assembled radio is sold to the retailer for $25.00, and the retailer sells the radio to the public for $32.95. The value of production is not $67.95, but rather the sum of the **value added** at each stage of production. The value added is the difference between the price of the output at that stage and the cost of the goods purchased from suppliers. The assembler sells the radio for $25.00 but bought the materials for $10.00, so he has added $15.00 of value. The retailer sold the radio for $32.95 and bought it for $25.00. The value of his retailing services is $7.95. The $10.00 of transistors and plastic, the $15.00 of assembly, and the $7.95 of retailing produce a total of $32.95, the value of the final product net of intermediate output.

The reason for worrying about value added is partly because goods may be made in one year and sold in the next. If the radio is assembled in 1975 and sold in 1976, the radio would not contribute $25.00 one year and $32.95 the next. The 1976 contribution to GNP would be $7.95. Removing intermediate transactions, including rent and interest paid within the business sector, leaves compensation of employees, net interest paid to other sectors, and the capital consumption allowances, plus other nonfactor costs.

Now we can examine factor and nonfactor costs. The most important factor cost, or source of national income, in the GNP account, compensation of employees, totaled $707.1 billion in 1972. Compensation includes direct payments of wages and salaries ($627.3 billion), plus supplements ($79.7 billion) such as the employer's contributions to social security.

The net interest figure in the GNP account reflects the payment by the corporate sector to the noncorporate sector of interest for the use of funds, minus interest received. That portion of interest payments paid to or received from other corporations disappears in the aggregation process just as the rental costs for the individual firms disappear. Thus, if a corporation paid interest of $400 to another corporation and $6,000 to a private individual, the $6,000 would be a contribution to the aggregate net interest entry in the GNP account, while the $400 would disappear in the aggregation process. In 1972, net interest payments by the business sector to the personal sector were $45.2 billion.

Major nonfactor costs of the business sector are business transfer payments, such as bad debts and legal corporate gifts ($4.6 billion in 1972); indirect business taxes, such as sales taxes and excise taxes, which are included in the selling price of the good ($107.8 billion in 1972); and finally, the capital consumption allowances ($102.4 billion).

The capital consumption allowances represent an estimate of the capital used up during production, including investment in new computers to replace obsolete models or in automated, suburban plants to replace downtown mills. This allowance is not simply the cost of replacing the machine or building; machinery and buildings wear out (or depreciate) over many years, and the wearing out (or depreciation) is spread over these years rather than taken all at once in the year of replacement. Over time the sum of these allowances will provide a better estimate of total capital replacement than the figure for any one year, since the annual figure is a reflection of accounting practices and tax laws rather than an accurate estimate of the real value of replaced goods.

Looking at corporate profits and inventory valuation adjustment, we see that in 1972, when costs of the business sector were deducted from the receipts on the output of the sector, the residual stood at $98 billion. This represents total corporate profits before taxes. Taxes on these profits took $42.7 billion, and $26.0 billion was given over to the individual stockholders in dividends. (Dividends to corporations holding stocks are excluded just as interest and rent within the sector are.) The remaining $29.3 billion represents retained earnings, a part of the savings of business. The inventory valuation adjustment recognizes that a change in inventory prices represents a windfall profit or sudden loss, not a change in output, and is therefore deducted from total corporate profits.

Two items on the left-hand side represent nonbusiness income, proprietors' income and rental income of persons. Proprietorships are unincorporated enterprises, including self-employed people such as doctors. Because the money paid to the proprietor is not readily broken down into a salary and a profit component as in most businesses, their income is kept in a separate category in the national account.

The second major item reflecting the economic activity of individuals is rental income of persons, distinguished from rental paid by corporations to other corporations (which disappears in the aggregation process leading to GNP). As mentioned earlier, housing services are a component of personal consumption on the right side of the GNP account. These services include an imputed value for the services provided to home owners by the stock of privately owned housing. Just as personal consumption expenditures for rented housing are balanced on the left side of the statement by the wages and salaries used to pay those rents, so the personal consumption expenditures for owner-occupied housing must be balanced on the left by an income entry, namely rental income of persons.

Finally, because the income side (left) of the account is calculated independently of the expenditure side (right), "statistical discrepancy" is included on the left-hand side of the account to balance the totals.

Measuring Market Activity

National income accounts use market prices to measure the level of economic activity. Although this is both logical and convenient, behind it are all the assumptions of microeconomic theory about price reflecting cost and value. When markets are not competitive, can we say that price reflects the value of the output or does it include a hidden transfer payment to the producer? When a tariff raises the price of imported cars, should GNP be increased?

The use of price is also complicated because a number of items in GNP have no market price and must be imputed. The output of the nonprofit sector, and in particular, government, is measured by cost rather than market value, as we have seen. The services of banks and other financial intermediaries are measured neither solely by the charges to the customer nor by the costs of handling the accounts, but instead by an imputed interest flow. This is calculated by adding the amount of interest that the money earns from investment, which is not in fact paid to account holders, to the amount of the service charge as the income generated by banks or other financial services. Other items, such as compensation in kind, the value of food kept by farmers for their own use, and the imputed rental of owner-occupied homes, are calculated using the price of equivalent products that are sold in the market.

Adjusting for Price

When GNP goes up, it may be due to an increase in production or it may mean that the price of the output has gone up. We have already encountered this problem to some extent in the inventory valuation adjustment. In order that the measure of value not simply reflect a rise in price, GNP in current dollars is deflated by what is known as **implicit price deflator,** a weighted average of price changes in the four sectors which comprise GNP. This results in a measure of real output expressed in "constant dollars." The Commerce Department has been using 1958 as its constant dollar year for over a decade, but it is revising its estimate based on 1967. For example, GNP in 1972 was $1155.2 billion in 1972 current dollars but only $790.7 billion in constant 1958 dollars because the implicit price deflator is 146.1. Thus

$$\frac{\text{Current Dollars}}{\text{Price Deflator}} \text{ or } \frac{\$1155.2}{146.1} \text{ equals Constant Dollars } (\$790.7)$$

The implicit price deflator shows that if there had been no inflation since 1958, total GNP in 1972 would have been $790.7 billion. The GNP deflator is not the same thing as the consumer price index. The consumer price index starts with (i.e., uses for weights) the quantities of the *base year* included in the representative market basket and multiplies by current prices to get current cost of living, whereas the deflator starts with the *current* quantities and multiplies by base year prices to get real output.

Price comparisons can still be misleading, however; not only does the quality of goods change but also people's needs and wants change. Some commodities such as spats fall into oblivion while others such as dashikis appear. This problem is particularly troublesome when the proportion of measured to unmeasured activity changes over time. GNP does not include the value of home-produced goods and services but only the value of goods purchased by the household. It also does not include capital gains and losses on real estate, stocks, and the like or, perhaps most important, the market value of illegal activities. When state lotteries were introduced, millions of dollars that probably flowed into illegal (and uncounted) channels before then, suddenly appeared in government coffers and in the income accounts. GNP appeared to grow, when in fact the change was one of definition.

With the increase in working women, a similar transfer from uncounted to counted categories is occurring. If the output of housewives and volunteers were to be imputed, this would solve one problem of the shift between measured and nonmeasured sectors, but it would raise technical problems of how to value such services. The amounts involved are large, according to John Kendrick, who has been working on this problem for a number of years. Housewives' services would have increased GNP by more than 40 percent in 1929 and 20 percent in 1965. Volunteer activities in the same period grew more than 15 times in dollar value and would have more than doubled their importance to GNP (from .9 percent to 2.1 percent).[2]

Adjusting for Population

Even if the output of an economy measured in dollars is growing, the average citizen may not be increasingly well off if the population is growing faster than output. A bigger pie divided among more people may mean that everyone ends up with a smaller slice. To take into account the growth of population, output may be divided by the population to obtain real income per capita. The total real GNP for the United States in 1970 was $722.1 billion; per capita real income was $3,524, of which $2,603 was disposable income. In Latin America, GNP totaled $142.1 billion, or one-fifth of U.S. GNP; the per capita income was only $510 in 1970, or one-seventh of a U.S. citizen's. Measures of welfare based on the notion of per capita GNP assume that each person receives an equal share of national income. In a country where in 1972, 26 million people received less than what the Department of Labor considered a "minimum adequate income" ($4,275 for a family of four), it is clear that the per capita figure is a rough index at best, which should be adjusted to take account of the distribution of income.

Per capita GNP also fails to reflect growth needs. It assumes that all output is consumed at once, with no investment for following periods. The measure of net national product makes an allowance for capital needs, but as William Nordhaus and James Tobin indicate in a recent book which questions the adequacy of GNP as a measure of economic welfare, even this underestimates future capital needs as the population expands: "Per capita consumption cannot be sustained with zero net investment; the capital stock must be growing at the same rate as population and labor force." Tobin and Nordhaus distinguish between actual and sustainable measures of eco-

2. National Bureau of Economic Research, *47th Annual Report*, 1967, p. 11.

nomic output; the sustainable measure is "the amount that could be consumed while meeting both capital consumption and growth requirements."[3]

Environmental and Social Overhead: A Depreciation Issue

The costs of living in an urban environment—dry cleaning, carfare, tranquilizers—have been calculated by Tobin and Nordhaus. They see higher wages in urban areas as something close to combat pay, an incentive to put up with "urban disamenity." The difference between wages in cities and in smaller towns represents the costs of urban disamenity. They find that such costs do act as a drag on the growth of national income measures but not to the extent that many have feared.

A broader approach to the environment examines the social costs of industrialization, which include poisoning the environment, overloading it with wastes, and depleting natural resources. As GNP goes up, so does the burden on the environment. The deterioration and the expense of halting it can be seen as a form of depreciation analogous to the capital consumption allowance, and can be deducted to show the true costs of economic progress. For example, the C-111 project, a canal in southern Florida that would have transported barges to an Aerojet plant, would have increased Aerojet's contribution to GNP but would have upset the ecological balance of a large part of a major estuarine belt, whose waters hatch over 150 species of fish as well as other wildlife. The destruction of this habitat is surely worth more than simply the decline in the contribution of GNP in the Florida fishing industry that such a project would have caused. An environmental depreciation allowance, based on an imputed value of the lost services from a healthy environment, would decrease net national product and national income.

Another of the preconditions for production is a relatively stable, healthy society. But are the expenditures to maintain that society intermediate or final? Or less abstractly, should the accounts include missile silos, police gear, and sanitation trucks? Right now, they do; defense expenditures alone amount to nearly 6 percent of GNP.[4] But clearly Japan or Switzerland, who are covered by our nuclear umbrella and who devote only a minuscule amount to defense, are able to spend more resources on consumption and investment that provide consumer satisfaction and industrial vigor.

3. William Nordhaus and James Tobin, "Is Growth Obsolete?" in *Economic Growth*, Fiftieth Anniversary Colloquium V (New York: National Bureau of Economic Research, 1972), pp. 6–7. Note that this measure is similar to that of J. R. Hicks, referred to earlier, except that it adds the item "growth requirements" to the amount which must be netted out of GNP.

4. *Economic Report of the President January 1974*. GNP for 1973 was $1.29 trillion and national defense outlays were $74.2 billion. Other analysts would include more government expenditures in defense categories, raising the percentage further.

Commentary: Measuring the General Welfare

Article I, Section 8 of the Constitution states that "the Congress shall have power to lay and collect taxes . . . to . . . promote the general welfare of the United States." This clause has empowered the Congress to pass legislation establishing national economic and social policy in such areas as employment opportunities, civil rights, welfare, price control, regulation of trade and monopolies, and a vast array of other areas affecting every aspect of the economic and social life of the nation, together with the set of agencies and commissions which carry out these policies. Analysis of the effectiveness of any of these programs in improving the social or economic life of the country must surely begin with the programs' stated goals and then proceed to the issue of the relationship between those goals and the "general welfare."

The data used both to define the problem each program is designed to ameliorate and to determine program goals are taken primarily from the figures provided by the Departments of Commerce and Labor: specifically, the national income accounts, the U.S. censuses of population and housing, and the unemployment surveys taken by the Department of Labor. Goals are expressed in terms of increases in monetary incomes, taxes paid by beneficiaries of worker training programs, numbers of dwelling units constructed, etc. For example, the Economic Opportunity Act, which established the Office of Economic Opportunity (the "war on poverty") defined "poverty" purely in terms of family income, and defined the goals of the program in terms of increasing the monetary incomes of those families to a level above an arbitrarily defined "poverty line." (Not surprisingly perhaps, the long-term effectiveness of this act in helping poor families has been seriously questioned by administrators and participants alike.[1]) Although the general aim of these programs is to increase the "general welfare," that welfare is empirically defined purely in terms of monetary income. One tends, instinctively perhaps, to suspect that the actual aim of these programs and policies is more complex and less quantifiable. Policymakers are forced to use GNP and per capita income and housing units built as "proxies" for the real variables which make up the general welfare.

In a speech made a short time before his death, Senator Robert F. Kennedy protested that "the Gross National Product does not allow for the health of our youth, the quality of their education or the joy of their play. It does not include the beauty of our poetry or the strength of our marriages, the intelligence of our public debate or the integrity of our public officials. It measures neither our wit nor our . . . learning, neither our compassion nor our devotion to country. It measures everything, in short, except that which makes life worthwhile."[2]

Clearly Senator Kennedy was groping for some measurement which would tell him more about the state of the general welfare than that provided by the Gross National Product. In fact, of course, there is no way to measure "the beauty of our poetry" or the extent of the compassion of the American people, even though one may also feel, again instinctively, that these too are somehow components of the welfare which Congress is empowered to promote.

Surely what we are seeking is a middle course—a measure more inclusive than those provided by the national income accounts,

1. See Sar A. Levitan, *The Great Society* (Batlimore, Md.: Johns Hopkins, 1969) and Daniel P. Moynihan, *Maximum Feasible Misunderstanding* (Glencoe, Ill.: Free Press, 1969).
2. *The Times*, London, February 10, 1968.

but one which does not defy quantification under any circumstances. One approach to the problem is to broaden GNP by developing social correlations. Nancy and Richard Ruggles of the National Bureau of Economic Research have been synthesizing what they call a "micro data set" for the household sector, containing economic, social, and demographic characteristics. After merging the data from various sources, social scientists may be able to examine more precisely, for example, "the impact of inflation and unemployment on the income of households with different social and demographic characteristics."[3]

A broader search for a more comprehensive set of social indicators has been organized under the auspices of the Office of Management and Budget. "Social Indicators 1973" consists of a series of 165 charts designed to display trends in eight areas: health, public safety, education, employment, income, housing, leisure, and population. By starting from various generally accepted assumptions about what is desirable, the study charts what progress (or decline) has been experienced in each area. The objectives include good health, readily available medical care, long life, freedom from crime and fear of crime, the necessary education to make the most of one's abilities and play a full part in society, the opportunity to do a worthwhile job, enough money for life's necessities and the chance of earning more, a comfortable house, and leisure. In time, the hope is to find a measure of social progress which will become what the concept of Gross National Product is to economics.

Clearly, these are a step in the right direction, although they finesse the problem of defining the social progress in terms which can be directly susceptible to measurement. Thus, while the goals of various social and economic programs can be stated in terms of changes in these social indicators, it is virtually impossible to determine whether, in fact, the programs themselves have *caused* any of the changes discovered at a later period of time.

An example may be instructive; an increase in national or per capita income per se does not indicate whether the recipients of the increase had to work more hours to get it, or whether it was a result of increases in wages and/or other benefits, such as health insurance. The persons involved may have worked 60 hours a week (as is often the case in the automobile industry at the beginning of the production year) or 35 hours a week (civil servants in the city of Detroit, for example). Thus, an increase in the gross national income of Detroiters may reflect a reduction in the amount of leisure among some, an increase in leisure among others (an automobile worker going to work for the city), or no change at all.

Certainly, an increase in total income of Detroiters is an increase in their general welfare—there can be little argument with the idea that increases in income provide the potential for increases in the amount and perhaps in the quality of education, health care, and other benefits available to the population at large.[4] On the other hand, a given increase in income accompanied by a reduction in total leisure time available to the population results in a lower increase in that welfare than that same increase in income provides when there is no reduction in leisure time available.

Leisure time can be estimated by comparing per capita income with income per hour worked; an increase in per capita income unaccompanied by an increase in income per hour worked (wage rate) is obviously an indicator of a decrease in leisure. Data are available which would enable one to make an estimate of the total change in leisure for the workers in Detroit's automobile plants over a given period of time, and some data are available which would make it possible to estimate

3. National Bureau of Economic Research, *53rd Annual Report*, September 1973, p. 47.

4. Thus, the low rate of increase in GNP during the late 1950s was an issue in the 1960 presidential campaign, precisely because the national income (and thus taxes paid) had not been growing rapidly enough to permit needed improvements in the educational, health, and welfare systems of the country.

these changes for other workers in the Detroit area. Thus, some indication of the change in the general welfare of Detroiters due to the combination of changes in income and changes in leisure could be computed. An estimate of the total value of leisure has also been made by James Tobin and William Nordhaus.[5] This values leisure at $90.1 billion in 1929 (when current-dollar GNP was $103.1 billion) and at $775.5 billion in 1965 (when current-dollar GNP was $684.9 billion). The implication of this is that leisure grew more rapidly than total output.

Many other components of the general welfare do not allow such immediate computation. The quality of working conditions is an example; it is surely difficult to argue with the proposition that a worker whose safety and health is endangered by his job is worse off than one for whom this is not the case. It is equally sure that an improvement in working conditions is an improvement in the quality of life. Unfortunately this is a difficult improvement to measure, although efforts have been made. For example, Robin C. O. Matthews has suggested the development of a "hedonic price index" which would measure the improvement (or deterioration) in working conditions.[6]

In general, then, measurement of the "general welfare" requires the development of a definition of the term and a set of quantifiable indicators of social progress over time. Ultimately it may also be possible to develop ways of determining the effect upon such progress of particular social and economic programs and policies.

5. "Is Growth Obsolete?" in *Economic Growth*, Fiftieth Anniversary Colloquium V (New York: National Bureau of Economic Research, 1972).

6. "Discussion," in *Economic Growth*, p. 89.

One alternative way of looking at these expenditures for defense and public safety is to classify them as regrettable necessities, a form of social overhead that represents an intermediate output in the production of a stable society. This is the approach of Tobin and Nordhaus, who find that such expenditures rose in importance from 8 percent of GNP in 1929 to 16 percent in 1965. (Another approach is that of Kenneth Boulding, who maintains that our military stance encourages the likelihood of nuclear war and half-seriously suggests that such a cost should somehow be deducted from our national product.)

Tobin and Nordhaus have reclassified the remaining government expenditures as consumption and investment, a change that is seconded by many but has not been adopted by the Department of Commerce. Under investment come such items as education, public housing, and mass transportation expenditures.

A New Account?

The sum of the changes by Tobin and Nordhaus produces a new kind of account, what they call the measure of economic welfare (MEW). Economist Paul Samuelson promptly renamed it NEW, net economic welfare, a name that has stuck. NEW is a measure not of production but of the annual real consumption of households. It adjusts for price changes, population, urban costs, and technological change, and includes leisure and nonmarket activities. Table 3.3 shows that these adjustments raise the size of national economic activity appreciably, and also shows that GNP or NNP have grown faster than NEW.

The question posed by such changes is: Is GNP to be a measure of production, as it has traditionally been designed to be, or is it to be considered a measure of welfare? However laudable studies of the value of leisure or housewives' time may be, they may simply not belong in a measure whose reliability is founded on the ready signal of exchange value price. Moreover, such changes would deceive people into believing welfare could be measured by GNP.[5] The real objection to changing GNP, however, is not simply conceptual but practical: experimenting with alternatives and adjustments is extremely costly.[6]

The Sector Accounts

GNP measures expenditures on national product but does not look at that part of income that is not spent, namely saving. Breaking income and expenditure down into four sector accounts—business, personal, government, and foreign—enables us to look at GNP in terms of income and product

5. Arthur N. Okun, "Social Welfare Has No Price Tag," *Survey of Current Business* 51 (July 1953): 129.
6. Simon Kuznets, "The Penalties of Success," ibid., p. 115.

Table 3.3 Comparing GNP, NNP, and MEW (billions of 1958 dollars)

		1929	1954	1958	1965
1.	Gross national product	203.6	407.0	447.3	617.8
2.	Capital consumption	−20.0	−32.5	−38.9	−54.7
3.	Net national product	183.6	374.5	408.4	563.1
4.	Regrettables and intermediates[a]				
	a. Government	−6.7	−57.8	−56.4	−63.2
	b. Private	−10.3	−16.4	−19.9	−30.9
5.	Imputations for items not included in GNP				
	a. Leisure	339.5	523.2	554.9	626.9
	b. Nonmarket activity	85.7	211.5	239.7	295.4
	c. Disamenities	−12.5	−24.3	−27.6	−34.6
	d. Services of public and private capital	29.7	48.9	54.8	78.9
6.	Additional capital consumption	−19.3	−35.2	−27.3	−92.7
7.	Growth requirement	−46.1	−63.1	−78.9	−101.8
8.	Sustainable MEW	543.6	961.3	1047.7	1241.1
9.	NNP per capita (actual dollars)	1545.0	2305.0	2335.0	2897.0
10.	Sustainable MEW per capita (actual dollars)[b]	4462.0	5898.0	5991.0	6378.0

SOURCE: William Nordhaus and James Tobin, "Is Growth Obsolete?" in *Economic Growth*, Fiftieth Anniversary Colloquium V (New York: National Bureau of Economic Research, 1972), p. 12.

a. Government regrettables and intermediates include all outlays using resources for purposes "other than consumption or capital formation supportive of future consumption," such as national defense, business subsidies, and police protection. Personal intermediates include personal or business expenses plus one-fifth of personal transportation expenses for commutation.

b. Assumes leisure has not been augmented by technological progress but other nonmarket activities have.

originating in each sector and to examine the role of saving directly. Using the sector accounts, we can also examine the flow of transfer payments excluded from the GNP account. Refer to the numbers in parentheses following each entry in Table 3.4: those preceded by a letter indicate items of counterentry within the sector accounts; those not preceded by a letter refer to items in the GNP Account, Table 3.2.

The Business Sector

The business sector comprises the more than 10 million proprietorships and partnerships, the 2 million corporations, the more than 15,000 banks and other financial institutions, the close to 2,000 life insurance companies, plus government enterprises like the Post Office and the municipal water and sewage system—in short, all organizations producing goods and services at a price intended to cover the costs of production.

The business sector retains part of its funds as savings. Although gross business saving is not an entry on either the sector or GNP account, it can be derived from their entries. The capital consumption allowances, undistributed profits, and inventory adjustment together form the bulk of gross business saving. Because so much of the activity in the modern economy is derived from these businesses the total amounts of the various entries are close to, and in some cases identical with, the corresponding statistics in the national income and GNP accounts. For this reason, the Commerce Department no longer compiles a separate account for the business sector.

The Personal Sector

The personal sector represents both the single largest market for the business sector's product and the single largest recipient of its expenditures, in the form of corporate wages, salaries, and dividends. Furthermore, the personal sector receives payments from the government, both of interest and social security benefits, and also pays the government taxes. Being a type of payment for which goods and services are not exchanged, transfers are not considered productive income and as such are not listed as part of the GNP. Still, they represent an important source to the personal sector. The sum of the right-hand side of Table 3.4A constitutes personal income which is spent on the three general categories of consumption, savings, and taxes, represented in the left-hand column. More precisely, personal outlays include: total personal taxes, wage payments (primarily by non-profit institutions), personal consumption expenditures made to the business and foreign sectors, and interest paid by consumers. Subtracting expenditures from personal income leaves personal savings.

The Government Sector

Table 3.4B shows the national income accounts' summary of government receipts and expenditures. The activities of agencies like the Post Office, which offers a marketable service, are not included except for subsidies they receive or surpluses they add to the government treasury. When purchases, transfers, interest, subsidies/surpluses are deducted from receipts of the government, the residual is the government's surplus or deficit. This residual is equivalent to saving or dissaving in the other sectors. This account must be distinguished from the federal budget. Because the consolidated government account includes state and local units, it eliminates intergovernmental transfers, a substantial item that is growing with the advent of revenue sharing. The consolidated account is also calculated on a calendar year rather than the July 1–June 30 fiscal year used by the federal government. The deficit and surplus on the national income account is therefore different from the federal deficit or surplus that has such a large effect on fiscal policy.

Table 3.4   Sector Accounts (billions of dollars)

A. Personal Income and Outlay Account, 1972			
1. Personal tax (G10)	142.2	7. Wages and salary	627.8
2. Personal outlays	747.2	8. Other labor income	40.7
3. Personal consumption expenditures (18)	726.5	9. Proprietors' income (4)	74.2
		10. Rental income of persons (5)	24.1
4. Interest paid by consumers (P15)	19.7	11. Dividends (9)	26.0
		12. Personal interest income	78.0
5. Personal transfer payments to foreigners (net) (F5)	1.0	13. Net interest (12)	45.2
6. Personal saving (IS3)	49.7	14. Net interest paid by government (G5)	13.0
		15. Interest paid by consumers (P4)	19.7
		16. Transfer payments to persons	103.0
		17. From business (14)	4.6
		18. From government (G3)	98.3
		19. Less: Personal contributions for social insurance (G15)	34.7
PERSONAL TAXES, OUTLAYS, AND SAVINGS	939.2	PERSONAL INCOME	939.2

C. Foreign Transactions Account, 1972			
1. Exports of goods and services (29)	73.5	3. Imports of goods and services (30)	78.1
2. Capital grants received by the U.S. (IS10)	.7	4. Transfer payments from U.S. Government to foreigners (net) (G4)	2.7
		5. Personal transfer payments to foreigners (net) (P5)	1.0
		6. Net foreign investment (IS2)	7.6
RECEIPTS FROM FOREIGNERS	74.2	PAYMENTS TO FOREIGNERS	74.2

The Foreign Sector

When U.S. firms buy or build overseas subsidiaries, they derive profits which add to the profits of the parent companies. If foreign companies establish subsidiaries in the United States, the employees they hire locally receive wages which add to the flow of personal income in the United States. Although such flows represent only a very small proportion of total activities, and could be consolidated as items in other sector accounts, they involve a somewhat different mechanism of exchange and receive their own account.

The foreign sector's current transactions are presented in Table 3.4C. On the left-hand side are listed the various sources of income to the United

B. Government Receipts and Expenditures Account, 1972

1.	Purchases of goods and services (31)	255.0	10.	Personal tax (P1)	142.2
2.	Transfer payments	101.1	11.	Corporate profits tax liability (8)	42.7
3.	To persons (P18)	98.3	12.	Indirect business tax (15)	109.5
4.	To foreigners (net) (F4)	2.7	13.	Contributions for social insurance	73.7
5.	Net interest paid (P14)	13.0	14.	Employer	39.0
6.	Subsidies less current surplus of government enterprises	1.7	15.	Personal (P19)	34.7
7.	Surplus or deficit (−) (IS9)	−2.8			
8.	Federal	−15.9			
9.	State and local	13.1			
	GOVERNMENT EXPENDITURES AND SURPLUS	368.2		GOVERNMENT RECEIPTS	368.2

D. Gross Saving and Investment Account, 1972

1.	Gross private domestic investment (22)	178.3	3.	Personal saving (P6)	49.7
2.	Net foreign investment (F6)	−7.6	4.	Gross business saving	124.4
			5.	Undistributed corporate profits (10)	29.3
			6.	Inventory valuation adjustment (11)	−6.9
			7.	Capital consumption allowances (16)	102.4
			8.	Government surplus or deficit (−) (G7)	−2.8
			9.	Capital grants received by the U.S. (F2)	.7
			10.	Statistical discrepancy (17)	−1.5
	GROSS INVESTMENT	170.6		GROSS SAVING AND STATISTICAL DISCREPANCY	170.6

SOURCE: U.S. Department of Commerce, *Survey of Current Business* 53 (July 1973), Table A.

States; on the right-hand side are listed the various categories of U.S. expenditures abroad. Imports of goods and services includes not only the purchase domestically of foreign goods, but also the expenditures of U.S. tourists overseas. Transfer payments refers to the payment made with no product or service received in exchange, which are therefore ignored in the GNP account. In this case, it means both personal and governmental forms of international assistance, from CARE packages to U.S. government economic and military aid.

The category of the net foreign investment on the left side of the account is analogous to the category of gross business saving in the business sector account, of personal saving in the personal sector accounts, and of surplus

Table 3.5   Balance of Payments Summary 1953–1973 (billions of dollars)

(Credits + Debits −)	1935	1937	1939	1946	1950	1955	1958	1965	1968	1970	1971	1972	1973
1. Current account													
Exports	3.3	4.6	4.4	14.9	14.4	22.5	25.5	41.0	50.7	62.9	66.3	73.5	102.0
Imports	−3.1	−4.3	−3.4	−7.0	−12.0	−17.8	−20.9	−32.3	−48.2	−59.3	−65.5	−78.1	−96.2
Balance	0.2	0.3	1.0	7.9	2.4	4.7	4.6	8.7	3.3	3.6	0.8	−4.6	5.8
2. Capital account													
U.S. private capital	—	—	—	−0.6	−1.3	−1.3	−2.9	−3.8	−5.4	−6.9	−10.1	−8.5	
Foreign capital	—	—	—	−1.0	1.9	1.4	1.3	0.4	9.4	5.9	22.5	20.8	
Balance	1.5	0.9	1.5	−1.6	0.6	0.1	−1.6	−3.4	−4.0	−1.0	12.4	12.3	
3. Unilateral transfers													
Private	—	—	—	−0.7	−0.5	−0.5	−0.6	−0.7	−0.8	−1.0	−1.0	−1.0	
U.S. government (net)	—	—	—	−5.3	−4.2	−4.9	−5.0	−5.4	−7.3	−6.4	−7.6	−8.5	
Balance	−0.2	−0.2	−0.2	−6.0	−4.7	−5.4	−5.6	−6.1	−8.1	−7.4	−8.6	−9.5	
4. Errors and omissions	0.4	0.4	0.8	0.2	−0.2	0.4	0.4	−0.6	−0.8	−1.2	−10.8	−3.1	
5. U.S. official reserves													
(increase −)	−1.9	−1.4	−3.1	−0.5	1.9	0.2	2.2	1.3	−0.9	2.5	2.3	0ª	0.2

SOURCE: U.S. Department of Commerce, *Survey of Current Business* 53 (June 1973), Table 2; 54 (February 1974), Table 12.
a.   Less than $50 million.

or deficit in the governmental sector account. In all cases, the category represents a sum needed to account for the difference between expenditure and income.

The foreign transactions sector of the national income and product account should not be confused with the balance of payments account, also published by the Commerce Department. The foreign transactions account deals only with U.S. exports, imports, and transfers. The balance of payments account, shown in Table 3.5, adds to that a category of capital transactions (building plants abroad or buying foreign stocks and bonds relative to foreign investment in the United States) in order to obtain a comprehensive statement reflecting the overall net change in the nation's purchases (or sales) of goods, securities, real investment, transfers, and services with regard to the rest of the world. The net result is reflected in changes in monetary reserves, or in the case of the United States, changes in borrowing from foreign central banks. Since early 1973 it has become an accepted practice to allow large reserve changes to signal the need for a change in the relative prices of national monies. This "floating" exchange rate system will be discussed in Chapter 18. The final entry represents the net position of all these flows—trade, capital, and transfers.

Saving and Investment Account

The fifth sector account is intended to show how gross saving, or the income not consumed, equates to gross investment, or the product not consumed. Table 3.4D demonstrates how the four previous sectors interrelate by taking from each the "balancing" item which served to show how much that particular segment of the economy had augmented (or decreased) the capital stock of the economy as a whole.

Actual investment is summed up on the left-hand side of Table 3.4D, consisting of net foreign investment, and gross domestic private investment.

The right side of the ledger is composed of the saving items identified in each sector account: personal saving and gross business saving, government surplus or deficit, and statistical discrepancy. The gross saving and investment account, like those of each individual sector, is intended to balance— without the addition of a specific "balancing" item. (Actually, inventory accumulations act to balance out the two, increasing when saving is high and spending is low, but declining when saving decreases and spending picks up.) When this balance is achieved, income equals expenditure and investment equals savings, the conditions of equilibrium in the national economy.

Income Identities

The flows we have been working with can be readily summed up in a few mathematical statements. First of all, we have seen that expenditure (GNP) equals consumption (C), plus gross private domestic investment (I), plus government purchases (G), plus exports minus imports $(X - M)$. In the following section we will assume for the purposes of our model that the economy is closed, that is, exclusive of foreign trade, so that $X - M = 0$ and therefore $GNP = C + I + G$. (If we want to make this net, we subtract depreciation, D, from GNP, or $Y = GNP - D$.)

We also know that the flow in the left-hand account goes either to individuals as disposable income, Y_d, to government as personal, corporate, or indirect business taxes, T, or to business as undistributed profits, a form of business savings, S_b. Since both sides of the GNP account are equal

$$\text{Income side} = \text{Expenditure side}$$

$$Y_d + T + S_b = C + I + G \tag{3.2}$$

Further, disposable income (Y_d) is either saved (S_p) or consumed (C); that is, $Y_d = C + S_p$, so that

$$C + S_p + T + S_b = C + I + G \tag{3.3}$$

Consolidating private savings (S_p) and business savings (S_b) we may write $S = S_p + S_b$, so that

$$C + S + T = C + I + G \tag{3.4}$$

Subtracting C from both sides of (3.4) leaves

$$S + T = I + G \tag{3.5}$$

which states that income equals expenditure if total income-related leakages out of expenditure $(S + T)$ equal total non-income-related injections of expenditure $(I + G)$.

Finally, with no government sector, or one that never runs a surplus or deficit, the simplest equilibrium condition with G = T = 0 is:

$$S = I \qquad (3.6)$$

This equation seems straightforward, but it contains no hint of how the two sides operate. If both sides respond to the same thing (or more formally, are functions of the same variable), the two can be brought into line by a change in that variable. If the two are functions of different variables, then bringing them into line is more complex. Two main schools of economics are based on that difference in interpretation (among other things). The classical school held that saving and investment are both functions of the interest rate and would therefore be automatically equated by changes in the interest rate. The Keynesian school, on the other hand, believes that savers and investors are two different groups. Savers base their decisions on the amount of income they have, whereas investors calculate their return against the prevailing interest rate. The implications and theoretical bases of this macroeconomic debate can be explored only over a series of chapters, and Parts II and III will unfold the argument in its entirety.

Questions and Exercises

1. If we counted up all the transactions in an economy, the figure would be far higher than GNP. How can this be if GNP measures the economy's output?
2. Many Americans buy a new car every year or two—or at least they did before the "energy crisis"—and planned obsolescence is a part of the marketing strategy for many consumer durables. What would happen to GNP if such goods were treated as part of investment? What would happen to NNP?
3. Which of the following would contribute to the GNP account:
     Receipts of a state lottery
     Receipts from the numbers racket
     Dividends from AT&T stock
     Proceeds from the sale of AT&T stock
     Rent paid to a landlord by a business firm
     Rent paid to a landlord by a person
     Implicit services furnished by owner-occupied dwellings
     Implicit services furnished by housewives
   Explain the reasons for inclusion or exclusion.
4. In Alphabetania and Betabetania gross private domestic investment is the same—$50 billion. Alphabetania, however, has a net investment of $45 billion whereas its neighbor has $32 billion in net investment. Calculate the capital consumption allowances for each nation. Which one probably has newer plants and machinery? If both countries have the same GNP and GPDI this year, why is one likely to grow faster than the other in subsequent years?
5. Calculate the value added at each stage of production and the final contribution to GNP. (Assume that any other intermediate costs are final costs for this exercise.)

Value added

A ton of iron ore is mined and sold to a steel mill for $50. _____
The mill produces sheet metal from the iron ore and sells it
to an auto body manufacturer for $125. The auto body manu- _____
facturer shapes it into the body of a Vega and sells it to a
Chevrolet plant for $250. Chevrolet makes a Vega and sells it _____
to a dealer for $2000. The dealer puts the Vega in his show- _____
room and sells it to a teenager for $2500. What is the total _____
contribution to GNP of these transactions? _____

Would GNP increase if the student used the car for a summer job, then sold the
car in the fall for $2000 to get money for college tuition? Explain.

6. During the Depression real GNP (based on 1958 prices) was higher than the
actual GNP dollar level. Today the opposite is true. Explain why.

7. Deflators may be calculated for the components of GNP as well as total GNP.
Calculate the real value of personal consumption using the following data:

Year	Personal consumption	Deflator	Real personal consumption
1929	$ 77.2 billion	55.3	_____
1933	45.8	40.6	_____
1943	99.3	59.9	_____
1953	230.0	91.7	_____
1963	375.0	106.1	_____
1972	726.5	137.9	_____

8. In 1973 the price deflators for the components of personal consumption were
durables 114.5, nondurables 146.8, and services 160.0. In which sector was
inflation greatest? If services are a rapidly growing component of GNP (and they
are), what are the prospects for controlling inflation?

9. For every dollar of gross income not spent on the purchase of final goods and
services there is a dollar of final goods left unconsumed. Explain this proposition using the income identities in the chapter.

10. Here is an abbreviated account for the personal sector:

Personal taxes	100	Compensation	500
Personal outlays	530	Proprietors' income	45
Personal saving	40	Rental income	20
		Dividends	20
		Personal interest	50
		Transfer payments	60
		Less: Social	
		insurance contributions	25
Total:	670		670

What is the personal income level in this economy? What is the level of disposable income?

[illegible] Tobacco products (n.d.c.)	[illegible]	[illegible]	[illegible]	[illegible]	[illegible]	[illegible]	[illegible]	[illegible]	[illegible]	[illegible]	[illegible]	[illegible]	[illegible]	[illegible]	[illegible]	[illegible]
Clothing, accessories, and jewelry	11,193	9,713	8,217	6,042	5,438	6,562	7,010	7,661	8,092	7,991	8,406	8,852	10,509	13,061	15,993	17,466
1. Shoes and other footwear (n.d.c.).	1,675	1,375	1,207	1,022	887	1,072	1,031	1,145	1,279	1,257	1,226	1,265	1,446	1,793	1,872	1,958
2. Shoe cleaning and repair (s.)	164	141	114	100	98	102	106	113	122	118	114	[illegible]	[illegible]	[illegible]	223	218
3. Clothing and accessories except footwear.[3]	7,682	6,659	5,713	4,022	3,731	4,585	4,982	5,403	5,546	5,495	5,893	[illegible]	[illegible]	[illegible]	[illegible]	[illegible]
a. Women's and children's (n.d.c.).	4,662	4,100	3,528	2,446	2,254	2,801	3,080	3,226	3,277	3,337	3,607	[illegible]	[illegible]	[illegible]	6,940	[illegible]
b. Men's and boys' (n.d.c.)	3,020	2,559	2,185	1,576	1,477	1,784	1,902	2,177	2,269	2,158	2,286	[illegible]	[illegible]			
4. Standard clothing issued to military personnel (n.d.c.).	12	11	9	10	11	7	9	12	13	14	16	32	[illegible]19			
5. Cleaning, dyeing, pressing, alteration, storage, and repair of garments including furs (in shops) not elsewhere classified (s.).	473	420	352	252	230	265	302	339	383	391	397	423	492			
6. Laundering in establishments (s.).	475	458	392	310	252	262	272	304	323	308	312	340	397			
7. Jewelry and watches (d.c.)	560	513	328	252	172	198	233	265	333	323	355	409	550			
8. Other[4] (s.)	152	136	102	74	57	71	75	80	93	85	93	106	131			
Personal care	1,116	1,039	979	817	660	760	802	864	961	951	1,004	1,036	1,162			
1. Toilet articles and preparations (n.d.c.).	591	515	504	420	320	377	374	395	428	442	486	507	607			
2. Barbershops, beauty parlors, and baths (s.).	525	524	475	397	340	383	428	469	533	509	518	529	555			
Housing	11,530	11,050	10,291	9,011	7,907	7,602	7,702	8,011	8,533	8,936	9,139	9,446	10,167			
1. Owner-occupied nonfarm dwellings—space-rental value[5] (s.).	5,868	5,552	5,101	4,416	3,844	3,643	3,646	3,759	3,950	4,104	4,179	4,310	4,706			
2. Tenant-occupied nonfarm dwellings (including lodging houses)—space rent[5] (s.).	4,500	4,397	4,200	3,753	3,296	3,158	3,199	3,365	3,639	3,870	3,994	4,154	4,438			
3. Rental value of farmhouses (s.)	913	865	775	664	614	640	683	693	733	745	741	744	767			
4. Other[6] (s.)	249	236	215	178	153	161	174	194	211	217	225	238	256			
Household operation	10,735	9,585	8,425	6,779	6,466	7,209	7,737	8,821	9,525	8,865	9,624	10,479	11,951			
1. Furniture, including mattresses and bedsprings (d.c.).	1,201	937	796	509	462	514	666	848	923	827	949	1,060	1,320			
2. Kitchen and other household appliances[7] (d.c.).	768	671	565	344	408	518	614	[illegible]	845	711	774	881	1,158			
3. China, glassware, tableware, and utensils (d.c.).	628	442	429	406	364	404	407	[illegible]	[illegible]	[illegible]	475	510	623			
4. Other durable house furnishings[8] (d.c.).	1,148	937	783	562	472	573	617	827	[illegible]	[illegible]	[illegible]	991	1,214			
5. Semidurable house furnishings[9] (n.d.c.).	717	570	497	374	391	449	478	591	639	568	[illegible]	[illegible]	913			
6. Cleaning and polishing preparations, and miscellaneous household supplies and paper products (n.d.c.).	485	471	419	328	332	386	403	449	488	485	508	[illegible]	[illegible]			
7. Stationery and writing supplies (n.d.c.).	143	133	103	71	69	87	101	112	131	129	149	162	191			
8. Household utilities	3,044	3,058	2,844	2,615	2,561	2,729	2,792	2,979	3,042	2,971	3,128	3,391	3,582			
a. Electricity (s.)	616	660	674	662	645	671	697	726	766	810	849	910	965			
b. Gas (s.)	542	560	556	537	495	494	503	516	528	523	538	573	575			
c. Water and other sanitary services (s.).	278	296	296	278	269	301	311	326	331	327	343	359	368			
d. Other fuel and ice (n.d.c.)	1,608	1,542	1,318	1,138	1,152	1,263	1,281	1,411	1,417	1,311	1,398	1,549	1,674			
9. Telephone and telegraph (s.)	569	577	554	482	436	443	472	511	542	542	576	615	695			
10. Domestic service (s.)	1,716	1,483	1,146	835	732	850	911	1,016	1,187	1,023	1,129	1,218	1,237			
11. Other[10] (s.)	316	306	289	253	239	256	276	299	328	337	347	358	411			
Medical care expenses	2,937	2,835	2,549	2,127	1,983	2,164	2,288	2,493	2,672	2,68[illegible]						
1. Drug preparations and sundries (n.d.c.).[11]	604	568	517	449	427	468	474	509	558	57[illegible]						
2. Ophthalmic products and orthopedic appliances (d.c.).	131	133	117	93	92	124	131	140	165	15[illegible]						
3. Physicians (s.)	959	924	819	661	617	678	731	820	854	83[illegible]						
4. Dentists (s.)	482	463	408	312	276	295	302	331	350	35[illegible]						
5. Other professional services[12] (s.).	250	233	201	154	138	145	151	165	168	16[illegible]						
6. Privately controlled hospitals and sanitariums[13] (s.).	403	404	395	386	363	369	406	422	454	46[illegible]						
7. Health insurance	108	110	92	72	70	85	93	106	123	13[illegible]						
a. Medical care and hospitalization (s.).[14]																
b. Income loss (s.)																
Personal business	4,158	3,704	3,311	2,875	2,832	2,860	3,043	3,231	3,430	3,26[illegible]						
1. Brokerage charges and investment counseling (s.).	756	495	318	224	340	195	213	263	243	17[illegible]						
2. Bank service charges, trust services, and safe-deposit box rental (s.).	76	79	80	78	79	92	104	116	126	13[illegible]						
3. Services furnished without payment by financial intermediaries except insurance companies (s.).	1,278	1,141	1,017	872	757	793	792	843	876	81[illegible]						
4. Expense of handling life insurance[15] (s.).	874	901	[illegible]	[illegible]	[illegible]	[illegible]	[illegible]	[illegible]	1,025	1,00[illegible]						
5. Legal services (s.)	40[illegible]	[illegible]	[illegible]	[illegible]	[illegible]	359	371	[illegible]	[illegible]	[illegible]						
6. Funeral and burial expenses (s.).	[illegible]	[illegible]	[illegible]	415	387	[illegible]	[illegible]	[illegible]	[illegible]	[illegible]						
7. Other[16]	165	144	[illegible]	[illegible]	[illegible]	[illegible]	[illegible]	160	250	26[illegible]						

Incomes reflect a spotty picture

[illegible] producing industries, where manufacturing employment and average hourly earnings declined. The declines were especially marked in the trans[portation] equipment industries, victi[mized] by both the trucking strike and [the] fuel crisis.

C[urrent spen]ding on consumer durables, which had shown a very sizable increase in the first quarter of 1973 and had remained essentially flat for the next six months, declined in the fourth quarter by $6 billion. Expenditures on passenger cars plummeted $7.1 billion (see table), a decline comparable in both current dollar and real terms to the drop that occurred during the auto strike of three years ago. Although some slowing in the pace of new car sales was widely anticipated well in advance of the launching of the 1974 models, the magnitude of the decline has surpassed most expectations. The Arab oil embargo and accompanying uncertainties as to the availability and cost of gasoline have taken their toll on the auto industry. They have not only weakened the demand for new cars beyond the amount of slippage that might otherwise have occurred, but have also precipitated a strong shift toward smaller vehicles. However, parts shortages and capacity limitations have constrained the production of smaller cars both at home and abroad and lengthened delivery times. Consequently, sales of new passenger cars—domestic types and imports combined—dropped from the record [an]nual rate of 12.6 million units reached this past March to a seasonally adjusted annual rate of 9.6 million units in December. In January, sales of new domestic cars, which had been at a seasonally adjusted annual rate of 7.9 million units in December, slipped to 7.7 million units. This compares with a fourth-quarter average of 8.4 million.

Measure of Labor Earnings

Personal income for February

State and region	February 1974	February 1973	Percent change versus year ago	Year to date	Percent change versus year ago
Millions of dollars (not adjusted for seasonal variations)					
NEW ENGLAND	$ 5,475	$ 5,067	+ 8.1%	$ 11,037	+ 8.6%
Connecticut	1,526	1,465	+ 4.2	3,129	+ 6.7
Maine	363	325	+11.7	725	+11.7
Massachusetts	2,695	2,464	+ 9.4	5,416	+ 9.1
New Hampshire	300	271	+10.7	597	+11.0
Rhode Island	420	390	+ 7.7	834	+ 7.3
Vermont	171	152	+12.5	336	+12.4
M[I]DDLE ATLANTIC	17,973	16,588	+ 8.3	35,908	+ 8.4
[Ne]w Jersey	3,748	3,415	+ 9.8	7,466	+ 9.4
New York	9,109	8,461	+ 7.7	18,204	+ 7.7
[Pe]nnsylvania	5,116	4,712	+ 8.6	10,238	+ 8.8
SOUTH ATLANTIC	13,460	11,937	+12.8	26,992	+14.5
Delaware	280	270	+ 3.7	558	+ 3.3
Dist. of Columbia	447	406	+10.1	896	+ 9.9
Florida	3,378	2,992	+12.9	6,763	+13.9
Georgia	1,864	1,637	+13.9	3,748	+16.4
Maryland	1,918	1,755	+ 9.3	3,844	+10.2
North Carolina	1,943	1,712	+13.5	3,902	+17.6
South Carolina	944	798	+18.3	1,894	+20.8
Virginia	2,065	1,808	+14.2	4,139	+16.2
West Virginia	621	559	+11.1	1,248	+16.2
EAST NORTH CENTRAL	18,586	17,382	+ 6.9	37,262	+ 7.5
Illinois	5,550	5,084	+ 9.2	11,118	+ 9.3
Indiana	2,304	2,116	+ 8.9	4,636	+ 9.8
Michigan	4,127	4,053	+ 1.8	8,241	+ 2.9
Ohio	4,702	4,398	+ 6.9	9,467	+ 7.4
Wisconsin	1,903	1,731	+ 9.9	3,800	+10.5
EAST SOUTH CENTRAL	4,539	4,087	+11.1	9,176	+12.4
Alabama	1,205	1,075	+12.1	2,415	+12.6
Kentucky	1,160	1,069	+ 8.5	2,372	+ 9.3
Mississippi	684	623	+ 9.8	1,415	+13.7

Consumer Debt Climbed a Bit in January, But Rise Was Sharply Below Year Ago's

By a WALL STREET J[OURNAL Staff Reporter]

WASHINGT[ON]—Consumer debt [a]ccelerated sl[ightly] in January from the slim [D]ecember increase, the Federal Reserve [B]oard reported.

Total consumer borrowing in January rose [a] seasonally adjusted $790 million, the board [sa]id, exceeding December's $704 million in[c]rease—the smallest in two years—but far be[hi]nd the $2.1 billion rise of January 1973.

Reserve Board analysts said that, despite [th]e pickup, the credit picture was still "fairly [we]ak" in January. "It wasn't a strong month," [d]eclared one analyst, who said the big decline [in] auto sales in recent months continues to af[fe]ct consumer borrowing.

Installment credit outstanding in January [ro]se an adjusted $917 million, with most of the [ri]se in nonautomotive consumer goods and per[so]nal loans. Auto credit edged up an adjusted [5]9 million after declining $23 million in De[cember] [illegible]

[illegible] [ch]arg[e] [ac]count balances and single-payment loans, fell an adjusted $127 million in January, the first such decline since September and the biggest drop since February 1972, when such credit slid $195 million.

Both extensions and repayments of consumer installment credit increased in January after falling in December. New extensions rose to an adjusted $13.71 billion from December's $12.68 billion, while repayments increased to $12.80 billion from $12.27 billion.

At the end of January, installment and non-installment consumer debt combined totaled $178.69 billion, up $21.46 billion from the year-earlier figure.

Short-term and intermediate-term consumer credit outstanding (estimates in millions of dollars):

Type of Credit	Jan. 31 1974	Change from Prev. Month Adj.	Change from Prev. Month Unad.	Change from Year Earlier
Installment cred. total	146,575	+ 917	− 862	+19,207
Automobile	50,617	+ 59	− 513	+ 6,264
Other consumer goods	47,303	+ 469	− 227	+ 7,351

Income Determination Model

4

The national income accounts in the preceding chapter introduced the concept of economic activity from which a flow of income is received and expenditures made. It is possible to examine or measure the total output of an economy either in terms of the expenditures that are made to purchase that output or in terms of the earnings or incomes that are derived in the process of turning it out. In both cases the same output is being measured, and it is clear that the value of national output measured as income must always equal the value of national output measured as expenditures, when savings equals investment, or if a government sector is included, when savings plus taxes equal investment plus government expenditure.

In any economy, there will be an infinite number of levels of output where $Y = E$ may hold, and in the next two chapters we will attempt to go behind the savings-investment equality condition and discover what determines the particular level of national output at which an economy will settle and how changes in this level come about. This chapter begins with an analysis of a very simple private-sector model, which includes only expenditures and income items within the private sector. The only variable affecting expenditure at this stage will be income. In Chapter 5 we will add the government sector, in which the effects of government spending, taxes, and transfer payments are added to the private sector spending and incomes, and later we will further expand our model to include exports and imports.

From our analysis of national income accounts in Chapter 3, we saw that the identity $Y = E$ can be broken down into the components of Y and E. In a private-sector economy, there are two groups who receive income. One group either uses its income for consumption spending or saves it. This group is normally composed of individuals and spends less than it earns. The other group, the business sector, may decide to invest and temporarily spend more than it earns. Total income is thus composed of either consumption or savings, whereas total expenditure is composed of either consumption spending or investment. Two equations summarize these concepts:

$$Y = C + S$$

and

$$E = C + I$$

It is the individual components of these equations—C, S, and I—that provide the key to understanding how the aggregates—income and expenditures—are determined and the conditions under which they can change.

The Consumption Function

The analysis presented here of the behavior of consumption is based largely on the work of John Maynard Keynes. In Chapter 6 this analysis will be modified, but it provides a convenient starting point. Keynes assumed that every individual needs a certain minimum level of expenditure to support life. He regarded this level of consumption spending as **autonomous,** or fixed: that is, it remained constant at all levels of income. All income up to this level will be consumed, and if income should equal less than this autonomous amount, the consumer would either delve into past savings or borrow against future earnings in order to maintain this necessary level of consumption.

Once income exceeded this autonomously determined minimum amount, however, Keynes believed that further increases in consumption spending would be tied closely to net income. "Men are disposed," said Keynes, "as a rule and on the average, to increase their consumption as income increases, but not by as much as the increase in their income."[1] This behavior of consumption spending is described as **induced,** because, in contrast to the autonomous spending mentioned above, it is dependent on the level of net income.

Keynes' overall view of consumption spending can be expressed by the equation

$$C = a + bY \qquad (4.1)$$

where a represents a constant, the minimum autonomously determined level of consumption spending, and b represents that portion of incremental income which will be spent as consumption. For example, if a is equal to $2000 and b to ¾, then the equation would tell us that a family with a total income of $12,000 would have a consumption spending level of $2000 + ¾ of $12,000 or $11,000 in all; at Y = $16,000, C would equal $14,000 ($2000 + ¾ of $16,000).

The equation $C = a + bY$ is known as the consumption function; it identifies that amount of consumption spending which will occur at every level of income with the change in income. The extent of each change in consumption will depend on b, referred to as the **marginal propensity to consume** (MPC). For example, if b is ¾, then a $100 increase in income will result in a $75 increase in consumption spending, but if it is ⅘, then a $100 increase in income will produce an $80 increase in consumption. The marginal propensity to consume, b, represents the relationship between the amount of change in Y and the amount of change in C and can be expressed

$$b = \frac{\Delta C}{\Delta Y}$$

The equation $C = a + bY$ is charted in Figure 4.1 in an example which uses income and consumption figures for an economy where a = $20 billion and b = ¾Y. Note that the line representing the consumption function ($C = a + bY$) intersects the vertical axis (consumption spending) at $20 billion, or a, illustrating that consumption spending will not go below this level regardless of the amount of income received. Point X indicates consumption spending of $110 billion at an income level of $120 billion, and point Z indicates consumption spending of $140 billion at an income level of $160 billion. Comparing point X with point Z, we see that there has been a change in C of $30 billion in response to a change in Y of $40 billion,

$$\left(\frac{\Delta C}{\Delta Y} = \frac{30}{40} \right)$$

reflecting the fact that $\Delta C = ¾ \Delta Y$ in this economy. When graphic analysis

---

1. J. M. Keynes, *The General Theory of Employment, Interest and Money* (New York: Harcourt, Brace, 1936), p. 96.

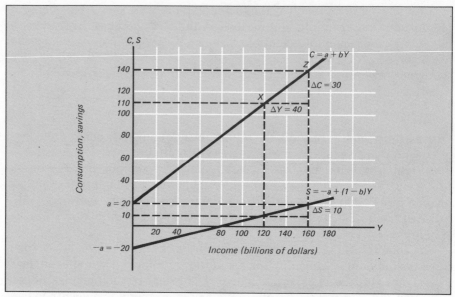

Figure 4.1 The consumption schedule and the savings schedule

is used to describe the consumption function, b is often referred to as "the slope of the consumption function" or, as noted, the marginal propensity to consume. A little experimenting with Figure 4.1 will demonstrate that a consumption function with a flatter slope or a lower marginal propensity to consume (that is, where b is a smaller fraction) would be one in which changes in income would produce relatively smaller changes in consumption spending. A consumption function with a higher marginal propensity to consume (where b is a larger fraction) would represent an economy where changes in income produced larger changes in consumption spending.

We have identified b as the relationship between changes in C and changes in Y, or the marginal propensity to consume. The marginal propensity to consume, a central concept in this model, should not be confused with the **average propensity to consume** (APC), or the portion of the total (rather than incremental) income that is consumed. For example, given the consumption function used in Figure 4.1, $C = \$20$ billion $+ \frac{3}{4}Y$, we saw that when $Y = \$120$ billion, $C = \$110$ billion. Thus, at $Y = \$120$ billion, the average propensity to consume would be $\$110$ billion$/\$120$ billion or .917. Using a similar approach, it can be shown that in this economy, the APC at $Y = \$160$ billion is $\$140$ billion$/\$160$ billion or .875. It is important to note that APC falls as Y rises, as we shall see later.

In short, consumption is the portion of expenditure that has an autonomous element a that is independent of income and an income-induced element bY. Combining these two elements as

$$C = a + bY \qquad (4.1)$$

gives the consumption function, which merely states the hypothesis that, given the parameters a and b, once Y is known, then C is known. In addition, the above equation yields a relationship between changes in Y and changes in C, or the marginal propensity to consume.

$$MPC = \frac{C}{Y} = b \qquad (4.2)$$

Strictly speaking, the marginal propensity to consume is the partial derivative with respect to Y of the consumption function. This is a mathematical term for the change in consumption, given a change in income, holding everything else constant. The average propensity to consume, APC, is simply the ratio of C to Y, which can be obtained by dividing both sides of the consumption function by Y:

$$APC = \frac{C}{Y} = \frac{a}{Y} + b \qquad (4.3)$$

Notice that since we have assumed that a is some positive number, equation (4.3) tells us that APC is greater than MPC by an amount a/Y. Since a is assumed to be constant, the difference between APC and MPC ought to fall as income rises since a/Y will fall as income rises. This means that the consumption function given by (4.1) implies that APC falls as income rises; as we shall see in Chapter 6, this fact suggests some troublesome implications for an economy.

For the purposes of this model, a consumption function has been assumed in which the MPC is a constant, that is, that the portion of additional income consumed is the same at all levels of income above a. Since MPC plays such an essential role in describing the behavior of consumption spending, this is a key assumption which at first glance does not appear to be consistent with intuition. For example, it seems probable that a household with an income of $100,000 will spend a smaller percentage of any incremental $1000 of income than a family with an income of only $15,000. Initially, Keynes suggested that this was so, that lower income families would have a higher MPC than higher income households, and he therefore believed that it would be necessary, in order to draw up a consumption schedule for an economy, to know not only the aggregate level of income earned in that economy but also how income was divided among various income groups. As we shall see in Chapter 6, subsequent studies have in one way confirmed Keynes' hunch, implying that, realistically speaking, an accurate consumption function for an entire economy *at one specific time* would suggest a lower MPC than would be revealed by a study of consumption spending for the economy as a whole *over an extended period of time.* In addition, empirical evidence confirms that MPC is constant over time for the entire economy in the long run, and for this reason, a consumption function with a constant MPC is generally used in economic forecasting.

The Savings Function

The savings function can be determined from the consumption function and the equation describing income as being composed of consumption and saving. If

$$Y = C + S$$

and

$$C = a + bY$$

then we can substitute C in the first equation and say that

$$Y = (a + bY) + S \tag{4.4}$$

Solving for S:

$$S = -a + (1 - b)Y \tag{4.5}$$

Notice the parallel between the savings function in this equation and the consumption function given by the equation (4.1). The autonomous portion of saving, $-a$, mirrors the autonomous portion of consumption a, since if you have zero income you must dissave at rate $-a$ in order to consume at rate a. The term attached to Y in the savings function $(1 - b)$ is, analogous to the consumption function, the **marginal propensity to save** (MPS). Notice that

$$MPC + MPS = 1$$

or

$$b + (1 - b) = 1 \tag{4.6}$$

since an increment in income is either consumed or saved.

The average propensity to save, or

$$APS = \frac{S}{Y} = -\frac{a}{Y} + (1 - b) \tag{4.7}$$

is larger than the marginal propensity to save $(1 - b)$, since $(1 - b)$ is greater than $-a/Y + (1 - b)$, again the mirror or reverse image of the case for consumption.

The most important point about the savings function for our purposes here is to notice that it completely identifies a relationship between S and Y once a and b are known. This is identically true for the consumption function, which could readily be derived from the income identity $Y = C + S$ and the savings function in equation (4.5) just as the savings function was derived from the income identity and the consumption function. Therefore, our analysis of the income determination process can concentrate either on the consumption function or the savings function without loss of generality since, given $Y = C + S$, one necessarily implies the other. For this reason we shall choose to concentrate on the savings function in our analysis of the income determination process.

The savings function has also been plotted on Figure 4.1. The line representing the savings function indicates that at all levels of income below $80 billion, savings will be a negative number, because households will be digging into their savings or borrowing in order to provide the funds needed to supply the minimum autonomous amount of consumption spending required to support life. Above this level, the amount of savings is determined by the savings function. Observe that at an income level of $120 billion where it was determined earlier that consumption spending would equal $110 billion, saving is $10 billion, while at Y = $160 billion, where C = $140 billion, S = $20 billion. We identified the marginal propensity to consume as $\Delta C/\Delta Y$ or the slope of the consumption function. The marginal propensity to save can be expressed similarly as $\Delta S/\Delta Y = 10/40$ or the slope of the savings function.

The Investment Function

In the simplest income determination model developed in this chapter, we are limiting consideration of factors affecting the components of consumption to income. In Chapter 7 we will see that investment is tied to a variety of factors, including technological change, size of corporate profits, and interest rates. But for the purposes of this chapter, investment is taken as an exogenous amount, determined outside the model. Thus it will remain constant regardless of changes in income.

Figure 4.2 illustrates the savings function together with investment, represented by a line horizontal to the income axis, reflecting the hypothesis that investment is independent of income.

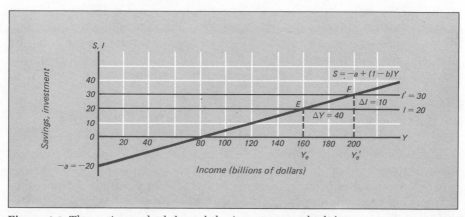

Figure 4.2 The savings schedule and the investment schedule

Equilibrium Income

Equilibrium income is the income level at which savings equals investment. In order to sustain an equilibrium level of income, savings, or nonexpenditure which rises with income, must be offset by investment expenditure. The level at which savings equals investment (equal to $20 billion) is identified on Figure 4.2 as Y_e, or $160 billion.

The equilibrium level of income determined by the savings-investment equality is the same as that where total income equals total expenditure. Since income reflects the cost of goods produced while expenditure reflects the proceeds from sales of goods, this is also the level at which all goods produced are purchased. The equivalence of $S = I$ to $Y = E$ can readily be seen by setting income equal to expenditure.

$$Y = C + S = C + I = E$$

Subtracting C from both sides leaves

$$S = I$$

It helps to understand the concept of equilibrium if we look at what would be happening on either side of point Y_e. To the right, given $I = 20$, savings is greater than investment. If income-induced leakages out of expenditure, S, exceed non-income-induced demand injections into expenditure, I, then all goods produced will not be sold and income will fall. Income must fall until savings falls to a level given by Y_e. Then $S = I$ and equilibrium income is reached. All goods produced are sold since non-income-induced demand injections into expenditure equal income-induced leakages out of expenditure. This is a level of income from which there is no tendency to move in the absence of exogenous changes. Conversely, to the left of point E, where investment temporarily exceeds savings, expenditure demand exceeds total current goods available, and income will rise until savings rises to a level at point Y_e, equal to I. This occurs because as more goods are produced in response to expenditure demand in excess of current goods available, the incomes of factors producing the goods are increased. Their higher incomes in turn result in more expenditure, as indicated by the consumption function, which further increases income until equilibrium is reached where $Y = E$ or, equivalently, where $S = I$ at point Y_e in Figure 4.2.

The Concept of Unintended Investment

It is, however, entirely possible that intended investment will not equal actual savings at every point in time. It may be true that investors will not plan to invest enough to equal savings implied by a given level of income. That is, the level of production must be sustained by sufficient demand in the form of consumption and investment. For example, in our economy in Figure 4.2, suppose that sales have been good and output grows to $180 billion worth of goods and services, implying a level of disposable income of $180 billion. Of this income, $155 billion will go to consumption and $25 billion to saving. But investment is fixed at $20 billion, making a total expenditure demand of $165 billion in consumption plus $10 billion of investment, or $175 billion, short of output by $5 billion. The amount of output which exceeds demand will be unintended investment in the form of inventory accumulation. This disequilibrium condition implies that production will be cut back in order to reduce inventories until the $Y = E$ or $S = I$ condition is restored at $Y_e = \$160$ (given no other exogenous changes).

Similarly, if businesses underestimate demand and production is only $140 billion, while investment remains fixed at $10 billion, disinvestment will result in the form of reduced inventories since consumption expenditure of $125 billion plus investment of $20 billion exceeds planned output by $5 billion. More production means more payments to factors of production, so income rises to Y_e. The point here is that savings must always be equal to intended investment plus unintended investment ($I = I_i + I_u$); only in equilibrium will intended investment equal savings.

The Multiplier

The impact of a change in investment, written as ΔI, upon equilibrium income involves a phenomenon known as the multiplier, or, more precisely, the **investment multiplier.** The term multiplier refers to the fact that given the income-expenditure model as we have specified it, the change in income resulting from a change in investment is some multiple of the original change in investment.

Let us examine the conditions under which this result will occur. Returning to Figure 4.2, we begin at point E with equilibrium income $160 billion determined by the intersection of the savings schedule with $I = 20$ at E. Suppose now that investment rises by $10 billion ($\Delta I = 10$) from I to I', as shown in Figure 4.2. In order for income to reach an equilibrium level equal to expenditure, we have seen that savings must equal investment. Given our savings function, income must rise in order to induce a rise in savings. In Figure 4.2 given a marginal propensity to save of $\frac{1}{4}$, we can see that an increase of $40 billion in income (from Y_e to Y_e') is sufficient to produce an increase in savings equal to the increase in investment. The new equilibrium income, $200 billion, is determined by the intersection of the savings schedule with the new level of investment at point F.

We can determine the investment multiplier from Figure 4.2. The slope of the savings function is $1 - b$. This is identical to $\Delta I/\Delta Y$ where, in Figure 4.2, $\Delta I = I' - I$ and $\Delta Y = Y' - Y$. If we know that

$$\frac{\Delta I}{\Delta Y} = 1 - b$$

then the multiplier is simply the inverse of $\Delta I/\Delta Y$, or $\Delta Y/\Delta I$. The inverse of any expression is obtained by dividing it into one. Therefore

$$\frac{1}{\Delta I/\Delta Y} = \frac{1}{1 - b}$$

or

$$\frac{\Delta Y}{\Delta I} = \frac{1}{1 - b} \tag{4.8}$$

The investment multiplier, or the change in income given a change in investment, is $1/1 - b$. Since we have already specified that b must lie between zero and one, $1/1 - b$ *must* be greater than one. Hence, $\Delta Y/\Delta I$ has a value of greater than one, which necessarily implies that ΔY is greater than ΔI. Consider an example: if $b = \frac{3}{4}$, then $1/1 - b = 4$. This suggests that the income-expenditure model as we have specified it here implies that if investment rises by \$10 billion, income will rise by \$40 billion, given that the marginal propensity to consume, or b, is equal to $\frac{3}{4}$. If b were to fall to $\frac{2}{3}$ from $\frac{3}{4}$, the implied multiplier falls from 4 to 3. Obviously, then, the size of the multiplier depends crucially upon the value assigned to the marginal propensity to consume.

A closer look at how the investment multiplier process comes about will enable us to understand how it works through time. So far, we have performed only what is called a comparative static analysis, starting at an initial equilibrium position, E, introducing a single change, ΔI, and observing the impact upon the new equilibrium, F. What we want to consider is precisely what is going on between E and F that causes Y to rise by $Y = (1/1 - b)\Delta I$.

The key to understanding the multiplier process is to recall the consumption function:

$$C = a + bY \tag{4.1}$$

This is the expression describing income-induced expenditure. Recall our expression for total expenditure:

$$E = C + I$$

In equilibrium, we have seen that

$$E = Y$$

Thus, at time 0:

$$Y_0 = C_0 + I_0$$

Now what happens to expenditure when investment rises by ΔI between time 0 and time 1? Expenditure rises by ΔI. We have then (in equilibrium) that

$$Y_1 = C_0 + I_0 + \Delta I \tag{4.9}$$

with $Y_0 = C_0 + I_0$ where Y_0, C_0, and I_0 are the initial levels of Y, C, and I given at point E in Figure 4.2. $Y_1 - Y_0$, the *initial* change in income, is equal to ΔI. The increase in investment represents an increase in expenditure, which in turn causes an increase in income. But the expenditure increase does not stop here. The non-income-induced expenditure increase causes income to rise and thereby causes income-induced expenditure to rise. Consumption rises by $b\Delta Y$ for every increase in income. Consumption would rise by *more* if b were to rise, which suggests a basis for our conclusion that the value of the investment multiplier rises with b.

To summarize, investment expenditure rises, causing an increase in income. The increase in income causes consumption to rise. But consumption is also an increase in expenditure, which *in turn* causes another consumption expenditure increase. Of course, this process takes time, and the subsequent expenditure increases may be said to occur in stages. As the stages continue, with an income-induced expenditure increase leading to a rise in income and yet another income-induced increase, the increases diminish.

For example, suppose investment rises by $10 billion—spent, say, on new factories and machinery. The first effect of this spending will be the receipt of $10 billion in additional income in wages, profits, rent, etc., by those directly involved in the process of turning out the new plant and equipment. Thus at the first stage, it is clear that an increase of $10 billion in demand will produce an increase of $10 billion in income. However, the effect of the original $10 billion will not stop here. Those who receive these wages, profits, etc., will use most of these monies for consumption spending, with the exact amount depending on the marginal propensity to consume in the economy. For example, in our model, the MPC is ¾; thus, of the original $10 billion received in income, $7.5 billion will be devoted by its recipients to consumption spending. This spending will, in turn, represent income to those who produce the $7.5 billion of output purchased by these recipients. In other words, to this point, the original $10 billion of incremental investment will create not merely $10 billion of income, but $10 billion + $7.5 billion. This process will continue, with the recipients of the $7.5 billion spending ¾ of that, or $5.625 billion, and the recipients of the $5.625 billion spending ¾ of that, and so on. Thus the total amount of spending from the initial $10 billion will be a sum of a series of numbers, each one of which represents the consumption spending resulting from the preceding round of income. This is illustrated in Figure 4.3.

The sum of all expenditure increases will, in equilibrium, be equal to the sum of all income increases because, as we have seen, the E = Y condition requires

$$E + \Delta E = Y + \Delta Y \tag{4.10}$$

We have also seen that the sum of Y depends on b, given I, and is given by

Commentary: Stimulating Aggregate Demand

In 1974 a recession loomed. Efforts to halt inflation during 1972 and 1973, including price controls, led to an increase in the unemployment rate to 5.6 percent by late 1973. This situation was worsened by the energy crisis—in particular, the shortage of petroleum. First to feel the pinch was the automotive industry, quickly followed by other industries which depend on petroleum, such as plastics. Cutbacks in production led to worker layoffs. Moreover, economists calculated that the rise in the retail price of gasoline produced a $4 billion decline in the amount of disposable income available to consumers for other uses. Policymakers searched for tools which were fast acting and would have maximum effect on the level of aggregate demand.

The 1975 budget, formulated to counteract this recessionary trend, increased spending in the areas of social security, unemployment compensation, and other welfare programs designed to increase the disposable income of consumers. The total budget allocation for these programs was $100 billion, or one-third of the total. A $6 billion rise in defense spending brought the total to $85 billion. The federal housing program was increased to $5.7 billion and $4 billion was allocated for energy research and environmental studies. Despite rumors that a tax cut was being considered as a measure of stimulating demand (a similar increase in 1964 is generally regarded as a triumph), the government ruled out a tax cut at that time. Surprisingly, a tax cut is not always politically feasible. In this case, projected increases in federal spending over the next five years indicated a need to maintain the revenue base. Moreover, it is extremely difficult to raise taxes after a period in which there has been tax decrease since citizens are unlikely to support the idea that they are protecting their future welfare by giving up present income.

Manipulating aggregate demand is not quite so simple as a look at the consumption function might suggest. One problem is that of the time required to enact fiscal policy. For example, when the oil shortage became apparent, considerable federal funds had already been appropriated for other uses, requiring the administration to go to Congress and request additional funds to counteract the recessionary trend. This process takes time, during which the economy can worsen. Moreover, once the government has obtained the funds, it usually takes about six months for the increase in government spending to have a direct effect on the income of consumers. Funds must pass from the Treasury to the federal agency to the state agency and finally to the individual. The time lag also hinders fiscal policy when a restrictive policy is required; often funds have been appropriated and projects are just getting under way when it becomes obvious that restraint is necessary. The issue then becomes a problem of weighing the benefits of continuing the program and the economic waste of abandoning something already underway against the costs of not applying the appropriate fiscal restraint.

The production of the entire federal budget suffers from this time lag. Budget discussions are begun on the basis of forecasts about the level of economic activity one year in advance. During the year significant changes in the economy can occur, and the various assumptions must be adjusted and approved by the authorized branches of the government. Since the effectiveness of fiscal policy as a countercyclical tool has become generally accepted, a major issue has been how best to use the federal budget to provide for the welfare of all citizens. The 1960s saw the development of the Great Society programs, which allocated federal funds for food stamps, Medicare, child care programs, educational assistance programs, and job retraining programs. By 1975 expenditures for these programs amounted to 15 percent of the total budget. The rise in expenditures created a corresponding increase in the federal bureaucracies needed to administer the programs, and administrative costs accounted for a large share of the expenditures. Many people began to question whether this centralized administration was the best way to deal with the problem of poverty. In his 1972 budgetary address President Nixon announced his New Federalism program, the long-run goal of which is to replace cumbersome federal welfare programs with cash payments directly to the individuals. Proponents of this plan argue for a negative income tax, which would create a minimum guaranteed income for low-income families. By providing cash instead of services, the government would be exerting less control over the individual's disposable income. Opponents of the program argue that it would be extremely expensive— a minimum of $25 billion would be needed to give low-income families an income of $4000 per year for a family of four—and would not guarantee that the money would be used to provide for basic needs. On the state level, the New Federalism's goal is to provide fewer services and more cash aid to states through the Revenue Sharing plan. The underlying theory of the program is that states are better able to use funds to provide for their needs than is the federal government.

Considerable controversy exists, however, over whether government spending should be directed toward individuals at all. Some economists maintain that government spending should be directed toward the private sector instead, arguing that only by increased economic growth can problems such as poverty, pollution, urban blight, and the need for mass transportation be solved. In *Retreat from Riches* (New York: Viking, 1973), Peter Passell

and Leonard Ross argue that economic growth in the private sector creates a dividend that trickles down to benefit all members of our society. Thus a policy which encourages private investment in high-technology industries would, through the trickle-down process, provide even unskilled workers with job opportunities, thereby increasing the level of aggregate demand. Passell and Ross take the position that income redistribution does not work, since it penalizes the most productive members of our society. They further argue that only by encouraging growth in the private sector can the appropriate technologies be developed which would solve pollution problems, create new sources of energy, and improve the economic condition of cities.

Opponents maintain that more expenditures in the public sector are needed in order to solve the crucial issues of our time. Since it may be difficult to induce private industry to adopt pollution controls or to develop new methods of urban transit, government should be prepared to shoulder the burden of achieving these goals. Economists such as John Kenneth Galbraith and Robert Lekatchman argue that the federal budget should be adjusted to provide for massive public expenditures, even in some cases subordinating the goal of economic growth. These economists argue that rather than relying upon a growth dividend, income should be redistributed in order to provide a basic equitable standard of living to poor families. Unlike Passell and Ross, they accept the basic rationale of the Great Society programs of the sixties and want to improve the administration and widen the scope of the programs.

Economists of both schools agree that the fiscal power of the government can be directed toward a wide range of economic goals. The question for the 1970s is how to order the priorities for achieving these goals.

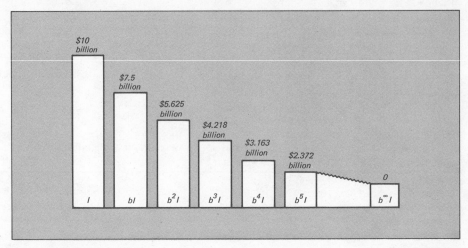

Figure 4.3 The increments of income that will result from a single increment of $10 billion of investment spending in an economy where b = ¾

$$\frac{\Delta Y}{\Delta I} = \frac{1}{1-b} \qquad (4.8)$$

or

$$\Delta Y = \frac{1}{1-b}\Delta I \qquad (4.11)$$

where 1/1 − b is the multiplier.

We will see in the following chapter that a change in government expenditure affects income in exactly the same way as a change in investment. Similarly, it should be noted also that a change in the autonomous portion of consumption will have a multiple effect on income identical to that of changes in C or I. An increase in savings, for example, which is the same as a decrease in consumption, will reduce income by a multiple amount, resulting in what is known as the "paradox of thrift."[2] But this holds true only if consumption falls *at every level of income.* That is, since part of consumption depends on income, specifically, that part designated as b in our equation C = a + bY, it is only a change in a, or autonomous consumption, that influences income via the multiplier, 1/1 − b. This can readily be seen by writing

$$Y = C + I$$
$$C = a + bY$$

---

2. This refers to a decision by consumers to reduce spending in order to save a greater proportion of income. The paradox arises because the resultant drop in income may actually lead to reduced savings.

and replacing C in the first equation with a + bY. Then

$$Y = a + bY + I \qquad (4.12)$$

This can be rearranged as

$$Y = \left(\frac{1}{1-b}\right)(a + I)$$

so that

$$\frac{\Delta Y}{\Delta I} = \frac{\Delta Y}{a} = \frac{1}{1-b}$$

Later chapters will considerably modify the model of income determination; the effect of most changes will be to lower the value of the multiplier.

MATHEMATICAL APPENDIX
The Complete Multiplier Analysis

A mathematical derivation of the multiplier is worth considering with some care because it makes clear the exact nature of the conditions that must hold in order to give the multiplier result that we derived in Figure 4.2.

Because investment is a flow of expenditure per unit of time, the rate of investment flows must be increased to a higher level and held there in order for the full multiplier effect to be felt over time; a one-shot increase in investment would produce only a once-and-for-all rise in income with income eventually returning to its original level. The necessary investment condition is shown in Figure A4.1.

A running faucet provides a good analogy for our discussion of the change in investment flows. The volume of water flowing out of a faucet per minute could represent the rate of investment flow. If the faucet opened further by one turn, so that the volume of water flowing out of the faucet per minute is increased, and the faucet is left in this position, we have the kind of flow change represented by the increase in investment associated with the full multiplier over time. If the faucet is instead opened more for a minute and then closed back to its original position, we have an analogy to the one-shot investment increase that will not produce the full multiplier effect on income.

In our discussion of the multiplier process, we shall be required to distinguish between income levels at different points in time. The starting point will be designated as Y_0, which reads "income at time zero." Of course, Y_1, Y_2, and so on, follow Y_0 as income at subsequent times indicated by the numerical subscripts. The last time period in our time series will be denoted by the subscript n, which represents some large number to which we need assign no particular value.

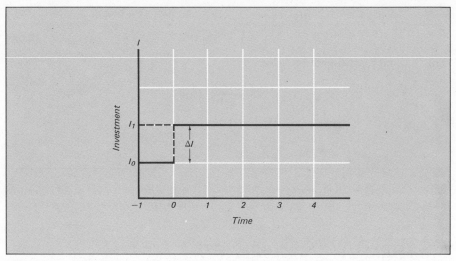

Figure A4.1 Investment shift over time required for a higher level of income over time

Suppose we begin with income equal to expenditure at time 0. We have seen that this condition may be written as

$$Y_0 = C_0 + I_0$$

Now we introduce an increase in investment, ΔI, which is to be continuously maintained. This gives

$$Y_0 = C_0 + I_0 + \Delta I$$

In the next time period, income will have risen by the amount of the expenditure increase, ΔI. This condition is written as

$$Y_1 = Y_0 + \Delta I$$

or

$$Y_1 = Y_0 = \Delta Y = \Delta I$$

In the next time period, ΔY arising from and equal to ΔI will have given rise to an *induced* expenditure increase, by way of the consumption function, equal to $b\Delta Y = b\Delta I$. So we have

$$Y_2 = Y_1 + b\Delta I = Y_0 + \Delta I + b\Delta I$$

The $b\Delta I$ change in expenditure will induce another expenditure increase, by way of the consumption function, equal to $b(b\Delta I)$, or $b^2\Delta I$. Then we have

$$Y_3 = Y_2 + b^2\Delta I = Y_0 + \Delta I + b\Delta I + b^2\Delta I$$

The expression on the right-hand side is an explicit statement of the starting level of income, Y_0, and of all the induced expenditure increases: ΔI, $b\Delta I$, $b^2\Delta I$. The induced expenditure process continues to operate until time period n, when we have

$$Y_n = Y_{n-1} + b^{n-1}\Delta I = Y_0 + \Delta I + b\Delta I + b^2\Delta I + \ldots + b^{n-1}\Delta I$$

We may write Y_n in terms of only the long form on the extreme right-hand side of the equation because things equal to the same thing are equal to each other. We also can collect I terms on the right-hand side. These steps give

$$Y_n = Y_0 + \Delta I(1 + b + b^2 + \ldots + b^{n-1})$$

Now we require some intermediate steps with which to get an expression for the multiplier, $\Delta Y/\Delta I$, out of this last equation. First we multiply both sides of the equation by b:

$$bY_n = bY_0 + \Delta I(b + b^2 + b^3 + \ldots + b^n)$$

Then we subtract both sides from Y_n as it is defined above:

$$Y_n - bY_n = Y_0 - bY_0 + \Delta I(1 - b^n)$$

This may also be written as

$$Y_n(1 - b) = Y_0(1 - b) + \Delta I(1 - b^n)$$

Subtracting $Y_0(1 - b)$ from both sides gives

$$(1 - b)(Y_n - Y_0) = \Delta I(1 - b^n)$$

Because we began with income, Y_0, and finished with Y_n, it is clear that $Y_n - Y_0$ defines ΔY.

$$(1 - b)\Delta Y = \Delta I(1 - b^n)$$

Dividing both sides by $1 - b$ gives

$$\Delta Y = \Delta I\frac{(1 - b^n)}{(1 - b)}$$

Dividing both sides of the resulting expression by I gives

$$\frac{\Delta Y}{\Delta I} = \frac{(1 - b^n)}{1 - b}$$

It would seem that this last condition ought to be identical to $1/1 - b$, which we have previously defined as the multiplier. The condition under which this holds true gives a firm idea of the notion of time associated with the multiplier. Remember that b is a fraction lying between zero and one. As n gets larger and larger, the fraction b raised to the nth power becomes smaller and smaller. For example, $3/4 \times 3/4 = 9/16 \times 3/4 = 27/64$, and so on. In fact, as n approaches the largest possible value, called infinity, b^n approaches zero. The implications of this condition are written in mathematical shorthand (where ∞ = infinity) as

$$\operatorname*{limit}_{n\to\infty} \frac{\Delta Y}{\Delta I} = \frac{1}{1-b}$$

This expression reads: the limit of the value of $\Delta Y/\Delta I$ as n, the number of time periods over which increased investment has been maintained, approaches infinity is $1/1 - b$.

Does this mean that it takes an infinite amount of time for investment to produce the multiplier effect on income? Not really, as further discussion will point out. We have not defined the *length* of time interval, n. Operationally, it ought to be the length of time that a change in expenditure takes to produce an income change, which in turn produces another expenditure change. This is a difficult matter to estimate. However, a more generally applicable statement about the length of time necessary to produce a nearly full multiplier effect can be made: although n must approach infinity for $\Delta Y/\Delta I$ to be exactly equal to $1/1 - b$, within the context of this model, if n reaches 10 to 15, nearly the full effect of the multiplier is felt. The impact of additional induced expenditure changes falls off rapidly at a rate suggested by ΔI, $b\Delta I$, $b^2\Delta I$, $b^3\Delta I$, and so on. Because b is a fraction, the *initial* ΔI is the largest with subsequent induced expenditure effects being less as indicated by $b\Delta I$, and so on.

It is conceivable, then, that if n were about four months, virtually all of the multiplier effect would be felt by the end of three years after the initial increase in investment. If n were one month, less than a year would be sufficient. This is really an issue that only measurement can resolve.

Questions and Exercises

1. If autonomous consumption is given as $40 billion and the marginal propensity to consume is two-thirds of total income of $900 billion, what is the indicated level of total consumption?
2. Give some specific subjective and objective factors of a nonincome nature which also might affect the level of consumption spending, besides the factor of income. Why, then, is consumption taken to be exclusively a function of income in the model of income determination?
3. Assuming the same set of facts as in question 1, if investment is given as $250 billion, will the $900 billion level of income be an equilibrium level? Why or why not?
4. What is meant by the "investment multiplier"? How may it be determined from the marginal propensity to consume? From the marginal propensity to save?
5. Assume the following possible range of values for the marginal propensity to consume and marginal propensity to save. Fill in the corresponding value of the multiplier for each level of the marginal propensity to consume and to save:

Marginal propensity to consume	Marginal propensity to save	Multiplier
0.90	0.10	_____
0.80	0.20	_____
0.75	0.25	_____
0.66⅔	0.33⅓	_____
0.50	0.50	_____

6. Explain why, although the marginal propensity to consume is constant, the average propensity to consume (average consumption) will decline as the level of income rises in a given consumption schedule. Does this mean that the average propensity to save (average saving) will also decline? Why or why not?

7. Explain the statement: "The actual totals of saving and investment *must* necessarily be equal in national income accounting. But desired totals may not be equal, and such inequality will lead to disequilibrium levels of income."

8. What is meant by "unintended investment"? Does it imply a condition of disequilibrium in income and output? Explain.

9. Will planned larger saving, in excess of given volume or planned investment, result in smaller actual saving? Explain this seeming paradox of thrift.

10. Explain why the "multiplier" works to increase income by a multiple rise in G or I. Why do you suppose G is not simply increased as much as possible if income is alleged to rise by three or four times the increase in G?

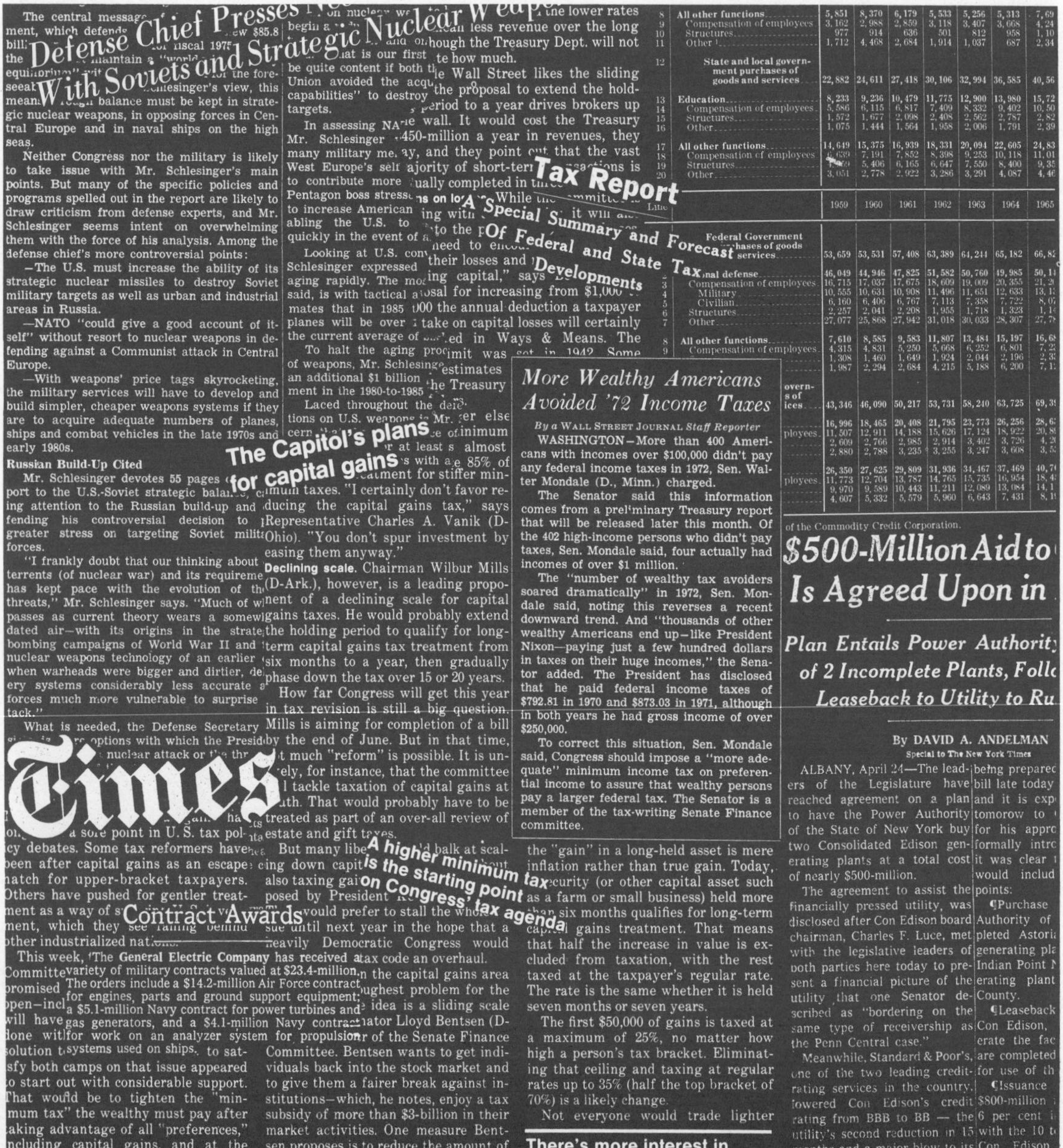

The central message of the report, which defends the spending on ... fiscal 197... the ... maintain a world equilibrium of ... foreseeable ... Schlesinger's view, this means ... balance must be kept in strategic nuclear weapons, in opposing forces in Central Europe and in naval ships on the high seas.

Neither Congress nor the military is likely to take issue with Mr. Schlesinger's main points. But many of the specific policies and programs spelled out in the report are likely to draw criticism from defense experts, and Mr. Schlesinger seems intent on overwhelming them with the force of his analysis. Among the defense chief's more controversial points:

—The U.S. must increase the ability of its strategic nuclear missiles to destroy Soviet military targets as well as urban and industrial areas in Russia.

—NATO "could give a good account of itself" without resort to nuclear weapons in defending against a Communist attack in Central Europe.

—With weapons' price tags skyrocketing, the military services will have to develop and build simpler, cheaper weapons systems if they are to acquire adequate numbers of planes, ships and combat vehicles in the late 1970s and early 1980s.

Russian Build-Up Cited

Mr. Schlesinger devotes 55 pages of his report to the U.S.-Soviet strategic balance, giving attention to the Russian build-up and defending his controversial decision to put greater stress on targeting Soviet military forces.

"I frankly doubt that our thinking about deterrents (of nuclear war) and its requirements has kept pace with the evolution of the threats," Mr. Schlesinger says. "Much of what passes as current theory wears a somewhat dated air—with its origins in the strategic bombing campaigns of World War II and nuclear weapons technology of an earlier ... when warheads were bigger and dirtier, delivery systems considerably less accurate ... forces much more vulnerable to surprise attack."

What is needed, the Defense Secretary says, is ... options with which the President, by the end of June. But in that time, ... nuclear attack or the threat ... much "reform" is possible. It is unlikely, for instance, that the committee will tackle taxation of capital gains at ... ith. That would probably have to be ... has ... treated as part of an over-all review of ... estate and gift taxes.

Chief Presses ... on nuclear we ... clear Weapons

Defense ... lesiecw $85.8 ... With Soviets and Strategic Nuclear ...

begin a ... an less revenue over the long ... and or ... hough the Treasury Dept. will not ... at is our first to how much.

be quite content if both the Wall Street likes the sliding Union avoided the acqu ... the proposal to extend the holding capabilities" to destroy ... period to a year drives brokers up targets ... wall. It would cost the Treasury

In assessing NATO Mr. Schlesinger $450-million a year in revenues, they many military me ... and they point out that the vast West Europe's self ajority of short-term ... ions is to contribute more ... ually completed in the ... Pentagon boss stress ... on lo ... While the committee to increase American ... ng with ... it will ... abling the U.S. to ... to the ... quickly in the event of ... need to ...

Looking at U.S. con ... their losses and ... Schlesinger expressed ... ing capital," says aging rapidly. The mo ... said, is with tactical ... sal for increasing from $1,000 mates that in 1985 ... 000 the annual deduction a taxpayer planes will be over take on capital losses will certainly the current average of ... ed in Ways & Means. The

To halt the aging pro ... mit was ... in 1942. Some of weapons, Mr. Schlesinger estimates an additional $1 billion ... the Treasury ment in the 1980-to-1985 ...

Laced throughout the ... tions on U.S. weapons ... Mr. er else cern ... at least ... of minimum ... with ... 85% of ... ument for stiffer minimum taxes. "I certainly don't favor reducing the capital gains tax," says Representative Charles A. Vanik (D-Ohio). "You don't spur investment by easing them anyway."

Declining scale. Chairman Wilbur Mills (D-Ark.), however, is a leading proponent of a declining scale for capital gains taxes. He would probably extend the holding period to qualify for long-term capital gains tax treatment from six months to a year, then gradually phase down the tax over 15 or 20 years.

How far Congress will get this year in tax revision is still a big question. Mills is aiming for completion of a bill

Times

... a sore point in U.S. tax policy debates. Some tax reformers ... ... been after capital gains as an escape hatch for upper-bracket taxpayers. Others have pushed for gentler treatment as a way of ... ment, which they ... railing behind other industrialized nations.

This week, ... The General Electric Company has received a variety of military contracts valued at $23.4-million. The orders include a $14.2-million Air Force contract for engines, parts and ground support equipment, a $5.1-million Navy contract for power turbines and gas generators, and a $4.1-million Navy contract for work on an analyzer system for propulsion systems used on ships.

Contract Awards

Committee promised open—incl will have done wit ... solution to satisfy both camps on that issue appeared to start out with considerable support. That would be to tighten the "minimum tax" the wealthy may pay after taking advantage of all "preferences," including capital gains, and at the same time scale down the taxes on investments that have been held for a number of years.

A major rationale for declining rates ...

The Capitol's plans for capital gains

A higher minimum tax is the starting point on Congress' tax agenda

Tax Report

A Special Summary and Forecast Of Federal and State Tax Developments

But many liberals balk at scaling down capital ... also taxing gains posed by President ... would prefer to stall the whole ... sue until next year in the hope that a heavily Democratic Congress would ... n the capital gains area ... ughest problem for the ... idea is a sliding scale ... ator Lloyd Bentsen (D-... of the Senate Finance Committee. Bentsen wants to get individuals back into the stock market and to give them a fairer break against institutions—which, he notes, enjoy a tax subsidy of more than $3-billion in their market activities. One measure Bentsen proposes is to reduce the amount of capital gains subject to taxation by 2% a year, until 80% is excluded for an asset held 16 years or more. Under such a system, a taxpayer in the 50% bracket

the "gain" in a long-held asset is mere inflation rather than true gain. Today, ... curity (or other capital asset such as a farm or small business) held more ... n six months qualifies for long-term capital gains treatment. That means that half the increase in value is excluded from taxation, with the rest taxed at the taxpayer's regular rate. The rate is the same whether it is held seven months or seven years.

The first $50,000 of gains is taxed at a maximum of 25%, no matter how high a person's tax bracket. Eliminating that ceiling and taxing at regular rates up to 35% (half the top bracket of 70%) is a likely change.

Not everyone would trade lighter

There's more interest in restructuring capital gains than reforming taxes

is simply a recognition that much of

More Wealthy Americans Avoided '72 Income Taxes

By a WALL STREET JOURNAL Staff Reporter

WASHINGTON—More than 400 Americans with incomes over $100,000 didn't pay any federal income taxes in 1972, Sen. Walter Mondale (D., Minn.) charged.

The Senator said this information comes from a preliminary Treasury report that will be released later this month. Of the 402 high-income persons who didn't pay taxes, Sen. Mondale said, four actually had incomes of over $1 million.

The "number of wealthy tax avoiders soared dramatically" in 1972, Sen. Mondale said, noting this reverses a recent downward trend. And "thousands of other wealthy Americans end up—like President Nixon—paying just a few hundred dollars in taxes on their huge incomes," the Senator added. The President has disclosed that he paid federal income taxes of $792.81 in 1970 and $873.03 in 1971, although in both years he had gross income of over $250,000.

To correct this situation, Sen. Mondale said, Congress should impose a "more adequate" minimum income tax on preferential income to assure that wealthy persons pay a larger federal tax. The Senator is a member of the tax-writing Senate Finance Committee.

of the Commodity Credit Corporation.

$500-Million Aid to

Is Agreed Upon in

Plan Entails Power Authority of 2 Incomplete Plants, Foll ... Leaseback to Utility to Ru ...

By DAVID A. ANDELMAN
Special to The New York Times

ALBANY, April 24—The leaders of the Legislature have reached agreement on a plan to have the Power Authority of the State of New York buy two Consolidated Edison generating plants at a total cost of nearly $500-million.

The agreement to assist the financially pressed utility, was disclosed after Con Edison board chairman, Charles F. Luce, met with the legislative leaders of both parties here today to present a financial picture of the utility that one Senator described as "bordering on the same type of receivership as the Penn Central case."

Meanwhile, Standard & Poor's, one of the two leading credit-rating services in the country, lowered Con Edison's credit rating from BBB to BB — the 6 per cent i ... utility's second reduction in 15 ... months and a major blow to its ... finances. In effect, it removed ... many institutions, such as savings and loan associations, from the market for Con Edison's ...

being prepared ... bill late today ... and it is expe ... tomorrow to ... for his appro ... formally intro ... it was clear ... would includ ... points:

¶Purchase ... Authority of ... pleted Astori ... generating pla ... Indian Point ... erating plant ... County.

¶Leaseback ... Con Edison, ... erate the fac ... are completed ... for use of th ...

¶Issuance ... $800-million ... 6 per cent i ... with the 10 t ... Con Edison ... have to pay ... sue. The leas ... Edison plus ... utilites of an ...

	8	All other functions	5,851	8,370	6,179	5,533	5,256	5,313	7,69
		Compensation of employees	3,162	2,988	2,859	3,118	3,407	3,668	4,24
	10	Structures	977	914	636	501	812	958	1,10
	11	Other	1,712	4,468	2,084	1,914	1,037	687	2,34
	12	State and local government purchases of goods and services	22,882	24,611	27,418	30,106	32,994	36,585	40,56
	13	Education	8,233	9,236	10,479	11,775	12,900	13,980	15,72
	14	Compensation of employees	5,586	6,115	6,817	7,409	8,332	9,402	10,50
	15	Structures	1,572	1,677	2,098	2,408	2,562	2,787	2,82
	16	Other	1,075	1,444	1,564	1,958	2,006	1,791	2,39
	17	All other functions	14,649	15,375	16,939	18,331	20,094	22,605	24,83
	18	Compensation of employees	6,539	7,191	7,852	8,398	9,253	10,118	11,01
	19	Structures		5,406	6,165	6,647	7,550	8,400	9,35
	20	Other	3,051	2,778	2,922	3,286	3,291	4,087	4,46
			1959	1960	1961	1962	1963	1964	1965

				Federal Government purchases of goods				
		services	53,659	53,531	57,408	63,389	61,244	65,182	66,85
		National defense	46,049	44,946	47,825	51,582	50,760	49,985	50,14
		Compensation of employees	16,715	17,037	17,675	18,609	19,009	20,355	21,3
		Military	10,555	10,631	10,908	11,496	11,651	12,633	13,1
		Civilian	6,160	6,406	6,767	7,113	7,358	7,722	8,0
		Structures	2,257	2,041	2,208	1,955	1,718	1,323	1,1
		Other	27,077	25,868	27,942	31,018	30,033	28,307	27,7
		All other functions	7,610	8,585	9,583	11,807	13,485	15,197	16,68
		Compensation of employees	4,315	4,831	5,250	5,668	6,252	6,801	7,2
			1,308	1,460	1,649	1,924	2,044	2,196	2,3
			1,987	2,294	2,684	4,215	5,188	6,200	7,1
		overnments of ices	43,346	46,090	50,271	53,731	58,240	63,725	69,39
		ployees	16,996	18,465	20,408	21,795	23,773	26,256	28,63
			11,507	12,911	14,188	15,626	17,124	18,922	20,80
			2,609	2,766	2,985	2,914	3,407	3,720	4,2
			2,880	2,788	3,235	3,255	3,247	3,698	3,5
		ployees	26,350	27,625	29,809	31,936	34,467	37,469	40,76
			11,773	12,704	13,787	14,765	15,735	16,954	18,4
			9,970	9,589	10,443	11,211	12,089	13,084	14,1
			4,607	5,332	5,579	5,960	6,643	7,431	8,1

Government Demand

5

A society can regulate and manipulate its own economy without government intervention. For hundreds of years in many countries governments made war and kept peace at home but did not play crucial roles in the daily operations of the economy. The twentieth century has changed all that. In the United States the federal government has taken an increasingly active role in attempting to control the economy and setting fiscal policy, especially since the crash of 1929. Table 5.1 indicates this growth.

While Gross National Product in current dollars has expanded six times since 1946, government purchases of goods and services have grown more than ten times, and government transfers (transfer payments, interest, and subsidies) have increased over seven times. As a result, total government expenditures (purchase plus transfers) have risen nine times, and the ratio of government purchases of goods and services to Gross National Product has jumped from 12.9 percent in

Table 5.1   Growth of the Public Sector in the United States (billions of current dollars)

	1929	1939	1946	1973 (preliminary)
Gross National Product	$103.1	$90.5	$208.5	$1,288.2
Government expenditures:				
Purchases of goods and services	$8.5	$13.3	$27.0	$277.2
Percent of GNP	8.2%	14.7%	12.9%	21.5%
Transfer payments, interest, and				
subsidies	$1.8	$4.2	$18.5	$130.2
Total expenditures	$10.3	$17.6	$45.5	$407.4
Government tax and nontax receipts	11.3	15.4	50.9	419.0
Surplus (+) or deficit (−)	+1.0	−2.2	+5.4	+11.6

SOURCE: Council of Economic Advisers, *Annual Report* (Washington, D.C.: Government Printing Office, 1974), p. 258

1946 to 21.5 percent for 1973. Government revenues (tax and nontax receipts) have also kept pace, with growth of over eight times for the period 1946 to 1973. Growth rates between 1929 or 1939 and the present are even more striking.

Many factors have accounted for this absolute and relative expansion in the public sector of the United States in modern times, not the least of which have been basic changes both in prevailing economic theory and policies about the economic role and importance of government expenditures.[1] Without the public sector, then, our income determination model would be theoretically and institutionally incomplete.

Introducing the government sector to the income determination model has the immediate theoretical effect of adding a new term to the income and expenditure equations, as follows:

$$Y = C + S + T$$

and

$$E = C + I + G$$

in which the new income term, T, stands for taxes, and the new expenditure term, G, stands for government spending for goods and services. Since income, Y, equals expenditure, E, the equations above determine a new equilibrium condition beyond the savings equals investment (S = I) equilibrium concept of the preceding chapter.

$$S + T = I + G \tag{5.1}$$

---

1. Students will find an interesting historical exposition of the growth of the public sector in Herbert Stein, *The Fiscal Revolution in America* (Chicago: University of Chicago Press, 1969).

The same equilibrium condition can be expressed as

$$S = I + (G - T) \tag{5.2}$$

where $G - T$ represents the government deficit (expenditure in excess of taxes) if $G - T$ is positive; and the government surplus (taxes in excess of expenditures) if $G - T$ is negative. Although we may speak of an increase in taxes or in government spending, we are really speaking of a net figure in which the injection of the government is greater than the leakage from income (deficit) or government leakage is greater than its injection (surplus).

The Uses of Fiscal Policy

We have seen that economic equilibrium occurs when income is equal to expenditure, a condition for which saving must equal investment, or $S = I$.

If consumer saving should grow more rapidly than the level of investment, perhaps due to apprehension about future economic conditions, then the equilibrium has been disturbed, and $S > I$. Fiscal policy may then be used to restore the balance; where $G > T$, so that $(S - I) = (G - T)$, we see that

$$S + T = I + G$$

Taxes are added to saving as a leakage from the income stream, while government spending is added to investment as an injection into the expenditure stream.

An equilibrium condition does not guarantee full employment and price stability, however. There may be a difference between the equilibrium level of total spending, or aggregate demand, and the level of spending needed to stabilize the economy at full employment. Thus this difference, or gap, can be either inflationary or deflationary. A deflationary gap occurs when actual expenditure is less than expenditure at the full-employment level of income; an inflationary gap occurs when total spending is greater than required for full-employment output.

The goal of fiscal policy is to maintain equilibrium income at a full-employment level. When the economy is below this equilibrium income level, an expansionary policy is used; when the economy is above this equilibrium income level, a contractionary policy is used. In either case, policy is "countercyclical" because it works to change the prevailing economic conditions.

Three government tools influence total expenditure and income levels in the economy: expenditures on goods and services, direct taxes, and transfer payments. An increase in government purchases, for example, will operate directly to increase the level of aggregate demand for goods and services, whereas an increase in personal taxes will operate *indirectly* to reduce this level by lowering the amount of disposable income consumers have to spend. Transfer payments, like tax increases, operate indirectly, but in the reverse direction. An increase in transfer payments gives more money to individuals and thus raises the level of total spending by raising personal consumption. These, then, are the tools which the government sector can manipulate in order to restore equilibrium and to close inflationary and deflationary gaps.

But before policymakers can devise adjustment measures, they must determine the magnitude of the effects of government purchases, taxes, and transfers upon total spending and the level of income. Their job is complicated because, like consumption and investment, government activities are subject to multiplier effects. Some of the major questions to be addressed are: Does an increase in government spending have the same stimulus as a tax cut of equal magnitude? Does a spending increase have the same stimulus as an increase in transfer payments? Why is an equal increase in government spending and taxation expansionary? Can an automatic counter-cyclical policy be devised or does the government have to rely on discretionary changes in spending and transfers?

Discretionary Tools

Discretionary fiscal policy refers to changes in the level of spending, taxation, and transfers not induced by changes in income. For example, in 1973, President Nixon vetoed new legislation authorizing $20 billion to $30 billion worth of new programs (including rural waste and water disposal grants, low-cost loans to rural cooperatives, federal aid to hospital construction, and manpower training), promising to defy any Congressional override by impounding the funds, as he had done with other programs. Clearly, this policy, intended to curb inflation, was not automatically put into effect as prices rose but was the result of a decision by the President to reduce government expenditure. Similarly, tax rate changes or increases in the amount of transfer payments decided upon by Congress are discretionary.

Government Purchases of Goods and Services

A primary role of government purchasing is to provide the society with public goods and services—a legislature, an army, a national museum, a highway system—the list continues. But the magnitude of such purchases may be used to some extent to correct an imbalance in the economy caused by either insufficient or excess demand. The government sector does not represent an addition to the expenditure stream, since such expenditures eventually would have been made privately had not the government commanded resources from the private sector by means of taxation. But government may spend at a time when the private sector might have saved, and its decisions are relatively centralized and subject to deliberate control rather than being made by hundreds of consumers and businesspeople, subject to the pressures of the marketplace. Government expenditure, to the extent that it is discretionary, may be employed to mitigate the impact upon the economy of sharp changes in private expenditure which may be destabilizing.

The level of government purchases of goods and services, like investment spending, is independent of the level of income, that is, they both are exogenous to the income-expenditure model. Accordingly, whenever government purchases of goods and services increase, the level of total spending shifts upward by the amount of government spending. The effect on income is exactly the same as if investment had changed, since $Y = E$ may be written as:

$$Y = C + I + G \qquad (5.3)$$

where

$$C = a + bY$$

Therefore:

$$Y = a + bY + I + G$$

$$Y - bY = a + I + G$$

$$Y = \left(\frac{1}{1 - b}\right)(a + I + G) \qquad (5.4)$$

and:

$$\frac{\Delta Y}{\Delta a} = \frac{\Delta Y}{\Delta I} = \frac{\Delta Y}{\Delta G} = \frac{1}{1 - b}$$

Where taxes are included, consumption depends on income after tax proceeds have been netted out, or

$$C = a + b(Y - T) \qquad (5.5)$$

Substituting this in the previous equation, we get

$$Y = a + b(Y - T) + I + G \qquad (5.6)$$

If we want to show the multiplier explicitly in this equation, we may write[2]

$$Y = \frac{1}{1 - b}(a + I + G - bT)$$

2. This follows from:

$$Y = a + bY - bT + I + G$$

$$Y - Yb = a - bT + I + G$$

$$Y(1 - b) = a + I + G - bT$$

$$Y = \frac{1}{1 - b}(a + I + G - bT)$$

or

$$Y = \frac{a + I + G - bT}{1 - b} \qquad (5.7)$$

For simplicity's sake, we shall assume initially that taxes equal zero, so that

$$Y = \frac{a + I + G}{1 - b}$$

Thus, given an identical increase in investment, government spending, or the autonomous part of consumption spending, the effect on income is the same. The multiplier for each of these non-income-induced injections is the reciprocal of the MPS, or $1/1 - b$. That is,

$$\frac{\Delta Y}{\Delta a} = \frac{\Delta Y}{\Delta I} = \frac{\Delta Y}{\Delta G} = \frac{1}{1 - b} \qquad (5.8)$$

Again taking the marginal propensity to consume to be ¾ as we did in Chapter 4, the MPS is ¼, and the multiplier is 4. An increase of $10 billion in government expenditures for goods and services therefore will lead to an increase in the level of income by $40 billion.[3]

Figure 5.1 portrays the government-spending multiplier at work. The I line shifts upward by $10 billion when this amount of government purchases is added. Since at equilibrium $S + T = G + T$, or leakages equal injections, the new equilibrium requires higher leakages given an increase in injections represented by ΔG. For this to occur, income must rise. Given $\Delta G = \$10$ billion, the required rise in the level of income is $40 billion, from Y_1 to Y_2. This is particularly desirable in this instance since Y_2 is the level of income (output) at which full employment occurs. The deflationary gap of $10 billion, necessary to reach full-employment equilibrium, has been closed through government spending. (Notice that the same impact on Y is shown by the upward shift of I to $I + G$, with a new equilibrium where $S = I + G$ at Y_2.)

At the $240 billion equilibrium level of income, Y_1, saving of $40 billion equals the combined total of investment ($20 billion) and government spending (also $20 billion). But the economy is not at full employment. Now if the government spending is increased by $10 billion, national income rises by a far greater amount to the full-employment level. This increase in income must be $40 billion, given an MPS of ¼. Thus, at the new (and full-employment) equilibrium level of income of $280 billion, the total investment and government spending is $50 billion, equal to the savings of $50 billion generated by the rise in income.

3. This can be shown mathematically as follows:

$$\Delta Y = G\left(\frac{1}{MPS}\right)$$

$$\Delta Y = 10\left(\frac{1}{\frac{1}{4}}\right) = 40$$

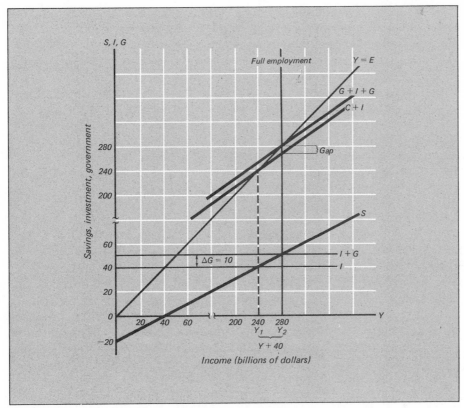

Figure 5.1 The government expenditures multiplier

The $10 billion in government spending did not just happen by chance. The government planners in this very simplified economy know that the gap between the full-employment level of income and the current equilibrium level is $40 billion. This is the change in Y that they want to attain. Therefore, they find the necessary level of government spending by dividing ΔY by the multiplier.[4] More abstractly, the planners calculate the deflationary gap between the level of expenditure at the original level of income and that necessary for full employment. Government purchases are then

4. Given $\frac{\Delta Y}{\Delta G} = \frac{1}{MPS}$, then $\Delta G \frac{1}{MPS} = \Delta Y$

This may be written as $\Delta G = \frac{\Delta Y}{\frac{1}{MPS}}$.

Inserting the figures used in the text:

$\frac{40}{\Delta G} = \frac{1}{.25}$; $\Delta G(4) = 40$; $\Delta G = \frac{40}{4}$; $\Delta G = 10$

used to close that gap. If the economy is troubled by an inflationary gap, the government-expenditures component of total spending can be reduced, thereby cutting national income by an even greater amount.

In an economy with a large government spending multiplier, small changes in government activity can have an explosive effect on the economy. Even in a huge and far more complex economy like that of the United States, some effects can be seen. During the years when the United States was waging the "war on poverty" and the war in Vietnam, the increases in government expenditures created an inflationary gap that began to push prices upward. The tool that the government turned to in this case (with much hesitation) was an increase in taxes.

Lump-Sum Taxes

In order to understand the simple tax multiplier we shall assume, first, that taxes are not proportional to income but are imposed as lump sums. Government expenditure, like investment, represents an injection into expenditure; taxation, like saving, represents a leakage out of expenditure. But as we noted, taxation does not affect expenditure directly. Some portion of taxes is paid from savings, and only a portion of it is taken from consumption. That proportion is the marginal propensity to consume times the taxes, or $-bT$. The effect on income thus occurs in two steps. First, aggregate demand is reduced by $-bT$, then the multiplier affects this amount.

The mathematics of this approach were begun in equation (5.7):

$$Y = \frac{a + I + G - bT}{1 - b}$$

To calculate a change in income caused by a change only in lump-sum taxes, we find that

$$\Delta Y = \frac{-b\Delta T}{1 - b}$$

The lump-sum tax multiplier is expressed

$$\frac{\Delta Y}{\Delta T} = \frac{-b}{1 - b} = \frac{-\frac{3}{4}}{\frac{1}{4}} = -3 \tag{5.9}$$

where $b = MPC = \frac{3}{4}$, and $1 - b = MPS = \frac{1}{4}$. Suppose, for example, that taxes of $10 billion are introduced. We know that part of the taxes would come out of saving and the remainder out of consumption. Since the MPS is $\frac{1}{4}$ and the MPC is $\frac{3}{4}$, $2.5 billion would be paid from reduced savings and $7.5 billion from reduced consumption. Withdrawing $7.5 billion from aggregate demand will produce a $30 billion drop in the level of income as follows:

$$\Delta Y = \frac{-\frac{3}{4}(10)}{1 - \frac{3}{4}} = \frac{-7.5}{\frac{1}{4}} = -7.5(4) = -30$$

Or simply,

$$\Delta Y = \frac{-b}{1 - b\Delta T} \text{ or } -30 = (-3)(10)$$

Figure 5.2 illustrates this process. Before taxes are introduced (S_1), the equilibrium income is $240 billion. Assume lump-sum taxes in the amount of $10 billion are imposed. Taxes and saving together raise the total withdrawal from the economy $(S + T)$ again. This does not occur until the economy has reached $210 billion, a $30 billion decrease in income.

Balanced Budget Multiplier

Combining our two examples, we find that the initial spending increase and the initial tax increase are the same ($10 billion), but the expansionary effect on income of an increase in spending ($40 billion) is greater than the contradictory effect on income ($30 billion) of an increase in taxes. A balanced budget $(G = T)$ in our simplified economy thus seems to be expansionary.

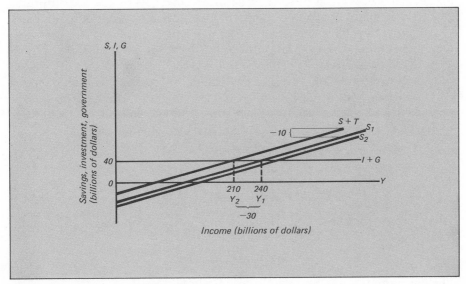

Figure 5.2 The tax multiplier

The reason for this is the difference in the effects of spending and taxes on total spending. As we have seen, the full increase in government spending raises total spending and thereby, income. The increase in taxes, however, is only partially reflected in a reduction in expenditure, and therefore the effect on income is smaller. In short, a balanced budget is expansionary because the effect of taxes is to take money away from private individuals, with an MPC of 3/4, and transfer it to the government, with an MPC of 1.

Equal changes in G and T are not mutually offsetting because of the differences in the resulting multipliers. The final change in income is the sum of the changes in G and T; mathematically expressed, this is

$$\frac{\Delta Y}{\Delta G + \Delta T} = \frac{1}{1-b} + \frac{-b}{1-b} = \frac{1-b}{1-b} = 1 \tag{5.10}$$

In this simplified economy we find that the balanced budget multiplier is always one, and therefore income always rises by the amount of the increase in government spending. This is what we mean by saying a balanced budget is expansionary. In a simplified economy, a government can stimulate the economy even if its budget is balanced.

Government Transfer Payments

Because government transfer payments consist of purely financial shifts of funds from government to households, they are not included in GNP. But their volume grew from $1.8 billion in 1929 to $130.2 billion in 1973; transfer payments now constitute nearly a third of total government expenditures. Thus, they cannot be ignored in any model of income determination.

Although transfer payments are a form of government expenditures, they do not create so powerful a stimulus to the economy as an increase in direct government purchases. Transfer payments, such as social security, unemployment compensation or welfare payments, are part of disposable income (DI). Instead of reducing DI, as do taxes, they increase DI. In effect, transfer payments are negative taxes, and are subject to an analogous multiplier.

To include transfer payments we may restate equation (5.4) as

$$Y = C + S + (T - T_r) \tag{5.11}$$

and

$$E = C + I + G$$

T_r represents transfers. Disposable income in this economy would include these transfers.

$$Y_d = Y - T + T_r \tag{5.12}$$

The consumption function would also include them

$$C = a + b(Y - T + T_r) \tag{5.13}$$

The equilibrium level of income would therefore become

$$Y = a - bT + bT_r + I + G$$

Making the multiplier explicit, we conclude with the equation

$$Y = \frac{a + I + G - bT + bT_r}{1 - b} \tag{5.14}$$

This equation indicates why an increase in transfer payments will not raise income by the same amount as an increase in direct government spending (or investment). As a "negative tax," transfer payments add to DI, but part of these transfer payments are saved, not spent. The proportion spent is determined by the marginal propensity to consume. The multiplier for transfers, therefore, is simply the positive version of the tax multiplier.

$$\frac{\Delta Y}{\Delta T_r} = \frac{b}{1 - b}$$

Or, using our figures,

$$\frac{3/4}{1/4} = 3 = \frac{\Delta Y}{\Delta T_r}$$

Since $Y/T = -3$, or more generally $Y/T = -b/1 - b$, it is clear that if increased transfers are financed by increased taxes, the budget will be balanced but no expansionary effect will occur.

Automatic Stabilizers: Proportional Taxes

Up to this point, changes in tax revenues or transfer payments or government purchases have not been induced by changes in income. This is hardly realistic, however, since an increase in the equilibrium level of income will bring in more taxes and perhaps may take people off the unemployment and welfare rolls. Sales taxes and excise taxes likewise vary with the level of income. If the tax rate is the same at all levels (a proportional tax system), then tax revenues rise as incomes increase, or are proportional to income as $T = tY$. Ignoring transfer payments, the consumption function then becomes

$$C = a + b(Y - tY) \tag{5.15}$$

and the equilibrium level of income is

$$Y = a + bY - btY + I + G$$

The multiplier can be made explicit as before:

$$\Delta Y = \frac{1}{1 - b + bt}(\Delta a + \Delta I + \Delta G)$$

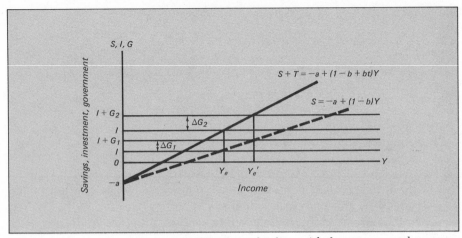

Figure 5.3 The government expenditures multiplier with lump-sum and proportional taxes

or

$$\Delta Y = \frac{\Delta a + \Delta I + \Delta G}{1 - b(1 - t)} \tag{5.16}$$

Obviously, the effects upon income of a given increase in any of the non-income-induced components (a, I, or G) are identical. When these injections increase, income rises to provide a source of offsetting leakages that restore equilibrium. Now, just as $1 - b$, or the MPS, represents the portion of each dollar of additional income that leaks into saving, the term $1 - t$, or the marginal propensity to tax, represents the portion of each dollar of income that flows into taxes. Together they measure leakages, or the amount of income that is removed at each stage. Because more is being removed with a proportional tax structure than without it, the value of the multiplier is smaller with proportional taxes than without.

Suppose, for example, that the MPC, or b, is ¾ and that the tax rate, t, is ⅓. Then the value of the multiplier is 2.[5] From Figure 5.3 we can see that with lump-sum taxes the leakage schedule may be written as

$$S + T = -a + (1 - b)Y$$

represented by the broken line. The rise in I or G required to increase income from Y_e to Y_e' is $\Delta Y = (\Delta G_1)(1 - b)$ where lump-sum taxes prevail.

With proportional taxes,

$$S + T = -a + (1 - b + bt)Y$$

5. $\dfrac{1}{1 - \frac{3}{4}(1 - \frac{1}{3})} = \dfrac{1}{1 - \frac{9}{12} + \frac{3}{12}} = \dfrac{1}{\frac{1}{2}} = 2$

and the required rise in G to move income from Y_e to Y_e' is $\Delta Y = \Delta G(1 - b + bt)$. Since ΔY is equal in both cases, $\Delta G > G$, because the proportional tax-expenditure multiplier $(1/1 - b + bt)$ is less than the lump-sum tax-expenditure multipler $(1/1 - b)$. The lower multiplier means that income is less volatile. It rises less when total expenditure increases and falls less when total expenditure declines. The proportional tax system, then, has a built-in dampener and is therefore an automatic stabilizer.

In theory a balanced budget with such a proportional tax system has the same expansionary effect as we noted earlier. We start with a form of equation (5.16)

$$Y = a + b(Y - tY) + I + G$$

Since a balanced budget implies $tY = T = G$, we may substitute G for tY in the above equation. Thus

$$Y = a + b(Y - G) + I + G$$

or

$$Y = a + bY + I + (1 - b)G$$

Making the multiplier explicit, we can see

$$Y = \frac{a + bY + I + (1 - b)G}{1 - b}$$

As we saw in equation (5.10),

$$\frac{\Delta Y}{\Delta G} = \frac{1 - b}{1 - b} = 1$$

Thus, the balanced budget multiplier seems to hold, but in practice things are not so simple. To predict the exact level at which the tax rate, t, will produce tax revenues, tY or T, that exactly equal G, we have to be able to predict Y. We cannot simply set T and G equal because every time G increases, this affects income which in turn affects tax revenues, since these are a proportion of income, tY. Planners are now shooting at a moving target and may well overshoot or undershoot.

Moreover, when government spending exceeds tax revenues, part of the ensuing deficit may be made up by the increased tax revenues collected from the rise in aggregate demand and income. For example, an increase of \$1 in government purchases produces \$2 in income, when the multiplier is 2. One-third of this income is collected as taxes (\$ .66). Thus, a \$1 increase in government purchases would actually cost only \$ .33. This is a mixed blessing, for although it reduces the deficit, it also reduces the stimulatory effect of government purchases. Such reductions are known as "fiscal drag."

Part of the tax structure in the United States has an even stronger counter-

Commentary: Tax Credit Policy

Because government not only spends but taxes in the interests of stability, the U.S. tax structure reflects a variety of policy measures designed to stimulate or dampen demand in both the personal and business sectors. In addition to direct tax cuts, for example, tax credits may be provided for certain kinds of expenditures. Two such credits are the investment tax credit and the foreign tax credit.

The investment tax credit, first instituted by the Kennedy administration as a loudly proclaimed use of fiscal policy to stimulate long-term growth, allows businesses to take off 7 percent of the price of capital purchases from their final taxes. In effect, this raises the rate of return on the plant and equipment and frees cash that otherwise would flow into the Treasury.

However, many business executives insist the effects of the investment tax credit are marginal, since the potential of the investment must be there in the first place. "No one is going to buy an expensive piece of equipment for the credit-saving alone and then have it sit in his yard," points out Norris Eckstrom, vice-president of Bucyrus-Erie Co.[1] Others stress that the tax credit may make the margin of difference in an investment decision, making more capital available.

When the economy is booming, however, such stimulus may be inflationary. Economist Arnold C. Harberger of the University of Chicago, for example, believes that business increased its relative share of GNP during the 1960s at the expense of the housing industry. With both mortgage seekers and businesses making capital investment competing avidly in the market for funds, one group could gain only if the other lost.[2]

The potentially inflationary effects of the tax credit made its use an intermittent affair during the late 1960s; it was lifted in 1966 in order to combat inflation, then reinstituted only five months later when the economy faltered slightly. In 1969 President Nixon waged a protracted battle with Congress to get the tax credit suspended as part of his war on inflation, only to temporarily revive the credit again in 1971 as part of the New Economic Policy.

The temptation to remove the tax credit during a boom is almost irresistible, because business investment climbs sharply during good times only to fall off abruptly during bad times. But this is in effect closing the barn door after the horse is stolen, since investment decisions are made several years in advance. Removing stimulus today will not substantially reduce spending already committed for, but may put the brakes on future commitments. Likewise, restoring the tax credit in a recession does not provide immediate stimulus. Thus the effects of the reinstated tax credit showed up not in 1971, when the economy was recovering from a sluggish period, but in 1973, when it was already overheated.

Not all investment is made at home. Increasingly, U.S. corporations have expanded abroad. In 1961 less than half of the top 100 firms had European branches; by 1965, 700 did. In 1967 one-quarter of our imports came from U.S. enterprises abroad. Because the income from foreign operations are taxed both here and abroad, corporations are allowed to use foreign tax credits to reduce U.S. tax liabilities on foreign income. This provision has recently come under the scrutiny of both Congress and the Internal Revenue Service.

The House Ways and Means Committee wants to limit the use of the foreign tax credit by the international oil companies. As U.S.

1. "Business Looks Warily at the Tax Credit," *Business Week*, October 2, 1971, p. 78.

2. Ibid.

law stands now, these companies—like all multinational corporations—figure their U.S. tax bill on foreign sources of income and then subtract the full amount of foreign taxes they have paid on that income. If their income is $100 million the U.S. tax rate is 48 percent, and foreign taxes amount to $10 million, then the corporation would have to pay only $38 million to the U.S. Treasury on its foreign income. (($100 × .48) − $10 = $38). If the oil company paid $48 million in foreign taxes, it would not be liable for any U.S. taxes on its foreign income.

The proposed way of treating these taxes is as a business deduction. The foreign taxes are subtracted from the income *before* the U.S. tax bite is taken. With the same income, U.S. tax rate, and foreign tax level, the deduction approach would make the multinational oil company's U.S. taxes $42.2 million (($100 − $10) × .48 = $42.2). To pay no U.S. taxes, the company would have to have used its entire foreign income for foreign taxes. The House would limit the tax credit to some percentage of the foreign income and use the deduction approach for the remaining taxes. In addition, excess tax credits could not be applied to the income from nonoil operations, and tax benefits from foreign losses could be recaptured by the United States in subsequent years if the oil company's foreign operations show a profit then. A final feature of the bill would eliminate the option of calculating foreign taxes and income on a country-by-country basis. This option permits heavy foreign taxes or losses in one nation to offset U.S. tax liabilities more than under the proposed system. The House bill would require all multinationals—not just oil companies—to aggregate all taxes or losses from foreign companies. In all, $500 million a year might be realized by the government from this proposed bill.

The Internal Revenue Service, on the other hand, wants to redefine the sources of income. Its proposed regulations take a harder look at domestic expenses such as administration and interest on loans for capital investment that produce revenues abroad. The prime example is research and development: if a multinational whose research facilities are entirely in the United States discovers a new product or process to sell here and overseas, the expenses are charged to its U.S. branch. By attributing a larger share of these expenses to its foreign operations, the company reduces its overseas income and tax liability. This would also reduce the tax credits the firm receives on its U.S. taxes, thereby increasing its U.S. tax bill. Such taxes on multinationals might increase by $100 million or more because of the proposed changes, and deter some companies from considering overseas expansion.

Companies with centralized management and research, such as those in the pharmaceutical industry, have the most to lose. Under the IRS proposals, they might face a 6 to 8 percent drop in after-tax income, as opposed to a 3 percent drop for the average multinational.

"If the Treasury insists on pushing ahead with these regulations," said Matthew P. Landers, treasurer of the drug company Pfizer, Inc., and head of the National Association of Manufacturers subcommittee on international taxation, "it will encourage multinationals to do R&D in foreign countries where they can get the tax deductions."[3] This move abroad in turn would affect U.S. tax revenues, employment levels, and balance of payments.

The Congressional bill and IRS regulations are simply proposals, the final form of which will probably be changed by industry pressure and further studies of their impact. But whether they are passed or not, they indicate a few of the complications introduced by an economy that is increasingly internationalized. To the problems of domestic tax policy, such as uncertain efficacy, differential effects, and lags, is added the question of whether the tax changes will provoke a flight of business abroad.

3. "A Tax Worry for Multinationals," *Business Week*, March 2, 1974, p. 52.

cyclical effect than a proportional tax system.[6] As incomes rise, taxpayers in our progressive tax system move into higher brackets, and income tax collections increase more than proportionately, thus restraining the upturn in consumption. On the other hand, as incomes decline, taxpayers move downward into the lower tax brackets, and income tax collections decrease more than proportionately, thus tending to dampen the downturn in consumption. Transfer payments in the United States also tend to decline automatically on upturns, as people go back to work and go off unemployment, and to increase automatically on downturns, as people are thrown out of work and begin collecting unemployment. A progressive tax system lowers the multiplier even further and provides even greater automatic stabilization. In fact, one study of recessions in the United States indicates that such stabilizers staved off one-third to one-half of the income declines that otherwise would have occurred.[7] However, these same stabilizers worked during booms to shave off a quarter or more of potential income growth, a striking demonstration of the problem of fiscal drag.

The Full-Employment Budget

The level of economic activity obviously affects federal revenues; with a given set of tax rates, the closer the economy is to full employment the larger government revenues will be. Thus, a level of government spending which would be in deficit at low levels of economic activity will be in surplus at full employment levels. The full-employment budget is thus defined as the level of government revenues and expenditures which would have occurred had the economy been functioning at full employment (4 percent). For example, President Nixon offered a budget in fiscal 1974 which called for spending of $269 billion with revenues of $250 billion. At full employment, this $19 billion deficit would have turned into a slight surplus.

The full-employment budget sorts out the effects of the level of income from the effects of policy. By focusing on the requirements of a full-employment economy, this budgetary approach eliminates misleading appearances created by income-induced effects.

Concluding Note

Thus far we have seen that introducing government to a two-sector income determination model requires adding an injection to expenditures, govern-

6. A recent study of the U.S. tax system has found that the total effect seems to be proportional despite the progressive tax structure and the presence of transfer payments. See Joseph A. Pechman and Benjamin A. Okner, *Who Bears the Tax Burden?* (Washington, D.C.: Brookings Institution, 1974).

7. Peter Eilbott, "The Effectiveness of Automatic Stabilizers," *American Economic Review* 56 (June 1966): 450–465.

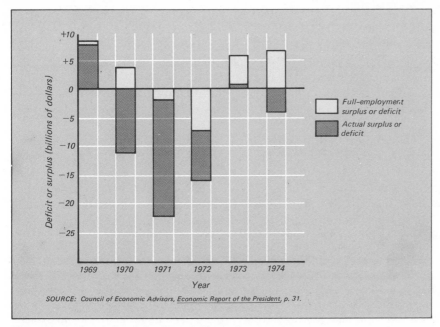

Figure 5.4 shown with axis labeled "Deficit or surplus (billions of dollars)" and years 1969 through 1974.

Legend:
- Full-employment surplus or deficit
- Actual surplus or deficit

SOURCE: Council of Economic Advisors, *Economic Report of the President*, p. 31.

Figure 5.4 The federal budget: full-employment (4 percent unemployment) and actual deficits and surpluses, 1969–1974 (calendar years)

ment purchases; a leakage from income, taxes; and an addition to income, transfer payments. The equilibrium level of income in such an economy is expressed:

$$Y = \frac{a + I + B - bT + bT_r}{1 - b}$$

When this economy is below full employment, the level of spending can be increased by (1) increasing government purchases, (2) increasing transfer payments, (3) cutting taxes, or (4) some combination of these. When this economy is suffering from an inflationary gap, spending can be reduced by (1) reducing government purchases, (2) decreasing transfer payments, (3) raising taxes, or (4) some combination of these.

Changes in government payments have the greatest unit effect of the tools. If policy dictated a balanced budget for this simplified three-sector economy, no stimulus could be achieved by increasing transfer payments while increasing taxes by the same amount because one would offset the other. Some stimulus would result, however, from increasing government purchases while increasing taxes by the same amount, since the balanced budget multiplier in this case is one.

Less stimulus from deficit spending is provided in an economy with a proportional tax system. In such a case income-induced leakages from increases in income would include both savings and taxes, and the value of the multiplier would be $1/1 - b(1 - t)$, far smaller than the multiplier for the previous system. The lower multiplier serves as a flywheel to regulate the swings of the economy, acting as an automatic stabilizer.

Federal surpluses and deficits result from both policy decisions and the level of income. The full-employment budget unmasks the income effects and shows the level of the budget if the economy were to achieve full-employment equilibrium.

But, one might ask, if the effect of all these alternatives is only to achieve the same, or less, effect on income as that created by investment, why complicate not only our model, but economic reality, by fiscal stimuli? The reason, as Keynes was not the first to point out, is that the modern capitalist economies may not, over time, generate sufficient income, and thus expenditure, to buy the goods produced; government spending is thus introduced to take up the slack. Keynes expressed this succinctly:

> If the Treasury were to fill old bottles with banknotes, bury them at suitable depth in disused coal mines which are then filled up to the surface with town rubbish, and leave it to private enterprise on well-tried principles of *laissez-faire* to dig the notes up again (the right to do so being obtained, of course, by tendering for leases of the note-bearing territory), there need be no more unemployment and with the help of the repercussions, the real income of the community, and its capital wealth also, would probably become a good deal greater than it actually is. It would, indeed, be more sensible to build houses and the like: but if there are political and practical difficulties in the way of this, the above would be better than nothing.[8]

Questions and Exercises

1. Calculate the level of national income when $a = 20$, $b = 3/4$, $I = 20$, $G = 0$, and $T = 0$. By how much does income increase if $G = 25$? By how much does income decrease if taxes are 25? By how much does income increase if $G = 25$ and $T = 25$?
2. Calculate the level of national income when $a = 20$, $b = 5/6$, $I = 20$, $G = 20$, and the tax rate is 20 percent. What is the multiplier if taxes are not proportional? What is the multiplier if they are proportional?
3. Calculate the level of national income when $a = 30$, $b = 2/3$, $I = 75$, $G = 40$, $T = 42$, and $T_r = 12$. (If your answer is less than 300, you have forgotten to employ the multiplier; if your answer is more than 500, you have added taxes rather than subtracting them.)

8. J. M. Keynes, *The General Theory of Employment, Interest and Money* (New York: Harcourt, Brace, 1936), p. 129. Unfortunately, government stimuli are generally highly inflationary, a problem with which Keynes was not greatly concerned. For an interesting account of the increasing difficulties of reconciling fiscal stimuli with inflation, see Paul M. Sweezy, "Keynesian Chickens Come Home To Roost," *Monthly Review* 25 (April 1974): 1–12.

4. The deflationary gap in the economy of question 3 is 10. Will increasing transfer payments by 10 close the gap? By how much will income rise if government purchases are increased by 10? If income rises by 30, how large an increase in transfer payments was needed to accomplish this?

5. Suppose that the President has impounded $1 billion in order to reduce government expenditures that are inflationary. Congress, upset at the insult to its prerogatives and fearing a recession, passes a tax cut of $1 billion. If the tax system is not proportional and the MPC is $3/5$, will Congress succeed in offsetting the President's reductions? Justify your answer.

6. State and local taxes are regressive, that is, as income decreases, the proportion of income taken in taxes increases. How might this affect stabilization?

7. When state legislatures see that tax revenues are falling and the budget deficit is rising because of a recession, they often pass a tax hike in order to reduce the deficit. Should Congress follow the lead of the state legislatures?

8. In 1973 some $9 billion in taxes overwithheld in 1972 was refunded to individuals. What was the immediate effect on disposable income, if the MPC = $2/3$? What was the effect on consumption? What was the effect on total income?

9. Any fiscal policy is developed within an institutional context. Although the President presents a budget reflecting his fiscal goals, Congress passes the individual bills authorizing spending and revenues. Congress assigns the responsibility for overseeing appropriations and the responsibility for authorizing revenue bills to two distinct committees. What effects might these institutional arrangements have on discretionary policy? On automatic stabilizers?

10. Government activities may affect the consumption and investment functions. For example, if the MPC of the rich is lower than the MPC of the poor, a tax system that redistributed income might raise the MPC for the economy. What would be the effect on the multiplier if this occurred?

Ghetto Fraud On the Installment Plan

Commodities
Nixon Administration Takes Passive Stance On Stiff New Round of Food-Price Increases

Minimum-Wage Bill With Two-Step Rise Approved by Senate

CONSUMER REPORTS Knows What's Best for Us All

present income

with T.V. back cracked notify company to come have fix. Company claimed misplace T.V. sent repossed T.V. 1949 had to stick in hanger to get reception — two weeks after that broke down. Called to _____ moved T.V. still pay _____ ment — left job o _____ garnishment which ef _____ relation as the garnishee took away from our expenditures food clothing and rent. Which for which my wife was forced to except welfare and I left to establish myself again T.V. paid $500 never received T.V."

Louis-Ferdinand _____ conceit that life wa _____ on the installment pl _____ in New York City, _____ close to being literally true.

Six years ago sociologist David Caplovitz of Columbia's Bureau of Applied Social Research published a book called *The Poor Pay More*. The book is a landmark in the literature of consumer problems, right out there with *The Jungle* and *Unsafe at Any Speed*. As a result, Caplovitz has become witness-in-residence at a host of committees and subcommittees where he talks about the lack of "scope" which keeps poor people from leaving their neighborhoods in search of _____

By a WALL STREET JOURNAL *Staff Reporter*
WASHINGTON—The Senate passed a new minimum-wage bill, bringing closer another test of wills _____ dent Nixon and Congress.

The 69-to-22 vo _____ House, whe _____ Education _____ mittee pla _____ it next Wednes _____ subcommitte _____ has _____ approved a version m _____

The Senate bill would increase _____ $1.60-an-hour federal minimum wage to $2 _____ most workers soon after enactment, and to $2.20 a year later. The bill also would expand coverage of the minimum wage law's provisions to an additional seven million workers, mostly government employes, household domestics and smaller retail employes.

This is the third time around for an attempted minimum-wage increase within three years. From the outset the Nixon administration has agreed that the $1.60 pay floor should be raised, but at a slower timetable than Congress wants. An even more important cause of the three-year deadlock is the refusal of Congress to let employers pay teenagers less than the adult minimum, a provision which Mr. Nixon again _____ last week and which is again omit _____

A typical story: "It said the payment book in the mail it was for $1,306. Well, I gritted my teeth and paid on it until I owed $508. But I missed a payment, so they call my job and say they'll take $6.80 a week. I went to the marshal and he said if I would send him $16 every two weeks he wouldn't call my job anymore."

Mr. Nixon vetoed last year _____ House failed to override him. But the passage of time during the long wrangle has made the $1.60 pay floor more vulnerable to erosion fr _____

better-quality junk. Birch? maple? dowels? glue? fabrics? veneers? Fe it—*shlock* is _____ of gum _____ flakeboard, k _____

_____ comn. The _____ *shlock* _____ are strictly W. & J. _____ ntages of _____ 0 per cent _____ —they tal _____ er wholesale _____ pers" _____ ber is 100 per ce _____ _____ a _____ _____ three or _____

_____ buy *shlock*? Because the *shlock* emporia will give terms: "Easy credit." "Easy credit" means that as long as you are working and have wages that can be attached in _____ event that you _____ _____ say. "Easy cre _____ eur Bar-rac _____ the _____ into store _____ _____ eferer who _____ says _____ yc wa _____ give _____ desan a part your salary, the salesman will come back from the phone smiling and try to hustle you into $1,1 By MITCHELL C. LYNCH month and ap *Staff Reporter of* THE WALL STREET JOURNAL rd there WASHINGTON—The Nixon administration apparently intends to weather the new food-price storm with a policy hovering between await-and-see and hope-and-pray.

This, at least, is the way some economists in the White House and Agriculture Department see things as the government battens down the hatches for another stiff round of farm and store-shelf price boosts caused by tight supplies.

"Sure, we saw this coming," said Gary L. Seevers, a member of the President's Council of Economic Advisers. "But the question is, what you do about it."

The answer: nothing. "A new situation doesn't automatically mean you do something _____ The market itself can solve many of _____ Mr. Seevers said.

_____ economists are _____

_____ said. "You _____ _____ not p _____ _____ er prob _____ ment, by Presi _____ food prices are going to rise sha _____ July. Many see this as ironic becau _____ lieve a major factor in the anticipated pric _____ spiral was the series of government actions last year aimed at keeping prices down.

A Passive Policy

President Nixon acknowledged this passive policy at his press conference last week when he said the only solution to higher fo _____ p _____ to "get the supplies an _____ s _____ _____ een found wanting." _____ t year's government action included the temporary lid on meat prices, the export embargo on soybeans and the fertilizer-price review. _____ ment officials said the freezer cost $897 on the paper, but when the supplies _____ _____ d _____ d _____ Furthermore, said Mr. Seevers _____ these uncertainties are interrelated _____ ple, some lesser-developed countric _____ dieting better harvests this year th _____ with fertilizer prices skyrocketing _____ tries mightn't be able to afford eno the _____ _____ caused ma _____ paying overseas market.

walnut finish bachelor chest, matching mirror, full size bed, with 1 pc. Firestone comb. mattress, 16 pcs. dishware, 16 pcs. cutlery, 8 towels, 11 pc. salad set, 29 table access.

But once they've spent the money to get you into the store, they can't let you out with only a miserable $198 worth of *shlock*. That is only the bait end of bait-advertising. By the time the _____ ves, he should have put his _____ ock on the dotted line for at least $1,000. To cause this takes more than just an old-fashioned bait-and-switch. It requires nothing less than that balletic extravaganza of salesmanship known to the trade as the "turnover" or "tossover," code name "T.O." The salesman starts by showing the customer a pile of junk for $198. One store keeps its bait furniture piled in a dark corner, lit by a naked lightbulb. It is painted battleship gray, _____ "You don't want this stuff," I'll take it." "You don't want this stuff," he say _____

The personal income of Americans topped a trillion dollars last year for the first time. It has more than doubled in less than a decade. And thereby hangs a tale you seldom hear much about in the inflation story. Both prices *and* incomes have soared in the inflation whirlwind. And the incomes have far outclimbed the prices. It means two things. For the consumer, it means any expectation of a sizable decline ahead in high prices will likely prove unwarranted. For the businessman, it means he should not bet too heavily on a big weakening in consumer buying power.

It is strange, but apparently eternally true, that people should expect prices to stand still while their wages rise. They remember the prices of the "good old days"—not the lean paychecks. High wages are the very stuff of which high prices are made. The auto worker's high pay is the plumber's high cost of owning a car. And the plumber's fat fee is the auto work-er for getting a pipe fixed.

Of all the figures poured out of the official statistical mills, there is none so widely publi-regularly noted as that representing the cost of living—the index of consumer _____ ed on the 1967 price level as 100. The _____ of the wage-price coin, the size of _____ aychecks, gets less attention.

_____ the inflation record for nearly a _____ s, the table below traces both the _____ price index and the average weekly _____ of production and nonsupervisory _____ manufacturing industries, as com-480: Department of Labor. The 1973 fig-for December.

Personal Income

What's in the shopping basket?

Price index weighting

**mer Prices Vs Weekly Wages
1962 to 1973**

	Prices	Wages
	90.6	$ 96.56
	92.9	102.97
	97.2	112.34
	104.2	122.51
	6.3	133.73
	5.3	154.28
	8.5	173.86

rains, of course, FOOD he wages have s the prices. The entire 1962-73 pe-

at inflation is a good it is brutal to the in-ncome increasing as erage." And it is es-ching retirement, HOUSING ain largely un-teen climbing.

paycheck ladder History's record _____ ion is bad medicine for him too.

example may be cited in the dec-eceding the inflationary era chron-While prices and wages both rose, _____ from 1952 through 1962 saw inflation _____ ely restrained. And here is what hap-

**Consumer Prices Vs Weekly Wages
1952 to 1962**

Year	Prices	Wages
1952	79.5	$67.16
1954	80.5	70.48
1956	81.4	78.78
1958	86.6	82.71
1960	88.7	89.72
1962	90.6	96.56

Over the decade of relatively mild inflation the record adds up to:

PERSONAL INCO _____ a seasonally adjusted _____ trillion year _____ TRANSPORT month earlier, the Co _____ reports.

CLOTHING ETC

1963
1952
1973

AUG SEP OCT NOV DEC J _____

HEALTH & RECREATION

Dow Jones Futu _____
5.39; last year, 198.20
Dow Jones Spot-
year 201.26.

_____ om—1451.6, up _____ als 100).

Consumption

6

The Keynesian treatment of the consumption function, summarized as

$$C = a + bY$$

in Chapter 4, is known as the absolute income theory, primarily because it hypothesizes that consumption is solely a function of real disposable income. Keynes did, however, recognize various subjective and objective factors, in addition to income, which might affect consumption. He summarized eight subjective factors as precaution, foresight, calculation, improvement, independence, enterprise, pride, and avarice. The strength of the subjective factors would also depend on such social factors as: (1) the institutions and organization of the economic society; (2) spending and saving habits fostered by race, education, convention, religion, and current morals; (3) present hopes and past experiences; (4) the scale and technique of capital equipment; (5) prevailing distribution of wealth; and (6) the established standards of life. Objective factors include: (1) changes in wage and price levels; (2) changes in accounting practices, with respect to depreciation, etc.; (3) windfall gains or sudden losses; (4) changes in fiscal policy; (5) changes in expectations; (6) substantial changes in the rate of interest.

In Keynes' judgment, however, the subjective factors which affect consumption spending change only slowly over time. Moreover, extensive social change, secular change, and changes in the distribution of wealth would cause, even more gradual shifts over time. Particular objective factors of an abnormal or extraordinary nature, such as wars, strikes, etc.; major changes in the tax structure; and exceptional sudden gains or losses, would not be likely to be of more than transitory or secondary importance in causing shifts in the marginal propensity to consume. Moreover, Keynes did not attach much importance to changes in the rate of interest as an influence on consumption, except indirectly.[1]

Thus, for the absolute income theorists, the sole influence on consumption expenditure was taken to be real disposable income. The simplicity of this theory made it a welcome contribution to macroeconomic theory: knowing the level of income made it possible to predict the level of consumption. And consumption, along with investment and government expenditure, constitutes a major element of aggregate demand. Moreover, if the relationship between income and consumption is stable, then estimates of future income levels can give accurate forecasts of future consumption.[2]

The theory also seemed to make sense, at least "common sense," because the observed economic behavior of family units (households) appeared to correspond to what the theory led economists to expect. That is, when household income increases, most households increase their level of consumption, but by a percentage smaller than the prior increase in income. They also increase their levels of saving when income increases. Conversely, when household incomes drop, at least in the short run, their consumption drops by less than the drop in income, and dissaving may occur in an effort to maintain consumption levels.

When long-run empirical studies were conducted to test the absolute income theory, however, economists found that the concept of absolute income did not seem to account adequately for the macroeconomic behavior of specific economies. This led to the formulation of alternative theories to

1. John Maynard Keynes, *The General Theory of Employment, Interest and Money* (New York: Harcourt, Brace, 1936), especially pp. 107–110. See also Alvin H. Hansen, *A Guide to Keynes* (New York: McGraw-Hill, 1953). The original Keynesian formulation has been modified in modern restatements pursuant to the formulation suggested by J. R. Hicks in his article "Mr. Keynes and the 'Classics': A Suggested Interpretation," *Econometrica* 5 (April 1937): 147–159.

2. Arthur Smithies developed Keynes' hypothesis and applied it in this manner in "Forecasting Postwar Demand," *Econometrica* 13 (January 1945): 1–14; so did James Tobin in "Relative Income, Absolute Income, and Saving," in *Money, Trade, and Economic Growth* (New York: Macmillan, 1951), pp. 135–156. For a discussion of theories of the determinants of consumption, see R. Ferber, "Research in Household Behavior," *American Economic Review* 52 (March 1962): 19–63.

reconcile the contradictory evidence produced by the short-run and long-run studies. One such alternative theory was the relative income theory, developed by James Duesenberry, who suggested that households gear their consumption to that of other households in their own income group. Rather than having an absolute standard for their consumption pattern, Duesenberry suggested that households watch what other "similar" households are buying and try to "keep up with the Joneses." Another economist, Milton Friedman, offered the permanent income theory, which hypothesizes that household consumption patterns are determined by more long-run considerations of expected total lifetime earnings, including future expected earnings. Finally, economists have suggested other factors, not related to levels of income at all, that may affect the level of consumption. One such factor is the interest rate. Another is the distribution of income in the economy. Price levels and expectations with regard to price changes also seem to have their effect on consumption.

This chapter will examine the absolute, relative, and permanent income theories in the light of the available data. It will also consider the major nonincome factors mentioned above that appear to influence expenditure decisions by consumers.

The Absolute Income Theory

The absolute income theory has some implications that make one wonder, in retrospect, why it was so enthusiastically accepted for many years. Recall that in Chapter 4 the portion of income saved, or average propensity to save implied by the absolute income theory was:

$$APS = \frac{S}{Y} = -\frac{a}{Y} + (1 - b)$$

Given that $C = a + bY$, the average propensity to save, S/Y, increases, therefore, as disposable income increases. It follows that the average propensity to consume, or C/Y, decreases as income increases if the absolute income theory is correct.

One implication of the theory, however, was disturbing. If an economy in fact behaved the way individual households seemed to do in the short run, then as a country became more wealthy the ratio of saving to income, S/Y, should increase steadily. Under such conditions, planned (intended) investment must increase also, or else income would tend to fall. During the depression of the 1930s economists feared that investment might not be able to expand enough to keep up with the increasing S/Y ratio as the economy recovered and income increased. They thought this might lead to secular stagnation, a long-run shortage of investment relative to saving which would tend to perpetuate the depression. Economists took this danger quite seriously and proposed that federal deficit spending might be the only remedy, compensating for the shortage of investment (relative to saving) by injecting large doses of government spending into the economy.

Fortunately, the world did not behave as theory had led the economists to expect. Simon Kuznets conducted an exhaustive study of aggregate saving and consumption behavior in the United States over a long period and found that there was no tendency for S/Y to increase over time as income rose.[3] Instead, he found that the portion of disposable income saved remained near constant over the long run (1869–1938) despite enormous increases in income. This led economists to question the original assumptions of the absolute income theory.

Economists intensified their search for empirical evidence to help understand the factors underlying consumption behavior. Two empirical approaches, cross-sectional and time-series, produced contradictory results. Cross-sectional studies are those conducted for a single point in time. They tended to support the absolute income theory, because they showed that at any single point in time households with incomes below the mean level of income consumed a larger portion of their disposable incomes than households that were above the mean. Time-series analysis demonstrated the relationship between *aggregate* (not household) disposable income and aggregate consumption over a long period of years. Some early time-series studies seemed to support the absolute income theory. But in 1946 Kuznets published a new set of time-series data which conflicted with the absolute income theory and seemed to indicate that the average propensity to consume or C/Y, remained constant at all income levels. By dividing the 70-year period from 1869 to 1938 into short-run periods (to minimize short-run influences such as recessions), Kuznets found that the average propensity to consume remained constant over time.

Consider Figure 6.1, which shows hypothetical long-run and short-run analyses.

Averaging out each short-term period, as Kuznets did, we would find that the long-run consumption function (which is traced out by the average points X, Y, and Z for each short-run period) looks like C_L. It increases with disposable income, but the APC is constant, not declining. In other words, over the long haul the portion of an economy's income that is consumed remains steady. But if we conduct a cross-section analysis for each short-run period we may find that owing to cyclical effects, the consumption functions look like C_{S_1}, C_{S_2}, and C_{S_3}. Within each short-run period, during "lean" (depression or recession) years all or nearly all disposable income will be consumed, while during the "fat" (boom) years more will be saved and a relatively smaller portion of disposable income will be consumed. So, the short-run cross-section studies tend to support the absolute income theory, while the long-run analysis tends to contradict it.

3. Simon Kuznets, *National Product Since 1869* (New York: National Bureau of Economic Research, 1946), p. 119. Raymond Goldsmith's findings confirmed and expanded those of Kuznets. See *A Study of Savings in the United States*, Vol. 1 (Princeton, N.J.: Princeton University Press, 1955), p. 78.

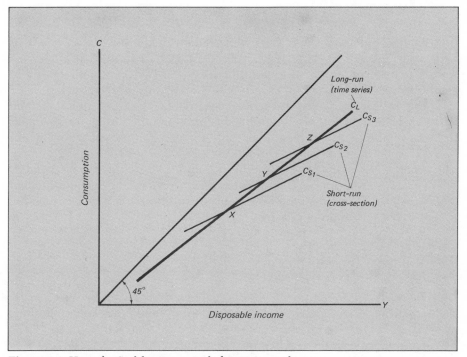

Figure 6.1 Hypothetical long-run and short-run analyses

Economists committed to the absolute income theory stated that several intruding factors had upset the consumption function and that the long-run function, C_L, does not represent a true map of the relationship between consumption and income, but is rather an illusory line which happens to intersect points such as X, Y, and Z as it drifts upward. The factors which the absolute income theorists considered as disturbing the "true" consumption function were based on empirical observation. One factor was drawn from the recognized tendency of urban dwellers to save a smaller portion of their incomes than do rural dwellers. Accordingly, the steady shifting of population from rural areas to the cities was cited as contributing to the "consumption drift." Similarly, improvements in medical care have led to an increase in the percentage of the population that is elderly. Although people reaching retirement generally experience a sharp decline in income, they still tend to consume as much as before. This allegedly tended to shift the consumption function upward over time. The third and probably most important factor which modified the consumption function was the accumulation of wealth over time. According to these theorists, this accumulation permitted households to spend relatively more of their current incomes because prior savings already provided sufficient protection against unexpected future expenses.

What the absolute income theorists argued, therefore, was that if these subjective and objective factors had not intervened, the consumption function would have looked like C_{S_1} and extended indefinitely to all levels of disposable income. Instead, it has drifted upward gradually. But, they asserted, the consumption drift described by the line C_L is not essentially significant, as it is caused by factors which are historically unique.

These arguments failed to satisfy opponents of the absolute income theory, who argued that the long-run consumption function, C_L, represented the true relationship between disposable income and consumption, while C_{S_1}, C_{S_2}, and C_{S_3} were cyclical functions reflecting misleading extraneous or temporary factors. This continuing debate led to the formulation of the relative and permanent income theories. Each rejects the absolute income theory and each considers the long-run consumption function, C_L, to be the true one, but for different reasons.

The Relative Income Theory

James Duesenberry attempted to reconcile the contradictory results of cross-sectional (household budget) studies and time-series (aggregate) studies, as well as the results of short-run and long-run time-series studies.[4] His prime assumption in the relative income theory is that increased income is perceived only against the backdrop of other households' incomes. Hence, if all incomes for a given group of households are increasing at roughly the same rate, none of the individual households will notice a change in income and therefore no change will occur in the percentage of income devoted to consumption. According to Duesenberry, if all (or most) households move steadily upward into higher absolute income brackets, they will tend to consume the same percentage of the increase as they did of the original income, and thus more than the absolute income theory would have led us to predict. Studies have shown that over the long run this is the pattern for families in the United States.

The exception to this orderly theory comes in the case of a household which experiences an increase in income which jumps the household into a relatively higher income bracket. In such a case, Duesenberry hypothesizes that the household would tend to increase its individual rate of savings, thereby increasing its consumption by a smaller proportion than the increase in income. Specifically, the household thrust into a higher income bracket

4. James S. Duesenberry, *Income, Saving, and the Theory of Consumer Behavior* (Cambridge, Mass: Harvard University Press, 1949). For a similar but independent interpretation, see also F. Modigliani, "Fluctuations in the Savings-Income Ratio: A Problem in Economic Forecasting," in *Studies in Income and Wealth* 11 (New York: National Bureau of Economic Research, 1949).

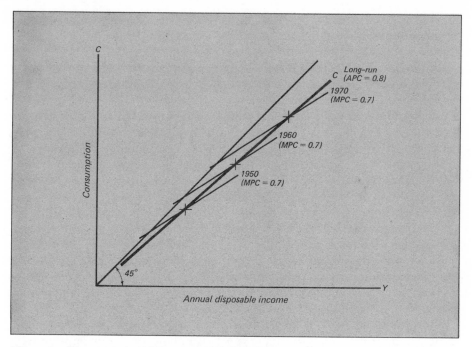

Figure 6.2 Cross-sectional consumption functions and the relative income theory

will, in the short run, feel relatively wealthy and will tend to save the new windfall, rather than to spend it.

The relative income theory does not entirely contradict the absolute income theory for the short run. Cross-sectional studies for specific years still show that those households with large incomes consume a smaller proportion of their disposable income than those with lower incomes.[5]

Consider the hypothetical case of Figure 6.2. For each year (1950, 1960, 1970) the graph shows a cross-sectional consumption function representing many households and their consumption patterns. The Xs represent the average propensity to consume (for all households, averaged out, for each of those years). As we see in the graph, over the long run the APC remains constant (as some fixed proportion of disposable income such as 0.8). But for each individual year the cross-sectional approach shows us that marginal

5. Even here, though, Duesenberry did demonstrate that relative economic status is crucial to households. He found that white and black families with identical disposable incomes behaved differently in consumption. At each level of income, the blacks consumed less and saved more than did the whites, presumably because they were better off (relative to their peer group) than the whites were at the same income level. This is not the only possible interpretation. James Tobin looked at the same data and concluded that the reason was that the white family felt more secure, and therefore did not have to save as much. See Tobin, "Relative Income, Absolute Income, and Saving."

propensity to consume is less than the average propensity to consume. That is, those households with incomes above the long-run trend in a given year consume a smaller portion of disposable income than would be indicated by the long-run APC. Conversely, households with relatively low incomes in a given year consume a larger portion of disposable income than would be indicated by the long-run APC.

What happens if there is a recession and incomes fall in the short run? Duesenberry argued, just as the absolute income theorists did, that households would try to defend their standards of living by reducing their rates of saving (or even by dissaving), thereby reducing their consumption much less than the fall in income. If we add together the consumption patterns of all households, we find that the aggregate consumption function for an economy when national income is falling is similar to that proposed by the absolute income theorists. Figure 6.3 shows both long-run and short-run aggregate consumption functions.

Duesenberry maintained that as long as income was steadily increasing, the consumption function would be as indicated by the long-run consumption function, C_L. That is, there would be a marginal propensity to consume equal to the average propensity to consume with an intercept at 0. This fits Kuznets' long-run studies. But, Duesenberry argued, if national disposable income should drop (say from Y_{d_1} to Y_{d_2} in Figure 6.3), consumption will not drop back along C_L. Instead, households will try hard to maintain the consumption patterns to which they are accustomed, moving downward along C_{S_1} from C_1 to C_2. They may even dissave in order to do so, and their

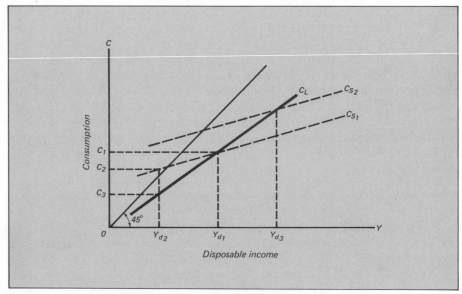

Figure 6.3 Long-run and short-run consumption functions

MPC will therefore be less than their APC. The aggregate consumption function for the short run (the duration of the recession) will therefore look like C_{S_1}. Duesenberry also argued that the consumption function will not resume its long-run configuration until the highest previous level of income is once again reached.

This means that during periods of economic expansion the economy will move upward along C_L. If at income level Y_{d_1} a recession occurs, consumption will drop back along the short-run consumption function C_{S_1}. Income may drop drastically, to Y_{d_2}, for example. Consumption will drop much less drastically, to C_2 rather than C_3. When recovery occurs, according to Duesenberry, consumption will move back up along C_{S_1} until income reaches Y_{d_1} again, and then the long-run consumption function will be followed. The next time there is a recession (for example, after income level Y_{d_3} has been reached) consumption will again fall back, but this time along short-run consumption function C_{S_2}. Again, the long-run function will not be resumed until recovery is complete. This pattern of long-run consumption growth at an MPC equal to APC, and short-run decline along consumption functions with a lower MPC, is known as the **ratchet effect,** since it resembles the ratchet behavior of a car jack or other tool. The breaking point in the graph (where the short- and long-run consumption functions meet) is permitted to shift upward (to higher levels of income) but never to decline.

The relative income theory appears to resolve some major problems observed in cross-sectional and time-series data. It also takes into account both short-run and long-run phenomena. But it presents problems of its own, by failing to differentiate between large and small increases in disposable income. If families are slow to respond to drastic increases in income (i.e., if their MPC is less than their APC), this should also be true for the economy as a whole. This latter problem was tackled by Milton Friedman in his permanent income theory, to which we now turn.

The Permanent Income Theory

Despite the advances of the relative income theory some economists question whether theories based on a measure of current income adequately explain economic behavior, pointing out that spending should be a function of some more fundamental index of economic well-being. Few people gear their expenditures to current income with no thought of future or past changes in income.[6] A young person recently out of college will be inclined to spend a large proportion of his income because he expects that his income will increase in the future so that he does not have to save a large proportion

6. R. M. Fisher found that groups with variable incomes, such as self-employed people or farmers, tend to save a higher proportion of their incomes than do groups with "safer" incomes. See "Explorations in Savings Behavior," *Bulletin of the Oxford University Institute of Statistics* 18 (1956): 201–278.

for future needs. A man of sixty, at the peak of his earning power, will spend a smaller proportion of his income in order to save money for his retirement.

Milton Friedman therefore formulated the permanent income hypothesis in order to account for the tendency for individuals to adjust consumption spending over time to their average income flow.[7] In Friedman's model, current income is broken down into two parts: permanent and transitory income. Permanent income is the "normal" income which an individual expects to have. Transitory income is a temporary addition or subtraction to permanent income due to some unforeseen event. For example, assume that an individual who usually earned $120 per week received a paycheck of $100 because he had missed time on account of illness. His current income is $100, while his normal or permanent income is $120, since the -20 is only a transitory element. Had the same individual received a bonus of $20, making his current income $140, his transitory income would be $20 above permanent income.

Friedman has attempted to quantify consumption based on permanent income. An individual's calculation of permanent income at a given time, t, is based on observed levels of his past measured income. In short, an individual averages out the observed levels of past measured income in periods previous to time t in order to determine his permanent income at time t. This statement of the permanent income notion is based on the hypothesis of how an individual modifies his notion of permanent income in the face of observed changes in measured income. Thus,

$$Y_t^P - Y_{t-1}^P = B(Y_t - Y_{t-1}^P) \text{ where } 0 < B < 1 \tag{6.1}$$

which states that the notion of permanent income is adjusted by some fraction, B, of the difference between current measured income, Y_t, and permanent income one time period ago, Y_{t-1}^P. Equation (6.1) is a first-order difference equation, and while the procedure for solving it lies beyond the scope of this book, a solution to equation (6.1) clearly shows permanent income to be a declining, weighted average of past values of measured income. The solution to equation (6.1) is presented as equation (6.2)

$$Y_t^P = BY_t + B(1 - B)Y_{t-1} + B(1 - B)^2 Y_{t-2} + \ldots + B(1 - B)^n Y_{b-n} \tag{6.2}$$

where B defines the weights attached to past values of measured income, Y_t equals measured income at time t, Y_{t-1} is measured income one year previous, Y_{t-2} is measured income two years previous, and Y_{t-n} measured income n years previous. The first terms of the right-hand side of the equation

---

7. Milton Friedman, *A Theory of the Consumption Function* (Princeton, N.J.: Princeton University Press, 1957). A related theory was developed independently by Franco Modigliani and Richard Brumberg which states that savings is dependent on the average income for a lifetime. See "Utility Analysis and the Consumption Function, an Interpretation of Cross-Sectional Data" in Kenneth K. Kurihara, ed., *Post-Keynesian Economics* (New Brunswick, N.J.: Rutgers University Press, 1954), pp. 388–436.

Table 6.1   Implied Weights Used in Calculating Permanent Income from Measured Income

Y_t B	Y_{t-1} $B(1-B)$	Y_{t-2} $B(1-B)^2$	Y_{t-3} $B(1-B)^3$	Total weights
0.7	0.21	0.063	0.0189	0.9919
0.6	0.24	0.096	0.0384	0.9744
0.5	0.25	0.125	0.0625	0.9375
0.4	0.24	0.144	0.0864	0.8704
0.3	0.21	0.147	0.1029	0.7599
1.0	0	0	0	1.0000

are large, the nth term of the right-hand side very small. This reflects the fact that more weight is given to measured income during the most recent years.

The actual value assigned to B determines the weight given to the measured incomes. Table 6.1 gives different values for B. Notice that the larger the weight given to current measured income, B, the more rapidly do the weights given to past values of measured income decline. Where B = 0.4 the four most recent observations of income exhaust about 87 percent of the total weight given to past values of measured income. Friedman found, in fact, that the weighting pattern implied by B = 0.4 gave the best predictions when applied to his statistical data. This means that an individual's assessment of permanent income at time t is determined primarily by averaging the level of measured income over the four previous time periods. Simple manipulation of equation (6.1) shows that permanent income at time t is actually a weighted average of permanent income at time t − 1 and present measured income.[8] That is:

$$Y_t^P = BY_t + (1-B)Y_{t-1}^P \qquad (6.3)$$

Perhaps the most significant aspect of the permanent income formulation is its ability to resolve the apparent discrepancy between the absolute or relative short-run formulations and the long-run formulation. Since per-

8. This year's permanent income is expressed by the equation:

$$Y_t^P = BY_t + B(1-B)Y_{t-1} + B(1-B)^2Y_{t-2} + B(1-B)^nY_{t-n} \qquad (1)$$

Last year's permanent income can be expressed as:

$$Y_{t-1}^P = BY_{t-1} + B(1-B)Y_{t-2} + B(1-B)^{n-1}Y_{t-n} + B(1-B)^nY_{t-n+1} \qquad (2)$$

Equations (2) and (1) can be combined as follows:

$$Y_t^P = BY_t + (1-B)Y_{t-1}^P + B(1-B)^nY_{t-n+1}$$

Ignoring the last term, which approaches zero as n approaches a very large number,

$$Y_t^P = BY_t + (1-B)Y_{t-1}^P \qquad (6.3)$$

manent income is taken to determine consumption entirely, we may write:

$$C_t = wY_t^P \tag{6.4}$$

Substituting into the above equation the expression for permanent income given by equation (6.3), we find:

$$C_t = wBY_t + w(1 - B)Y_{t-1}^P \tag{6.5}$$

Equation (6.5) defines a relationship between measured consumption and measured income given some additional term that depends on an index of past overall economic well-being, or $w(1 - B)Y_{t-1}^P$. Equations (6.4) and (6.5) are represented in Figure 6.4. Notice that the $w(1 - B)Y_{t-1}^P$ is analogous to the a of $C = a + bY$ while wB is analogous to the b. The long-run marginal propensity to consume out of a rise in permanent income, w, is greater than the shorter run marginal propensity to consume out of measured income, wB, since B is less than one and positive in sign.

In order to understand the distinction between permanent and measured income, suppose that measured income rises by XZ in Figure 6.4. From equation (6.3) we know that permanent income rises by less since

$$\frac{\Delta Y_t^P}{\Delta Y_t} = B = \frac{XY}{XZ}$$

This rise in permanent income, measured along $C = wY_t^P$ is XY, less than XZ, since $B = XY/XZ$ and $0 < B < 1$. When measured income rises by XY, the permanent income formulation claims that measured consumption rises because of the (less than XZ = XY) rise in permanent income. Because the change in measured income overstates the rise in permanent income the marginal propensity to consume is set too low, at wB, because it is wrongly assumed that it is the rise in measured income which gives rise to the increase in consumption. In short, measured observations would give a line like $C = w(1 - B)Y_{t-1}^P + wBY_t$, analogous to $C_t = a + bY_t$, while, properly specified, the consumption function would be $C = wY_t^P$.

If Y_t remains at point Z, over time Y_{t-1}^P will rise so that the measured consumption function would shift up to intersect the permanent consumption function at point U in Figure 6.4. This would explain the "consumption drift" or general consumption function-shift phenomena found in earlier studies.

In spite of difficulties in measurement, the permanent income formulation of the consumption function is probably the most desirable, both on theoretical and empirical grounds. Theoretically, it is more satisfying to hypothesize that consumption depends on a more comprehensive measure of economic well-being than current income. Empirically, both the long-run consumption function and the shifting short-run consumption function are readily explained within the framework of the permanent income formulation.

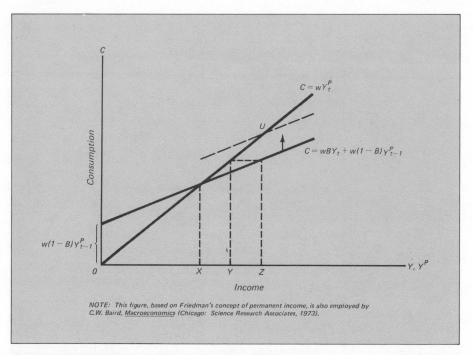

Figure 6.4 The relationship between measured consumption and measured and "permanent" income

Interest Rates

Interest rates as determinants of consumption behavior entered into classical theory as a direct influence, and into Keynesian theory as an indirect influence. Although most empirical evidence so far tends to show the role of interest rates to be insignificant in comparison to other influences,[9] it is interesting to examine this theory. The typical consumer has a positive time preference: that is, he would rather consume now than defer his consumption for a future date. A high interest rate provides the consumer with a motive for giving up present consumption and saving to buy future goods. If he can obtain additional income because of a higher interest rate, then by waiting for a given period of time, say a year, he can purchase more goods. The indifference curve shown in Figure 6.5 indicates the consumer's preference map for present and future goods. All points on curve I_1 represent

---

9. See Lawrence R. Klein, "The Empirical Foundations of Keynesian Economics," in Kurihara, ed., *Post-Keynesian Economics*; and especially Daniel B. Suits, "The Determinants of Consumer Expenditure: A Review of Present Knowledge," in *Impacts of Monetary Policy* (Englewood Cliffs, N.J.: Prentice-Hall, 1963).

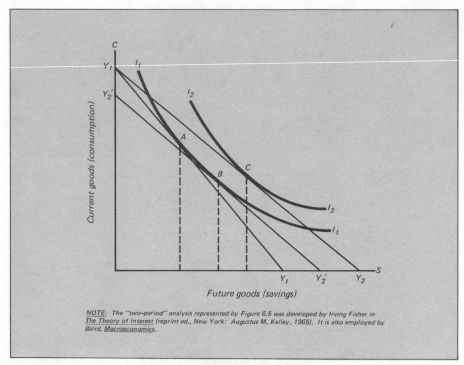

NOTE: The "two-period" analysis represented by Figure 6.5 was developed by Irving Fisher in *The Theory of Interest* (reprint ed., New York: Augustus M. Kelley, 1965). It is also employed by Baird, *Macroeconomics*.

Figure 6.5 Effect of a rise in the interest rate on consumption (or savings)

combinations of present and future goods which give the consumer a given level of satisfaction. If the consumer can have no more than the total quantity of goods in selection I_1, he will be indifferent to whatever point on the curve at which he finds himself. Current and future goods are substitutes, since I_1 says that the individual will remain as well off, given less current goods, with more future goods. I_1 also says that the rate at which current goods must be increased given a loss of future goods to maintain indifference, rises as the share of current goods rises. Line Y_1Y_1 represents the original budget line in Figure 6.5, which describes the various combinations of current and future goods which consumers *can* buy given their income at level Y. The slope of the budget line is given by the price of current goods divided by the price of future goods, or $1/1 + i$ where i is the interest rate.

If the interest rate rises, the price of current goods relative to future goods falls, as shown by line Y_1Y_2, since the return to giving up current consumption, in terms of the future goods one could buy, rises as the interest rate rises. Line $Y_2'Y_2'$ is drawn parallel to line Y_1Y_2 to identify the point, B, along I_1 which would be selected at the new relative price of future goods. The movement from A to B represents what is known as a **substitution effect,** substituting current goods for future goods, due to a rise in their relative price. In addition to the substitution effect, an individual lender would experience a positive **income effect,** or **scale effect,** from higher interest rates. This is represented by the move from point B to point C. However, for the economy as a whole, the lender's gain is the borrower's loss, so the scale effect nets to zero, leaving only the substitution effect, which states that savings (or purchases of future goods) rises with the interest rate while consumption (purchase of current goods) is reduced by a rise in the interest rate. This concept will be explored in greater detail in Chapter 8.

Other Nonincome Determinants of Consumption

Income Redistribution

Almost all economists have recognized that other nonincome-related factors may affect the average propensity to consume. It is generally recognized that an economy with a relatively equal distribution of income where 25 percent of the total disposable income is held by the richest 10 percent will have a higher APC than an economy where the wealthiest 10 percent have 40 percent of the nation's income. Keynes maintained that a redistribution of income will increase the APC of an economy.

Keynes' theory regarding MPC and the level of income has not been confirmed by the data.[10] While it may be true that a poor family will, on the average, spend every penny of its income, this does not mean that it will treat an income increment in the same manner. Cross-sectional statistics show quite substantially that measured APC varies inversely with measured income level, but they are far less conclusive in defining what happens to MPC. Of course, as we have seen, the permanent income theory suggests that the sensitivity of APC to the level of income may be due to an illusion arising from a misspecification of the consumption function.

Prices

Economists have recently begun to reemphasize the effect of price expectations on consumption. The Keynesian model holds that price increases will not cause the level of consumption to decline so long as wages increase proportionately with prices. Recent experience, however, has shown that wages do not increase as rapidly as prices. Economists have begun to focus on expectations of changes in price level and their relationship to consumption.[11] For example, an expectation that prices will rise higher and higher, as during an inflation, may cause the consumer to make extra purchases

10. See R. A. Musgrave and M. S. Painter, "The Impact of Alternative Tax Structures on Personal Consumption and Saving," *Quarterly Journal of Economics* 62 (August 1948); also H. Lubbell, "Effects of Redistribution of Income on Consumers' Expenditures," *American Economic Review* 37 (March 1947): 930.

11. Prices at time t can be viewed as a weighted average of prices in previous time periods. Using a formulation similar to that employed when analyzing permanent income, one gets

$$P_t = BP_t + B(1 - B)P_{t-1} + B(1 - B)^2P_{t-2} + \ldots + B(1 - B)^nP_{t-n}$$

Commentary: Consumer Boycotts

In March 1973 consumer organizations all over the country planned a nationwide meat boycott for the first week of April of that year. Their protests were directed against the rapid increase in the price of meat during the first three months of 1973. From January to March the retail price of beef had increased 20 percent and the price of pork increased 16 percent. The organizations felt that by encouraging consumers to boycott the meat counters they would be able to lower the skyrocketing retail prices. By the end of the boycott week little price reduction was evident. The boycott, along with the AFL-CIO's threat to demand wage increases above the 5.5 percent guideline if prices were not lowered, prompted the administration to impose price ceilings on the retail price of meat. It was hoped that in six months the prices would be rolled back to a more suitable level.

By September 1973, however, it was obvious that the price ceilings and boycott had not produced major price reductions; farmers, economists, and government officials concluded that the consumer would just have to get used to paying more for meat. The boycott provides an opportunity for assessing the potential for consumer action as resources become scarcer in the decades to come. Its failure suggests conclusions about effects of individual consumers and price controls on our growing economy.

The high price of meat in early 1973 was attributed to the rapid increase in disposable income in the economy in 1972. From 1971 to 1972 disposable income increased from $770.5 billion to $850.9 billion, a 10.4 percent rise which was the sharpest in twenty-five years. Several factors accounted for this rise. The first was the increase in overall business activity during 1972, which created a sharp decrease in the number of people unemployed. The vast increase in federal outlays for food assistance programs also increased disposable income. The period from 1969 to 1972 saw a rise in the number of food stamp recipients from 3.2 million to 13.2 million, and an increase in social security benefits put $12 billion in purchasing power in the hands of the elderly. Newly employed workers, food stamp recipients, and the elderly are precisely the consumers most likely to better their diet by increasing their consumption of meat. The vast increase in demand during 1972 was not, however, accompanied by an increase in supply.

The supply of beef was not adequate to meet the unusual demand conditions of 1973. First of all, because of rising standards of living abroad and the devaluation of the dollar, there was a 26 percent increase in the amount of American beef exported in 1972. This dramatic increase in exports reduced the supply available for domestic consumption. Moreover, bad weather caused tremendous delays in bringing cattle to the slaughterhouse during the early part of 1973, creating for the short term further pressure on the supply. Most importantly, the economics of beef production are not capable of meeting rapid rises of demand. It takes two years for a steer to mature to the point where it is profitable to slaughter the steer for meat production. Thus the farmers in 1973 were essentially responding to the demand conditions in 1971 when they brought their herds to slaughter. During 1971 demand was considerably lower. The economy was in a downturn and farmers accordingly made their decisions to increase their 1971 herds with those factors in mind. The production decision made in 1971 was for a supply sharply lower than the demand of early 1973.

In view of the economics of cattle production it is easy to see why boycotts and price controls are ineffective methods for reducing the retail prices of meat production. A boycott for a short term does nothing to increase the supply, since that decision, having been made two years previously, is effectively out of the control of the farmer. Even the farmers were not able to take short-term action against the boycott. Some farmers threatened to withhold sending cattle to be slaughtered so long as the boycott and price controls were in effect. But given the high costs of feed, it is unprofitable to let cattle keep eating for more than two years before slaughter. Therefore, by withholding cattle from the processors the farmer would be taking an additional beating. The boycott therefore could affect neither the prices nor, in the short run, the supply of cattle available for slaughter.

Price controls also have little effect on the short-term price structure and may decrease the supply in the long run—thus causing an increase in prices. Since the supply of cattle was predetermined when the decision to institute price controls was made, the price controls had little effect on the supply of beef for the rest of 1973. Moreover, since the existence of artificial constraints on prices influences the farmer's future expectation of income, he is less likely to plan to increase the size of his herd, and thus the supply of meat available two years in the future, when he feels that prices might be lower. The long-run result of price control is to decrease the supply available two years from their institution.

The farmer's income is determined by the price he can get for his animals from feedlot operators. Feedlot operators purchase the heifers and calves from the farmer and fatten the animals for six months before slaughter. In 1972 and 1973 the price of all grains increased dramatically, particularly soybeans, which are used extensively by the feedlot operators. The feedlot operators were caught in a squeeze. The prices which they could get for the slaughtered cattle from packing houses were fixed; at the same time, their operating costs soared. The feedlot operators are not in the long run able to get the farmers to accept the lower prices which they must pay if they are to make a profit on their feedlot operations. The result is that farmers find it increasingly less profitable to produce cattle for feed lots.

It does not seem likely that the upward pressure on meat prices will decrease in the years to come. Classical price theory would hold that the cattle producers would simply increase their production in response to the stimulus of higher prices until the supply reached the level of demand. Then, as larger numbers of farmers switched into cattle production a glut would develop on the market and prices could be expected to decline after equilibrium was reached. However, given the rapid rise in demand, this seems unlikely. There is continual pressure to increase the amount of benefits paid to the elderly under social security and the number of people receiving food stamps. Combined with expected increases in the level of employment, the disposable income of consumers is likely to continue to increase, and with it the demand for meat. There is a finite amount of grazing land in this country and the large cattle ranches are already operating at capacity. Increases in supply will have to come from increased output of smaller, less efficient producers which, because of higher costs, will increase prices. Since demand is likely to increase faster than supply, prices in the future will undoubtedly tend to be even higher. Moreover, with the general rise in world living standards and increasing demand for exports of soybeans and other grains traditionally used in the feedlots, the cost of producing meat will increase dramatically, resulting in a long-run increase in the price of meat.

As the prices of meat continue to rise, choices will have to be made in order to protect the purchasing power of the consumer's dollar. Producers may respond to the high costs of meat production by supplying less expensive protein substitutes for meat. The tastes of individuals for meat will undoubtedly be affected if, over the long run, the real price of meat rises. It is too soon to predict the responses on the demand and supply sides of the market, but preliminary evidence suggests that some demand shift away from meat is underway. This shift will be restricted, however, by its limited impact on meat prices.

before prices rise even higher, causing an increase in consumption. Some individuals claim that an increase in prices during an inflation will anger consumers, causing them to reduce rather than stockpile goods,[12] thus decreasing consumption. An important study by the University of Michigan's Survey Research Center shows that expectations of a higher future income will cause consumers to spend more and save less.[13] By and large, however, the relationship between price expectation and consumption has not been well defined.

Wealth

Studies have also been conducted on wealth as a possible determinant of the level of consumption. For example, a person with a measured income of $10,000 per year and assets of $200,000 is probably going to spend more than a person who earns $10,000 per year and has no financial assets. Friedman, in formulating his permanent income hypothesis, analyzed wealth effects. In his model, wealth is broken down into two categories, human and nonhuman wealth. Nonhuman wealth consists of assets which can readily be converted into cash should the need arise. Human wealth, on the other hand, consists of an individual's earning power, which is a function of his education and experience. The higher the ratio of nonhuman to total wealth, the greater the amount of permanent income which an individual would be willing to consume.

The relative income theory, examined earlier, is also concerned with wealth effects, since an individual's consumption decisions are determined by his income and by the observed wealth of other individuals in the same income category. So far, economists have not been able to isolate wealth effects from income effects in order to determine the relationship between wealth and consumption. James Tobin has used wealth to explain the connection between short-run budget studies and long-run studies such as that of Kuznets.[14] Tobin argued that the growth of wealth over time in the United States has caused an upward shift in the cross-sectional consumption functions. In Tobin's view, the upward movement has traced out the observed growth in long-run APC and MPC curves. To date, the evidence indicates that wealth has an indirect role in causing changes in consumption, since wealth is so closely tied to income.

While all of these factors play some role in determining consumption expenditure, the fundamental determinant in general theoretical treatments of the economy has been found to be measured income or some variant thereof, such as relative or permanent income. Most disputes concern only the *manner in which* income changes affect consumption. Therefore, con-

---

12. E. Mueller, "Consumer Reactions to Inflation," *Quarterly Journal of Economics* 78 (May 1959): 246–262.

13. George Katona, *Psychological Aspects of Consumer Behavior* (New York: McGraw-Hill, 1951).

14. Tobin, "Relative Income, Absolute Income, and Saving," pp. 135–136.

sumption is the portion of private expenditure which is relatively easy to predict. This will become clear in the following chapter as we examine the theory of investment, the other portion of private expenditure.

Questions and Exercises

1. The absolute income theory of consumption assumes that spending levels are dependent on disposable income. How might it be possible for per capita income to drop and consumption to remain more or less at the same level without contradicting this theory?

2. How would a general rise in price levels affect the real income of the household? What response would be predicted by the absolute income theory of consumption? What about a decrease in the general price level?

3. The same form or source of income may be permanent or transitory income depending on the expectations of the recipient. Under what circumstances would an inheritance be transitory income? Are there any circumstances under which it may be included as permanent income? Explain.

4. The efforts to conserve energy and the environment in 1973–1974 seemed to have some effect in reducing consumption, or at least the rise in consumption, of some types even though incomes continued to rise. How might the relative income hypothesis have explained such a phenomenon?

5. The Nixon administration attempted to reduce the consumption of energy, particularly gasoline, in 1973–1974 by allowing prices to rise. What was the income effect? How would the change in income be reflected in consumption patterns? (Recall the characteristics of short-run consumption functions.) Would it make much difference if people believed the shortage to be temporary or permanent? How?

6. The equation for the permanent income of a very young worker might have a higher value for B than that for an older worker. Why? How would you compare the values of B in the permanent income equation for a union worker of high seniority with that of an independent small business proprietor? Why might they be different?

7. Although the rate of consumption is believed to be affected by substantial changes in the interest rate, it may also be that the primary activity in such cases is changes in the form in which assets are held, not necessarily in the rate of saving. Do you agree or disagree? Why?

8. If the time-series consumption function is the most accurate one, what are the implications for the savings available for expansion as an economy grows? The likelihood of a glut developing as an economy grows?

9. One of the criticisms of the Friedman permanent and transitory income hypothesis is that consumers may also be expected to engage in transitory spending. How would you explain the criticism? How might transitory spending invalidate the proposed relationship between spending and permanent income?

10. In the early 1970s, as the Nixon administration attempted to deal with the problem of inflation, Milton Friedman noted that one of the objectives of government economic policy was to reduce "inflation psychology." What did Friedman mean? How would it have affected the location of the short-run consumption function?

in periods of expansion relative to periods of recession.

During the 71 postwar quarters of business cycle expansion (completed expansions), nonfarm personal income nationally increased at an average annual rate of 7.6 percent with individual quarterly changes ranging from an increase of 28 percent to a decline of nearly 1 percent. During the 17 quarters of recession (5 completed recessions), nonfarm personal income increased at an average annual rate of 1.9 percent, with quarterly changes ranging from a decline of 3 percent to a gain of 11 percent. The difference between the expansion and recession averages is 5.8 percentage points, which is called the "cyclical swing," in this article. The expansions and recessions are timed by peaks and troughs in real quarterly gross national product (GNP),[2] because the article deals with quarterly personal income as an integral component of national

Construction Outlays In January Fell 2.3% From Month Before

WASHINGTON — Construction spending sagged in January, falling 2.3% from a December total that was revised to show a slim increase, rather than a sizable drop, from November, the Commerce Department said.

January construction outlays fell to a seasonally adjusted annual rate of $133.2 billion from December's revised $136.3 billion. January's total was 1.8% below the year-earlier $135.7 billion rate.

December's revision, mainly reflecting larger-than-estimated construction outlays by state and local governments, raised that month's spending 0.3% above November. Originally, the department reported December construction spending fell 2.3% from the prior month.

The current home-building slump caused total private construction spending in January [...] large as to suggest [...] ficulty [...] labor, materials and capacity [...] at whatever is postpon [...] to the [...] in that [...] up busi [...] prospec [...]

Price Rises

The survey reported [...] facturers pect prices they charge to rise % in from 1973 and they anticipate a further 15% increase by 1977. Last year's actual rise in prices for manufactured goods was 7.7%, according to the Bureau of Labor Statistics.

Reporting on particular industries, the survey said petroleum companies [...] 17% rise in their prices thi [...] this may already [...] Greenwald s [...]

The cyclical swing was positive in all regions and in 48 States. [...] the sw [...] than 1 [...] in Michigan and Indiana to less than 1½ percentage

cyclical [...] state and regional busi cycles, because the measures of pro tion necessary for such a calcula do not exist.

First Quarter Performance of Selected Companies
(Dollar figures in millions)

Company	First Quarter Earnings (Loss)			First Quarter Sales			Profit Margin	
	1974	1973	% change	1974	1973	% change	1974	1973
Alcoa	$45.4	$21.1	+115	$653.8	$495.9	+32		
Anaconda	26.3	14.6	+98	414.0	294.0			
Armco	37.6	24.1	+56	680.5	531.9	+28	5.5	4.5
A.T.&T.	799.4	700.4	+14	6,310.0	5,620.0	+12	12.7	12.5
Avon	17.7	20.3	-13	242.2	220.8	+10	7.3	9.2
Beth. Steel	43.1	40.5	+6	1,130.0	967.4	+17		4.2
Braniff	5.7	4.0	+43	126.0	99.0	+27	4.5	4.0
Burl.gton	28.0	20.2	+37	589.9	561.9	+14	4.8	3.9
C.	40.6	55.3	-21	553.3	425.0	+30	7.3	13.0
Du.nt		138.0	+4	1,612.0	1,400.0	+15	8.9	9.9
Ex.	5.0		+39	9,945.0	6,239.0	-59	7.1	8.1
G.te	122.3			2,909.3	2,547.4	+14	4.2	4.5
G	23.7			285.5	231.9	+23	8.3	9.0
G.year		45.3		30.0	1,070.0	+10	3.9	4.2
.ay		7.4	+64	6.2	193.8	+12	1.3	3.8
I.b.	4	340.		.000.0			14.4	13.9
NCR			+6	38	367.4		3.1	2.0
Phil. Morris	37		+1		570.6	+13		5.7
Polaroid	9.9		-12	.7	135.3	+8	6.	8.4
P. & G.	95.9	86.6	+11	.9	1,024.3	+3		8.5
Rockwell	37.7	34.3	+10		801.3	-	.5	.6
Texaco	589.4	264.0	+123		2,494.0		1.9	0.6
T.W.A.	(47.3)	(14.8)	—	3		-1		
Un. Carbide	94.1	66.3	+42	1,109.6	905.5	+2	8.5	
Westinghouse	29.4	40.9	-28	1,452.0	1,268.0	+15	2.0	

U.S. Industry Increases '74 Spending Plans 19%

By HERBERT KOSHETZ

American industry plans to spend $119.1-billion for new plant and equipment this year, an increase of 19.4 per cent compared with 1973, McGraw-Hill Publications said yesterday.

Douglas Greenwald, chief for McGraw-Hill, in a capital- taken pointed ment i-the-1974. Our survey cts a ion of rising appro heavy backlogs of capital orders and of contracts dustrial and commercial in bon as well as signifi r price increases said.

said, spending this year in real terms would show an increase of about 8.5 per cent.

He pointed out that 1974 investment plans had been stepped up since last fall. A survey taken in October indicated a 13.5 per cent increase and a recheck in early March showed an 18.5 per cent rise in ning plans.

howed that the one

group, p crease in their cap this year, with the biggest centage gain in nonferrous metals where manufacturers plan a 71 per cent increase.

The auto industry, however, hit hard by a drop in demand

they did during 197 companies plan a ag outlay of $8.28-billion i capital spending, or 52 pe more than they spent lastose in Spending plans for the 22.6 billion in January. Un industry are up 49 per cen expenditures of $2.77-b

government-sponsored private corporation was created in 1972 to help channel funds into student loans through secondary market and warehousing activities. It currently plans to sell 234,000 common shares at $150 a share to qualified financial and educational institutions that are eligible to participate in the student loan program, a spokesman said. Last July, Sallie Mae announced plans to raise $105 million through the sale of 700,000 common shares. Instead of the common stock offering, however, Sallie Mae sold two issues of $100 1 of 182-day discounts li c market last cover. Its debt securities are backed by the Treasury.

Proceeds will be used to fund Sallie Mae's existing warehousing operations and its new loan-purchase program, and for general corporate purposes. Under the warehousing program, Sallie Mae accepts guaranteed student loans as collateral, and advances funds to the institutional lenders so they may make additional student loans, the spokesman added.

Underwriters led by Lehman Brothers Inc., Bank of America, First National Bank of Chicago, Merrill Lynch, Pierce, Fenner & Smith Inc., Morgan Stanley & Co. and Salomon Brothers will handle the sale, expected to take place April 10.

Inventories and Backlogs

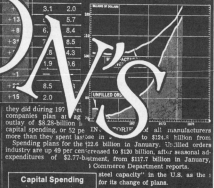

all manufacturers to $124.8 billion from creased to $120 billion, after seasonal adjustment, from $117.7 billion in January, Commerce Department reports.

steel capacity" in the U.S. as the for its change of plans.

Operation in 1978

It declined to specify either the the furnaces or the total cost of the ment, but did say that the new facilit expected to be in operation during n added that the necessary pollution will be installed on supporting facilit

The decision was made despite t ure of the Pennsylvania legislature s pass a package of pending bills—fre referred to as the "Bethlehem bills" would provide the company certai ances from antipollution laws. The noted that under the new pr federal environ year. tems up co only one it cut ted "changing

Capital Spending
$120 in billions of dollars
110
100
1973
Planned
80
70

Capital and Investment

7

To the policymaker responsible for achieving stabilization goals, the investment component of expenditure is of special interest. On the one hand, investment is by far the most volatile component of expenditure, showing much sharper year-to-year changes than personal consumption, and it is therefore generally assumed to be an important force behind economic fluctuations. On the other hand, important as it is, any analysis of investment spending is likely to be much more difficult than a comparable study of consumption. Consumption spending has been seen to be largely determined by disposable income or some variant thereof. Conversely, investment spending is not generally related in a stable way to any one factor: a whole series of variables, including interest rates, the level or change in national income, business expectations, and the introduction of innovations are likely to affect investment demand. Complicating the problem further, many of these factors, such as expectations and innovations, are very difficult to measure and even more difficult to offset.

As a result, policymakers find themselves in a peculiar dilemma. Changes in investment spending significantly affect the success of attempts at maintenance of a high-employment, stable economy, but at the same time are difficult to predict. Since it is difficult to anticipate changes in investment expenditure, it is difficult to design policy responses to offset any destabilizing implications of such changes. For example, an economist who believes that investment spending is dependent on expected corporate profits will advocate a cut in the corporate tax rate as the best way to encourage such spending, whereas one who feels that investment is closely tied to changes in national income or introduction of new innovations may recommend completely different measures. This chapter will introduce and explain some of the most widely accepted explanations of investment demand; Chapter 11 will discuss the policy implications which logically follow from the alternative explanations.

Capital and Investment: A Few Definitions

Investment spending is subdivided into three separate categories, as shown in Figure 7.1: business fixed investment (nonresidential structures plus expenditures for plant and equipment), residential construction, and business inventories. Each of these components is influenced by different factors. Private housing, for example, is closely tied to demographic factors (i.e., the rate of new family formation) and interest rates, and is only distantly affected by changes in corporate profits; inventory investment is related to changes in the level of national income and corporate profits and expected price changes; and plant and equipment expenditures are influenced by all these factors and some others as well. Because housing and inventory investment constitute only about one-third of total investment and spending, the discussion which follows will concentrate exclusively on investment spending devoted to plant and equipment, which represents about two-thirds of the total investment component.

The terms **capital** and **capital stock** designate the supply of plant and equipment owned by business; **gross investment** is the total amount which is spent on new capital stock in a given time period. However, during any period some of the existing capital stock wears out or is used up in the ongoing process of depreciation. During some periods, gross investment will exceed depreciation, causing the total capital stock to increase; in such cases, **net investment** occurs. When depreciation is larger than gross investment, **disinvestment** occurs, and the stock of capital will fall.

The Decision to Invest

In a market economy such as that of the United States, earning a profit is the purpose of a business enterprise. The decision to invest, therefore, is

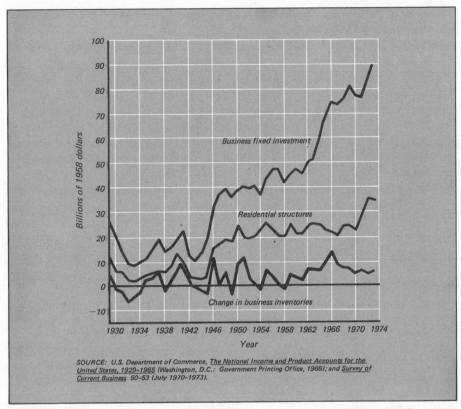

Figure 7.1 Components of gross private domestic investment, 1929–1973 (constant 1958 dollars)

directly related to the profits an executive hopes to make from the additional capital stock acquired by such investment spending. This is complicated by the fact that in most cases the earnings, and therefore the profits, to be obtained from an additional unit of capital stock are spread out over several years—four or five in the case of a new truck or piece of machinery, perhaps as many as twenty or thirty in the case of a new factory. However, as one might imagine, earnings to be received four years or twenty years from now are not as valuable as earnings received immediately. It is therefore necessary to find some way of valuing the future returns to be obtained from an investment in terms of their current or present value. How do we go about expressing the value of a dollar to be received some time in the future in terms of the value of a dollar on hand now?

The Present Value of a Future Asset

The simplest approach to the question of present value is to attack it through the familiar concept of compound interest. Assume you deposit $1,000 at 6 percent in a bank where interest is credited once a year. At the end of one year, you have your original deposit, $1,000, plus 6 percent of $1,000, or $1,060 in all. We can express this relationship in an equation where P_1 is the amount you will get back at the end of the year, P_0 is the original deposit, and i is the rate of interest paid.

$$P_1 = P_0 + P_0(i) \text{ or } \$1,060 = \$1,000 + (\$1,000 \times 6\%)$$

This equation may be rewritten as

$$P_1 = P_0(1 + i) \tag{7.1}$$

At the end of the second year, the total principal, P_2, will be equal to this $1,060, P_1, plus 6 percent of $1,060, or $1,123.60; that is

$$P_2 = P_1 + P_1(i)$$

which may be rewritten as

$$P_2 = P_1(1 + i)$$

Substituting for P_1 from equation (7.1) we find:

$$P_2 = P_0(1 + i)(1 + i)$$

or

$$P_2 = P_0(1 + i)^2 \tag{7.2}$$

This equation can be generalized to apply to a sum of money left at compound interest for any number of years by substituting the number of years for the exponential 2 in the above equation. For example, the formula for the principal at the end of five years would be $P_5 = P_0(1 + i)^5$, and the formula for the principal at the end of n years would be $P_n = P_0(1 + i)^n$.

These formulae explain how it is possible to determine the *future* value, P_n, of a present sum, P_0, left at interest, i. However, as explained earlier, it is necessary for a business executive to find some way of expressing the *present* value of the future sums of money he expects his investment to produce, and to determine, based on this information, whether the investment is desirable. The equations developed above suggest a method through which this objective can be accomplished.

We have shown how $1,000 left on deposit at 6 percent compound interest is worth $1,123.60 at the end of two years. We can reverse this, given the future sum, the time period, and the rate of return, to get the present value of a future sum. Given that $P_n = P_0(1 + i)^n$, we divide each side of the equation by $(1 + i)^n$, arriving at the new formula

$$P_0 = \frac{P_n}{(1 + i)^n} \tag{7.3}$$

Substituting the figures for a two-year deposit, we find that the present value, P_0, of $1,123.60, P_n, to be obtained two years hence, given an interest rate of 6 percent, is indeed $1,000.

$$P_o = \frac{1123.60}{(1 + .06)^2} = \frac{1123.60}{1.1236} = 1,000$$

Net Present Value, Future Value, and the Rate of Return

The concepts of **net present value, future value,** and **rate of return** can be employed in several ways in making investment decisions. As a practical matter, firms usually know in advance the cost of a projected investment, P_o, and have some idea of the total return of income to expect the investment to yield over its life, P_n. Using these figures in the equations developed above, a firm can estimate the rate of return that each investment can be expected to produce, then discard as uneconomic certain investments, and list the others in order of preference. Unless an investment will provide a rate of return which is higher than the prevailing interest rate, it is not profitable to invest. This is true whether the firm must actually borrow the money or whether it has the funds available from its own resources. For example, if interest rates are 10 percent, and the rate of return on an investment is estimated to be only 8 percent annually, an investor would lose money on the investment. The same applies if he had, say, $1,000 of his own money in hand; in this case he would be able to lend the money to others and earn $100 rather than use it to make the investment and earn $80.

Ranking investments by rates of return can be used to determine the order in which to proceed with investments given only limited funds (or borrowing power). Given a list of investments, all of which provide rates of return higher than the current interest rate, those with the highest rates are, of course, preferable, given that the anticipated risks on each of the projects under consideration are the same.

We shall see that, given

$$P_o = \frac{P_n}{(1 + i)^n}$$

it is useful to be able to calculate the value of i which satisfies the above equation, knowing P_o and P_n. There is no direct mathematical way to solve for i in those cases where the life of the asset is more than two years, that is, where n is greater than 2. The usual approach is to estimate—to take a value of i, substitute it in the right-hand side of the equation, and given P_n and P_o, see if the equation balances. For example, given an asset with a net present value or purchase cost of $2,000 ($P_o$ = $2,000) that is expected to produce $3,000 in income over a five-year period (P_5 = $3,000), an i of 8.5 percent looks about right. Thus:

$$2,000 = \frac{3000}{(1 + .085)^5} = \frac{3000}{1.504}$$

It is also possible to use compound interest tables to determine the inter-

Table 7.1 Amount of 1 at Compound Interest

Year	8.1%	8.2%	8.3%	8.4%	8.5%
1	1.08100	1.08200	1.08300	1.08400	1.08500
2	1.16856	1.17072	1.17288	1.17505	1.17722
3	1.26321	1.26672	1.27023	1.27376	1.27728
4	1.36553	1.37059	1.37566	1.38075	1.38585
5	1.47614	1.48298	1.48984	(1.49673)	1.50365
6	1.59570	1.60458	1.61350	1.62246	1.63146
7	1.72496	1.73616	1.74742	1.75874	1.77013
8	1.86468	1.87852	1.89246	1.90648	1.92060
9	2.01572	2.03256	2.04953	2.06662	2.08385
10	(2.17899)	2.19923	2.21964	2.24022	2.26097

est rate. These tables are set up so that one can read the value of 1 at compound interest, varying rates for varying periods. In the sample given in Table 7.1, for example, we see that 1, compounded at 8.1 percent, will equal 2.178 at the end of ten years, or that if 1 grows to 1.496 in five years, it is compounding at 8.4 percent. In terms of the equations presented earlier, 1 is equal to P_0, the compound interest rate is equal to i, and the number in the table is the equivalent of P_n.

Note that in order to find i through these tables, it is necessary to know both P_0 and P_n, and to reduce the equation to those terms where $P_0 = 1$. Thus, in the problem given above, where we are attempting to find that rate of compound interest at which $2,000 increases to $3,000 in five years, we must divide both numbers by $2,000 in order to produce a problem in the terms the table can solve. The new problem then becomes one of finding that rate of compound interest at which 1 will grow to $1\frac{1}{2}$ in five years, and the table shows us that this is roughly 8.5 percent. In practical terms this would mean that a firm would consider this investment only when interest rates were at or below 8.5 percent, and that all other things being equal, it would rank this investment before others with rates of return lower than 8.5 percent but after those with interest rates of less than 8.5 percent.

The Marginal Efficiency of Capital (MEC)

We have defined r as that rate of return which would make P_0 equal to P_n in n years. Keynes defined the **marginal efficiency of capital** (MEC) as that rate of discount which would make the net present value of the returns expected from the capital asset during its life exactly equal to its supply price. If a firm's borrowing rate is equal to its MEC, that firm may be shown to possess its **optimum stock of capital.** A smaller stock of capital would mean MEC exceeds i (given diminishing returns to capital). The firm could raise total profits by adding capital. If, on the other hand, i exceeds MEC, the firm holds capital yielding a negative return. For example, a firm with an initial capital stock of $10 million and facing a cost of capital of 10 percent will decide to invest only in new plant and equipment with MECs of at least 10 percent; if these projects total $1 million, its optimum capital stock will be $11 million. On the other hand, if it decides to invest in plant and equipment with MECs as low as 8 percent, because of a lower cost of borrowing equal to 8 percent, and selects $3 million of such projects, its optimum stock would be $13 million. This is shown in Figure 7.2.

Combining the MEC schedules for all individual firms, we arrive at an MEC schedule for the entire economy, shown in Figure 7.3. Note that the MEC curve has a negative slope, indicating that the higher the MEC required of new investments, the smaller the optimum capital stock.

Generalizing Net Present Value

Understanding the concept of the marginal efficiency of capital allows us to look more closely at the investment decision. It is necessary to examine each of the factors which can affect the marginal efficiency of capital; then we can confront the problem of increasing costs of producing more capital goods, implicit in an investment decision to add to the capital stock.

In considering the factors which may affect MEC, recall that MEC is the value of i which makes net present value (NPV) equal to 0, where:

$$NPV = \frac{R_1}{(1 + i)} + \frac{R_2}{(1 + i)^2} + \frac{R_3}{(1 + i)^3} + \ldots + \frac{R_n}{(1 + i)^n} - P_K K \qquad (7.4)$$

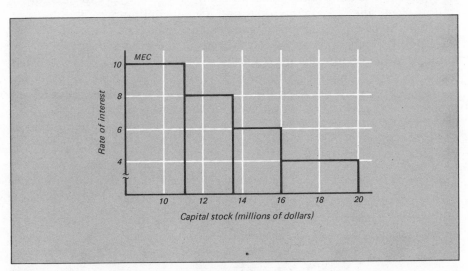

Figure 7.2 MEC schedule for an individual firm

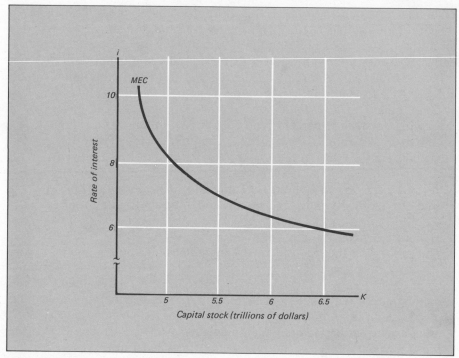

Figure 7.3 MEC curve for an economy

for a project with a life of n periods where R_i (i = 1 . . . n) is expected future returns from capital, P_K is the price, and K is the optimum capital stock, or that quantity of capital currently being considered for purchase.

The NPV expression can be generalized for the economy as a whole by noting that the Rs in equation (7.4) represent the money value of expected output associated with a given quantity of capital and labor. In order for the formula to hold, the Rs must be constant over time. Since these Rs are to represent the portion of output going to the owners of capital, the stream of returns to labor, or P_nN, must be subtracted from total output to obtain the return to capital. It can be shown that as n goes to infinity, the present value calculation simplifies to:

$$PV = \frac{\text{Annual return}}{i}$$

With these concepts in mind, NPV for the capital stock of the economy, which is assumed to last forever, will be:

$$NPV = \frac{P \cdot y(K, N) - P_nN}{i} - P_KK \tag{7.5}$$

where output, y, is expressed as some function of the quantity of capital, K, and labor, N, available in the economy: $y = y(K, N)$.

The price of capital when the capital stock is optimum will be obtained when adding to K adds nothing to NPV, or

$$0 = \frac{P \cdot MP_K}{MEC = i} - P_K \tag{7.6}$$

This equation may be rewritten in terms of the price of capital as:

$$P_K = \frac{P \cdot MP_K}{MEC = i} \tag{7.7}$$

The MEC will be the value of i which satisfies the above equation, since that value of P_K implies a maximum value for the next present value of decisions to add to the economy's stock of capital:

$$MEC = i = \frac{P \cdot MP_K}{P_K} \tag{7.8}$$

Scarcity of Capital Goods

Necessary to a full understanding of the investment decision is recognition of the scarcity of resources, which implies an increasing marginal cost of adding to the capital stock, or investing in plant and machinery, in terms of noncapital goods or consumption goods. This condition is represented by a trade-off, known as a **production transformation surface**, between capital goods and consumption goods (where these two types of goods are assumed to exhaust the classes of goods being produced). Two features of the production transformation surface, represented in Figure 7.4 by the curve $T_K T_C$, are important. First, more capital goods can be produced only if fewer consumption goods are produced; and second, the cost of producing an additional unit of capital goods, in terms of units of consumption goods foregone, rises with the share of production devoted to capital goods.

Looking at Figure 7.4, we can see the implied trade-off between production of current and capital goods by first noting that at point T_C on the C axis, only consumption goods are produced. Output of C is OT_C while (foregone) output of capital goods is OT_K, implying zero output of K. Moving along the production transformation surface to point H represents a reduction in the output of consumption goods by GT_C and an increase in production of capital goods by OE. Notice that Figure 7.4 is drawn so that point E divides the distance OT_K into two equal parts, or $OE = ET_K$. In moving from point T_C to point H along curve $T_C T_K$, the ratio of the rise in the output of capital goods to the fall in the output of consumption goods is OE/GT_C.

The notion of the increased cost of capital goods, K, in terms of consumption goods given up, C, may be illustrated by moving further along the pro-

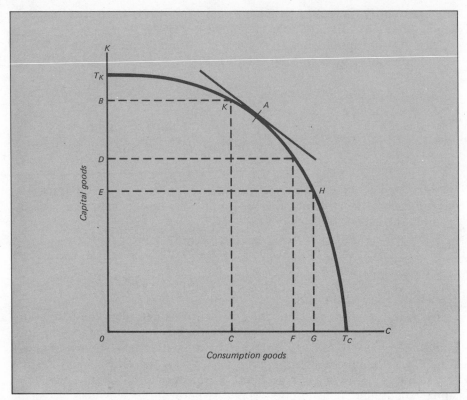

Figure 7.4 The production transformation surface between capital goods and consumption goods

duction transformation surface to point T_K. In this case the output of consumption goods falls by OG to zero, while the output of capital goods rises by ET_K, which, as we have seen, is equal to OE. The distance OE represents, as we have seen, the initial increase in K obtained at a cost, in terms of C, equal to only GT_C. The marginal cost, in terms of C, of producing additional K in the amount of ET_K = OE has risen from GT_C to OG. In fact, it is the "bowed out" shape of T_KT_C relative to point O, that represents the likely economic fact of an increasing marginal cost, in terms of consumption goods, of producing more capital goods, or investment. As more production is devoted to capital goods, increasing quantities of consumption goods must be given up in order to free the necessary resources. This is because C and K are not perfect substitutes in production. If they were, the relative resource inputs required to produce K would be identical to those required to produce C. The production transformation surface would be a straight line, and C and K would be identical goods from the standpoint of the resources required to produce a unit of each good.

Relationship Between the MEC and the Decision to Invest (MEI)

In order to analyze the relationship between the MEC and the decision to invest presented in Figure 7.5, we must recall the discussion of increasing marginal cost and the requirements for i = MEC. In looking at four-quadrant diagrams such as Figure 7.5, it is important to remember that all movement away from the center represents an increase in the variable being measured along each axis. Movement toward the center represents a decrease.

Quadrant A identifies the initial capital stock at K_0. The downward sloping schedule in quadrant A represents the present discounted value of the value of the marginal product of capital or:

$$P_K = \frac{P \cdot MP_K}{i} \tag{7.9}$$

where P_K is the price of a unit of capital goods and MP_K is the marginal prod-

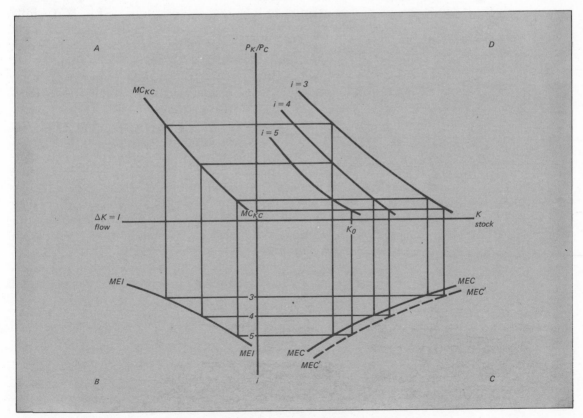

Figure 7.5 Determination of MEC and MEI and their interrelationship

uct of capital. Each schedule is drawn for a given interest rate, i, shifting up as i falls, since the rate at which returns from capital are discounted is thereby reduced.[1] The vertical axis of quadrant A represents the price of capital goods in terms of consumption goods, a reminder that the price of capital goods, expressed in terms of consumption goods, is the most economically meaningful or "real" price of capital goods.

MC_{KC} in quadrant B represents the increasing marginal cost of increasing the stock of capital goods expressed in terms of consumption goods, or P_K/P_C. Notice that the higher the level of investment, expressed as ΔK, the larger the increase in P_K/P_C required for a given ΔK. This is consistent with the "bowed out" production transformation surface shown in Figure 7.4.

The **marginal efficiency of investment** schedule (MEI) in quadrant C describes the relationship between investment and the interest rate. Its inwardly bowed shape reflects the increase in the rise in P_K as i falls, or the positive second derivation of P_K with respect to i in equation (7.7) as reported in footnote 1.

The marginal efficiency of capital schedule (MEC) for a given price of capital goods, is represented in quadrant D. If P_K falls to P_{K_1}, MEC shifts outward to MEC' at each interest rate since, as can be seen from equation (7.5), a fall in P_K requires the purchase of more units of capital at a given interest rate and a given marginal product of capital, MP_K, to keep the net present value equal to zero. This is equivalent to saying that, given i and given MP_K, the optimum capital stock rises as the price of capital goods falls.

We can now examine the relationship between MEC and MEI in order to see the implications for these schedules of changes in the interest rate, the price of capital goods, and the marginal product of capital. In quadrant A a set of schedules for the present discounted value of the value of the marginal product of capital are drawn for different interest rates, but, initially, for given values of MP_K and the price of output. The MEC is derived as the relationship between i and the optimum *level* of the capital stock for given values of P_K, MP_K, and P. The MEI is derived as the relationship between i and the optimum *change* in the capital stock, given MP_K and P. Notice that P_K/P_C varies with movement along MEI, since investment defines a *change* in the production of capital goods which, as was seen in the analysis of the production transformation curve, requires a change in the price of capital goods in terms of consumption goods.

1. The upward shift in the schedule may be derived by differentiating equation (7.7) with respect to i:

$$\frac{\partial P_K}{\partial i} = \frac{-P \cdot MP_K}{i^2} < 0$$

The result indicates that as i falls, equilibrium P_K for a given capital stock rises. The upward shift rises for each subsequent fall in i since the second derivative of P_K with respect to i is positive—or the change in the rise in P_K for each fall in i gets larger.

$$\frac{\partial^2 P_K}{\partial i^2} = \frac{2P \cdot MP_K}{i^3} > 0$$

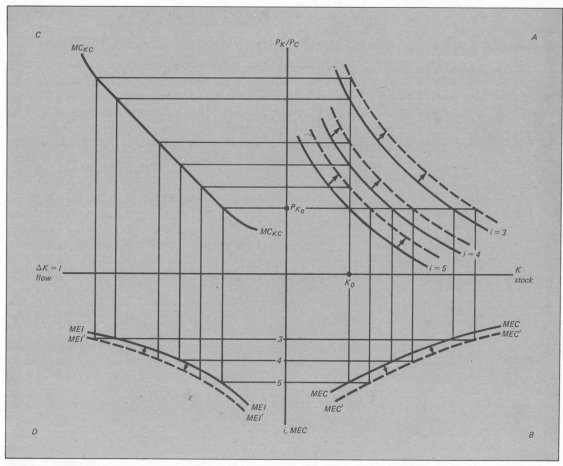

Figure 7.6 Effect of a higher price, P, or higher marginal product of capital, MP_K, on MEC and MEI

Shifts in MEC and MEI

Shifts in MEC and MEI are shown in Figure 7.6, which reproduces Figure 7.5. Given a rise in the marginal product of capital, or the price at which goods produced with capital can be sold, each schedule in quadrant A representing the discounted present value of the value of the marginal product of capital shifts up. This results in an upward shift of both MEC and MEI, which is consistent with the expectation of an increase in the optimal stock of capital at each interest rate, given a higher value of the marginal product of capital. The same change would result in a higher rate of investment at each interest rate, as reflected by the outward shift of MEI.

The Stock-Flow Problem and Shifts in the MEI

The relationship we have just examined between investment as the change in the capital stock and the actual capital stock presents a difficulty

Commentary: More Investment at Higher Interest Rates - Invalidation of Theory?

Early 1974 saw the highest interest rates in twenty years. The prime rate, which is the interest rate banks charge to their best customers, soared to over 11 percent, while yields on government securities increased to over 9 percent. Economic theory holds that when interest rates increase, investment declines, given that other factors influencing investment remain unchanged. However, a survey of twenty-six leading industries taken early in 1974 shows that most firms planned to increase their capital spending.[1] According to the survey, businesses planned to spend $119.1 billion for new plants and equipment, an increase of almost 20 percent and the largest increase in eighteen years. The planned increase in investment in the face of rapidly rising interest rates and, thus, rising cost of borrowing money suggests that, indeed, other factors influencing investment behavior have not remained unchanged and in addition have changed more sharply than anticipated. The upturn in capital spending surprised economists who had predicted a recession for early 1974 and forced them to revise their predictions. Most economists now agree that if the expenditures are made as planned, a recession can be averted during the latter part of 1974.

One reason for the decision to increase investment is the widespread general lack of capacity in the economy. During late 1973 and early 1974 output of both durable goods (particularly iron and steel, but also nonferrous metals, such as aluminum) and nondurable goods (chemicals, rubber, and especially paper) were insufficient to meet consumer demand. Shortages naturally resulted, and in some industries, especially those which depend on steel, such as the small machine industry, the shortages caused additional cutbacks in production. The survey indicates that with the end of price controls, industries are aware that in order to take advantage of rising prices, it is necessary to increase their productive capacity; of the expenditures surveyed, 53 percent were to go for plant expansion, and it was estimated that in 1975, 56 percent of the capital expenditures were to go for increasing capacity rather than for simply maintaining present facilities. Many of the firms surveyed indicated that they planned to increase capacity regardless of the level of consumer demand. An economist for an aluminum company observed, "You would have to have a collapse in the economy to make us pull back, and I am not sure that we would pull back even then."[2]

Inflation, and the fear that it will get worse, lies behind many decisions to invest; businesses feel it is better to borrow now rather than be forced to pay higher rates in the future. The president of one firm observed, "While some of our machines look expensive now, if inflation keeps going they are going to look cheap within a year or two."[3] A related explanation is that some firms, particularly those in the petroleum industry, earned higher profits in 1974 because of the energy crisis. Accordingly, they can afford to increase their investment in explorations for new sources of oil and in finding better and cheaper methods to refine oil. The decisions to expand investment are based less upon present market conditions than upon future expectations of prices and interest rates. In the case of steel, produc-

1. McGraw-Hill Economics Department, *Business Plans for New Plants and Equipment: 1974–1977* (New York: McGraw-Hill, 1974).

2. *Business Week*, May 4, 1974, p. 21.
3. Ibid.

ers both underestimated world demand and mistakenly took sufficient capacity for granted. The profits generated from the consequent pricing of steel were not such as to encourage expanded capacity. However, with increased production in the country generally, and thus increasing demand for steel and steel parts, steel producers have reassessed the situation and, with the end of price controls, have boosted the price of steel so that profits to generate additional production should no longer be a problem; increases of 10 percent on most and 20 percent on some steel products are expected in 1974. As a result, the major steel producers have announced plant construction plans to produce nearly 20 million tons of raw steel capacity by 1980.[4]

In fact, the coincidence of high investment and high interest rates is readily "explained" (although not necessarily predicted) by economic theory. The distinction which must be made is between a movement *along* the investment demand schedule and a *shift* in the entire investment schedule. Consider the diagram opposite. The schedule for the supply of funds (which, remember, is equivalent to a demand for bonds) has remained fixed. The demand for funds by investors (who are bond suppliers), or MEI schedule, has shifted sharply outward at each interest rate due to sharply rising prices for products and perhaps to an increase in the expected marginal product of capital, in view of heavy excess demand in some sectors of the economy. Recall that a rise in prices of output, or MP_K, resulted in an upward shift of the MEI schedule (see Figure 7.5). The result of an upward shift in the MEI schedule to MEI' is a rise in the interest rate from i_0 to i_1 while investment rises from I_0 to I_1. This result does not invalidate the negative or inverse relationship between changes in investment and the interest rate *along* the MEI schedule which takes all other factors influencing investment to be fixed. It merely reflects the impact of changes in other variables which make investors willing to invest more even at higher

4. *Business Week*, May 11, 1974, pp. 118–119.

interest rates. The interest rate must rise in the face of a shift in the investment demand schedule in order to convince lenders to lend more funds. This is reflected in a movement along the loan supply schedule.

Although the coincidence of higher interest rates and higher levels of investment is consistent with theory, theory does not enable us to predict when and by how much the MEI schedule will shift. Indeed, all of the causes of such shifts are not known. In short, there is no necessary connection between a good theory which "explains" past investment behavior and accurate prediction of investment behavior. The latter requires, first, an ability to predict behavior of volatile factors like business expectations and, second, an accurate measure of the link between changes in variables affecting investment behavior and investment behavior itself. Empirical studies of past investment behavior have gone a long way toward supplying the second element, while the first element remains largely unfathomed. This means that government stabilization policy still faces the combined difficulties of unpredictable changes in investment and considerable lags in implementing fiscal policy measures designed to offset the impact of such changes on the economy.

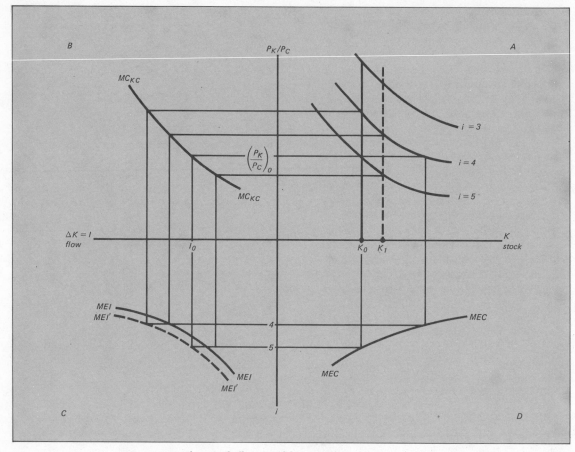

Figure 7.7 The stock-flow problem

in strictly determining the MEI. Notice that the MEI is derived, in each case, for $K = K_0$. But if I is defined as ΔK, it is, strictly speaking, inappropriate to assume the capital stock to be fixed once investment is underway. Keynes recognized this problem and dealt with it by specifying that he was interested in short-run changes in investment. Since over the short run (say, one year) $I = \Delta K$ would be tiny relative to the entire capital stock, the impact of I on K could be safely ignored. Annual investment for the United States is currently about 7.7 percent of the total physical stock of capital.[2] But ignoring the impact of investment upon the capital stock makes the MEI schedule appear to be more responsive to interest rate changes than it may, in fact, be. As we can see in Figure 7.7, which reproduces Figure 7.5, if we

2. Anatol Balbach, "Foreign Investment in the United States—A Danger to Our Welfare and Sovereignty," Federal Reserve Bank of St. Louis *Review*, October 1973, pp. 10–13.

can incorporate the impact of investment upon the capital stock, we introduce systematic, if small, downward pressure on the entire MEI schedule. If I_0 at $i = 5$ implies an annual increase in the capital stock of $K_1 - K_0$, the larger capital stock requires a lower P_K/P_C for equilibrium at $i = 5$ and $i = 4$ in quadrant A. The lower level of P_K/P_C reduces the production of capital goods at each interest rate, as reflected by the curve labeled MEI′ below MEI in quadrant C.

Theories of Investment Demand

Optimum capital stock, and therefore investment demand, can be affected either by those factors that produce a move along the MEC curve or those factors that shift the curve. Moves along the curve come about only through interest rate changes; shifts of the curve, however, may be caused by a variety of factors.

The Acceleration Principle

The acceleration principle holds that investment demand is dependent on increases in output, because such increases put pressures on firms to expand their stocks of capital goods.

The exact relationship between changes in output and investment spending depends on the **capital-output ratio**—the amount of capital needed to turn out a stated level of production. For example, a stocking manufacturer may need one knitting machine and other equipment with a total cost of $150,000 to turn out $50,000 worth of stockings per year. The capital-output ratio for this firm will be 3; that is, $3 worth of capital goods, K, are required for each $1 of output, y, or, assigning the symbol w to the capital-output ratio, $K = wy$ ($150,000 = 3 \times $50,000). This equation can be used to indicate how changes in output, y, will affect optimum capital stock, K, and consequently, investment spending, I. Given an existing level of y which can be supplied with the existing level of K, there will be no need for any increases in K, and therefore no net investment spending.[3] Increases in y beyond this level, however, will lead to additional increments of I.

In other words, if output increases over two periods of time, from y_1 to y_2, optimum capital will increase from K_1 to K_2, and the net investment spending needed in the second period, I_2, to produce the higher output will be the difference between the desired level of capital in the second period, K_2, and the original capital, K_1, or

$$I_2 = K_2 - K_1 \qquad (7.10)$$

If prices are taken to be fixed, national income, Y, equals the value of out-

3. Note that there may actually be some investment spending during the period in order to replace equipment that has worn out or depreciated. However, since there is no need for a higher level of *net* capital, there will be no investment spending *on a net basis*.

put, P_y. Then, given $K = wy$ where w is the capital-output ratio, we can substitute wy for K in the above equation:

$$I_2 = wy_2 - wy_1$$

or

$$I_2 = w(y_2 - y_1) \qquad (7.11)$$

Equation (7.11) indicates that the net investment spending during a period of time is equal to the change in output (income) during the period of time multiplied by the capital-output ratio. Thus, in a plant with a capital-output ratio of 3, an increase in output from $1 million to $1,100,000 would require net investment spending of $300,000.

Equation (7.11) assumes that there is no excess capacity during the first period. If there is, we must adjust the equation by subtracting such excess capacity, X_1, from the right-hand side, leaving

$$I_2 = w(y_2 - y_1) - X_1 \qquad (7.12)$$

which states that investment spending equals the capital-output ratio times the increase in output but less the amount of excess capacity existing during period 1. In the above example, investment spending, which we had calculated at $300,000, would be only $175,000 if the firm had had excess capacity of $125,000 during the initial period. Note that if excess capacity, X_1, equals the increment of additional capital required to turn out the higher output, $X_1 = (y_2 - y_1)$, there will be no net investment despite the increase in output.

We can also adjust the equation to show gross or total investment, I_G, rather than net investment, by adding to the net investment figure that amount of investment spending required to replace depreciated capital goods, D_2, giving us

$$I_2 + D_2 = I_{G_2} = w(y_2 - y_1) - X_1 + D_2 \qquad (7.13)$$

Thus the gross or total investment spending of the stocking company would be that additional capacity required to supply the additional output, $w(y_2 - y_1)$, less excess capacity existing during the first period, X_1, plus whatever amounts the company had to spend to replace depreciated capital stock that could no longer be used, D_2.

The sets of equations just developed are significant for two reasons. First, they indicate the casual relationship between changes in output and investment spending. Second, they point up the fact that the investment spending resulting from a change in output is very likely to be larger than the change in output that caused it. This will be true for every case where w is higher than one; that is, where the amount of capital needed to produce a given output is larger than the value of the output. This concept lies at the heart of the acceleration principle and will become clearer if we examine the operation of the principle in a hypothetical firm.

Table 7.2   Investment Spending for a Hypothetical Firm

Year	Output	Optimum Capital	Actual Capital	Net New Capital Required[a]	Replacement Demand	Gross Investment Spending
1967	1,000,000	3,000,000	3,000,000	—	300,000	300,000
1968	1,000,000	3,000,000	3,000,000	—	300,000	300,000
1969	1,100,000	3,300,000	3,000,000	300,000	300,000	600,000
1970	1,200,000	3,600,000	3,300,000	300,000	300,000	600,000
1971	1,400,000	4,200,000	3,600,000	600,000	300,000	900,000
1972	1,600,000	4,800,000	4,200,000	600,000	300,000	900,000
1973	1,700,000	5,100,000	4,800,000	300,000	300,000	600,000
1974	1,700,000	5,100,000	5,100,000	—	300,000	300,000
1975	1,600,000	4,800,000	5,100,000	−300,000	300,000	—

a. Net new capital required represents the difference between the optimum capital and the actual capital.

Take as an example the stocking firm introduced earlier, which has a capital output ratio of 3. Assume that the plant operates at capacity in 1967, producing $1,000,000 of stockings with $3,000,000 of capital, and that the average life of the capital goods is ten years, so that the company must invest $300,000 each year to replace the equipment that wears out. This information is presented in the first line of Table 7.2, where we see that total or gross investment spending for the firm will equal $300,000 in 1967.

Sales remain constant at $1,000,000 in 1968. The only investment spending required is the $300,000 to replace existing capital. In 1969, sales increase by 10 percent, or $100,000, to $1,100,000. Because the capital output ratio is 3, the firm will need capital of $3,300,000 to produce this output. As a result, gross investment spending will increase from $300,000 to $600,000, of which $300,000 represents replacement demand and $300,000 additions to net capital.[4] Observe that although output has increased by only 10 percent, investment spending increases by 100 percent; this accelerated change in investment in response to an initial increase in output is the basis of the acceleration principle.

In 1970, the firm's sales advance once again by $100,000 to $1,200,000, at which level $3,600,000 of capital stock is required. Existing capital at the end of the previous year was $3,300,000; the firm must therefore spend an additional $300,000 for new capital plus $300,000 for replacement capital,

---

4. It is possible to reach this same figure for gross investment spending with the formula given earlier, using w = 3, and the information in the 1969 line of the table.

$$I_{1969_g} = w(Y_{1969} - Y_{1968}) - X_{1968} + D_{1969} \text{ or}$$

$$\$600,000 = 3(\$1,100,000 - \$1,000,000) - 0 + \$300,000$$

or $600,000 in all. Note that although the firm has experienced an increase in output identical to that of the previous period ($100,000), its investment spending has remained constant at $600,000. It is not until 1971, when the improvement in output increases from $100,000 to $200,000, that any further increases in investment spending will occur. In 1971, this $200,000 jump in output will mean that an additional $600,000 of new capital is required; when added to replacement demand of $300,000, we reach a gross investment spending total of $900,000.

The 1970 and 1971 experience of this firm illustrates a very important tenet of the acceleration principle. Investment demand, which is quite volatile, will increase only in those years when the absolute increase in output increases (as it did in 1971): if the increment of output remains the same (as it did in 1969 and 1970, when output increased each year by an identical $100,000) then investment spending will level off.

The company has another good year in 1972, increasing its output from $1,400,000 to $1,600,000. Since, however, the amount of the increase ($200,000) is identical with the increase achieved in the previous year, investment spending remains unchanged. The company's experience in 1973 shows what happens to investment spending in those years when business is still good, with output increasing but by a smaller absolute amount than the previous year. In 1973, output advanced by $100,000 to $1,700,000; in the previous year it had increased by $200,000. This new 1973 level of output requires more new capital goods, it is true, but only $300,000 more rather than the additional $600,000 required in the previous year. As a result, when 1973 new capital-goods requirements are combined with replacement demand, gross investment spending reaches only $600,000, compared with the $900,000 level of 1972. In other words, even if output keeps increasing, once there is a decline in the absolute amount of the increase, investment spending will fall.

The company's output is unchanged in 1974, requiring no new additional capital goods, so investment demand is limited to $300,000, which represents a very sharp drop in the level of investment spending. In 1973, sales fall modestly, from $1.7 million to $1.6 million, or by about 6 percent. Investment spending, however, is completely eliminated, because the firm needs no new equipment and can forego its usual replacement demand by using some of the new capital goods purchased in the previous year (but not required for current production) to replace the worn-out equipment.

From this example it is possible to draw some conclusions about the performance of investment demand in the economy as a whole. Given an economy operating close to capacity, relatively minor increases in output will result in relatively large increases in investment demand. In order for further increases to occur, however, the absolute amount of the increase in output must increase. The economy must grow at an *ever-increasing rate* in order for investment demand to increase at all.

It can be seen from the action of the acceleration principle that investment and output follow a cyclical pattern. Numerous statistical studies reveal that investment spending is characterized by more extreme fluctuations than any other sector of the economy. Wesley Mitchell, for example, estimated that consumption spending rose by 15 percent during periods of business expansion, while investment spending rose by 55 percent; and that consumption spending dropped by only 10 percent during recessions, while investment spending dropped by 49 percent.[5] The acceleration principle is clearly useful in explaining these fluctuations because it shows how a relatively modest increase in consumption spending and output can lead to huge increases in investment spending and vice versa. We will examine how the accelerator interacts with the multiplier to further accelerate fluctuations in the appendix to this chapter. Expressed in terms of the MEC curve, the acceleration principle holds that an initial increase in the demand for output will cause an upward shift in each of the schedules in quadrant A, resulting in upward shifts of the MEC and MEI schedules due to a rise in the marginal product of capital and/or the price of output. Further upward shifts will occur only if the absolute amount of the rise in output increases from one time period to the next.

The Profits Theory

Whereas the acceleration principle links investment to changes in the level of output, the profits theory ties investment to the level of current profits, postulating that firms will increase investment spending when profits are high and will cut such spending when profits decline. Higher current profits lead to higher estimated future profits—the Rs in the net present value equation—resulting, in turn, in higher levels of investment at each interest rate.

The profits theory maintains that current profits are an important indicator of future profit levels. Thus, in computing the MEC of projected investments with a life span of several years. a business executive operating in a very profitable business environment will be more likely to estimate high future profits and, therefore, a higher MEC schedule. Conversely, in a year characterized by low profits, he will be less optimistic in his estimates of future profits and rate of return to be earned on any new investment. Figure 7.5 shows this as a shift to the right of the MEC and MEI curves in response to high current profits and increased expected prices, or MP_K. Of course, reverse shifts would occur if lower current profits reduced expected P or MP_K.

There are certain pitfalls in the profits theory. If the increase in current profits is due to conditions that are temporary, it would be foolish to build higher MEC and MEI schedules based on these profits. Even for companies with current profits not tied to special transitory conditions, it is often risky to project the future in terms of the present. Although profits for many automobile companies reached new all-time highs in 1973, it became clear by

5. Data from Wesley C. Mitchell, *What Happens in Business Cycles* (New York: National Bureau of Economic Research, 1951), p. 154.

late 1973 that the profitability of any future investment would be severely affected by the energy shortage and the expected shift to smaller cars. As a practical matter, most firms recognize that more than a simple extrapolation of current profits is necessary to construct an MEC or MEI schedule; for this reason, the profits theory, by itself, does not appear to offer a complete explanation of investment demand.

There is, however, one additional reason for believing that the current level of profits may have an important effect on investment. Funds for investment come either from internal or from external sources. The external sources involve either borrowing or selling new stock; an important internal source of funds is profits. Many companies will be reluctant to finance externally even if the MEC of the projected investment would make such financing worthwhile. They may feel, for example, that the stock market is unrealistically low or too demoralized for an offering of new stock and/or that they already have so much debt that it would not be conservative to borrow any more funds. Thus a high level of current profits, which provides large sums of internal funds, may encourage investment spending and may provide another explanation for a possible link between current profits and investment spending. Of course, firms must expect to earn more by reinvesting profits than they could earn in alternative uses of the funds if such a decision is to be viewed as strictly rational.

The acceleration principle and the profits theory have been recently reexamined and put into the framework of a flexible accelerator model in a review of the empirical studies of investment behavior which we will take up in the next section. First, however, let us consider the role of interest rates, central to the Keynesian model with which we began, and the role of finance.

Interest Rates and Investment Demand

The initial response of many economists to Keynes' concept of the marginal efficiency of capital was to try to draw the same close relationship between interest rates and investment demand as they had between income and consumption demand. However, further analysis, plus forty years of empirical observation and/or measurement have shown that interest rates are a relatively unimportant determinant of investment spending, as we shall see in the following section.[6] Business expenditures on fixed capital

6. In recent years many attempts have been made to evaluate and quantify the relationship between investment spending and interest rates. In "A Study of Industry Investment Decisions," *Review of Economics and Statistics* 49 (May 1967): 151–164, Michael K. Evans concluded that a 1 percent interest rate change produced a change in investment expenditures of only ¼ to ½ of 1 percent. Other studies seem to confirm this modest assessment of the importance of interest rates. Economists E. Kuh and J. R. Meyer concluded that although the relationship between interest rates and investment spending was presumably "something greater than zero," all available evidence suggested that "interest elasticity of demand (was) not large." See "Investment, Liquidity and Monetary Policy," in Commission on Money and Credit, *Impacts of Monetary Policy* (Englewood Cliffs, N.J.: Prentice-Hall, 1963), pp. 340–341. See also James Duesenberry, *Business Cycles and Economic Growth* (New York: McGraw-Hill, 1958).

are fairly inelastic as far as interest rates are concerned. An elastic demand schedule would show a sharp increase in investment expenditures with every decline in interest rates; most investment demand schedules, on the other hand, suggest that only limited amounts of additional investment spending are activated by any drop in interest rates.

Three circumstances characteristic of business operations in a complex industrialized economy appear to limit the elasticity of investment demand with respect to the interest rate. The first concerns the relatively fixed relationship between capital and the other factors of production which often exist in a business operation. We will examine the substitution between labor and capital in Chapter 10; for now, an example will suffice. Assume that a bus company requires one bus driver for each bus. Regardless of the decline in the cost of capital, it cannot substitute additional capital goods (buses) for the labor content of its output (drivers): its investment will increase only if demand for bus service increases. In other words, investment for this company will be fairly unresponsive to small changes in the interest rate.

The second factor concerns the durability of a projected investment. Although a drill press or stamping machine may be durable enough from a physical standpoint to last for many years, in general, improved equipment or changing production methods will probably render these investments obsolete before they actually wear out. Therefore, a relatively short life span is used to compute the flow of profits because it is assumed that the funds used to finance will be recouped quickly. For example, a drop in interest rates from 6 percent to 5 percent will be more important on a loan of $1000 for 20 years than on a loan of $1000 for 2 years; although the change in rates is the same in both cases, the dollar saving is $200 in the first case ($10 × 20 years) but only $20 in the second. This observation is confirmed by the fact that housing, which is usually financed by long-term loans, is much more responsive to changes in interest rates than business investment, where the investment must be paid off much sooner.

The Role of Finance in Dampening Investment Fluctuations

Up to this point, we have treated the interest rate prevailing at any one time as a single fixed rate and have assumed that unlimited quantities of funds would be available at this rate. In fact, if investment demand rises, more funds must be made available in order to increase the flow of loans to finance the higher level of investment. A higher interest rate is required to induce such additional lending. This can be seen in Figure 7.8, where a positively sloped supply schedule for loans is superimposed upon the MEI schedule which represents a demand for the funds supplied by lenders. As the MEI schedule shifts out at each interest rate to MEI', the interest rate must rise from i_0 to i_1 to induce the additional supply of funds to finance a rise in investment from I_0 to I_1. It is important to notice that if loan funds were available in unlimited quantities at i_0 the shift from MEI to MEI'

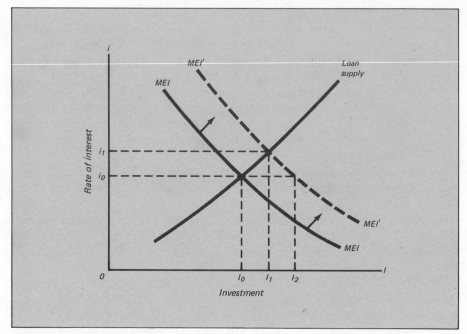

Figure 7.8 Increased cost of borrowing dampens ΔI as MEI shifts upward

would have increased investment by a larger amount to I_2. However, since most lenders are not indifferent about the rate of interest they are paid, higher rates must be paid to induce them to forego more current consumption and lend more. This fact is reflected in the positively sloped loan-supply schedule, producing a dampening effect on investment fluctuations.

Empirical Analysis of Investment Behavior

Efforts by economists to identify and measure the determinants of investment behavior for the purpose of predicting the rate of investment have met with some of the most difficult problems encountered in empirical analysis of economic phenomena. Although investment is the type of expenditure for which prediction is most necessary for purposes of controlling income in the Keynesian framework, it has proven to be the very type of expenditure most difficult to predict. Indeed this fact has been used to suggest that the system of macroeconomic control implied by the Keynesian framework may encounter great difficulties. Among the primary reasons for the problems in predicting investment are the large role which difficult-to-measure expectations play in determining investment, the stock-flow problem alluded to in the previous section, the difficulty of accurately measuring the capital stock in view of its inhomogeneity over time and across industries, and the problem of accurately determining the pattern of response by investors to a discrepancy between actual and desired stocks of capital. A model based on the acceleration principle may provide the most realistic explanation of how and why investment demand changes.

A review of the most significant recent empirical studies of investment behavior has been undertaken by Dale W. Jorgenson.[7] This review includes analysis not only of what determines investment or desired capital, but also of the time structure involved in the investment process and the role of replacement investment. Jorgenson selects as a framework for his analysis a model which concentrates on the time structure of investment and expands it into a complete theory of investment which is consistent with the empirical studies. This is the flexible accelerator model developed by H. B. Chenery and L. M. Koyck.[8] The essential feature of the model is a form of the **distributed lag formulation** which explains how changes in desired capital are transformed into actual investment expenditures. The actual change in capital stock from time $t - 1$ to time t (say over a year) represents some fraction (λ) of the difference between the *desired* capital stock in time t, K_t^d, and the *actual* capital stock in time $t - 1$. This specification, known as the Koyck lag, is written as:

$$I = K_t - K_{t-1} = \lambda[K_t^d - K_{t-1}] \qquad (0 < \lambda < 1) \qquad (7.14)$$

It is, of course, necessary to identify K_t^d in terms of observable variables; that is, we need to know what determines desired capital stock. Recall equation (7.9):

$$P_K = \frac{P \cdot MP_K}{i}$$

This may be rewritten employing an expression for the elasticity of output with respect to capital, E_{yK}:

$$E_{yK} = \frac{K}{y} \frac{\Delta y}{\Delta K} = \frac{K}{y} MP_K \qquad (7.15)$$

E_{yK} is the ratio of the percentage change in output to the percentage change in the capital stock. Since

$$\frac{K}{y} MP_K \frac{y}{K} = MP_K = E_{yK} \frac{y}{K}$$

7. See Dale W. Jorgenson, "Economic Studies of Investment Behavior: A Survey," *Journal of Economic Literature* 9 (December 1971): 1111–1147.

8. See H. B. Chenery, "Overcapacity and the Acceleration Principle," *Econometrica* 20 (January 1952): 1–28 and L. M. Koyck, *Distributed Lags and Investment Analysis* (Amsterdam: North-Holland, 1954).

equation (7.9) may be rewritten as:

$$P_K = \frac{\dfrac{Py}{K} E_{yK}}{i} \qquad (7.16)$$

Multiplying both sides of equation (7.16) by K gives:

$$K \cdot P_K = \frac{PyE_{yK}}{i} = \frac{YE_{yK}}{i} \qquad (7.17)$$

Dividing both sides of equation (7.17) by P_K gives:

$$K^d = \frac{YE_{yK}}{iP_K} \qquad (7.18)$$

The term K on the left-hand side of equation (7.18) is K^d, the desired capital stock, since equation (7.18) is only a reformulation of equation (7.9) which was derived for the optimum capital stock where the level of net present value with respect to changes in the capital stock was at a maximum.

Now it is possible to use equation (7.18), which expresses the desired capital stock in terms of observable variables, in equation (7.14) to express an equation for predicting investment. Recall that the *change* in capital stock, or $K_t - K_{t-1}$, defines investment. Therefore the left-hand side of equation (7.14) is I_t, and we have:

$$I_t = \lambda \left[\frac{YE_{yK}}{iP_K} \right] - \lambda K_{t-1} \qquad (7.19)$$

Notice that equation (7.19) says that investment, at a given i, rises with P or MP_K (since E_{yK} rises with MP_K given K/Y). Investment is also shown to fall with an increase in the capital stock in the previous time period, given the $-\lambda K_{t-1}$ term. This is consistent with the analysis of the impact of a change in the capital stock on the MEI schedule in Figure 7.7. Of course, equation (7.19) also confirms the shape of the MEI schedule, with I_t falling as i rises.[9]

The flexible accelerator model is extended by Jorgenson to include a model of replacement investment, as replacement investment constitutes a significant portion of total aggregate investment.[10] The model most consistent with the evidence is known as the **geometric mortality distribution**, in which replacement is proportional to actual capital stock.

9. The slope of MEI or the change in investment given a change in the interest rate, holding all else constant, is the partial derivation of I_t with respect to i in equation (7.19)

$$\frac{\partial I_t}{\partial i} = \frac{-\lambda YE_{yK}}{i^2 P_K} < 0$$

10. According to Jorgenson, "capital consumption has dominated gross capital formation" since 1919. See Jorgenson, "Economic Studies," p. 1112.

The Chenery-Koyck flexible accelerator model most adequately explains the evidence put forward in empirical studies. Jorgenson divided this evidence into determinants of investment, time structure of investment, and replacement investment. Looking first at the determinants of investment, Jorgenson identifies three areas: (1) the capital output ratio, or capacity utilization, (2) internal funds, and (3) the cost of external finance.

The flexible accelerator model was developed as an alternative to both the accelerator model of J. M. Clark,[11] in which desired capital is proportional to *output*, and the profits theory discussed earlier. A modification of this theory, in which the constraint of funds, both internal and external, is the principal determinant of investment, is also significant.[12]

Although the relative importance of each group varies among the studies reviewed, capacity utilization, or real output, was the most significant explanatory variable in all but three of the studies, and exclusive in many of them. In an economy operating at close to full capacity, changes in demand and output appear to be the single most important factor in determining investment expenditures.[13] It is important to note that *pressure on capacity* is the key factor in translating increases in output into increases in investment spending. When the firm or the economy is *not* operating close to full capacity, it would appear that the availability of internal funds becomes of prime importance. This occasioned a modification of the flexible accelerator model. However, further evidence shows that internal funds are far less significant than external finance.[14]

As to the second problem of current empirical investigation, the time structure, some form of distributed lag formulation is used by all of the studies. Evidence shows that although it varies among manufacturers, the

11. J. M. Clark, "Business Acceleration and the Law of Demand: A Technical Factor in Economic Cycles," *Journal of Political Economy* 25 (March 1917): 217–235.

12. J. Tinbergen, "Statistical Evidence on the Acceleration Principle," *Economica* 5 (May 1938): 164–176; J. Tinbergen, "A Method and Its Application to Investment Activity" in *Statistical Testing of Business Cycle Theories*, Vol. I (Geneva: League of Nations, 1938); L. R. Klein, *Economic Fluctuations in the United States, 1921–1941*, Cowles Commission for Research in Economics, Monograph No. 11 (New York: Wiley, 1950) and "Studies in Investment Behavior" in *Conference on Business Cycles*, Universities-National Bureau Conference Series, No. 2 (New York: Columbia University Press for the National Bureau of Economic Research, 1951).

13. See J. R. Meyer and R. R. Glauber, *Investment Decisions, Economic Forecasting and Public Policy* (Cambridge, Mass.: Harvard University Press, 1964). The study by Evans concluded that every change of 1 percent in output leads to an average change of 1½ percent to 2 percent in investment over a two-year period.

14. See J. S. Duesenberry, *Business Cycles and Economic Growth* (New York: McGraw-Hill, 1958); J. Meyer and E. Kuh, *The Investment Decision* (Cambridge, Mass.: Harvard University Press, 1957); see also the theory of finance developed by Franco Modigliani and M. H. Miller in a series of articles, most significantly "The Cost of Capital, Corporation Finance, and the Theory of Investment," *American Economic Review* 48 (June 1958): 261–297; "Reply to Rose and Durand," *American Economic Review* 49 (September 1959): 655–659; "Corporate Income Taxes and the Cost of Capital: A Correction," *American Economic Review* 53 (June 1963): 433–443; and "Some Estimates of the Cost of Capital to the Electric Utility Industry, 1954–57," *American Economic Review* 56 (June 1966): 333–391.

average lag between the decision to invest and actual expenditure is from one and a half to two years.[15]

Finally, the evidence conclusively supports the geometric mortality distribution for replacement, which implies that replacement is proportional to capital stock. The concept of replacement investment will be examined more fully in our discussion of business cycles in the appendix to this chapter.

Role of Expectations

As Jorgenson notes at the conclusion of his empirical survey, in a broader sense, "the most important open question in the study of investment is the integration of uncertainty into the theory and econometrics of investment.[16] Any investment projection is affected not merely by the forecasts based on current profits and losses, but also by general expectations about the future. A sense of optimism (and therefore a higher MEC schedule) may accompany a change of administration in Washington because businesses may feel that the new administration will deal with them more kindly. Conversely, a wave of pessimism may sweep over the entire business community following a relatively small, and possibly temporary, downturn in sales. Once underway, these expectations may tend to snowball, and minor increases or decreases in investment spending turn into booms or busts. For example, the boom in investment spending in 1972 and 1973, following a flat 1970 and 1971, was probably at least in part attributable to the climate of confidence and optimism created by President Nixon's New Economic Policy speech in August of 1971. The uncertainty and pessimism resulting from the combination of Watergate and the energy crisis in 1974 may have dampened the investment spending surge that might otherwise have occurred in that year.

The problem, as Jorgenson notes, is that it is exceedingly difficult to simultaneously determine production, investment, financial policy, and security prices. An equation like (7.19) can be employed to predict investment behavior given that an estimate of E_{yK} is available along with data series on Y, i, P_K, and K. The last two series are the most difficult to obtain since existing data are in terms of the value of capital, or $P_K \cdot K$. Accurate estimates of capital units, K, must be obtained in terms of the actual services from capital, in order to disentangle P_K from $P_K \cdot K$. As the ability to predict investment behavior improves, so will the ability of policymakers to obtain target values for macroeconomic policy goals like full employment, income, stable prices, and interest rates consistent with orderly capital formation.

---

15. See Jorgenson, "Economic Studies," p. 1142.
16. Ibid. Jorgenson notes that Modigliani and Miller have done this to some extent.

Questions and Exercises

1. Assume that an inventor develops a gadget that will make existing equipment more productive. What would you predict for orders of the gadget itself? Would there be any change in orders for existing equipment? How would you show changes from the gadget in the MEC curve?

2. The role of expectations can be seen in the equation for the discounted rate of return (r). Where?

3. Some gasoline companies have been advertising that they need increased profits for further expansion. How would you defend or criticize this point of view? Would additional profits necessarily be spent on expansion? Why or why not?

4. As a result of the energy crisis it would be reasonable to predict a relatively large number of innovations in energy production, such as the mining of shale oil. How would such innovations affect investment? What factors would either encourage or discourage related investment?

5. Until 1973 plans for producing additional energy with atomic plants were met by considerable lack of enthusiasm. By 1974, however, the construction of such plants were projected in relatively great numbers. What explanation would you offer? What are the implications for the innovation theory of investment?

6. The home-building industry is characterized by small business units controlling only a very small portion of the market. Yet the record of innovation in this industry has been relatively poor when compared to that of other industries. Would you have expected great innovation? Why or why not?

7. In an effort to stimulate a rather sluggish economy during the early 1960s, the Kennedy administration pressed Congress for a cut in corporate taxes. The cut is believed to have been responsible for stimulating a period of rapid expansion with low unemployment. Why? Might this policy have been more or less effective in stimulating an expansion of output and employment than expansionary monetary policy leading to a reduction in interest rates?

8. In the midst of the Arabian oil embargo of 1973–1974 and for some time thereafter, the profits of some oil companies rose dramatically while the price of their stock continued to drop. How would you explain this phenomenon? Assuming that the stock market reflects business expectations, what use would you predict for the additional profits? Why? Under the circumstances, oil companies seeking expansion would be likely to use money from what source?

9. As the United States moved into the early months of the energy crisis in 1973, it became evident that shortages could easily develop in exploration and drilling equipment for oil and natural gas. Using the acceleration principle and this industry as an example, how would you describe growth and contraction for the industry?

10. Some investment ventures are undertaken even though the return expected is only $\frac{1}{4}$ of 1 percent above the cost of investing. Other ventures are undertaken only when the expected return is significantly above the cost of investing. What explanation would you offer? On these grounds, how responsive would you expect investment to be to small changes in the interest rate? Why?

Appendix: Business Cycles

For many centuries, observers have noted that economic activity is not constant—whether its variation is due to crop failures or seasonal cycles in an agricultural society or to the more complex variables of a technological world. In modern times, economists have observed the repetitive pattern of peak, contraction, revival, and expansion to be a regular cycle of about seven to ten years' duration.[1]

Explanations which have been advanced to explain the instability of the economy cover a wide range—from the notion that they are linked to spots on the sun to an attempt to explain them in terms of business innovations to a restatement of the adage that "what goes up must come down." In general, these theories can be divided into two basic categories: exogenous theories, which find the cause of cycles to be outside of the economic system, and endogenous theories, which see the cycle as being generated by forces within the economy itself.

---

1. This seven-to-ten-year pattern was first observed by Clement Juglar in the 1860s, but it is not the only business cycle which economists recognize. A long-term cycle of thirty to fifty years was identified by N. D. Kondratieff in 1922, and in 1923 Joseph Kitchin noted a much shorter forty-month cycle.

Exogenous forces that may turn a slump into a revival or a boom into a depression include wars, political developments, natural disasters, or great innovations. There is no question that political developments of 1973, including the Watergate revelations and the Arab oil embargo, were major forces in simultaneous economic troubles in the United States. Exogenous forces like these are unpredictable, but explanations of the cycle have also been formulated around predictable exogenous events. William Stanley Jevons (1835–1882) linked the business cycle to the appearance of sunspots every seven to ten years, on the assumption that the accompanying abnormal radiation affected crops and thus the economy.

Endogenous theories find the cause of business cycles within the economy itself. The fluctuations of the economy are seen as predictable and not caused by the random intervention of outside forces. Perhaps in a desire to believe in the efficacy of theory to deal with erratic behavior, but also based on accumulated evidence, most modern economists subscribe to endogenous explanations.

In general, endogenous theorists can be classified into two groups: the overexpansionists and the underconsumptionists. According to the former, depressions and expansions are self-generating. Recession is caused simply by overproduction, and a revival follows naturally from a depression. The reasoning behind goes as follows: during a boom, expectations and spending are high. The consumer is optimistic, so he borrows money to purchase a new house or a color TV; business is spurred by high sales to expand inventories and plant capacity. But this cannot go on indefinitely. Soon the consumer will own all the durable goods he needs; furthermore, he will be more heavily in debt. Business will soon find itself with higher costs and excess plant capacity, so it will halt investment. The recession picks up momentum as cuts in income and investment continue. But the slump will not last indefinitely, for consumer durable goods and business capital wear out, and the expansion of the market caused by purchase of replacement items soon causes economic activity to pick up. The cycle then repeats itself.

Critics of the overexpansionists think that their philosophy borders too closely on the puritan ethic. They disagree that recessions follow booms just as inevitably as a hangover follows a night on the town and that the belt-tightening of a depression will eventually be rewarded by an upswing in the economy. In the view of the underconsumptionists, depressions can easily become chronic in a laissez-faire economy, and the intervention of the government can effectively prevent business slumps. As evidence, they point to the economy of the post-war period. While there were three recessions during the 1950s, there were none at all from 1961 to 1969, and the recession in 1969–1970 occurred, it is charged, because it was probably induced deliberately by monetary policy in an effort to curb inflation. Indeed, the increased role of government in recent decades has made many of the assumptions of the overexpansionists obsolete.

The social responsibility of government to intervene to maintain a healthy level of employment is a central feature of underconsumptionist theory. John Maynard Keynes argued that a mature economy like that of the United States tends toward underconsumption, letting savings lie idle rather than using them to stimulate the economy,[2] so government must intervene. In fact, the Employment Act of 1946 amounts to a legislated responsibility for the U.S. federal government to take steps to maintain full employment of labor. Of course, there is a price to pay for this artificial control, and underconsumptionists recognize chronic inflation as a necessary evil.

In the remainder of this appendix, we will examine several theories of the causes of business cycles. After a discussion of the interaction of the accelerator and the multiplier, a relationship first perceived by economist Paul Samuelson, we will examine representatives of two major types of endogenous theory: real and monetary. The former include the works of J. R. Hicks, who presents a sophisticated model of accelerator-multiplier interaction, and Joseph Schumpeter, who sees periodic technological innovations as the key to cyclical activity. These real theories find the sources of instability in the regular interaction of parts of the economic system, specifically the volatile nature of investment. Monetary theories, on the other hand, give primary credit to the activities of financial institutions which regulate the supply and velocity of money.

The Acceleration Principle

The key to a number of explanations of the business cycle in the post-World War II era is the accelerator, described in Chapter 7, whereby a small change in consumer demand (equivalent to business output) will give rise to a much greater change in producer demand for capital investment goods such as machinery. The accelerator, referred to in discussions of business cycles as the acceleration principle, describes an important element of instability in the economy, for it says in effect that a period of prosperity can turn into a recession simply because demand levels off at a high point instead of continuing to rise at a constant rate.[3]

Investment demand is extremely sensitive to fluctuations in aggregate demand. This is because in most major industries it takes a huge investment in new capital to produce a modest net increase in output. For the example given in Chapter 7 (see Table 7.2), the capital/output ratio was 3 to 1. A

---

2. J. M. Keynes, *The General Theory of Employment, Interest and Money* (New York: Harcourt, Brace, 1936).

3. One of the most famous presentations of the acceleration principle is J. M. Clark's "Business Acceleration and the Law of Demand," *Journal of Political Economy* 25 (March 1917): 217–235. Since World War II, the acceleration principle has received considerable attention through its combination with the Keynesian consumption function in accelerator-multiplier models, which will be discussed later in this appendix.

$100,000 increase in demand for the hypothetical firm's output necessitated a net investment (beyond that required to replace the existing capital as it depreciated) of $300,000 by the firm. Moreover, because capital wears out slowly, the magnitude of investment demand aimed only at replacing capital as it wears out (which is all that is needed if aggregate demand remains unchanged over time) is slight compared with the investment demand required to expand production in a boom period. In the example from Chapter 7, a 10 percent increase in firm output required a 100 percent increase in the rate of investment. In short, investment demand is extremely volatile.

This volatility also works to cut investment demand sharply as soon as aggregate demand begins to level off. Only a constant absolute growth in aggregate demand can sustain a given level of investment demand beyond the replacement level, and only a steadily increasing rate of growth in aggregate demand can sustain an increasing level of investment demand. Therefore, as soon as a boom begins to level off, investment demand begins to drop (in absolute terms), *even if aggregate demand continues to grow* but less rapidly than before. The effect of the accelerator is to sharpen the extremes of the business cycle. A small increase in aggregate demand is accelerated into a business boom. Then, when the pace slackens only slightly, the accelerator turns what might have been a mere leveling off into an economic contraction. At the bottom of the resultant downswing, investment demand is so low for a time that little existing capital is even replaced. Then, as capital depreciation accumulates, some firms increase their investment demand from zero to the replacement level, and the accelerator produces another upswing.

Sometimes the additional investments induced in one boom period have a delayed effect and help amplify growth during a subsequent boom. This is because most investment occurs during the upswings of the business cycle, and the new capital has a limited durability. After a certain period (ten years for the example in Chapter 7) it must be replaced, and if the original investment purchases were clustered within a relatively short time span, the capital equipment may tend to wear out all at once and have to be replaced within a relatively short time span as well. This phenomenon is known as a **replacement wave.** In a complex economy such as that of the United States, and in most businesses which plan ahead for growth, replacement waves are not too pronounced. But the phenomenon is quite discernible as one aftereffect of such severe shocks as war in economies which have only a few major industries.

The Inventory Accelerator
It should be noted here that the acceleration principle not only magnifies the relationship between investment in capital equipment and sales; it also amplifies the functional relationship between inventory investment and sales. Peaks and troughs of the business cycle caused by variations in the levels of inventory have become apparent in the United States since World

War II. In order to further understand business cycles, it is therefore important to explain the causes of increases and decreases in stocks of goods maintained by businesses. Although several factors are involved, including price expectations, perishability of stocks, interest rates, and obsolescence, the most important factor is the level of sales, for business will not accumulate stocks unless it expects to turn them into finished products.

A firm's inventory orders consist of two parts. The first, the replacement of stocks which have been turned into finished products and sold, is determined by the *level* of sales. The second, which consists of adjustments to increase or decrease inventory levels, depends upon *change* in the level of sales, for if sales are growing rapidly, then inventory levels will grow even faster in anticipation of continued increases, in a pattern similar to the investment growth shown in Table 7.2. If the rate of growth of sales slows down—even though the absolute level of sales is still rising—the result will be a decline in the rate of inventory accretion and probably in overall inventory orders. Thus, the inventory accelerator works in the same way as the investment accelerator, enabling a small change in the level of sales to cause far greater shifts in levels of inventory.[4]

The acceleration principle explains the basic character of the functional relationship which exists between output and investment. But as many critics have pointed out, the acceleration principle must include several qualifiers.[5] Most importantly, the strength of the accelerator is diminished if the economy or firm is operating at less than full capacity. If excess machinery exists, then an increase in demand may simply result in fuller utilization of existing capital rather than purchase of new equipment. The accelerator is also altered if the capital/output ratio is not constant. If a firm can change that ratio (e.g., in response to demand changes it expects will be short-lived), the accelerator is weakened. It may prefer to use capital more intensively (thereby shortening its life span) rather than invest in new capital. And if the acceleration principle is used to explain the cyclical nature of the whole economy rather than the behavior of a particular firm, even more difficulties arise. Not all types of businesses have the same capital/output ratio, and most likely there are times when mainly those businesses with high accelerators feel heavy demand and other times when mainly those businesses with low accelerators experience such demand. This means

4. For a more detailed explanation, see Lloyd A. Metzler, "The Nature and Stability of Inventory Cycles," *Review of Economic Statistics* 23 (August 1941): 113–129.

5. One of the most crucial criticisms is that of the necessity for the economy to be working at full capacity. See D. Streever, *Capacity Utilization and Business Investment* (University of Illinois, Bureau of Economic and Business Research, Bulletin No. 86, 1960). W. J. Baumol points out that under some circumstances investment may fluctuate *less* than final demand in "Acceleration Without Magnification," *American Economic Review* 46 (June 1956): 409–412. Inconsistencies in the relationship between consumption and investment were found by Jan Tinbergen in "Critical Remarks on Some Business Cycle Theories," *Econometrica* 10 (April 1942). And A. D. Knox concluded that the acceleration principle was inadequate by itself to explain the cycle in "The Acceleration Principle and the Theory of Investment: A Survey," *Economica*, New Series 19 (August 1952): 269–297.

that the economy as a whole may have a high accelerator at one time and a low accelerator at another, preventing any meaningful average.

Finally, the acceleration principle assumes that increased output and the rise in investment occur simultaneously, when in fact a sudden rise in demand may long precede a response in investment levels. In order to compensate for this, more sophisticated models of the accelerator incorporate a time lag, such as the flexible accelerator model presented in Chapter 7, which enables the economist to create a more realistic approximation of the behavior of the variables.

The Interaction of the Accelerator and the Multiplier

The acceleration principle indicates that the level of investment reached by an economy is a function of the rate of increase of expenditure which is proportionate to income. The accelerator, or capital-output ratio, works so that an increase in consumption will cause an increase in the level of investment.

Neither the multiplier nor the accelerator can act alone. In effect, the two forces combine in a series of endless possibilities, depending on the values of the accelerator and the marginal propensity to save. In simplest terms, the relationship can be expressed as follows:

$$\Delta I_a \rightarrow (\text{mult.}) \rightarrow \Delta Y \rightarrow (\text{accel.}) \rightarrow \Delta I_b \rightarrow (\text{mult.}) \rightarrow \Delta Y \rightarrow \ldots .$$

where an initial increase in autonomous investment (I_a) works through the multiplier to cause an increase in income (Y), and this works through the accelerator to cause a greater change in induced investment (I_b), which in turn increases income still more, and so the interaction continues. The process is supercumulative because one initial increase (or decrease) will set off a snowball effect where income and investment interact to magnify the impact at each successive level.

But income and investment will not keep climbing higher and higher indefinitely because two forces work to cause an eventual leveling off. First, the marginal propensity to save and other leakages, such as taxes, reduce the rate of growth of consumption at each stage. While income continues to grow, so does the proportion of additional income which is saved rather than spent, until consumption finally ceases to increase at all. And, second, the initial increase in autonomous investment soon exhausts itself, for as the capital stock grows during the period of expansion, the marginal efficiency of capital is likely to fall until investment is no longer profitable. Thus, while the interaction of the multiplier and the accelerator magnifies economic expansion, it also acts to set its own limits through the eventual reduction of consumption and autonomous investment.[6]

6. This discussion pertains only to certain values of the accelerator and the multiplier, as is shown later in this appendix. For a further discussion of this case, see Alvin H. Hansen, *Business Cycles and National Income* (New York: Norton, 1951), pp. 177–178.

Paul Samuelson studied the interaction of the multiplier and the accelerator and derived a model in which a series of equations express the way in which the two forces interact to affect income, consumption, and investment over time.[7] Subscripts t in the following equations indicate time periods. Thus if t is a given time period, $t - 1$ is the previous period, $t + 1$ is one period in the future, and so on backward and forward in time. Starting with time formulations for income, consumption, and investment,

$$Y_t = C_t + I_t + G \qquad (A7.1)$$

$$C_t = bY_{t-1} \qquad 0 < b < 1 \qquad (A7.2)$$

where b is the marginal propensity to consume, and

$$I_t = w(C_t - C_{t-1}) \qquad w > 0 \qquad (A7.3)$$

where w is the capital-output ratio; more spending implies a need to build more capacity to satisfy growth in demand.

If we substitute equation (A7.2) into equation (A7.3) for C_t and if $C_{t-1} = bY_{t-2}$, we find:

$$I_t = w(bY_{t-1} - bY_{t-2}) = wb(Y_{t-1} - Y_{t-2}) \qquad (A7.4)$$

Substituting from equations (A7.2) and (A7.4) into equation (A7.1) for C_t and I_t (all in terms of Y), gives:

$$Y_t - bY_{t-1} + wb(Y_{t-1} - Y_{t-2}) = G$$

or

$$Y_t - b(1 + w)Y_{t-1} + wbY_{t-2} = G \qquad (A7.5)$$

Shifting "time" subscripts two periods ahead:

$$Y_{t+2} - b(1 + w)Y_{t+1} + wbY_t = G \qquad (A7.6)$$

Equation (A7.6) is a second-order difference equation which describes a path for Y through time in response to changes in G. The path may move away from the initial value of Y (unstable) or move away and then return (stable). It may rise and fall (oscillate) as it moves either away or away and back. The pattern of movement depends on values of w and b. We can see this more clearly by looking at Figure A7.1.

The actual method for solving equation (A7.6) for the time path of Y lies beyond the scope of this book, but the significance of the solution can readily be seen. First, the solution for Y with no induced investment, or $w = 0$, is simply

$$Y = \frac{1}{1 - b}G \qquad (A7.7)$$

with the familiar $(1/1 - b)$ multiplier. With induced investment $(w \neq 0)$

7. Paul Samuelson, "Interactions Between the Multiplier Analysis and the Principle of Acceleration," *Review of Economic Statistics* 21 (May 1939): 75–78.

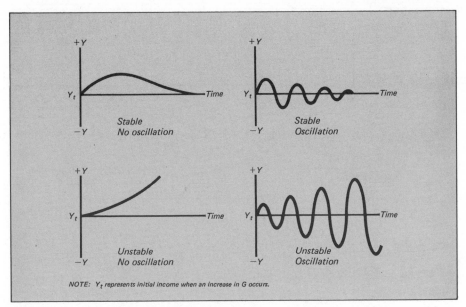

Figure A7.1 Alternate time paths for Y given a change in G

it is necessary to check the solution for Y for stability and oscillation. Stability requires that wb < 1. If wb > 1 the value of Y never returns to its original level once a disturbance is introduced by ΔG. Oscillation does not occur if

$$b > \frac{4w}{(1 + w)^2}$$

while

$$b < \frac{4w}{(1 + w)^2}$$

implies oscillation.

These conditions, in terms of b and w, are represented in Figure A7.2. The solid line satisfies the condition $b = 4w/(1 + w)^2$. Above it no oscillation occurs, while below it oscillation occurs. The broken line satisfies the condition wb = 1, and above it the path of Y is unstable, while below it the path of Y is stable.

If w = 3, a value of b < ⅓ is required for stability, since otherwise wb > 1 will hold, violating the stability condition. Since b is usually taken to lie between 0.7 and 0.8, as is shown in Figure A7.2, values of w between 1.25 and 1.43 would be "typical" values of the acceleration coefficient consistent with stability.

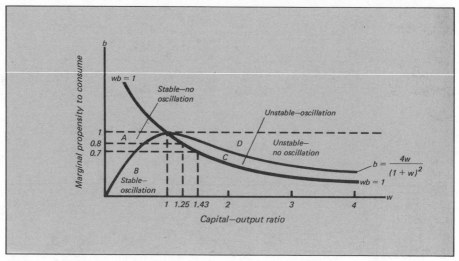

Figure A7.2 Implications of values of b and w for the path of Y

Hicks' Theory of Business Cycles

Starting from the hypothesis of the interaction of the accelerator and the multiplier, J. M. Hicks developed one of the better known theories of business cycles.[8]

Hicks' model is a fairly simple application of the interaction of the accelerator and the multiplier. Hicks hypothesized that the value of the accelerator must be such that it will produce explosive or unstable curves if left unhindered. Since observation tells us that no "explosion" has in fact occurred, Hicks concludes that the pattern of fluctuations is not that of a free cycle, such as would occur with unconstrained, unstable oscillations of the sort shown in Figure A7.1. Rather, the pattern of fluctuations is constrained by a "full-employment ceiling" and an "investment floor," which prevent income from following a path of explosive growth (or contraction, depending on the direction of the initial shock). These constraints act to prevent income from following a path of unconstrained oscillations, and the result is a cyclical pattern of bouncing back and forth, like that shown in Figure A7.3.

Hicks thus assumes that the value of the accelerator falls within region C

8. J. M. Hicks, *A Contribution to the Theory of the Trade Cycle* (Oxford: Oxford University Press, 1940). For discussions of Hicks' theory see James Duesenberry, "Hicks on the Trade Cycle," *Quarterly Journal of Economics* 44 (August 1950): 464–476; see also S. S. Alexander, "Issues of Business Cycle Theory Raised by Mr. Hicks," *American Economic Review* 41 (December 1951). Richard Goodwin also sees the accelerator-multiplier interaction as the force behind the business cycle. See "The Nonlinear Accelerator and Persistence of Business Cycles" *Econometrica* 19 (January 1951): 1–17.

or D of Figure A7.2. This means that its interaction with the multiplier will cause income to rise at a faster rate than the growth rate of the full-employment ceiling; thus, returning to Figure A7.3, at point t_1, the two lines intersect. What happens at point t_1 is simply a repetition of the same kind of pattern we saw in Table 7.2. The mere fact that output ceases to increase at a growing rate (it is still growing, but only at the level of the economy's overall growth) is enough to cause an absolute decrease in total output. Because the change in output between periods t_1 and t_2 subject to the ceiling constraint is less than that from t_0 to t_1, an absolute decrease in investment is inevitable.

But the curve of output does not bounce off the ceiling line as soon as it hits. Instead, there is a lag from t_1 to t_2 between expansion and contraction. This lag acts according to the lagged form of Samuelson's formula which we discussed in the previous section, so that the level of investment is determined by the change in demand in the two previous periods. Thus, it takes some time for the leveling off of output to start the process of disinvestment, or negative investment, which accompanies the recession.

Contraction is the inevitable result of expansion in Hicks' constrained cycle. As soon as disinvestment starts at point t_2, the cumulative interaction of the multiplier and the accelerator causes output to plummet, overshooting the equilibrium line for income, E. At this point, t_3, income reaches the floor and can fall no more. In fact, it is actually rising, for even during de-

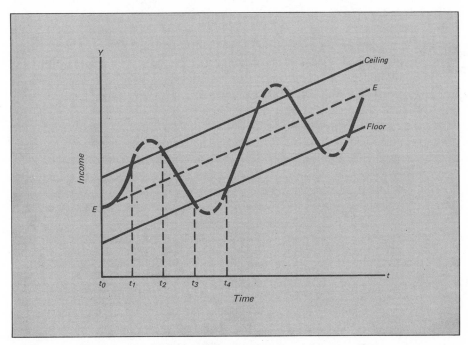

Figure A7.3 Hicks' constrained oscillations, income rising over time

pression, $t_3 - t_4$, the floor, which is determined by autonomous investment levels, follows a path of growth over time.[9]

How long the economy remains in the state of depression depends in part upon the rate of technical progress. The growth of autonomous investment is partly dependent on advances in technology: obsolescence of old equipment is one reason for depreciation and replacement. Since the burden of starting up the interaction of the multiplier and the accelerator in a revival depends upon the renewal of replacement investment, it is evident that the rate of progress is a very crucial factor in determining the length of a depression. Another factor, of course, is the amount of surplus capital accumulated in the preceding boom. When worn-out and obsolete machinery lower capital levels to a point where replacement is necessary, investment spending begins again, pushing income up and activating the accelerator to produce the same general pattern we saw in the first phase of the cycle.

Schumpeter's Theory of Innovations

Hicks' theory provides a neat explanation of the business cycle, and many of its critics attack the point that it is indeed too neat. There is no mention of monetary disturbances, rates of profit, speculative atmosphere, or a score of other potentially primary causal factors which may not be purely endogenous.[10] Joseph Schumpeter developed another endogenous theory, but his approaches the phenomenon from a diametrically different angle: it pinpoints as the key to the business cycle a factor that almost every other theorist considers to be exogenous, that of innovation.[11]

Innovation can be defined as putting new processes to commercial use, as distinguished from invention, which is the discovery and development of a new process alone. Innovations are not limited to a single advance in one industry. Instead, one successful innovation on the part of a daring entrepreneur will engender a whole cluster of innovations in that particular industry, and each advance is followed by a secondary wave of innovations in other industries. Schumpeter noticed that it is the rare entrepreneur who is willing to take the risks involved in offering a new process or product to the market, but if an innovating entrepreneur is rewarded by success, he is soon followed by a "herdlike" wave of other entrepreneurs eager to imitate

9. Hicks recognizes that the absolute level of autonomous investment varies considerably, and that its rate of growth is likely to decline during a depression. But even so, he maintains that autonomous investment is still positive, and that its level still follows a relatively constant growth rate over time.

10. See for example, Duesenberry, "Hicks on the Trade Cycle." Hicks' model relies heavily on the assumption that changes in income and consumption are principle determinants of investment. As we saw in Chapter 7, however, recent studies have indicated that a more flexible model is indicated.

11. Joseph Schumpeter, *The Theory of Economic Development* (Cambridge, Mass.: Harvard University Press, 1934), and *Business Cycles* (New York: McGraw-Hill, 1939).

and share the profits. Indeed, in many cases it is a matter of economic survival to imitate, for if the new process can cut costs considerably then the innovator will soon command a disproportionate share of the market if others can't compete. (The spate of imitations following a highly successful film like "The Godfather" exemplifies such "herdlike" imitative behavior.)

The pattern followed by the business cycle derives from periodic clusters of innovations and their repercussions. To Schumpeter, innovation was the force behind both economic progress and the economic instability of depressions and booms. The production of the automobile, for example, spurred development of several products, from steel to rubber, asphalt, gasoline, oil, and glass. One innovation can thus be the cause of an economy-wide spurt of growth. However, Schumpeter also saw the boom as a basic disruption of the economic system which, if left undisturbed, would remain in the "neighborhoods of equilibrium." Depression is a necessary consequence of booms, a period of readjustment which allows the economy to adjust its price system, production levels, and incomes.

Eventually the boom turns into a depression, primarily because sooner or later all of the secondary innovations that are to follow from one major advance will have been put into effect. At the same time, the burst of investment spending required to put new processes into commercial practice will be reduced to a trickle because all of the capital equipment needed for production will have been purchased. In addition, the favorable climate for risk-taking during the expansion will have engendered a number of financial disasters as well as successes, and the effect of these will contribute to the general downswing which accompanies the drying-up of funds. The economy thus sinks into a painful period of depression, where bank credit is low and many firms which were unable to adjust to the abnormal situation of the boom go bankrupt. Eventually expectations rise again, and another entrepreneur dares to innovate—and the entire process begins again.

Although Schumpeter's perspective is intriguing, some empirical evidence indicates that it is the business cycle which creates innovations, and not the reverse. Few entrepreneurs are willing to take the risk to innovate unless the climate is right, just as the exploitation of new processes which follows an innovation depends largely on the availability of funds for investment and research. In sum, it appears that it is the conditions which characterize a period of economic upswing that set the stage for investment—not the investment that creates revival.

Monetary Theories of Business Cycles

We have seen that the interaction of the accelerator and the multiplier is central to business-cycle analysis: the influence of banks and their regulation of money supply is also important. A change in the policy of the central bank or in the behavior of money holders or financial intermediaries has a direct effect on the aggregate level of income and the cyclical activity of the economy.

Indeed, some theorists consider the regulatory activities of financial institutions to be central to any theory of the business cycle. Among these was Frederick von Hayek, who felt that any change in real factors, such as the accelerator-multiplier interaction, first must be "translated" into the money and price system before it could affect economic activity.[12] This process of translation magnifies any disruptive impact into a major expansion or contraction.

According to Hayek, the power of the banks to artificially expand money supply through easing credit is the ultimate cause of first booms and then depressions. Imagine an economy in equilibrium, where all resources are employed and where banks maintain a 100 percent ratio of reserves to deposits. Under these circumstances, the level of savings of the community will determine the funds available to entrepreneurs for investment, because only the amount of money deposited in the bank can be released by the bank for investment. Thus, if the community maintains a high marginal propensity to consume, relatively little will be put into savings banks, demand for credit will be higher than reserves, and interest rates will be high. In contrast, if the community tends to save a high proportion of its income, more funds can be released for investment, and interest rates will be lower.

Hayek distinguishes between voluntary and forced savings. The former is the level of savings the community will deposit in banks, as determined by the propensity to save. Forced saving, however, results when banks artificially ease credit, freeing more funds to investors than are deposited by savers. The easy credit offered by banks creates the illusion that it is a profitable time for business to invest in capital and lengthen the structure of production (illusory because any monetary expansion beyond the rate of voluntary savings cannot long be sustained). Artificial easy credit leads businesses to overinvest, which results in rising prices, which lower real income and thus consumption; and the result is that the community is forced to save more than usual.

While forced savings release more money for investment, the amount is limited, and while further increases in investment mean that consumer prices will rise still more, the process will ultimately act to take money from savings. If investment is artificially stimulated too far beyond profit expectations, this is likely to magnify the impact of any ensuing slowdown in economic activity.

Hayek's theory has pitfalls. In addition to ignoring real factors, it draws too rigid a picture of monetary policy's effect on cyclical behavior, concluding, for example, that forced saving always brings recession. In fact, there are instances where long-term capital requirements cause investment to

12. Frederick von Hayek, *Prices and Production* (London: George Routledge, 1931). An excellent discussion of both Hayek and Hawtrey's theories is provided in Hansen, *Business Cycles and National Income*, pp. 377–393.

exceed the level of the marginal propensity to save (in the absence of the income-redistributional effect of monetary expansion), and in such cases it is possible to prolong a situation of constant, percentage growth almost indefinitely, barring interference of other factors.

Another economist, R. G. Hawtrey, focused upon the effect of changes in interest rates on inventory levels.[13] There are two main parts to Hawtrey's thesis. First, a change in credit will bring a change in the ratio of stocks to sales desired by business, for easy credit encourages entrepreneurs to purchase inventories when "the price is right" and so build up more stocks than are actually needed. Second, a loosening of credit which increases income is not immediately accompanied by increased spending or a higher level of public cash holdings. Instead, there is a time lag between a change in bank credit and an increase or decrease in the level of cash holdings and transactions in the community. Banks, according to Hawtrey, fail to predict the long-range impact of their activities and overcorrect by either tightening or easing too far. But because of the lag in the currency flow, the banks continue to keep interest rates high throughout the recession. This adds to the slump and causes the contraction to overshoot equilibrium. The economy sinks into a depression and stays there until sufficient money has flowed back to cause excess reserves. At this point, credit is loosened, and the cycle begins again.

Hawtrey's thesis presents a rather distorted picture. Whereas, to him, expansion is accompanied by low interest rates, real business booms are characterized by a high level of demand for credit and therefore high interest rates. In turn, during a real recession, there is little demand for loans in relation to the money supply, and so credit is far more likely to be loose. Again, Hawtrey maintains that credit rates alone are sufficient to raise and lower the desired ratio of stocks to sales, but common sense tells us that this is not so, for real factors which stem from the behavior of the consumer are responsible for sales expectations, and their influence cannot be ignored in any theory.

Finally, Milton Friedman has documented a monetary theory of business cycles for the United States in a highly influential study with Anna Schwartz.[14] The basic thesis is that rapid changes in the rate of growth of the money supply induce cyclical changes in income. Since the variability of growth in the United States money supply has increased since the Federal Reserve System came into operation in 1914, Friedman argues that a reversion to monetary "rules" would be desirable whereby the rate of growth of the money supply is set at some stable level. More attention will be given to the analytical basis for Friedman's views in Part III.

13. R. G. Hawtrey, *Good and Bad Trade* (London: Constable, 1913); also *Currency and Credit* (London: Longmans, Green, 1919).

14. Milton Friedman and Anna J. Schwartz, *A Monetary History of the United States, 1867–1960*, National Bureau of Economic Research (Princeton, N.J.: Princeton University Press, 1963).

U.S. Monetary Dilemma

Burns Pledges to Curb... Terms Inflation Problem 'Dangerous'

House Votes Bill To Audit the Fed But Limits Scope

By a WALL STREET JOURNAL *Staff Reporter*

WASHINGTON—The House sharply watered down, and then approved, a bill to establish the first independent audit Federal Reserve System.

In the key decision, the... to 139 to limit any such audit... Accounting Office to "administe..." operations, thus excluding any examination of monetary policy operations. The House went on to pass the measure, 333 to 20.

The vote to limit the audit was a severe setback to House Banking Committee Chair-

It's not surprising for a housing central banker of whatever nationality to plea... tence... "It... of the Fed thinks it can...

...me foe of the Fed. Rep. Patman... gled for years to set up an outside audit of the Fed in hopes of curtailing its indep... dence.

After the vote, Mr. Patman express... "regret that the weakening... mea... passed," but predicted that... gress "will support a... countability and... The Texas Democ... ...al version is "a... of accountability...

...r of bankers and even Reserve ...air. Chairman Arthur Burns lobbied diligently against the measure, contending it would subject the independent Federal Reserve to short-run political and economic pressures.

Mr. Burns, in particular, hoped to avoid any audit, but clearly found the watered-down version much more acceptable, because it wouldn't cover the system's policy

...insist, the Fed can do plenty of good or evil right now to shape the economy during the second h... year and into...

That's... ...on (R., Ohio). ...ve arm of Congress the Fed's administrative practices as long as it didn... ous adverse effect" on mone...

Even this weaker version have trouble clearing Cong week, the Senate Banking feated a move to establish the Federal Reserve, and whether the issue will be re... Senate now.

Also included in the E... was a provision extending... the Fed's authority to purch... lion of Treasury public debt the bill increases to $140 million the amount the... System may spend for build...

...this year, supplying enough new credit to help the econ... omy out of the doldrums but

Federal Reserve Statement

	Daily Averages for the weeks ended:		
(Millions of dollars)	May 1, '74	Apr. 24, '74	May 2, '73
Reserve position, all member banks—			
Required reserves	$36,682	$35,919	$32,271
Total reserves held, including vault cash	36,840 A	36,109 A	32,502
Excess (deficit) reserves	158 B	190 B	233
Less: borrowings at Federal Reserve Banks	2,083	1,884 R	1,875
Equals: free or (net borrowed) reserves	(1,925)	(1,694) R	(1,624)
Reserve position, 8 major New York banks—			
Excess (deficit) reserves	79	333	105
Borrowings at Federal Reserve	107	55	182
Net federal funds purchases	2,938	2,622	1,753
Basic reserve surplus (deficit)	(2,966)	(2,644)	(1,831)
Federal Reserve credit outstanding—			
Governments and agencies:			
Held outright	81,637	80,996	75,830
Under repurchase	1,094	693	319
Float	1,902	2,491 R	2,166
Other assets	1,289	1,191	1,120
Other factors affecting reserves—			
Gold stock	11,567	11,567	10,410
Special drawing rights	400	400	400
Currency in circulation	72,042	72,308	66,133
Treasury deposits	2,460	1,666	4,084
Government securities held for foreign central banks			
(Wednesday figures)	27,484	27,158	30,384
12 Major New York Banks			
(Selected balance sheet items in millions of dollars: Wednesday figures)			
Total loans adjusted	67,358	65,102	55,244
Commercial and industrial loans	34,878	34,295	28,832
United States Treasury securities	4,116	4,004	3,769
Tax-exempt securities	7,516	7,584	6,869
Demand deposits adjusted	23,807	22,136	21,056
Total time deposits excluding large certificates of deposit	14,608	14,424	12,904
Large negotiable certificates of deposit	23,452	25,373	18,494
Eurodollars	1,789	1,645	1,801

*As reported: not adjusted for transfers of loans to affiliated companies.
**Over $100,000.
Adjusted to include $58-million of reserve deficiencies on which penalties have in connection with changes in regulation J.

WASHINGTON,
Arthur F. Burns,...
of the Federal Re...
said today that the...
money and credit...
omy had been grow...
rapidly than the...
"wished or intende...
pledged to slow...
sion.

Dr. Burns spoke...
at a briefing...
to a new decisi...
serve to publish...
tion about the... Currency outside banks...
gets" decided... Other Federal Reserve...
by the Federal... liabilities and capital...
Committee. But... Total "market" factors...
on interest rates...
arose, Dr. Burns a...
in strong languag... Net Federal Reserve credit...
He called the...
blem "grave and... market operations...
ous" and said of...
"We are not going... light holdings:...
and prepare a mon... securities...
to the continuance... acceptances...
inflation—on the contra... cy obligations...
hope to do our part in...
during it."

Matters of 'Concern'

The recent "explosion" obligations...
business loans made... bank borrowings...
as well as "excessive" borrowings...
etary "aggregates"... Federal Reserve assets...
money supply are...
"deep concern to reserves"...
the Federal Reserve...
Dr. Burns said.

Factors	Jan. 2	Jan. 9
	— 316	— 624
	— 741	+ 983
	— 722	+ 202
	27	— 73
	+ 290	+ 531
	+ 4	+ 571
	— 196	+ 496
	—1,037	+ 59
	+ 705	— 23
	+ 879	+ 428
	9	— 4
	+ 117	+ 5
	— 195	— 338
	— 68	— 48
	— 37	— 66
	+ 172	— 134
	— 4	— 12
	92	+ 7
	+ 969	— 449
	— 88	— 390

Bank Rate Raised To 8% by Reserve

Rise From 7½% to Record Level Strong Signal of Board's Anti-Inflation Policy —Increase in Bank Credit Cited

Special to The New York Times

WASHINGTON, April 24—The Federal Reserve Board, in a strong signal of its anti-inflation policy, raised its discount rate today to a record level of 8 per cent.

The increase was from 7½ per cent, itself a record, established last August. The discount rate is the interest rate charged to banks temporarily short of funds that need to borrow from the Federal Reserve.

In a brief announcement the board said: "The action was taken in... light of a recent rapid rise in money and bank credit... recognition of increases that have already occurr... er... rm interest rates. The problem of inflation continu... seriou... rn to the board."

Technically, the board approved to... higher discount rate from seven of the 12 regional Reserve banks—those of New York, Philadelphia, Clevela...

Richmond, Kansas City, Dallas and San Francisco. The others are expected to follow shortly.

An increase in the discount rate sometimes brings increases in other interest rates, but more often in recent years it has simply followed other rates upward.

Below Prevailing Rates

Even at 8 per cent, it will be well below the "cluster" of other money-market rates that now prevail, includi... per cent prime bank rate to business. Thus today's move may not by itself lead...

Chart 1
GROWTH IN MONETARY AGGREGATES
Seasonally adjusted annual rates

M1 = Currency plus adjusted demand deposits held by the public.

M2 = M1 plus commercial bank savings and time deposits held by the public, less negotiable certificates of deposit issued in denominations of $100,000 or more.

Adjusted bank credit proxy = Total member bank deposits subject to reserve requirements plus nondeposit sources of funds, such as Euro-dollar borrowings and the proceeds of commercial paper issued by bank holding companies or other affiliates.

Source: Board of Governors of the Federal Reserve System.

Is the Fed a $500-Billion Weakling?

Word from Washington that the Federal Reserve Board is determined to continue money-s... a restri... regardless of ...t effect... as hou... build...

Credit Markets: yesterday. The evidence was sufficiently plain in the rise of the basic lending rate of the First National Bank of Chicago (one of the 10 biggest banks in the country) to 10.4 per cent from the 10.1 per cent it had been quoting for the last week and... Although the Federal Reserve additional funds into ...three-day... and later for both one-day...

deposit were being quoted at 10.4 per cent.

Prime-Rate Action

After the close of business yesterday, the Franklin Nation... announced that effec... raising its ...per cent.

...Franklin hau... cent. The... announce a 10½ po... was the Citizens and Southern National Bank in Georgia, which last week said it was charging a dual rate: 10¼ per cent on existing loans and 10½ per cent on renewals or new loans.

In Philadelphia yesterday, John R. Bunting, chairman of the First Pennsylvania Corporation, told stockholders at the bank holding company's annual meeting he believes there is a... prime rate will ...larly neglect...

High Interest Rates Slow...

Market Profile
Wednesday, April 24, 1974
New York Stock Exchange
Volume: 16,010,000 shares

Up 241 — 303 Unchanged

ISSUES TRADED 1,793

Down 1,249

	Jan. 2	Jan. 9
Required reserves	...,190	...,192
Excess reserves		
...sonal borrowings	31	19
...rrowed reserves	34,446	35,414
...rry-over, excess or (—)		
	229	15...

Money
and
Interest

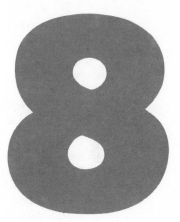

Our study of macroeconomics thus far might be termed "Keynes without money"; it has been confined to an analysis of how an economy reaches product-market equilibrium, or that level of national income where income equals expenditure. A role for money has sometimes been implied, particularly in discussions of the way in which interest rates affect savings and investment, but the interest rate has been assumed as given, without any investigation of how it is determined or why it changes. We will now attempt to fill this gap.

To most economists, the interest rate represents the price of money, and the price of money, like the price of any other commodity, settles at the equilibrium level where supply equals demand. Thus, to understand how interest rates are established, it will be necessary to explore the factors underlying demand and supply in the money market. Similarly, to understand how and why interest rates change, it will be necessary to analyze the forces that produce changes in the demand and supply curves for money. This chapter will elaborate on our original macroeconomic model, which was limited to a study of product-market equilibrium, by introducing the concept of money-market equilibrium—that rate of interest where the supply of money equals the demand for money. The following chapter will examine how product-market equilibrium and money-market equilibrium interact.

Money in the United States Economy

Money in use in the United States today consists of two varieties: currency (both paper money and coins) and demand deposits. Currency represents less than one-fourth of the total money supply. Commercial bank demand deposits, or checking account balances, make up the other three-fourths. Government efforts to control the money supply are generally implemented through actions which operate upon the quantity of demand deposits held by the public since they comprise the largest part of the money supply.

Money has been defined as that which is generally and directly accepted in a community as payment for goods and services and for repayment of debts—that is, as a **medium of exchange.** It is important to keep this definition in mind in differentiating between money (currency and demand deposits) and near monies or other interest-bearing assets which include time deposits, short-term government debt, bonds issued by business corporations, savings and loan shares, or government savings bonds. These interest-bearing assets can be converted into currency or checking account balances quickly and with insignificant loss. But they must first be converted and therefore do not qualify as part of the money supply defined in the narrow sense as a medium of exchange. Like money, however, interest-bearing assets serve the function of a **store of value.** For store of value purposes, a household or business can choose to hold its assets either in the form of money or in the form of interest-bearing assets. Clearly, the demand and supply of money, and consequently the interest rate which represents the equilibrium level at which the demand and supply meet, will depend at least in part on such decisions. It is money's role as a medium of exchange which makes it a unique asset, but as an asset it also serves as a store of value and therefore is a substitute for many other assets, such as time deposits, savings and loan shares, and bonds.

A final function of money is its use as a convenient **unit of account,** or standard in which the value of all other goods and services can be expressed. This function greatly simplifies economic decision-making by providing the prospective buyer or seller with a common unit (dollars) with which he can compare the relative cost of a wide variety of otherwise heterogeneous items.

The Demand for Money

The demand for money is determined by the desire of individuals and businesses to hold part of their assets in the form of money. In order to measure the demand for money, it is necessary to understand the reasons that people want to hold money rather than use it to buy other assets.

Most economists offer a combination of a scale and a substitution argument to explain changes in the demand for money. The **scale argument** refers to the impact of the level of income or wealth upon the demand for money. The demand for money is directly related to the level of income; the higher the income level, the greater will be the effective demand for currency or demand deposits. The **substitution argument** refers to the relative attractiveness of assets that can be substituted for money. It suggests, for example, that when alternative assets such as bonds are relatively unattractive (for example, when they offer very low interest rates or appear unusually risky) people will prefer to keep their wealth in the form of money, and the demand for money will increase. The scale and substitution arguments provide a useful framework for understanding the nature of the demand for money, which can be broken down into transactions demand (which classical economists considered the sole reason for holding money), precautionary demand, and speculative demand (both originally identified by J. M. Keynes).

Transactions Demand for Money

The **transactions demand** springs from the function of money as a medium of exchange because money is used as the method of payment in most exchanges of goods and services. But since the act of buying usually is not perfectly synchronized with the receipt of income, it is necessary to keep some assets in the form of money in order to have the means of paying for goods and services that will be purchased in the future. This can be seen in the example of a household with an annual income of $12,000, received in monthly installments. On the first of the month, $1,000 is placed in a checking account, which is gradually drawn on during the month. On the average, this household will be holding $500 in idle money balances over the year even though it does not actually save any money. This $500 is the family's transactions demand for money, L_T.

The transactions demand for money is closely related to the level of income. This can be seen by example. A family with an income of $2,000 a month will make more transactions involving larger amounts of money than a family with an income of $1,000; accordingly, its demand for transaction balances will be higher. The household that keeps average transaction money balances of $500 when its monthly income is $1,000 may hold average transaction-money balances of $600 if its monthly income should then

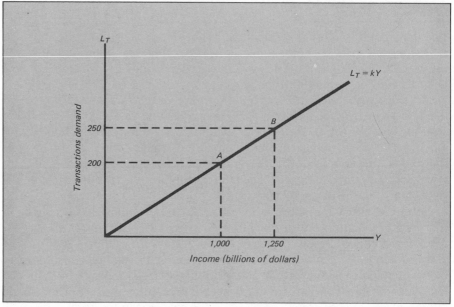

Figure 8.1 The transactions demand for money

increase to $1,200. This concept can be stated algebraically as

$$L_T = kY \qquad (8.1)$$

where L_T represents transactions demand, k the portion of income which is kept as transaction balances, and Y, income. This formulation is often called the "Cambridge-k" equation after the group of economists at that university responsible for its origin. This equation is illustrated in Figure 8.1, which shows transactions demand in an economy where $k = \frac{1}{5}$. Thus, at point A, where annual national income is $1,000 billion, the demand for transaction balances would be $200 billion, while at point B, where Y = $1,250 billion, transactions demand would be $250 billion.

An important addition to the theory of transactions demand has been made by two post-Keynesian economists, William J. Baumol and James Tobin.[1] Their findings have indicated that interest rates are an important determinant of transactions demand. Moreover, they have demonstrated that the relationship between transactions demand and income is not the direct linear relationship postulated by Keynes, that is, that transactions demand does not increase or decrease by the same amount as changes in

1. William J. Baumol, "Transactions Demand for Cash: An Inventory Theoretic Approach," *Quarterly Journal of Economics* 66 (November 1952): 545–556; and James Tobin, "The Interest Elasticity of the Transactions Demand for Cash," *Review of Economics and Statistics* 38 (August 1956): 241–247.

income; rather, changes in income produce proportionately smaller changes in transactions demand.

Baumol's work is based on an analysis of the reasons people hold a given inventory of money for transaction purposes. He noted that transaction balances are held because income and expense are not synchronized; offset against the convenience of holding these monies for future transactions is the fact that they represent a loss of potential income which could be generated by investing in interest-paying assets rather than holding non-interest-paying money. Baumol suggested that the rational individual would at all times try to minimize the level of his transaction balances in order to maximize the interest that his assets could earn if they were not tied up in such transaction balances. For example, a household receiving $36,500 once a year, on January 1, and spending this income at a steady $100-a-day rate, might ideally prefer to purchase 365 units of $100 bonds immediately after payday, and then sell one back each successive day of the year. In this way, the household would have practically all of its available assets earning interest and would have eliminated the need for any transaction balances. It would do a better job at maximizing income than the family that deposited its entire paycheck in the checking account on January 1 and wrote checks against it as needed during the year; the second household would maintain an average annual transaction balance of $18,250, compared to $100 for the first.

Unfortunately, the bond-buying procedure outlined above, which would produce over $900 of interest during the course of the year, is impractical. Apart from the costs involved (brokerage fees, mailing expense, daily transportation to and from the safe deposit box), it would be cumbersome to buy, store, and cash in such a large number of individual securities. This does not mean, however, that all attempts to minimize transaction balances are doomed to failure. A compromise alternative might be to divide the $36,500 on January 1 into four equal amounts, leaving one-quarter in cash but investing the remainder in bonds which will be sold in three equal parts on April 1, July 1, and October 1. Under such a plan, transaction balances would be at a maximum $9,125 on the first day of each quarterly period, an average of $4,062.50 throughout the year. This is considerably less than the average transaction balance ($18,250) of the household that made no attempt to invest any part of its paycheck.

Figure 8.2 illustrates the three alternative programs. In section (a) the household has invested all of its assets in bonds on January 1, liquidating one bond each day. Since its idle transaction balances are at a minimum, it has maximized the income to be earned on its assets. In section (b), the household leaves its entire paycheck in the form of non-interest-earning transaction balances. In section (c), the household divides its assets between bonds and money, arranging a subsequent sale, in three equal parts, of the bonds purchased.

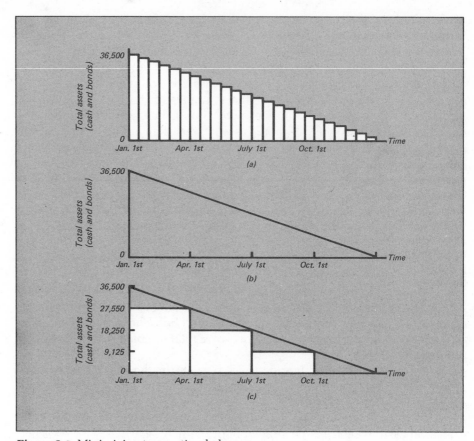

Figure 8.2 Minimizing transaction balances

This analysis makes clear the importance of interest rates in determining the size of the money inventory that a household will carry for transaction purposes. If interest rates on bonds are very low, the interest foregone by *not* investing will be insignificant; thus there will be little motivation for reducing transaction balances. Conversely, as short-term interest rates are high, individuals and businesses will find it profitable to exchange money balances for investments and will therefore attempt to lower transaction balances.

Baumol's approach also brings out a second important observation regarding the behavior of transaction balances. We have noted that an investment program based on the *largest* number of individual bond purchases would provide a household with the highest earnings from its assets and the lowest possible average transaction balance. But every purchase involves costs (brokerage fees, mailing, safekeeping) which the investor must pay. He must therefore balance the income to be foregone by engaging in relatively fewer bond purchases (and thus maintaining higher transaction balances) against the expenses incurred through the larger number of bond purchases required to permit him to minimize his transaction balances. To a certain extent, this decision will be based on interest rates, for, obviously, the higher the interest rates, the more expense the investor can absorb. But the decision is also related to the size of the dollar amounts involved, since many of the costs involved in purchasing and selling securities are relatively fixed and do not vary much with the size of the transaction. For example, a bank may have a minimum $25 charge for each bond purchase and/or sale, and under such circumstances, it would not be sensible, given an interest rate of 5 percent, for an investor to divide up an annually paid income of $12,000 into twelve individual bonds. A little arithmetic will show that although in theory such a practice would minimize his average nonearning transaction balance, the brokerage costs of $325 (one purchase and twelve sales at $25 each) would more than eat up the entire interest income (about $300) from the purchases.

When the sums involved become larger, economies of scale come into play, and the results may be very different. The costs required to make a given number of bond transactions stay the same, but the interest earned is higher because the face value of each bond is higher. (For example, it would cost the same amount to buy and sell twelve $10,000 bonds as it does to buy and sell twelve $1000 bonds, but the income received will be ten times as much.) As a result, a higher-income household is in a better position to engage in the larger number of bond purchases that are required to maximize income. These facts suggest that the proportional relationship suggested by the Cambridge-k equation between increases in income and increases in transaction balances may not be accurate. It is true that the transactions demand for money will increase as income increases because more transactions occur at higher income levels, but the demand will not increase as fast as the increase in income because of the economies of scale that encourage bond investment as an alternative to transaction balances when larger sums resulting from higher incomes are involved. Specifically, Baumol concluded that the transactions demand for money would change at one-half the percentage rate at which income changed; for example, a 10 percent increase in income would result in a 5 percent increase in transaction balances.

The consensus today is that transactions demand is a function of both income and interest rates, a concept which can be expressed algebraically as $L_T = L_T(Y, i)$. Because we are dealing with two sets of variables—income and interest rates—it is impossible to show this equation as a single curve as we did in Figure 8.1, where transactions demand was shown as a function of a single factor, income. Instead, economists often use a series of curves, *each* of which represents transactions demand at different interest rates, while holding income constant. This is shown in Figure 8.3, where Y_1 indicates transactions demand (L_T) at various interest rates when national income equals $1,000 billion, and Y_2 and Y_3 represent L_T at other levels of

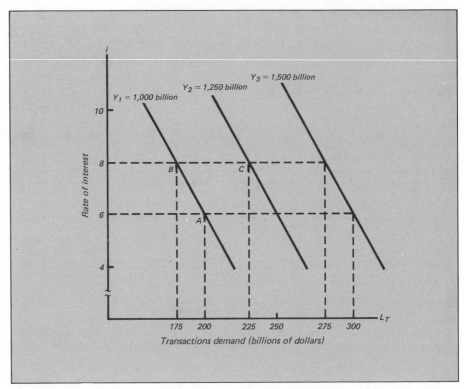

Figure 8.3 The transactions demand for money at different interest rates

national income. Point A, for example, indicates that transactions demand would be $200 billion in an economy with a national income of $1,000 billion when interest rates stood at 5 percent. In this economy L_T would decline to $175 billion (point B) if interest rates rose to 8 percent. The figure also shows that transactions demand would be $225 billion if interest rates were 8 percent in an economy where national income was $1,250 billion (point C).

The Precautionary Demand for Money

While recognizing the importance of transactions demand, Keynes identified a second component of the total demand for money as **precautionary demand.** Keynes defined precautionary cash balances as those which are kept for sudden emergency expenditures as well as unexpected expenditure opportunities. Since there are always uncertainties regarding the receipt of future income and the need for future expenditure, the prudent person will allow for such uncertainties by maintaining an extra money reserve. Keynes suggested that precautionary demand was, like transactions demand, closely tied to income. At higher income levels, individuals and households feel there are a greater number of contingencies in which a readily available supply of money might be useful, either to prevent a disaster or to take advantage of an opportunity. For example, a family with two automobiles and a boat and a snowmobile is more likely to have unexpected repair bills than a family with only one car. Post-Keynesian economists suggest, however, that precautionary demand, like transactions demand, responds inversely to changes in interest rates. At high interest rates, a household may be willing to accept the risk that it may run short in an emergency and be forced to liquidate invested assets or borrow; at very low interest rates, it may not.

Because precautionary demand responds like transactions demand to changes in income and interest rates, analysis of the total demand for money usually combines transactions demand and precautionary demand in the single equation $L_T = L_T(Y, i)$.

The Speculative Demand for Money

One of Keynes' most innovative breaks with classical economics was his identification of a third component of total demand for money, the **speculative demand.** Classical economists generally held that the demands for money would be limited to those based on transaction grounds and that once such demands were filled there could be no reason why a rational person would seek to keep his assets in the form of nonearning assets rather than bonds. Keynes, on the other hand, pointed out that there might be very good motives, aside from the transaction and precautionary ones, for keeping one's assets in the form of money. This is tied to the substitution argument: if one believed that the substitution of bonds for money might result in a loss of assets (for example, when bond prices seemed to be sinking, so that a loss might be incurred when the bonds were sold), then it would indeed be preferable to forego the interest and keep one's assets in money.

This speculative demand for money, based on the fear of loss of assets, is derived from the store of value function of money. Thus we might assume that the demand for money will increase when individuals and businesses feel that money, rather than bonds, represents a better store of value for their assets.

Under what circumstances will money prove a better store of value than bonds? These circumstances are closely related to expectations about bond prices. If investors believe currently low bond prices are going to rise, they will prefer bonds to money. However, if they feel that bond prices are currently high and will decline in the future, then they will prefer to keep assets in the form of money and avoid the loss that would be incurred in the future by buying bonds now. In order to understand how expectations about bond prices are established, we must examine the forces that determine changes in the price of bonds.

Assuming a bond on which there is no appreciable credit risk, such as a bond issued by the U.S. government or a high-grade corporate borrower such as AT&T, the price of the bond reflects the relative attractiveness of its interest payment in comparison with interest available from alternative comparable investments. For example, during the 1950s, the U.S. Treasury sold billions of dollars of $3\frac{1}{2}$ percent bonds due in 1990. Each of these bonds paid $35 a year in interest, and each was sold at a price of about $1,000, reflecting the fact that, at the time, $3\frac{1}{2}$ percent was a reasonable rate of return on government securities. By the 1970s, however, the entire level of interest rates had changed, and the government was forced to offer $75 a year in interest, or $7\frac{1}{2}$ percent, to sell a new issue of bonds coming due at about the same time as those sold at $3\frac{1}{2}$ percent. At this point, no one would pay $1,000 for the $3\frac{1}{2}$ percent bonds with their modest $35-a-year interest payments since they could get a $7\frac{1}{2}$ percent bond (or $75 a year in interest) for the same $1,000. Instead, the price of the old bonds fell until it reached a level (about $750) at which the bonds provided a rate of return comparable to that of the new ones.[2]

As this example illustrates, bond prices move inversely to interest rates. An increase in interest rates will produce a decline in bond prices; if interest rates decline, then bond prices will rally. For example, in 1970, AT&T sold an issue of 8.7 percent bonds at a price of around $1,000. By 1973, when interest rates had dropped, these bonds sold for as much as $1,120.

Keynes explained the speculative demand for money in terms of a "normal" long-term interest rate which he believed existed in the minds of investors. When the market rate of interest was above this normal rate, Keynes believed that investors would "expect" it to fall; in other words, they would expect bond prices to rise. Thus, they would be eager to exchange cash balances for bonds, and the speculative demand for money would fall. Conversely, if the market rate were below the normal rate, investors would anticipate higher rates and lower bond prices. They would therefore avoid bonds, preferring to leave their assets in money balances, and the speculative demand for money would increase.

This concept can be expressed algebraically as $L_S = L_S(i)$, which indicates the amount by which the speculative demand changes in response to changes in interest rates *and is an inverse function of i*. The equation is shown graphically in Figure 8.4 where we see that at point A, with a 6 percent interest rate, the speculative demand for money would be $15 billion, while at point B, at 8 percent, it would be only $10 billion.

Observe the shape of the curve in Figure 8.4. At very high rates of interest, it is almost vertical and close to the zero level of speculative demand. This

2. In determining the price level for an old, low interest rate bond, we take into account not only the actual annual interest payment, but also the difference between the current market price and the eventual redemption price. In other words, at $750, the $3\frac{1}{2}$s of 1990 provide a yield comparable to the $7\frac{1}{2}$s of 1988 at $1000, if we include not merely the $35 in interest to be paid each year but an annual proportionate share of the gain of $250 which will be received when the bonds are repaid in 1990. This concept is called "yield to maturity" and it is the yield to maturity of comparable bonds which must be approximately the same at any time in the bond market.

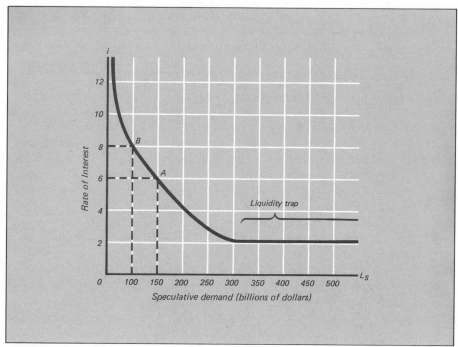

Figure 8.4 The speculative demand for money, or the liquidity preference curve

implies that at certain interest rates, investors believe that rates are so high that they cannot go any higher, or, in other words, that bond prices *must* rise. At these levels, the speculative demand for money is almost nonexistent—everyone prefers bonds.

At the other end of the interest spectrum, at very low rates, the behavior of the curve is also significant. Here the curve becomes horizontal. This can be interpreted as the reaction of investors to an interest rate level so low they feel it can go no lower: interest rates are bound to rise, and consequently bond prices are bound to fall. At such rates of interest, no one will buy bonds because they feel that purchase of bonds will mean certain loss. As a result, there is an unlimited demand for money in preference to bonds at this interest rate, and all additional monies that find their way into this economy will be held as speculative balances. These monies will not be invested in bonds as long as interest rates remain so low, because individuals will be waiting for interest rates to return to normal and bond prices to fall. This area of the speculative demand for money curve is called the **liquidity trap** area. The entire speculative demand curve, $L_s = L_s(i)$, is often called the **liquidity preference curve** in reference to its role as an indicator of investor preference at various interest rates for liquidity (money balances) rather than bonds.

The importance of Keynes' analysis of speculative demand will be seen in the discussion of the limitations of monetary policy in Chapter 12. Nevertheless, some of the implications of the notion of liquidity preference should be mentioned here. We have noted that in the classical model the demand for money was confined largely to transactions demand, which was regarded primarily as a function of income. According to this view, if income remains constant, the total demand for money will remain fairly constant, and any infusions of money into an economy will have to affect either prices or quantities of goods produced.[3] If, however, as Keynes demonstrated, some of the increases in the money supply are absorbed by an increase in the demand for money because of a liquidity preference, such increases in the money supply may have no effect on prices or quantities. The liquidity preference theory explains why increases in the supply of money, which, under the classical theory, should be an effective way of increasing production and employment, may, under some circumstances, have no effect at all on the level of employment.

Professor James Tobin of Yale has developed an explanation of liquidity preference which appears somewhat more realistic than that put forward by Keynes, since it does not depend on expectations about future interest rates as compared with a hypothetical normal rate, but rather on the trade-off between income and potential loss that exists for every bond purchase at every interest rate.[4]

Tobin divides all those who own assets into two categories: risk-averters and risk-lovers. Extreme risk-lovers (a definite minority) would almost never hold speculative money balances; they would prefer at all times to accept risk of loss in exchange for the income to be obtained by buying bonds. Risk-averters, on the other hand—and Tobin claims that most wealth-holders are in this category—would prefer to avoid the risk of loss that comes with holding bonds rather than money. In other words, they have an intrinsic preference for liquidity, a preference that can be offset only by increasingly higher interest rates. A high interest rate operates as an incentive to risk, whereas a decline in the interest rate will make people less willing to accept the risk inherent in bond purchases as opposed to cash balances.

Are you a risk-averter or risk-lover? Consider the following proposition: Would you rather have a certain gift of $1,000 or a chance to pick from two "prizes," one of zero dollars and one of $2,000, with an equal chance of getting each prize? Those taking the $1,000 can be called risk-averters since they have avoided the alternative—a "fair" bet with an expected value of $1,000, because $.5(0) + .5(\$2,000) = \$1,000$. Those who go for this alternative are risk-lovers. Viewers of the television show "Let's Make a Deal" are

---

3. This is just another way of restating the basic classical quantity of money equation familiar to all beginning economics students: if $MV = Py$ and V is a constant, then changes in M must result in changes in either P or y, where P is the average price of commodities in terms of money and y is the number of units of commodity output available.

4. James Tobin, "Liquidity Preference as Behavior Towards Risk," *Review of Economic Studies* 25 (February 1958): 65–86.

constantly treated to the agonies of contestants who are ambivalent regarding their attitude toward risk. Often if the "prize" is large enough, as in a lottery where the quantity risked is small but the likelihood of winning is even smaller, people will behave as risk-lovers. This is necessary for lotteries to be profitable for their organizers.

Although Tobin agrees with Keynes that liquidity preference is closely dependent on interest rates and that it moves inversely with interest rates, Tobin bases his explanation on the role of interest as an incentive to overcoming risk aversion rather than on expectations about future interest rates.

The Total Demand for Money

We can synthesize the transactions and precautionary demands for money, L_T, together with the speculative demand for money, L_S, into a single equation. Given

$$L_T = L_T(Y)$$

which explains that transactions demand is a function of income, and

$$L_{TS} = L_{TS}(i)$$

which explains that both transactions demand and speculative demand are functions of interest, we find that combining the two:

$$L = L(Y, i)$$

where L represents both L_T and L_S or the total demand for money. This equation is indicated graphically in Figure 8.5 as a series of curves, each of which shows how the demand for money responds to changes in interest rates at a given level of income.

Curve L_1 represents a hypothetical total demand for money where Y = $1,000 billion. It shows that at the $1,000 billion level of national income, demand for money would be $250 billion at 4 percent interest but only $200 billion at 6 percent. In an economy where Y = $1,250 billion, ($L_2$), a 4 percent rate would produce a demand for money of $300 billion, and a 6 percent rate would produce a demand of $250 billion; both demand levels are substantially higher than for comparable interest rates at the lower income level. This reflects the fact that the transactions-demand component of total demand increases with income. Curve L_3 represents demand for money in an economy where Y = $2,000 billion. Note that the three curves converge and flatten out at the extreme right. This is the Keynesian liquidity trap area; the graph points out that at the low interest rate of 2 percent, the demand for money is infinite. Another way of phrasing this same concept would be to say that at 2 percent there is no demand for money substitutes since the risk of loss of principal is so great and/or the income to be earned from bonds is so small.

A recent post-Keynesian addendum to the analysis of the demand for money is found in the modern quantity theory postulated by economist

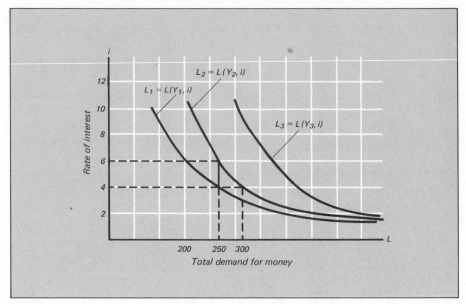

Figure 8.5 The total demand for money in response to the interest rate

Milton Friedman. Friedman suggests that the demand for money is not merely a function of income and interest rates, but also varies directly with total wealth. As wealth in the hands of individuals and businesses reaches higher levels, larger amounts of assets will be kept in money balances. We will examine Friedman's theory of wealth in more detail in Chapter 13. Here it will be sufficient to indicate that if wealth is assigned a role as a determinant of the demand for money, then the entire demand for money equation will read

$$L = L(Y, i, W)$$

The Supply of Money

Thus far we have taken the money supply as given, assuming that it was exogenously determined by the monetary authorities. At this point it will be useful to examine the methods through which the size of the money supply is established and the way in which changes are brought about by the monetary authorities.

Two kinds of money comprise the money supply (M_1) in the United States: currency (including coins) and bank deposits. Figure 8.6 maps out the behavior of the money supply in the United States from 1940 to 1973.

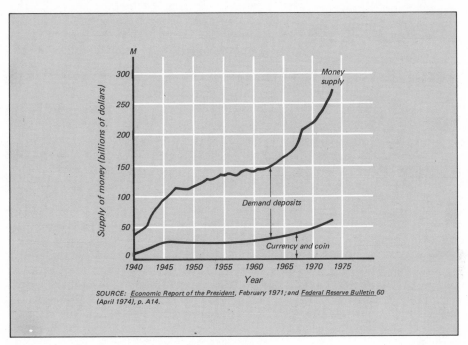

Figure 8.6 The U.S. money supply, 1940–1973

The size of the currency component is not directly subject to monetary authority control but is determined by the choice which the public and the banks make at any time between bank deposit balances and cash. However, with the exception of monetary crises, such as the bank panic of 1933, the relationship between deposits and cash remains fairly constant, so that any action by the monetary authorities to affect the bank deposit component usually has a predetermined consequence for the currency component. An essential first step in defining this relationship is some understanding of commercial bank operations.

The Commercial Banking System

In the United States, commercial banks are privately owned business organizations, whose objectives are to maximize profits by the most efficient use of assets. Typically, a commercial bank balance sheet will show that the bank owns three main kinds of assets: loans (which are IOUs for monies the bank has lent out to its customers), investments (which are mostly government bonds), and reserves (which are monies the bank owns, but which it is keeping at its district Federal Reserve bank). Liabilities, or the source of the funds which the bank has used to acquire these assets, are primarily the demand deposits which customers have in their checking

Commentary: How Much Money Is There Anyway?

Keynesians and monetarists continue to dispute the degree to which money matters in an economy, but both sides generally agree that money has some influence on major aggregate economic variables. Prices, for example, including even the price of money itself, i.e., the interest rate, and thus ultimately the general output of the economy are directly influenced by the money supply.

Thus, someone has to be in the counting house, finding how much money is sifting through the economy and deciding if the supply should be increased, decreased, or allowed to go along in benign neglect. Since it is the job of the Federal Reserve System (through its powers to conduct open-market operations, to raise or lower the reserve requirements of member banks, or to alter discount policy) to make these decisions, it falls to this institution to know what the money supply actually is. In recent years this has been increasingly difficult to judge accurately as more banks have either left the system or chosen not to affiliate, so that the supply of money which they controlled could be only loosely approximated.

Yet the money in nonmember banks is just as much a part of the monetary river flowing through the economy as comparable accounts in member banks and can influence the state of the money supply. The problem becomes even more acute when there are changes in the existing patterns of money accumulation in different sections of the country. This happened in 1973, when farm income in agricultural areas bulged as a result of the bulge in demand and in prices for farm products. Since many of the rural banks were not part of the Reserve System, the Fed's money count for the year was less accurate than usual. The Fed seized the occasion to again ask Congress, as it has done off and on since the founding of the system, to impose uniform reserve requirements on all the nation's banks, whether or not they were part of the system.

The major argument repeatedly put forward by the Federal Reserve is that in order to function as the nation's money manager, it must be able to control the money supply through its control of the assets held as reserves by the banking system. The Fed emphasized that the *size* of the reserve requirements is not the key issue, since many state requirements are similar to their own; what is significant is the *kinds* of assets which banks are required to hold. Because nonmember banks are able to hold more of their reserves in assets that either yield interest or buy services from correspondent banks, the nonmembers have a competitive advantage. The result, one top officer of the Fed pointed out, is that $1 of reserve in a member bank supports $7 in demand deposits whereas the same $1 in reserves supports $50 of demand deposits in a nonmember bank.

Nonmembers enjoy additional advantages: they don't need to buy stock in the Federal Reserve and are not subject to the same bank audits. The result is a trend toward "dropouts" from the system and the consequent decline of the Fed's ability to get accurate estimates of the money supply and therefore to influence that supply.

The Fed also maintains that Congressional imposition of uniform reserve requirements would help reduce some additional inequities both within the system and among various banking institutions, such as the savings and loan associations and savings banks. Some of these were eased in 1973 by changing the classifications of banks' reserve requirements according to geographical location. Under the new standards the requirements are based on size rather than location, with a graduated scale ranging from 10 to 22 percent for reserve city banks and from 7 to 14 percent for other banks.

None of these issues, however, are free of political considerations. A growing feeling in Congress is the view that the Federal Reserve should be shorn of some of its independent power. Presidents and Congress tend to feel policy tools—both fiscal and monetary—belong in their hands, and an independent monetary authority, with the power to refuse requests for easy or tight money, is a growing irritant. This view prevails in the powerful House Banking Committee, particularly under the strong chairmanship of Wright Patman (despite the fact that in 1961 he was chairman of a Congressional committee that recommended uniform reserve requirements for all banks, member and nonmember). Another Congressional obstacle is the fear that a uniform reserve requirement would be the beginning of the end of the state-national dual banking system, which has many devoted and influential supporters.

But since the questions of the supply of money and its control will not go away by themselves and since the current trend is toward disassociation from the system—86 percent of commercial bank deposits were in member banks in 1945 compared with 80 percent in 1970 and 78 percent in 1973—the Federal Reserve is faced with the necessity to take some kind of action in order to maintain a high degree of control over the money supply. Failing an ability to impose uniform reserve requirements on all U.S. banks, the Fed may wish to experiment with some means, such as variable reserve requirements for member banks as credit conditions change, in order to stabilize the share of deposits in member banks. Such an action might stop the decline in the system's membership, encourage dropouts to return, inspire new banks to join, and thus improve the statistics that the Fed has to work with.

accounts at the bank. Savings deposits also make up a large part of commercial bank liabilities, but these assets are not generally considered as part of the money supply. We can focus on the demand deposit portion of commercial banks' liabilities without loss of generality. Assets and liabilities for Bank A are shown in the hypothetical Balance Sheet No. 1.

Balance Sheet No. 1   Bank A

ASSETS		LIABILITIES	
Reserves	$ 400	Deposits	$1,800
Loans	$1,000		
Investments	$ 400		

Suppose that this bank holds reserves in excess of those required by the Federal Reserve System. When the bank makes a new loan, it obtains a new asset—the IOU from the borrower—and a new liability—the demand deposit balance which it gives the borrower. The balance sheet consequences of a new loan are shown in Balance Sheet No. 2.

Balance Sheet No. 2   Bank A makes a loan of $100

ASSETS		LIABILITIES	
Reserves	$ 400	Deposits	$1,800
Loans	$1,000		+$ 100
	+$ 100		
Investments	$ 400		

Customers who have checking accounts at one commercial bank (Bank A) often write checks against these accounts which are given to people who deposit them in another bank (Bank B). Bank B then sends the checks to the Federal Reserve bank, which, in turn, subtracts the amount of the check from the reserve account of Bank A and adds it to the reserve account of Bank B. The effect of such a transaction on Bank A is to decrease a liability (the checking account balance of the check-writing customer) and to decrease an asset (Bank A's reserve account at the Fed).

Balance Sheet No. 3   Customer of Bank A writes a check which is deposited in another bank.

ASSETS		LIABILITIES	
Reserves	$ 400	Deposits	$1,900
	−$ 100		−$ 100
Loans	$1,100		
Investments	$ 400		

The reverse occurs when a customer deposits a check drawn on another bank in his account at Bank A. After this check clears through the Federal Reserve bank, Bank A finds itself with an increased balance in its reserve account at the Fed and with an increase in the deposits held by its customers.

Reserves held at the Fed, in addition to their use as a mechanism to facilitate the clearance of checks drawn on different banks, perform a more significant function: they constitute the basis of a device, known as the **fractional reserve system,** through which the Fed operates to control the money supply. In the United States commercial banks are required by law to keep minimum reserves equal to a certain percentage of deposits. For example, if this reserve requirement is 20 percent, a bank with deposits of $5,000 would have to keep reserves of $1,000; or to phrase it somewhat differently, a bank with reserves of $2,000 could not carry deposits of more than $10,000.

Occasionally, a bank will find itself with more reserves than it is legally required to carry at the Fed. Assuming reserve requirements of 20 percent, Balance Sheet No. 1 above illustrates such a situation, for here we see a bank with $1,800 of deposits (which would require 20 percent of $1,800, or $360 of reserves) and reserves of $400. Such reserves over the required level are described as **excess reserves.** Since the objective of a commercial bank is to maximize profits, and since loans are the best source of profits, the normal response of a bank to an excess reserve position is to increase loans. A bank with $400 of reserves would recognize that legally it could carry a larger volume of deposits than $1,800, and it would try to bring up its deposit total by making additional loans. (Recall the discussion of Balance Sheet No. 2 above.)

Let us now summarize the implications of the fractional reserve system in the execution of Federal Reserve Board policy. We have seen that demand deposits represent the most important part of the money supply and that the level of demand deposits is determined by the reserve position of the commercial banks. Banks with excess reserves will increase their demand deposits (and thus the money supply) by increasing loans; banks that find themselves with no excess reserves, or worse yet, in a negative reserve position, will find it impossible to increase their demand deposits (they may actually be forced to refuse to renew loans in order to cut back their demand deposits), and the net effect will be to slow down or reverse any growth in the money supply. By controlling the reserve position of the commercial banks, the Federal Reserve Board can effectively control the size of the money supply, given a constant ratio of demand deposits to reserves and a constant desired ratio of demand deposits to currency.

Federal Reserve Operations

Open-market operations are the most important means by which the Federal Reserve can control the reserve portion of the commercial banks. These operations involve purchases and sales of government bonds by the

Federal Reserve banks and are carried out in the open market. Each time the Fed buys bonds, it pays for them by giving the seller a check drawn on itself. The seller then deposits this check in his own bank. When the check clears, the net effect for the bank is an increase in its deposits and also an increase in the bank's reserve account at the Fed.

Let us consider an example of an open-market operation. Suppose the Fed buys $1 million of bonds held as an investment by Prudential Insurance, and Prudential deposits the Fed's check at Chase Manhattan Bank. Chase will find itself with $1 million of additional demand deposits in the Prudential account and with an additional $1 million of reserves. Since under a 20 percent reserve requirement, the Chase need have only $200,000 of additional reserves at the Fed to carry the $1 million of new demand deposits, it now has $800,000 of *excess* reserves and will be encouraged to make new loans and thus increase the money supply. Through purchases of government bonds from the public, the Fed can create additional reserves for the commercial banks and therefore lead to an increase in the money supply.

Balance Sheet No. 4   The Federal Reserve buys $1 million of government bonds from Prudential and Prudential deposits the Fed's check in its account at Chase Manhattan Bank

Chase Manhattan Bank		
ASSETS		LIABILITIES
Reserves	+ $1 million	Deposits (in Prudential's account) + $1 million
Excess reserves	+$800,000	

What will be the total increase in the money supply resulting from any single increase in reserves? We have seen that the initial impact of the Fed's purchase of the bonds held by Prudential was to leave Chase with $800,000 of excess reserves, which it lent to customers. The commercial banking system, of which Chase is a part, could increase total demand deposits by a multiple of the initial increase in Chase's reserves. To see this, suppose that the checks written by Chase's customers are deposited in the recipient's own banks. Actually, checks written by Chase's customers will end up in a group of banks, but assume for simplicity that all of these $800,000 of checks are deposited in the Bank of America. Once the checks clear, Bank of America will find itself with $800,000 of additional deposits and $800,000 of additional reserves. Since it needs only $160,000 of reserves to carry the new $800,000 of deposits, Bank of America now has $640,000 of excess reserves and can comfortably make new loans of $640,000.

Balance Sheet No. 5   Chase Manhattan lends $800,000 to customers, who write checks for the entire $800,000, which are then deposited by recipients at Bank of America

Bank of America

ASSETS		LIABILITIES	
Reserves	+$800,000	Deposits	+$800,000
Excess reserves	+ 640,000		

If all these lenders at Bank of America write checks which are then deposited at Continental Illinois, the Chicago bank will experience an increase of deposits and reserves of $640,000, providing it with $512,000 of excess reserves, which it will then use for additional loans. This chain of loan creation could continue throughout the banking system, with each succeeding group of banks obtaining an increment of excess reserves and writing new loans.

In all, the entire banking system could eventually create additional deposits of five times the initial increase in reserves, a change equal to the reciprocal of the reserve requirement. This can be seen in Table 8.1. Note that the net addition to the money supply resulting from this $1 million purchase of bonds is $5 million, consisting of $1 million in deposits placed directly in the Prudential's account at Chase and an additional $4 million

Table 8.1   Possible Effect of $1 million Purchase of Government Bonds by Federal Reserve System as the New Reserves Created by This Purchase Move Through the Banking System

	Increase in Deposits	Net Increase in Reserves	Increase in Loans
Chase Manhattan	$1,000,000	$800,000	$200,000
Bank of America	800,000	640,000	160,000
Continental Illinois	640,000	512,000	128,000
First National Bank of Houston	512,000	409,000	105,000
Putnam Trust Company	409,000	327,000	82,000
Cleveland Trust	327,000	261,000	66,000
Girard Trust	261,000	210,000	51,000
Chemical Bank	210,000	168,000	42,000
.			
.			
.			
etc.			
Bank n	0	0	0
	$5,000,000	$4,000,000	$1,000,000

of deposits created through loans by banks throughout the system. This relationship between any increment of reserves injected into the banking system, ΔR, and its maximum effect on demand deposits, ΔD, is called the **money multiplier.** The money multiplier is derived through the equation:

$$D = \frac{1}{RR}R \qquad (8.2)$$

The money supply is equal to 1 divided by the reserve ratio times R since $R/D = RR$. From equation (8.3) it is easy to derive the money multiplier which states that the change in the money supply will be equal to the change in reserves times 1 divided by the required reserve ratio.[5]

$$\Delta D = \frac{1}{RR}\Delta R \qquad (8.3)$$

Given these equations, we see that in the banking system described above, with a reserve requirement of 20 percent, the maximum money multiplier is 5, and an additional infusion of $1 million in reserves through the purchase by the Fed of $1 million of government bonds could lead to an increase of as much as $5 million in the money supply.

Open-market sales of government securities by the Fed have precisely the opposite effect as purchases. For example, assume the Fed sells $1 million out of its inventory of bonds to the U.S. Steel pension fund, and the pension fund pays for these bonds by writing a check on its bank, Mellon National Bank and Trust, made out to the Fed. When this check clears, Mellon will find that its deposits (the U.S. Steel pension account) have declined by $1 million, and its reserves have also declined by $1 million.

---

5. A formal derivation of equation (8.3) is as follows: let D_0 stand for the initial stock of the demand deposits, L_0 for the initial stock of loans, R_0 for the initial stock of reserves, D_i for the stock of demand deposits at the end of Phase I ($i = 1 \ldots n$), ΔR for the initial change in reserves, RR for reserve requirement, and $v = (1 - $ the leakage rate)—expressed as a decimal; for reserves only this is (1 − reserve ratio), or $(1 - .15) = .85$. Initially we have

$$D_0 = L_0 + R_0$$

because assets (R_0 and L_0) equal liabilities (D_0). At the end of Phase I we must include the impact on the balance sheet

$$D_1 = D_0 + \Delta R$$

That is, $D_1 - D_0 = \Delta R$, or $\Delta D = \Delta R$, the change in reserves equals the change in demand deposits. Continuing on to later phases we have

$$D_2 = D_1 + v\Delta R = D_0 + \Delta R + v\Delta R$$

$$D_2 - D_1 = \Delta D \text{ in Phase II is equal to } v\Delta R$$

$$D_3 = D_2 + v^2\Delta R = D_0 + \Delta R + v\Delta R + v^2\Delta R$$

$$D_n = D_{n-1} + v^{n-1}\Delta R = D_0 + \Delta R (1 + v + v^2 + \ldots + v^{n-1})$$

Multiply both sides by v

Balance Sheet No. 6   Effect on Mellon National Bank and Trust Co. when Fed sells $1 million of government bonds to U.S. Steel pension fund, and the fund pays for these bonds by writing a check on its account at Mellon

Mellon National Bank and Trust

ASSETS		LIABILITIES	
Reserves	− $1 million	Deposits	− $1 million (decline in U.S. Steel pension account)

Assuming Mellon had no excess reserves before this transaction, it would now find itself in a negative reserve position of −$800,000. Since a $1 million decline in reserves implies the need for a $5 million decline in deposits,[6] and since the Mellon so far has lost $1 million in deposits, the likelihood is that the bank will be under pressure to reduce its loans in order to further reduce deposits and bring its reserve/deposit ratio back to the required level.

To summarize, sales of bonds by the Fed reduce bank reserves and lead to reductions in loans and in the money supply. Since the contraction of reserves caused by such a sale moves through the banking system just as the expansion of reserves procedures outlined above, the net contraction for the entire banking system could be the amount of the initial sale by the Fed times the monetary multiplier, i.e., a $1 million sale could lead to a $5 million decline in the money supply.

Although open-market operations are the most important means by which

$$vD_n = vD_0 + \Delta R (v + v^2 + v^3 + \ldots + v^n)$$

Subtract both sides from $D_n = D_0 + \Delta R (1 + v + v^2 + \ldots + v^n)$

$$D_n - vD_n = D_0 - vD_0 + \Delta R (1 - v^n)$$

$$D_n (1 - v) = (1 - v) D_0 + \Delta R (1 - v^n)$$

$$(1 - v)(D_n - D_0) = \Delta R (1 - v^n)$$

$D_n - D_0 =$ total change in demand deposits $= \Delta D$. Therefore

$$(1 - v)\Delta D = \Delta R (1 - v^n)$$

$$\Delta D = \Delta R \frac{1 - v^n}{1 - v}$$

$$\lim_{n \to \infty} \Delta D = \frac{1}{1 - v}\Delta R$$

Because $(1 - v) = (RR)$

$$\Delta D = \frac{1}{RR} \Delta R$$

If $D_0 = R_0 = 0$, then $D = \frac{1}{RR} R$

6. Assuming that this bank had no excess reserves.

the Fed can regulate the reserve position of commercial banks, there are other options. First, the Fed can change the reserve requirement itself. For example, a banking system with $300 billion of deposits, a 20 percent reserve requirement, and $60 billion of reserves has no excess reserves. If, however, the reserve requirement were reduced to 18 percent, required reserves would be only $54 billion and the system would find itself with $6 billion of excess reserves, or enough to create additional loans (or money supply) of almost $35 billion. Second, the Fed can alter the **rediscount rate,** which is the interest rate paid to the Fed by commercial banks when they seek to make up inadequate reserves by borrowing from the Federal Reserve.

Member bank borrowing involves adjustment of excess reserves to what is known as **free reserves.** Whereas excess reserves are total reserves less required reserves, free reserves are excess reserves less total commercial bank borrowing from the Federal Reserve System, called "member-bank borrowing." Free reserves are particularly significant because their level is often taken as an indication of the posture of monetary policy: a low level of free reserves is taken to reflect monetary "tightness," as it discourages borrowing, and a high level is taken to reflect monetary "ease," encouraging members to borrow from the Fed. This is misleading, however, because it ignores the factors affecting desired free reserves.

Basically the determinants of desired free reserves are (1) uncertainty about net deposits over withdrawals and (2) the relationship between market interest rates and the rediscount rate at which commercial banks can borrow

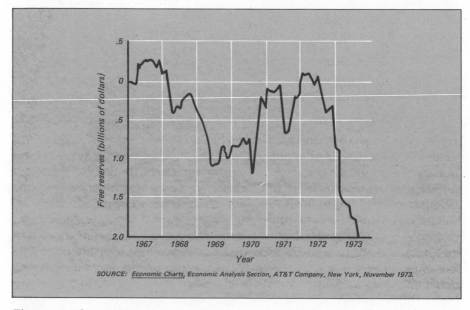

Figure 8.7 The performance of free reserves in the United States from 1967 to August 1973

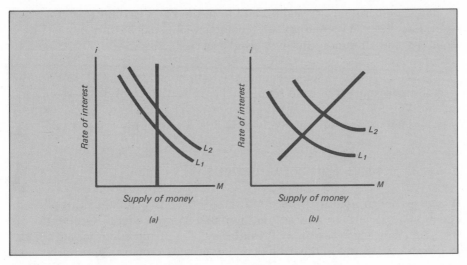

Figure 8.8 The supply of money

from the Federal Reserve System. If, given free reserves of $100 million and a discount rate of 7 percent, market interest rates rise from 8 percent to 9 percent, monetary policy has effectively eased, since desired free reserves will fall and commercial banks as profit maximizers will be attempting to expand their lending activities. Free reserves may even be negative, with member-bank borrowing in excess of excess reserves, when market rates are particularly high, as in 1973 and 1969. Negative free reserves are generally referred to as **net borrowed reserves.** The level of free reserves in recent years is represented in Figure 8.7.

Interest Rate Level and the Money Supply

Thus far, no attempt has been made to incorporate possible effects of the interest rate on the money supply. The supply of money has been represented as a vertical line, the same at every rate of interest, implying that M will settle at that level predetermined by the Fed regardless of the interest rate, as shown in section (a) of Figure 8.8. The responsiveness of excess reserves or desired free reserves (and therefore responsiveness of the supply of money to changes in the interest rate) suggests, however, that the M curve would be more accurately shown as a positively sloped supply curve, with higher amounts of M appearing at higher interest rates. This is shown in section (b).

Such a money-supply curve reflects the fact that as market interest rates rise, commercial banks become more aggressive as intermediaries between lenders and borrowers. In general, higher market lending rates occur before higher borrowing rates must be paid by commercial banks. This is due to the ability of commercial banks to attract either demand deposits at zero interest rates or savings deposits bearing relatively low interest rates as a "tie-in" or "one-stop-banking" appeal. In addition, the Fed discount rate often lags behind market rate increases and so commercial banks borrow more heavily from the Fed (inducing net borrowed reserves) in periods of particularly tight money.

The result of more aggressive intermediation by commercial banks in the face of higher market interest rates will be a larger stock of demand deposits outstanding for a given quantity of reserves. Therefore, the money supply may be seen to respond positively to higher levels of the interest rate.

Federal Reserve Policy Limitations

It is essential to note that there are several oversimplifications implied in equation (8.3) and in the assumption that every Federal-Reserve-Board-inspired change in reserves will result inevitably in a predetermined change in the money supply in the form of an increase in demand deposits. A number of structural factors within the monetary system limit the effectiveness of Federal Reserve Board policy and make it difficult to establish the money supply at the level it deems most desirable. Our original model assumed that all excess reserves would inevitably be used by the banking system to create additional loans and therefore increase the money supply or, in other words, that banks are always in a zero excess-reserve position. Such an approach appears rational at first glance because it would seem to maximize bank profits. In some cases, however, bankers will often be reluctant to use all their excess reserves to make loans. In periods of economic uncertainty, such loans may appear uncomfortably risky. Recent studies by economist R. L. Teigen indicate that there is also a relationship between the level of excess reserves and interest rates.[7] As has been noted, when interest rates rise, the opportunity cost of keeping "idle" excess reserves also increases and bankers are more willing to accept the risks involved in using these reserves to create additional loans. Therefore excess reserves decline and the money supply increases. In brief, Teigen found that excess reserves and interest rates moved inversely. With no change in the total amount of reserves in the banking system, a higher interest rate will provide a larger supply of money, whereas a lower interest rate will mean more excess reserves and a lower supply of money.

Another simplification was our initial interpretation of equation (8.3), which implied that ΔR, or the change in reserves, was purely a function of Federal Reserve activities. It is possible, however, for the banking system to circumvent the Fed at times by finding outside sources of reserves. In recent years it has done this on several occasions when the Fed was trying to cut reserves. Commercial banks, for example, have from time to time persuaded their customers to switch funds already in the banks from demand

7. R. L. Teigen, "The Demand for and Supply of Money," in W. L. Smith and R. L. Teigen, *Readings in Money, National Income, and Stabilization Policy* (Homewood, Ill.: Irwin, 1970), pp. 74–111.

deposit accounts, which require high percentage reserves at the Fed, to time deposits, which carry a much smaller reserve requirement. These banks have induced large domestic investors to lend them substantial sums of money by offering to pay very high interest rates known as certificates of deposit and have borrowed extensively from Americans and foreigners who had dollar balances in Europe (Eurodollar loans). The net effect of these and similar operations was to provide the banking system with additional reserves despite the Federal Reserve Board's policies.

It is true that the Fed could, and did, clamp down on many of these activities once they became significantly large. But the intriguing thing to many observers has been the ability of the banking system to develop an alternative source of reserves every time the Fed eliminated an old one. When the Fed made it impossible for the banks to raise funds by selling certificates of deposit, the banks exploited the Eurodollar market; when this source was closed down, the banks raised billions through the commercial paper market, a previously untapped source of money. The implication is strong that bankers are increasingly unwilling to submit passively to Fed attempts to keep the money supply under restraint when they have customers ready and eager to borrow money at high rates and that the role of the Fed in regard to reserves must be reevaluated with this in mind.

Money-Market Equilibrium

Students of microeconomics know that equilibrium in any product market will settle at that price level where supply equals demand. In the money market, the interest rate (or price) at which the market will settle is that

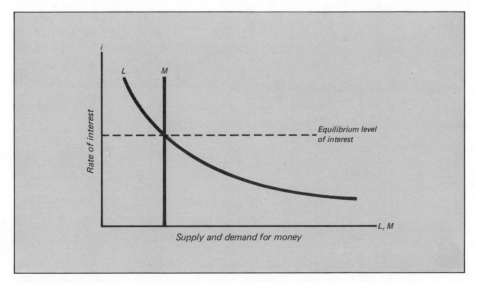

Figure 8.9 Monetary equilibrium: a simple model

quantity of money where the total demand for money equals the total supply. A very simple graphic representation of this concept in Figure 8.9 places monetary equilibrium at the intersection of a single demand schedule for money, L, and a supply schedule for money, M. The single demand curve shows demand for money at one given rate of national income; the supply line is vertical, implying that the supply of money is an inelastic amount established by the monetary authorities and independent of interest rates. The interest rate at the point of intersection would be the equilibrium level of interest in the economy.

Changes in the equilibrium level of interest will occur as the result of changes in the demand for money (L curve) in response to shifts in the supply of money (M line). If open-market operations by the Fed or changes in reserve requirements increase the supply of money, this will produce a shift in M to the right, from M_1 to M_2, as indicated in Figure 8.10. Assuming there is no change in the demand for money, M will then intersect L at a lower interest rate. Note however, that once changes in the supply schedule cause it to intersect the demand schedule in the liquidity trap area, moving from

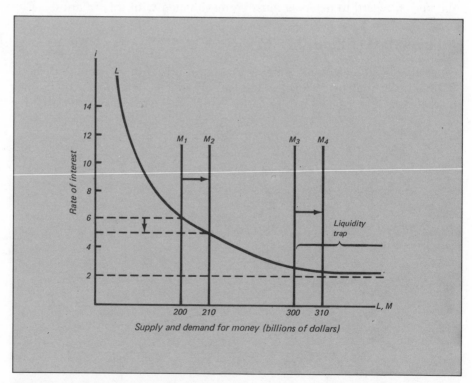

Figure 8.10 Changes in equilibrium rate of interest resulting from changes in the supply of money

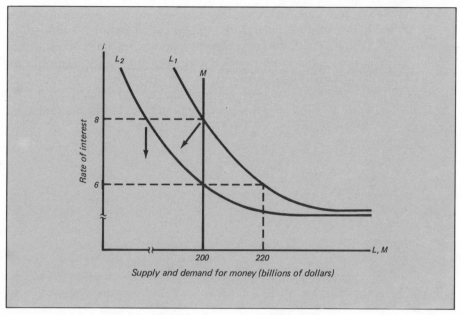

Figure 8.11 Changes in equilibrium rate of interest resulting from changes in income

M_3 to M_4 in Figure 8.10, additional increments in the supply of money will have no further effect on interest rates. In other words, shifts in M that move it along the elastic portion of the L curve produce significant changes in the equilibrium rate of interest, but shifts that occur in the liquidity trap area do not.

Changes in the equilibrium rate of interest will also occur as a result of shifts in the supply schedule, M, in response to changes in the level of income. At lower levels of income, the need for transaction balances falls, and therefore the demand for money is lower at every interest rate. For example, if national income falls from $1,400 billion to $1,300 billion, the public will need and hold smaller cash balances at every interest rate. This is shown graphically in Figure 8.11, where the equilibrium level of interest, given a money supply of $200 million, falls from 8 percent to 6 percent as a result of a shift from L_1 to L_2 caused by a decline in national income.

Although the simplified model of monetary equilibrium presented in Figure 8.9 is useful as a preliminary device for showing how changes in equilibrium occur, a more complete model would provide a more accurate picture. The supply schedule for money, for example, might be sloped, rather than vertical, reflecting the fact that as interest rates increase, excess reserves decline, and the money supply tends to rise. A more complete picture also would include a series of demand curves, instead of one, each of which would indicate the demand for money at a different income level.

This more complete model is necessary to point up the interrelationships among all the factors that determine supply and demand for money, including the policy of the central monetary authority, interest rates, and income levels. It will therefore provide a view of the way the equilibrium level of interest rates is established, as well as the way in which equilibrium values of other variables, such as national income, are determined. This model, known as the IS/LM model, will be developed in the following chapter.

Questions and Exercises

1. General bank credit cards charge no interest if the balance is paid within fifteen to twenty days from receipt of the statement. How does the existence of such cards affect the transactions demand for money? Would the demand for money tend to become more or less responsive to interest rates? Why?

2. At various times, the House Banking Committee has entertained the idea of allowing interest payments on checking accounts. How would this change affect the strict definition of the money supply? Would the definition be likely to change? Why or why not?

3. What is the prevailing belief concerning bond prices when in the liquidity trap range of the L_s curve? Most economists who believe there is such a region, believe it to occur only at very low rates of interest, say from 2 to 3 percent as in the 1930s. Is it possible to have a trap at say, 5 percent? Under what circumstances?

4. The early 1970s were years of relatively high rates of inflation. Potential bond buyers wanted not only a return for risk-taking, but an additional return to compensate for expected loss in dollar buying power. What effect would you predict for the demand for money with an expectation of continued rising prices?

5. Assume that you are offered a sure $50 or a chance in a lottery. In the lottery, you will have odds of 10 to 1 of getting $500 or $0. Is this a "fair" return? Why or why not? Would a risk-averter be inclined to take the chance on the lottery? Why or why not?

6. Assume that the Fed buys $2 million in Treasury bonds from the Bank of America and that the reserve requirement is 25 percent. What would be the maximum amount of money created or destroyed by this transaction? What would be the effect on the money supply of the same operation if the reserve requirement were 20 percent?

7. In the spring of 1974 when the Fed was engaging in tight money policies, the volume of consumer credit purchases (financed by installment loans and credit card purchases) rose significantly. Would you expect such purchases to be elastic or inelastic with respect to the interest rate? What factors would be likely to affect the level of consumer credit?

8. Suppose banks have an aversion against borrowing from the Federal Reserve system, resorting to such borrowing only on a short-term basis to correct their reserve positions. What would be the implication for the effectiveness of the "discount rate" policies of the Fed if banks lost such an aversion? Why?

9. Suppose that the Fed sells a large issue of government bonds. What would be the effect on the money supply schedule? If it purchased a large number of bonds? If it raised the reserve requirement? What factors, if any, would tend to reduce the effects of these policies?

10. Science fiction writers and others have periodically painted a picture of a future economy in which salaries and other payments to individuals are made directly to a central banking authority which in turn pays bills directly by debiting accounts. Other bills are paid simply by dialing a code on the telephone which automatically debits one account and credits another. What would be the implication for the money demand schedule, if any?

A blip that unsettles the Fed

The end of the Arab oil embargo and other good news have diminished the threat of recession to the U.S. economy. But for the Federal Reserve, the change has only meant more freedom to move against the country's other major dilemma: a new surge of inflation threatened by a surprising rise in the money supply.

To be sure, there are some pretty obvious limits to how tough the central bank can get. It news that the money supply —— en by $3.7-bil——n in the —— ——ing a steep, —— the beginning of ——— immediate response in fin—— kets —— terest rates shot up all across the —— curve in —— the belief the Fed would —— min—— for some weeks unt—— money —— co—————

The ne—— rates was paced by —— night interbank borrowings—— reserves—federal funds—which the central bank's trading desk closely controls. Fed funds bounced from a 1974 low of around 8¾% to 9⅝% at one point this week. Following suit, three-month Treasury bills, selling for 7.81% a week ago, were trading at 8.03% by the middle of this week.

On the same track, spurred in part by extraordinary loan demand, the prime lending rate of big commercial banks has started climbing back from its February declines. At midweek, Bankers Trust Co. of New York raised its prime rate to 9%.

Resistance. But the question remained whether the central bank's Federal Open Market Committee (FOMC), meeting Tuesday, would decide to maintain this upward pressure on interest rates for long, and whether the money supply could resist the Fed's controlling efforts enough to force FOMC to do so.

The answer seemed to be that for the next few weeks the Fed will continue to lean relatively harder in the direc-——n of firming rates. After that, be—— use of the expectation that the U.S. —— ——t to more exp——ive and still ——pli——, ——ight resume —— dec—— ——ttom by summer. O—— —— Richard Thomas of —— Bank of Chicago, "We think this is a little blip in a downward movement, ——gh it may last for a month or so."

—— w—— But this week's FOMC —— —— by greater ——— w——les —— omy—higher —— api—— spending, stronger housing unemployment rate rising slower —— feared—added a new element of uncertainty: Suppose the economy snaps back so ebulliently that inflation, instead of slowing down, keeps right on roaring ahead? Treasury Secretary George Shultz this week said the second half of 1974 "will be a crossroads for the future of inflation in America. We could get a step-up in the inflation rate from which it would be hard to retreat." If that happens, interest rates will be trending up all year.

So far, even inflation hawks at the Fed probably do not buy that view. As recently as Feb. 21, Fed Chairman Arthur Burns projected that unemployment would still be at 6% by yearend. The consensus at the Fed is probably that, so far, upbeat news only signifies that the danger of a cumulative downward spiral in the economy is unlikely. The conventional forecasts still look for a slow pickup in the second half of 1974, held back by sluggish consumer spending.

What the Fed would like most is for that forecast to come true, so that over next winter inflation can be sweated out of an economy that is almost stationary. Yet with the business cycle in the process of turning around, the Fed cannot be sure what policy will produce that result. Observes an economist at one New York securities firm: "I don't think it has a long-term plan right now, since it doesn't know how weak the recovery is." ∎

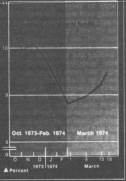

Interest rates begin to creep up again

Oct. 1973-Feb. 1974   March 1974

10

9

8

O N D J F 8 15 18
1973 1974   March

▲ Percent

Data Salomon Bros.

The current inflation is confusing not only consumers and businessmen. It's confounding economists as well.

Consumer prices in the past year have sailed upward by more than 10%, a rate not approached since the Korean war. The phenomenon, moreover, extends far beyond the U.S. As Arthur Burns, the Federal Reserve Board chairman puts it, "Inflation now is the dominant economic force in every major nation around the world."

The consequences, economists agree, could be pretty dismal. In the view of Henry

This is the first of two stories on U.S. inflation. This article examines the growth of the price problem. A second story will look at the prospects for a ——turn to price stability.

Kaufman of Salomon Brothers, the brokerage firm, they could easily include "domes—— ——rest, militant strikes, consumer uprising—— wage and price inequities $2.5 billion. Lending activity in January was —— ——fully rectified."

The question is more —— ——mic cause, as Karl Brunner of —— ——versi Rochester says in a recent study, "An i—— ——rly conceived explanation of in—— ——ot yield useful suggestions for in—— ——ffe—— ——nd successful ——d-inflationary ——cke—— ——mese? ——T—— ——er economists —— nor —— ——e or—— tion—or even —— ——col—— planations.

The Controls Debate

Some analysts argue that the price —— sion stems in part from the econo—— ——tions created by wage-price —— others are more disturbed by —— rush to dispose of those same —— controls are scheduled to die

Bond Markets

Prices Little Changed But the Trend Is Down, With Very Few Sales

By LINDLEY B. RICHERT
Staff Reporter of THE WALL STREET JOURNAL

NEW YORK — Bond prices were little changed in unusually light trading.

Though so few transactions took place the bias was decidedly downward, dealers said. Market-makers are openly disappointed that last week's successful $500 million offering by American Telephone & Telegraph Co. failed to spark any significant follow-through buying in seasoned issues.

Now a 30-day calendar of over $2.4 billion new corporate issues, "working in conjunction with high short-term interest rates and a damaging rate of inflation, could conceivably dampen the fantasies of even the most imaginative bond salesman," said the Bank of New York.

The best short-term borrowing rate available at First National Bank of Chicago jumps today to 11.75% from 11.40%. Should other commercial lenders move to that level from their just-established 11.50%, it would be the 12th general rise in the banking industry's base lending fee since mid-March.

Burdened Calendar

An already burdened calendar of negotiated tax-exempt offerings rose $109 million after underwriters accelerated to Thursday, from next Tuesday, a sale of South Carolina Public Service Authority revenue bonds. Rated single-A by Moody's and double-A by

S&L Savings Inflow Climbed in January, Home Loans Fell

By a WALL STREET JOURNAL *Staff Reporter*

WASHINGTON — The flow of money into savings and loan associations increased sharply in January but mortgage-lending by S&Ls fell to a two-year low, the Federal Home Loan Bank Board said.

Federally insured S&Ls had a net savings inflow of $2.05 billion in January, up from $406 million in December and the largest surplus since $3.11 billion in January 1973.

Mortgage loans closed at S&Ls totaled $2.29 billion, down 7% from December's $2.46 billion and a substantial 36% below the year-earlier $2.6—— billion. Lending activity in January was the —— —— st since February 1971, when $1.83 billion —— ans were closed.

—— R. Bomar, bank board chairman, —— —— part of th—— funds to —— —— —— that was dra—— —— months of savings o—— —— has declined i—— six of the se—— ——ce last June, when loans totaled $5.59 billi——.

Commitments outstanding for future mortgage lending increased $200 million in January —— —— However, the in—— ——ase was —— ——al January ——, and total —— ——sla —— ——ments at the end of the month w—— —— year earlier, the bank

---

Chart II
SHORT-TERM BUSINESS BORROWINGS AND RELATED INTEREST RATES

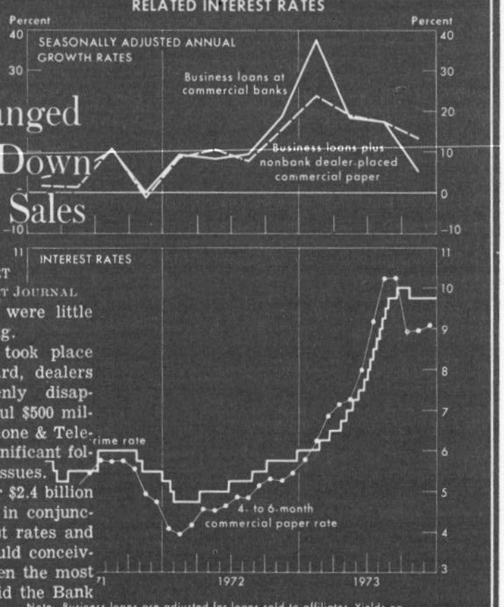

Percent   Percent
40   40

SEASONALLY ADJUSTED ANNUAL
GROWTH RATES

Business loans at
commercial banks

Business loans plus
nonbank dealer-placed
commercial paper

INTEREST RATES

11   11

10   10

me rate

4- to 6-month
commercial paper rate

'71   1972   1973

Note: Business loans are adjusted for loans sold to affiliates. Yields on
four- to six-month commercial paper are monthly averages of daily figures.
—— rate is the interest rate posted by major commercial banks on

utilities'' delayed until Thursday today's planned $58.4 million sale to finance pollution-abatement facilities for Detroit Edison Co., underwriters said.

Normally negotiated sales exert less upward pressure on market rates than do competitive offerings, because underwriters have the luxury of time to more carefully tailor terms to investor interest. But, one specialist said, the bulk of those negotiated items on the calendar are "yield situations," or lesser-quality issues commanding higher interest rates.

INTEREST RATES (latest Wednesday, except bond yields, which are previous Friday)

International comparisons (% per annum)	America	Britain	Belgium	France	Germany	Italy	Netherlands	Switzerland	Japan
Money market rates:									
Day-to-day money*	10⅜	10.00	9½	12⅞	8⅞	n.a.	n.a.	12.00	11⅜
Three-month money*	9.00	13⅛	9.70	12⅞	7¾	n.a.	n.a.	9¼	6⅞
Commercial bank rates:									
Prime lending*	11.00	13½	11.00	13.70	12⅜	14.00	11¼	7¼	11–11¼
Three-month deposits (large amounts)	11.00*	13.66*	12.10	11⅛	9¾	4¾	11¼	6.00	5⅛
Bond market yields:									
Government long-term bonds	7.12	12.85	n.a.	n.a.	10.92	8.07	9.90	7.40	8.16
Corporate prime bonds	8.41	15.69	n.a.	n.a.	11.30	8.40	10.31	7.66	8.39
Eurobonds (by currency)	9.43	—	—	—	9.85	—	9.85	7.50	—
Exchange rates									

Equilibrium in the Product and Money Markets

9

Earlier chapters have defined product-market equilibrium as that level of national income where savings equals investment (S = I) and money-market equilibrium as that level of interest rates where the demand for money equals the supply of money (L = M). But even as these theories were presented, there were indications that they involved oversimplifications. Our analysis of product-market equilibrium included no provision for variations in interest rates, and yet it is clear from Chapter 7 that investment spending is a function of interest-rate levels and will change with changes in interest rates. Similarly, the simple L = M monetary equilibrium equation initially ignored the question of income level, although we saw earlier that the transaction component of the demand for money was very definitely a function of income. In brief, it appears that if a more realistic model of the economy is to be developed, some method must be found by which equilibria of the product and money markets are expressed in terms of income and interest-rate levels. In this way a general equilibrium can be found where, for unique values of income and the interest rate, product and money markets are simultaneously in equilibrium. Once we have developed this model, we can use it to analyze the potential effects of monetary and fiscal measures on the economy. We will begin with an examination of product- and money-market equilibria in a simple two-sector economy; subsequently, we will add a government sector.

The IS Schedule

Chapter 4 established the notion that product-market equilibrium exists where I = S. Such a condition exists in Figure 9.1 at point A, where savings and investment are each $200 billion at a national income level of $1,300 billion. We should remember from the analysis of investment spending in Chapter 7, however, that investment is probably at least in part a function of interest rates. Therefore, the investment level of $200 billion represented by line I_1 in Figure 9.1 must be an investment schedule which *assumes a given interest rate*—a schedule that will change if interest rates change. For example, if I_1 assumes an interest rate of 5 percent, a new higher schedule would emerge if interest rates were only 4 percent. This new investment schedule, I_2, would intersect the savings line at a higher level, and the final result would be a higher equilibrium level of income, represented by point B, where Y = $1,400 billion. Conversely, a rise in interest rates from 5 percent to 6 percent would depress investment spending to only $150 billion,

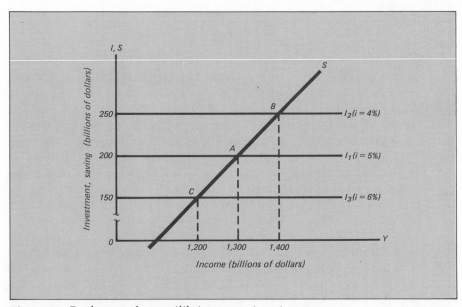

Figure 9.1 Product-market equilibrium at various interest rates

and the investment line I_3 would intersect the spending line at point C, where $Y = \$1,200$ billion.

As this example illustrates, aggregate product-market equilibrium cannot be expressed merely in terms of the behavior of S and I at various income levels alone; it must be determined as a set of pairs of values of interest rates and income levels where savings as a function of income is equal to investment as a function of the interest rate. Once we recognize this, it becomes evident, as Figure 9.1 indicates, that there may be product-market equilibrium at many different income levels, each of which represents a particular combination of income and interest rates.

Using the data developed from Figure 9.1, it is possible to draw up a schedule listing those combinations of i and Y at which $S = I$ in this economy, as follows:

I = S WHEN	
i EQUALS	Y EQUALS
4%	$1,400 billion
5%	$1,300 billion
6%	$1,200 billion

This information is shown graphically in Figure 9.2. The resulting line,

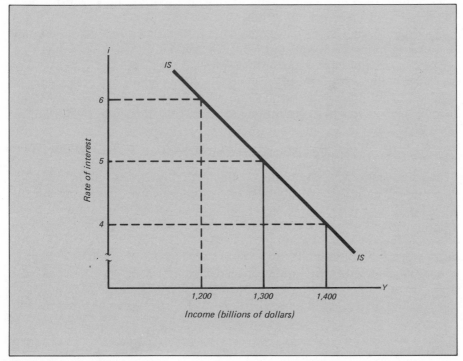

Figure 9.2 The IS schedule

which indicates all the possible i-Y combinations where I = S, or where product-market equilibrium exists, is called the IS schedule.

A similar but more complete derivation of the IS schedule was first developed by J. R. Hicks.[1] It explores in greater detail the interrelationships between interest rates, investment, product-market equilibrium, and income and will be particularly useful later in this chapter when we discuss the step-by-step processes through which changes in income or interest rates can be effected. Hicks' work is best illustrated through a four-quadrant diagram, represented by Figure 9.3. Figure 9.3 should be read from quadrant A, in the upper left-hand corner, counterclockwise to quadrant D, in the upper right-hand corner. When looking at four-quadrant diagrams of this type, remember that movement away from the center always represents an increase in the variable measured along each axis.

Quadrant A shows investment demand at various interest rates. It is simply the investment demand, or MEI, schedule studied earlier, in which investment spending moves inversely with interest rates. We see, for example, that I = $250 billion when i = 4 percent and that I = $200 billion when i = 5 percent. Quadrant B ties each of the investment spending totals from quadrant B to that level of savings that would occur at equilibrium. Of course, since product-market equilibrium exists only where S = I, the savings total in each case in quadrant B will be equal to the investment total. In other words, if quadrant A tells us that investment at 5 percent will be $200 billion, then quadrant B tells us that, if we are to be at equilibrium, savings must also equal $200 billion.

Quadrant C shows the relationship between the levels of savings illustrated in quadrant B and the levels of national income. We know that saving is a function of income, or that there is a single level of saving that is consistent with every level of income. Quadrant C indicates that a savings total of $200 billion would occur in an economy with an income of $1,300 billion, that savings of $250 billion would imply an economy with an income of $1,400 billion, and so on.

The information developed in the preceding three quadrants is summarized in quadrant D as the IS line. To understand this, let us retrace our steps from quadrant A, assuming an interest rate of 5 percent. In quadrant A, we saw that a 5 percent interest rate produced investment spending of $200 billion; in quadrant B we noted that investment spending of $200 billion required savings of $200 billion at equilibrium; in quadrant C we observed that savings of $200 billion occurred only in an economy with income of $1,300 billion. Tying all this together, the IS line in quadrant D points out that, given the original interest rate of 5 percent, savings will equal investment only where income is $1,300 billion. It also indicates all the other i-Y combinations where S = I (i.e., i = 4 percent, Y = $1,400

1. J. R. Hicks, "Mr. Keynes and the 'Classics': A Suggested Interpretation," *Econometrica* New Series V (April 1937): 147–159.

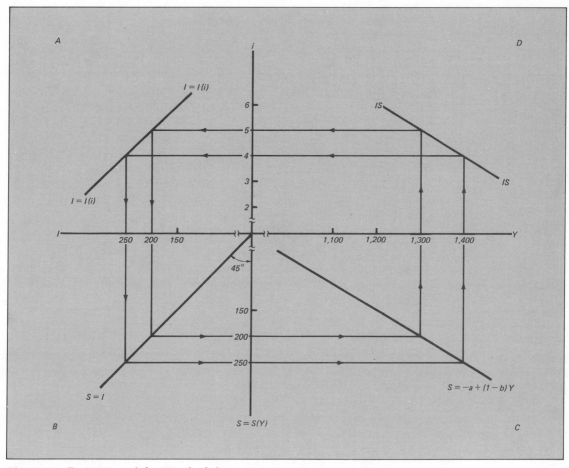

Figure 9.3 Derivation of the IS schedule

billion), emphasizing the fact that there are many levels of income, rather than one, at which product-market equilibrium may settle, depending on the interest rate.

Slope of IS

The use of the four-quadrant diagram as a foundation for the final IS line is particularly useful as a device which highlights the interrelationships between interest rates and investment (quadrant A), investment and savings (quadrant B), savings and income (quadrant C), and income and interest (quadrant D) and thereby explains the negative slope of IS. The IS line has a negative slope because S rises with Y and I falls as i rises. If S = I is to be maintained, say, when Y rises inducing a rise in S, then i must fall at the same time in order to induce a rise in I. Therefore, S = I requires changes in i and Y in opposite directions, producing a negative slope for IS.

The LM Schedule

The original simple model of money-market equilibrium introduced in Chapter 8 showed equilibrium as that interest rate at which a single demand schedule, L, and a supply schedule, M, intersected. However, by the end of the chapter, a more complex model had been suggested which included not one but a series of L schedules, each of which represented demand for money at a different income level, and each of which intersected the M schedule at a different interest rate. This new model, presented in Figure 9.4, recognizes the fact that the transaction component of the demand for money, L_T, is a function of income, and that therefore the entire demand schedule must vary with changes in income.

What are the implications of the money-market equilibrium model illustrated in Figure 9.4? Clearly, it points out that money-market equilibrium cannot be described merely in terms of the intersection of the L and M schedules *at a given interest rate*. Rather, it must also include a reference to the level of income, because monetary equilibrium will exist at different interest rates given different income levels. For example, as Figure 9.4 indicates, for a given money supply ($M_S = \$250$ billion) when national in-

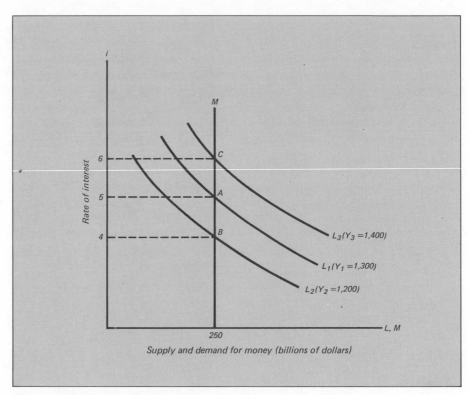

Figure 9.4 Money-market equilibrium at various income levels

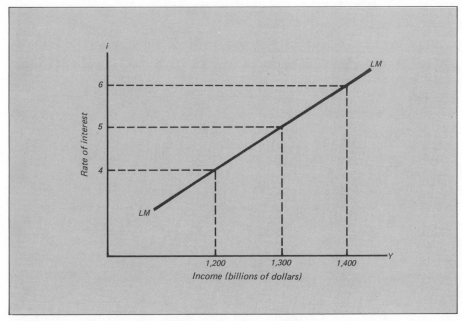

Figure 9.5 The LM schedule

come is $1,300 billion, L_1 is the demand curve for money, and monetary equilibrium will settle at point A, or 5 percent, but monetary equilibrium is also possible at other interest rates (point B, point C), given other levels of Y and consequently other L curves.

The information presented in Figure 9.4 can be summarized in a schedule which shows the various i-Y combinations where monetary equilibrium will exist, as follows:

	L = M WHEN
i EQUALS	Y EQUALS
4%	$1,200 billion
5%	$1,300 billion
6%	$1,400 billion

This is shown graphically in Figure 9.5 as an LM line, which describes money-market equilibrium in terms of Y and i values just as the IS schedule developed previously shows all the possible combinations of interest rates and income where I = S, or where product-market equilibrium exists.

The derivation of the LM schedule can be traced in more detail through the use of the four-quadrant diagram in Figure 9.6, which follows the same procedure employed in Figure 9.4 to derive the IS schedule. Quadrant A, in the upper left-hand corner, shows another variant of the demand for

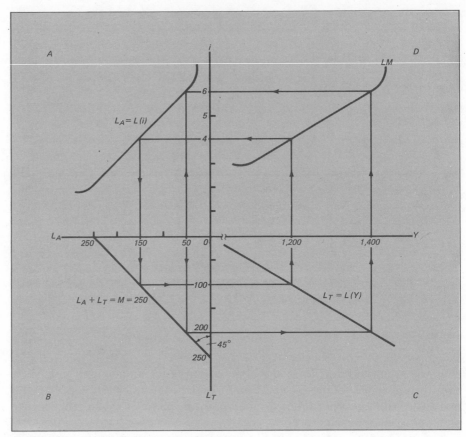

Figure 9.6 Derivation of the LM schedule

money, the **asset demand for money**, L_A. Similar to the speculative demand, the asset demand represents the interest sensitivity of transactions, precautionary, and speculative demands for money as varying inversely with the interest rate. Here we see, for example, that $L_A = \$50$ billion if the interest rate is 6 percent, $100 billion at 5 percent, $150 billion at 4 percent, and so on. In quadrant B, monetary equilibrium and a money supply of $250 billion are assumed and based on these assumptions, the demand for money is divided into its two components, transactions demand, L_T, and asset demand, L_A; that is, if asset balances are $50 billion, then transaction balances must be $200 billion. In quadrant C, the relationship between transaction balances and income is explored. We know that transaction balances vary with income. In this model, transaction balances of $200 billion are consistent with income of $1,400 billion.

Finally, in quadrant D, the LM schedule emerges, in which the interest rates postulated in quadrant A are tied to the income levels derived from quadrant C in those combinations required to produce the money-market equilibrium postulated in quadrant B, where the demand for money equals the supply of money. We see, for example, that the conditions necessary for money-market equilibrium can be met by a combination of Y = $1,400 billion and i = 6 percent, because this combination will provide the asset balances ($50 billion) and transaction balances ($200 billion) needed to satisfy the equation for money-market equilibrium, $L_T + L_A = M$ ($250 billion). It is also obvious, however, that there are other i-Y combinations where monetary equilibrium can settle, or where speculative and transaction balances will total $250 billion (i.e., Y = $1,200 billion, i = 4 percent, and so on) and these are all identified as points along the LM schedule.

Slope of LM

The LM schedule in Figure 9.6 is drawn for a given money supply. It slopes positively in terms of i and Y. This is because LM describes values of i and Y where money demand equals a given money supply. If Y rises, the demand for money rises; to maintain money demand equal to fixed money supply, i must rise, too, in order to counteract the increase in money demand induced by a rise in Y.

General Equilibrium

The IS line indicates all the combinations of Y and i where product-market equilibrium can settle. There is, however, only one combination of Y and i at which both the money market and the product market will be in equilibrium, or in other words, where I = S and L = M. We can find this combination by superimposing the IS line on the LM curve in the space bounded by the i (vertical) axis and the Y (horizontal) axis. The point where the two schedules intersect will represent general equilibrium in both the product market and the money market.

The IS and LM schedules derived earlier in Figures 9.3 and 9.6 are combined in Figure 9.7. Here general equilibrium settles at an interest rate of 5 percent and a national income of $1,300 billion. Note that there are other i-Y combinations where either product-market or money-market equilibrium can occur, but there is no other point on the chart where both markets will be in equilibrium.

The Role of Government

What are the consequences of adding government to the private-sector model developed to this point? As we saw in Chapter 5, the inclusion of government in the model changes the equation for product-market equilibrium from S = I to S + T = I + G. This expanded equation states that equilibrium can occur only when leakages from the income stream, which with a government sector include both savings and taxes, are equal to injections into the income model, which with a government sector include both in-

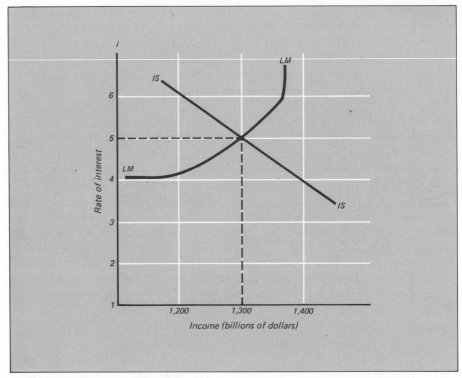

Figure 9.7 General equilibrium

vestment and government spending. Therefore, once we add government to the model, the IS schedule is no longer merely a representation of those possible combinations of i and Y where I = S; instead it becomes a line showing those combinations of i and Y where I + G = S + T, with the levels of G and T set by policymakers where taxes are taken to be lump sum.[2]

Since the LM schedule remains unchanged, general equilibrium now becomes that level of i and Y where LM intersects an IS schedule which (although we will continue to refer to it as an IS schedule) now represents product-market equilibrium in an economy that includes not just private sector consumption, investment, and spending, but also government spending and taxation.

Shifts in General Equilibrium

As Figure 9.7 implied, changes in the interest-rate and/or income components of general equilibrium can occur as the result of shifts in the IS schedule and/or the LM schedule. Since the IS line represents product-

2. With proportional taxes, T = tY, income determines tax proceeds, and taxes, like savings, become an income-induced leakage out of expenditure. As we saw in Chapter 5, proportional taxes affect the multiplier. The effect of proportional taxes on general equilibrium (IS/LM) multipliers is demonstrated in the appendix to this chapter.

market equilibrium at those levels of i and Y where $I + G = S + T$, shifts in the IS schedule may be caused by changes in the level of investment at each interest rate, the level of savings at each income, or by shifts in government expenditure or tax rates. Shifts in the LM schedule will come about largely because of changes in the money supply, unless the demand schedule for money shifts for given levels of Y and i.

Shifting the IS Schedule

Changes in Investment

In Chapter 7 we examined how changes in expectations, in profits, or in technology could lead to changes in the amount of investment that would occur at every interest rate. Assume that such a change in investment develops, shifting the investment demand curve so that it is $50 billion higher at every interest rate. This is shown in quadrant A of Figure 9.8 as a shift

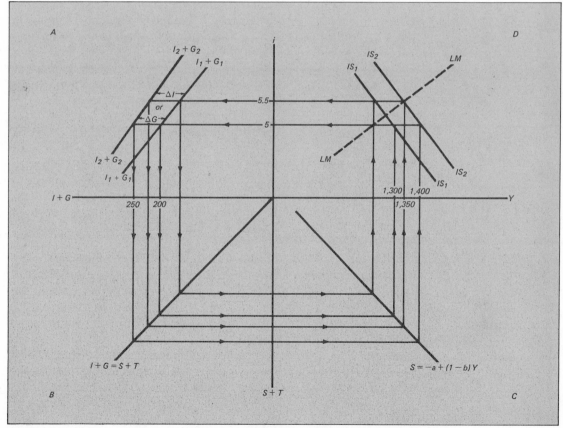

Figure 9.8 Shifting the IS schedule through a change in I or G, leading to a new equilibrium level of Y

from I_1 to I_2. Ignoring government activity for now, we see that under these new conditions, investment demand will equal $250 billion, at a 5 percent rate of interest, rather than $200 billion, as under the original I_1 schedule. Tracing the effect of this higher level of investment spending through the diagram, we see that the $250 billion of savings required at equilibrium will occur only in an economy where Y = $1,400 billion.

If we follow this same procedure for every interest rate on the new I_2 line, it can be shown that the equilibrium level of Y along the IS line emerging in each case in quadrant D is higher than the original I_1 line. This is shown by line IS_2, derived from the I_2 line in quadrant A together with the schedules in quadrants B and C. In other words, as a result of a shift upward in the investment demand schedule, the IS line has shifted upward also, and product-market equilibrium at each interest rate will therefore settle at a higher level of national income. In short, if investment is higher at each interest rate, savings must be higher as well, and this result can only be induced by a higher level of income indicated by an upward shift of IS.

The amount by which the Y component of this new IS_2 line will exceed the Y component of IS_1 at each interest rate depends on the size of the multiplier in the economy. In quadrant C, we see that the MPS in this economy is $1/2$, or that the multiplier is 2. Since we know that the change in income (ΔY) resulting from any change in investment is equal to the change in investment (ΔI) times the multiplier $(1/1 - b)$ it is clear that an increase of $50 billion in I ($\Delta I = \$50$ billion) will produce an IS schedule the Y component of which must be $100 billion higher at every interest level ($\Delta Y = \$100$ billion).

Given the new product-market equilibrium schedule, IS_2, and assuming no change in the LM curve derived from Figure 9.6, where will general equilibrium now settle? This can be determined by superimposing the original LM schedule in quadrant D of Figure 9.8. We see that general equilibrium now settles at a level like Y = $1,350 billion with i = $5^{1}/_2$ percent. Note that the income level at the new general equilibrium is somewhat lower than that suggested by the earlier analysis of the initial impact of the increase in I. This occurs because of the interaction between any increase in income and interest rates. Once an additional amount of investment spending is injected into an economy and income begins to rise, the demand for transaction balances also begins to rise.[3] Since the supply of money is fixed for a given LM schedule, this higher demand for transaction balances can be met only by a decline in asset balances, which requires an increase in interest rates.[4]

Of course, as interest rates rise, investment spending declines. The overall effect is that the total increase in income projected initially on the basis of the original estimate of investment demand never occurs because rising interest rates keep the final increment of investment spending below the

3. Because $L_T = L_T(Y)$.
4. Because $L_A = L_A(i)$.

original estimate. This analysis emphasizes the point noted before that increases in investment spending do not take place in a vacuum, but are accompanied by increases in interest rates, and that these higher interest rates will tend to limit the extent of the final increase in investment and income introduced by any initial upward shift in the investment demand and IS schedules.

A downward shift in the investment demand schedule, resulting from a decline in expectations or in profits, would have precisely the opposite consequences. It would produce an IS line with a lower Y component at every interest level. However, because of the expansive implications of the decline in interest rates that would occur as a result of an initial drop in investment spending and income, neither investment spending nor income would decline as much as the downward shift would suggest. Instead, a new general-equilibrium level would emerge, showing both a relatively modest decline in income and a decline in interest rates.

The precise extent of the changes in the equilibrium level of interest rates and income resulting from any change in investment spending depends on how investment spending responds to changes in interest rates (that is, the slope of the MEI schedule) and the shape of the LM schedule, which is in turn determined by the response of money demand to changes in income and the interest rate. This will be examined in more detail at the end of this chapter.

Changes in Investment: Fiscal Policy 1

Changes in government spending have the same effect on the IS schedule as changes in investment. Government expenditure can be viewed for analytical purposes as public investment. Recall that in Chapter 5, $\Delta Y/\Delta I = \Delta Y/\Delta G$. Referring back to Figure 9.8, we see that an increment of $50 billion from G_1 to G_2 would shift the original I + G line in quadrant A just as the increment of I discussed in the previous section did, and this increase in government spending would also lead to an upward shift in the IS line and to a new level of general equilibrium. The key point to remember is that, once again, the equilibrium level of income at which the economy will finally settle will not reflect the entire increase implied by the application of the multiplier to the increment of government spending. Instead, as we explained in our analysis of the effect of an increase of investment spending on national income, part of the expansionary implications of the increase of G will be dissipated because of the higher interest rates that will accompany increases in income. These higher interest rates will occur because of the equilibrium requirement in the money markets, and their effect will be to lower private investment.

Changes in Savings

The preceding paragraphs traced the steps through which higher levels of investment or government spending would produce an upward shift in the IS schedule and a higher general-equilibrium level for both income and interest rates. A similar pattern will emerge if, for some reason, there is an increase in consumption spending (or a decline in savings) at every income level. Recall from Chapters 4 and 5 that $\Delta Y/\Delta I = \Delta Y/\Delta G = \Delta Y/\Delta a$. During the early days of the Korean War in 1950, for example, consumers, fearing a repetition of the shortages of World War II, increased their consumption spending, with a corresponding decline in savings. Graphically, such a reduction in savings would show up as a downward shift in the savings function in quadrant C of Figure 9.9, indicating, for example, that savings would equal $200 billion instead of $250 billion in a $1,400-billion economy. (Remember that S + T decreases as it moves upward toward the center in quadrant C.) The final effect, seen by deriving IS_2 from $S_2 + T_2$ would be to shift the entire IS schedule to IS_2 in quadrant D, and assuming

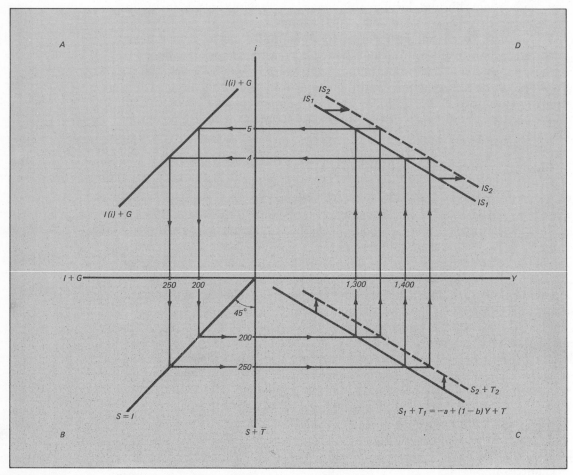

Figure 9.9 Shifting the savings-plus-tax schedule through a change in S or T in a general-equilibrium setting

no change in the LM schedule, this would result in a general-equilibrium level with higher i and Y components. Conversely, a decline in consumption spending (or an increase in savings) induced by such factors as overall pessimism or large stocks of consumer goods, will shift both the savings schedule and the IS schedule downward, resulting in an equilibrium level with lower national income and interest rates. Of course, the modification of the results arising from inclusion of the LM schedule is the same as in the cases when shifts of IS were due to ΔI or ΔG.

Changes in Taxes: Fiscal Policy 2

Changes in lump-sum taxes will also shift the IS schedule. A cut in lump-sum taxes is comparable to a decline in the savings function because both produce an increase in consumption spending and therefore a higher level of income. Graphically, the effect of a lump-sum tax cut would show up in Figure 9.9 as a downward shift in the IS_1 line in quadrant D, where the new IS_2 line would have a higher Y component at every level of i. The exact amount of the increase in Y at each interest rate in response to the cut in lump-sum taxes would depend upon the size of the tax cut and the marginal propensity to consume.[5]

Assuming no change in the LM schedule, the economy will settle at a new higher general-equilibrium level because IS_2 will intersect the original LM line at a higher Y. Once again, however, note that the final equilibrium level of national income will not increase by the full amount implied by a shift in the IS line introduced by a cut in savings or taxes. This occurs because part of the expansionary effect of the cut in taxes or savings will be dissipated by the higher interest rates that accompany the initial increases in national income and depress investment spending.

Figure 9.10 summarizes the conclusions reached in Figures 9.9 and 9.8, in which we examined how changes in the several components of the IS line can shift IS and affect general equilibrium. Changes that produce higher spending levels—that is, a reduction in the level of savings at each level of income or a reduction in lump-sum taxes—will shift the IS schedule upward. If there are no changes in the LM schedule, the general-equilibrium level resulting from this upward shift will include both a higher level of interest rates and a higher level of income, as shown in Figure 9.10(a). It is especially important to remember that the *full* effect of the increase in spending is not reflected in the increase in national income; instead, part of the increase in spending shows up as higher interest rates. The implications of this statement will be explored in more detail shortly; basically, however, Figure 9.10(a) suggests that fiscal policy alone (that is, shifting IS through changes in G or T) is less expansionary in terms of increasing

---

5. In this economy, the marginal propensity to consume is $\frac{1}{2}$. The formula for the tax multiplier is $(b/1 - b)$, giving a tax multiplier of 1. This would mean that any tax increase would shift the Y component of the final IS schedule by the amount of the tax increase.

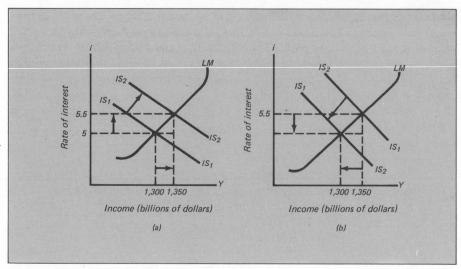

Figure 9.10 Shifting the IS schedule and the level of general equilibrium

national income than fiscal policy combined with monetary policy that simultaneously shifts the LM schedule.

Figure 9.10(b) shows how changes in general equilibrium result from downward shifts of the IS line superimposed on an unchanged LM schedule. These downward shifts may be brought about by a decline in the investment demand schedule or in government spending, or by an increase in the savings function or in taxes. Following such a shift in the IS line, general equilibrium settles at a point where both interest rates and national income are at a lower level.

One further point should be noted. In the examples used in this section, we have so far ignored those cases where IS intercepts the LM schedule in either the horizontal or vertical range, as shown in Figures 9.6 and 9.7. These extremes require special consideration and will be discussed at the end of this chapter.

Shifting the LM Schedule

In practice, changes in the money supply will be the most usual source of shifts of the LM schedule, but it is worthwhile to consider implications of both demand and supply changes for the LM schedule.

Changes in the Demand for Money

The L_T schedule for an economy shows the demand for transaction balances that will exist at each income level. Changes in payment practices, however, may produce a new transaction balance schedule. In recent years, for example, the increased use of credit cards with prearranged lines of credit available to holders of such cards may have slightly reduced the demand for transaction balances at every level of national income. Graphically, this would show up in quadrant C of Figure 9.11 as an upward shift in the transaction balance line from L_T to L_T', indicating, for example, that transaction balances of $150 billion would be demanded in an economy with a national income of $1,400 billion. This shift in the L_T line would be reflected in a downward shift at each income level from LM_1 to LM_2 in quadrant D, or in an LM schedule where equilibrium in the money market would exist at a higher level of national income for every interest rate. This occurs because, at a given rate of interest, with a given money supply, if the

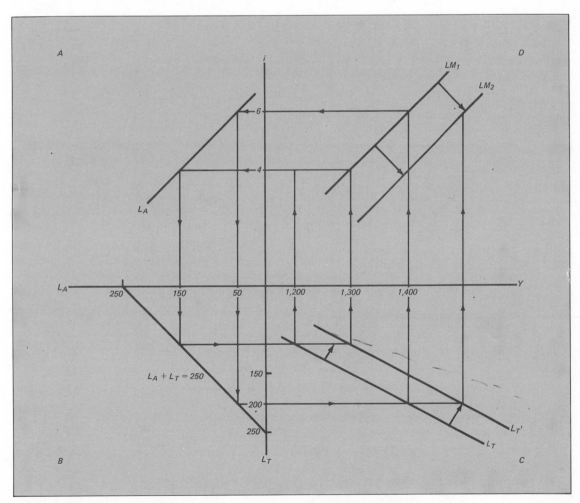

Figure 9.11 Impact of a reduction in the transactions demand for money

demand for money at each given income level falls, higher income is required to keep money demand equal to money supply.

Figure 9.12 indicates the result of a change in the asset demand for money.
If expectations about inflation change, there will be a change in the asset
demand for money at every interest rate. For example, in an economy where
the expected rate of inflation rises, money holders anticipate an increase in
the rate at which their money depreciates in terms of goods. L_A would
shift down at each interest rate (L_A to L_A' in Figure 9.12) and LM_1 would
shift to LM_2.

If the asset demand for money, L_A, falls at every interest rate, then, for
a given money supply, income must rise to maintain money demand equal
to money supply. This fact is reflected by the downward shift from LM_1 to

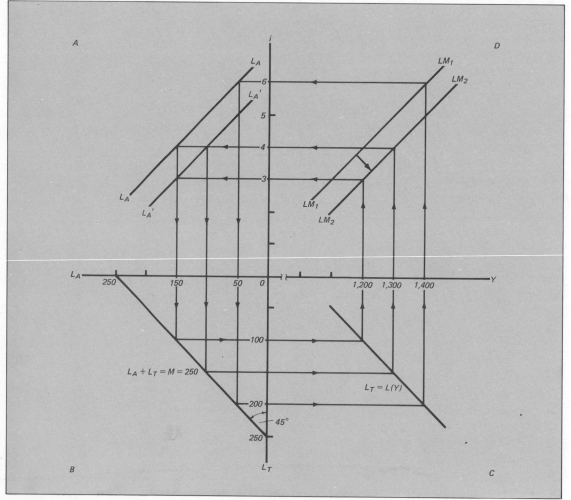

Figure 9.12 A drop in asset demand for money due to a rise in expected inflation

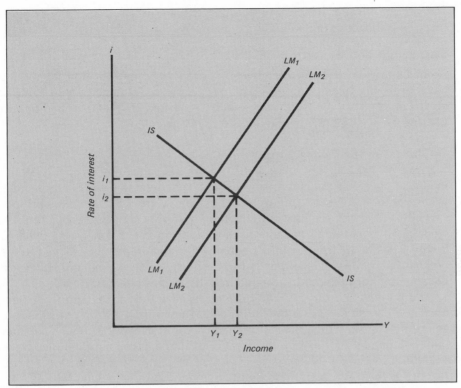

Figure 9.13 General equilibrium after a shift in LM

LM_2 at each level of income in Figure 9.12. Notice also that the result of such an LM shift would stimulate demand by lowering interest rates and raising income (given a negatively sloped IS schedule). Such an increase in demand could put upward pressure on prices. It is possible that an increase in ex-*pected* inflation can lead to results that make the expected increase in inflation more likely to occur. Since actual inflation increases may in turn generate expected increases in inflation, it may be said that inflation feeds upon itself.

To summarize, we can say that any changes in psychology, technology, or institutional practices that reduce demand for money at every interest rate will shift the transactions demand for money upward and the LM schedule downward, as done in Figure 9.11. Such a downward shift in LM means that monetary equilibrium will settle at a higher level of national income for every interest rate. Conversely, changes that increase the demand for money at every interest rate shift the L_T line to the left and the LM schedule to the left. Note, however, that when the original IS line is super-imposed on these new LM lines in quadrant D of Figures 9.11 and 9.12, the result will look like Figure 9.13, where the broken line indicates the general-equilibrium level at which the economy will settle.[6] This level does not reflect the full change in national income implied by the shift in the LM schedule. Instead, the new equilibrium level includes both changes in income and changes in interest rates (Y_1 to Y_2 and i_1 to i_2), indicating that part of the expansionary or deflationary effects of changes in the demand for money have been dissipated in interest rates. This performance is, of course, analogous to that we observed when we shifted in the IS schedules in Figures 9.8 and 9.9, while leaving LM unchanged.

Changes in the Money Supply

The most typical reason for a shift in the LM schedule is a change in the money supply. Assume, for example, that the Federal Reserve Board decides to pursue open-market operations that expand M from $250 to $300 billion. The effect of such an increase in the money supply is traced in Figure 9.14, where LM_1 is assumed to have been derived in the manner employed in Figure 9.6. The L_A line remains unchanged in quadrant A, since we project no changes in the expectations that underlie speculative demand. However, the equation for the schedule in quadrant B has now changed from $L_T + L_A =$ $250 billion to $L_T + L_A = $300 billion, because the money supply is now $300 billion rather than $250 billion. In quadrant D, a new LM schedule emerges (LM_2) on which the i component is lower at every income level than the i component of the original LM_1. For example, given national income of $1,300 billion and a money supply of $250 billion, the equilibrium interest rate is 5 percent. With an increase in the money supply to $300 billion, LM_2 can be derived. Along LM_2 the equilibrium interest rate when income equals $1,300 billion is 4 percent. This is because an increased money supply means that monetary-sector equilibrium requires a higher demand for money at each interest rate. This can only be induced by higher income, so LM must shift down from LM_1 to LM_2.

To determine the effect of the shift from LM_1 to LM_2 on general equilibrium, we can superimpose the original IS schedule on the two LM lines in quadrant D. A new general-equilibrium point emerges: $i = 4\frac{1}{2}$ percent, $Y =$ $1,350 billion. Observe that the decline in interest rates at general equilibrium is less than the 1 percent decline implied by the shift in LM. This reflects the fact that the initial effect of any fall in interest rates is to stimulate investment spending and therefore income. Any increase in income, however, requires higher transaction balances which in turn limits the amounts available for speculative balances and therefore puts an upward pressure on interest rates. In other words, it appears that, assuming no change in the IS schedule, the full effect of any increase in the money supply will not be reflected completely in a decline in interest rates, but rather, will show up in part in a higher level of national income. Thus, declines in the total money

6. A shift in either L_T or L_A, as indicated in Figures 9.11 and 9.12, will produce equilibrium where $i = 4\frac{1}{2}$ percent and $Y = $1,350 billion. We have chosen to shift L_T, as shown in Figure 9.11.

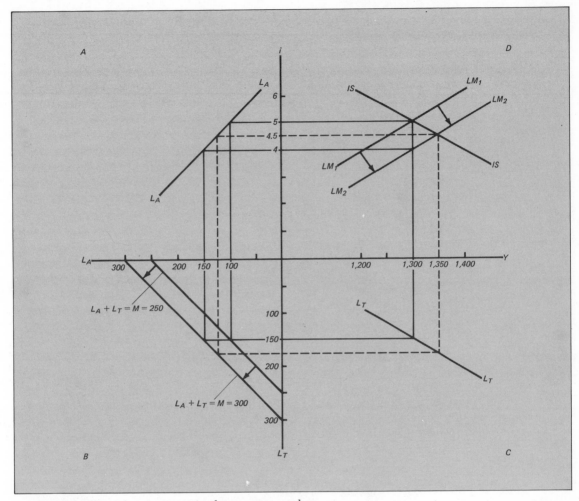

Figure 9.14 Effect of an increase in the money supply

supply ($L_A + L_T$) shift LM upward, and assuming no change in IS, produce a general-equilibrium level characterized by higher interest rates and a lower level of national income.

Simultaneous Shifts in the LM and IS Schedules

We have noted that while changes in I, G, or T will shift the IS schedule, the final effect on equilibrium national income is dissipated in part by higher interest rates, if the LM schedule is left unchanged. The implication of this is that if the government wishes to move general-equilibrium income to a

Commentary : Econometric Models

Running a tidy experiment in macroeconomics is virtually impossible. For one thing, few people are in a position to manipulate economic variables: although the President can do so in some instances, often he cannot afford the political heat of an experiment that fails, and in any case he lacks another economy to serve as a control with which to compare the results. But suppose an imaginary economy could be constructed, one that behaved like our own. Then it would be easier to try out different government policies or play with alternative marketing strategies without worrying about the imaginary people out of work or the imaginary business failures if the worst ensued from the experiment.

These imaginary versions of the economy exist today in about a dozen forms around the country. They go beyond the graphs of the IS/LM models to construct a mathematical replica of economics processes. In computers at the Federal Reserve Board, at Wharton School of Business, at the Brookings Institution—to name a few—large-scale econometric models have been constructed and are being refined. The Brookings model requires 359 equations to describe the activities of the U.S. economy. This model is so complex that it has never been run all at once; a simpler version of "only" 216 equations is used to simulate short-term changes in the economy and to analyze the effects of different policies.

The models translate the kinds of theory with which we have been working into something closer to reality. The tools used to build these models are those of econometrics. Econometrics is the link between the cool, clear world of theory and the untidy world of actual economies. Most economic relationships can be specified by equations. For example, consumption is a function of income, production a function of factor inputs, liquidity preference a function of interest rates and income, investment decisions a function of interest rates and assets. An econometrician takes the available data and tries to specify and measure the equation which explains the economic behavior. For example, to get an equation for the relationship between the demand for money and explanatory variables like interest rates and income, the econometrician would feed raw historical data about interest rates, income levels, and money holdings for a large number of economic units into a computer. The computer would perform a sophisticated computation called regression analysis, which would find the mathematical equation which best fits the data. The resulting equation would presumably describe a numerical relationship between the demand for money, which is the dependent variable, and the variables which are taken to be "explanatory": income and the interest rate.

The results do not always possess the neat properties suggested by pure theory, but they may be better fitted to the real world of disturbances and individuality. For example, it has been suggested in Chapters 4 and 6 that consumption is a function of disposable personal income:

$$C = a + bY_d$$

However, if we look at the consumption expenditures and income for a group of households for any given year, it would be sheer coincidence if all homes with identical incomes had identical consumption expenditures. The discrepancy between the theory and the actual behavior may result from the individuality of the households, from another set of determining variables (some of which were considered in Chapter 6), from the sheer indeterminancy of human behavior (which we fervently hope is not the case), or from inaccurate data. Whatever the source, a "disturbance term" can be introduced which acts as a catch-all for the effects of unspecified variables on the dependent variables, so that

$$C = a + bY_d + E$$

On the average, E should equal zero if the theoretical formulation is to hold. Intense analyses of the disturbance or error term are employed by econometricians to check for the adequacy of their specified explanatory variables. One of the major problems in econometric modeling is to decide how much to aggregate and how many explanatory variables to employ. An economist could produce a unique equation for every transaction within an economy and show the links between them. But no computer could hold this model. To simplify, the economist creates aggregates of similar transactions. Purchases of beer—and other consumer nondurables—can be lumped with purchases of automobiles—and other consumer durables—and with purchases of haircuts or airplane tickets—and other services—to form consumption expenditures. For some purposes, this aggregate works; for others, the economist may want to disaggregate into the components—nondurable, durable, and services. Or consumption may be disaggregated in some other way. (In the Brookings model five equations take care of consumer demand.) The components cannot be arbitrarily selected but must be specified and related in a coherent way. Thus, the model builder must know how a sector operates.

Actually, the large-scale models, such as the Brookings model, are the product of many economists. No one researcher could readily acquire the intimate knowledge of all sectors that are required to build a large-scale model. Sector specialists set to work creating equations and verifying them, and only later are these sectors put together and reconciled into a model.

Sector models are often useful by themselves. For instance, during the energy crunch of 1973–1974, William Nordhaus of Yale University employed an econometric model of energy use to see what the future held. The model included both present and future sources of energy with estimates of their changing availability and cost. Nordhaus found that if the United States insists on going ahead with "Project Independence" or some other program to achieve self-sufficiency in energy, the cost of meeting energy demand over the next twenty years will be 50 percent higher (or a total of $320 billion) than with free trade. However, free trade takes cooperation; the costs to the United States of monopolistic pricing and prolonged embargoes by supplying nations might justify developing the abundant domestic resources. If the country could count on only sporadic interruption of imports, it might be cheaper to rely on free trade (with stockpiles of domestic oil to tide the country over embargo periods) than to become self-sufficient.

Whatever the scenario, in the future petroleum and natural gas will give way to various forms of coal, shale oil, and nuclear power, with breeder reactors supplying most of the world's energy by the year 2000. Because of the capital investment necessary, energy will be expensive. But the prices will not continue to double or triple as they did during the energy crunch. From 1970 to 2010 the price increases would range from 1.1 percent per year for electricity to 3.5 percent per year for transportation fuels. In essence, Nordhaus' model shows "long-run alternatives to present energy sources are available at reasonably predictable prices."[1]

The predictions of such a model are only as good as its specificity. Sector specialists develop equations from historical data of varying degrees of completeness and accuracy. Those equations are constantly being revised. Equations that may work well in explaining past conditions may be less successful in tracking conditions in today's economy. The reason is not always poor data or poor equations. Often structural changes in the economy itself will alter the relationships of the variables. For example, should the scarcity of

1. Brookings Institute, "An Optimistic Outlook on Energy," *The Brookings Bulletin* 11, no. 1 (Winter 1974): 4.

energy lower the capital-output ratio, it would be necessary to change this value in the investment equations. Some changes, such as a strike or oil embargo, can be accounted for by a dummy variable which, like the disturbance term, reflects the mathematical effect but does not explain the processes at work.

An exact replica of the economy may never be possible. For one thing, even an exact copy might not remain so, not only because of structural changes but because of unpredictable elements like "entrepreneurial animal spirits" that affect investment decisions along with more calculable factors. There is substantial progress, however. A survey of eleven econometric models found that the solution errors are now within "reasonable bounds, and that there is relatively uniform agreement about the pattern and magnitude of fiscal impacts."[2] For example, both the Brookings and the Wharton models forecast an upturn in the economy during the latter part of 1974.

Where knowledge about the relationship between monetary- and fiscal-policy measures and a single, major variable like national income is desired, there is an alternative to the large-scale models. The so-called single-equation models, such as that developed at the Federal Reserve Bank of St. Louis, directly attack the problem of measuring the impact on national income of changes in government expenditure, taxes, or changes in the money supply by fitting regression equations like:

$$Y_t = a_0 + a_1 G_{t,t-1} + a_2 M_{t,t-1} + E$$

In this equation, a_1 and a_2 measure the impact upon current income, Y_t, of current or lagged changes in government expenditure, $G_t G_{t-1}$,

2. Gary Fromm and L. R. Klein, "A Comparison of Eleven Econometric Models of the United States," *American Economic Review*, May 1973, p. 393.

and the money supply, $M_t M_{t-1}$. More detailed attention is devoted to the St. Louis model in Chapter 14, but here it can readily be seen that such an approach precludes discovery of any detailed information regarding the parameters involved in a model such as IS/LM. As such, it is a highly aggregated, reduced form approach. "Reduced form" refers to the fact that the parameters which define $\Delta Y/\Delta M$ or $\Delta Y/\Delta G$ are not specified in the single equation. Their combined effect is instead lumped together in a_1 or a_2.

The St. Louis model has done about as well as the large Wharton or Brookings models in predicting the behavior of national income. Of course, the more detailed information on disaggregated sectors and model parameters require the larger models. In general, a model should be designed to yield desired empirical information as simply as possible. The single-equation model sacrifices detailed information for simplicity and low cost of estimation, while the large models obtain more detailed information but only with a loss of simplicity and low cost. Econometric models which take the middle road between these extremes also exist, and their strengths and weaknesses reflect such compromise.[3]

3. A ten-equation Keynesian model, for example, is contained in Michio Morishima and Mitsuo Saito, "A Dynamic Analysis of the American Economy, 1902–1952," *International Economic Review* (May 1964): 125–164.

higher level than is possible with shifts in IS alone, it must accompany fiscal measures, which shift the IS schedule upward, with an increase in the money supply so that LM will also shift up. In this way, the higher transaction balances that accompany a higher level of income will be satisfied by the higher money supply rather than through an increase in interest rates that depresses investment spending. Graphically, the effectiveness of simultaneous shifts in LM and IS is shown in Figure 9.15. In section (a) only the IS line is shifted; assume that the effect on general equilibrium is an increase of $50 billion in Y ($\Delta Y = $50 billion) and an increase of $\frac{1}{2}$ of 1 percent in interest rates ($\Delta i = .5$ percent). In section (b) the same changes in I or G or T produce the same shift in IS, but because the monetary authorities have increased the money supply, the LM schedule shifts too. Given an appropriate LM shift, such as that shown in section (b), interest rates remain unchanged, and the full extent of the increase in spending implied by the shift in IS shows up in the increase in national income, say, $\Delta Y = $100 billion.

In summary, Figure 9.15 emphasizes the interrelationship of fiscal and monetary policy. Expansionary fiscal policies cannot achieve their full potential unless they are accompanied by expansionary monetary policy; an administration that wishes to increase national income most efficiently must combine tax cuts and/or increases in government spending with an expanding money supply. Conversely, declines in government spending (leftward shifts in the IS line) introduced in an attempt to slow down the inflationary pressures produced by a too-rapidly growing national income may be only modestly effective on their own. Combined, however, with a tight money policy (a shift to the left in the LM schedule) that restrains the

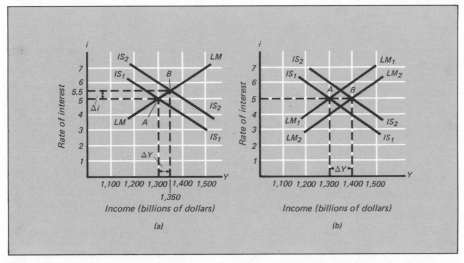

Figure 9.15 New general equilibrium. Section (a) shift in IS; section (b) shift in IS and LM

growth of the money supply and produces higher interest rates, these fiscal measures may prove much more useful.

It must be remembered at this point that prices have been assumed to remain constant in our analysis of the effect of simultaneous upward shifts of IS and LM. This really amounts to wishful thinking; the impact of allowing prices to vary will be explored in Chapter 10. Suffice it to say for now that a simultaneous rise in G and M is likely to be highly inflationary due to the additive impacts upon aggregate demand. Indeed, a good part of United States inflation in the 1973–1974 period was due to just such actions by United States policymakers.

Another Look at Slope

Keynes' analysis of the speculative demand for money indicated that at very low interest rates the demand for money became perfectly elastic. This occurred because wealth holders, believing that interest rates could go no lower and bond prices no higher, kept all additional increments of wealth in cash. Such behavior produced a demand-for-money curve that was absolutely flat at very low interest rates at the extreme right (see Figure 8.9) which, in turn, produced an LM curve with a similar horizontal slope at the extreme right. This area, where the equilibrium interest rate for the monetary sector remains unchanged even as the income component changes, is called the **Keynesian range**, shown again in Figure 9.16. At the opposite extreme the asset demand for money may be insensitive to the interest rate. Reflecting this, the L_A schedule is vertical in this area, as is the resultant vertical LM curve. This area of the LM curve is called the **classical range**. The **intermediate range** of the LM curve is that area where changes in monetary equilibrium involve both changes in interest rates and changes in income. The significance of the different ranges of the LM curve becomes apparent when we examine the effect of shifts in the IS or LM schedules that occur within the several ranges.

If the economy is operating within the Keynesian range, then changes in the money supply are ineffective as a tool for increasing equilibrium national income—since LM does not shift in the Keynesian range when the money supply is altered. For example, a shift from LM_1 to LM_2, as illustrated in Figure 9.17(a), will produce no change in general equilibrium. In such an economy, trapped within this Keynesian range, monetary measures will prove useless. Instead, if policymakers wish to move the economy to a higher level of national income, they must adopt expansionary fiscal measures that shift the IS schedule. This is shown in section (b).

In the intermediate range shown in section (c), shifts in either the IS or LM curves will affect general equilibrium national income. As indicated earlier, the change in income will be most sizable where shifts in IS are combined with shifts in LM. Section (d) shows the effect of shifts in IS once

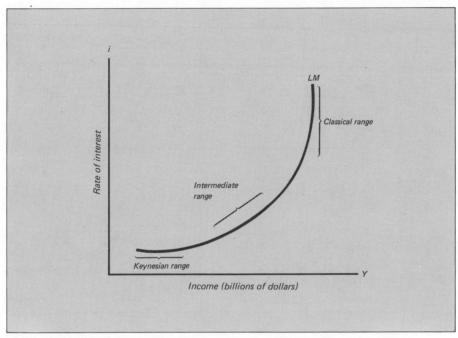

Figure 9.16 The shape of LM: classical, Keynesian, and intermediate ranges

the economy has reached the classical range. Here, IS shifts have no effect on national income; they merely produce higher interest rates. If, for example, the government were to increase spending at this level, without providing for any increase in the money supply (that is, with no shift in the LM schedule), then the additional demand would be reflected entirely in higher interest rates. This in turn would lead to a lower level of private investment and an unchanged level of national income since the lower private investment would just offset the higher government expenditure. In the classical range, increases in national income can be accomplished only through upward shifts in the LM schedule brought about by increasing the money supply, as shown in section (e). None of any such increases in the money supply will be absorbed by increases in asset balances, since they are insensitive to interest rate levels. The result is a higher quantity of money available for transaction balances that can support a higher level of national income. In essence, sections (d) and (e) demonstrate why fiscal measures are ineffective stimuli to national income in the classical range, and why monetary policy becomes the only effective tool in this area.

A summary of the effects of monetary sector parameters on the slope of LM is found in the appendix to this chapter, together with the effects of such parameters on money and expenditure multipliers.

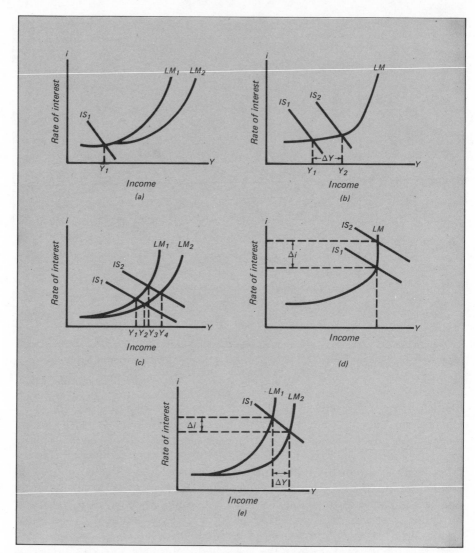

Figure 9.17 Fiscal and monetary policy: the shape of IS and LM

We noted that the effectiveness of monetary and fiscal policy as devices to shift equilibrium national income depends to a large extent on the range of the LM schedule in which the economy is operating. This effectiveness is also determined by the slope of the IS schedule. The IS schedule used up to this point in this chapter has been one that slopes downward to the right; that is, changes in product-market equilibrium along the curve are characterized by increases in income in response to declines in interest rates. Because IS schedules with flatter or steeper slopes carry different policy·implications, we must therefore consider at this point the determinants of the slope of the IS schedule.

The slope of the IS schedule is determined by two factors. The first is the slope of the MEI curve, or how responsive investment spending is to changes in interest rates. If investment is relatively insensitive to changes in interest rates (i.e., expectations, technological change, etc.), then the MEI curve will be almost vertical, indicating that changes in interest rates will have little effect on investment, as shown in quadrant A of Figure 9.18. Under such circumstances, the final IS line must be nearly vertical because if investment does not change with interest rates, income will not be required to change in order to keep savings equal to investment. This is shown in quadrant D.

The slope of the IS line is also affected by the marginal propensity to save: the lower the MPS, the flatter will be the IS line, since as i falls and I

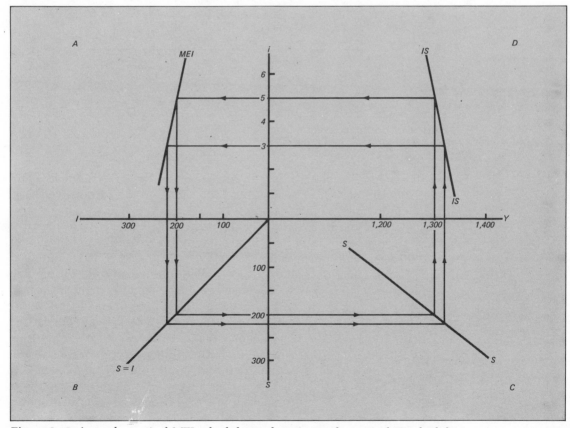

Figure 9.18 A nearly vertical MEI schedule produces a nearly vertical IS schedule

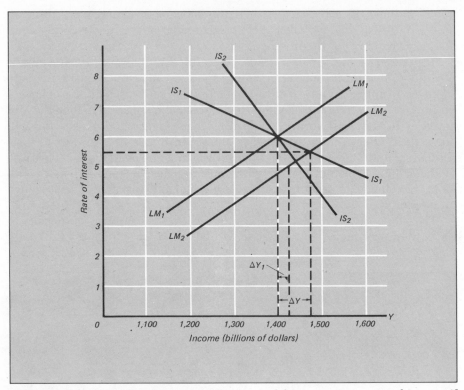

Figure 9.19 Shifts in LM are a more effective tool for increasing national income if the IS schedule is relatively flat

rises, the more income will have to rise to restore I = S. To summarize, the slope of the IS schedule falls as the MPS falls and the responsiveness of investment to changes in the interest rate rises.

The slope of the IS schedule, or the degree of its elasticity in regard to interest, is especially important in evaluating the potential significance of shifts in LM as far as changes in national income are concerned. Figure 9.19 compares the effect of a shift in LM on both a relatively flat IS line (IS₁) and a relatively steep IS line (IS₂) in an economy operating in the intermediate range. In an economy with a relatively flat IS line, the shift in LM will produce a substantial shift in Y; in an economy with a relatively vertical IS line, the shift in LM will have almost no effect on Y.

This pattern has significant policy implications. An economist who believed that investment was interest inelastic creating a relatively steep IS line (and Keynes was among these) would have little faith in the ability of monetary measures to shift the economy to a different level of national income. He would feel, for example, that increases in the money supply and lower interest rates would not stimulate investment spending and therefore incomes during a recession. Nor would he believe that monetary stringency and higher interest rates would be effective anti-inflationary devices should the need arise to depress investment spending and income. In other words, those who see the IS line as relatively steep will find themselves unable to place much confidence in monetary measures, and they will advocate the use of fiscal measures as the primary stabilization tool, while those who believe the line is fairly flat will be more sympathetic to a combination of fiscal and monetary policy. We will examine these conflicting assumptions about the shape of the IS schedule in Chapter 12, where we consider fiscal and monetary policy in greater detail.

MATHEMATICAL APPENDIX
Slopes of IS and LM

Slope of LM

Recall the monetary sector equilibrium condition:

$$M_S = L(Y,i) \tag{A9.1}$$

Along the LM schedule the money supply does not change, so obtaining an expression for the change of both sides of equation (A9.1), we have:

$$0 = \Delta M_S = L_Y \Delta Y + L_i \Delta i \tag{A9.2}$$

where:

L_Y is the impact of a change in income on the demand for money, holding i constant

L_i is the impact of a change in the interest rate on the demand for money, holding Y constant.

From Chapter 8 we know that L_Y is positive and L_i is negative. Since the LM schedule is located within a coordinate system where the vertical axis measures i and the horizontal axis measures Y, its slope is given by $\Delta i/\Delta Y$. Based on equation (A9.2), the slope of the LM schedule is:

$$\left(\frac{\Delta i}{\Delta Y}\right)_{LM} = -\frac{L_Y}{L_i} > 0 \tag{A9.3}$$

From equation (A9.3) it is readily apparent that the slope of LM is positive (>0). It is also apparent that in a liquidity trap, where L_i approaches infinity, the LM schedule will have a zero slope (a flat or horizontal shape). Conversely, if the demand for money is insensitive to the interest rate so that $L_i = 0$, the LM schedule has an infinite slope (a vertical shape).

Slope of IS

The equilibrium condition along IS is given by:

$$I(i) + G = S(Y) + T \tag{A9.4}$$

Obtaining an expression for the change of both sides of equation (A9.4) gives us the expression:

$$I_i \Delta i = S_Y \Delta Y \tag{A9.5}$$

where:

$\Delta G, \Delta T = 0$

I_i is the impact of a change in i on investment (holding all else constant)

S_Y is the impact of a change in Y on savings (holding all else constant).

In Chapters 4 and 7 we have seen that S_Y is positive (the MPS) and that I_i is negative.

Since the IS schedule is also located within a coordinate system bounded by i and Y in exactly the same manner as the LM schedule, its slope is also given by $\Delta i / \Delta Y$. Based on equation (A9.5), the slope of IS is therefore given by

$$\left(\frac{\Delta i}{\Delta Y} \right)_{IS} = \frac{S_Y}{I_i} < 0 \tag{A9.6}$$

Equation (A9.6) confirms a negative slope for the IS schedule. If $I_i = 0$, the IS schedule is vertical. As S_Y falls, the IS schedule approaches a horizontal shape.

Expression of Multipliers in Terms of Parameters

Solving for the impact of ΔM and ΔG on ΔY and Δi requires simultaneous solution of equations (A9.2) and (A9.5), where ΔM_S and ΔG do not equal zero. Given:

$$\Delta M_S = L_Y \Delta Y + L_i \Delta i \tag{A9.2'}$$

$$\Delta G + I_i \Delta i = S_Y \Delta Y \tag{A9.5'}$$

We can solve for the value of i that satisfies (A9.2'):

$$\Delta i = \frac{-L_Y}{L_i} \Delta Y + \frac{\Delta M_S}{L_i}$$

If we substitute this term into equation (A9.5'), we find:

$$\Delta G + I_i \left[\frac{-L_Y}{L_i} \Delta Y + \frac{\Delta M_S}{L_i} \right] = S_Y \Delta Y$$

Collecting the ΔY terms on the left-hand side, we have:

$$\Delta Y \left[S_Y + \frac{I_i L_Y}{L_i} \right] = \Delta G + \frac{I_i \Delta M_S}{L_i} \tag{A 9.6'}$$

Finally, solving for the government-expenditure multiplier where LM is constant ($\Delta M_S = 0$) gives:

$$\left(\frac{\Delta Y}{\Delta G}\right)_{\Delta M_S = 0} = \frac{1}{S_Y + \dfrac{I_i L_Y}{L_i}} > 0 \tag{A9.7}$$

If $\Delta G = \Delta M$:

$$\left(\frac{\Delta Y}{\Delta G}\right)_{\Delta G = \Delta M} = \frac{1 + \left(\dfrac{I_i}{L_i}\right)}{S_Y + \dfrac{I_i L_Y}{L_i}} > 0 \tag{A9.8}$$

Notice that in the liquidity trap case, where $L_i = \infty$,

$$\left(\frac{\Delta Y}{\Delta G}\right)_{\Delta M_S = 0} = \frac{1}{S_Y} = \frac{1}{MPS} = \frac{1}{1 - MPC}$$

Of course, equation (A9.8) indicates that the impact on income rises if G and M are increased together.

Letting $\Delta G = 0$, which assumes that IS is not shifting, equation (A9.6′) gives:

$$\left(\frac{\Delta Y}{\Delta M}\right)_{\Delta G = 0} = \frac{\dfrac{I_i}{L_i}}{S_Y + \dfrac{I_i L_Y}{L_i}} > 0$$

It is useful to restate this expression by multiplying the numerator and denominator by (L_i/I_i), which yields:

$$\left(\frac{\Delta Y}{\Delta M}\right)_{\Delta G = 0} = \frac{1}{\dfrac{L_i S_Y}{I_i} + L_Y} > 0 \tag{A9.9}$$

Notice that if $L_i = 0$, as in the classical case, we have:

$$\frac{\Delta Y}{\Delta M} = \frac{1}{L_Y} > 0$$

If $L_i = \infty$, as in the liquidity trap case (or if $I_i = 0$), we have:

$$\frac{\Delta Y}{\Delta M} = 0$$

Values for the impact of ΔM_S and ΔG and Δi may be obtained by solving equation (A9.2′) for Y and substituting the result into equation (A9.5′):

$$\Delta Y = \frac{\Delta M_S - L_i \Delta i}{L_Y}$$

$$\Delta G + I_i \Delta i = S_Y \left[\frac{\Delta M_S - L_i \Delta i}{L_Y}\right]$$

We can collect the Δi terms on the left-hand side as follows:

$$\Delta i \left[I_i + \frac{S_Y L_i}{L_Y} \right] = -\Delta G + \frac{S_Y}{L_Y} \Delta M_S$$

Therefore:

$$\left(\frac{\Delta i}{\Delta G} \right)_{\Delta M_S = 0} = \frac{-1}{I_i + \dfrac{S_Y L_i}{L_Y}} > 0 \qquad (A9.10)$$

And:

$$\left(\frac{\Delta i}{\Delta M_S} \right)_{\Delta G = 0} = \frac{\dfrac{S_Y}{L_Y}}{I_i + \dfrac{S_Y L_i}{L_Y}} = \frac{1}{\dfrac{L_Y I_i}{S_Y} + L_i} < 0 \qquad (A9.11)$$

Finally:

$$\left(\frac{\Delta i}{\Delta G} \right)_{\Delta M_S = 0} = 0 \text{ if } L_i = \infty \text{ in the liquidity trap case.}$$

$\left(\dfrac{\Delta i}{\Delta G} \right)_{\Delta M_S = 0}$ also rises as I_i, S_Y, L_i fall and as L_Y rises.

$\left(\dfrac{\Delta i}{\Delta M_S} \right)_{\Delta G = 0}$ rises in value as L_Y, I_i, and L_i fall and as S_Y rises

Questions and Exercises

1. Why does equilibrium in the money market need to be related to the level of national income? Similarly, why does equilibrium in the product market need to be related to the rate of interest?

2. Draw and label the four-quadrant curves for the product market. Determine the effect on product equilibrium levels if the MEI curve shifts downward by $40 billion for all rates of interest.

3. Assume an economy in which the MEI curve shifts upward by $10 billion and the MPS for the economy is 0.4. On which curve do you see the effects of the multiplier? Where would the new general equilibrium level for the economy fall? Why would there be a smaller rise in income than that indicated by the multiplier?

4. Suppose that there is a shift in the MEI curve to the left. What will eventually happen to interest rates? Why? Will the drop in investment be as high as originally anticipated? Why or why not?

5. Show the effects of a reduction in government expenditures on the IS curve and on the equilibrium level for the economy as a whole. What would tend to happen to interest rates? What would tend to occur if the economy were in the classical range of the LM curve? The Keynesian region?

6. Assume that rising optimism by businessmen is also accompanied by an increase in the money supply by monetary authorities. What effects would you predict?

7. Assume that investors revise their estimates of a "normal" rate of interest from 7 to 8 percent. What would be the effect on the L_S schedule? The level of income?

8. If the innovation theory of investment is essentially correct, and there is a significant technological breakthrough in the production of usable energy, what changes would you predict for the MEI curve? The equilibrium level of income? Interest rates?

9. Assume that the Federal Reserve Open Market Committee sells Treasury bonds in the amount of $10 billion. Show the effects of this policy on the LM schedule. How much of a change in the money supply would occur?

10. In the midst of continued inflation in early 1974, Senators Kennedy and Mondale cosponsored a bill that would have provided tax relief primarily for families earning less than $10,000 per year. The administration argued that such tax cuts would be inflationary, while the sponsors and their chief advisor, Paul Samuelson, believed that they would not be inflationary.* Under what circumstances would each view be correct?

*"A Vision of Sugarplums," *Newsweek*, May 6, 1974, pp. 66–67.

The Changing Role of Women: Implications for Planners

The Great American Wage Puzzle

Joblessness Held At Its 5.2% Rate During February

Non-Union Employes Invited to Complain

In Colorado, Bad Days for a Cattleman

Economy May Have Seen the Worst

the year America changes the way it treats its retired workers. And so, at an un_____ but clearly _____ but _____ actly wh_____

The I_____-member_____ nation's l_____ serve__ a turn _____ "landmark_____ on Friday when it announced a _____ment on its first big contra__ of the year, with the aluminum _____ nating story of week'_____ co-operation a_____ lation lies behind the settleme_____ steelworke__ say.

One of t_____ lab__ in decades, _____ multifaceted plan that ins_____ for the first time in a _____ trial package a partial cost-of-living escal_____ and it lowers the full-pension retirement age to 62 from 65 years. The plan is effective next Feb. 1 but covers all retirees as of last weekend.

About as significant, says I. W. Abel, the dy-

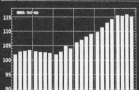

Man-Hour Output

PRODUCTION per man-hour (private, nonfarm) in the fourth quarter of 1973 fell to as 115.1% of the 1967 average from 115.9% recorded in the third quarter, the Labor Department reports____, believe that most of this year's downturn in the American economy has already taken place.

H_____ver, _____ nece_____ _____ now-show-the 1_____ ing declining output for at least another month. Figures for March and the first quarter will not be published until April and even May.

The Government normally makes an official forecast only once a year — at the time of the President's economic report to Congress in late January or early February. But the Government regularly updates its forecast without publishing the results. The latest updating was nearing completion last week, with most of the main February statistics in hand.

Without revealing specific numbers, officials now concede a sizable decline in the "real" gross national product in first quarter. They beli_____ ___tlook for the secor_____ very sma__ direction—that is, for an __ sentially flat economy.

For the second half, they are projecting what is probably a somewhat stronger recovery than the "standard" private forecast. It is

Economic signs turn upward and lifting of Arab embargo aids confidence that recovery will strengthen.

with or without the end of the embargo. The embargo's end removes some of the _____side risk in t____ _____ _____ps _____ _____n half."

In other words, the lifting of the Arabs' embargo on oil shipments to the United States has not significantly changed the Administration's

is thoroughly designed for the worker's benefit. Mr. Abel says that the steel accord and other accomplishments in his eight-year presidency pale in comparison to it.

"Twenty-five years ago the United Steelworkers in this city went about establishing the right of employes to have pensions," the 65-year-old labor leader said Friday. "I would hope and I have reason to believe that the establishment of an escalator revision to secure these pensions will find its way into other labor agreements in other industries."

That remark smacks of understatement. ____only _____ven million other workers cur_____ _____nsi__ escala__ r when ____ab_____ ____ for ___ation this year, bu_____ ____vi____ rect say in the settlements for a t____ _____ That's because almost 700,000 are Steelworkers in "other industries"—can making, nonferrous metals and basic steel. The aluminum pact itself, a 40-month contract that supersedes the final months of the old three-year document that was to have expired May 31, will cover almost 55,000 workers in the USW and the Aluminum Workers International Union after it is extended to "me-too" settlements later this year. The contracts signed Friday _____ Reynolds Metals and Kaiser _____

From $100 Monthly Up—and H___

Until last week there wa_____ suspect that the aluminu_____ would improve o ATLANTA — Delt_ Air the auto, rubber Lines, with _____ and frugal _____ _more money in 1973 than ___many other domestic airline ____ever made in any year.

c__ Whatever happens to this ir profit, Delta seems unlikely s to squander any of it. At b Hartsfield Airport here, whenever a Delta jet takes off or lands it rattles the t walls of a r__ of unpreno_____ ____ they look as if they c could be garages — actually w they contain Delta's execu-n tive suite.

Absent from the office ti walls are costly paintings like in those sometimes seen at other ly trunk airline headquarters. A a company spokesman told u a visitor that W. Thomas th Beebe, the Delta chairman le and chief executive officer, prefers travel agency posters p (extolling Delta's services) to di any Frederic Remington glor-S ifications of early-day travel G perils from man and beast. Se In a wide-ranging inter-th view the other day, Mr. de Beebe said it was too soon rec to predict what effect the ex-sti pected increase in rates (an __average of 6 per cent across re the board) would have on air str travel generally. But he said bar he was "really bothered" by oil he C.A.B.'s call for higher Gu fares __short hauls of 250 to be _____ _____ta_____ et,_____ce yourself out o__ u_____ita ye_____eader said. "Last December, ge_____when the regulatory agency He authorized a 5 per cent domestic fare increase, Delta

example of what early planning, early lines and a responsible attitude by truly sional negotiators can accomplish." He hopes the settlement "will set a stand negotiations throughout this important

The package contains numerous for the USW and the Aluminum Workers dition to the pension program. It im medical insurance, providing a limited plan for the first time in the industry. It sickness and accident benefits in all years and raises supplementary unemplo benefits. An extra holiday has been add the second year and longer vacations i third year for employes with at least 17 of service Also, the contract "rolls in" cos ____ ____ustments to increase the wo _____ ____evi__ ____ figu____ _____of that means nig____ment in other pay-related benefits. it now will take only a 0.3-point Consum Price Index rise—instead of a 0.4-point boos to get an extra penny an hour in wages.

The USW did fall short on some of its of course ___ s generally are exul ___ ____ the chances for pu _____ements through in other u industries. Only one of 48 local USW preside _____nin__ package, acc ___next ___ _____ rec_____ ___ an companies, w_____ _____ contract-clu_____ ____ _____ 1,251 _____ 303 _____ ___remaining _____ steelworkers: retirement incom "matches" working wages and is covered full cost-of-living rises.

WAGE SETTLEMENTS

First-year changes in wage rates alone and in wages plus benefits. Major collective bargaining settlements.

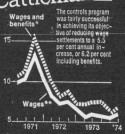

Wages and benefits*

The controls program was fairly successful in achieving its objective of reducing wage settlements to a 5.5 per cent annual increase, or 6.2 per cent including benefits.

Wages**

1971 1972 1973 '74

*Wage and benefit figures cover agreements for 5,000 workers or more.

**Wage figures cover agreements for 1,000 workers or more.

Source: Department of Labor

didn't raise the fare on flig of 300 miles or less.

But this time, Mr. Bee said, he expects the C.A to enforce its ruling. If as and if it also requi the South and Southeast wit the Mid____ ____ and which ha_____ seems ____ ___in ___ ____ be a very serious misjudg Mr. Beebe said. "I'm not rier on a number of all sure it won't be adve England

to the airline industry.

Until it acquired Northeast Airlines in August, 1972 Delta was often referred to as "that line which connects the South and Southeast wit the Mid____ ____ and which has-the __re clause," calling for a be__ on which _____vious retirees getting the ____me ____nts and providing ____rs, down to $15 on a

A Goal for Other Bargainers

isn't new to Mr. Abel. von praise for another experimental negotiating U.S. steelmakers—a pact nion's right to a nation-

us $230 monthly until re-ters idled by shutdowns or alf a full pension) for the employe.

34,170	35,499	38,507	39,597	38,203
2,986	3,013	3,106	3,083	2,949
2,862	2,878	2,981	2,924	2,807
124	135	125	159	142
822	840	897	955	859
60	71	92	119	95
106	99	98	98	89
431	443	457	470	416
163	165	180	192	192
62	62	70	76	67
806	866	1,104	1,082	1,055
8,364	8,904	9,645	10,591	9,131
4,777	4,963	5,185	5,461	5,046
1,085	1,157	1,157	1,223	1,166
112	108	109	111	108
1,139	1,196	1,218	1,263	1,092
699	768	829	843	807
		300	325	301
		554	594	578
				383
				131
345	352			277
				53
3,587	3,941	4,460	5,130	4,085
320	360	415	459	398
289	329	364	398	342
262	281	317	356	310
917	996	1,147	1,317	1,026
220	249	277	313	256
505	577	664	791	626
319	338	385	461	353
101	105	137	171	141
433	464	492	580	363
231	242	262	284	270
		2,121	2,240	1,973
			1,251	1,061
		303		281
				324
				141
				13
				26
				130
391	390			420
379	376	393	422	400
15	14	17	20	21
409	414	442	458	444
386	392	418	437	423
23	22	24	21	21
5,567	5,707	6,155	6,674	6,547
1,492	1,507	1,612	1,770	1,767
4,075	4,200	4,543	4,904	4,780
1,332	1,352	1,401	1,445	1,436
286	279	278	287	288
101	89	103	101	82
126	129	135	138	122
355	372	376	392	405
132	136	139		142
327	347	371	388	307
4,766	4,936	5,267	5,538	5,310
591	618	670	397	398
330	370	658	694	661
2,004	2,095	2,240	2,374	2,166
15	17	20	22	21
207	207	241	246	249
72	72	72	73	73
217	159	178	193	187
193	190	205	224	201
403	420	456	491	516
109	113	114	118	122
23	25	29	31	33
234	240	244	251	259
438	434	441	424	424
6,752	7,072	7,958	7,088	8,078
2,106	2,076	4,845	3,924	4,809
1,747	1,702	4,464	3,537	4,405
357	449	521	517	507
250	263	290	313	326
1,140	990	3,653	2,707	3,572
359	374	381		404
4,646	4,996	3,113	3,164	3,269
4,326	4,870	2,978	3,024	3,129
3,122	3,152	1,174	1,206	1,239
1,570	1,621	1,713	1,762	1,871
	2,097	91	56	19

Housing Starts

(Seasonally adjusted annual rate, millions of units)

2.5

1968 1969 1970 1971 1972 1973

Industrial Production

(Seasonally adjusted, 1967=100)

130

U.S. Auto Sales

(Retail deliveries of vehicles made in U.S. and Canada and sold in U.S. only. In thousands)

1,000

Aggregate Supply and Demand

10

Up to this point our analysis has focused almost exclusively on macro-economic relationships; we have not paid specific attention to how output is produced, which is equivalent to how income is earned. We have been building a model to explain such essential real-world phenomena as national income, the level of employment (full or unemployment), and interest rates. The income determination model constructed in Chapter 4 was the basis, to which were added the modifications required by consideration of the money market in Chapters 8 and 9. This analysis has emphasized the components of *demand*—consumption (Chapter 6), investment (Chapter 7), and government expenditures (Chapter 5)—which yielded the basic equation for the equilibrium level of national income excluding foreign trade: $Y = C + I + G$. This emphasis on the demand side reflects the initial Keynesian assumption that it is the commodity market that determines the level of output. If equilibrium national income is at a level lower than that required for full employment, then, the argument goes, demand must be insufficient. The policy prescription is to increase demand through fiscal and/or monetary policy.

Keynes' emphasis on demand was appropriate for the conditions prevailing in the industrialized world at the time he wrote: high unemployment, steady prices, and wages that rose only as a result of increased productivity. The present industrialized, capitalist world, however, faces somewhat different problems. Modern Western economies are much closer to full employment, and there is a strong inflationary tendency with both wages and prices rising rapidly. To take account of these conditions, our model must be improved through more precise consideration of the supply side of the equation. As full employment is approached, aggregate supply becomes important, especially if we are to know to what extent shifts in aggregate demand $(C + I + G)$ will result in real changes in output and to what extent they will merely lead to changes in prices (inflation, for example) without changes in real physical output.

Implied in this shift of emphasis from demand to supply is the need to relax the earlier assumption of an unchanging price level. We are still concerned with shifts in the aggregate demand function. But such shifts—leading, for example, to an increase in national income, Y—may be accompanied by higher price levels, P, or increased real physical output, y, or both (where $Y = Py$). How much of such an increase will be in prices and how much in real output is a crucial question which can only be answered by finding the economy's equilibrium level of national income, taking into account fluctuating price and wage levels as well as money-market conditions and any barriers to automatic, self-regulating adjustment in the economy. Answering the question requires the use of some of the powerful tools derived from microeconomics, especially supply and demand curves. We will construct, first, aggregate supply and demand curves for labor and then aggregate supply and demand curves for the economy as a whole. This will nearly complete the neo-Keynesian model for general equilibrium in an economy.

Labor as a Factor of Production

The relationship between a nation's output and the resources upon which it can draw is called a **production function.** Typically, these resources include labor, N, capital, K, land, L, and the stock of know-how embodied largely in sophisticated labor and capital known as technology, A. Each of these is considered a **factor of production** and each can affect the level of output in an economy.

Since one of the primary concerns of macroeconomic policy is full employment of the labor force in the short run, the role of labor is one of the most important factors of production for macroeconomic theory. Thus we will assume that the stock of land is fixed and that technology is constant over the period of time under investigation. The stock of capital will be taken to be fixed also, which amounts to assuming that new investment in capital equipment is just sufficient to replace worn-out capital. While this assumption would obviously do some violence to the facts if held to over a long period of time, for the one or two years involved in the time horizon of the policymaker it will not be misleading. The annual addition to the U.S. capital stock, which is given by annual net investment, was about $89 billion in 1971.[1] This constituted about 3 percent of the total stock of reproducible capital of about $3,000 billion. Assuming such a small change to be zero over a year is a compromise made in the interest of simplicity and of highlighting the role of labor in a macroeconomic setting.

If N represents the total quantity of homogenous labor in the economy, taking the capital stock, technology, and land to be constant, the aggregate production function may be written as

$$y = y(N) \tag{10.1}$$

where the physical quantity of output, y, is a function of the quantity of labor. Equation (10.1) may be written in terms of income at the current price level, P, as

$$Y = Y(N) \tag{10.2}$$

where $Y = Py$, or money income equals the money value of output produced by labor.

Holding all factors of production other than labor constant, as the quantity of labor emphasized is increased, each additional unit of labor has less and less capital, land, and technology with which to work. The law of diminishing returns suggests, therefore, that the *additional* output produced by the last unit of labor employed, or the **marginal product of labor,** falls as more and more labor is employed. The diminishing marginal product of labor is shown by the aggregate production function relating output to the quantity of labor in Figure 10.1. When a unit of labor is added, from N_1 to N_2 the resulting increase in output, Δy_1, exceeds the increase in output, Δy_2, that arises when a further addition to the labor force is made from N_6 to N_7. In Figure 10.1 capital, land, and technology are explicitly noted as fixed by the bar over each. Although this assumption will be retained, it will not be explicitly noted hereafter.

The significance of the production function for our purposes is that it links the quantity of labor employed with output, or income. Therefore, once we specify the demand and supply schedules for labor, the full-employment quantity of labor will be determined by the intersection of labor demand and supply. The fully employed quantity of labor in turn identifies a full-employment level of income. This provides a useful target for policymakers; fiscal and monetary policy measures can be used to shift the IS and LM schedules so that they intersect at the full-employment level of income.

1. Gross private domestic investment of $150.8 billion less corporate capital consumption allowances or depreciation of $61.9 billion equals $88.9 billion.

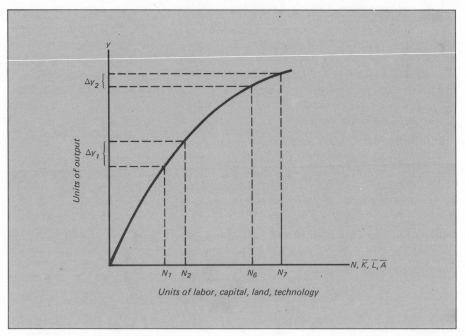

Figure 10.1 The aggregate production function with a diminishing marginal product of labor

Much of the rest of this chapter will be devoted to presenting a theory of employment. Essentially, the level of employment is determined by the supply and demand curves for labor. But the problem is more complex than simply plotting these curves together. We need a theory of the relationship between employment and output which takes into account the effect of changes in price and wage levels: that is, one which analyzes the extent to which increases in national income, Y, are due to either price-level increases, P, or increases in real physical output, y.

The Supply of Labor

Since aggregate economic activity derives, ultimately, from the behavior of millions of individuals, in order to determine the aggregate supply curve for labor it is necessary first to consider—on a microeconomic level—the supply curve of labor for the individual.

In the absence of compulsion (such as labor conscription) the model assumes that the individual makes free choices as to how much to work based only on a "rational" weighing of his or her personal needs and preferences and on the economic incentives offered by the employment opportunities. An economically rational individual is assumed, in microeconomic theory, always to prefer higher earnings to lower for a given number of work-hours per week at a particular job. That is, when more lucrative employment than presently available is offered to the individual, that person will prefer it and will not continue working at the lower wage rate for sentimental or other reasons (such as loyalty). At the same time, work is not an end in itself. Rather, work must involve sacrifice. It means passing up desired leisure-time activities (such as sleeping late or going fishing). Therefore, a rational individual's employment choices always involve balancing the **opportunity costs** of working against the desirable opportunities forfeited by working.

The model further assumes that the opportunities sacrificed are "precious," i.e. there is a scarcity value involved which dissipates somewhat when the opportunity concerned is available in increasingly abundant amounts. Thus, for example, an extra (marginal) unit of leisure time, such as a week's vacation, is assumed to be more valuable psychologically to the pressured executive who works $11\frac{1}{2}$ months a year than to the leisurely academic who may enjoy a 3-month-long summer vacation. As the individual's work time (in hours per week or weeks per year) increases, there is an increasing discomfort or psychological sacrifice (the microeconomic term is "disutility") attached to each additional unit of time worked. Thus, at least beyond some point, the individual will have to be compensated at a higher and higher rate of pay to get him or her to put in additional work-hours, since the psychological value of leisure time increases as it gets scarcer and the opportunity cost of working additional extra hours, therefore, increases.

In effect, as the wage rate or salary offered to an individual increases, two effects pull him in opposite directions. A higher wage means that the opportunity cost of leisure (not working) has increased so that the individual tends to substitute more work time for leisure time out of the 24 hours available each day. Therefore, the substitution effect operates to increase the quantity of labor supplied as the wage rate rises. On the other hand, at a higher rate of pay an individual has more income. He may feel he needs the money less or that to earn more money would be foolish if no time remains to enjoy spending it. In this case the income effect operates to reduce the quantity of labor supplied as the wage rate rises. It appears that for a normal work week time period the substitution effect for workers outweighs the income effect; after this, the income effect begins to operate. Such a transition was discovered in World War II, when higher overtime wages failed to consistently attract labor for more than 60 hours a week.

Given these considerations, we would expect the rational economic individual's supply curve for labor to look like the one represented in Figure 10.2, where income effects outweigh substitution effects; due to an increasing **marginal disutility of labor,** the curve slopes upward to the right. Higher wages must be paid to coax more work-hours out of the individual. In real-world terms, we can find this institutionalized in time-and-a-half pay

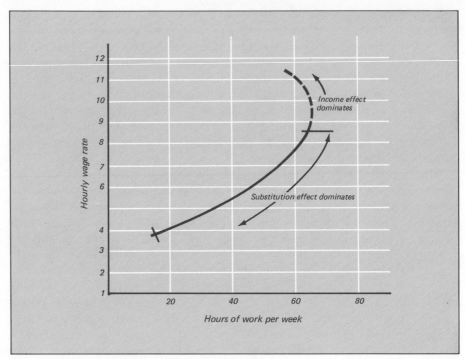

Figure 10.2 The individual supply of labor

for ordinary "overtime" work (beyond 35 or 40 hours per week) and some-times double pay for working on Sundays or holidays. And since an indivi-dual's leisure time is scarce and increasingly valuable as the work week lengthens, the supply curve climbs more steeply (i.e., it is concave when viewed from above) as the number of work-hours per week increases. As income effects begin to dominate, the curve necessarily begins to rise more steeply, and the individual's supply curve for labor bends backward toward the left (as represented by the broken line).

Having determined the shape of the individual's supply curve for labor, we now derive the aggregate supply curve by summing the number of work-hours supplied by all individuals in the economy at each wage rate. They may have different individual supply curves (some may be willing to work only 20 hours at a $2 wage while others will work 40 hours), but for our theoretical purposes it makes no difference. The shape of the curves is what matters. If they follow the pattern shown in Figure 10.2, the aggregate supply curve will resemble N_S in Figure 10.3.

Note that along the vertical axis the wage rate is now designated "real wage," rather than a specific monetary wage. This will be of importance later when we consider the effects of changes in the price level. For now, it is enough to say that we assume workers will only work harder if their real wage (money wage divided by price level) increases. If price levels increased as much as money wages did (during an inflationary period, for example), we would not expect workers to put in more work-hours since it takes real material compensation to offset the sacrifice of enjoying less leisure time.

The Demand for Labor

Just as the aggregate supply curve for labor was derived from the microeconomic behavior of the many individuals who supply labor, so, likewise, the aggregate demand for labor is based on the behavior of the numerous firms that demand labor. The microeconomic analysis of firm behavior requires the following assumptions:

1. The firm operates under conditions of perfect competition. That is, it is one of so many small firms that no single firm can have a noticeable effect on the market prices of the factors of production it employs. Specifically, with regard to hiring labor, we assume that the individual firm hires a negligible percentage of all available labor. Likewise, the firm sells such a small part of the total market sales of the product it produces that it cannot significantly influence the selling price. For such a firm the prices of labor and output are both given by market conditions.
2. Since we are interested in the short-run demand for labor by the firm, we assume that the only factor of production which can be varied in the short run is labor. All the other factors (capital, land, and technology) are constant in the short run.

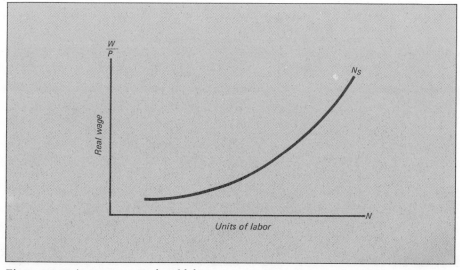

Figure 10.3 Aggregate supply of labor

3. The firm's behavior will be rational in terms of a single goal: to maximize its profits (or minimize its losses). It will adjust its level of output and its hiring of labor (the only variable factor it can control in the short run) in order to maximize profits.

The question for the firm, then, is: How much labor shall we hire? To answer this it is necessary first to review the most basic principles of the microeconomic theory of the firm. A perfectly competitive firm maximizes profits when the price of output equals the marginal cost of producing the output. This is written as

$$P = MC \qquad (10.3)$$

The **marginal cost** of an extra unit of output is, therefore, the wage paid to an additional laborer divided by the number of extra units of output, or **marginal physical product,** produced by an extra unit of labor. That is,

$$MC = \frac{W}{MP} \qquad (10.4)$$

where MC is marginal cost, W is the wage rate, and MP is marginal physical product. The marginal revenue, MR, brought to the firm by an extra unit of output produced is the same as the price, P, at which it is sold. So: $MR = P$.

If increasing amounts of labor are used with fixed amounts of other factors of production, beyond some point diminishing returns set in, and the marginal cost curve for extra units of labor inputs rises, as shown in Figure 10.4. The firm will hire additional units of labor at the prevailing wage even though their marginal physical product declines (each new

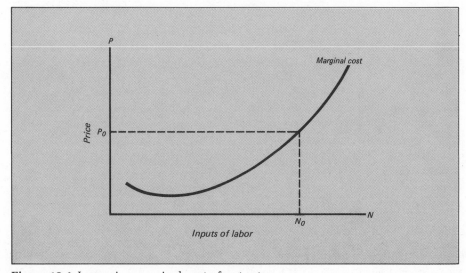

Figure 10.4 Increasing marginal cost of output

work-hour added yields a smaller increase in output than the previous one)
up to the point where the rising marginal cost equals the marginal revenue
(price, P_o, of output). Beyond that point it would be irrational (i.e., against
the rule of profit maximization) to hire additional units of labor since their
marginal costs would exceed the value of the additional production. So
the profit-maximizing output level occurs where:

$$MR = P = MC$$

or

$$P = \frac{W}{MP} \tag{10.5}$$

This profit-maximizing output also determines the amount of labor the
firm hires. The firm's output and amount of labor hired will change if the
wage rate, price obtained for the firm's product, or marginal product of labor
changes. Equation (10.5), the firm's profit maximizing condition, may be
rewritten as

$$\frac{W}{P} = MP \tag{10.6}$$

which states that a firm maximizes profits when the real wage of labor, W/P,
is equal to its marginal product.

The output of a firm in perfect competition depends on its profit-
maximizing calculations of how best to deal with factors beyond its control,
namely the market price of its product and the prevailing wages for available labor. The amount of labor hired depends on these same factors. But
what happens if the market price of the product changes? If it increases, the
firm will hire more labor and expand output, since it is not profitable to
cover even higher (rising) marginal costs. If the market price declines, the
firm will reduce output and lay off some workers. If higher prices prevail
for a long time, the firm may not only keep the additional labor hired because of short-run profit-maximizing conditions, but it may also invest in
new capital to provide the additional labor with the machinery needed for
more efficient (and profitable) production.

What happens, though, if prices decline and employment and output
have to be cut back? Consider the situation where there is a sharp reduction in investment in the economy as a whole. This would occur during a
depression, i.e., a drop in overall output because of a lack of demand, aggravated by the acceleration principle (see Chapter 7). For a while all firms
producing the product our model firm turns out would try to keep selling
their full, normally scheduled output. But with reduced overall demand,
this would glut the market and bid down the product's price. Our model
firm would have no independent control over the price and would have to
accept the new, lower prices. It would adjust accordingly and reduce output.
It would also begin to lay off workers. How many is a complex question that

demands a more precise look at another aspect of firm behavior—the firm's option to change the ratio between capital and labor in use.

Consider first a firm producing its product at what it considers the most efficient ratio of capital to labor given the prevailing factor costs of each. How does it calculate the most efficient ratio? The costs of capital are based on a calculation of the long-run needs of the firm. In the short run, capital need not enter a firm's cost calculations because its availability is fixed, but in the long run it must be gradually replaced (as it wears out), so its factor cost to production must be taken into consideration in the firm's production decisions.

The optimum ratio of capital to labor depends both on the technological requirements of production *and* on the relative costs of each. Other things being equal, a firm will use as little of the most costly factor and as much of the cheaper factor as possible to produce the desired output. Technological requirements of most productive processes are not rigid. While it is true that one seamstress can only use one pair of scissors (capital) at a time and any additional scissors would be redundant, in most productive processes there is at least some interchangeability (trade-off) of capital and labor possible for a given output. In most factories, a reduction of capital could be compensated for by an increase in labor (and vice versa) to produce a given output. This trade-off of factors is represented in Figure 10.5, where different combinations of capital and labor are used to produce set levels of output.

Consider the curve labeled y_1. We see that beyond certain limits, increases

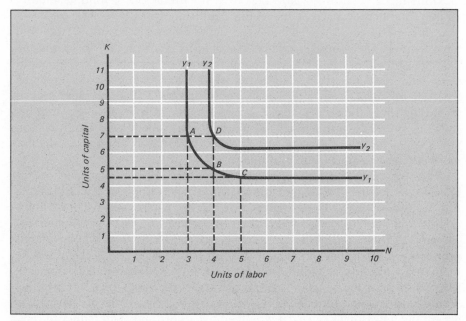

Figure 10.5 Isoquant curves

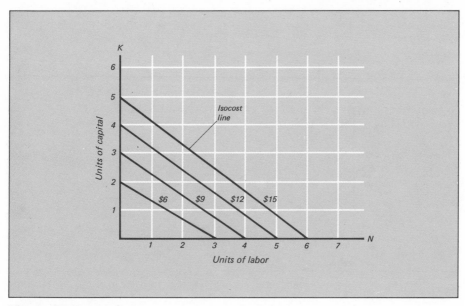

Figure 10.6 Isocost lines

in capital or labor have no effect on output. But there is a range (the curved area) where there is a trade-off. Output y_1 can be produced with 7 units of capital and 3 of labor (point A), or with 5 units of capital and 4 of labor (point B), or with 4½ units of capital and 5 of labor (point C). If 7 units of capital are combined not with 3, but with 4 units of labor, total output will increase to y_2 and be at point D on a higher curve. We can imagine a whole series of such curves, called **isoquants** (or equal-product curves), which plot all combinations of capital and labor that yield a given level of output.

For a given output level, which combination will a firm choose? That depends on the relative costs of each of the factors of production. A firm will gear its production process to minimizing the total costs of any given level of output. A graphic illustration of the way the firm solves this problem is to plot a series of parallel lines that represent equal total costs of combinations of capital and labor. Look at Figure 10.6. If a unit of capital costs $3 and a unit of labor costs $2, all the lines represent combinations of capital and labor that add up to specific total costs (such as $6, $9, etc.). These lines are called **isocost** (equal cost) **lines.** Their numerical slopes are equal to the ratio of the labor cost to the capital cost, or ⅔. If we now put isoquants and isocost lines together in one diagram, we get Figure 10.7.

The rational, cost-minimizing firm will use the amount of each factor of production that produces the desired output, y, at the least total cost. This occurs where the isocost line is tangent to the isoquant y. This is the lowest cost combination of factor inputs that will yield the desired output at the prevailing factor prices for labor and capital. Of course, if factor prices

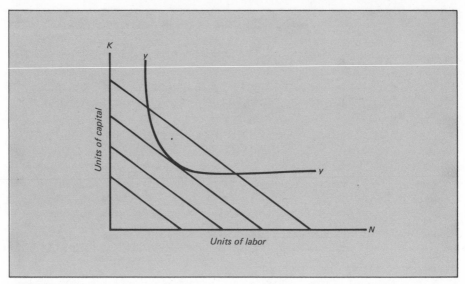

Figure 10.7 Isoquants and isocosts

change, the isocost lines will have a different slope, and the appropriate (lowest) one will be tangent to the isoquant at a different point. We now see that the level of employment (of labor by a firm) cannot be determined solely by knowing its level of output; "factor mix," or ratio of labor and capital utilized, must be known as well.

Returning to our earlier discussion, let us see what happens if a firm is forced to cut back the level of output that it has been accustomed to for a long time. Since it is a rational firm, it has been producing with the ratio of capital and labor that yields its output in the least costly way. Looking at Figure 10.8, assume that initially the firm is producing an output represented by the isoquant y_0, and the economy as a whole is at full employment. The isocost line tangent to this isoquant (at point A) has a (negative) slope with a numerical magnitude equal to the ratio of the labor cost to the capital cost P_N/P_K, and the amounts of each factor used are K_0 and N_0. Now assume that due to a recession and falling prices for the firm's product there is a sharp cutback in output to isoquant y_1. If this situation were to prevail indefinitely, in the long run the firm would lay off some of its labor, fail to replace some of its capital, and seek to produce output y_1 at the same capital and labor ratio as it did y_0 (assuming the factor prices do not change relative to each other). This is represented by the broken isocost line parallel to the first and tangent to y_1 at point B. But in the short run we know that capital and labor are not equally variable. Labor can be cut back from N_0 to N_2. If done for all firms in the economy, this might represent a recession level of output, with sizable unemployment. But, in fact, the firm will, in the short run, cut back its employment even more.

The reason for this is that capital cannot be laid off the way labor can. It is a long-run cost already incurred, already "sunk" into the firm's plant and machinery. Since it cannot readily be salvaged or redeemed in the short run, for the firm its marginal cost can be regarded as zero. Under these conditions, the firm will try to use as much of its cheapest factor (capital) and as little of its most expensive one (labor) as possible to produce the new, reduced output y_1. Thus, there will no longer be a factor price line parallel to our old one at output y_0. Instead, there will be a new, vertical factor price line tangent to y_1 at point C. The firm will utilize K_1 of capital and N_1 of labor to produce y_1. Note, however, that this does not utilize all of the firm's stock of available capital. Some capital will be redundant. Machines will lie idle, even though men are unemployed. Employment of labor will drop far below N_2 and N_1 as capital replaces labor in the production process. The firm will produce output y_1 in the most efficient and profit-maximizing (or, perhaps, loss-minimizing) way it can, but for the labor force this may be disastrous, and such high unemployment (with its resultant loss of buying power from workers and further decline in aggregate demand) may plunge the economy into a deep depression. Clearly a particular level of output does not imply a single, uniquely determined level of employment.

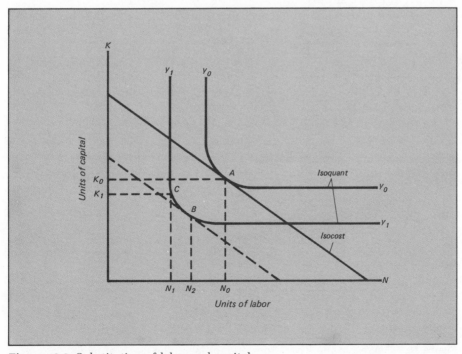

Figure 10.8 Substitution of labor and capital

The Firm's Demand Curve and the Aggregate Demand for Labor

One conceivable remedy would be to try to stimulate investment by lowering the interest rate. But as we saw in Chapter 7, this will not work since $K_0 - K_1$ already represents excess capital lying idle. No matter how low the interest rate, there is no reason for the firm to invest in new capital. Thus, monetary policy will have no influence within this framework. Only an injection of demand into the economy (through additional government expenditure, for example) might be able to raise output from y_1 to y_0 and restore the original level of employment and utilization of capital.

Initially we saw that a firm's demand for labor seemed to depend on the marginal productivity of labor, the cost of labor, and the price of the product. For the economy as a whole (with many different firms, millions of workers, various prices and wage rates) we could sum the firms together and express the aggregate demand for labor in terms of average wage rates (confronting all firms) and average prices, or price levels (for all products). Thus, we could say that aggregate demand for labor was a function of wage levels and prevailing price levels or, more simply, the demand for labor, N_D, is some function of the real wage.

$$N_D = N_D\left(\frac{W}{P}\right) \tag{10.7}$$

This was the "classical" economic view and is shown in Figure 10.9 along with the aggregate supply curve for labor from Figure 10.3.

The model presented in Figure 10.9 shows that the equilibrium level

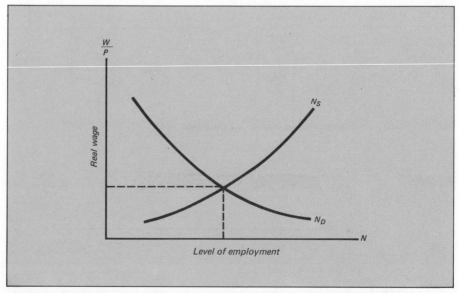

Figure 10.9 Aggregate supply and demand for labor: the classical model

of employment would occur where the aggregate supply and demand curves for labor intersect. The classical view provided a mechanism to assure full employment. If employment dropped, real wages could fall (and would, in fact, drop as unemployed labor bid down money wages faster than price levels fell) until full employment was restored.

But from our discussion of firms underutilizing capital, we can see that the aggregate demand for labor is more complex. Demand for labor is a function not only of real wages, but of aggregate demand in the economy, and regardless of the labor supply curve, there is no single, unique equilibrium level of employment. Clearly, we need a more sophisticated model of the economy, one which takes into account determinants of the demand for output in addition to the real-wage rate, if we wish to understand fully the determinants of the level of employment and discover policy alternatives that can assure full employment.

The Aggregate Supply Curve

So far the classical model for equilibrium national income and level of employment has been alluded to but not presented in detail. Figure 10.9, as we have just seen, expresses the classical view that the level of employment is uniquely determined by labor market equilibrium. But we have also seen that, according to the microeconomic theory of the firm, demand for labor can be insufficient (that is, it can remain at less than full-employment levels in the short run) because capital can be used to replace labor in the production process.

This is not necessarily contradictory. Up to now we have simply avoided exploring the linkage between our microeconomic and macroeconomic theories. In our discussion of the microeconomic theory of the firm we took as given the prices obtained for the firm's product and the money wage it paid its labor. But these can, and in the real world obviously do, fluctuate in the short run. Look at Figure 10.9 again. The labor market's equilibrium level of employment is determined by the supply and demand curves for labor. Each of these curves is a function of the real wage, and real wage is simply the ratio of money wage to price level. So price and wage levels, which may fluctuate in the short run, affect not only the labor market, but also the microeconomic behavior of firms hiring labor. In this next section we will elaborate on the classical model and then present an important Keynesian refinement to it. We will see that each model employs a different aggregate supply curve. An aggregate supply curve represents the relationship between national income and the price level. The difference between the classical and Keynesian models is that in the classical model money wages are assumed to be flexible upward and downward. That is, there is perfect competition in the labor market, with money wages free to fluctuate according to supply and demand for labor. The Keynesian model assumes the downward rigidity of money wages. That is, money wages are free to increase, but not to decline, so there is no longer perfect competition in the labor market. The reason for this assumption, as well as its validity, will be discussed later.

The Classical and Keynesian Aggregate Supply Schedules

The aggregate supply schedule can be derived with a four-quadrant diagram as shown in Figure 10.10, remembering that increases in variables are measured by movement away from the center, here represented by point Q. Quadrant C depicts the labor market. It is the same as Figure 10.9 except that now the real wage is on the horizontal axis and the level of employment is on the vertical axis. Quadrant D presents the aggregate production function, and is identical to Figure 10.1, except that national income is on the horizontal axis and the level of employment is on the vertical axis. Quadrant A

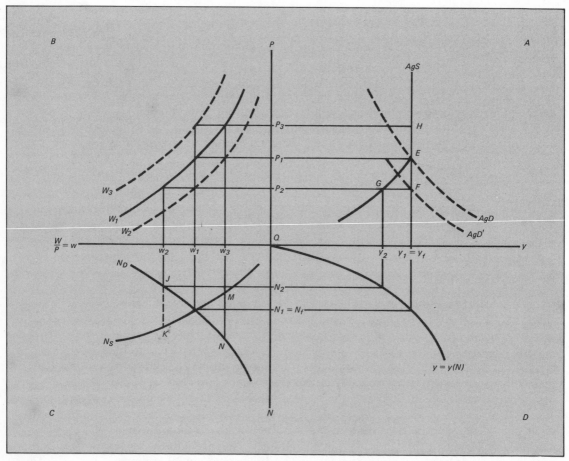

Figure 10.10 Aggregate supply with money wages rigid downward or freely flexible

presents the aggregate supply curve (which has not yet been derived). Quadrant B shows a series of constant money-wage curves shaped to indicate the inverse relationship between the price level and the real wage which is inherent in the definition:

$$\text{real wage} = \frac{W \text{ (money wage)}}{P \text{ (price level)}}$$

The curve says

$$\frac{W}{P} \cdot P = W$$

The classical economists assumed that full employment would always be assured by virtue of the flexibility of money wages. An excess supply of labor would result in a fall in money wages sufficient to reduce real wages to a level consistent with full employment, such as w_1 in Figure 10.10. Similarly, an excess demand for labor would raise money wages to a level consistent with w_1. In contrast, Keynes observed that money wages were slow to fall even in the presence of unemployment and an excess supply of labor due to workers refusing to accept work at lower rates of pay. Keynes thus introduced the assumption that money wages are rigid downward but flexible upward—that is, they will rise in the case of an excess demand for labor. Classical and Keynesian assumptions regarding the flexibility of money wages carry different implications for the shape of the aggregate supply schedule.

Start at point E in quadrant A of Figure 10.10, where $P = P_1$, and $W = W_1$, implying w_1 and $N_1 = N_f$, or full employment of labor, in quadrant C. This in turn implies full-employment output, $y_1 = y_f$, in quadrant D. Let aggregate demand fall.[2] If, for example, a gloomy business prognosis depresses investment expenditure by shifting the MEI schedule to the left, aggregate demand would fall at every price level so that the aggregate demand schedule would shift downward to AgD′. The price level would fall to P_2, due to the new intersection of aggregate demand and supply at point F. Under classical assumptions, if the fall in P raised real wages to w_2, the resulting excess supply of labor (JK in quadrant C) would quickly lower money wages to W_2 so that $w_2 = W_1/P_2$ would return to w_1, where

$$\frac{W_1}{P_1} = \frac{W_2}{P_2}$$

At w_1 full employment of labor will be restored and full-employment output, $y_1 = y_f$, will be maintained at P_2. On the other hand, if an increase in aggregate demand (not shown) were to increase the price level to P_3, the real wage $w_3 = W_1/P_3$ would rise to w_1 because the excess demand for labor (MN in quadrant C) would raise money wages to W_3. So

2. Aggregate demand is represented in Figure 10.10 by a broken line since we have not yet explained its derivation. We are mainly concerned with the shape of the aggregate supply schedule here and will derive an aggregate demand schedule in Chapter 11.

$$\frac{W_1}{P_1} = \frac{W_3}{P_3}$$

At w_1, given $N_1 = N_f$, full-employment output would be restored at $y_1 = y_f$. Thus, with money wages flexible both upward and downward, the classical aggregate supply schedule becomes a vertical line passing through points F, E, and H. This is evident from the fact that y remains at $y_1 = y_f$ for P_1, P_2, and P_3 as long as money wages are freely flexible in both directions.

If money wages are rigid downward, as Keynes suggested, however, the aggregate supply schedule will have a positively sloped portion like that shown running through point G to point E in quadrant A of Figure 10.10. To see how this arises, suppose P falls from P_1 to P_2. If wages remain rigid at W_1, real wages rise to $w_2 = W_1/P_2$. At a higher real wage, firms will hire less labor, so N_1 falls to N_2. Less labor produces less output, as indicated by the production function at y_2. The intersection of P_2 and y_2, as a result of downwardly rigid wages, is point G, a point on the Keynesian aggregate supply schedule. Since Keynes considered wages to be flexible upward (as indeed they are), if the price level rises, the result is identical to the classical case with W_3 implying $w_1 = W_3/P_3$ and N_1 implying $y_1 = y_f$. Therefore, the Keynesian aggregate supply schedule is defined by a positively sloped portion passing through point G to full employment at point E, and a vertical portion, identical to the classical case, above point E.

The Aggregate Production Function and the IS/LM Model

Although we shall return to the aggregate supply schedule, it is worthwhile at this point to tie up our discussion of the labor market and the production function with the IS/LM analysis. This is done in Figure 10.11,[3] where output is represented in current prices as $Y = Py$. The direct link between equilibrium in the labor market at point U, where $w_1 = W/P$ and $N_1 = N_f$, to full-employment income at $Y_1 = Y_f$ is evident by way of the production function. Looking at Figure 10.11, we can consider the relationship between changes in the labor market, on the production side of the model, and general equilibrium, as indicated by the IS and LM schedules on the demand side of the model. Problems can arise even when wages are fully flexible, as we shall see.

Assume that money wages are *not* rigid downward. Consider what would happen if there were a sudden influx of new workers into the economy that was already at full employment. The situation is depicted in Figure 10.11 by a shift from N_S to N_S'. Point Y_1 represents equilibrium national income at the original full-employment level. Point Y_2 is the new national

3. This figure is derived from R. A. Mundell, "An Exposition of Some Subtleties in the Keynesian System," *Weltwirtschaftliches Archiv* (December 1964), pp. 301–314.

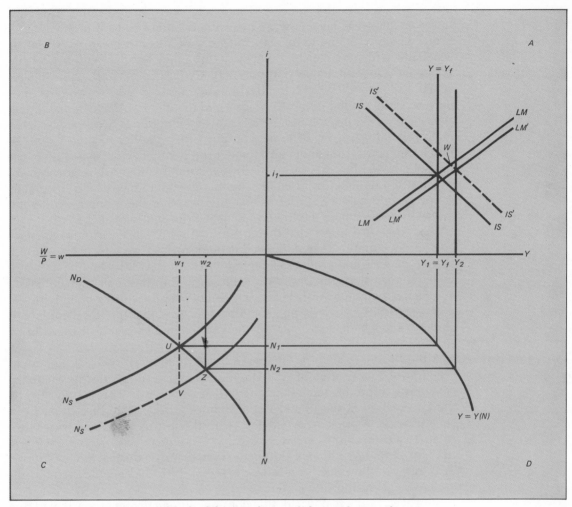

Figure 10.11 The IS/LM model, the labor market, and the production function

income that would be produced if all the new labor were employed with the labor market clearing at w_2N_2, or point Z. For purposes of simplicity, we assume also that there are no government expenditures or taxes at Y_1, given w_1, there would be an excess supply of labor equal to UV. According to our classical model (Figure 10.9), a fall in real wages should eliminate this. But real wages only fall as the result of a decline in money wages (with steady prices) or a rise in prices (with money wages fixed) or some combination of the two. In any case, money wages must fall more, proportionally (or rise less, proportionally), than prices if real wages are to fall.

In a perfectly competitive labor market, money wages are free to drop; "involuntarily unemployed" labor will bid down money wages. Initially prices will remain the same, and real wages will also decline. The new, lower money-wage level at w_2 reduces the marginal costs of production for firms, which will tend to increase output, and thus income, to Y_2. So far, so good. But will firms be able to sustain these new levels of output and employment? Only if the new output is actually purchased, or the new income actually spent, and here's the rub. Let us suppose for now that w_1 falls to w_2 only because of a fall in money wages, and that the price level remains constant. (As we shall see in Chapter 11, this assumption is necessary to determine the LM schedule.) The new output which implies income Y_2 will be purchased, and Y_2 therefore sustained, only if either the IS schedule or the LM schedule shifts. A shift of the IS schedule due to a rise in government expenditure or a shift in the LM schedule due to an increase in the money supply would suffice, but let us examine whether the economy will automatically settle where the IS and LM schedules intersect at Y_2.

The possibility arises that the larger quantity of labor will raise the marginal product of the heretofore fixed capital stock. As we saw in Chapter 7, a rise in the marginal product of capital will shift the MEI schedule outward, which in turn shifts the IS schedule outward. This development would then automatically tend to shift the IS schedule toward an intersection with LM at Y_2, say to IS'. There is no guarantee, however, that the IS schedule will shift far enough right to intersect the LM schedule at Y_2, at least within a reasonable period of time.

If the IS schedule shifts rightward but falls short of intersecting the LM schedule at Y_2, say at point W, a situation of excess supply results where the economy can produce more at Y_2 than it is able to sell. This is indicated by the intersection of the IS and LM schedules at a point to the left of Y_2. In such a case the price level may fall (with the impact upon real wages nullified by a continued downward flexibility of money wages). As we will see in Chapter 11, LM will then shift to the right, because the real money supply, M/P, rises as the price level falls. Such a shift, to LM', could restore full-employment equilibrium at Y_2.

However, in the real world, this does not automatically occur, in part due to institutionalized resistance to wage cuts. This means that in an excess supply of labor situation, such as UV at w_1 in quadrant C of Figure 10.11, full employment requires a cut in real wages, which can only take place through a price increase.

This problem may be eased somewhat by the existence of money illusion in the labor market. Keynes argued that because of money illusion, the supply of labor is a function not of real wages but of money wages, at least in the short run. According to Keynes, for a certain amount of time even if prices rise employed workers will continue to work just as hard (or just as many hours per week) at their customary money-wage rate. This will permit real wages to drop and additional workers to be employed. In such a case, what has really happened is that the labor supply curve has shifted downward and to the right, to S_N' in Figure 10.12, which represents quadrant C of Figure 10.11 under the assumption of money illusion.

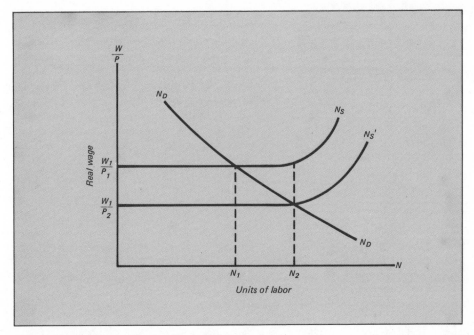

$$\frac{W}{P}$$

Figure 10.12 Money illusion in the labor market

The labor supply curves consist of a flat segment at the historically given money-wage rate, W_1, and a sloped tail section with the breaking point coming at full employment. Behind the shape of these curves is the assumption, essential to money illusion, that at a prevailing *money* wage (to which workers have become accustomed) any number of workers from none to all would be willing to work. That is, up to full employment (the breaking point at N_2), additional workers can be hired at the same money-wage rate. When full employment is reached, the curve bends up sharply since the bargaining position of the entire labor force then drastically changes. Workers would require higher wages to supply labor beyond N_2.

In Figure 10.12, at the original money-wage and price level, W_1/P_1, there is a certain amount of involuntary unemployment, $N_2 - N_1$, since labor offers N_2 but only N_1 is employed. But with the price level rising from P_1 to P_2, this unemployment is absorbed as workers, subject to money illusion, continue to offer N_2 at the new, lower real wage, W_1/P_1, at which firms desire to hire N_f, the full-employment quantity of labor. The labor supply curve has shifted without the labor force noticing it. To sweeten the pill, money wages may also rise, but not as fast as prices, so real wages still decline. The result is the same. This pattern (inflationary spirals) is increasingly observable in modern Western economies. The question is: What policy measure will raise the price level in order to shift the labor supply schedule to N_S'? In order to answer this question we must develop a model of aggregate demand and supply by which the price level can be determined.

Commentary: The Problem of Unemployment

The problem of unemployment has been a long-term one for the U.S. economy. In the past twenty years, the unemployment rate has fallen below the target 4 percent only once, in 1953, and the average rate since 1945 has been just over 4.5 percent.

Moreover, a certain level of unemployment may be built into the structure of the labor market; such structural unemployment cannot be dealt with by manipulating levels of output or demand. Even if we assume that aggregate supply and demand are balanced at full employment, it is possible that some workers may be temporarily out of work when demand shifts from the products of one industry to those of another. Consider the case of a depressed industry such as Appalachian coal mining. Thousands of unemployed workers are still living near the coal mines where they (or their fathers) used to work when the coal industry was booming. There may be jobs elsewhere in the country, but for personal reasons (including fear of discrimination against "hillbillies") families stay near the mines. Department of Labor studies indicate that nearly 20 percent of the population changed residence on an annual basis since the Second World War and that a majority of these moves were primarily job-related, reflecting individual's perceptions (correct or not) of labor-market demands in their home region and elsewhere. Age, however, is the single most important determinant of mobility, which declines sharply after twenty-five with the attendant rise in family formation, home ownership, and involvement in the community. Older workers, in particular, are often reluctant to move even to a good job they know of elsewhere because of moving costs and personal preferences.

In part this may be due to inadequate channels of information by which employees and employers can find each other. In the natural course of their lives, workers may seek new opportunities, and employers may discover that they need new, hard-to-find categories of workers. Each may search for the other (through newspaper ads, employment agencies, and other avenues), but the search will take time. Thus a certain level of frictional unemployment will be attributable to persons temporarily out of work while looking for jobs. This is sometimes called the "natural" unemployment rate, and it is considered responsible for the target rate of 4 percent.

Other factors have contributed as well, among them: shifts or cutbacks in government and private spending; industry relocation to new geographic areas; changes in international competitive conditions; and the sheer rapidity of technological change (and sometimes the lack of it) in a fast-changing global economy.

Shifts in the level and pattern of government military and space outlays, for example, are estimated to have affected about 2 million jobs between 1968 and 1971. Over the past twenty years, lower labor costs, natural regional advantages, state and local tax and other development incentives have all figured heavily in new plant-location decisions and in movement of manufacturing and assembly operations from one region to another.

Sharp increases in imports of high-style, low-priced footwear and of synthetic textiles and apparel helped precipitate the closing of some smaller domestic factories between 1966 and 1971, due in part to failure to anticipate competition and changing consumer tastes, in part to undercapitalization which precluded a shift into new lines. Decisions by U.S.-based multinational companies to manufacture or assemble components or equipment abroad for sale in the U.S. market also led to some domestic plant shutdowns—conspicuously so in the consumer electronics field. A few recent paper and chemical plant closings have stemmed from inability of firms to comply at "reasonable" cost with antipollution or other environmental regulations.

Another form of structural unemployment occurs when skills that workers have learned are no longer in demand. Demand for blacksmiths, for example, fell much faster than the rate at which trained blacksmiths died off after the automobile was invented. Each of these developments has, temporarily at least, produced regional or local "pockets" of high unemployment, despite ample growth in alternate job opportunities at other locations or in other segments of the economy.

Another structural aspect is the changing composition of the labor force over the past ten years. More teenagers, women, and minorities are seeking jobs now than ever before. In 1961, the participation rate for teenagers in the work force was 47 percent; in 1971, it was 52 percent. For women the growth rate grew from 38.1 percent to 43.9 percent in the same period. And unemployment rates for these groups are higher than for adult white males: in 1971, adult white male unemployment was 4.4 percent against 5.7 percent for women, 9.9 percent for nonwhites, and 16.9 percent for teenagers of both sexes. Only half of the unemployed individuals in 1971 were unemployed because they had lost their jobs; the remainder had quit, recently entered the job market, or never worked before.[2]

Thus the most accurate picture of unemployment in the United States today is not one in which there is a shortage of jobs, but rather one in which a variety of obstacles prevent individuals from getting and keeping the kinds of jobs they want—or which the economy can offer. One way to reduce unemployment due to immobility and lack of information is to combat it with concerted state-financed efforts, as is done in Norway and Sweden. In Sweden, for example, the government not only provides a centralized employment exchange to shorten searches for new jobs but requires employers to give two to six-months' advance warnings of perspective mass layoffs to the state and the union, and one to

six months' notice of individual dismissal to employees, the latter varying with age. Displaced workers receive free training or retraining; liberal compensation, rent, and travel allowances during the training period; and relocation allowances or compensation for travel to jobs outside the home district. The state will also purchase owner-occupied dwellings if a move is made to a new area.

In the United States a number of states have recently instituted free worker-training programs, most notably Alabama, which according to a report in The Wall Street Journal trained 8,000 workers in new specialized plants in the first two years of operation. The program has not only helped to attract specialized new industry to the state, but also cut its unemployment outlays. Other states have devised less direct incentives. Massachusetts, for example, offers a tax credit to industries for each employee hired from welfare rolls. At the federal level, the Comprehensive Employment and Training Act of 1973 provides for the development of a "comprehensive system of labor-market information" including a computerized job-data bank. It provides payment of usual unemployment compensation (and a small allowance for dependents) during the training period. Relocation and home purchase allowances, however, have not been provided, nor is there provision for a national exchange to facilitate interregional labor transfers.

These measures offer an auspicious beginning to minimizing structural unemployment problems; others which certainly could be tried include travel, relocation, and home purchase arrangements to induce workers to accept jobs outside their home areas; early retirement under Social Security for older workers; amendment of tax laws to provide more liberal deductions for moving expenses and to permit deduction of education costs that lead to new job skills; more affirmative programs in education, job discrimination, and child care facilities.

Prices and Aggregate Demand

We have seen that the price level is an important factor underlying aggregate supply; it has an equally important role in the modern theory of aggregate demand both directly and via the mechanism of the money market. As we suggested in connection with the shift of LM in response to price level changes in Figure 10.11, the role played by prices in affecting aggregate demand is crucial in rescuing the economy from a potential underemployment situation. Keynes, however, was skeptical about the workability of wage and price flexibility as a means to rescue the economy from an underemployment equilibrium.

Keynes discussed the suggestion, made by some economists, that reducing money wages might be an antidote for economic depression via resulting increases in aggregate demand. The argument for reduced money wages assumes that firms would hire more labor at lower wages because of lower costs and that this would induce greater output. The counterargument is that, while this might work for a single firm or industry, if it happened throughout the entire economy the workers with reduced money wages, who are also consumers, would be unable to purchase the increased output, so the price level would have to decline as well. There would be lower wages and prices again, but no net increase in output and, therefore, no improvement in the level of employment.

Keynes argued that such price-level changes would have no appreciable *direct* effect on aggregate demand, because they would not change the levels of consumption or investment that underlie aggregate demand. If incomes and prices fell proportionally (for example, if they were both halved), Keynes argued that consumers would make the same decisions, since real purchasing power is what matters to them. Likewise, government expenditures and investment decisions would not change. So the commodity market would not be affected by changes in the price level, and the location of the IS curve would not change.

Keynes did recognize, however, that the money market would be affected by a price-level change in a way that indirectly affects aggregate demand. A lower price level would lead to an increase in the value of real money balances held. That is, a given quantity of money balances would be worth twice as much if all prices are cut in half. Therefore, a fall in the general price level increases the real money supply.

The effect of a lower price level on the real money supply and thereby on the LM schedule is shown in Figure 10.13. Suppose that initially the price level is at 1 with a money supply of 200 units. Since the price level, P, represents the price of a unit of output or goods in terms of money, 1/P represents the price of a unit of money in terms of goods. Therefore the "real" or goods value of money is given by

$$M \cdot \frac{1}{P} = \frac{M}{P} \tag{10.8}$$

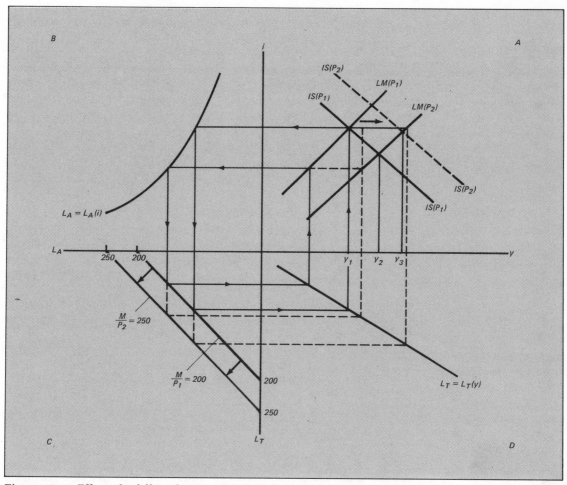

Figure 10.13 Effect of a fall in the price level on the real money supply and the LM schedule

If P falls from 1 to, say, .8, the real supply of money rises from 200/1 to 200/.80 = 250. The effect on real money balances is identical to what it would be if M rose by 50, holding P constant, which is precisely the way in which LM has been shifted in previous discussions. The result of a fall in P is an outward shift of $LM(P_1)$ to $LM(P_2)$ as shown in Figure 10.13. A different LM schedule exists for every price level.

The outward shift in LM caused by a fall in the price level results in an increase in aggregate demand. The IS schedule is included in quadrant A as a reminder that as the real money supply expands, an excess supply of money results. Keynes, of course, recognized that, consistent with his view of close substitutability between money and bonds, the excess supply of money would create an excess demand for bonds. As a result, bond prices would be bid up or, equivalently, the interest rate would fall, leading to an increase in investment which represents an increase in aggregate demand. This positive but indirect impact upon aggregate demand arising from a lower price level is known as the **Keynes effect.**[4] It should be emphasized that while Keynes himself saw this as a logical possibility that could work to increase aggregate demand in an unemployment situation, he argued against a policy of relying on a deflationary solution to unemployment on grounds of social justice and social expediency. He pointed out that such an effect would be too slow to work to relieve chronic unemployment. Furthermore, in the event of a liquidity trap the LM schedule would not be shifted by a lower price level over the liquidity trap range. And during a depression, as we have suggested in the discussion of Figure 10.8, redundant capital might exist so that investment would not respond, at least in the short run, to a lower rate of interest.

The Keynes effect is not the only possible interpretation of the impact of changes in the price level upon aggregate demand. A number of economists, the most frequently cited of whom is A. C. Pigou,[5] have argued that price-level changes could provide an antidote for unemployment by way of a direct effect on expenditure which could bypass the difficulties implied by a liquidity trap or unresponsiveness of investment to the interest rate. Pigou argued that since cash and bonds increase in value if price levels drop, a consumer who already has sizable holdings in cash and bonds will realize an increase in the real balance (wealth) held, given a fall in the price level. This result is known as the **Pigou effect,** or **real-balance effect.** Pigou further argued that this will lead some consumers to allocate an increased portion of their income to consumption, since now, with a lower price level, they are already richer (in real terms) than they previously had expected to be (before the price level dropped) and can afford to spend more on consumption and less on saving. Looking again at the consumption function, $C = a + bY$, or the savings function, $S = -a + (1 - b)Y$, the value of a (the portion of consumption savings not related to income) is influenced by the real-balance effect. As we saw in Chapters 4 and 5, a shift in a has the same multiplier effect as a shift in I or G. Therefore, the IS schedule shifts as a changes in response to the real-balance effect. If the price level falls, a rises, and $IS(P_1)$ shifts to $IS(P_2)$ in Figure 10.13. This describes a direct increase in aggregate demand resulting from the impact upon real balances of a lower price level.

The results of our discussion regarding the impact of the price level upon aggregate demand are presented in Figure 10.14, which we will examine in

4. For a fuller discussion of the Keynes effect and for the most competent discussion of the economics of Keynes, his disciples, and critics, see Axel Leijonhufvud, *On Keynesian Economics and the Economics of Keynes* (New York: Oxford University Press, 1968).

5. A. C. Pigou, "The Classical Stationary State," *Economic Journal* 53 (December 1943): 343–351, and "Economic Progress in a Stable Environment," *Econometrica* 14 (August 1947): 180–188.

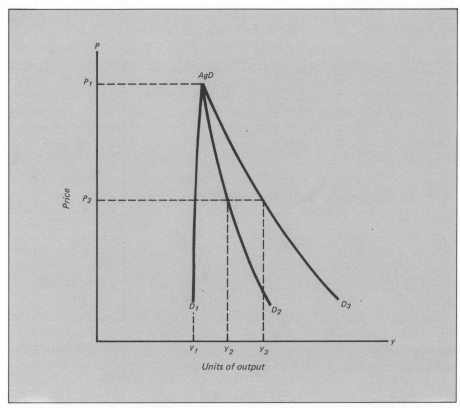

Figure 10.14 Three views of the impact of price level changes on aggregate demand

connection with Figure 10.13. Line D_1 describes the situation where no Keynes effect occurs, due for example to a liquidity trap or to the unresponsiveness of investment to the interest rate. In this case either the LM schedule will not be shifted by an increase in real balances or the IS schedule will be vertical to indicate the unresponsiveness of investment to the interest rate. Line D_1 may also be viewed as a short-run aggregate demand schedule where the Keynes effect is seen to operate. Notice that a fall in the price level from P_1 to P_2 results in demand at Y_2, as indicated by the shift from LM(P_1) to LM(P_2) in Figure 10.13. Finally, line D_3 represents the combined impact of the Keynes effect and the real-balance effect. The fall in the price level from P_1 to P_2 results in demand at Y_3, as indicated by the combined shifts of LM(P_1) to LM(P_2) and IS(P_1) to IS(P_2) in Figure 10.13.

Returning to the original question of whether money wage cuts and a resulting fall in the price level can eventually restore full employment, we have identified two mechanisms, the indirect Keynes effect and the direct Pigou effect, or real-balance effect, which operate to restore full employment by way of an increase in demand. The objections to relying on the real-balance effect have already been alluded to with regard to the Keynes effect: the price-level cuts might have to be large, and the time required for them to occur and have an effect could be extremely long. If they had to be repeated, consumer purchasing and firm investment decisions might be deferred in the speculative hope of further price-level drops. Institutionalized downward wage rigidity has already been discussed as an impediment to implementing such a policy. Deflationary pressure is operative in restoring equilibrium in theory, but in practice it may be too slow to operate where the policy goal is year-to-year full employment or where wage rigidity is prevalent.

Shifts in Aggregate Supply and Demand— Changes in the Price Level

We can now consider aggregate supply and demand together and examine the causes of related changes in the price level. Look at Figure 10.15, which combines quadrant A of Figure 10.10 with an aggregate supply curve consistent with the assumption of wage rigidity, and the aggregate demand curve D_3 from Figure 10.14, which includes both the Keynes effect and the real-balance effect. The aggregate demand curve represents the amount of national income that is purchased at each price level. The intersection of the aggregate demand curve with the aggregate supply curve determines the equilibrium national income and the price level at a particular point in time. Since the lower portion of the aggregate supply curve is positively sloped and the upper portion of the aggregate supply curve is vertical, an increase in demand may lead to an increase in the level of income and the price level, or it may simply lead to an increase in the price level with no increase in real national income.

Assume that the economy is initially in a recession at output level y_1 and price level P_1; y_f represents the full-employment level of national income, given AgS_1. In this situation any increase in demand (a shift of the aggregate demand curve to AgD_2) would lead to a price-level increase to P_2. This would be the full-employment equilibrium at the lowest possible price level. Below that price level there would be unemployment. Above it the level of output cannot increase. If aggregate demand should increase again (with the curve shifting to AgD_3), the price level would increase to P_3, but the real level of output (and employment) would remain at y_f. If this situation (excess aggregate demand) were to persist, continued price increases, or inflation, would be the result. If the new price level, P_3, were to persist long enough, upward pressure on money wages (caused by the excessive demand that pushed prices up to P_3) would raise money wages enough to restore the fixed equilibrium ratio of money wages to price level which is called the real wage. Recall from Figure 10.10 that there is only one long-run real-wage level that is consistent with full employment and equilibrium in the labor market. The effect of money illusion may last a while, but sooner or later workers will insist that their wages be brought in line with price increases. At this point the curved section of the aggregate supply curve will shift up to P_3 (as shown in Figure 10.15 by the broken curve). Now if there should be a decline in aggregate demand to AgD_2, not only will there be a decrease in the price level (though not all the way to P_2), but some unemployment will also appear. So there is a built-in inflationary ratchet in this model. When demand is insufficient, increases in demand risk causing inflation if they overshoot their mark. On the other hand, if demand is considered excessive but the economy has already adjusted to the new price level (through a shift in the aggregate supply curve), any reduction in demand will lead to recession, accompanied by only a small reduction in the price level.

The twin problems of unemployment and inflation seem to be built into our relatively sophisticated and realistic macroeconomic model. Is there any way, within this model, to avoid sitting on the horns of this unemployment-inflation dilemma? Look at Figure 10.15 again. At the initial price level, P_1, and with the initial aggregate demand curve, AgD_1, and aggregate supply curve, AgS_1, the national income generated at y_1 was at a level that implied unemployment. We have assumed a fixed aggregate production function and a fixed money-wage rate. But if the productivity of labor could be increased, then a new aggregate production function would result. This could permit the full-employment aggregate supply function to shift to the right, say to

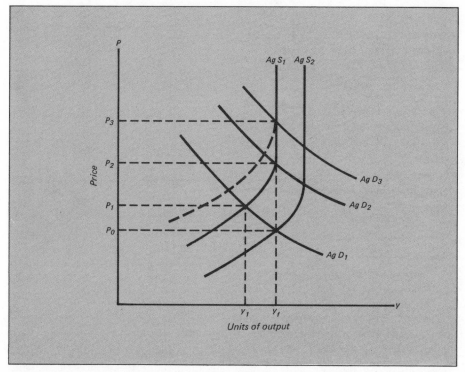

Figure 10.15 Aggregate supply and demand: wages rigid upward and downward

AgS_2. That would allow a full-employment level of real income to be attained at y_f without a price increase. In fact Figure 10.15 shows the price level decreasing to P_0 as a result of the aggregate supply curve shifting to the right. Employment would increase because, the marginal physical productivity of labor having increased, firms would demand more labor at every real wage to maximize profits while increasing output.

The impact on aggregate supply of an increase in labor productivity which shifts the firm's demand for labor outward at each real wage can be determined from Figure 10.10, reproduced here as Figure 10.16. In quadrant A, the aggregate supply schedule AgS is derived from N_D and therefore N_1 and N_2 in quadrant C, and Y_1 and Y_2 in quadrant D, for price levels P_1, P_2, and P_3. If an increase in the productivity of labor results in N_D' as in Figure 10.16, AgS' can be derived analogously to AgS. The new full-employment position

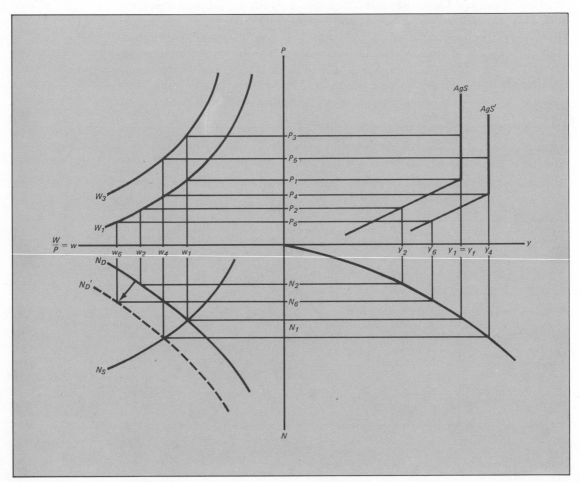

Figure 10.16 An outward shift in aggregate supply due to an increase in labor productivity

is $P_4 y_4$. If P_4 rises to P_5, W rises to W_3 so real wages stay at w_4 and y is unaffected. If P_4 falls to P_6, real wages rise to w_6, so y falls to y_6. Thus, a labor productivity increase may act as a damper on inflationary pressures and may reduce the burden the Keynesian model places on government expenditures (injections of demand) to assure full employment. Of course, if labor productivity should decline, the aggregate supply curve would shift upward and to the left, causing both higher prices *and* unemployment. To combat this there then might have to be Keynesian-type increases in demand to restore full employment, but this would be at even higher price levels.

Whereas our previous treatment of wage and price levels (where demand for labor is a function of real wages) assumed a fixed labor productivity, we now see that if wages increase only as much as labor productivity does, a steady price level and level of employment can be maintained. The opposite side of this coin is that whereas inflationary pressures can be dampened if labor productivity increases (relative to wages), such pressures can also be encouraged if labor productivity fails to increase as much as wages do. This analysis treats price rises from two distinct points of view. One cause is excessive demand, with the aggregate demand curve shifting too far to the right (as in Figure 10.15), leading to **demand-pull increases.** Over time, this type of shift will cause inflation in the model once full employment has been reached. The other point of view attributes price rises to shifts in the aggregate supply function due to wage levels that rise faster than labor productivity. In such situations, stable price levels cannot be maintained along with full employment, so prices have to rise along with wages. Whenever increased prices are attributed to rising costs of firms, which shift the aggregate supply curve, economists call this **cost-push increases.** If wages increase more than labor productivity, this is a special case of cost-push increases known as **wage-push increases.** Like demand-pull increases, over time these price-level changes lead to inflation.

Let us consider cost-push price rises more closely. Total costs, to a firm, reflect the cost of all factors of production, especially labor and capital. To increase production and profits (at a given price level), a firm must increase labor productivity. This is done by increasing the amount of capital that the firm's workers use in production. The cost of capital must also be covered, however, so with increased labor productivity the earnings of non-labor factors (especially capital) must also increase proportionally if the firm is to maximize profits.

Since productivity gains vary greatly from industry to industry and firm to firm, some firms (and industries) will have greater productivity gains (over time) than the national average, and others will have smaller gains. To keep prices stable (on the average for the whole economy) a policy of wage-price guidelines set by the government is one tactic to stem inflation while maintaining full employment. Under such guidelines, firms (or industries) with greater-than-average productivity increases that grant wage increases equal to the national average productivity increase (a percentage calculated by the government and set forth in its guidelines) are required to reduce prices. Firms with lower-than-average productivity increases are permitted to increase prices to compensate for any wage increases granted that are in excess of their own productivity increases. Thus, overall price stability can be maintained while wages (on the average) increase along with labor productivity.

By the yardstick of a national wage-price guideline, we can view cost-push increases as the result of violations either by labor or by firms. If labor, through union power, demands and is able to obtain wage increases that exceed productivity increases, we have the wage-push inflation mentioned above. Likewise, if firms, seeking to increase profits, insist on raising prices beyond the amount provided for in the guidelines, or fail to lower prices when productivity increases exceed wage increases, we have **profit-push increases.** This latter case is possible, of course, only in monopolistic or oligopolistic industries, where firms are able to influence their prices (as they cannot do in industries where perfect competition exists). But major sectors of the economy are dominated by firms that can to some extent "administer" prices (energy, steel, autos, and communications are good examples), so profit-push inflation is a potential problem posed by the concentration of economic power on the side of business, just as wage-push inflation is a problem posed by the concentration of economic power in labor unions.

Most discussions of cost-push inflation blame labor unions more than they do oligopolistic or monopolistic firms. This is because whereas firms must fear that excessive price increases will lead to a decrease in sales (and therefore, perhaps, profits), labor union officials care mainly about the well-being of their already-enrolled rank-and-file members. They would like as large wage increases as possible (up to the point where they cause layoffs), so they make demands that violate the wage-price guidelines. If this is done throughout an industry or in the whole economy, such wage settlements cause wage-push inflation over time. Wage increases for unionized workers may also spill over and lead to wage increases for nonunion labor. Nonunion firms and industries may have to pay workers more to prevent them from flocking to unionized ones or forming their own unions. So unionization and the resulting labor demands are the major causes of cost-push inflation, even though firms may be prompt to respond to wage increases by raising prices and passing on the burden to the economy as a whole (in the form of inflation), rather than absorbing a reduction in profits.

Demand-pull price rises are more likely to continue indefinitely (and therefore lead to inflation rather than one-time price increases) if aggregate demand continues to increase as fast as prices rise. But for this process to continue the money supply must expand. Otherwise, the increased prices will reduce the real money supply and lower aggregate demand by way of the Keynes effect and the real-balance effect. On the other hand, to prevent inflation by limiting the growth of the money supply is to risk unemployment. And full employment with inflation may be more acceptable, politically, than stable prices and high unemployment. This possible trade-off between unemployment and inflation will be examined more carefully in Chapter 16.

This analysis of the labor market and how it affects the aggregate supply and demand curves adds sophistication and completeness to our macro-economic model at the same time that it raises new problems. Of particular concern is the question of whether or not the economy can automatically return to full employment once a full-employment equilibrium has been disturbed by a sharp exogenous change, such as a drop in private invest-ment. In the next chapter we will return to the IS/LM equilibrium model and reconsider it in the light of our new assumptions about the labor market, while permitting the price level to fluctuate. This analysis will provide some answers about the theoretical ability of the economy to automatically obtain full-employment equilibrium.

Questions and Exercises

1. Assume that a firm has experienced a drop in the price received for its product by 10 percent. What actions would you predict in the short run? Illustrate the adjustments on the isoquants for labor and capital.
2. With selective price and wage controls in the early 1970s, it might be argued that for those firms under controls, the effects would be the same as if they had suffered a decline in the price for their products. What are those effects? Agree or disagree? Why?
3. By 1974, the general price level was rising significantly faster than wages. What would be the effect on employment in the presence of money illusion? No money illusion?
4. This chapter has reviewed an example of what might happen in an economy if there is an increase in the supply of labor. Again assume an economy without government. Would the same reasoning apply if the economy were to lose a portion of its labor force? Why or why not? Where would the economy tend to settle if investment did not change?
5. Could it be argued that a drop in the general price level tends to benefit the rich? Why or why not?
6. Why did Keynes argue that the drop in prices necessary to substantially affect aggregate demand might have to be enormous? How about the elasticity of de-mand for money? The elasticity of investment with respect to the interest rate?
7. Could you argue that it would be fruitless to try to return price levels to some previous lower levels? Why or why not?
8. One criticism of the wage-price guideposts is that wage rates relative to one another throughout the economy would be fixed, thus fixing any inequities that exist at the starting point. Agree or disagree? Why?
9. Some critics of the so-called energy industries have argued that these industries have contributed to a type of profit-push inflation. Under what circumstances could this view be defended?
10. Throughout the early 1970s interest rates marched continually upward with very few and only minor reverses. Do these increases provide some evidence for the belief that IS and LM schedules may have been shifting to the right over time? Why or why not?

ork Times

Think about it for a minute — one thing you'll have to admit right off is that the celebration of the body and its pleasures ... consume much fuel. Just suppose ...

Industrial Output Down 0.5% in March, Drop Smallest of Any in 4-Month Slide

...can population ... stay-at-home hedonism or ...

Hugh He... ...-room beds that revolve at the push of a button, quadraphonic stereo and Aegean cruises). The energy-demand curve would flatten out in no time.

And as implausible as it may sound, the theory of energy conservation through hedonism is no joke. It has been seriously suggested as one of the alternate future paths that would lead American society away from the energy-intensive culture we live in today. And the theory's not to be dismissed lightly, either, because it was suggested by a serious and scholarly man —Amitai W. Etzioni, the author and Columbia University professor of sociology.

Mr. Etzioni presented his provocative view of "The Conserving Society" to a group of ... government offic... cians who baronial s... cious Ha... atop a forested mountain... which now is used by Columbia as a seminar center. The professor's purpose wasn't to predict where the energy crisis will lead us ("only fakirs predict the future") but to examine the profound questions the crisis poses and to sketch out some possible alternative answers.

"What is at stake is the central project of our society," Mr. Etzioni told the group. And what is the central project? Well, if a lunar tribe sent a spaceship down to earth to ... up to, the ...oonmen would ... that the central project of U.S. society seems to be ...

The great oil squeeze has put unemployment back in the news again. Layoff stories have splashed into the headlines for weeks now. And each one has been dramatically reported in TV newscasts. Automobile makers, airlines, hotel and motel operators, retail gasoline distributors have been especially hard hit. Other areas of the economy have been affected to a small degree. And there are probably more layoffs to come. Thus an in-perspective look at justiety is where we stand on the employment front may be in order.

The latest official tally places the unemployment "rate" at 5.2% of the labor force. It was in the 5% zone all through the first four months of last year but slipped as low as 4.6% last fall.

But the unemployment rate figure and the layoffs get far more attention than the hirings by big and little businesses all over the country. While they don't make the headlines, the hirings are going on all the time. And in this decade they have built up to an enormous army of nearly 86 million gainfully employed people.

The table below, using Department of Labor figures, traces the great growth in the total number of civilians at work just since 1970. Figures through 1973 are yearly averages.

---

goals so that we can fill our gas tanks, vacation homes and two-car garages.

History has never known another central project so demanding of energy resources. "The main question for the future," says the Columbia professor, "is whether we will go on with the production-... project ... ...gists see an inter... ...-slo... ...le, ...n greater emhas an opposite vision... ...drive for more production, a waning of the appetite for consumption, both stemming

---

The central project of U.S. society seems to be the production of resources during working-hours and the consumption and destruction of them in leisure time.

---

from what he calls "a thinning out of the commitment to our central project."

...scholar isn't thinking about hippies ... talks of a thinning significant, how... stops taking home a briefcase full ... on weekends, or the worker who decides to take early retirement at age 62. These gradually-accumulating signs of "people losing their commitment to working hard and consuming hard" are the significant indicators of change, he believes.

These straws in the wind make few headlines. But societies rarely change directions like a band on a football field, doing an about face and marching off to a new tune. A switch away from our central project could result, Mr. Etzioni contends, through just such a gradual and subtle erosion of commitment to production and consumption.

If that happens, what would Am... pursue as their new central proj... Etzioni ... ...nativ... ...thinks. Loss of commitment production would lead to "the celebra... of the body." A noticeable minority of Americans already is pursuing this proj... ...havi... ...rd—at ...nistic v... But th... bilized 4 ... that ...barbarian ...—A re... ...stic pu... ...und y... Furth... year's 0... more i... ...lan o... ...age ...pt. ...ast O...

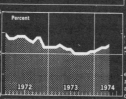

Jobless Married Men

Percent

1972 1973 1974

UNEMPLOYMENT —among married... from 2.4% the preceding month, the Labor Department reports.

This is the background of where we stand ... to now. And it is clear that if there is any ...ntraction in overall employment ahead, it will certainly be from a very high level. The ...

---

good vase that satisfied you personally.
—Sensitivity-group society. In this kind of central project, the important pursuit in life would be to deeply understand ourselves and others and to strive for empathy. "There already are several million Americans who make this their central project," says Mr. Etzioni. The rise of encounter groups, sensitivity training and ... empathy efforts give evidence of ... leanings in this direction.

...olitical society. This alternative ... find a society organized around the ... of public affairs and the improvement of government. The focus probably wouldn't be big politics, but small politics —community groups, school boards, neighborhood uplift. The millions of people who spend their evenings and weekends on such pursuits would make them their first priority.

An Unavoidable Distraction

What, all the alternatives have in common, the professor notes, is a downgrading of producing and consuming. Surely, even the hedonists, artisans, sensitivity-groupers and small-bore politicians would have to produce and consume to some extent. But this wouldn't be their whole life. It would be just an unavoidable distraction, to be limited to a bare minimum while the new central project takes precedance.

...Columbia sociologist isn't ... ...natives ... erosion of ... spending ethic.

Whether this erosion will broaden out into a fundamental change is essentially unpredictable, because this will depend on an accumulation of millions upon millions of individual decisions — much like the course of population growth. But zero energy growth doesn't seem to be any less plausible a notion than did zero population growth a few years ago, and today there is evidence that millions upon millions of individual decisions by Americans ... ...have pointed th... ...s a possible answer to the energy crisis doesn't seem so silly. In fact, some of the more conventional wisdom seems sillier. The Arden House conferees were deluged with fancy econometric projections of future energy demand, oil industry capital needs, synthetic fuel proand the like—all of which relied on the assumption that the future ...bon' copy of the past, but in tripli...

...sillier to think that 6% of the people can indefinitely go on con... a third of its energy and other re... than to think that millions upon ... of Americans will find ways to ...om the oil squeeze, home building has been in steep slide since the early part of last year.

If all this adds up to the beginning of a re... ...ession—as it may—we can look for some guidnce to what happened to total employment ... ...ast recessions. There have been five slow ...owns in the past quarter century officially ...classified as recessions. And their impact on ...Apri...total employment was less than some think. Here's what happened. Labor Department figures trace declines in total civilian employment from the start to the end of each slump. Figures represent thousands.

Employment and Recessions

Recession	Start	End	Down
1948-49	58,417	57,269	1,148

Rise of $1 Billion In Jobless Benefits Proposed by Nixon

Plan Would Help Those Who Used Up Aid, Extend It to Some Not Currently Eligible

By a WALL STREET JOURNAL Staff Reporter

WASHINGTON—The Nixon administration proposed new unemployment benefits for workers who have exhausted theirs and for many who aren't currently eligible.

The program would add $1 billion to federal jobless benefits in the fiscal year that starts July 1, Labor Department officials estimate. It would end when the fiscal year did, on June 30, 1975.

The new program seeks to head off efforts in Congress to enact special benefits for workers who lose their jobs due to the energy crisis. The pending emergency energy conservation bill, for instance, would provide benefits for up to a year for energy-related joblessness.

Labor Secretary Peter Brennan stressed that the Nixon administration's proposal would ...orker who had exhausted other un... ...would "make it un... ...cial legislation de... ...of workers ...harmed ...

Most stat... ...up to 26 weeks of unemployment benefit... ...kers. In addition, a federal-state program of extended benefits provides another 13 weeks of payment when states meet certain "trigger" points. Extended benefits currently are being paid in Massachusetts, Rhode Island and Washington State, and New York State likely will begin ... payments the week of Feb. 24, the Labor ...artment officials say.

...nder the new plan, the trigger points would be less stringent, and, localities as well as states could qualify.

Current Triggers

Currently, an extra 13 weeks of payments are triggered by one of two circumstances. First, joblessness among those covered by unemployment compensation must be 4½% or more nationally for three months. Or second, this "insured" unemployment rate in a particular state must average 4% or more for any 13-week period and must also exceed 120% of the average rate over the like period in the two previous years. (Congress has waived the 120% rule for the 1974 first quarter.)

States with pre... ...lessness have joi... meet, so the new p... ...Instead of a natio... ...paid whe... ...more in a... ...for the m... ...irement ...le 13-we... ...Sept. 30, ...d to refle...

...d unempl... ...percentag... ...al unemp... ...sured une... ...ied Jan. 1... ...rate wa... ...sis. While

Business Sales and Inventories
Revised series, seasonally adjusted.

Billions of dollars

$235
230
225
220 Inventories
215
210
205
200
195

$165 Billions of dollars

Full-Employment Equilibrium

11

The IS/LM model developed in Chapter 9 enables us to consider the notion of general, or simultaneous, equilibrium in the commodity and money markets; equilibrium in the labor market and determination of real output have been examined in Chapter 10. This chapter will combine these models into an IS/LM model that is extended to identify full-employment general equilibrium in the commodity and money markets. Operationally, the general equilibrium we will develop here requires that the IS and LM schedules intersect at a level of income (output) at which the labor force is fully employed.

We cannot extend the IS/LM model developed in Chapter 9 by simply appending a full-employment level of income onto it, because of the importance of an additional variable—the price level. The price level was taken to be fixed in the simple IS/LM model, but we saw in the discussion of the labor market that the price level is crucial in the determination of aggregate supply and demand. With rigid money wages, real wages fall as the price level rises. More labor is hired at a lower real wage, and output rises until "capacity" is reached at the level of output implied by full employment of the labor force. (See Figure 10.10) At the capacity level of output, wages and prices are assumed to rise together if aggregate demand is increased. Therefore, since the price level varies in the analysis of full-employment output and the labor market, before we can extend the IS/LM model we must first look at the impact of price-level changes on the IS and LM schedules.

It is important to note that the price-level changes considered here are assumed to be one-shot events; current price changes are assumed not to generate any expectations regarding future price behavior, and therefore do not describe inflation, which is a rate of change of prices occurring over time. This assumption is necessary because the extended IS/LM model is a comparative statics apparatus; it cannot consider the behavior over time of variables like the price level. Note also that when prices enter into a model the distinction between **real variables,** expressed in terms of physical or commodity units, and **nominal variables,** expressed in terms of money, becomes very important. For example, in considering income or output when the price level was fixed, there was no need to distinguish between a change in real income or output, y, and nominal income or output, Y, since where

$$Y = Py$$

$$\Delta Y = P\Delta y$$

The change in nominal income or output, ΔY, is identical to the change in real income or output, Δy, evaluated at a constant price, P. In order to incorporate a flexible price level into our model, however, we must make this distinction: all variables will be expressed in real terms, which accounts for the impact of changes in the price level. Thus real output, y, is equal to nominal income or output divided by the price level

$$y = \frac{Y}{P}$$

Impact of Price-Level Changes upon IS and LM

If price-level changes are of the one-shot variety, we can also assume at this stage that the IS schedule does not change in response to price-level changes in the absence of the real-balance effect. We saw in Chapter 10 that the real-balance effect, or the Pigou effect, refers to the impact on expenditure (or savings) arising from changes in the real value of the money stock. As the price level falls, real balances are worth more in terms of what they can buy; money holders feel better off and consequently spend more at each level of real income.

We will consider the result of a change in expenditure brought about by the real-balance effect later in this chapter. Leaving this aside for now, the IS schedule describes a set of values of real incomes and interest rates at which real savings equals real investment or, if a government sector is included, real savings plus real taxes equals real investment plus real government expenditure. Both sides of the equation $(S + T = I + G)$ may be put into real terms by dividing by the price level. Thus

$$\frac{S}{P} + \frac{T}{P} = \frac{I}{P} + \frac{G}{P} \tag{11.1}$$

Writing equation (11.1) in functional form with lowercase letters employed to indicate real variables gives

$$s(y) + t(y) = n(i) + g \tag{11.2}$$

Lowercase terms in this equation stand for nominal variables expressed in real terms, and n stands for real investment, or I/P, in order to avoid confusion with lowercase i, which represents the interest rate. Equation (11.2) states that real savings, s, which is some function of real income, y, plus real taxes, t, which is some function of real income, y, equals real investment, n, which is some function of the interest rate, i, plus real government expenditure, g.

When the price level was taken to be fixed, the LM schedule indicated a set of values of income and interest rates where money demand equaled money supply. With a fixed price level, there was no need to distinguish real money demand, real income, and real money supply from the nominal values of these concepts. When the distinction between real and nominal values in the monetary sector is made, the most obvious change is in the inverse relationship between the real money supply, M/P, and the price level. This is perhaps better understood by recalling that

$$\frac{M}{P} = M \cdot \frac{1}{P}$$

where M is the number of units of money, and P is the price of a commodity unit in terms of money. Therefore, 1/P is the price of a unit of money in terms of commodity units. Multiplying M by the price of money in terms of commodities gives M/P, the "real" (or commodity) value of money balances. Since the real value of the money supply moves inversely with the price level, there exists a different LM schedule in real terms for every price level. The exact impact of price-level changes on the LM schedule is demonstrated in Figure 11.1.

Suppose the LM schedule is derived for a real money supply of $250 billion (as in Chapter 9) where the price level is 1. This gives $LM(P_1)$ in quadrant D of Figure 11.1. If P_1 rises to P_2 (from 1 to 1.25), the effect on the real money supply is identical to that which would occur if P remained at 1 and M fell from $250 billion to $200 billion. There follows a fall in the real money supply and a leftward shift of the LM schedule to $LM(P_2)$. Therefore,

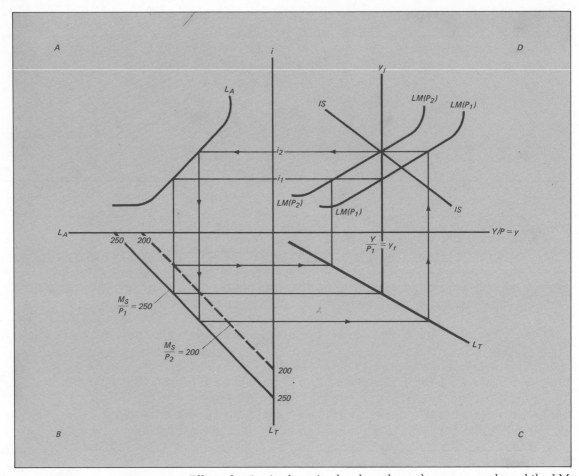

Figure 11.1 Effect of a rise in the price level on the real money supply and the LM schedule

a different LM schedule may be seen to exist for every price level. LM would shift to the right if the real money supply were increased to, say, $300 billion by a fall in P to 0.80.

The Labor Market and the Shape of the Aggregate Supply Schedule

We saw in Chapter 10 that the aggregate supply schedule describes the relationship between the price level and output (for a given capital stock) that is implicit in the assumptions made about the workings of the labor market. With money wages rigid downward, the aggregate supply schedule is positively sloped up to full employment and vertical at full employment.

The derivation of the aggregate supply schedule is reproduced in a slightly different perspective in Figure 11.2, which places the aggregate supply schedule in quadrant A, the labor market in quadrant C, and the production function in quadrant D. Quadrant B represents the rigid wage assumption along W_1. Starting at P_1, if the price level falls to P_2 and money wages remain rigid at W_1, then real wages rise from W_1 to W_2, labor demanded and hired falls from N_1 to N_2, and output falls from y_1 to y_2. Notice that if the classical assumption of freely flexible wages is followed when P_1 falls to P_2, then the excess supply of labor at W_2 would lower money wages to W_2, in turn maintaining W_1, N_1, and therefore y_1. In short, the aggregate supply schedule is vertical at y_1 under the assumption of freely flexible wages. Of course both cases coincide above P_1 as wages are flexible upward under both Keynesian and classical assumptions. A rise of the price level to P_3 creates an excess demand for labor which raises W to W_3 so that W_1, N_1, and y_1 are all maintained at P_3.

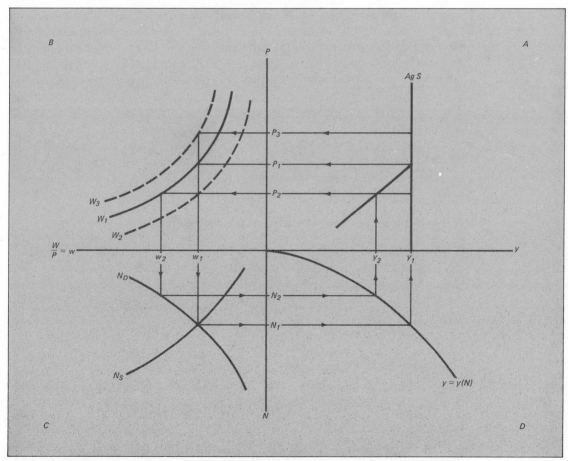

Figure 11.2 Aggregate supply with money wages rigid downward or freely flexible

IS/LM Analysis with Flexible Prices and No Real-Balance Effects

The level of full-employment output identified in Figure 11.2 is represented on the y axis in Figure 11.3. Figure 11.3 shows an IS/LM model expressed in real terms. Notice that the LM line is drawn for a given price level, P_1. Point E is no more than a happy coincidence since commodity-market and money-market equilibrium just *happen* to occur coincidently at the level of output, y_1, which requires full employment of the labor force earning full-employment income, y_f.

Suppose now that IS_1 is shifted to IS_2 by an increase in government expenditure or private investment. Line IS_2 will intersect the LM schedule at point Q, above full-employment output. This represents a level of aggregate demand which exceeds the capacity of the economy to produce. Consequently, the price level rises to P_2, inducing the LM schedule to shift backward, and a new equilibrium is established at point G. In this case the result of an increase in government expenditure or investment would be a higher *nominal* level of income since the price level has risen also. There is no effect, however, on real income above y_f, since that represents the supply constraint in terms of the ability of the economy to produce. The final equilibrium at point G occurs at a higher price level which effectively produces a contraction in the real money supply. This results in an increase in the inter-

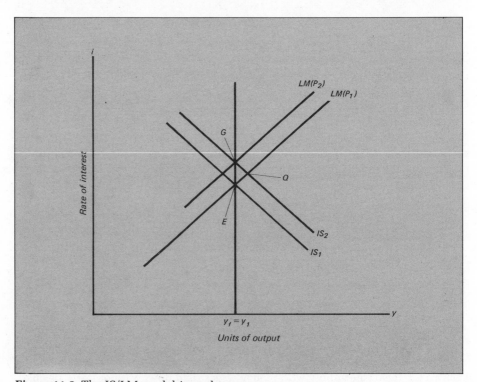

Figure 11.3 The IS/LM model in real terms

est rate, which in turn lowers investment. Thus equilibrium is restored in the commodity sector with the return of expenditure to the original level consistent with output available at y_1.

Figure 11.3 can also be employed to consider the impact of an increase in the money supply at full employment. Suppose original equilibrium occurs at point G. If the LM schedule is shifted rightward by an increase in the money supply (rather than by the equivalent, for the real money supply, of a fall in the price level to P_1), the excess demand equilibrium at point Q results. Excess demand raises the price level until the LM schedule returns to its original position, intersecting IS_2 at point G. In this case, the only result of an increase in the money supply is a rise in prices. The intimate link between changes in the money supply and the behavior of the price level will be analyzed in detail in our discussion of monetary theory and policy in Part III. At this point we can see that at the full-employment level of income predictions based on the IS/LM model closely approximate monetarist predictions of a close relationship between changes in the money supply and changes in the price level when wages are flexible in both directions.

Thus we can see that at the full-employment level of income, both expansionary fiscal policy in the form of increased demand and expansionary monetary policy in the form of an increase in the money supply will be inflationary. The two exceptions, which we will examine in greater detail below, are the liquidity trap case or the case where investment does not respond to changes in the interest rate. In the liquidity trap situation, an increase in the money supply will not reduce interest rates as money holders will choose to hold on to more money rather than invest in interest-bearing assets at low rates of return. In the second case, a climate of pessimism due to a recent economic downturn or a fear that rates of return will be very low will discourage investment even at lower interest rates. In both instances expansionary monetary policy at full employment would only increase money in the hands of money holders. There would be no effect on prices since demand would not be affected.

However, suppose that due to an onset of business pessimism investment is reduced so that IS_1 shifts down to IS_2 in Figure 11.4. At P_1, the result is an equilibrium below full employment at point F. If, however, the excess supply of output at lower levels of demand results in a fall in the price level to, say, P_2, $LM(P_1)$ shifts out to $LM(P_2)$ and output increases toward the full employment level. The new equilibrium, point G, is selected arbitrarily between point F and full-employment output because there is nothing to *guarantee* that the price level will fall far enough to produce an increase in the real money supply sufficient to lower the interest rate by enough to restore total expenditure to a full-employment level. Moreover, as prices are generally rigid downward (or very slow to fall), this result may occur far too slowly for anyone concerned with unemployment (or those put out of work by the absence of demand for the goods they produce). The eventual fall in prices, however, brings into force the phenomenon known as the **real-**

balance effect. This, as we will see, accelerates the consequent rise in expenditure and lessens the amount by which the real money supply must be increased in order to restore a full-employment level of demand.

The Role of the Real-Balance Effect

Real-balance effects resulting from the change in price level will produce a different IS schedule for each price level. As the price level falls, real balances held by money holders are increased, and these money holders reduce the level of savings at each level of real income. The impact upon the IS schedule is shown in Figure 11.5.[1] The real savings function, $s = s(y, m)$, is written assuming real balances $m_1 = M_1/P_1$ with the nominal money supply given at M_1 and the price level at P_1. These conditions, along with the real investment schedule and the equilibrium condition $s = n$ (or $\Delta S/\Delta P = \Delta I/\Delta P$) give rise to the IS line $IS(P_1)$, in quadrant D, where real savings equals real investment at price level P_1. Without real-balance effects, line $IS(P_1)$ is undisturbed by a change in the price level, since neither the real investment

1. This reproduces Figure 9.3 with the addition of price-level changes; that is, in real terms.

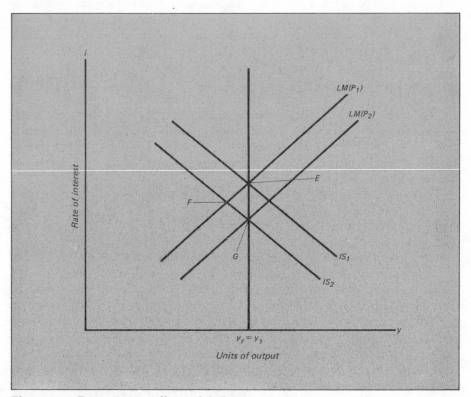

Figure 11.4 Expansionary effects of deflation

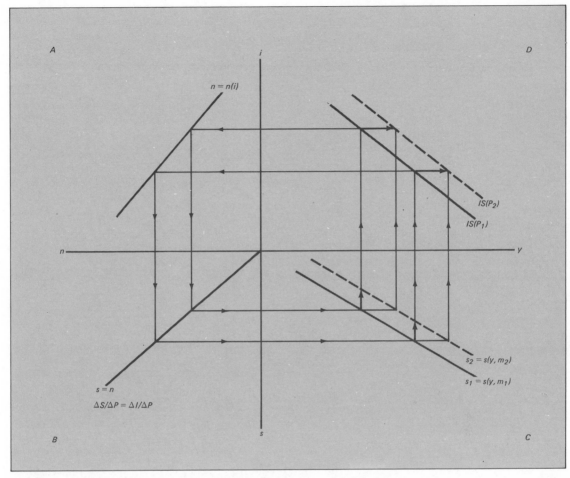

Figure 11.5 Impact upon the IS schedule of a change in real balances

schedule in quadrant A nor the real savings schedule in quadrant C is affected by a price-level change.[2] But the operation of the real-balance effect means that saving behavior is not completely determined by income. In quadrant C, a different schedule relating real saving to real income exists for

2. Strictly speaking this condition requires that if we begin with the IS line equilibrium condition written in nominal terms as

$$I(i) = S(Y)$$

then dividing both sides by the price level, letting n represent the lowercase form of I, to obtain

$$n(i) = s(y)$$

does not affect equilibrium (i is unaffected since it is written in percentage terms, and in equilibrium the behavior of the price level should not affect the *rate* of return). When the transition from nominal to real terms does not affect equilibrium, the equilibrium equation is said to be homogeneous of degree one.

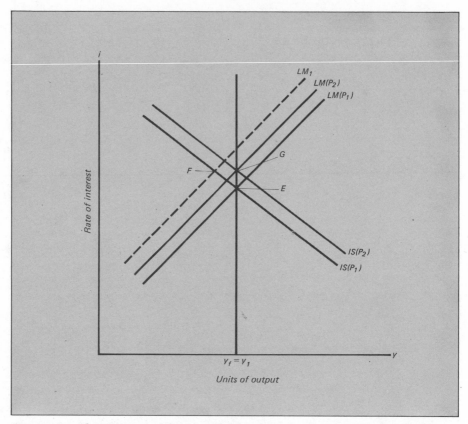

Figure 11.6 The IS/LM model with a flexible price level and real-balance effects

every price level. If the price level falls from P_1 to P_2 so that the real value of money assets has increased rising to m_2, savings is cut at each level of income and line $IS(P_1)$ shifts out to $IS(P_2)$ in quadrant D. Falling prices can be expansionary insofar as they increase real balances and thereby cut savings. In order to restore savings to the level at which they equal investment for any given interest rate, income must be higher at each interest rate. This new equilibrium requirement is reflected by the rightward shift in the IS schedule from $IS(P_1)$ to $IS(P_2)$. Of course, if the price level rises, the real-balance effect will shift the IS schedule back to the left.

Now let us consider the role of the real-balance effect in the context of the IS/LM model with full employment. In Figure 11.6 both IS and LM are defined at given levels for a single price level, taken to be P_1. Suppose that the general equilibrium at point E is disturbed by a reduction in the money supply so that the LM schedule at $LM(P_1)$ shifts back to LM_1 (initially, the price level is unaffected). If the price level falls at point F, with aggregate demand below full-employment output, two effects occur. First, the fall in the price level raises real money balances and shifts line LM_1 rightward to $LM(P_2)$. Second, the positive real-balance effect shifts line $IS(P_1)$ rightward to $IS(P_2)$. The final equilibrium, shown in Figure 11.6 at point G, occurs back at full employment with a higher interest rate since the money supply is now lower in real terms with P_2 greater than P_1. With the real-balance effect included, it is no longer necessary for the price level to fall by enough to return LM to its original position in order to restore full employment. The direct expansionary impact upon expenditure (through reduced saving) of a positive real-balance effect shifts the IS schedule to the right and reduces the gap to be filled by an expansion of the real money supply.

The real-balance effect also reduces the expansionary effect of monetary- and fiscal-policy measures undertaken to move the economy to full employment. Assume the economy is at an equilibrium level of real income, below the full-employment level, such as at point A in Figure 11.7. Suppose that an increase in government expenditure is undertaken to shift the IS schedule rightward and move the economy toward full employment. If the aggregate supply schedule has a positive slope, as between y_2 and y_1 in Figure 11.2,

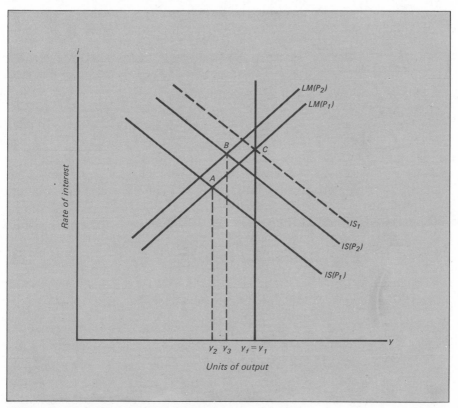

Figure 11.7 A higher price level cuts the real multiplier

the increase in aggregate demand represented by a higher level of government expenditure will lead to a higher price level. If the initial shift in the IS schedule before the price level rises is to IS_1, intersecting $LM(P_1)$ at point C, the subsequent rise in the price level, say to P_2, results in $LM(P_2)$ and $IS(P_2)$ and an IS/LM equilibrium real-income level at point B. The distance from y_1 to y_3 represents the reduction in the real multiplier induced by the effects of higher prices upon the IS and LM schedules. A similar reduction in the money multiplier also results from an induced higher price level.

Although another round of increases in government expenditure could narrow the gap between y_3 and y_1 (at y_f), this would involve more inflation and less increase in real output per unit increase in government expenditure, since, as can be seen from Figure 11.2, the aggregate supply schedule gets steeper as full employment is approached.

The policy implications of the real-balance effect lie in its theoretical ability to rescue the economy from the chronic unemployment that could occur if a government were reluctant to increase expenditure and if monetary policy would not work due either to the liquidity-trap situation or to the failure of investment to respond to changes in the interest rate. In a liquidity trap, the interest rate cannot be reduced since liquidity preference is infinite, and in the case where investment fails to respond to the interest rate, reducing the rate is futile. Monetary policy efforts to stabilize the economy by changes in the interest rate would therefore fail. But the real-balance effect says that a change in the real quantity of money, however it occurs, affects expenditure *directly* and not only by means of first reducing the interest rate and thereby inducing more investment expenditure.

In Figure 11.8 it is assumed that both a liquidity trap *and* an unresponsiveness of investment to the interest rate plague the economy. Either is sufficient to render monetary policy ineffective without the real-balance effect. Neither will do so with the real-balance effect. Assume that initially the economy is at point A below full employment with the IS and LM schedules intersecting at y_2 given a price level P_1. With expenditure below the full-employment level of output, the price level falls, say to P_2, shifting line $IS(P_1)$ to $IS(P_2)$ and intersecting LM at point B. The price change affects the LM schedule only in sloped range, as shown by the shift from $LM(P_1)$ to $LM(P_2)$ where LM is not horizontal. Economists who argue against Keynesian fears of chronic underemployment, due either to a liquidity trap or unresponsiveness of investment to the interest rate, point out that there is *some* price level, shown as P_3 in Figure 11.8, at which real balances would be large enough to return expenditure to a full-employment level at point C, even in the absence of an increase in government expenditure.

The strength of the real-balance effect is therefore a subject of considerable debate.[3] Although this point has considerable theoretical significance,

---

3. See the commentary in Chapter 15 for a review of empirical studies of the real-balance effect.

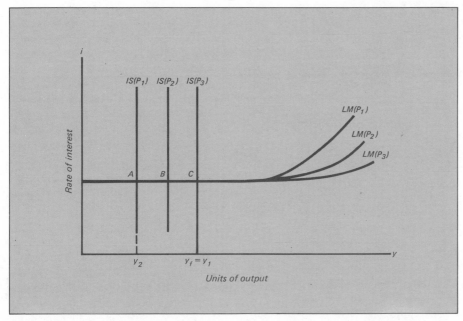

Figure 11.8 The real-balance effect escape from chronic underemployment

however, it has been of little practical interest to policymakers charged with maintaining a steady level of high employment over time. Given the quantitatively small size of the real-balance effect and the downward rigidity of many prices, the time required to restore full employment based solely upon the operation of the real-balance effect would likely be considerable.

The Full-Employment IS/LM Model: Concluding Note

We have seen that if the price level is permitted to vary in the IS/LM model a different LM schedule and a different IS schedule are needed for each price level, resulting in a more awkward analysis, geometrically, than in the case where the price level is assumed to be fixed. This is because IS/LM is essentially a two-variable model, requiring only two equations. With the price level taken to be fixed, IS represents the equilibrium equation in the commodity market and LM represents the equilibrium equation in the money market, thus allowing a single equilibrium. One point represents equilibrium values of the two endogenous variables, the interest rate and nominal income. That equilibrium would only be disturbed by a change in some exogenous variable, such as a change in the money supply, government expenditure, or investors' expectations, which altered the level of investment at each interest rate.

Commentary: Suffering Stagflation

Inflation is always painful. It erodes the real income of anyone whose salary is not automatically adjusted, and it eats away at hard-earned personal savings. This hits hardest at old and retired persons of modest means. In 1973, for example, the rate of inflation was 6.2 percent, and buying power (measured by real income) dropped 4 percent on an average because some wages increased. But for people whose wages did not rise, buying power fell a full 6.2 percent. In a recession, when inflation is combined with a fall in real incomes, the decline in buying power increases because there is less money at hand with which to buy. In the first quarter of 1974 the U.S. economy experienced the double hardships of inflation (running at an approximate 12 percent annual rate) and recession (a fall in real output at an approximate 6 percent annual rate), a situation sometimes referred to as "stagflation."

Inflation is usually attributed to excess aggregate demand (demand-pull), which normally occurs during periods of boom rather than bust. Yet it has been suggested that the high rate of inflation may, in itself, have contributed to the drop in real output. A high rate of expected (future) inflation pushes up interest rates, which chokes off credit and hits hard at certain decentralized industries with small capital reserves, such as housing construction. The soaring interest rates in 1974 lured money away from mortgages into higher interest-earning assets, and the consequent rates on mortgages scared off many home buyers. Housing starts in April 1974 were off 32.4 percent from the previous year, and building permits (which usually precede housing starts by two months) fell 19 percent in May. Moreover, a continuing high rate of inflation means union leaders demand large wage increases when labor contracts are renegotiated, and this may lead to increased labor unrest, strikes, and lost workdays for the economy.

If inflation and recession can coexist, and if one contributes to the other, economic policymakers face particularly difficult choices. Citing higher oil prices as a major cause of 1974 inflation, the *Economist* (London) has chided major Western countries for failing to reflate demand:

> No major country has reflated demand with indirect tax cuts to offset the effect of higher oil prices . . . . Most countries have allowed oil costs to push up consumer prices, so deflating demand. They have compounded this by increasing monetary stringency and higher interest rates.[1]

Advocating both a loose fiscal policy (which is implied by the recommended tax cut) and a relaxed monetary policy may seem odd under high inflation conditions. But falling real output is the crucial indicator: combined with high inflation, it is a sure sign of supply-induced, or cost-push, inflation, as opposed to the more common demand-induced variety.

The policy dilemma can readily be seen in the diagram, which represents the aggregate demand schedule, D, and the aggregate supply schedule, S. If, starting at point A, aggregate demand shifts from D_1 to D_2, prices and output rise. If demand pressure halts at point B, capacity output is reached with full employment of the labor force. Suppose, however, that a subsequent exogenous shock—an example might be the 1974 increase in the price of both domestic and foreign oil—occurs at this point. Such a cost-push phenomenon means that less output is forthcoming at each price level, and the aggregate supply schedule shifts leftward from S_1 to S_2. (Notice that capacity, or full-employment, output is not changed by the shift. It simply occurs now at a higher price level.) The result of moving from

1. The *Economist*, London, June 1, 1974.

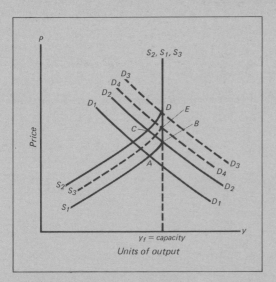

Units of output

the full-employment equilibrium at point B to point C is a drop in real output at the same time that prices rise higher, reaching a level above that induced by demand-led inflation.

At point C, policymakers are faced with a difficult situation. Real output has fallen to a level below full employment at the same time that prices have risen even further than they had in the demand-led shift from point A to full employment at point B. What makes the situation more difficult for policymakers is the likelihood that they probably had induced a significant part of the demand shift from D_1 to D_2 in their willingness to suffer some inflation in order to attain full employment. But the inflation that was considered tolerable when it led to full employment has been exacerbated by cost-push phenomena. This situation arose during the 1973–1974 oil crisis, when cost-push pressure was added to demand-led pressure in many countries, including the United States.

If taxes were cut or monetary policy eased, aggregate demand could be shifted to D_3, achieving a new full-employment equilibrium at point D. But the danger is that such a move would tend to fulfill and reinforce the inflationary expectations of consumers and producers; the shifts from point A to B to C to D illustrate a true inflationary spiral. These inflationary expectations induce cost-push phenomena which shift the aggregate supply schedule to the left, and the whole process of further inflation accompanied by a fall in real output may repeat itself. Even in the absence of resource shortages, the demands of labor for increased wages to offset the expected impact of inflation on real purchasing power could be expected, and businesses are equally likely to respond to inflationary expectations by raising prices. This was especially true in the first half of 1974 when wage and price controls were suddenly lifted.

To avoid this, policymakers may choose to remain for a time at a point like C (with less than full employment, a fall in real output, and inflation still underway) in the hope that if aggregate demand is held steady, inflationary pressure will subside. Once inflation relaxes a bit, aided perhaps by some fall in cost-push forces (for example, a growth in the stock of capital or in the labor force at given prices) which shifts aggregate supply to S_3, aggregate demand will be cautiously increased to D_1. The result of these moves might initially be some point like E, possibly followed by a shift in demand which moves the economy toward full employment at only slightly higher prices.

The reasons for proceeding cautiously are clear. If demand is reflated too soon, inflationary expectations will be reinforced, and another round of inflation will threaten with the possibility of continued unemployment. This was the fear of the U.S. administration early in 1974. If demand is reflated too late, unemployment and inflation-sapped purchasing power may precipitate a reduction in aggregate demand which exacerbates recessionary tendencies. This is the fear expressed by the *Economist*. The situation is particularly difficult because the correct choice requires information about the speed at which labor and commodity markets adjust and the precise manner in which inflationary expectations are formed. Such dynamic information is not readily available, and it is, consequently, the subject of intensive research by many economists.

When the price level is permitted to vary, however, the macro model has three endogenous variables—the interest rate, real income or output, and the price level. The two equilibrium equations represented by IS and LM are no longer sufficient to determine a single equilibrium. Although the solution presents no theoretical difficulty, a geometric solution is awkward in two-dimensional space. A three-equation IS/LM model with a flexible price level is presented algebraically in the mathematical appendix.

In addition to a variable price level, the full-employment IS/LM model includes the constraint that in order to reach full-employment equilibrium, the IS and LM schedules must cross at the single level of real income which absorbs full-employment output. We have seen that such an equilibrium can be attained automatically both in the liquidity trap case and in the case where investment fails to respond to the interest rate, providing our model includes the operation of the real-balance effect. However, the automatic restoration of full employment with falling prices inducing positive real-balance effects requires that money wages be flexible downward. If money wages are rigid downward, due to resistance of workers to accept work at lower rates of pay, lower prices will simply raise the real wage rate. Unemployment will then *increase* as firms hire less labor at a higher real price. Therefore, even in the presence of the real-balance effect, a chronic underemployment situation is possible. (Of course, in the presence of prolonged unemployment, it is likely that money rates will eventually fall, as workers are forced to accept lower rates of pay.)

Thus, although the operation of the real-balance effect reduces the threat of chronic unemployment in the Keynesian liquidity trap case (where an increase in the money supply will not lower the interest rate) or in the case of investment failing to respond to the lower interest rate, we see that it can only work by a cut in money wages. This result is somewhat ironic, as has been noted by Professor Harry Johnson in a discussion of Keynesian theory.[4] As we have seen repeatedly in discussion of the workings of the IS/LM model, the Keynesian system suggested two major flaws on the demand side of the IS/LM macro model: that an increase in the money supply may fail to lower the interest rate in the case of a liquidity trap and that, even if effected, a lower interest rate may fail to stimulate investment. But the operation of the real-balance effect provides the means for an eventual return to a full-employment level of output even in these situations. The only remaining rationale for a chronic underemployment situation is rigidity of money wages. The irony arises from the fact that the implication of this analysis is that full employment can be restored by a cut in money wages, which is equivalent to the classical economists' argument that underemployment equilibrium is impossible with flexible wages.

However, it is important to distinguish between a theoretical argument

---

4. Harry G. Johnson, "Monetary Theory and Keynesian Economics," in *Money, Trade and Economic Growth* (London: Unwin University Books, 1962).

and appropriate policy in a case where steady high employment is a primary goal. Although both concepts are important, they may not be fully compatible. Keynes, like most economists, found himself in the somewhat ambivalent role of theoretician and practitioner. The gap between the two is likely to be largest in cases where one is employing a comparative statics model such as the IS/LM model that is devoid of specific content regarding the time required for adjustment to equilibrium. The fact remains that over the short run, at least, downward rigidity of wages is an observable fact, thus restricting the already slow operation of the real-balance effect in restoring full employment. For these reasons, policymakers employ a mixture of fiscal and monetary measures. The effectiveness of the policy measures depends on the accuracy of their assumptions about the responsiveness of the IS and LM schedules, as we shall see in the following chapter.

MATHEMATICAL APPENDIX
The IS/LM Model with a Flexible Price Level

The model presented here extends the fixed-price IS/LM model presented in the mathematical appendix to Chapter 9. For those who find mathematics a simpler form of expression, we can describe the model in real terms with three equations to determine three endogenous variables—the price level, P, real income, y, and the interest rate, i. Thus we have

$$n(i) + g(G, P) = s(y, P) + t(y) \qquad \text{(A11.1)}$$

$$m(M, P) = L(y, r) \qquad \text{(A11.2)}$$

$$y = y(P) \qquad \text{(A11.3)}$$

Equation (A11.1) describes the equality between real investment, n, plus real government expenditure, g, and real savings, s, plus real taxes, t, required for equilibrium in the commodity sector. Notice that real government expenditure, g, is written as some function of nominal government expenditure and the price level. Since $g = G/P$

$$\frac{\partial}{\partial G(g)} = \frac{1}{P} = g_G > 0$$

$$\frac{\partial}{\partial P(g)} = -\frac{G}{P^2} = g_P < 0$$

Equation (A11.2) describes the equality between the real money supply and the real demand for money. The real money supply, m, analogous to real government expenditure, is written as some function of the nominal money supply and the price level. Since $m = M/P$

$$\frac{\partial}{\partial M(m)} = \frac{1}{P} = m_M > 0$$

$$\frac{\partial}{\partial P(m)} = -\frac{M}{P^2} = m_P < 0$$

P is absent from the real demand function for money since the price level only affects the demand for nominal money balances.

Equation (A11.3) describes the positively sloped portion of the aggregate supply schedule derived in Figure 11.2 (assuming that money wages are rigid downward). Of course, when capacity output is reached at full employment,

$$\frac{\partial y}{\partial P} \text{ or } y_P = 0$$

We wish to find solutions for the impact of changes in government expenditure and changes in the money supply upon each of the endogenous variables, y, i, and P. Differentiating our three equations and collecting terms into a matrix format gives:

$$\begin{bmatrix} v_y & -n_i & u_P \\ L_y & L_i & -m_P \\ 1 & 0 & -y_P \end{bmatrix} \begin{bmatrix} dy \\ di \\ dP \end{bmatrix} = \begin{bmatrix} g_G dG \\ m_M dM \\ 0 \end{bmatrix} \qquad (A11.4)$$

where:

$$v_y = (s_y + t_y) > 0$$

$$n_i < 0$$

$$u_P = (s_P - g_P) > 0$$

$$L_y > 0$$

$$L_i < 0$$

$$m_P < 0$$

$$y_P > 0$$

In this matrix, v_y represents the marginal propensity to save plus the tax rate ($sy + ty$); n_i represents the impact of changes in the interest rate on investment holding all else constant, or $\partial n/\partial i$; s_P represents the impact of changes in the price level on savings holding all else constant, or $\partial s/\partial P$; u_P is s_P plus the impact of changes in the price level on real government expenditure, g_P; L_y and L_i represent the impact on the real demand for money of changes in real income and the interest rate, holding all else constant, or $\partial L/\partial y$ and $\partial L/\partial i$; m_P represents the impact of changes in the price level on the real money supply holding all else constant, or $\partial m/\partial P$; and y_P represents the impact of changes in the price level on real output, or $\partial y/\partial P$. Equation (A11.4) may be compactly written as $Hj = k$, where H is the matrix of parameters, j is the vector of changes in endogenous variables, and k is the vector of changes in exogenous variables. Notice that $s_P > 0$ represents the Pigou effect since as the price level rises and real balances fall, savings rises. Employing Cramer's rule[1] to solve equation (A11.4) yields the following solutions (where the determinant of matrix H, or $|H| = -[v_y L_i y_P + n_i(L_y y_P - m_P) + u_P L_i] > 0$):

$$\frac{dy}{dG} = \frac{-L_i y_P g_G}{|H|} > 0 \qquad \frac{dy}{dM} = \frac{-n_i y_P m_M}{|H|} > 0$$

$$\frac{di}{dG} = \frac{(L_y y_P - m_P) g_G}{|H|} > 0 \qquad \frac{di}{dM} = \frac{(-v_y y_P - u_P) m_M}{|H|} < 0$$

$$\frac{dP}{dG} = \frac{-L_i g_G}{|H|} > 0 \qquad \frac{dP}{dM} = \frac{-n_i m_M}{|H|} > 0$$

The results all carry expected signs.

The extreme classical and Keynesian results obtained for the price exogenous model in the appendix to Chapter 9 are generally preserved in the price-endogenous model. If $L_i = 0$, indicating the classical case where the interest rate does not affect the demand for money, then the impact of a change in government expenditure on both real output and the price, and therefore on $Y = Py$, is zero.

$$\frac{dy}{dG} = 0$$

$$\frac{dP}{dG} = 0$$

The impact of a change in G on the interest rate remains positive

$$\frac{di}{dG} = -\frac{1}{n_i} > 0$$

The money multiplier with $L_i = 0$ and $m_M = 1$ becomes

$$\frac{dy}{dM} = \frac{1}{L_y - \dfrac{m_P}{y_P}} > 0$$

which differs from the fixed price result only insofar as $m_P \neq 0$. The impact of a change in the money supply on the price level

$$\frac{dP}{dM} = \frac{1}{L_y y_P - m_P} > 0$$

carries the expected positive sign. And, given $L_i = 0$ and $m_M = 1$ we have

$$\frac{di}{dM} = \frac{v_y y_P + u_P}{n_i(L_y y_P - m_P)} < 0$$

---

1. For an explanation of how to apply Cramer's rule, see A. C. Chiang, *Fundamental Methods of Mathematical Economics* (New York: McGraw-Hill, 1969), pp. 113–117.

In the liquidity trap case where $L_i = \infty$ and $g_G = 1$ the impact of a change in government expenditure on real output and on the price level is given by

$$\frac{dy}{dG} = \frac{1}{v_y + \dfrac{u_P}{y_P}} \qquad \frac{dP}{dG} = \frac{1}{v_y y_P + u_P}$$

which, recalling $v_y = s_y + t_y$ puts dy/dG close to the price-exogenous multiplier case. Here the multiplier is smaller due to the real-balance effect since $u_P/y_P > 0$ adds to the size of the denominator of the expression for dy/dG. The impact of a change in G on the interest rate, di/dG, remains zero in the price-endogenous liquidity trap case as it is in the price-exogenous case. Of course, given $L_i = \infty$,

$$\frac{dy}{dM} = \frac{dP}{dM} = 0$$

since L_i appears only in the denominator of these expressions. Also, in the liquidity trap case di/dM remains zero as in the price-exogenous model. This result confirms the ineffectiveness of monetary policy in the liquidity trap case where real-balance effects are absent.

If $n_i = 0$ as some Keynesians suggest, and letting $g_G = 1$

$$\frac{dy}{dM} = \frac{dP}{dM} = 0$$

$$\frac{dy}{dG} = \frac{1}{v_y + \dfrac{u_P}{y_P}} > 0$$

$$\frac{dP}{dG} = \frac{1}{v_y y_P + u_P} > 0$$

These results show that the zero money multiplier given a zero impact of changes in the interest rate on investment remains intact in the price-endogenous case.

Finally, given $n_i = 0$ and $g_G = 1$, we have

$$\frac{di}{dG} = \frac{L_y Y_P - m_P}{-L_i(v_y y_P + u_P)} > 0$$

$$\frac{di}{dM} = \frac{1}{L_i} < 0$$

The signs are unaltered from the price-exogenous case.

Questions and Exercises

1. Why must we first gauge the impact of the price level on changes in the IS and LM schedules before we can extend the IS/LM model at full employment?

2. Assume that the price level has just risen by 10 percent. Normally this would generate expectations of future price rises. Why must we assume, however, that such a price-level change is a one-shot event, when we are working with the extended IS/LM model?

3. What does the IS equation describe? How does it vary when expressed in terms of money and in real terms?

4. In Figure 11.2, we see that when the price level falls from P_1 to P_2, money wages remain rigid at W_1, while real wages rise from W_1 to W_2. Why do real wages rise? What underlying assumption is made about wages which dictates that the aggregate supply schedule remains vertical at y_1?

5. Can you show, by means of the graph in Figure 11.4, that in the absence of government intervention there is nothing to guarantee a full-employment level of spending? Why doesn't the price level keep falling until such a level is attained?

6. Why does the real-balance effect produce a different IS schedule for each price level?

7. How does the real-balance effect reduce the expansionary effect of monetary- and fiscal-policy measures taken to move the economy to full employment? How can the real-balance effect rescue the economy from chronic unemployment in the Keynesian liquidity trap case? In the case of investment failing to respond to a lower interest rate?

8. Why is the strength of the real-balance effect a subject of considerable debate?

9. Can you trace the impact of an increase in the money supply on the price level by means of the graph in Figure 11.3? Why is the LM schedule shifted rightward by the money supply increase?

10. How do downward rigidity of prices and money wages limit the ability of the real-balance effect to guarantee full employment? To what extent are prices and money wages rigid downward in today's economy? How do these conditions compare with those of the 1920s and 1930s?

Clinging to the old game plan

incentives, the amount of saving ... level and natt... ... ... dis... ... of resources and lead to inefficiencies. Finally, the level and structure of taxes determine the level of disposable income, and the *distribution* of after-tax income among ... groups.

Th... ... ... he investigati... ... ...ive effects of taxes. In a general way incidence theory is applied distribution theory in which the focus is on how various tax regimes affect factor returns and commodity prices. The distributive impacts of some taxes are fairly straightforward, while the effects of others are quite complex. For example, the burden of a proportional income tax, that is imposed on all income, is proportional to household's share in national income. O... the other hand, taxes that do not apply to all types of income, or to all commodities, change relative commodity prices, influence

Changing Course

Nixon's Budget Shows Effects of Watergate And Economic Woes

He Drops Austerity Plans, Pledges to Use Spending In Fight Against Recession

Sacred Cow or Dead Horse?

By JAMES P. GANNON
Staff Reporter of THE WALL STREET JOURN...
WASHINGTON — Preside...
get, unvei...d yeste... ...
woes o...? ... ...conomic di...
forcing ... ...everse cours...

Gon...l ... ...ent of austerity, ...critics and Congress last y... w...h cuts in social programs, veto threats and rigid spending ceilings. Now Mr. Nixon appears as a conciliatory, politically weakened compromiser—dusting off some once-discarded liberal initiatives to try to appease his would-be impeachers and ready to bust his own budget with a federal spending splurge to sto\p a recession.

The co...rast between the budget that ... Nixon se...t to Congress yesterd...y and ...

Stor...
on page ...
budg...t o... ... on page 20.

that he preser...s a year ...
starker—in ... ...
thrust. Thus ... ...ures the precipitous p'... ... ...ne presidency of Richard M. Nixon

Then and Now

Flexing his massive 1972 electoral mandate, Mr. Nixon a year ago confidently mapped out the course he wanted his second term to take:

...act commodity prices at profit maximizing levels. A large part of this review is devoted to incidence theory built on these neoclassical assumptions. Initially a set of simplifyi... ass...mptions ... ...t commo... ...ete ... in ... ...cts; (2) ...t there is no for-...gn trade; (3) that factors of production are perfectly mobile (shiftable) between different industries; and (4) that the *total* supplies of all factors are in perfectly inelastic supply to the economy as a whole. Then, whenever possible, the assumptions will be relaxed. We shall review the literature on dynamic incidence which allows for longer-run effects of tax policy through

Economic-Panel Democrats Ask Tax Cut Of $10 Billion to Halt Looming Recession

By a WALL STREET JOURNAL *Staff Reporter*
WASHINGTON — The U.S. economy is slumping into a recession that should be countered with a $10 billion tax cut and a new public-employment program, the Joint Economic Committee of Congress declared.

"It is of the utmost importance that measures be taken immediately to counter the recession which is already emerging," said the annual report of the Democratic-dominated panel of Congressmen and Senators. The minority report of its Republican members, reflecting the Nixon administration's stand, rejected a tax cut to offset economic weakness but said the administration's standby contingency plans to pump up spending should be readied for use by late spring if the economy remains sluggish.

"The U.S. economy is in a seriously troubled state" and prospects for an early upturn "are poor," the panel's majority contended. Charging that the admini... has overstated likely ... ... underestimated ... ...

... ...cent econo... ... ...ittle doubt tha...
...nly has a'... ... ...ession
... ...ll."

...mmittee, which can't initiate legislation, also said in its report that the nation's unemployment rate, which stood at 5.2% of the work force when last counted in February, will approach 6% by midyear and will remain at or above that mark for the rest of 1974. The Nixon administration's forecast is that joblessness will average about 5.7% for the year and won't top 6% in any month.

Inflation Rate of 8% or ...

Rising food pri... ... of higher
... ...l ... ...mounting
... ... of 8% or more" for 197...
That would be higher than the "7' rat...
cast by the Nixon admini...t... ...y
... ...index, the
... ... gauge.

To stimulate the economy and help offset inflation's pinch on consumers, the panel majority recommended "a tax cut of approximately $10 billion, aimed primarily at lower-income taxpayers." About $6 billion of this cut, they added, could be offset by re\nue raised through "loophole pluggi\g" tax-law changes, such as repeal of the 22%

interest rates, President Nixon's eco...
nomic advisers this week urged him to hang tough with the current "steady as you go" policy. As has happened re-peatedly ... ...however, they may

... ...o favors the "bold stroke" in economics as well as international affairs, wants his economic advisers to

'We are sticking to our anti-inflation policy,' says Stein

dent policy of monetary restraint.

But to observers outside the Administration, the housing action emphasizes that the major burden of fighting inflation is already on the Fed, and it may not be able to cope (page 34).

Chart III
SELECTED INTEREST RATES

Percent 11
10
Federal funds 9
Aaa-rated corporate bonds 8
7
6
Tax-exempt bonds 20-year maturity 5
3-month Treasury bills 4
3
1969 1970 1971 1972 1973

Note: Rates for Federal funds (effective rate) and three-month Treasury bills (market yield) are monthly averages of daily figures. Yields on Aaa-rated corporate and twenty-year tax exempt bonds are monthly averages of weekly figures.

Sources: Board of Governors of the Federal Reserve System; Moody's Investors Service, Inc.; and The Bond Buyer.

second quart... ...
the health ind... ... ...
Living Council as ... u...
agency, is pending ... ...

The report said ... ...
because they have lost ... ...
effective only in the short run and b...
the current economic slowdown provides the "appropriate time" to remove them.

The majority recommended that a permanent anti-inflation agency be created to administer a "largely voluntary price-wage review system." Such an agency could mon-reduce taxes by $68 for a four-person family with an income of $6,000, and the saving would range upward to $280 for a four-person family in the high-over $200,000 tax bracket.

Tax Incidence Theory: The Effects of Taxes on the Distribution of Income

What's Wrong with American Economics?

Capitol Weighs Tax Cuts As Anti-Recession Move

Stopping Inflation

inflation — "bread-and-butter issues" —than about im-peachment. When asked what he thought should be done to stop the inflation, Mr. Brennan he had been "appointed, not anointed." And he added, "I don't have any real answer, other than that we all have to try to find the answer."

Economic Analysis

Was Mr. Brennan saying that the Administration had no plan for dealing with inflation? Well, yes and no, the Secretary indicated. The Administration had "no clear program to solve it tomorrow." But it was "working on it every day."

Who was doing that? "Many people," said Mr. Brennan. "Economists."

The Secretary of Labor appeared to take only rueful comfort in the thought that the economists were figuring out the answers. "I was not ...d with all their ability ...ains," he said, "but I ...at I can get in trouble ... own without having help me."

...ously, the time has come ... good men and women ...bond to Secretary Bren...lea and come to the aid ...r country (this being a ...san issue) by providing s to the following mul-...poice questions:

What is the cause of in-
?

...igher demands by labor ...ges. ("True," says Mr ...n.)

...igher increases in prices ...ofits — "greedy profits." ...Brennan puts it. (Also ...he says.)

...Deficit in the Federal ...(Likely to exceed $10-...this year.)

...oo much military spend-...ational defense outlays ... $6.5 billion, to $81.9 ...in the new fiscal year ...ions to come.

...axes are too low and ...s increased. (Conven ...ice-prsion answer.)

...axes are too high and ...he ratio of ...lin\oven ...l Democratic liberal au-

...ss than one tent\.")
...en just one mar... The stock of money has ...important to ...eased too fast. (In the last ...ly. M-1 — demand deposits ...oney in circulation — ...s not been ... 6 per cent. But ...y ... W ...ches M-1 plus time ...so classified is ... ...es deposits — in ...ent.")

Actually, conside... ...ge of food ...ployed are pe\ ...nd the world, and the wip-A great man\cks, out of United States surplus ...'t worked or so... Quadrupling of oil prices ...ave recently de...the Organization of Petrole-...t to legislation chang... um Exporting Countries.

...y which the House Wa\ 10. Distortions produced by ...Means Committee is sch...Nixonian wage-price controls ...to start considering next and the "bubble" now develop-...If a tax reduction meas...ing with the lifting of controls.

...ed by the Finance 11. Floating exchange rates, ...ould probably which release nations from the ...discipline of having to set their

Fiscal and Monetary Policy

12

The relative effectiveness of monetary and fiscal policy is a current issue of debate among economists. But "effectiveness" is itself a vague concept which must be defined in terms of more concrete policy goals such as full employment, stable prices, and satisfactory economic growth. There is, moreover, another dimension to "effectiveness," namely the speed with which policy instruments have their desired effects. If a theoretically effective automatic response, such as the real-balance effect, takes months or years to have its impact, how "effective" can we consider that as a remedy for the problems of a real-world economy?

One way to avoid these conceptual difficulties is to redefine our policy goals in terms of economic stabilization. A stabilization policy seeks to keep the economy within a desired range of optimum levels of employment, rate of inflation, rate of growth, etc. Any shift that moves the economy away from such stability must be counteracted, and as quickly and precisely as possible. The goal of stabilization policy is to "fine tune" the economy to the greatest possible degree, while also cushioning it as much as possible from exogenous disturbances. Both the magnitude of response to a particular policy tool and the rapidity of response are important. It is here that supporters of fiscal and monetary policy disagree over policy tools.

The Shape of IS and LM

But underlying the debate is the question of the importance of money in an economy. To see why, let us review briefly where our macroeconomic model has led us. In the last chapter we saw that there were certain cases within the Keynesian framework in which the ability of monetary policy to increase output and employment in the absence of a real-balance effect was thrown into doubt, at least on a theoretical level. Specifically, in the case where investment fails to respond to changes in the interest rate, resulting in a vertical (perfectly interest-inelastic) IS schedule and in the case of a liquidity trap, where increasing the supply of money will not further lower the interest rate, resulting in a horizontal (perfectly interest-elastic) LM schedule, efforts to effect investment by way of changes in the money supply leading to a change in the interest rate would not work. (We saw that the operation of the real-balance effect counteracts this to some extent, but only if workers are forced, over time, to accept a wage cut.) In both these cases, changes in the supply of money in an economy would have no effect on "real" variables, such as income, employment, and the rate of interest. Thus in addition to the role of the real-balance effect, a major policy debate centers around the shapes of these IS and LM schedules. The shape of these schedules depends, as we have seen, on assumptions about the parameters in the money and commodity sectors, namely on those parameters which determine the responsiveness of the demand for money to changes in income and the interest rate, the magnitude of the MPC or the MPS, and the responsiveness of investment to changes in the interest rate.

In this chapter we will study the Keynesian and classical assumptions about these parameters. We will then examine the available empirical evidence, which tends to confirm a position somewhere between the two, a position in which money can affect real variables but to a limited extent. Finally, we will review the fiscal and monetary policy tools available to government authorities, and their application in the postwar period. The monetarists will be treated from a different point of view in the next chapter.

Keynesian Assumptions

Extreme Keynesian economists have shown that in a liquidity trap situation the LM schedule becomes horizontal, and many argue that the demand for money approximates the liquidity trap closely enough to imply a nearly horizontal LM schedule. If the LM schedule is horizontal, or nearly so, the interest rate cannot fall further, so monetary policy cannot be effective in lowering the interest rate and encouraging investment. As we saw in Chapter 8, Keynes explained the liquidity trap situation primarily on the basis of the speculative demand for money. If the interest rate gets low enough (so that the price of bonds gets very high), it may reach a point, at some positive value, at which investors will be convinced it can go no lower. (Equivalently, they may be convinced that the price of bonds must fall.) Since the speculative demand for money refers to holding money in anticipation of purchasing bonds (a close substitute for money) at a favorable price, if investors expect the price of bonds to fall at some low interest rate they will simply hold any additional cash in the hope of converting it into bonds when the interest rate rises (or when the price of bonds falls).

This results in a horizontal LM schedule over the range of the liquidity trap, as shown in Figure 12.1. We can see from Figure 12.1 that the horizontal portion of the LM schedule cannot be affected by a change in the money supply—whether due to actions of the monetary authority or due to responsiveness of the money supply to changes in the interest rate. For example, if the money supply is increased from MS_1 to MS_2 in quadrant B, there will be no impact upon the horizontal portion of LM in quadrant D. If the IS schedule crosses the LM schedule in the horizontal range, equilibrium could occur at point A, for example, with income at Y_1 and the interest rate at i_1, and an increase in the money supply will have no impact upon endogenous variables, i and Y. The impact of the increase in the money supply upon the vertical portion of LM is as normally expected and is represented in Figure 12.1 by LM'.

Extreme Keynesian economists argue that due to more aggressive intermediation by commercial banks as the interest rate rises, the money supply is positively related to the interest rate. This results in a flatter LM schedule, along which the money supply is not fixed. In Figure 12.2, the LM line is derived assuming the money supply to be unresponsive to the interest rate, as in Figure 12.1. However, if the money supply rises when i rises from i_1 to i_2, as shown by the outward shift from $M_S(i_1)$ to $M_S(i_2)$ in quadrant B, the resulting LM schedule will be that shown as LM' in quadrant D. Movement along the LM and LM' schedules can be described as follows. As Y rises from Y_1 to Y_2, the transactions demand for money rises. Along LM with a given money supply, i_1 would have to rise to i_3 in order to reduce the demand for money enough to keep money demand fixed and equal to a fixed money supply. However, if the money supply rises with i (along LM'), the increase in the interest rate required to maintain money-market equilibrium is reduced. This is because the money supply has risen enough to meet part of the increase in the transactions demand for money induced by the rise of income from Y_1 to Y_2. In short, the more responsive the money supply is to a rise in the interest rate, the flatter is the resulting LM schedule. This appears to imply that the result of an increase in government expenditure will

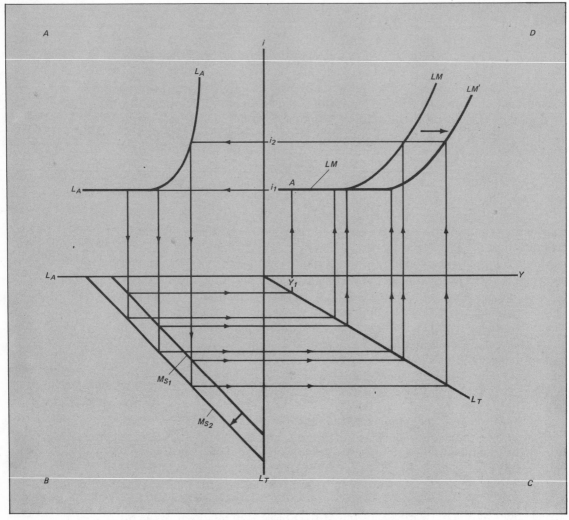

Figure 12.1 A horizontal segment of the LM schedule based upon a perfectly interest-elastic asset demand for money (liquidity trap)

be similar to the liquidity trap. However, the money supply will not in fact remain constant, so that part of the impact of a change in government expenditure upon Y or i will be due to an endogenously induced increase in the money supply.

The money supply might respond positively to the interest rate if the monetary authority attempts to peg the interest rate at a fixed level. In such a case, any increase in income and transactions demand will occasion an exogenous, or policy-induced, increase in the money supply. The increased demand for money will thereby be satisfied, and no rise in the interest rate

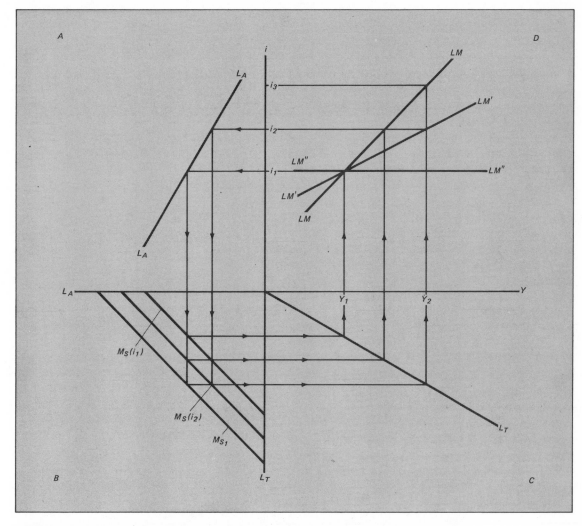

Figure 12.2 Impact of the money supply rising with the interest rate upon the LM schedule

will be necessary to keep money demand equal to money supply. In Figure 12.2 this result is shown along LM″ at i_1. The rise in income from Y_1 to Y_2 results in a policy-induced increase in the money supply to MS_1 so that no rise in the interest rate is required.

Classical Assumptions

Those who believe correct monetary policy to be a powerful macroeconomic tool share the assumption that the LM schedule is vertical, or close enough to vertical to deprive fiscal policy of its potential effectiveness. This

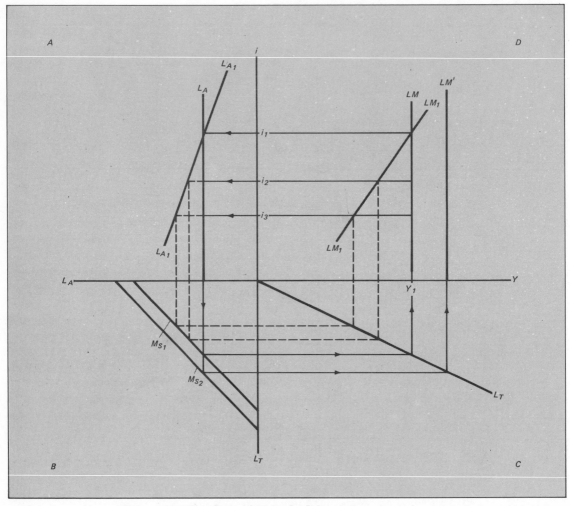

Figure 12.3 The classical LM schedule

assumption is based on the classical assumption that money is primarily a medium of exchange rather than an asset which is highly substitutable for other financial assets like bonds. Given this assumption, the demand for money is highly interest-inelastic. Major changes in the interest rate will have little effect on the demand for money. Figure 12.3 illustrates this situation. Since the asset demand for money is interest-insensitive, changes in the interest rate do not affect the demand for money during vertical movement along the LM schedule. Therefore, since the money supply is given along a single LM schedule, line LM simply identifies the level of income Y_1 at which transactions demand for money plus some interest-insensitive asset demand is equal to a given money supply M_{S_1}. The level of income Y_1 equates money demand to money supply for any interest rate, i_1, i_2, or i_3, since i does not affect the demand for money. A change in the money supply, such as an increase from M_{S_1} to M_{S_2}, shifts the LM schedule to LM′ in the absence of the real-balance effect, so that a vertical IS schedule due to the insensitivity of investment to the interest rate is the only thing which could render monetary policy ineffective. Of course, if the asset demand for money is only slightly interest-elastic, as shown by L_{A_1}, the LM schedule will be nearly vertical, as shown by LM_1, and the results of the extreme classical case will be slightly modified. A nearly vertical LM schedule means that large shifts in the IS schedule can have only minimal influence on the equilibrium level of income, no matter what the shape of the IS schedule. In the extreme case where the LM schedule is vertical and fixed at a certain level of income, income remains constant, and a shift in the IS schedule in response to changes in government expenditure or investment will affect only the interest rate. Even if the LM schedule is only highly interest-inelastic, such as LM_1 in Figure 12.3, large shifts in the IS schedule will have only minor effects on the level of income.

Policy Implications

So far, we have stated the most extreme cases. The policy debate hinges not so much on proving that one extreme, hypothetical case is possible, but rather on making realistic estimates of the parameters which determine the slopes of the IS and LM schedules. We may learn that both monetary and fiscal policy *can* be effective stabilizing measures in certain circumstances, but the crucial point is to learn which is more effective (or, to raise another issue, which is quickest to have its effect) and under what conditions each is most effective.

As we have already seen, extreme Keynesians have little faith in monetary policy to help alleviate recessions. We have seen why this might be so not only in the extreme case of the liquidity trap, but also in the case of business investment failing to respond to changes in the interest rate, especially if excess capacity exists. The liquidity trap is a special condition of the LM schedule. Keynesians maintain that not only is the LM schedule highly interest-elastic (perfectly so in the liquidity trap), but that the IS schedule is also highly interest-inelastic, i.e., close to vertical, where investment is relatively insensitive to changes in the interest rate.

This insensitivity concerning investment is not to be confused with the speculative demand for money. A sharp distinction must be made between the "real" and monetary sectors of the economy. Whereas businesses may well be sensitive to interest rates in their asset demand for money, when considering real investment we have seen (in Chapter 7) they may be relatively insensitive to changes in the interest rate, particularly if excess ca-

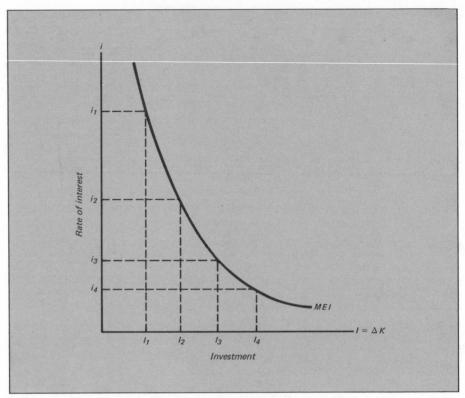

Figure 12.4 An MEI schedule with an interest-insensitive range

pacity exists. This is because investment occurs only when there is an imbalance between the firm's existing capital stock and its optimal desired capital stock. This imbalance, as we have seen, is related to the firm's production function and capital-labor ratio. No level of the interest rate will encourage a firm to invest if it does not have to do so. Only at the margin, where firms would like to invest but could be deterred by excessively high interest rates, would the interest rate play an important role. Therefore, a case can be made for the view that large changes in the interest rate have small effect on business investment.

In effect, Keynesians suggest that the marginal efficiency of investment (MEI) may be relatively insensitive to changes in the interest rate over some range. The MEI curve is shown in Figure 12.4. Assume initially that the prevailing interest rate is i_1, at which rate, according to the MEI curve, firms will invest a total of I_1. A major drop in the interest rate, to i_2, will, according to this MEI curve, increase I only slightly, to I_2. Keynesians assume that the MEI curve is of this nature in the range of interest-rate values where the IS and LM schedules intersect. They therefore see the possibility that a shift in LM would have little effect on income, since an interest-inelastic MEI implies a vertical IS schedule. Monetarists, however, hold that the MEI curve indicates a high level of sensitivity of investment to the interest rate over the relevant range of values. For example, if we start at i_3 and drop the interest rate to i_4 (where $i_3 - i_4 = i_1 - i_2$), investment increases dramatically from I_3 to I_4. An equivalent drop in interest rates from i_3 to i_4 instead of from i_1 to i_2 produces a much larger increase in investment ($I_4 - I_3$) in the elastic range of MEI than in its inelastic range ($I_2 - I_1$).

If the MEI schedule is interest-insensitive, the IS schedule which derives from it will be nearly vertical, since changes in the interest rate will have only a small effect on investment and income will not have to change by much to maintain the S = I condition. In such a case, the Keynesians would have a double argument for the relative effectiveness of fiscal policy over monetary: not only is the LM schedule highly interest-elastic (horizontal or nearly so), the IS schedule is highly interest-inelastic (vertical or nearly so) as well. Adding a nearly horizontal LM schedule to Figure 12.5 reflects

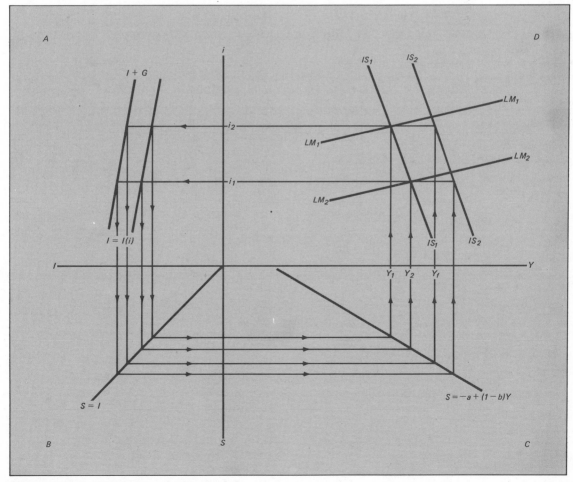

Figure 12.5 Keynesian IS and LM schedules

these assumptions. The policy implications are clear. A major shift in the LM schedule (the result of an expansionary monetary policy) from LM_1 to LM_2 can increase income only slightly (from Y_1 to Y_2). This is not enough to bring about a full-employment level of income, Y_f, in Figure 12.5. Fiscal policy, on the other hand, will be effective. A major shift in the IS schedule (brought about by an increase in government spending) is capable of producing a full-employment level of income, as shown by the shift from IS_1 to IS_2 in Figure 12.5.

Another important policy implication of the Keynesian assumptions is the absence (or weakness) of the self-regulating mechanisms in the economic model. If we start with the curves IS_1 and LM_1 the economy is far below full employment. If the monetary and fiscal authorities do nothing, as we saw in Chapter 11, the falling price level caused by unemployment may shift the LM schedule to LM_2. But this would not be enough to restore full employment. So, neither automatic adjustment in the money market nor deliberate monetary policy will be effective in raising income to a full-employment level, whereas fiscal policy will have a direct effect, *if* the Keynesian assumptions about the elasticities of the IS and LM schedules are correct.

It is clear from our discussion of the parameters determining the shapes of the IS and LM schedules that the theoretically derived conclusions about the relative effectiveness of monetary and fiscal policy are based largely upon the values assigned to such parameters as the responsiveness of investment and the demand for money to interest-rate changes. The marginal propensity to consume and the effect of income upon the demand for money are also important. The role each of these parameters plays in determining the impact of changes in exogenous government expenditures and the money supply upon endogenous income and the interest rate is expressed mathematically in the appendix to Chapter 9. The appendix to Chapter 11 considers the price-endogenous case. Because the values assigned to these parameters are crucial in determining the impact of monetary and fiscal policy measures, determination of the actual values is extremely useful; the theoretical debate must become an empirical one. A number of empirical studies have been undertaken, which we shall review briefly.

A Look at the Empirical Evidence

None of the empirical studies of such questions as the interest elasticities of money supply and demand is by itself conclusive, since each presupposes a definition of money and a choice of the interest rate to be used that could be regarded by hostile critics as arbitrary, if not capricious. Furthermore, the studies are not analogous to carefully controlled laboratory experiments, since they are based on real-world historical data, which consist of measurements of real economic events which cannot be manipulated or repeated. Thus, it is not always certain, when fitting a regression line to a time-series data set, whether the data represent a single schedule or a shifting set of schedules, although every effort is made to control studies for shifts in schedules. Nevertheless, there is considerable empirical evidence showing that neither the extreme Keynesian nor the extreme monetarist positions hold up under empirical scrutiny. Instead, results fall in a middle range of values, requiring a third, intermediate theoretical and policy position to take account of them.

The elasticity of the demand for money has long been a bone of contention between the extreme Keynesians on the one hand and the extreme monetarists on the other. The issue hinges upon the extent to which changes in the interest rate lead funds to be put into (or withdrawn from) other close substitutes for money, such as bonds and time deposits. If expansionary monetary policy increases the supply of high-powered money and pushes down the interest rate, it is important to know how much of the additional money will find its way into the real sector and how much will simply be absorbed as individuals abandon bonds or time deposits in favor of holding money, the most liquid asset, at lower interest rates.

An empirical study by Milton Friedman concludes that there is no stable, significant statistical relationship between the rate of interest and the demand for money.[1] His study has been criticized for its inclusion of interest-bearing time deposits in the definition of money, on the grounds that these constitute the main form of near-money that is influenced by changes in the interest rate. These critics claim that inclusion of time deposits in the definition of money obscures a large part of what would be a large response of money holdings (defined exclusively of time deposits) to changes in the interest rate. Other economists have used a narrow definition of money which includes only currency and demand deposits in commercial banks. When this definition of money supply is plotted against short-term interest rates over time, the interest elasticity of money demand is found by various researchers to lie somewhere in the range from −0.12 to −0.41.[2] The elasticity, of course, has a negative sign because of the inverse relationship between the interest rate and the quantity of money demanded. But it is the magnitude of elasticity that interests us. It is neither so high as to support the Keynesians, nor so low as to support the extreme monetarists. Thus, it falls in an intermediate range.

Similar studies of the elasticity of the supply of money with respect to the interest rate produce results with a range from 0.20 to 0.66, using the

---

1. Milton Friedman, "The Demand for Money: Some Theoretical and Empirical Results," *Journal of Political Economy* 67 (August 1959): 327–351.

2. See: H. R. Heller, "The Demand for Money: The Evidence from Short-run Data," *Quarterly Journal of Economics* 79 (May 1965): 291–303; Tong Hun Lee, "Alternative Interest Rates and the Demand for Money: The Empirical Evidence," *American Economic Review* 57 (December 1967): 1168–1181; David E. W. Laidler, "The Rate of Interest and the Demand for Money— Some Empirical Evidence," *Journal of Political Economy* 77 (December 1966): 543–555; Martin Bronfenbrenner and Thomas Mayer, "Liquidity Functions in the American Economy," *Econometrica* 28 (October 1960): 810–834.

same definition of money and short-term interest rates.[3] This, again, is in an intermediate range of values, far from either extreme. If these money supply and demand functions are taken into account, it is difficult not to conclude that the resulting LM curve must be relatively interest-elastic, although some of the elasticity may be due to the fact that the money supply responds positively to a rise in the interest rate due to commercial or central bank actions. In any event, there is little doubt that money matters, but it is not the whole story.

The other part of the story is the shape of the IS curve and its implications for the real sector. Here, too, it is interesting to examine the results of empirical studies investigating the relationship between the interest rate and the expenditures (both consumption and investment) that constitute aggregate demand. The notion that monetary policy affects investment (and thus aggregate demand) via the interest rate and the MEI curve is not new. One empirical study of the United States economy over the time period 1953–1965 has shown that a 1 percentage point fall in the interest rate leads to a $3.3 billion rise in investment after two quarters. The relationship was not found to be highly stable, however, suggesting that it may not hold over time.[4] It should also be noted that several studies have demonstrated that a significant inverse relationship exists between the interest rate and the level of consumption, especially of durable goods.[5] Probably this is because many consumer durables are purchased with credit, so the level of interest rates can affect this type of consumer demand. In addition, the results of computer simulation studies show that injections of high-powered money may affect consumption spending not only via the interest rate, but also more directly via increases in household wealth.[6] The transmission mechanism

3. See: Karl Brunner and Allan H. Meltzer, "Some Further Investigations of the Demand and Supply Functions of Money," *Journal of Finance* 19 (May 1964): 240–283; Ronald Teigen, "Demand and Supply Functions for Money in the United States: Some Structural Estimates," *Econometrica* 32 (October 1964): 476–509; Stephen M. Goldfeld, *Commercial Bank Behavior and Economic Activity* (Amsterdam, 1966); Stephen M. Goldfeld and Edward J. Kane, "The Determinant of Member-Bank Borrowing: An Econometric Study," *Journal of Finance* 21 (September 1966): 499–514; and Frank de Leeuw, "A Model of Financial Behavior," in James Duesenberry et al., eds., *The Brookings Quarterly Econometric Model of the United States* (Chicago: Rand McNally, 1965).

4. J. R. Moroney and J. M. Mason, "The Dynamic Impacts of Autonomous Expenditures and the Monetary Base on Aggregate Income," *Journal of Money, Credit and Banking*, 1972; see also articles cited by Dale Jorgenson in "Economic Studies of Investment Behavior: A Survey," *Journal of Economic Literature* 9 (December 1971): 1111–1147.

5. Colin Wright, "Saving and the Rate of Interest," in A. C. Harberger and M. J. Bailey, eds., *The Taxation of Income from Capital* (Washington, D.C.: Brookings Institution, 1969), pp. 275–299; and Michael J. Hamburger, "Interest Rates and the Demand for Consumer Durable Goods," *American Economic Review* 42 (December 1967): 1131–1153.

6. Frank de Leeuw and Edward M. Gramlich, "The Channels of Monetary Policy," *Federal Reserve Bulletin* (June 1969): 472–491; and Franco Modigliani, "Monetary Policy and Consumption: Linkages via Interest Rate and Wealth Effects in the FMP Model," *Consumer Spending and Monetary Policy: The Linkages* (Boston: Federal Reserve Bank of Boston, 1971), pp. 9–84.

appears to be as follows: a large injection of high-powered money (through open-market operations by the Federal Reserve) pushes up the price of bonds (lowers the interest rate); the high price of bonds pushes up the price of common stocks, since with lower interest rates on bonds, stocks become more attractive as investments; households with portfolios of stock find themselves wealthier than before and therefore increase their consumption spending.

Taken together, the above studies appear to confirm the monetarist assumption that the IS schedule is interest-elastic due to a responsiveness of aggregate demand to changes in the interest rate. The level of investment moves inversely with the interest rate, as does the consumption of consumer durables. Direct injections of new money increase wealth and, indirectly, consumption. So monetary policy may have an influence on both sides of the IS/LM model. The empirical evidence is not conclusive, in part because the empirical techniques have not yet been perfected, and disagreements inevitably arise. Some economists see monetary policy influencing consumption, others see it influencing the level of investment. Still others deny that it influences significantly the level of investment. Perhaps the safest conclusion is that the empirical evidence which has been analyzed so far appears to support a middle position on the impact of monetary policy, somewhere between the assumptions of the monetarists and those of the Keynesians.

The Synthesists

By now the reader may have the feeling that our presentation of the extreme Keynesian and monetarist positions serve as straw men, diametrically opposed to each other and serving mainly to illuminate the policy implications of each set of assumptions. This is the motive, in part, although proponents of each view would argue vehemently against treating their assumptions as far-fetched or unrealistic. There is, however, a large group of economists occupying the middle ground that, as we have just seen, enjoys considerable empirical support. We will refer to them as "synthesists." They have studied the arguments of each side, examined the empirical evidence, selected among the assumptions, and synthesized a theory based on the best of classical and Keynesian analyses. Though this is by no means a homogenous group, it is possible to outline their main areas of agreement among themselves.

The synthesists accept one major classical assumption: that money is important not only because of its utility for transactions, but also as a store of value. This implies a role for the real-balance effect and at least a moderately price-elastic aggregate demand schedule. The synthesists in some cases also include certain categories of near-money, especially time deposits (such as savings accounts), in their calculations of the money supply. Some also argue that both the supply of and demand for money are interest-elastic, which means that the synthesists envisage a relatively interest-elastic LM curve, and the interest-elastic LM curve combined with the assumed real-balance effect yields a relatively price-elastic aggregate demand schedule.

Lest we assume that the synthesists are supporters of monetary policy alone, we must point out that most emphasize the Keynesian assumption that monetary policy only affects the real sector *indirectly*, although some recognize the direct impact on expenditure implied by the real-balance effect. Money matters, largely insofar as it affects the level of income in the commodity market by way of interest rate effects. If monetary policy is used to lower the interest rate, firms will expand investment. This presupposes, of course, that the MEI schedule is at least somewhat interest-elastic. The expanded level of investment will then lead to the usual increase in consumption spending via the multiplier. There may also be an additional increase in consumption spending due to lower interest rates. The synthesists have taken into account the relatively recent upsurge in consumer credit spending. Since many consumer durables (such as automobiles) are purchased with credit, some consumption may be directly responsive to changes in the interest rate. With both consumption and investment responding positively to a fall in the interest rate, the synthesists see monetary policy as an important indirect means of influencing aggregate demand.

Synthesists are also supporters of fiscal policy, however. We have seen how the extreme Keynesians believe that only fiscal policy is effective and how they expect it to produce the full multiplier on income. The synthesists also believe that fiscal policy is effective, since they share the assumption that the LM schedule is interest-elastic. They point out, however, that the level of investment is sensitive to the interest rate, since they doubt that the MEI schedule is perfectly interest-inelastic. This means that fiscal policy will lose some of its effectiveness in practice. Fiscal policy may shift the IS schedule upward and to the right, which will tend to increase consumption but will drive up the interest rate at the same time. At a higher interest rate there will be somewhat less investment, so the multiplier effect resulting from fiscal policy is diminished by the effects of an interest-elastic MEI schedule.

In summation, the synthesists to some extent bridge the broad gap between the extreme Keynesians and the extreme monetarists. They assume that the elasticities of the IS and LM schedules are both somewhere between the two extremes, neither highly interest-elastic nor highly interest-inelastic. This results in a somewhat price-elastic aggregate demand schedule which, in reality, is even more elastic because of the real-balance effect. The policy implications are clear: both monetary and fiscal policy are important; they are interrelated, and the traditional Keynesian multiplier effect for fiscal policy is dampened. Monetary policy is seen to have both an indirect and a direct influence via the real-balance effect on income and employment.

Fiscal and Monetary Policy Time Lags

Another important issue concerning the relative effectiveness of monetary and fiscal policy to stabilize the economy hinges upon the speed with which they may be applied and upon the predictability of the speed with which they effect desired changes. Clearly, a policymaker must perceive a problem such as unemployment before trying to solve it. The time required for a solution depends upon the speed with which a policy instrument may be activated and the speed with which it acts upon the economy once activated. If the total time lag from perception to actual impact of a policy measure is too long, intervening changes in the economy itself may have obviated the need for a policy action before it can produce its effect. In some cases, these changes may reverse the situation, so that the problem that called for an expansionary fiscal policy in August of 1973 may have become a problem requiring tight fiscal policy in August of 1974, just at the time the expansionary fiscal policy is taking hold.

The **enactment lag,** or **inside lag,**[7] which represents the time required to enact a policy once a problem is perceived, is probably shorter for monetary policy. The Federal Reserve is not subject to the Congressional debates and compromises so frequently required to enact tax changes or large discretionary stabilization-oriented changes in government expenditure. Later in this chapter we shall see that automatic stabilizers can to some extent avoid the fiscal lag problem, however.

The **impact lag,** or combined **intermediate** and **outside lags,** represents the time required for fiscal and monetary policy measures to affect the economy once enacted. This depends in theory upon assumptions of how monetary and fiscal policy work. If policymakers assume that monetary policy must operate *indirectly* upon expenditure through its effect on the interest rate, a change in government expenditure which affects aggregate demand *directly* will have a shorter impact lag than a change in the money supply. If policymakers regard the real-balance effect as significant, changes in the money supply will also affect aggregate demand directly, and impact lags for monetary and fiscal policy measures will be comparable. Once again, the issue revolves around problems of measurement. While the literature in this area is extensive and sometimes complex, we can get an idea of the magnitudes involved by looking at a representative supporting study for each assumption.

In a widely read study of the relative importance of monetary and fiscal policy actions in effecting economic stabilization, L. C. Andersen and J. L. Jordan present empirical evidence suggesting that monetary policy exerts

7. For a fuller discussion of inside lags as well as intermediate and outside lags discussed below, see Albert Ando and Stephen M. Goldfeld, "An Econometric Model for Evaluating Stabilization Policies," in Albert Ando, E. D. Brown, and A. F. Friedlander, eds., *Studies in Economic Stabilization* (Washington, D.C.: Brookings Institution, 1968).

a larger, more predictable, and faster impact on GNP than fiscal policy.[8] These economists found that a change in the money stock exerts a large and almost equal impact on GNP over each of the four quarters after it is enacted, whereas the response to fiscal policy measures is uniformly smaller and less reliable; further, the maximum impact on GNP of a fiscal policy measure usually occurs during the third quarter following its enactment.

Frank de Leeuw and John Kalchbrenner criticized the Andersen-Jordan results and tested a modified approach.[9] Their criticism was based largely upon the question of whether the monetary and fiscal variables required by the specifications of the Andersen-Jordan model were actually exogenous. In order to deal with this problem, they specified some modified indices of monetary and fiscal policy actions. They also extended to eight quarters the period over which the impact on GNP of policy actions was to be tested. Basically, de Leeuw and Kalchbrenner found longer impact lags for monetary and tax policies than for government expenditures. In general, they concluded that the Andersen-Jordan finding that monetary policy measures completely dominate fiscal measures in their impact upon GNP was unwarranted.

While this account of an exchange between analysts of the relative impacts of monetary and fiscal policy by no means exhausts the literature in the field, its content is typical of the type of debate which characterizes it. Disputes generally hinge on the methodology employed to measure the effects under investigation and upon the variables employed to measure exogenous policy actions. This observation holds in many cases where more elaborate models are employed to investigate price, employment, interest rate, and other effects of policy measures. The complete dominance of either monetary or fiscal policy measures has not been conclusively established by any of these studies, which suggests that they tend to confirm the intermediate approach to policy evolved by the synthesists.

We should note here that the strict monetarist view regarding impact lags of monetary policy as espoused by Milton Friedman is that these lags are so long and variable as to make countercyclical monetary policy unworkable and potentially destabilizing. Friedman maintains that the impact lags of monetary policy are highly unstable, and the effects of monetary policy measures occur at some uncertain and fairly remote future time. Expansionary monetary policies, for example, might begin to work during some future boom that was not anticipated at the time the policy measures were enacted. A fuller discussion of impact lags will be presented in Chapter 14,

---

8. L. C. Andersen and J. L. Jordan, "Monetary and Fiscal Actions: A Test of Their Relative Importance in Economic Stabilization," Federal Reserve Bank of St. Louis *Review*, November 1968, pp. 11–24.

9. Frank de Leeuw and John Kalchbrenner, "Monetary and Fiscal Actions: A Test of Their Relative Importance in Economic Stabilization: Comment," Federal Reserve Bank of St. Louis *Review*, April 1969, pp. 6–11.

following an examination of the theoretical underpinnings of monetary policy. In order to better understand the problems of enactment lags, we shall look briefly at fiscal and monetary policy tools.

Fiscal and Monetary Policy Tools

Economic stability generally includes the goals of stable prices, a steady rate of unemployment as close as possible to the 4 percent full-employment goal, steadily increasing GNP, and balance of payments equilibrium. Until after World War II an annually balanced budget was also considered a goal of economic stabilization policy, and fiscal policy, or government spending and taxation, was generally directed toward this goal: when government spending exceeded tax receipts, creating a deficit, a tax increase was aimed at raising government revenue; combined with lower government spending, this would balance the federal budget. In the postwar period, however, budget deficits have frequently been designed as a means of raising total demand and thereby lowering unemployment levels and increasing wages and prices. Although many economists and more politicians regard deficit spending as preferable to unemployment and sluggish growth, as high levels of inflation have become increasingly chronic, a tighter budget may once again be seen as a policy goal. But the very acceptance of fiscal policy—whether designed to stimulate or to dampen economic activity—has created a new series of problems.

Fiscal Policy Tools

Today it is meaningful to speak of the U.S. economy as having a fiscal structure of its own; a set of automatic stabilizers which as we saw in Chapter 5 respond directly to certain fiscal situations. Included are the present withholding tax system, a relatively high marginal rate of taxes on personal earnings, and a flat 48 percent tax rate on corporate profits. If there is a sudden upsurge in GNP, the effect will be muted somewhat, since taxes will cut heavily into the marginal earnings (of individuals and corporations) and prevent the total GNP increase from being passed on as disposable income. This, in turn, severely dampens the multiplier effect, since taxes cut into each successive round of earnings. If GNP should drop, the same mechanism cushions the effect on disposable income and minimizes the recessionary effects. Automatic stabilizers may have helped prevent recessions and inflationary periods from being more extreme since World War II, but by dampening the multiplier effect the fiscal structure may also inhibit recovery from a recession and slow down the economy's short-run growth rate, resulting in a phenomenon known to economists as **fiscal drag,** an unintended deflationary pressure. Long-term budget balancing replaced the goal of annually balanced budgets in the late 1940s. It was hoped that automatic stabilizers

Commentary: Handling Stagflation

The year is 1974. The time is spring, following the announcement of double-digit inflation and a drop in real GNP for the first quarter. Unemployment is up to 5.2 percent from 4.6 percent the previous fall; real income has declined 4.7 percent from the previous year; it is an election year for Congress, and the pressure is on to give the people some relief. A proposal to pass a $6.6 billion tax cut, an acceptable stimulant in any ordinary recession, represents in today's inflationary recession a large gamble that output will be stimulated more than price hikes.

Economists and politicians are divided over the proposal, which takes the form of an increased personal deduction from $750 to $825, with the option of substituting a $190 tax credit instead. The controversy seems to focus on three key areas: whether the cause of the downturn is insufficient supply or insufficient demand, whether the inflation will be fueled by a tax cut, and whether the budget already contains enough stimulus to combat the sluggishness of the economy.

The administration position is that the drop in GNP is a fallout from the energy crisis and is like such sudden one-quarter drops as in 1959, when a steel strike sent GNP from a growth of 10 percent in the second quarter to one of −4 percent in the very next quarter. In 1974 plummeting auto sales and dislocations due to energy shortages accounted for much of the decline. The Bureau of Labor Statistics points out that although about 500,000 people were thrown out of work by the energy crisis, the number of people employed actually rose in the first quarter. (The unemployment rate went up because the labor force grew even faster than the number of jobs.) In April, Herbert Stein, then chairman of the Council of Economic Advisers, insisted, "The downturn is not spreading, is not cumulative, and may be near the bottom. The fact that job losses have not spread elsewhere is evidence of the underlying strength of the economy."[1] He cited the optimistic plans of business for capital spending, the sectors of the economy operating at near full capacity with backlogs of orders, and the expectations for a rebound in autos and housing, two of the hardest hit sectors. The forecast for 1974 has been for a slow first half with a stronger second half of the year, and Stein saw no reason to change the forecast or to pump in $6.6 billion. Secretary of the Treasury William Simon seconded this: "We just feel a tax cut at this time would be highly inflationary. We have a problem of supply now, not demand."[2]

The administration's antirecession plans include speeding $22 billion in tax refunds and urging federal agencies to time spending for the early part of the year. The administration is also requesting Congress to eliminate tax provisions that cause overwithholding, which would free another $6 billion this year. The 1975 budget itself calls for an additional $30 billion in spending and a $9.4 billion deficit, both measures to stimulate the economy.[3] If the upturn fails to materialize, there are contingency plans to "bust the budget," but right now inflation is Public Enemy Number One, and the economic guns are trained on it.

Proponents of the tax cut also see inflation, particularly from the energy crisis, as a bane,

---

1. "Hands Off for a While Longer," *Business Week*, March 30, 1974, p. 22; and "Stein Sees Limit to Economic Slide," *New York Times*, March 25, 1974, p. 42.
2. "The Senate Edges Toward a Tax Cut," *Business Week*, April 27, 1974, p. 42.
3. Murray Weidenbaum of St. Louis University believes this very much underestimates the total stimulus. By correcting for political vicissitudes, higher unemployment compensation, and "off-budget" agencies, he finds the deficit around $20 billion. "Why Taxes Shouldn't Be Cut Now," *Wall Street Journal*, April 9, 1974, p. 20.

but not in quite the same way. To them inflation is eroding consumers' incomes and confidence, which will keep the economy depressed unless something is done. Richard N. Cooper of Yale estimates that the quadrupling of oil prices during the oil embargo will mean U.S. consumers have $15 billion less to spend on other goods, which is equivalent to a 10 percent increase in federal payroll and income taxes. Little of this $15 billion is going to be returned to the U.S. spending stream this year in the form of orders for U.S. goods by oil sheiks or higher dividends and capital outlays by domestic oil companies. Thus, the oil crisis raises prices and depresses demand. Cutbacks have come in the purchase of consumer durables: nondurables have kept only slightly ahead of inflation; and retail sales have not really risen over the past year. Periodic surveys of consumer confidence by the University of Michigan detect a recession mood with people afraid to make large spending commitments. Although the savings rate is down from a relatively high 7.3 percent to 6.5 percent in the first quarter—normally a sign of more spending and therefore a stronger economy— the reasons might simply be a shift from savings accounts to higher interest investments by some and the necessity of spending more just to live by many others.

Inflation affects taxes, too. The value of the $750 individual deduction is 20 percent less than when it was passed in 1972, due to progressively higher tax rates on incomes made higher in real terms, but not money terms, by inflation. And inflation is putting the poverty line so high that people well below it are beginning to be liable for taxes because there has been no adjustment in the tax tables. If inflation keeps up at 6 percent (an underestimation if we follow administration predictions for 1974 of 7 percent), a five-person family will begin to pay taxes while their income is about $700 below the poverty line in 1974. The loss of real income to inflation, according to tax-cut advocates such as George Perry at Brookings Institution, creates further inflationary pressures as people try to catch up by demanding higher and higher wages. A tax cut could re-store disposable income without raising the wage bill, thereby reducing, not intensifying, inflation.

Tax-cut advocates maintain that the economy still is plagued by deficient demand. According to Walter Heller, professor at the University of Minnesota and former chairman of the CEA under Kennedy and Johnson, "inflation in 1974 has a life of its own, nourished . . . mainly by a variety of cost factors beyond the reach of fiscal and monetary management." These include food and fuel shortages that have sent prices skyrocketing, "a lagged response to the boom in world commodity prices in general . . . , the sharp rise in unit labor cost," and the price bulge caused by the elimination of price controls. Heller maintains that excess demand is not the cause of the current inflation, and further asserts: ". . . the great bulk of the stimulus of a prompt tax cut would therefore express itself in higher output, jobs, and income, not in higher prices."[4] But he does not indicate why the second follows from the first.

The final decision as to appropriate policy steps is not easily made. Inflation itself is an onerous tax. Demand stimulation is risky in that it is predicated for its success upon anticipated increases in income and output that are expected to result from its application. Continuation of a "steady as she goes" policy contains the danger that the effective demand sapped from the economy by rapid price increases of the past year will result in a downward spiral. Behind the positions on each side probably lies an implicit willingness of tax-cutters to accept more inflation and of non-tax-cutters to accept a higher level of unemployment. Macroeconomics is not a precise enough instrument to mandate the outcome of the dispute; politics, which is even more imprecise, will play a large part in determining policy.

4. Walter Heller, "The Case for Fiscal Stimulus," *Wall Street Journal*, March 11, 1974, p. 14.

would produce a budget surplus in years with a high pace of economic activity (and a tendency toward inflation) which would balance the budget deficits of slower years, especially those in which recession cut drastically into government tax receipts. It must be remembered that the economic conditions were viewed as *creating* the surplus or deficit, not the other way around. This was not a discretionary (consciously applied, short-run) policy, but one which depended on the effectiveness of the automatic stabilizers.

The negative long-range effects of the fiscal structure became increasingly obvious during the 1950s as economic growth slackened and the economy was operating at far from peak capacity. In order to compare actual performance with the economy's potential, President Kennedy's economic advisers devised the concept of "full-employment surplus," the imaginary but calculable budgetary surplus that would exist if the economy were operating at full employment.[10] During the Kennedy-Johnson administrations the significance of the full-employment surplus was taken to be that it showed just how restrictive automatic stabilizers had become. Ideally, the economy should operate at full employment, and there should be neither a large surplus nor a large deficit. If, at full employment, there were a large surplus it would show that the economy was geared to budget balancing at a level of income far below full employment. But as soon as that level is exceeded, automatic stabilizers tend to dampen further expansion.

Monetary Policy Tools

Monetary policy basically consists of Federal Reserve measures to control the growth of the money supply. These include increasing or decreasing the level of reserve deposits required of member banks, increasing or decreasing the rediscount rate (the rate of interest on Federal Reserve loans to member banks), and open-market operations (buying and selling government bonds in the open market). Thus the Federal Reserve can expand the money supply by (1) increasing the ability of commercial banks to make loans by lowering reserve requirements and/or the rediscount rate or (2) purchasing government securities held by commercial banks and thereby increasing the banks' stock of liquid assets, inducing them to make more loans. As we shall see in Chapter 14, the money supply will expand when commercial banks increase their loans. Similarly, the Federal Reserve can restrict the growth of the money supply by raising reserve requirements and/or the rediscount rate or by selling government securities to commercial banks. The stabilizing and destabilizing effects of these measures will be examined in detail in Chapter 14, when we look at the policy applications of monetarist theory. An understanding of Federal Reserve operations, however, will enable us to consider the relative effectiveness of fiscal and monetary policy in the United States since the end of World War II.

---

10. See Chapter 5 for a review of this concept.

Stabilization Policy in Operation, 1945–1970

Having examined the theoretical assumptions which underlie the choice of fiscal or monetary policy measures, we can briefly review the operation of both fiscal and monetary policy during the postwar years in order to consider their relative effectiveness in practice. This chapter will carry the record through the 1960s; Chapter 20 will then take it into the 1970s.

It is always difficult to generalize from the historical record. In theory, the policy stabilization record in the United States in recent years should provide a showcase in which the effectiveness of monetary and fiscal policy measures could be evaluated. In practice, however, the use of stabilization tools is often determined by other than stabilization requirements. Political, social, and military objectives may on occasion interfere with stabilization objectives. In 1931–1932, for example, when extremely depressed domestic economic conditions might have suggested a policy of monetary ease and low interest rates in order to stimulate business investment, the New York Federal Reserve bank raised the discount rate on eligible paper from 1.5 percent in May 1931 to 3.5 percent in October 1931 in an attempt to attract foreign deposits and discourage the outflow of gold from the United States. In fiscal 1968, on the other hand, although the economy was operating at a high level with clear evidence of serious inflationary pressures—conditions that would normally call for restraints in government spending and perhaps a budget surplus—military expenditures were permitted to escalate by $10 billion to $80 billion and final budget figures showed a substantial deficit.

A number of measures are used to evaluate economic stability and progress in achieving goals; these include GNP, the unemployment rate, the consumer price index, and budget surpluses and deficits. Table 12.1 charts the annual performance of various economic indicators since 1945. The discount rate, which fluctuates significantly within each year, is shown in Figure 12.6, together with the prime rate, the rate of interest which commercial banks charge borrowers with the highest credit ratings. Because of the difficulty in drawing firm conclusions about the theoretical effectiveness of fiscal and monetary policy measures from their performance to date, however, we will not try to pronounce judgment on either.

The Post–World War II Period: 1945–1949

Economic policy during the immediate postwar period was significantly influenced by nationwide fears that the country would suffer a severe depression once the economic stimulus provided by the war was over. By contrast, there was relatively little concern about inflation, at least initially. Almost at once, wartime wage and price controls were removed, and monetary policy was dominated by Federal Reserve open-market operations, the device through which the central bank bought enough government bonds in the open market to keep interest rates on the federal debt low and thus simplify Treasury debt management problems. However, a release of pent-up

Table 12.1   Selected Economic Indicators, 1945–1973

Year	Consumer Price Index (1967 = 100)	Unemployment rate (percent of labor force)	Real GNP (billions of 1958 dollars)	Real GNP index (1967 = 100)
	(1)	(2)	(3)	(4)
1945	53.9	1.9[a]	$355.2	52.6
1946	58.5	3.9[a]	312.6	46.3
1947	66.9	3.9	309.9	45.9
1948	72.1	3.8	323.7	47.9
1949	71.4	5.9	324.1	48.0
1950	72.1	5.3	355.3	52.6
1951	77.8	3.3	383.4	56.8
1952	79.5	3.0	395.1	58.5
1953	80.1	2.9	412.8	61.1
1954	80.5	5.5	407.0	60.3
1955	80.2	4.4	438.0	64.9
1956	81.4	4.1	446.1	66.1
1957	84.3	4.3	452.5	67.0
1958	86.6	6.8	447.3	66.2
1959	87.3	5.5	475.9	70.5
1960	88.7	5.5	487.7	72.2
1961	89.6	6.7	497.2	73.6
1962	90.6	5.5	529.8	78.5
1963	91.7	5.7	551.0	81.6
1964	92.9	5.2	581.1	86.1
1965	94.5	4.5	617.8	91.5
1966	97.2	3.8	658.1	97.5
1967	100.0	3.8	675.2	100.0
1968	104.2	3.6	706.6	104.6
1969	109.8	3.5	725.6	107.5
1970	116.3	4.9	722.1	106.9
1971	121.3	5.9	741.7	109.8
1972	125.3	5.6	790.7	117.1
1973	133.1	4.9	837.4	124.0

a. Based on population aged 14 and over; remaining data based on population aged 16 and over.

b. M_1 = currency plus demand deposits; figures based on December stock.

c. Calendar year (National Income Accounts) basis.

d. Balance on current account.

e. Manufacturing utilization rate—output as percent of capacity.

Annual percentage growth of real GNP	Index of money stock $(M_1)^b$ (1967 = 100)	Budget surplus or deficit^c (billions of dollars)	Balance of payments^d (billions of dollars)	Capacity utilization rate (manufacturing)^e
(5)	(6)	(7)	(8)	(9)
−1.7	na	−42.1	na	na
−12.0	na	3.5	4.885	na
−0.9	60.5	13.4	8.992	na
+4.4	59.6	8.4	1.993	92.7
+0.2	56.5	−2.4	.580	83.8
+9.6	62.2	9.1	−2.125	91.9
+7.9	65.6	6.2	.302	95.1
+3.0	68.2	−3.8	−.175	92.8
+4.5	68.9	−7.0	−1.949	95.5
−1.4	70.8	−5.9	−.321	84.1
+7.6	72.3	4.0	−.345	90.0
+1.8	73.2	5.7	−1.722	88.2
+1.5	72.7	2.1	−3.556	84.5
−1.1	75.5	−10.2	−.005	75.1
+6.4	76.7	−1.2	−2.138	81.4
+2.5	77.2	3.5	1.801	80.1
+1.9	79.6	−3.8	3.069	77.6
+6.6	80.7	−3.8	2.456	81.4
+4.0	83.9	.7	3.199	83.0
+5.4	87.6	−3.0	5.783	85.5
+6.3	91.6	1.2	4.306	89.0
+6.5	93.8	−.2	2.320	91.9
+2.6	100.0	−12.4	2.051	87.9
+4.7	107.8	−6.5	−.443	87.7
+2.7	111.6	8.1	−1.050	86.5
−0.4	118.4	−11.9	−.416	78.3
+3.2	125.8	−22.2	−2.790	75.0
+6.1	136.8	−15.9	−8.353	78.6
+5.9	144.7	.9	3.041	83.0

SOURCES: Column (1): Department of Labor, *Handbook of Labor Statistics 1973*, Table 121, and *Monthly Labor Review*, April 1974. Column (2): Department of Labor, *Employment and Earnings* 20 (June 1974). Column (3): Department of Commerce, *National Income and Product Accounts, 1929–1967*, supplement to *Survey of Current Business*, and *Survey of Current Business* 50 (July 1970) and 54 (July 1974). Columns (4) and (5): Column (3). Columns (6) and (9): *Federal Reserve Bulletin*. Columns (7) and (8): Council of Economic Advisers, *Economic Report of the President*, 1974, Table C-67 and Table C-68.

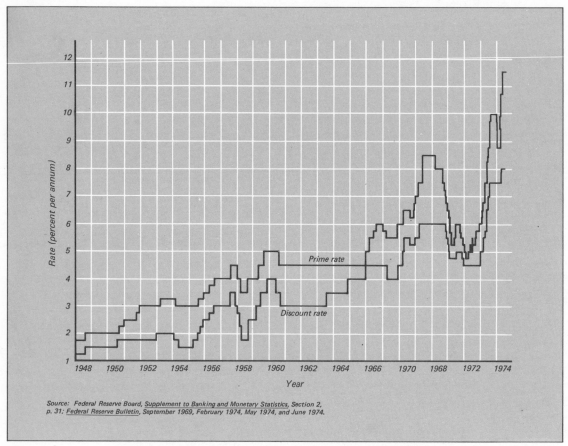

Figure 12.6 The discount rate and the prime rate, 1948–1974. Federal Reserve Bank discount rates on loans to member banks under Sections 13 and 13a.

demand for consumer goods and for business investment in plants and equipment began to be felt, encouraged by substantial liquid balances that had accumulated during the war years. Very shortly the inflationary consequences of these facts became clear—from 1946 to 1947, the consumer price index rose from 58.5 to 66.9 (1967 = 100), an increase of over 11 percent, and further price jumps occurred in 1948. The boom continued until late 1948. Then the 1948–1949 recession saw unemployment increase from less than 4 percent in 1948 to almost 6 percent in 1949, and prices finally stabilized, with the CPI actually declining during part of 1949.

During most of the expansionary phase of this cycle (1946–1948), federal fiscal policy was deflationary; large federal budget surpluses occurred in calendar years 1946, 1947, and 1948,[11] largely as a result of the tremendous

11. There are two ways of measuring federal budget surpluses and deficits: the fiscal year basis and the calendar year, or National Income Accounts, basis. Unless otherwise stated, figures are based on the calendar year.

drop in government spending from almost $85 billion in wartime 1945 to $29.8 billion in 1947. It should be noted, however, that some small part of the deflationary consequences of these federal surpluses were nullified because of large deficits in state and local budgets during the same period, deficits that reflected "catch-up" spending on building projects deferred during the war. In May 1948, however, Congress passed a 10 percent income tax cut, overriding President Truman's veto and ignoring the inflationary implications of such an action. The full effects of this tax cut were not felt until later that year, fortunately, by which time the economy had cooled off. The tax cut combined with some increase in government expenditures meant the 1949 budget was a deficit one, which probably contributed in part to the recovery which set in later that year. Monetary policy during the expansionary phase of this cycle included several increases in the discount rate and the imposition of higher reserve requirements, but much of the deflationary significance of such measures was weakened by the previously mentioned open-market operations. During the recession phase, the Fed reduced reserve requirements.

The Korean War Period and Its Aftermath: 1950–1954

A mild expansion was already underway when the Korean War began in June 1950. Remembering the shortages of World War II, consumers and businesses rushed out to buy. Government military spending also increased sharply, and major inflationary pressures appeared almost at once. Consumer prices spurted by 8.8 percent from June 1950 to June 1951, and the wholesale price index was up even more. Unemployment declined rapidly, holding steady at about a 3 percent level during most of 1951–1952. By mid-1951 prices began to stabilize, and during the next two years the United States enjoyed the enviable combination of both full employment and stable prices. Then the Korean War with its military spending ended in July 1953 and a recession set in. The index of industrial production declines by almost 6 percent from 54.8 in 1953 to 51.9 in 1954 (1967 = 100), and unemployment moved back up from 3 percent to 5.5 percent. The recession lasted for about a year, until August 1954.

Fiscal policy tools were used actively during this period. Higher taxes were imposed almost at the onset of the Korean War; as a result, the budget was in surplus during 1951, a measure which probably helped restrain the price inflation. Moreover, the same taxes that were introduced at the beginning of the war were permitted to expire in late 1953 and 1954, after the war ended, and these tax cuts are generally considered to have been a significant factor in keeping the 1953–1954 recession a mild one. Monetary policy was dominated by the "accord" of March 1951, in which the Treasury and the Federal Reserve finally agreed that the Fed would no longer be required to purchase government bonds on the open market in order to keep Treasury financing costs low but could instead buy and sell these bonds in accordance with stabilization requirements. The Fed used this additional flexibility to some extent during the expansionary part of the cycle, selling government bonds in an attempt to restrain the growth of member bank reserves. It also raised the discount rate during this period. Once the economy turned down in mid-1958, the Fed became even more aggressive, buying bonds in open-market operations, cutting reserve requirements twice, and reducing the discount rate.

The 1954–1958 Business Cycle

The expansionary phase that lasted from mid-1954 until mid-1957 was dominated by a boom in investment spending in the private sector, with total investment (GPDI) increasing by 43 percent from the first quarter of 1954 to the third quarter of 1957 and inventories showing a gain of 18 percent. The decline in economic activity, when it appeared in mid-1957, was also reflected in the investment figures, with total investment declining from $67.9 billion in the third quarter of 1957 to $52.4 billion in the first quarter of 1958 and the change in inventories during the period moving from +$2.7 billion to −$6.9 billion.

An important characteristic of this cycle was that, for the first time, both the unemployment figures and the price figures showed signs of the sticky performance which was to bedevil economic planners during the late 1960s and 1970s. Despite the sharp recovery experienced by the economy during the 1954–1957 period in terms of GNP, unemployment never fell below the 4.2 percent level. Although prices remained steady in 1954, they began to increase in 1955 and throughout the rest of the period, both during the expansion and during the downturn.

The Eisenhower administration was philosophically committed to the concept of "fiscal integrity," or a balanced budget, and fiscal policy in this period was primarily devoted to accomplishing these goals. The budget showed surpluses in the years 1955, 1956, and 1957, which were probably helpful in restraining the inflationary forces at work in the economy at the time, although the effectiveness of these surpluses was limited to a considerable extent in this case by concurrent deficits in state and local government budgets. Instead of cutting taxes when the economy turned down in 1957, government fiscal policy was directed primarily to some speeding up of highway construction and public works expenditures plus an extension of the time period for which unemployment insurance benefits would be paid. As a result of these measures and some decline in government receipts due to the slowdown in business, the budget did show a relatively large deficit in 1958 (−$10.2 billion).

Monetary policy during the first part of the expansion (1953) was fairly expansionary. In 1954 the discount rate was lowered. Then between early 1955 and 1957 the discount rate rose seven times, climbing from 1.5 percent in late 1954 to 3.5 percent by mid-1957, and the reserves of the banking system in general were restricted. The Federal Reserve did not respond immediately to the beginning of the recession in 1957, but by November it embarked on a series of rate reductions, and by May of 1958 the discount rate had declined to 1.75 percent. (Although it then began to rise again.) Open-market operations and reductions in reserve requirements were also used in attempts to expand bank reserves.

April 1958 – February 1961: The Fourth Postwar Business Cycle

The recovery that began in mid-1958 lasted for about two years, during which time real GNP increased by about 11 percent. Nevertheless, the recovery seemed to lack much of the vigor of other turnarounds and it was, in addition, somewhat shortlived. Although unemployment declined from 7.6 percent in August 1958 to 4.9 percent in June 1959, subsequently it began to rise and it remained at about 5.5 percent during most of the rest of the expansion. Similarly, the capacity utilization rate for manufacturing firms, which had reached 90 percent during the 1954–1957 expansion, never exceeded 84.4 percent in this cycle. Prices continued to increase slowly but persistently, and many began to question the viability of an economy which was growing at an average rate of only 3–4 percent and was faced with substantial underutilization of both human and physical resources even during its boom periods. The expansion ended in the second quarter of 1960, followed by a minor recession. Real GNP fell by 1.4 percent during the ensuing nine-month downturn between April and December, unemployment rose to over 6 percent, and creeping inflation continued.

Macroeconomic policy choices during the period were affected by persistent balance of payments problems, with the U.S. gold stock declining from about $22 billion in 1955 to less than $18 billion by the end of 1960. Continuing and growing payments deficits suggested that this gold outflow would continue. As a result, monetary authorities began to recognize that in the future, interest-rate policy would have to be set in accordance with balance of payments considerations as well as domestic economic requirements. As we shall see in Chapter 18, applying monetary policy to more than one goal at a time is not likely to be workable unless policymakers keep their goals flexible.

Many authorities credit both the lack of vigor shown by the recovery and the subsequent recession to the absence of aggressive fiscal measures on the part of the Eisenhower administration. For example, in the recession year 1960, the budget on a National Income Account basis showed a surplus of $3.5 billion. (On a full-employment basis, the surplus was about $13 billion.) This reflected the administration's preoccupation with the concept of the balanced budget; thus, when the 1959 figures showed that the budget was $1.2 billion in deficit, the response of the administration in 1960 was to reduce expenditures and increase taxes despite the fact that the economy was turning down.

Monetary policy during the expansion involved major increases in the discount rate (from 1.75 percent in April 1958 to 4 percent in September 1959) plus open-market operations directed at restraining the growth of the money supply, with interest rates throughout the economy rising to their highest levels since the 1920s. Some efforts were made to reduce interest rates and expand reserves once the expansion ended, but because of balance of payments problems, the Fed felt obliged to keep short-term rates fairly high in order to discourage short-term capital outflows to foreign money centers offering higher rates. In an attempt to balance these foreign considerations with domestic economic needs, a new policy, "operation twist," was adopted by the money managers, in which the Open-Market Committee sold short-term government debt (thus keeping short-term rates up in order to attract foreign borrowing and help the balance of payments position), and bought long-term bonds (thus keeping long-term rates down in order to encourage capital formation and growth). The operation was never completely satisfactory, however: gold outflows continued, and the refusal of the Fed to encourage short-term rates to decline significantly in 1960 was probably one factor contributing to the sluggishness of the recovery. The failure of "operation twist" was preordained by the fact that investors adjust the term structure of their portfolios according to the term structure of the interest rates. If the Fed acts to raise short-term rates and lower long-term rates, investors will respond by lending more short and less long,[12] which cancels the impact of Fed actions on the term structure of interest rates.

The Soaring Sixties

The recession of 1960–1961 was just about over when President Kennedy took office in January 1961; by the end of the year, unemployment had dropped from 7 percent in May 1961 to 6 percent, and capacity utilization had inched up from 74 percent to 81 percent. Most of the stimulus for this improvement came from the private sector, with inventory building providing the main impetus. In general, government action was limited to expansion of transfer payments and higher public works expenditures and farm supports. The expansion continued throughout 1962; real GNP showed an increase of 9.2 percent between mid-1961 and end of 1962, but unemployment never dropped below 5.5 percent and capacity utilization never rose above 81 percent, and by mid-year there were indications that the expansion was beginning to lose steam. At this point, two important innovations occurred: the Treasury introduced new permissible depreciation schedules that resulted in lower current tax payments, and Congress passed the investment tax credit, a measure which permitted businesses to subtract 7 percent of the cost of most new capital investments from their tax bills and thus encouraged investment spending. In addition, disturbed by the continuing high level of unemployment and the signs of slowdown, President Kennedy recommended to Congress a tax program that would cut both individual and corporate taxes. The measure found little support in Congress, particularly among those financial conservatives who pointed out that the budget was

---

12. If investors lend short, they accumulate a large quantity of assets to mature in 90–180 days; lending long generally refers to assets maturing in more than a year.

already in deficit even without a tax cut, but it was introduced again in 1963. This time the original package of tax cuts and tax reforms was accompanied by requests for substantial increases in government spending. Congressional foes immediately attacked proposed expenditures, and by late 1963, Kennedy's aggressive fiscal solution for economic sluggishness seemed to have little chance of passage.

Following the President's death in November 1963, however, Congress quickly adopted many of the Kennedy fiscal measures it had refused to consider earlier. These included mass transit legislation, the Economic Opportunity Act of 1964, and, most important, an $11 billion tax cut. Reductions in withholding taxes were implemented immediately, giving a major boost to the economy. Almost at once, the economy began to show significant signs of improvement, and by the first half of 1965, real GNP was growing at an annual rate of nearly 6 percent, unemployment was below 4.5 percent and capacity utilization reached 88 percent. Prices, moreover, remained relatively stable: the CPI moved up by only 1.1 points in 1963 and by 1.2 points in 1964 (1967 = 100). Increased prosperity throughout the economy created much higher government revenues—total federal revenues were almost $10 billion higher in calendar 1965 than in calendar year 1963.

In mid-1965 President Johnson sent a message to Congress asking for additional funds to fight the war in Vietnam. Over the next four years larger and larger sums were requested, appropriated, and spent, with total military expenditures reaching $80 billion in fiscal 1968. During this period, only modest attempts were made to reduce nondefense spending, and the economy which had been operating at a high level without this additional stimulus, suffered escalating inflationary pressures. The consumer price index was up 2.7 points in 1966, 2.8 in 1967. 4.2 in 1968, and 5.6 in 1969. Unemployment declined sharply, remaining below 4 percent from late 1965 through 1969, and capacity utilization reached the 90 percent level. Despite these indications of overheating, which were clear as early as 1965, political considerations such as the 1966 election and the unpopularity of the war kept the administration from requesting a tax increase in 1965 or 1966—indeed, excise taxes were actually cut in 1965.

The main brunt of the fight against inflation during those years was left to the monetary authorities, who increased the discount rate from 4 percent to 4.5 percent in December 1965, kept money supply growth at a minimum, and permitted interest rates to reach their highest levels in more than 35 years: the rate on prime commercial paper, for example, which had been around 3 percent in 1960–1963, reached 6 percent in 1966. Contradictory economic signs appeared in early 1967. Real GNP fell slightly during the first part of the year (from $668.1 billion in the fourth quarter of 1966 to $666.6 billion in the first quarter of 1967) and climbed only a modest 2.6 percent for the entire year.

Capacity utilization dropped, but unemployment stayed below 4 percent, although the inflation rate actually increased. The Fed, apparently viewing the situation as one with recessionary possibilities, adopted expansionary monetary policies, increasing the reserves of commercial banks with open-market operations, cutting the discount rate, and permitting the money supply to increase by 6.6 percent from December 1966 to December 1967. The administration, on the other hand, appeared more worried about the inflationary implications of the continuing federal deficits (over $12 billion in calendar year 1967) and the climbing consumer price index, and finally requested a tax increase from Congress. This was not passed in that year, however. By late 1967, clear signs of economic improvement began to appear, the Fed raised the discount rate, and as inflation became an increasingly serious problem, Congress granted the President a 10 percent tax surcharge in mid-1968. Further increases in the discount rate were introduced throughout 1968 and 1969. The Fed also attempted to some extent to control the growth of the money supply through the traditional open-market operations and reserve requirement changes. The banks, however, found ways of circumventing each new regulation (some banks were able to attain additional reserves through operations in the eurodollar market—i.e., the dollar market outside the United States), and the money supply continued to grow during 1968 (7.8 percent) and the first half of 1969.

When President Nixon took office in 1969, GNP was still moving up briskly, unemployment was 3.3 percent, and the CPI was rising at a rate of 5 percent a year. The fiscal 1968 budget showed a $25 billion deficit (although the calendar year deficit was only −$.3 billion). Nevertheless, the new President modified the tax program recommended by the departing President Johnson, who had asked for a one-year extension of the 10 percent tax surcharge from its original expiration date of June 30, 1969. President Nixon initiated a six-month extension at the 10 percent rate and then the imposition of a 5 percent surcharge from January 1, 1970 to June 30, 1970. However, he also obtained the repeal of the investment tax credit. Higher social security taxes were also collected beginning January 1, 1969, so that on balance little tax relief was granted during 1969. In addition, in mid-1969 the Federal Reserve Board tightened monetary policy significantly, allowing almost no growth in the money supply during the last six months of the year and permitting the prime rate to rise to 8.5 percent. By late 1969 there were some signs that a downturn was imminent, and by mid-1970, with the capacity utilization rate in the mid-70s, unemployment over 5 percent, and real GNP actually down for the year, it was clear that the extended prosperity of the soaring sixties was over.

The ineffectiveness of high interest rates during this period as a vehicle for controlling inflation may raise questions about the responsiveness of expenditure to changes in interest rates, although GNP did finally drop. A full understanding, however, requires analysis of the interrelationships between deficit budgets on the part of the government, interest rates, and the money supply and price expectations. If the government runs a large deficit which must be financed through borrowing, such borrowing will tend to lead to higher interest rates. This was the situation during 1967, for example, when the federal calendar year budget showed deficit of over $12 billion. If, however, the monetary authorities wish to keep interest rates down at the same time, as they did in 1967, their only alternative is to increase the money supply. This in turn puts upward pressure on prices, and the eventual consequence of several repetitions of this pattern is that inflationary expectations begin to dominate the money market, and lenders begin to demand ever-higher interest rates in order to compensate for the expected inflation. The result is a spiraling inflation, which can be traced to the increases in the money supply which were themselves the consequence of the original budget deficits.

Questions and Exercises

1. Describe the differences in the shape of the LM curve envisioned by the extreme Keynesians, the classicalists, and the synthesists. What is the rationale for each?
2. What factors would contribute to the elasticity or inelasticity of the IS curve?
3. Use the IS and LM curves to describe the effects the extreme Keynesians would expect from either expansionary fiscal or monetary measures.
4. Assume that an economist believes that maximum effect on the economy is produced only by the use of both monetary and fiscal measures. What specific point of view is he expressing?
5. What condition is described by "fiscal drag"? Are there any circumstances in which it might be viewed as a desirable effect? If so, what circumstances?
6. Assume you are a manager for Best Housekeeping Home Appliances, and you read in the *Wall Street Journal* that the Federal Reserve Board is considering selling a large issue of Treasury notes. What might be the consequences, if any, for the volume of sales for your business? Why?
7. Why is the definition of money so important in the determination of the elasticity of demand for money? Assume that a researcher includes savings accounts and short-term notes, such as 90-day Treasury bonds, in his definition of money. What would be the consequences for his findings? Why?
8. What economic problems in general faced the Eisenhower, Kennedy, and Johnson administrations, and what were the major methods used to deal with them?
9. It has been pointed out that though an individual firm may have a smaller capital stock than desired, its rate of acquisition may not be so easy to predict. Under certain circumstances, for example, we presume that the firm will wish to expand its stock of capital, but such an objective may be met by net investment rates of almost zero to near infinity. What are the implications of this point for the controversy concerning the slope of the IS curve? Is it possible that the slope of the IS curve is very specific to a given set of circumstances?
10. We have noted that changes in interest rates may affect the wealth of many consumers. How? Is there any similar effect that you might suggest occurring for a business that owns capital equipment? Assume a drop in interest rates. What happens to the opportunity cost of investing directly in a business as opposed to holding bonds? How does the change in attractiveness of holding capital stock affect the price of the capital?

Classical and Monetarist Macroeconomic Theory

PART III

Money

"NEW YORK — International Investors Inc., the 'gold bug' fund, says business is so good it can't handle any more, at least for the time being. Most of the fund's assets are in gold stocks. The fund says it won't accept any new sales for two weeks while it beefs up its staff, increases office space and 'improves its administrative system.' However, shareholders wishing to liquidate stock can do so.

"Stephen Zarlenga, sales director, says the fund transacted some 6% of all mutual fund busi U.S. in the first quarter. swelled to $156.6 million fro million at year-end, and per net (asset value) rose 54% to from $14.27. The fund is expec resume normal operations May

They never ring a bell, goe old Wall Street adage, when it's

Friedman Sees Wide Usage as Inflation Curb

By SOMA GOLDEN

Milton Friedman is at it again. The renowned economist from the University of Chicago has proposed a policy for beating inflation that has stirred his profession. What's more, the spunky con- servative says his idea will eventual triumph despite in the profession's initial resistance.

Economic Analysis

"It's only a question of when— not if," he predicted in a recent interview, with a self-assurance almost unmatched these days among economists.

Follows Brazilian Plan

The professor is proposing a plan — modeled he says after the recent Brazilian experience —to protect Americans against inflation through the use of a comprehensive system of escalator clauses throughout the economy.

Under the Friedman plan, wages would be per cent adjusted for rises or drops in the cost of living.

¶Interest rates on time deposits, Federal debt, corporate bonds, mortgages, and the like, would be supplemented by a similar 100 per cent inflation adjustment.

¶Income tax brackets and personal exemption levels would be readjusted every year to make sure that people do not have to pay Uncle Sam more taxes because of incomes artificially swollen by inflation.

¶Business accounting practices—such as depreciation and the valuation of fixed assets— would be changed to reflect the impact of rising prices.

Easier, 'Not Harder'

Most economists — confused by inflation and not familiar

ments is apt to change overnight; the Thursday-Friday rally in bullion and shares may well prove a flash in the pan. Yet there is reason to doubt whether gold, as a usually astute observes, so to speak, to the market week, has been "put on ice." For one thing, according to Richard Russell, eminent Dow theorist, the short interest in six listed gold stocks (four on the NYSE, two on the Amex), has increased steadily. At last count ued 235,133 shares, up fro t the end Techni t's bu

As ner the re ecisi Econo Econo r gold n the mark key the mai at e s emai n, tl n, can inance the com- mon y and monetary value alike of the precious metal. Finally, the U.S. Treasury, after a welcome changing of the guard, at long last may be ready to yield some of its indefensible positions, notably the ban on American citizens' ownership of gold. At $165 an ounce—a price few thought would ever be reached— gold will have its ups and downs. But in a day and age of currency debasement, as even Keynesians perforce must admit, the "barbarous relic" plays a vital role.

In the process it has done very well by patient holders. From a low of approximately $90 an ounce last November (when Arthur Burns touched off a momentary panic among the uninformed and unwary by disclosing, in terms calculated to mislead, the formal end of the so-called two-tier system), bullion shot up to a recent high around $18 more than four times th par. Similarly mon F imes Gold surged from 140 to over

Trends in Brazil: Inflation and Output

(Annual Change In Per Cent)

Wholesale Prices

out the idea. But virtually no one thought the proposal could be ignored, now that Professor Friedman had become its champion. George P. Shultz, Secretary of the Treasury, was typical: Milton Friedman is always worth listening to, he said.

The reason is reflected in recent economic history that without doubt been altered by Professor Friedman's campaigns. He has banged away at his fellow economists for years arguing primarily for more attention to the critical role of monetary policy in stabilizing the economy and for a switch from fixed to floating exchange rates in the international monetary system. The professor has made headway on both fronts and seems, at age 61, eager for the next battle.

'The argument for indexing is precisely the same as the

shares—Durban Deep, East Driefontein, East Rand Proprietary, Harmony, Kinross, Loraine, Southvaal, Randfontein, Winkelhaak—did even better.

Meanwhile, run-of-the-mill investments, stocks and bonds alike— not to mention cash in the bank—relentlessly declined in pur power. Small wonder tha nars becar the r tern ng i has yers ned anal h b going a land- s. The Frankfurter All- g me Zeitung last month reported: "The gold mania which has stricken West Germany and other countries can only be explained by panic buying by thousands of investors

Rise of the Gold Bugs

By WILLIAM H. PETERSON

For decades gold advocates and investors were dismissed as "gold bugs."

Who needs gold anyway? Lenin said gold should be used for building public lavatories. Keynes said gold is a "barbarous relic." Keynesians perforce must admit the "barbarous relic" plays a vital role.

Big Drop Posted In Federal Funds Rate to 10½%

Fed Bid to Aid Small Banks In Wake of Troubles at Franklin National Cited

A WALL STREET JOURNAL News Roundup

Efforts by the Federal Reserve Bank of New York to help small banks in the wake of Franklin National Bank's financial troubles apparently triggered a sharp decline in the rate on federal funds, a key short-term money-market interest rate.

The rate on those overnight loans of un committed reserves banks lend each other fell to 10½% in afternoon trading yesterday from 11⅜% Friday. Borrowing in the fed eral funds market is an important source o credit banks use to support lending opera tions.

Dealers attributed the lower funds rate to several factors:

—A heavy infusion of cash into the bank ing system last week by the nation's money managers.

—Stepped-up borrowing from the Fed's discount window, presumably banks h Diffi sing of where. ranklin Nation al's fina have made investors highly selective, to the detriment of many smaller, but financially sound banks.

—A sharp drop-off in the purchase of fed

fruitful alternative use for th funds.

So fresh weakness, which wo shake out the timorous and impr the market's technical positi should come as no surprise. Long range prospects are bright. Desp all efforts onetize the ial, ed by such doc s Pa A. Volcker, Un of t Treasury for Mo s, exchange value, cen as well as priv inve multiplied. No W ern g it would give up nce 0. Now the Europ economi mmunity, faced w the need finance heavy oil curred p ments deficits, agreed t value its gold holdi to ket-related" level. Dut ster of Finance is tak decision to Washington, whi with Shultz gone and Volcker goi may well ease its adamant stan the IM

cluding the United States—through a greater buildup of SDRs in the world's reserves.

So does conferee John Exter, former Citibank senior vice president, who holds that SDRs are even worse than today's major currencies. These sorry currencies, he argues, are simply paper IOUs, which exhibit a powerful tendency to multiply in volume and divide in value; but the similarly irredeemable SDR, without any obligor, "is not even an IOU, but a Who Owes You." He is alarmed, declaring:

"Incentives to maintain exchange rates are gone. We are in a world of competitive exchange-rate depreciation. To weaken its currency a central bank must make it more abundant, create more, which means competitive world-wide expansionism, which in turn means world-wide inflation on a scale hitherto unknown in history."

Gold-foe conferee David Meiselman of Virginia Polytechnic Institute, a student of Milton Friedman, takes issue with this line of reasoning and puts forth the case against gold. He argues gold does not in sure price level or economic stability; nor

Inflation accounting

SIR—Your article on inflation and accounts (April 27th) pleads for reform on what are, at first sight, persuasive grounds: when assets appreciate, their replacement brings awkward cash problems if the income account shows the gain and thus causes bigger payments of tax and dividend. Unfortunately, the case must, I suspect, be put less simply if it is to be convincing.

The case is strong for nominal appreciation, due to general price rise. It is weak for real appreciation, ie, the excess of special rise (in the price of the given asset) over gener rise

Su ost special price moves are fairly stable. that it falls. Here wealth has been lost and, if accounts are to be useful, surely they must show a drop in income. Yet (to be consistent) the crude reformist argument must state that the accounts should not tell the owner of his loss, and that he should get no tax relief—because he

Escalator Clauses Backed

Store of Value

Monetarism: Old and New

13

This chapter will examine the modern reemphasis on money and monetary policy as principal influences upon economic activity and as principal mechanisms for controlling inflation or deflation. We begin with an early formulation of the quantity theory of money and trace subsequent development of monetary theory to the more sophisticated monetarism of today.

Fisher's Equation of Exchange

In classical monetary theory during the nineteenth and early twentieth centuries, the primary function of money was considered to be as a medium of exchange. Consequently, the demand for money was considered to be based upon its unique ability to facilitate the exchange of goods and services. Attention centered on money's medium-of-exchange role to the exclusion of its store-of-value role, thus ignoring its services as an alternative to other assets for liquidity purposes in portfolio holdings as well as purposes of risk aversion.

An early formulation of the demand for money as a medium of exchange is Irving Fisher's equation of exchange,[1] which states

$$MV = PT \qquad (13.1)$$

in which M is the quantity of basic money (coin and currency in public circulation); V is its velocity or turnover in a given period, say a year; P is the average price level at which total transactions occur; and T is the total of all transactions in the given period. Fisher's concept of transactions included *all* transactions in the economy for the given period, not just those involving Gross National Product, which is the market value of all final goods and services. Thus transactions for intermediate goods were also included.

Fisher expanded the money-supply side of the equation of exchange to include M_1 (bank deposit currency, i.e., demand deposits subject to check withdrawals) and V_1 (velocity of such demand deposits), as follows:

$$MV + M_1V_1 = PT \qquad (13.2)$$

or, dividing through by T in order to find P,

$$P = \frac{MV + M_1V_1}{T} \qquad (13.3)$$

Thus expanded, Fisher's equation of exchange indicates that the price level (P) is dependent upon three factors: (1) the quantity of basic money (M) and bank demand deposits to checks (M_1); (2) the intensity of usage of the money supply (M and M_1) in serving as media of exchange, or velocity of each (V and V_1); and (3) the total volume of transactions of all kinds (T).

Fisher's introduction of M_1 and V_1 was appropriate because it recognized the increasingly predominant use of the bank check as a convenient means of payment instead of cash. Moreover, it expanded the concept of the money supply to include bank demand deposits subject to checks, or in modern reference, M_1 (currency plus demand deposits), which today is just one of the conventional measures of the money supply (the others being M_2, or M_1 plus time deposits at commercial banks other than large certificates of deposit; and M_3, or M_2 plus deposits at nonbank thrift institutions).

The most important question raised by Fisher's equation of exchange concerns what values of V and V_1 will make it hold true. If the Vs are generally steady and if T is unchanged, then changes in M yield proportionate changes in P; that is, a 10 percent increase in the money supply would produce a 10 percent rise in the price level. As Fisher pointed out, the equation of

---

1. Irving Fisher, *The Purchasing Power of Money*, new and rev. ed. (1922; reprint ed., New York: Augustus M. Kelley, 1963), pp. 149–183. The first edition was published in 1911.

exchange is a particularly useful truism for considering the impact of an increase in the quantity of money on prices, given the conclusion which follows from assuming steady values of the Vs and T.

Fisher qualified the assertion that the proportional relationship between changes in the money supply and changes in the price level would hold by noting that when M is increased, V and V_1 might rise for a short time during a transitional period due to the negative impact of rising prices upon the demand for money. This follows naturally because rising prices represent a fall in the purchasing power of money. Fisher's example is perhaps most illuminating:

> We all hasten to get rid of any commodity which, like ripe fruit, is spoiling in our hands. Money is no exception; when it is depreciating, holders will get rid of it as fast as possible. As they view it, their motive is to buy goods which appreciate in terms of money in order to profit by the rise in their value. The inevitable result is that these goods rise in price still further.[2]

Fisher goes on to point out that the upward pressure on prices is eventually terminated by higher interest rates. The rise in interest rates reflects the increased rate of depreciation implied by inflation for the purchasing power of the dollars being received as interest lenders.

> If prices are rising at the rate of 2 percent per annum, the boom will continue only until interest becomes 2 percent higher. It then offsets the rate of rise in prices [which has artificially depressed the real cost of borrowing]. The banks are forced in self-defense to raise interest because they cannot stand so abnormal an expansion of loans relative to reserves. As soon as the interest rate becomes adjusted, borrowers can no longer hope to make great profits, and the demand for loans ceases to expand.[3]

Fisher's description of the forces operating to end inflation via interest rates and the resulting pressure on the banking system is highly suggestive as an interpretation of the situation in the United States in 1974. Whereas Fisher spoke of a once-and-for-all increase in the money supply, the United States has experienced steady increases over time, partly to adjust the money supply for the needs of a growing economy (the equivalent of a rising T, or transactions volume). Over time, a change in the rate of growth of the money supply in a growing economy is equivalent to a change in the quantity of money in a static economy. From February 1970 to January 1972, the U.S. money stock (M_1) rose at an average annual rate of 6.2 percent. From January 1972 to March 1974 that rate rose to 7.4 percent while the growth of real output (as approximated by industrial production) fell from about 12.4 percent during 1972 to 3.8 percent during 1973 and to about an annual rate of about −6.0 percent during the first quarter of 1974. The rapid acceleration of inflation (measured by the consumer price index at annual rates) during

2. Ibid., p. 63.
3. Ibid., p. 64.

these periods from 3.2 percent during 1972 to 9.0 percent during 1973 and about 14.0 percent during the first quarter of 1974, even though exacerbated somewhat by the effects of the "oil crisis," is entirely consistent with Fisher's predictions based upon his "useful truism."

So too is the rapid increase in interest rates. Inflation rose by 5.8 percent during 1973, while during the same period interest rates on six-month commercial paper rose by nearly 5.0 percent. If the rate of growth of the money supply is held constant or reduced after the first quarter of 1974, at some point the rise in interest rates will outstrip the willingness and ability of borrowers to pay such rates, and interest rates as well as prices will stabilize. If the rate of growth of the money supply is continually increased, the economy will remain fixed in Fisher's "transition period" with a continuation of rising prices and interest rates.

As the discussion of Fisher's "transition period" should make clear, he was careful to qualify the proportional relationship suggested by the equation of exchange between changes in the quantity of money and changes in the price level. In short, Fisher's quantity theory does *not* claim that V or V_1 never change, as many critics have charged. Fisher readily acknowledged that given a rise in the money supply, other changes occurring simultaneously might affect the Vs or T and thus break the proportional relationship between changes in M and changes in P. But the impact of M by itself on P, holding everything else constant, is strictly proportional. Fisher's quantity theory is not invalidated by observations on the rate of change of prices that are not equal to contemporaneous rates of change of the money supply.

In fact, Fisher considered in detail the factors likely to affect values of V and V_1. These factors, which reflect his concentration upon the role of money as a medium of exchange, include: (1) the habits of the individual as to thrift and hoarding and the use of credit and checks; (2) the system of payments employed in the community as regards the frequency and regularity of receipts and payments; and (3) general causes like population density and the rapidity of transportation.

Probably the major shortcoming of Fisher's theory of money lay in the emphasis placed upon the role of money as a medium of exchange. This tended to weaken his analysis of the transition period and to restrict the factors which were considered to have an effect upon velocity. While the role of money as a medium of exchange is perhaps its most obvious one, it must be realized that money must be able to store purchasing power over time and over distance if it is to serve as a medium of exchange. For example, the U.S. dollar does not store or carry purchasing power beyond the borders of the United States and therefore cannot be employed as a medium of exchange in other countries. Hence, the store of value of money, while less obvious, is an essential role which must be fulfilled if money is to serve as a medium of exchange. And once the store-of-value role of money is recognized, it becomes easy to view money on a continuum with other financial

assets like savings accounts, savings and loan shares, and bonds and stocks.
All assets, not only financial but also physical—like land, buildings, or factories—are stores of value or, more generally, wealth, and as such may be viewed as having something in common with money. Money is an asset to its owner, just as a plot of land or an apartment building is an asset to its owner.

We shall see that it is the fundamental view of money as a store of value (wealth) which characterizes the approach taken by prominent monetarist Milton Friedman to the analysis of the role of money in the economy. Before turning to the analytical foundation of Friedman's approach, it will be useful to consider a proximate representation of a simple quantity theory in national income form. This model is employed by Friedman and others for the purpose of considering the simple quantity theory with figures derived from the national income accounts in place of the total money value of transactions (or PT) employed by Fisher. After a brief look at a related equation describing the relationship between money and income known as the Cambridge-k equation, we will consider Friedman's approach to the demand for money as an asset, his permanent income theory of the demand for money. This theory supplies the theoretical basis for some of Friedman's monetary policy recommendations.

The Quantity Theory in National Income Form

With the development and availability of national income accounting and data, it has become more meaningful analytically to express the quantity theory as a relationship between the quantity of money and national income expressed in terms of money. Recall that national income is the market value of all final goods and services produced in the economy in a given period, usually a year. Thus financial transactions (those involving existing capital assets), intermediate transactions, and nonmarket transactions are excluded. Fisher's version of the quantity theory included *all* transactions; modification is therefore necessary to express the quantity theory in national income form. Starting with the identity

$$Y = Py \qquad (13.4)$$

where Y stands for national income in current dollars, P in this context stands for the price index used in estimates of the national income in current dollars, and y is national income in constant dollars, or the number of units of output produced by the economy where each unit has an average price, P. Deflating national income from current dollars to constant dollars by dividing each side of equation (13.4) by P, equation (13.4) becomes

$$y = \frac{Y}{P} \qquad (13.5)$$

Introducing the money supply, M, and its income velocity, V_y, which equal national income, Py, we get the basic equation for the quantity theory in national income form:

$$MV_y = Py \qquad\qquad (13.6)$$

in which Py replaces Fisher's PT (average price times total of all transactions). Similarly, V_y now replaces V (total velocity of *all* transactions) of the transactions approach, and is defined as

$$V_y = \frac{Py}{M} = \frac{Y}{M} \qquad\qquad (13.7)$$

Thus V_y is the average number of times in the national income accounting year that a unit of money (M) is employed in income transactions.

Thus restated in national income form, the quantity theory is conceptually more satisfactory for meaningful monetary analysis, since it relates the money supply times its income velocity to the national income. In structure, the national income form of the quantity theory is still a definitional equation and thus subject to the same strengths and weaknesses as the transactions version. Moreover, all of the propositions regarding the conditioned proportional relationship between changes in the quantity of money and the price level still hold true in this form. Dividing both sides of equation (13.6) by y, and rearranging to solve for price level, P, we see

$$P = \frac{MV_y}{y} \qquad\qquad (13.8)$$

thus implying a proportional increase in the price level, P, if the money supply rises while the physical volume of the national income or output, y, remains constant.

It is useful for analytical purposes to formalize equation (13.6) and to differentiate with respect to time in order to clearly demonstrate the relationship between the percentage rate of change in the money supply, M, plus the percentage rate of change in income velocity, V_y, and the percentage rate of change in prices, P, plus the percentage rate of change in real output, y. This is expressed by equation (13.9).[4]

4. A little calculus will show how equation (13.9) is determined. Differentiating $MV_y = Py$ with respect to time will result in

$$M\frac{dV_y}{dt} + V_y\frac{dM}{dt} = P\frac{dy}{dt} + y\frac{dP}{dt}$$

which may be rewritten as

$$\frac{V_y}{V_y}M\frac{dV_y}{dt} + \frac{M}{M}V_y\frac{dM}{dt} = \frac{y}{y}P\frac{dy}{dt} + \frac{P}{P}y\frac{dP}{dt}$$

or

$$MV_y\left(\frac{1}{V_y}\frac{dV_y}{dt}\right) + MV_y\left(\frac{1}{M}\frac{dM}{dt}\right) = Py\left(\frac{1}{y}\frac{dy}{dt}\right) + Py\left(\frac{1}{P}\frac{dP}{dt}\right)$$

Since the percentage rate of change in a variable, x, is (1/x) (dx/dt), which can be indicated

$$\hat{M} + \hat{V}_y = \hat{P} + \hat{y} \qquad (13.9)$$

From equation (13.9) it is clear that if income velocity, V_y, and real output, y, are fixed, so that $\hat{V}_y = \hat{y} = 0$, $\hat{M}$ will equal $\hat{P}$. The proportionality between percentage rates of change in the money supply and in prices as postulated by Fisher holds for the modern quantity theory in national income form as well.

Notice also in equation (13.9) that if velocity is constant, $\hat{V}_y = 0$, then if $\hat{M} = \hat{y}$ the result is that $\hat{P} = 0$. In words, if velocity is constant, prices will be stable ($\hat{P} = 0$) if the money stock grows at the same rate as real output ($\hat{M} = \hat{y}$). This result is the basis for the "4-percent rule" suggested by Milton Friedman. Reasoning that on the average, the real rate of growth of the U.S. economy is about 4 percent, and citing evidence of his own[5] which suggests that V_y changes only slowly over time, Friedman suggests that if stable prices are desired, they could on average be achieved over time by setting the rate of growth of the money stock at 4 percent, equal to the average rate of growth of real output. Stable prices would require maintaining M constant at 4 percent with no changes in response, say, to interest-rate changes or changes in the level of unemployment. A combination of skepticism as to the workability of the Friedman plan and an unwillingness on the part of the Fed to forego its ability to alter rates of growth of the money supply in response to changes in money and labor market conditions has so far precluded a test of this proposal. But Federal Reserve policy recently shows greater concern with the rate of growth of the money supply as an indicator of monetary policy than previously, when the behavior of interest rates was taken to be the primary indicator. It might also be said that the rate of inflation in the 1960s and 1970s would have been lower had the 4 percent rule been consistently adhered to. While most economists would not disagree with this, many point out that following the 4 percent rule would impose heavy costs upon the economy in terms of higher rates of unemployment and perhaps more credit-market stringency, a claim Friedman denies.

Because the national income version of the quantity theory views money as an asset with utility relative to other assets, it has come to be regarded as a "way station" between the Fisher transactions version and the Cambridge cash-balances approach.[6]

in mathematical notation as $\hat{x}$, the above equation can be rewritten as

$$MV_y \cdot \hat{V}_y + MV_y \cdot \hat{M} = Py \cdot \hat{y} + Py \cdot \hat{P}$$

and dividing the left-hand side of this equation by MV_y, and its right-hand side by its equivalent, or P_y, will finally result in

$$\hat{M} + \hat{V}_y = \hat{P} + \hat{y}$$

This says that the rate of change in the money supply plus the rate of change in income velocity, equals the rate of change of prices plus the rate of change of real output.

5. Milton Friedman and Anna J. Schwartz, *A Monetary History of the United States, 1867–1960* (Princeton, N.J.: Princeton University Press, 1963).

6. Milton Friedman, "A Theoretical Framework for Monetary Analysis," *Journal of Political Economy* 78 (March/April 1970): 200.

The Cambridge Cash-Balances Approach

The term "Cambridge school" is applied to a group of British economists which includes Alfred Marshall, considered to be the founder of the school not only in monetary theory, but also in general economic analysis; A. C. Pigou, R. G. Hawtrey, D. H. Robertson, and John Maynard Keynes himself.[7] Although these economists differed in detail in their approach to monetary theory, all may be said to have sought to replace what they viewed as the mechanical ex post (realized) nature of velocity in the Fisher version of the quantity theory with an *ex ante* (predicted) concept of demand for cash balances held by people and firms, both for current purchases and as a store of future purchasing power, relative to given income. Such an *ex ante* concept of the demand for money implied volition in determination of the holding of cash balances relative to income and thus viewed monetary theory as akin to price theory, wherein individual decision making plays a key role.

The following formulation is a conventional representation of the Cambridge cash-balances approach to analysis of the demand for money:

$$M_D = kPy \qquad (13.10)$$

where M_D represents the desired quantity of money which, in equilibrium, is equal to the supply of money; P is the price index; and y is national income in constant dollars or real output. The new term, k, represents the ratio of cash balances desired relative to the national income, thus emphasizing the role of money as a store of value. The Cambridge cash-balances equation stresses the role of money as an asset, whereas the transactions approach stresses the use of money as a circulating medium to effect transactions.

Although the concepts of k and V in the Cambridge cash-balances approach and in the transactions approach differ in basic conceptual nature, they are really equivalent expressions. The ratio of cash balances, k, to national income can be shown to be the reciprocal of V_y in the national income version of the quantity theory. The national income version of the quantity theory, $MV_y = Py$, may be rewritten as

$$M = \frac{Py}{V_y} \qquad (13.11)$$

by dividing both sides by V_y. Note that kPy is also equal to M in equation (13.10), as indicated by

$$M_D = M = kPy \qquad (13.12)$$

Since expressions both equal to M are equal to each other, we have $kPy = Py/V_y$. Dividing each side of this equation by Py, we obtain:

7. See, for example, Alfred Marshall, *Money, Credit and Commerce* (New York: Augustus M. Kelly, 1965), pp. 38–39, 44–45; A. C. Pigou, "The Value of Money," *Quarterly Journal of Economics* 32 (1917/1918): 42; R. H. Hawtrey, *Currency and Credit* (London, 1919), pp. 39–41; D. H. Robertson, *Money* (London, 1922), p. 31; and John Maynard Keynes, *A Tract on Monetary Reform* (New York, 1924), pp. 83–85.

$$k = \frac{1}{V_y} \tag{13.13}$$

thus proving that k is the reciprocal of V_y. Therefore, the Cambridge-k equation is no more than a mathematical transformation of equation (13.6) which represents the national income form of the quantity theory, which is in turn equivalent to the transactions version of the quantity theory in its predictions regarding the proportional relationship between the rate of change of the money supply and the rate of changes of prices. Not surprisingly therefore, we have that

$$\hat{M} = \hat{k} + \hat{P} + \hat{y} \tag{13.14}$$

If $\hat{k}$ and $\hat{y}$ equal zero, then $\hat{M} = \hat{P}$, which is the quantity theory result.

The formal similarity between the quantity theory and the Cambridge-k approach should not obscure the fundamentally different roles for money that each of these theories emphasizes, however. In suggesting a theory of the demand for money balances, the Cambridge cash-balances approach strongly suggests the role of money as an asset. It therefore implies that rates of return on alternative assets where cash is viewed as part of a portfolio of financial assets ought to affect desired cash holdings. A typical demand function lurks behind $M = kPy$, where income represents a scale factor operating on the demand for money and factors like rates of interest on other financial assets are substitution or relative price variables affecting the level of desired money balances. The role of k is not portrayed as a highly stable element like V_y. Rather, k is viewed as a function of other variables, such as interest rates and even income. If this suggestion is allowed to manifest itself explicitly we may write

$$M = k(y, i)Py \tag{13.15}$$

where now

$$k = k(y, i)$$

k is some function of real income and the interest rate, i. A further application of the methodology developed in footnote 4 gives:

$$\hat{M} = E_{ky}\hat{y} + E_{ki}\hat{i} + \hat{P} + \hat{y} \tag{13.16}$$

which may be rewritten with P as the dependent variable as:

$$\hat{P} = \hat{M} - \hat{y}(1 + E_{ky}) - \hat{i}E_{ki} \tag{13.17}$$

where E_{ky} is the elasticity of k with respect to y or $\hat{k}/\hat{y}$ and E_{ki} is the elasticity of k with respect to i or $\hat{k}/\hat{i}$. Recalling that $k = M_D/Y$, if E_{ky} is zero then $M_D = Y$, implying a unitary income elasticity of demand for money balances. E_{ki} ought to be negative since, given Y, as interest rates rise the opportunity cost of holding money rises and the quantity of money desired falls.

Equation (13.17) gives the proportional relationship between $\hat{M}$ and $\hat{P}$ if k is invariant as y and i change, if $E_{ky} = E_{ki} = 0$, and if $\hat{y} = 0$. If, however,

$E_{ki} < 0$ (holding $E_{ky} = 0$ for now) a given increase in the money supply becomes less inflationary if i falls (more inflationary if i rises). Recall that in the Keynesian IS/LM framework, increases in the money supply do lower i. In fact, as E_{ki} gets very large, the liquidity-trap case is approached. This would mean that increases in the rate of growth of the money supply would have no inflationary impact where real output is fixed (as in the Keynesian full-employment case with a horizontal LM schedule).

Turning to E_{ky}, if $E_{ky} > 0$ holds, the meaning is that the income elasticity of the demand for money is greater than one, so that $k = M_D/Y$ rises with income. This result would reduce the inflationary impact of an increase in the money supply since part of any increase which raises Y (due either to $\hat{P}$ or $\hat{y}$ greater than zero) would be demanded and held. Conversely if $k = M_D/Y$ falls as income rises, $E_{ky} < 0$ is the result, and the inflationary impact of increases in the money supply is exacerbated by the implied reduction in the demand for money relative to income as income rises.

Thus the Cambridge-k equation is suggestive of modifications which break the proportionality between the rate of changes in the money supply and prices suggested by the quantity theory. Indeed it suggested and led to, in the fertile mind of J. M. Keynes, the sort of liquidity preference schedule

$$L = L(Y, i)$$

which was discussed at length in Chapter 8 and incorporated in subsequent chapters into the general equilibrium setting of the IS/LM model.

It is tempting at this point to say that we have come full circle from the early quantity theory back to the sort of monetary theory developed in Part II. In a sense this is the case, but the story does not end here. It remains to develop a theory of the demand for money which takes the view of money as an asset to its logical conclusion: money is a part of wealth (or the sum of all assets) and its role in the economy is reflective of this fact. These concepts are developed in Friedman's modern quantity theory.

The Demand for Money and the Permanent Income Theory

Stimulated by the Cambridge cash-balances approach to the quantity theory and its emphasis on the role of money as a store of value and hence as an asset, a number of theoretical formulations and empirical studies have been done on the demand for money. One of the most innovative is Milton Friedman's theory that the demand for money is largely a function of permanent income, in which the concept of permanent income in this context is used as a substitute for wealth because of the difficulties in obtaining aggregate data on wealth.[8]

---

8. See Friedman, "A Theoretical Framework for Monetary Analysis." Milton Friedman earlier developed the concept of permanent income for his theory of the consumption function in *A Theory of the Consumption Function*, National Bureau of Economic Research, General Series 63 (Princeton, N.J.: Princeton University Press, 1957).

The key to Friedman's demand-for-money function is his view that money is one kind of asset—one way of holding wealth by individuals and one kind of productive resource for business enterprises—which provides utility and productive services of its own. Friedman lists a number of variables that could affect the demand for money.[9]

$$M_D = M_D\left(P, i_b - \frac{1}{i_b}\frac{di_b}{dt}, i_e + \frac{1}{P}\frac{dP}{dt} - \frac{1}{i_e}\frac{di_e}{dt}, \frac{1}{P}\frac{dP}{dt}; w; \frac{Y}{i}; u\right) \quad (13.18)$$

where M_D is the demand for money; P is the price level; $i_b - (1/i_b)(di_b/dt)$ represents the market interest rate on bonds minus any change in the price of bonds; $i_e + (1/P)(dP/dt)$ represents the cash dividend rate on equities plus any change in price of equities; $(1/i_e)(di_e/dt)$ represents the capitalized value of equities times any change therein caused by change in cash dividend rates; $(1/P)(dP/dt)$ represents the level of purchasing power for money times any change caused by change in general price level; w is the ratio of nonhuman wealth to human wealth, or of income from nonhuman wealth to income from human wealth (such as embodied skills); Y/i is total wealth; and u represents all other utility-determining variables that affect tastes and preferences for money.

Dividing both sides of equation (13.18) by P, it can then be written in "real" terms as follows:

$$\frac{M_D}{P} = M_D\left(i_b, i_e, \frac{1}{P}\frac{dP}{dt}, w, \frac{Y}{P}, u\right) \quad (13.19)$$

Equation (13.19) merely lists the variables that influence the demand for real balances without indicating their relative importance in affecting the demand for money, nor their cyclical behavior. Accordingly, Friedman has studied these variables for the United States and their relationship to the demand for money in an elaborate study of long-term time series data, covering about nine decades from 1870 to 1954.[10] His conclusions, various of which have led to considerable controversy among monetary theorists and empirical researchers,[11] included the following:

1. Rates of interest had the expected negative correlation relative to demand

9. Milton Friedman, "The Quantity Theory of Money—A Restatement," *Studies in the Quantity Theory of Money*, Milton Friedman, ed. (Chicago: University of Chicago Press, 1956), p. 9.

10. Milton Friedman, "The Demand for Money: Some Theoretical and Empirical Results," *Journal of Political Economy* 67 (August 1959): 327–351.

11. See, for example, Allan H. Meltzer, "The Demand for Money: The Evidence from the Time Series," *Journal of Political Economy* 71 (June 1963); H. R. Heller, "The Demand for Money—The Evidence from the Short-Run Data," *Quarterly Journal of Economics* 79 (May 1965); David Laidler, "The Rate of Interest and the Demand for Money—Some Empirical Evidence," *Journal of Political Economy* 74 (December 1966). Friedman's departures from customary data techniques included use of cyclically averaged data rather than unaveraged chronological data. He broadened the definition of the concept of money to include time deposits in addition to coin and currency and bank demand deposits. A comprehensive survey of empirical evidence on the demand for money up to 1969 is contained in David Laidler, *The Demand for Money: Theories and Evidence* (Scranton, Pa.: International Textbook Co., 1969).

for money, but this was "too small to be statistically significant." Thus, in his simplified equation (13.20) below, Friedman omitted interest rates as a variable.

2. The rate of change in prices as a variable was omitted in equation (13.20) below because of the difficulty of formally isolating an effect.

3. Wealth, represented by the capitalized value of permanent income, is the most important variable, on a per capita basis, affecting demand for money. Accordingly, Friedman simplified his demand for money function to the following:

$$\frac{M_D}{NP} = \gamma\left(\frac{Y^P}{NP}\right)^\delta \tag{13.20}$$

in which M_D is demand for money; N is population; Y^P is aggregate permanent income in current dollars; γ and δ are behavioral parameters (constants) in this exponential equation, and P is the price level.[12]

As simplified, equation (13.20) indicates that a single variable, the per capita permanent income in constant dollars will satisfactorily explain demand for money per capita in constant dollars. Friedman employed an equation similar to equation (13.20) in an empirical study[13] aimed primarily at earlier critics of the quantity theory. Observing that measured velocity tends to rise and fall with the business cycle, these critics had contended that this instability of velocity invalidated the notion of a stable demand function for money.[14] In effect, Friedman's contention was that a permanent income version of the quantity theory which yielded a concept of permanent velocity would erase the instability of the demand function for money that was implied by such "procyclical" behavior of velocity.[15] Friedman was then

12. The exponential symbol, δ, measures the permanent income elasticity of the demand for real money balances.

13. Friedman, "The Demand for Money: Some Theoretical and Empirical Results."

14. Critics of the quantity theory attributed the cyclical behavior of velocity largely to cyclical behavior of interest rates. As a boom heats up, higher interest rates would lead money holders to economize on money balances, as suggested by the Keynesian theory of the demand for money. Lower money balances for a given level of income imply a rise in velocity where $V = y/m$. During a slump, with interest rates lower, the quantity of money demanded at a given level of income would rise and velocity would fall.

15. Some manipulation of equation (13.20) will clearly indicate the basis for Friedman's position. Rewriting equation (13.20) with $m^P = M/P^P$, or real money balances, and $y^P = Y^P/P^P$ or permanent income in real terms, gives

$$m^P = \gamma N\left(\frac{y^P}{N}\right)^\delta$$

Taking N out of the parentheses gives:

$$m^P = \gamma N^{1-\delta} y^{P\delta}$$

Dividing both sides by y^P gives an expression for the inverse of permanent velocity:

$$\frac{1}{V^P} = \frac{m^P}{y^P} = \gamma N^{1-\delta} y^{P\delta-1}$$

Inverting gives

able to compute a theoretical series on measured velocity for the period running from 1870–1957 that was highly correlated with observed or actual measured velocity, suggesting that a permanent income theory of the demand for money could readily account for the actual path of velocity.

Friedman's result can perhaps more easily be grasped with an intuitive approach. As we saw in footnote 15, measured velocity is to permanent velocity as measured income is to permanent income:

$$\frac{V}{V^P} = \frac{y}{y^P} \qquad (13.21)$$

The implied relationship between V and V^P throughout a business cycle is shown in Figure 13.1. As the economy moves toward a peak, since y^P rises more slowly than y (we shall examine reasons for this below) then measured velocity (y/m) rises above permanent velocity (y^P/m). At a peak, measured velocity overstates permanent velocity. As y falls, y^P falls more slowly, so measured velocity falls more than permanent velocity. The net result is an observable procyclical behavior of measured velocity which masks a far steadier path of permanent velocity. In the very long-run period Friedman did detect a downward trend to permanent velocity due to an income elasticity of demand for money balance with respect to permanent income of greater than one.[16]

The downward trend to permanent velocity, as well as Friedman's failure to detect a significant statistical role for interest rates in determining the demand for money, is probably due to Friedman's use of a money concept which includes currency, demand deposits, and interest-bearing time or

$$\frac{y^P}{m^P} = V^P = \frac{1}{\gamma}\left(\frac{y^P}{N}\right)^{1-\delta}$$

In order to compute measured velocity on the basis of this theory of the demand for money and the resulting expression for V^P, it is necessary to know the relationship between permanent and measured velocity. This can be seen from the following:

$$V = \frac{y}{m} = \frac{y}{y^P}\frac{y^P}{m} = \frac{y}{y^P}V^P$$

Therefore

$$V = \frac{y}{y^P}V^P$$

$$\frac{V}{V^P} = \frac{y}{y^P}$$

Then

$$V = \frac{1}{\gamma}\left(\frac{y^P}{N}\right)^{1-\delta}\frac{y}{y^P}$$

16. Work on this has also been done by William J. Baumol, "The Transaction Demand for Cash: An Inventory Theoretical Approach," *Quarterly Journal of Economics* 66 (November 1952). As we saw in Chapter 8, Baumol's inventory theoretic approach to the demand for money suggests an elasticity of demand for money with respect to transactions volume (proxied by income) of only one-half.

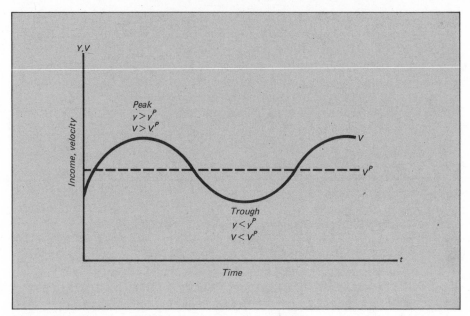

Figure 13.1 The procyclical path of measured velocity

savings deposits at commercial banks. Friedman's reason for this definition of money arises from the fact that time and savings deposits were not reported separately in the United States until 1914. Therefore, in order to obtain a continuous series on the money supply running back to 1870, the broader definition of the money supply, including time deposits, was employed.

A theory of the demand for money (or equivalently for the behavior of velocity) that defines the money supply as only cash and demand deposits would be a more useful predictive tool if it included some interest rates as explanatory variables.[17] This condition holds even if the permanent income concept is employed. Even the last seven years of Friedman's study began to show what many have suggested are signs of omitted interest-rate variables in understating velocity in the 1950s. In addition, institutional changes—such as a rapid growth of money substitutes in the form of savings and loan shares—may have led to some substitution out of money balances not detected by the simple permanent income formulation. This last effect, suggested by economists John Gurley and Edward Shaw, will be examined in more detail in Chapter 14, particularly in terms of its implications for monetary policy.

17. See T. H. Lee, "Alternative Interest Rates and the Demand for Money: The Empirical Evidence," *American Economic Review* 57 (December 1967): 1168–1181, and Dennis Starleaf, "The Specification of Money Demand-Supply Models Which Involve the Use of Distributed Lags," *Journal of Finance* 25 (September 1970): 743–760.

Most contemporary theorists have acknowledged that permanent income is a more comprehensive index of economic well-being than measured income in determining the demand for an asset like money, as it is for the consumption function. However, they would also include interest rates as an explanatory variable in the demand function for money, particularly where money is defined to include only currency and demand deposits.

Monetary Policy Implications of the Permanent Income Formulation

A theory of the demand for money like that represented by equation (13.20) may be shown to have some powerful implications for monetary policy. Consider an equation similar to equation (13.20), depicting in a simplified manner the relationship between the demand for money and permanent income:

$$m_{D_t} = aY_t^P \qquad (0 < a < 1) \qquad (13.22)$$

where the t subscripts indicate the date of each variable; m_D is the demand for real money balances; Y_t^P is real permanent income in period t, which is an approximation of the moneyholder's total wealth; and a, which is a constant, is the portion of wealth desired as money balances and is specified as being more than zero but less than one.

Since permanent income cannot be directly observed, it must be estimated from observable data. As we saw in Chapter 6, this may be done by hypothesizing the manner in which an individual's notion of his permanent income is altered. Equation (6.1) stated:

$$Y_t^P - Y_{t-1}^P = B(Y_t - Y_{t-1}^P), \text{ where } 0 < B < 1 \qquad (13.23)$$

An individual's notion of his permanent income may change from time $t-1$ to time t, by some weighted proportion, B, of the difference between current income, Y_t^P, and the previous period's permanent income, Y_{t-1}^P.

Since equation (13.23) is a first-order difference equation, it can be solved for Y_t^P in terms of past values of income as follows:

$$Y_t^P = BY_t + B(1-B)Y_{t-1} + B(1-B)^2Y_{t-2} + \ldots + B(1-B)^nY_{t-n}$$

$$(13.24)$$

Equation (13.24) says that current permanent income is a weighted average of current and past values of measured income with the weights all determined once the value of B is known.[18]

18. As we saw in Chapter 6, the value assigned to B determines the weight of the measured incomes. Table 6.1 showed the weights attached to measured income for each previous time period for different values for B. Using this table, we can compute the numerical value of the weight for each time period by following equation (13.24). For example, taking the value for B as 0.4, times $1 - B$, or 0.6, gives the 0.24 weight for $t - 1$.

The permanent income formulation of the demand for money thus adds precision to the Cambridge cash-balances formulation by representing the demand for money as determined by permanent income instead of current income. Like the Cambridge cash-balances version, the permanent income formulation has important implications for the effectiveness of monetary policy. The permanent income formulation not surprisingly suggests a theoretical rationale for Friedman's advocacy of monetary "rules" over "discretion," where the rules imply that the money supply be kept steady (or kept growing steadily, as indicated) in line with demand for money, in order to avoid induced fluctuations in income.

As we saw in Chapter 6, in order to make clear the analytical basis for the monetary rules approach suggested by the permanent income formulation we can rewrite equation (13.23) as

$$Y_t^P = BY_t + (1 - B)Y_{t-1}^P \tag{13.25}$$

Substituting equation (13.25) into equation (13.22) for Y_t^P, we get

$$m_{D_t} = aBY_t + a(1 - B)Y_{t-1}^P \tag{13.26}$$

Since demand for money (cash balances) in time period $t - 1$ is equal to the constant, a, times permanent income for the same time period, $t - 1$, or $m_{D_{t-1}} = aY_{t-1}^P$, we may rewrite equation (13.26) as

$$m_{D_t} = aBY_t + (1 - B)m_{D_{t-1}} \tag{13.27}$$

Finally, we may rewrite equation (13.27) to express income in terms of money, assuming equilibrium in the money market ($m_{S_t} = m_{D_t}$), as follows:

$$Y_t = \frac{1}{aB}m_{S_t} - \frac{(1 - B)}{aB}m_{S_{t-1}} \tag{13.28}$$

From equation (13.28) we can derive the impact upon current income of current and lagged changes in the money supply. The change in income given a change in the money supply, holding everything else constant, is given by the partial derivative of Y_t with respect to m_t or change in Y_t given a change in m_{S_t} in equation (13.28):

$$\frac{\delta Y_t}{\delta m_{S_t}} = \frac{1}{aB} > 0 \tag{13.29}$$

In the same manner the impact of a change in $m_{S_{t-1}}$ upon Y_t (called the "lagged" impact of a change in m_S on Y_t) is given by:

$$\frac{\delta Y_t}{\delta m_{S_{t-1}}} = -\frac{1 - B}{aB} < 0 \tag{13.30}$$

In words, equations (13.29) and (13.30) together suggest the following: the initial impact of an increase in the money supply is to raise income, as shown by 1/aB, which carries a positive sign and is greater than one, since both a and B are positive fractions, while the lagged impact is to lower income, as shown by $-(1 - B/aB)$. Taken at face value, this result is troublesome for monetary policy, because it suggests that the initial impact of an increase in the money supply is to raise income while the subsequent impact is to lower income. Furthermore, the size of the initial increase and the subsequent fall in Y_t increases as B falls so that the contrast between the period of rising Y and subsequently falling Y is increased sharply as B falls. Lower values of a will also increase the contrast, but a is a more familiar and probably more stable parameter than B.

These parameters determine the cyclical impact of changes in the money supply. Recall that a is the ratio of desired money balances to permanent income while B measures the rate at which the concept of permanent income is perceived to change, based upon a discrepancy between current measured income and past permanent income, as in equation (13.23). The parameter B deserves careful consideration here because, as we have suggested, it represents the key to understanding the cyclical impact upon measured income of changes in the money supply that is implied by the permanent income formulation. Equation (13.23) suggests a fundamental notion about the manner in which human perceptions change. One's notion of permanent income, or long-run wealth position, is modified when current measured income is larger than the previous period's permanent income. Suppose for example that perceived permanent income has been $10,000 per year, but current year earnings total $15,000. Equation (13.23) suggests that because measured income is currently higher than permanent income this will have some impact upon the current notion of permanent income, but permanent income will not change by the full amount of the difference between current measured and previous permanent income. This hypothesis is reflected by the value of B taken to lie above zero but *below* one $(0 < B < 1)$. In short, one's notion of permanent income is taken to change more slowly than measured income; just how much more slowly is determined by the exact value of B. The smaller the value of B, the lower the change in permanent income perceived on the basis of a discrepancy between current measured income and past permanent income. If B were 0.3, for example, the sum of weights by the time period $t - 3$ was reached would be less than .1029, whereas if B is 0.7, this sum would be .0189. More observations on past measured income would be required to determine current permanent income, reflecting the fact that Y_t^p changes more gradually as B falls.

What implications, then, does the value of B have for monetary policy? We have seen from equations (13.29) and (13.30) that the cyclical impact of changes in the money supply upon income rises as B falls. This can be understood by considering the response of money holders to a change in the money supply, based upon the permanent income theory of money demand. Starting from a position of equilibrium, suppose the money supply is increased by $1 billion. Initially, since permanent income is unchanged as we see in equation (13.22), money holders will perceive their money balances to be excessive and try to reduce money balances by exchanging them for bonds or goods, thereby leading to an increase in income. The initial spending wave induced by a rise in the money supply is based upon a perception of permanent income that is about to be changed by the spending wave itself; as income rises, permanent income rises but by less and more slowly.

During this initial phase, however, the pressure is for income to rise, leading to the situation suggested by equation (13.29). This phase goes on longer and produces a larger increase in income the smaller the value of B and the more slowly permanent income increases as a result of increases in measured income. Eventually, however, the increase in permanent income will induce money holders to add to money balances, since it is, after all, the level of permanent income which determines their demand for money.

In effect, then, money holders initially overestimate the redundancy of money balances at the time the increase in the money stock initially appears, due to a failure to anticipate the imminent increase in permanent income. As that increase materializes, money holders seek to add to their money balances and, in the absence of a subsequent increase in the money supply, can do so only by selling securities and goods, leading in turn to falling measured income. This phase is indicated by equation (13.30):

$$\frac{\delta Y_t}{\delta m_{s_{t-1}}} = -\frac{1-B}{aB} < 0$$

A fall in income in response to lagged money supply changes is larger as B falls. The lag in perceiving the initial overestimated redundancy of money balances and, subsequently, the proportions of the need for readjustment both rise as B falls.

This cycle may be repeated with less severe subsequent oscillations, as indicated in Figure 13.2. The major policy conclusion indicated by this

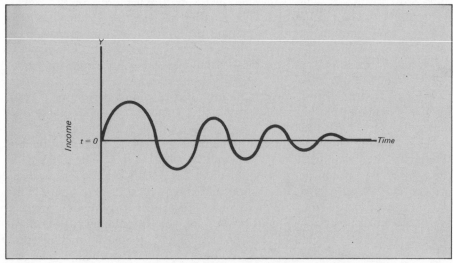

Figure 13.2 Time path of measured income in response to changes in the money supply as implied by the permanent income theory

examination of Friedman's permanent income formulation is that income levels will be kept stable by keeping the money supply steady in a static economy or growing steadily in a growing economy.

The Transmission Mechanism

The ways in which monetary changes exert an impact upon the economy are known as the transmission mechanism. The operation of this mechanism, which has been suggested by our discussion of the cyclical impact of changes in the money supply upon income, has been analyzed in detail by Milton Friedman.[19]

Assume that a situation of moving equilibrium obtains, in which real income per capita, the stock of money, and the price level are all changing at constant annual rates. The actual relation between these rates of change would depend upon such factors as whether real income is rising or falling; whether the ratio of wealth to income is constant, rising, or falling; the behavior of relative real rates of return on different forms of wealth; and the wealth elasticity of the demand for money. For example, if the rate of the rise in the nominal stock of money per capita is 4 percent, but the rate of rise in permanent income per capita is 2 percent, and the income elasticity of demand for money is $3/2$ (if ratio of wealth to income is constant, income elasticity of the demand for money also approximately indicates the wealth elasticity of the demand for money), then the rate of rise in the price level would be 1 percent, as follows:[20]

$$\hat{P} = \hat{M} - \gamma(\hat{y}^P) \text{ or } 1\% = 4\% - (3/2 \times 2\%) \qquad (13.31)$$

where $\hat{P}$ is the rate of rise in the price level; $\hat{M}$ is the rate of rise in the nominal stock of money per capita; $\hat{y}^P$ stands for the rate of rise in permanent income per capita; and γ is the income elasticity of the demand for money. For simplicity we are assuming that all interest rates in real terms (adjusted for price changes) and the ratio of wealth to income remain constant, so that the wealth elasticity of the demand for money is approximated by the elasticity of demand for money relative to permanent income.

Now suppose an unexpected rise occurs in the rate of increase in the stock of money ($\hat{M}$), and that this new rate of increase is maintained. If this increase resulted from an open-market purchase of government securities by the Federal Reserve,[21] it will affect the dynamic equilibrium level of income (to create a new dynamic equilibrium) in three ways: liquidity-portfolio effects, price-anticipation effects, and income-price-level effects.

19. Milton Friedman, "Money and Business Cycles," *Review of Economics and Statistics* 65 (Supplement, February 1963): 59–63.

20. Friedman indicates that these rates were roughly the actual values of $\hat{P}$, $\hat{M}$, and $\hat{y}^P$ over the years 1870–1960 in the United States. Friedman, ibid., p. 59 fn.

21. Open-market operations by the Fed will add to (or reduce) bank reserves and deposits. The bank reserves over and above the legal reserve requirements against the deposits are excess reserves, i.e., the bank reserves available for lending or investing.

Commentary: The Year of the Rising Interest Rates

1974 might be called "The Year of Rising Interest Rates"; not since the Civil War have interest rates reached such heights. Less than six months into 1974, prime rates hit almost 11.5 percent with predictions of further increases. A closely related development is the unchecked rate of inflation in the United States over the past twenty-four months, making the fear of two-digit inflation widespread among economists and policymakers.

Confusion among policymakers and the public as to the cause of the present difficulty is compounded by statements like the following: "Monetary policy in 1973 was basically restrictive . . . . For the year as a whole, the money supply grew at a rate of 5.7 percent."[1] This differs from a statement that appeared in a recent Chase Manhattan Bank report: "Money supply including time deposits, commonly called M_2, increased by 9.6 percent."[2] Monetary policy deemed restrictive in 1973 continued to be so in 1974. Then the New York Times stated, "The Federal Reserve has not eased monetary policy . . . . The money supply . . . stands at a seasonal adjusted rate of growth for the quarter ending May 29, 1974 of 9.2 percent, still well above the Federal Reserve target of 6 percent."[3] These statements point out the confusing nature of the money problem—a lack of unanimity as to what constitutes a definition of tight or easy monetary policy.

1. Report of the Joint Economic Committee (Washington, D.C.: Government Printing Office, 1974), p. 32.
2. Chase Manhattan Bank, Bi-monthly Report, April 1974, p. 5.
3. New York Times, May 31, 1974, p. 48.

Growth for 1974 as measured by Gross National Product (GNP) was projected to be approximately 8 percent, but actual figures for the first quarter showed a decrease of 5.8 percent in real growth. Putting it in money terms, the rate of money growth increased at a greater rate than actual production. One important reason may be the lack of capacity growth in various industries throughout the United States. (The recent energy crisis and lack of refining capacity is an example of being caught with "your capacity down.") A growth formula has worked well when a productive labor force combined with orderly growth of industrial capacity to accommodate a steady growth of aggregate demand along with the smoothly functioning transfer of funds from lenders to borrowers to keep the economy functioning smoothly. But new elements have been introduced in the seventies: Vietnam veterans and a changing labor force, the Watergate crisis, and accelerating inflation. Other disruptions have also occurred, due partially to a devaluation of the U.S. dollar against a number of other major currencies by something like 20 percent since early 1971, which has added to inflation and sharply altered the position of some U.S. industries with regard to their foreign competitors. Another sharp change during the first part of 1974 was the lifting of price controls; in many instances this induced firms to expand capacity after having been reluctant to do so for fear of not being able to charge prices consistent with a good profit for goods produced with new capital equipment. New solutions are required as industries try to readjust, reconvert, and in some cases expand. Many industries will find funds difficult to obtain. The rapidly rising prime rate during March and April of 1974 is a signal that the growth in the demand for loans is outrunning the growth in supply. In view of the fact that the rate of growth of the money supply during this period was about 9 percent, however, monetary policy cannot truly be considered to have been "tight." Rather it may be said that monetary policy restricted the flow of funds into the commercial banking system to a level below that which would equate the rapidly growing demand for loans with the supply of loans at an interest rate below about 11 percent. In effect, the Fed was "leaning against the wind" in the spring of 1974 in a manner designed to prevent exacerbation of an already serious inflationary trend.

In the face of a choice between inflation and recession, the Fed must strike a delicate balance between a reduction in the rate of monetary growth that is slow enough to prevent a serious recession, yet rapid enough to show some progress in the battle against inflation. The Fed considers the latter goal important for two reasons. First, it wishes to show some benefits of a relatively restrictive monetary policy before critics claim that it is engineering a recession by causing high interest rates and possibly higher unemployment levels; second, it wants to bring down the interest rate. If lenders perceive a reduced rate of inflation, they will anticipate a lower rate of depreciation in terms of purchasing power of their future interest dollars and will charge lower nominal interest rates. Interest rates at the 11–12 percent level have never occurred in times of stable prices.

A high rate of inflation throughout the world complicates the problem of assessing the real state of economies because most indicators are expressed in terms of money which is depreciating in terms of goods at the rate at which inflation proceeds. Recent suggestions that inflation should be "institutionalized" in the United States represents an attempt to adjust our money-denominated indices to real terms. Of course policymakers are likely to be hesitant to institutionalize a high rate of inflation which they have said for years they would reduce to a zero to 2 percent annual rate. Moreover, concern with the social aspects of full employment has tended to obscure the fact that workers at all levels and with varying skills may be adversely affected by inflation. As purchasing power falls due to unanticipated inflation, attempts to postpone, at least temporarily, a change in consumption patterns may lead households to look to the money markets to maintain old consumption levels. Credit cards, personal loans, education and contingency loans begin to expand, tending to accentuate upward pressure on interest rates. Inflation, whether acknowledged in advance or not, eventually becomes incorporated into people's expectations, leading to adjustments for anticipated inflation in the form of wage escalator clauses, higher nominal interest rates, and a general reluctance to enter into any long-term contracts with financial terms denominated in money terms. At a time when shops, supermarkets, and restaurants employ readily changeable price labels in the form of adhesive labels, mimeographed daily menus, etc., it is little wonder that corporate borrowers are undeterred by record high interest rates. With inflation expected to continue at a high rate, they can repay lenders with dollars which will have depreciated in terms of the quantity of goods they will buy.

Liquidity-Portfolio Effects

Both bank and nonbank sellers of the securities to the Fed would find their liquidity increased beyond desired levels—in the form of increased bank reserves for the banks derived from their own sales as well as from increased deposits of the nonbanks, and in the form of increased deposits for the nonbanks involved in the sales to the Fed. Both banks and nonbanks would therefore seek to reinvest the excess liquidity in similar securities but in so doing would tend to bid up the prices of such high-grade securities. Accordingly, banks would turn to loans or other bank-eligible securities and in the process of such expansion in loans and investments create additional deposits, thereby adding to the money stock further by a multiple of each dollar of excess reserves originally held.[22] Nonbanks would turn to other types of financial assets, such as higher-risk obligations, equities, etc., with similar liquidity and portfolio effects in turn upon the sellers of such assets.

As this process of turnovers in financial assets proceeds, the initial range of assets affected is widened, and their higher prices tend to raise wealth relative to income and to lower prevailing yields on financial assets. Issuers of obligations and equities are thus encouraged by the better terms and lower interest costs and yields to expand, and the original redundant liquidity concentrated in relatively few holders by the original open-market operations now becomes more diffused throughout the economy. Higher prices and lower yields would also tend to make financial assets more expensive and less attractive for portfolio adjustments than nonfinancial assets. The same cycle of purchases, increased liquidity, and adjustments in portfolios would in turn be reflected in nonfinancial areas, raising the demand curve in the commodity market and stimulating a rise in prices and interest rates in that market as well as a rise in money income.

To summarize, in the transitional period where the rate of change in the money supply has been altered so that it differs from its expected rate of change, rates of change in prices and real output will increase over their expected rates of change. This is because when rate of change in the money supply is not equal to desired rate of change in the money supply ($M_S \neq M_S^*$), money holders first are likely to purchase other financial assets such as bonds and equities. But in so doing they drive down the rates of return on bonds and on equities, thereby raising their prices, so that substitution of the excess money for goods and services begins in the manner emphasized by Fisher's early quantity theory.[23]

22. Bank excess reserves have been termed "high-powered," because the fractional legal reserve system against deposits means that for every dollar of excess reserves in the banking system, a multiple of dollars in loans and/or investments and hence in derivative deposits can result. For example, if legal reserve requirements against demand deposits average 15 percent, and maximum expansion (without leakages) occurs in the banking system, each $1 of excess reserves would create $6, two-thirds in loans and/or investments and hence in demand deposits ($1 in excess reserves divided by the 15 percent in legal reserve requirements).

23. Fisher, *The Purchasing Power of Money*, especially Ch. IV, pp. 55–73.

Price-Anticipation Effects

Whereas the increase in the rate of change in the money supply over its equilibrium rate of change initially results in lower interest rates, this is only a temporary "first round" effect, because the temporary fall in rates of return from financial assets will lead to the shift indicated for nonfinancial assets, thus increasing the demand for loanable funds and the demand for money for transactions purposes associated with the increase in expenditures for goods and services. We have seen that prices for both financial and nonfinancial assets will then rise above the previously anticipated rate of rise in prices, thus lowering real rates of return and real income. As the rise in prices proceeds, the anticipation that prices will continue to rise even further will lead to rise in interest rates and rates of return, as lenders and investors add a premium for price changes to their rates as compensation for the rise in prices and its shrinkage in real returns and asset values. This will be examined in more detail in Chapter 14.

Income-Price-Level Effects

As indicated, as money balances are built up beyond desired holdings and shift from money to financial assets and later to nonfinancial assets, prices of resources and of final goods and services will rise, thus resulting in rise in income.

Two characteristics of the connection between the money supply and income indicated by the transmission mechanism should be noted. First, the process of transition from one equilibrium path to another will involve a cyclical pattern of adjustment, rather than a smooth straight-line progression. One reason for this is that there will be a tendency to "overshoot" the new equilibrium path for the same reasons discussed earlier where changes in permanent income lag behind changes in measured income. As noted, there will be a tendency for price-anticipation effects to occur, as the result of expectations that the rise in prices, once begun, will carry on beyond the eventual equilibrium levels of rate of rise in price levels.[24] In addition, as the rate of growth of the money supply increases, demand for money will be less, relative to wealth and income, due to inflationary expectations, than it was originally, so that it will take a higher rate of increase in prices to achieve a rise in income. Finally, in the initial stages of the portfolio adjustment process, holders of money balances may underestimate the eventual extent of rise in prices as prices are slow to respond. As suggested earlier, money holders will initially overestimate the extent of monetary redundancy and therefore may overdo the extent of portfolio adjustments that will eventually be required at the new equilibrium.

A second major characteristic of the connection between the money supply and income is the lag between changes in the former and their impact

24. The same tendency to "overshoot" in the case of interest rates is traced in Milton Friedman's "Factors Affecting the Level of Interest Rates," in *1968 Conference Proceedings, Savings and Residential Financing Conference* (Chicago: U.S. Savings and Loan League, 1968).

upon the latter. As indicated in connection with the portfolio-liquidity effects, the initial effects of a change in money supply may be expected to occur in financial assets. This accounts for the fact that on the average movements in security market prices precede movements in business activity. Reasons for the lag may also be structural, including the delay before the cyclical situation and its need for appropriate action are recognized and the delay before the monetary actions taken become effective in impact. Monetary changes are never single and instantaneous but occur sequentially with a "feedback" effect in turn from business activity to money supply.

Moreover, the concept of "lag" is subject to various technical definitions, insofar as cyclical analysis is concerned. When Friedman refers to an "average lag," he means the average of weighted averages for several episodes of the interval between the action and its effects.[25]

On this concept of the lag, Friedman's empirical research led to the conclusion that monetary policy actions that produce a peak in the rate of change of the stock of money can be expected on the average to be followed by a peak in general business some sixteen months later; and conversely, monetary changes that produce a trough in business activity can be expected to achieve that slowdown in business some twelve months later.[26] Because of the inability to forecast the extent of lags, Friedman reemphasizes the advisability of the 4 percent rule for growth of the money supply. Because of the importance of estimating true lags in formulating monetary policy, we will look at this question in greater detail in the following chapter.

25. Milton Friedman, "The Lag in Effect of Monetary Policy," *Journal of Political Economy.* 69 (October 1961): 455.
26. Friedman, "Money and Business Cycles," pp. 32–64.

Questions and Exercises

1. The rapid introduction of new and significant quantities of gold and silver from the New World in the fifteenth century led to a period of rising prices gradually affecting most of Europe. How would the Fisher equation of exchange have accounted for this phenomenon?
2. Using the Cambridge cash-balances approach where $M_S = M$ and $M_D = kPy$, determine the value of k if the money stock set by the monetary authority is $50 billion and the value of goods sold is $200 billion. What would be the income velocity of money under these conditions?
3. Suppose that in the examples for question 2, the *ex ante* balance demand is .20. What would tend to happen to money income in the economy? Can you make any judgment as to whether the adjustment would be mainly in terms of P or Y? Why or why not?
4. According to the permanent income theory, the individual's demand for money is dependent upon his permanent income (wealth) or may be expressed as $M_{D_t} = aY_t^p$. Why is a specified as less than one but greater than zero?
5. Young families generally have a lower demand for cash balances than do older families, even when incomes are the same. Could you use the permanent income theory to explain this behavior? What difficulties, if any, do you find in expressing permanent income in terms of past income only?
6. Assume that the Federal Reserve Open-Market Committee elects to sell a large quantity of Treasury notes. Describe the liquidity-portfolio effects that you would expect. What might eventually happen to money income derived from the sale of real assets?
7. From a sale of bonds by the Federal Reserve Open-Market Committee, what price anticipation effect might occur? In the final analysis, might interest rates tend to fall? Why or why not?
8. Assume that the Federal Reserve takes expansionary action. Would it have reason to rest assured that the economy would smoothly reach a new equilibrium or moving equilibrium? Why or why not?
9. Lack of confidence in the official currency can produce changes in velocity. In 1973, a deepening international monetary crisis resulted in just such a drop in confidence in the American dollar. What effects might you predict for velocity? What effects would the Cambridge cash-balances formulation predict?
10. Assume that you are lucky enough to have had a grandfather who established for you a sizable trust fund. The fund provides you with the earning from the principal. The trust consists of long-term Treasury bonds. Assume now that interest rates began to fall—would you feel richer or poorer? If you were able to touch the principal, would you feel differently? Why or why not?

dollars of new offerings, gave what several specialists, felt to be a good account of themselves. The Treasury Department auctioned $1.8-billion one-year bills ... somewhat lower until the Federal Reserve made an appearance as a buyer for the systems account of Government coupon issues. The Fed's appearance as a purchaser of intermediate- and longer-term Government obligations helped to lift the market, specialists noted.

The Fed also made another appearance in the Federal funds market, which at one point during the day rose to as much as 14 per cent. Yesterday's action by the Fed in the funds market consisted of overnight or one-day repurchase agreements, carried out on a day that funds are often apt to move erratically, because it is the weekly settlement day for Federal Reserve member banks.

Before ... sury bill ... the mar ... turned to the Federal National Mortgage Association's $1.5-billion offering of debentures with coupon rates that were set at 8.45 per cent for $500-million of debentures due Dec. 10, 1976; 8.45 per cent for $650-million of debentures maturing Mar. 10, 1978, and 8.5 per cent on $350-million the first quarter of 1974—a decline in gross national product of 5.8% on an basis. It would probably be unfair to Fed's policy is fully responsible, but other hand, it would be difficult to lack of relationship.

On Monday Mr. Burns publicly that the Fed would continue to restr erately the growth of money and cr year. In the less than 100 hours si Burns spoke out, the already sky-hig rate has reached a record 10¾%, stock market has fallen 32 points, sured by the Dow Jones industrial

Hardly Enough Restraint

So far this year, the nation's mo ply—defined as currency and bank c accounts—has been growing at an rate of about 6.5%. Hardly anybod

Unmaking a Mess

Stopping the Inflation
Is Easy in Theory,
Painful in Practice

Tight Money Would Slow
The Economy & Cut Jobs
So Fed Tries 'Gradualism'

Mr. Friedman's Prescription

By LINDLEY H. CLARK JR.
Staff Reporter of THE WALL STREET JOURNAL
The Federal Reserve System, Chairman

---

bank and institutional buying said to be strong.

Meanwhile, the offering by the Federal Home Loan Banks of its $100-million consolidated discount notes also was portedly ... $100,- ... $1-million through five securities dealers, the notes bore the following rates: 8.8 per cent, on 30 to 59-day day maturities, and 8.75 per cent on 180 to 270-day maturities.

With all this to choose from, underwriters and investors involved in other sectors of the credit markets nontheless were able to report toward the close of the day anywhere from a fairly good to an excellent reception to additional new offerings.

Among these were an offering of $100-million of Chesapeake and Potomac Telephone Company of Maryland debentures, won by underwriters headed by ... corporation ... ese AAA-rated obligations were reported to be sold down to tag ends yesterday afternoon.

Also in the corporate market, a negotiated offering by underwriters headed by Morgan Stanley & Co. o ... lion of 8⅞ per cent ... of the General ... it.

On September 17 you asked Dr. Arthur Burns, the chairman of the Board of Governors of the Federal Reserve System, to comment on certain published criticisms of monetary policy. On November 6 the chairman replied on behalf of the System. This reply has been widely publicized by the Federal Reserve System. It was reprinted in the Federal Reserve Bulletin (November 1973) and in at least five of the separate Federal Reserve Bank Reviews.

The reply makes many valid points. Yet, taken as a whole, it evades rather than answers the criticisms. It appears to exonerate the Federal Reserve System from ...iable responsibility ... yet a close reading ... so, and other e ... does not refer, e ... the Fed has contributed to inflation.

According to the reply, "The severe rate of ...on that we have experienced in 1973 ...t responsibly be attributed to monetary ...jement" (italics added). As written, ...entence is unexceptionable. Delete the "severe," and the sentence is indefens-

The reply correctly cites a number of special factors that made the inflation in 1973 more severe than could have been expected from prior monetary growth alone—the world-wide economic boom, ecological impeded to investment, escalating farm energy shortages. These factors may xplain why consumer prices rose by 8% (fourth quarter 1972 to fourth quarter instead of, say, by 6%. But they do not n why ... h as t ... n why the fi ... years from 1968 to 1973. ...e reply recognizes that "the effec ...zation policies occur gradually ... and "that it is never safe to rely on ...ncept of money." Yet, the reply pres ...statistical data on the growth

---

Bay Transportation Authority revenue bonds and reoffered them at prices to yield from 5.25 per cent ... 1975 ne ... or's, the ...obligations were sold down to a balance of $49-million.

One offering that had been scheduled for yesterday, the New York Urban Development Corporation's $100-million of 12-month bond anticipation notes, was postponed due

By CAROL MATHEWS

The push is still on at the Federal Reserve to break back of inflation, as witness, the central bank's upping of the discount rate Wednesday to a record 8 per cent.

As as result, against the background of soaring interest rates, little relief is in sight for bond owners al... injured t ... de... a... te...

"It will be a couple of months with these rates up here, and if the Fed is serious about controlling inflation, that is the only way they can do it," said William Altschuler, portfolio manager of Lord, Abbett Bond Debenture

On today's calendar, two ... negotiated off ... ...ne earlier speculative sales ... headed by ...oldman, Sachs will be marketing $125-million of F. W. Woolworth Company debentures, rated A, which are expected to be priced at 99.25 with 9 per cent coupons to yield 9.08 per cent in 1999. A $150-million offering of Philip Morris, Inc., debentures, due from underwriters headed over the present ... the squeeze ... there is little solid ... to predict the limits of current rate rises.

The rate boosts have been so great already that po... tial investo... are tryi... decide whe... s bo... trea... ate... up further, our bonds will get sandbagged some more. But if rates go down, we're left with empty hands," lamented one institutional trader.

The dilemma is very real for institutions, it is pointed out, because they can miss a lot of income should rates decline and they have no bon... on hand, just short-

---

Bond Trading Active; Fed Is Buyer of U.S. Government Issues

Dollar Rallies on U.S. Interest Rate Rise, Possible Covering of Speculative Sales

Bonds: The Squeeze Is On

Bond Markets

Why Curbing Inflation Is the Fed's Job

Trading, though, was much quieter than during the middle of last week, when the dollar surged on reports of central bank intervention in support of the dollar and then fell on rumors that West Germany would break away from the few European currencies still tied in a joint float against the dollar.

In yesterday's trading, the dollar climbed 1.4% in Frankfurt, to 2.4820 West German marks from 2.4410 Friday. In Zu... U.S. currency rose 1.6% to 2.9410 ... 2.8775.

Eviden... ample that ...000 in six month certifica... of deposit at 11 per cent ... still leave an investor $100,000 on hand in Oc... ...er, plus interest, when rates for certificates of deposit may well be below 11 per cent.

By that ... bonds offered today at ... no longer be ... cause of a rate drop, and an... investor would have missedity, and certainly an opportunity to make not the other factor... only interest income on a ... bond, but price appreciation ...as well, as a whole, the Federal Reserve Sys...m has ...ised that responsibility in a way

an interest ...etrenchments from serves

Ban... dollar... to pur... that w... had n... marke... ery at ... Ger... are ex... forwa... excha... ny's ... and t ... Natior... excha... ...ed ...st rate. ... bond b... offered are in ... present situati... self," one obser... **The Treasury**

The confusio... raising some q... the upcoming funding of $4 ...as the ...ey; it ...he other factors... record is unmis... past three years

---

Movements in Money and Prices 1948-1973

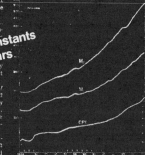

The reply makes many valid points. Yet, at an average rate of 4.6%; currently, they are rising at a rate of not far from 10%. The accelerated rise in the quantity of money has clearly been reflected, after some delay, in a similar accelerated rise in prices.

Paying with constants instead of dollars

However limited may be the Fed's ability to control monetary aggregates from quarter to quarter or even year to year, the monetary acceleration depicted in the chart, which has extended over more than a decade, could not have occurred without t... ...put ...year ... acceleration in the rate of inflation over the past decade could not ha... ...ithout the prior monetary ... may be the verdict on ...he short-run relations to which the reply re... ...run policies have

---

years as a whole but also for each of three ... sepa rately, as Table II shows. The one encouraging feature is the slightly lower rate of growth of M2 and M3 from 1972 to 1973 than in the earlier two years. But the tapering off is mild and it is not clear that it is continuing. More important, even these lower rates are far too high. Steady growth of M2 at 9% or 10% would lead to an inflation of about 6% or 7% per year. To bring inflation down to 3%, let alone to zero, the rate of growth of M2 must be reduced to something like 5% to 7%.

Table II: Recent Monetary Growth Rates			
Calendar Year	Annual % Rate of Growth		
	M1	M2	M3
1970-1971	7.0	11.8	12.8
1971-1972	6.4	10.2	12.5
1972-1973	7.4	9.5	10.6

For more than a decade, monetary growth has been accelerating. It has been higher in the past three years than in any other three-year period since the end of World War II. Inflation has also accelerated over the past decade. It too has been higher in the past three period ...pirical ng pre... monetary accelera... of the ...that ...nies ...the ...n in ...now... ...tical ...as

Loan demand soars along with inflation

For the first time in 43 years, this week Libbey-Owens-Ford Co. is going out. ...le the company to finance its spend... g plans, and President Robert G... ...ingerter is bitter about the steep inflation that has forced him to borrow now. He calculates that a year's rising prices have eaten up 11% of Libbey-Owens' net worth. "What the hell is left over... as for the investor when you have to bor...ebly re... to make up an inflation loss like ...re that?" he asks.

FEDERAL RESERVE BANK OF NEW YORK

Monetary Policy

14

We have looked in Chapter 12 at the controversy over the importance of money in the economy, with its implications for the proper role of monetary policy. At the center of the debate are two different views about how changes in the supply of money produce changes in the level of national income. In general, Keynesian economists believe that monetary policy affects national income indirectly by causing changes in the interest rate which in turn produce changes in consumption and investment, whereas economists generally referred to as monetarists, led by Milton Friedman of the University of Chicago, argue that changes in the supply of money produce changes in the level of national income directly. According to the monetarists, stable prices and a steady rate of real growth in GNP can only be attained by allowing the money supply to grow at approximately the anticipated real growth rate of GNP. Whereas Keynesians believe that monetary policy can be successful in keeping the economy on a steady growth path with low unemployment only when combined with the appropriate fiscal measures, monetarists believe that monetary policy is a much more important tool than fiscal policy. The theoretical differences among the Keynesians and the monetarists have fired the debate among economists, bankers, and politicians about the proper role of the Federal Reserve, the institution which determines the money supply in this country.

Another group of monetary theorists, the Radcliffe-Gurley-Shaw school,[1] has questioned whether a central banking authority like the Federal Reserve is actually able to control changes in investment and national income by way of the interest rate. Gurley and Shaw asserted that given the demand for money, the rate of interest may not be determined entirely by the rate of growth of the money supply; instead the interest rate may be powerfully affected by the rate of growth of financial intermediaries like savings and loan associations. In effect, they suggest that the growth of financial intermediaries may explain the long run upward trend in velocity (Y/M) in the United States since World War II. As we saw in Chapter 13, if velocity is not constant, either in the long run or through the business cycle, then the Federal Reserve power to control the rate of growth of the nominal money supply will not be an effective instrument for achieving stable prices and steady growth. Given

$$\hat{M} + \hat{V} = \hat{P} + \hat{y} \tag{14.1}$$

the implications of a steady M roughly equal to y will not be clear if V is unstable.

As we shall see in more detail later in this chapter, the work of the Radcliffe Commission in Britain and of economists John Gurley and Edward Shaw has therefore added a new dimension to the controversy over appropriate monetary policy.

Monetarists vs. Keynesians

The chief difference between monetarists and Keynesians is over the issue of how monetary policy works to produce changes in national income. Keynesians hold that contracting or expanding the supply of money works indirectly on the level of aggregate income by raising or lowering interest rates, which in turn influences the level of investment and expansion of credit in the economy. As we saw in Chapter 12, Keynesians therefore maintain that the effectiveness of monetary policy depends on the elasticity of the supply and demand for money with respect to the rate of interest and the responsiveness of consumption and investment expenditure to changes in the rate

1. See John G. Gurley and Edward S. Shaw, "Financial Intermediaries and the Saving-Investment Process," *Journal of Finance* 11 (March 1956): 257–276; and Committee on the Working of the Monetary System (Chairman: The Rt. Hon. Lord Radcliffe, G.B.E.), *Report* (London, 1959).

of interest. Monetarists maintain that the interest elasticity of expenditure with respect to interest-rate changes is not important. They hold that changes in the money supply have a direct effect on expenditure and therefore on national income, and thus an increase in the quantity of money produces an increase in GNP; a decrease in the quantity of money produces a decrease in GNP. Monetarists question the reliability of the Keynesian model since, as we have already seen, the IS/LM model typically postulates that the price level can be assumed to be fixed. They point out that this assumption is unrealistic in a world of rapidly changing prices and that their model is a better approximation of the real world since it allows for changes in prices.

Perhaps equally significant for the implied effectiveness of monetary policy is the difference between Keynesians and monetarists regarding the determinants and stability of the demand for money. As we saw in Chapter 8, the transactions, precautionary, and speculative demands for money all depend upon the level of interest rates. If interest rates rise, for example, the Keynesian model holds that people would be willing to sacrifice money and hence some of their liquidity in return for the higher yield of interest-bearing assets; if they fall, the public would be less willing to hold interest-bearing assets. Keynes also emphasized that investors might choose to hold their assets in the form of money regardless of the rate of interest, as in a depression. When investors have little confidence in the future of the economy, they may decide that it is virtually imperative to hold as much cash as possible in order to protect themselves from downward plunges in the value of their investments. In such circumstances monetary policy would be totally ineffective since velocity would be very unstable, simply falling if the money supply were increased, given $V = Y/M$.

Keynes perceived a substitution effect among money, financial assets, and real assets. Assuming that people were satisfied with their existing money balances, an increase in the supply of money would cause them to spend their additional money on financial assets. This forces down the interest rates and presumably results in an increase in investment expenditure, causing a rise in income by way of the multiplier, represented in its simplest form here as

$$\Delta Y = \frac{1}{1-b}\Delta I \qquad (14.2)$$

More generally, recall that

$$\Delta Y = m\Delta A \qquad (14.3)$$

where m is the multiplier, and A represents all autonomous expenditure, or $a + I + G$.

The effect upon yields on the assets which people wish to hold is the mechanism by which changes in money supply are transmitted into changes in the level of national income. As we saw in Chapter 12, the elasticity of the demand for money in relation to interest rates is at the center of Keynesian monetary theory. A change in the money supply can only affect GNP if it first changes interest rates and then only if consumption and investment are responsive to the changes in interest rates.

In contrast, the simple quantity theory allows for no interest elasticity of the demand for money. The simplest quantity theory states:

$$Y = MV \qquad (14.4)$$

where M equals the money supply, which is determined by the central bank, and V is the velocity of money. Quantity theorists hold that an increase in M produces an increase in Y since V is constant. Since Y may be thought of as being composed of prices times output, an increase in M produces a corresponding increase in either prices or output or some combination of the two. The predictive value of this theory holds only if V is a constant since if an increase in M caused a change in V, the formula would not explain changes in the level of Y. Equation (14.4) may be rewritten in a form linking changes in the nominal money supply to changes in nominal income in a manner analogous to the link between a change in nominal income and a change in autonomous expenditure expressed in equation (14.3).

$$\Delta Y = V \Delta M \qquad (14.5)$$

The basic constant of the simple Keynesian approach is the multiplier $\left(m = \dfrac{1}{1 - b} \right)$, while the basic constant of the simple quantity theory is velocity $(V = Y/M)$.

The difference between the simple quantity-theory model and the simple Keynesian model can be seen clearly by setting the definitions of income implied by these approaches equal to each other. Setting Y in the Keynesian equation $Y = mA$ equal to Y in the quantity theory $Y = VM$:

$$VM = mA$$

or

$$V = \frac{mA}{M} \qquad (14.6)$$

Equation (14.6) says that the velocity of money is equal to the level of income as determined by the Keynesian multiplier $(Y = mA)$ divided by the supply of money. To Keynesians velocity is not constant but is a function of the interest rate and adjusts according to changes in i. To reflect this, $V = mA/M$ would be rewritten as

$$V(i) = \frac{mA}{M} = \frac{Y}{M} \qquad (14.7)$$

The simple Keynesian theory would hold that in equation (14.7) it is velocity which adjusts, given changes in the interest rate to maintain the equality of equation (14.7), when the money supply, M, is changed. The simple quantity theory would hold that V is invariant in the face of changes in the money supply and that, rather, it is Y which adjusts to maintain the equality of equation (14.7) when the money supply is changed.

Monetarists and Keynesians have devoted considerable effort to measuring the impact of monetary policy upon income. A good deal of the analysis, which was conducted in the 1960s, focused not only upon monetary policy, but also upon a comparison of the effectiveness of monetary changes in general in explaining the behavior of income with the effectiveness of expenditure changes (including fiscal policy actions) in explaining the behavior of income. An econometric study by Milton Friedman and David Meiselman[2] supported the claim, suggested by equation (14.5), that changes in nominal income are better explained in most circumstances by the behavior of the money supply than, as suggested by equation (14.3), by the behavior of autonomous expenditure (including private investment and government expenditure). The only time the Friedman-Meiselman study showed autonomous expenditure outperforming the money supply as an explanatory variable of nominal income was during the Depression years. These results were challenged by Albert Ando and Franco Modigliani,[3] who criticized Friedman and Meiselman's definition of autonomous expenditure and demonstrated that inclusion of the war years biased the results against the autonomous expenditure variable. They also questioned Friedman and Meiselman's definitions of money. Ando and Modigliani proposed a criterion for the success of fiscal versus monetary policy that was different from the correlation coefficient criterion employed by Friedman and Meiselman. The complete dominance of monetary-policy over fiscal-policy effectiveness obtained by Friedman and Meiselman was held to be unwarranted by Ando and Modigliani, who concluded that a more balanced approach along with considerably more knowledge about how macro policy actually works were needed.

The debate between monetary- and fiscal-policy advocates continued throughout the 1960s and included a number of other studies. The question of what monetary and/or expenditure variables were appropriate for a test of their relative effectiveness as well as what criterion to use to judge their relative success continued to stimulate work by economists which, taken together, added considerably to the stock of knowledge regarding how the economy does respond to monetary- and fiscal-policy actions.

To support their view of the actual transmission process, the way in which changes in the money supply produce changes in wealth and thus in national income, monetarists have consistently chosen to rely upon

2. Milton Friedman and David Meiselman, "The Relative Stability of Monetary Velocity and the Investment Multiplier in the United States, 1897–1958," in Commission on Money and Credit, *Stabilization Policies* (Englewood Cliffs, N.J.: Prentice Hall, 1963).

3. Albert Ando and Franco Modigliani, "The Relative Stability of Monetary Velocity and the Investment Multiplier," *American Economic Review* 55 (September 1965): 693–728.

empirical evidence. Further support for the conclusions of his work with Meiselman has been provided by Friedman and his associates.[4] It has been found that there is a closer statistical correlation between money supply and GNP than between GNP and any of the Keynesian variables, such as government spending and investment. In the long run, changes in the money supply have always accompanied any changes in the level of the GNP.

Friedman's research has shown that while V is not a constant in the simple sense of the traditional quantity theory model, it can always be predicted so long as one knows certain other variables. Thus V is a stable function of the interest rates, prices, and wealth effects. Using this framework, Friedman concludes that changes in the supply of money might be somewhat offset by changes in the velocity of money that are also reflected in changes in price and output in the long run. In the short run, changes in the supply of money might also be slightly offset by changes in the velocity of money that are reflected in prices and output. Thus even though V might change, its change can be predicted, meaning that the essential predictive value of the simple quantity theory which we have examined is upheld: changes in the money supply can still be used to predict changes in the level of national income.

The policy implications of Friedman's analysis are straightforward. First, since there is a stable relationship between the quantity of money and the level of national income in the long run, the task of monetary authority is to let the money supply rise in accordance with the real growth rate of GNP. As we have seen in Chapter 13, the recommendation often mentioned in Friedman's work is that the Federal Reserve should gear the monetary supply to rise at the rate of 4 percent per year in order to produce a growth rate of 4 percent, 4 percent being close to the average real growth rate of the economy in the past 100 years.

In the short run, Friedman argues that the monetary authority should not tamper with the money supply in an effort to influence interest rates in order to produce changes in aggregate demand. This directly contradicts the Keynesian view that monetary policy should be directed toward finding the interest rate which will equate the level of investment with the level of full-employment saving in the economy. Friedman argues that changes in interest rates are not really a guide to the stance of monetary policy. In his view, an increase in the supply of money could cause interest rates initially to fall, as in the Keynesian model, but since people eventually increase their expenditures for goods and services in response to increases in the quantity of money, the resulting upward pressure on prices and incomes will eventually result in upward pressure on interest rates. If the money supply is increased, interest rates may also rise, because as production in-

---

4. Milton Friedman has set down his empirical analysis in "The Demand for Money: Some Theoretical and Empirical Results," *Journal of Political Economy* 67 (August 1954): 327–351; and, with Anna J. Schwartz, *A Monetary History of the United States 1862–1960* (Princeton, N.J.: Princeton University Press, 1963).

creases in response to higher levels of demand, the demand for capital rises, forcing up interest rates.

The real danger in aiming monetary policy at interest-rate levels, as Friedman sees it, lies in the inflationary potential of such a policy. If the Fed increases the money supply, expecting interest rates to fall, it will initially be correct in reading the attendant drop in interest rates as a signal of "easy money." But interest rates will subsequently rise, in Friedman's view, and if the Fed reads this rise as evidence of need for another injection of money, they will be misled into overexpansion of the money supply. If this overexpansion continues long enough, resultant inflation will lead to inflationary expectations which, in turn, will result in increases in the nominal interest rate as lenders attempt to protect the purchasing power of their interest earnings. If, in order to adjust for inflationary expectations, suppliers of labor and goods also reduce the level of services and goods they offer at given money prices, total output may fall. The result is an inflationary recession of the sort experienced in the first half of 1974. The possibility of this chain of events, arising from a misreading of interest rates as an indicator of monetary policy, leads Friedman to advocate the less discretionary steady-rate-of-growth-of-the-money-supply approach to monetary policy.

Friedman's empirical findings have been supported by the Federal Reserve Bank of St. Louis, which started to make extensive use of a monetarist model in the late 1960s for purposes of predicting GNP. The model assumed a growth rate in the money supply of 6 percent, based on an approximated rate of growth in money over the preceding three years. Its essential feature was the assumption that an increase in the supply of money by $1 billion would increase the level of GNP by $6 billion. The record of the St. Louis model compared to actual changes in GNP and to predictions based upon a model incorporating traditional Keynesian assumptions (consensus) is shown in Table 14.1.

The St. Louis model, particularly in predictions of price level and unemployment figures, appears to be more accurate than the predictions of the consensus model. While this test is hardly conclusive, the predictive value of the model tends to enforce the monetarist position. We will return to the predictive record of the monetarist model at the end of this chapter.

Monetarists vs. Other Monetary Theorists

While monetarists dispute Keynesians over the proper role of a monetary authority in controlling the supply of money, other economists have questioned whether a central banking authority is able effectively to control changes in investment and spending by altering the quantity of money. The Radcliffe Commission in Britain, which studied the growth and development of financial intermediaries in that country since World War II, con-

Table 14.1 The Record of Prediction

		St. Louis	Consensus	Actual
1969	GNP (billions)	$957.2	$940.0	$948.0
	Prices[a]	4.1%	3.5% (6.0)	5.1%
	Unemployment[b]	3.5%	4.1%	3.6%
1970	GNP	$997.2	$1007.0	$988.4
	Prices	4.6%	4.0% (5.6)	5.7%
	Unemployment	5.4%	4.6%	5.9%
1971	GNP	$1076.9	$1066.0	$1072.9
	Prices	4.0%	4.0% (3.3)	3.4%
	Unemployment	5.7%	5.6%	5.9%

SOURCE: Darryl R. Francis, "Has Monetarism Failed?" *St. Louis Federal Bank Review* 84, no. 3 (March 1972): 32–38. St. Louis predictions are based on the assumption of .6 percent money growth.

a. Rate of change of prices for St. Louis predictions is the change in the GNP deflator from fourth quarter to fourth quarter, and the "actual" figure is GNP deflator. Consensus' price predictions are for the consumer price index from December to December. Actual consumer price index changes are in parentheses.

b. The St. Louis predictions and the actual rate are for the fourth quarter, while the consensus prediction is for December.

cluded that the private sector had developed a marked ability to undercut actions by the Bank of England to control investment and spending through the development of money substitutes. In this country the work of John Gurley and Edward Shaw has produced similar conclusions. The central conclusion of the Radcliffe Committee and of Gurley and Shaw is that actions of the central bank play a smaller role in influencing investment and spending than suggested by a stable demand function for money of either the Keynesian or monetarist variety.

Radcliffe and Gurley-Shaw both view financial intermediaries as the culprits in preventing the central bank from carrying out an effective monetary policy. In a world in which everyone paid for his or her purchases out of current income and nobody wanted to buy more than current income allowed, financial intermediaries would not be important. But because some people always save part of their current income and others require additional funds to make capital expenditures, borrowing is an important aspect of the money flow. Financial intermediaries thus channel funds from net savers to those who desire to spend in excess of their current income. Commercial banks are the most important of these, but other financial institutions, including savings and loan associations, life insurance companies, common trust funds, pension funds, mutual savings banks, and government lending agencies, perform intermediation services. The intermediators use their funds to purchase what are called **primary securities.** Primary securities include government securities, primary and preferred stock, and mortgages. To obtain funds, intermediaries sell **indirect securities,** such as time deposits, savings and loans shares, insurance policies, and common fund stocks. The margin between what the intermediaries earn on their primary securities and the interest rates which they must pay to the holders of indirect securities provides them with sufficient compensation to justify their continuing to offer their services.

The development of financial intermediaries has several effects on the economy. Borrowers are able to obtain a larger quantity of funds from an intermediary than from a single investor. Lenders who provide funds to the intermediaries automatically have their risks diversified since the intermediary is able to invest their funds in a wide variety of projects. Moreover, since the net savers place their funds in savings accounts or common fund stock shares, they are not required to make long-term sacrifices in their liquidity. Intermediaries therefore provide a mechanism for economizing on the amount of money needed to support economic activity. The small saver has no need to hold money when he can readily convert his money into interest-bearing indirect securities such as savings accounts, which can readily be converted to cash should the need arise. In a world without intermediaries, the number of transactions which a given level of interest rates can support depends upon the money supply. With the spread of intermediaries, a given supply of money can support a larger number of transactions because of the liquidity effect of intermediaries. In other words, changes in the money supply can be offset by changes in the velocity of money. A cut in the money supply may lead to an increase in velocity, due to the ability of financial intermediaries to attract funds, as shown in equation (14.8).

$$\downarrow \hat{M} + \hat{V} \uparrow = \hat{P} + \hat{y} \tag{14.8}$$

If velocity rises while the money supply is reduced, it may neutralize the impact of the monetary change on the economy since $\hat{M} + \hat{V} = 0$ if $\hat{M} = -\hat{V}$.

The best way to understand this effect is by example. Suppose the monetary authority wants to check inflation by following a restrictive monetary policy. This could be accomplished by increasing reserve requirements of its member banks, which would dry up liquidity and reduce funds available for loans, in turn causing interest rates to rise and slowing down the expansion of the economy. As interest rates rise, an increased flow of funds into intermediaries could reduce the decline in total spending caused by the increase in interest rates. As interest rates on primary securities rise in response to the contraction of the money supply, intermediaries can raise the interest rates they offer to individual savers in order to attract more funds. Since deposits with financial intermediaries are close substitutes for money, the higher interest rates may induce savers to shift more money into such institutions, thus raising velocity. This shift increases the lending power of intermediaries, resulting in an increase in the supply of loanable funds. The intermediaries are therefore able to increase their purchases of primary securities, causing money to flow back into the commercial banks. The result is an increase in velocity, which substitutes for the reduction in the money supply, enabling a restoration of total spending to levels which existed prior to the monetary restriction. This undercuts the restrictive policy of the monetary authority. There is also evidence that intermediaries are able to undercut an expansionary monetary policy. In short, because the actions of financial intermediaries tend to offset the impact of changes in the money supply, by way of changes in velocity, their presence and growth may have weakened the power of the monetary authority to control economic activity.

The Radcliffe Committee concluded that since monetary policy is not really effective so long as intermediaries can undercut efforts to control the level of spending in the economy, it should be directed toward controlling the lending policy of the intermediaries. The Radcliffe Commission reasoned that such a policy was not politically feasible in Britain and hence argued that fiscal policy should be used to undercut the presumed effects of intermediaries. In this country, Gurley and Shaw have argued that the authority of the Federal Reserve should be extended to cover the actions of nonbank financial intermediaries.[5]

Keynesian opponents of the Radcliffe and Gurley-Shaw views argue that even though intermediaries can offset changes in the money supply, changes in the rate of interest can still operate to reduce the level of spending in the economy. Even though the use of money substitutes increases in response to increases in interest rates, it is impossible for the intermediaries to cause interest rates to settle back to their old level. Thus a tight money supply would still influence spending and, hence, income.

Money and Inflation

As we have seen, monetarists insist that the optimum monetary policy is one which allows the money supply to grow in proportion to the growth rate in GNP, pointing out that when the growth rate in money stock exceeds real growth in output, inflation becomes a problem. Clearly inflation has become one of the most serious problems facing our economy. Despite attempts to control the rate of inflation, it rose to 8.8 percent in the last quarter of 1973. Monetarists believe that a gradual return to a slower rate of money-supply growth is the best way to bring inflation under control.

In order to understand inflation, it is first necessary to differentiate between changes in relative price levels and an increase in the general price level. Changes in relative price levels provide an important economic func-

5. See John Gurley and Edward Shaw, "Financial Aspects of Economic Developments," *American Economic Review* 12 (September 1952): 515–538.

tion since they allocate resources in accordance with consumer demands. For example, if there was an increase in consumer demand for shirts rather than pants, the price of shirts relative to pants would tend to increase. Faced with the need to increase production, shirt manufacturers would be willing to pay higher prices for fabric and thread. Producers of fabric and thread would increase their sales to shirt manufacturers and decrease their sales to pants manufacturers. The result would be an allocation of resources in accordance with the wishes of consumers. In contrast to a change in relative prices, an inflationary price rise is a rise in the general level of prices. It is worth noting that if *all* prices and wages in the economy doubled overnight there would be no change in relative prices, and no one would be better or worse off. This can be understood by supposing simply that all of the dollar figures we have become accustomed to hearing, including our wage rates or salaries, were doubled tomorrow. No relative price changes would have occurred, and therefore no real economic effects would be felt. Having made this point, however, we must rapidly add that relative prices do not remain unaffected in inflation. Price changes do not all occur overnight. In fact they occur at considerably different rates in different markets, and this accounts, to some extent, for changes in relative prices during inflationary periods. Most individuals are concerned that during an inflation the price of what they sell, their labor services, will not rise as rapidly as the prices of the goods they buy and that therefore their real purchasing power will fall. It is for this reason that monthly figures on the increase (or fall) in the price of what "typical" consumers buy are published by the U.S. Department of Commerce in the Consumer Price Index. With these figures, individuals can adjust their earnings to real terms and perhaps bargain with their employer regarding maintenance of the purchasing power of wages or salary. With the distinction between inflation and relative price changes in mind, we can return to the discussion of inflation per se.

Given the distinction between relative price changes and changes in the general price level, it may be asked why inflation, which describes a general price increase, is bad. If, for example, P were to double, what might be the effects? First, it must be realized that a doubling of the general price level in no way guarantees that the individual prices which make up the general level would all double. Some might increase only 50 percent, others might triple. Usually wages do not rise as quickly as the price of consumer goods. If prices were to double and wages increased by only 50 percent, the wage earner would be worse off since his dollar would buy fewer goods and services. In the U.S. economy people whose income is fixed, such as old-age pensioners, suffer most severely during an inflation, as do the less-skilled or nonunionized workers, who are unable to secure wage increases. Members of large unions who may be able to get cost-of-living clauses in their contracts generally fare better.

Economists also draw a distinction between anticipated and unanticipated inflation. In an unanticipated inflation, borrowers benefit at the expense of creditors. Suppose a borrower owed $1,000 payable within a year. If during the year there was an inflation rate of 10 percent, at the end of the year the borrower would have to forego fewer real goods in order to repay the debt, because his dollar would buy less. The borrower's real wealth would have increased, while that of the lender would have decreased. In this sense, inflation can be said to have some effect on the redistribution of wealth. However, if the lender anticipated the inflation, he would charge the borrower a higher nominal interest in order to maintain the real purchasing power of his interest earnings. Anticipating a 10 percent inflation, the lender would charge 15 percent in order to make 5 percent in real terms.

In a sustained, but generally gradual, inflationary pattern such as the one experienced in this country from the 1950s to 1973, all sectors of the economy become adjusted to the idea of inflation. Thus, if workers anticipate a 4 percent price rise, they will demand a 7 percent wage increase in order to become 3 percent ahead of the game in real terms. Moreover, if they realize that the value of their money holdings is going to decrease over time, they are less willing to hold money and more willing to hold real assets. Economists sometimes refer to this behavior as a response to an inflationary tax on money. The difficulty with the response of money holders to the inflationary tax on their money balances is that it leads to further inflation. As money holders attempt to exchange their depreciating money assets for goods, they drive up prices. The proximate feelings accompanying such behavior are something akin to a desire to buy now before prices rise even further.

This behavior becomes extreme in the case of hyperinflation, where prices are rising so rapidly that money holders are literally racing to exchange their money for goods before it depreciates any further. Germany experienced such a hyperinflation shortly after World War I. Saddled with massive reparations payments to the victorious Allied powers of Europe, the German government tried to pay its bills by simply printing money. The resulting massive rate of increase in the growth of the money supply led to such a rapid inflation that workers were paid two or three times a day in order that they might attempt to exchange wheelbarrel-loads of nearly worthless money for goods before prices rose even further.[6]

In short, the value of money as a store of value and as a unit of account is seriously reduced by inflation. If inflation becomes rapid enough, deterioration of the store-of-value role becomes sufficient to impair the value of money as a medium of exchange since its acceptability in exchange for goods over time and space comes seriously into question. While the 8 percent to 10 percent rates of inflation experienced by the United States in 1973 and 1974 do not approach hyperinflation, such rates are high enough to impair the role of money as a store of value and a unit of account. Such damage is not entirely due to errant monetary policy, in view of the heavy price increases for petroleum products that have been exogenously imposed. But

---

6. See Phillip Cagan, "The Monetary Dynamics of Hyperinflation" in Milton Friedman, *Studies in the Quantity Theory of Money* (Chicago: University of Chicago Press, 1956).

given that such price increases have occurred, monetarists would contend that the path of price increases in the future is not likely to return to lower levels without a gradual reduction of the rate of growth of the money supply.

Monetary Policy Tools

The supply of money and credit in the U.S. economy is determined by the Federal Reserve in three ways: changing reserve requirements, rediscounting, and open-market operations. Clearly, one way to influence the creation of money in an economy is to control the level of required reserves member banks must keep against their deposits. If, for example, the Fed decides to increase reserve requirements and commercial banks are fully loaned up, the member banks will find themselves deficient with respect to their reserve requirements and will have to call in loans and sell some of their securities in order to build up their reserves. If the Fed decides to reduce reserve requirements, member banks will have excess reserves and will be able to increase their loans. Although fixing reserves is a powerful tool, it is used infrequently because it causes rapid dislocations in the economy. The raising of reserve requirements by only 5 percent causes an immediate contraction in the amount of credit in the economy. A sharp contraction could reduce the confidence of investors and further accelerate the contraction. For this reason, Congress has limited the extent to which the Federal Reserve can vary reserve requirements. As a policy tool it is used much less frequently than open-market operations and varying the discount rate.

Rediscounting refers to the process of lending funds to member banks, because the member bank has secured the loan by discounting the commercial paper and securities which it deposits with the Federal Reserve to secure the loan. Thus, by varying the rediscount rate the Federal Reserve can influence the amount of borrowing by member banks and in so doing can affect the power of the member banks to make loans. An increase in the rediscount rate reduces loans; a decrease in the rediscount rate increases loans.

Recently, economists have recognized that the Federal Reserve policy of changing rediscount rates may be destabilizing because it is not applied at the right time or with sufficient force. During the business cycle, short-term interest rates tend to fluctuate. If interest rates were rising and the Fed set a rediscount rate above the market rate, it would be pursuing a tight monetary policy. However, short-term interest rates fluctuate very quickly and quite often the rate rises above the rediscount rate, at which point it becomes cheaper for banks to borrow from the Federal Reserve. Thus, even though a restrictive policy was being followed, banks would find it increasingly attractive to borrow from the Fed. If, in response to this trend, the Fed were to lower the discount rate, interest rates could already be rising. Since it cannot produce changes in the rediscount rate as quickly as changes in short-term interest rates, the rediscounting ability of the monetary authority runs potentially counter to the business cycle, thus destabilizing the economy. A possible solution is for the Fed to peg its rediscount rate to the market rate of interest. Some economists have argued that the lags in Federal Reserve manipulation of the discount rate are so severe that the Fed should abandon this policy tool and concentrate on open-market operations.

Perhaps the most useful policy tool is the purchase and sale of securities on the open market. A Federal Reserve purchase increases money and credit, while a sale contracts it. The power to expand or contract credit is considerable—a purchase (or sale) of $1 billion in securities may result in an expansion (or contraction) of up to $5 billion in credit—but it is the most flexible tool and thus favored by most monetary economists.

Open-market operations of the Federal Reserve are entirely discretionary. The Federal Reserve Open-Market Committee decides whether to expand or contract credit on the basis of its own forecasts of the level of activity in the economy. While there are laws which specify the amount of reserves which must remain in the Federal Reserve, the Open-Market Committee has substantial discretionary authority. Moreover, as open-market operations are constantly going on, there is less of a problem with time lags between decision and implementation than exists with fiscal policy.

There are several secondary tools which the Federal Reserve has used from time to time. In recent years, Congress has given the Federal Reserve the authority to regulate the terms of installment credit loans. Under Regulation Q the Federal Reserve is also able to impose limits on the interest rates which banks can pay on time deposits. As a result of using this power, the Federal Reserve was probably responsible for complicating the credit crunch which hit the economy in 1966. Concerned about inflationary trends in the economy during 1965, the Fed used Regulation Q to increase the interest which commercial banks were able to pay on time deposits. But restrictions on the amount of interest paid by savings and loan associations, which are required by law to limit their lending to mortgages, was left unchanged. (Usually commercial banks pay slightly lower rates of interest on their time deposits.) The result was that money flowed out of the savings and loan associations into the commercial banks. Mortgage lending by savings and loan institutions declined by 60 percent in late 1966. Residential construction, accordingly, declined sharply. By interfering with the market interest rate, the Federal Reserve has often produced undesirable effects on the owners of small businesses and mortgage lenders who cannot adjust to increases.

Economists have also recognized that the Fed can influence the money market through what are called "announcement effects." The hint that the Fed might raise the rediscount rate has tremendous repercussions throughout the financial community. Because changes in the rediscount rate do not mean that the Fed is about to enter a long-term policy of either expanding or retracting credit, the announcement effects may tend to have a destabilizing influence on the economy. This indicates another advantage of the open-market operations: since the buying and selling of government securities is continuous, these operations do not provoke the same announcement effects of other policy measures.

Despite its technical independence, however, the actions of the Federal Reserve are not entirely free of constraint, primarily imposed by the pursuance of contradictory goals by fiscal authorities. The frequent frustration of attempts to stabilize the economy by the use of monetary policy was evident in our discussion of fiscal and monetary policy in Chapter 12 and will become increasingly clear in the remainder of this chapter.

Monetary Policy Problems

The focal point of this chapter has been the several approaches to the proper role of monetary policy. Since the Federal Reserve controls monetary policy in the United States, much of the debate centers around which policy the Federal Reserve should follow: should it be guided by *rules* and maintain a growth of the money supply that is even with the growth of output, or should it exercise *authority,* the power to use monetary policy as a countercyclical tool. Those who believe that the elasticity of the supply and demand for money with respect to interest rates determines the effectiveness of monetary policy argue that the Federal Reserve should intervene in the economy whenever interest rates indicate that stimulation or restraint is needed. Monetarists, on the other hand, argue that observed changes in interest rates are not valid indicators of the required monetary policy or of the state of the economy because it is difficult to tell what an observed change in interest rates actually signifies. A change in interest rates could be the result of a temporary fluctuation or it could signal the beginning of a long-term trend in the economy. For example, at the beginning of an inflationary cycle, interest rates start to increase in response to anticipated depreciation of future interest payments. If the Fed interpreted the rise in interest rates as indicating a need to increase the supply of money in the economy, it would be reinforcing the rise in spending and contribute to the inflationary spiral, as we shall see. For this reason, monetarists argue that it is impossible for the Fed to pursue a countercyclical monetary policy.

Another difficulty in using monetary policy as a countercyclical tool is due to the lag between the time the Federal Reserve decides to increase or decrease the money supply and the time the decision will be felt by different sectors of the economy. Monetarists point out that without the ability to forecast their effects, decisions regarding monetary policy are hazardous.

Empirical Studies of Time Lags and Monetary Policy

As we saw in Chapter 12, two main time lags should be considered in the implementation of monetary policy—inside lags and impact lags. Inside lags, which involve the Fed's internal decision-making process, include the **recognition lag,** or lag between the time at which appropriate monetary action is necessary and the time when the Federal Reserve recognizes that action is necessary, and the **decision lag,** the time between the Fed's recog-

Commentary: Bringing Down Inflation with Escalator Clauses

In the first quarter of 1974, prices in the United States climbed at an annual rate of 14.5 percent, creating an adjusted inflation level of 8 percent. Yet real GNP actually declined by 5.8 percent, the largest drop since 1958. Such conditions posed a dilemma for the Federal Reserve: by restricting the money supply, the traditional remedy for inflation, they ran the risk of seriously weakening an already faltering economy.

Monetary economist Milton Friedman admitted monetary policy alone could not solve both problems and advised the United States to look to Brazil for an alternative; there inflation is worse than ours, but real growth has continued at 10 percent per annum since 1968. In 1964, Brazil's economy was hardly rosy. Hyperinflation that year ran 91.9 percent.[1] The year before the rate was 80 percent. Capital markets had dried up. There were plenty of borrowers, eager for loans that they could repay with greatly devalued money, but few investors were willing to put up money for any length of time. Here was a classic consequence of the uncertainty caused by price instability.

Behind this instability lay huge government deficits, running twice the size of revenues and being financed by newly printed money. When the military took over the Brazilian government in 1964, they tried traditional fiscal and monetary stabilization methods—cutting the deficit and curbing the growth in the money supply. To this they added wage and price controls containing escalator clauses that provided a "monetary correction" for the effects of inflation, a measure also known as indexing. In the United States those unions that negotiate cost-of-living escalator clauses enjoy "monetary correction" since, as inflation rises, real income is protected by equivalent wage increases. This eliminates the pressure for unions to demand higher and higher wage contracts in expectation of inflation, since the effect of inflation is taken care of. But only about 5 percent of the U.S. work force has this protection. In Brazil this system has been applied to all workers. On May 1 every year the minimum wage is adjusted for the rise in the wholesale price index for the past year, the expectations for the coming years, and any productivity gains of Brazilian workers.

In addition, such things as interest rates, rents, mortgages, pensions, and fixed assets have escalator clauses. A government bond, for example, is issued at a fixed rate with a guaranteed monetary correction for inflation during the life of the bond. A $100 bond bought at an interest rate of 5 percent would yield $115 if inflation were 10 percent or $125 if inflation were 20 percent. Only the income from the fixed interest is taxed, however. Companies, too, need only pay taxes on real income and can deduct the appreciation in working capital due to inflation and the added depreciation of plants and equipment.

The goal of this system, according to its architect, Octavio Gouvea de Bulhoes, a former finance minister of Brazil and now president of one of its banks, has been to guarantee a real rate of return to stimulate economic growth. In effect, what the Brazilians have tried to do is separate out the unexpected ef-

---

1. For a full account of the Brazilian economic recovery and its implications for the United States, see Francis E. Hassey, *Inflation: The Need for a New Mentality* (Boston: State Street Bank & Trust, 1974). A short account by Hassey appeared in "Indexing: An Inflation Lesson from Brazil," *New York Times*, April 7, 1974, p. 14.

fects of inflation, or as one Brazilian business executive put it, "We don't fight inflation, we live with it."[2]

It is this elimination of uncertainty that Friedman feels is important in restoring stability. Israel and Argentina now use forms of indexing, and in the United States, social security increases are tied to inflation and commercial banks are tying interest rates to the rises in the prime rate. Friedman proposes that indexing be widely introduced to adjust:

—wages by 100 percent of the increase in inflation (that is, if the CPI goes up 10 percent, wages will go up 10 percent);
—interest rates on time deposits, corporate bonds, mortgages, etc., by 100 percent of the increase in inflation;
—tax rates to deduct all income that is solely the result of inflation;
—business accounting to separate out the effects of rising prices.

"The only way to cure inflation is to slow the growth of the money supply," he says, "but there will be side effects. Cost-of-living indexing will help to ease the effects."[3] When the brakes go on, according to Friedman, indexing "lets people out of the box on contracts and long-term commitments." He goes on, "If escalators are everywhere, the Government can slow down the economy without a deep recession, without widespread unemployment."[4]

Not everyone applauds Friedman's proposals. Some, like James Tobin of Yale University, agree that indexing federal bonds would be useful or call for other forms of partial indexing.[5] Others, like UCLA economist Benjamin Klein, argue that indexing would have been readily adopted before this if it could eliminate the uncertainty of inflation. Klein points out that business executives have been aware of this tool yet it has "failed the market test" because the uncertainties of the indices are greater than the uncertainties of inflation. In short, a reliable set of indices has yet to be found.[6]

The effectiveness of the Brazilian system has also been questioned. Brazil curbed most of its inflation between 1964 and 1967—before indexing was fully in operation. These measures trimmed the real wages 18 percent during that period, and over the decade ending in 1970 the wages of unskilled workers fell 30 percent, according to one Brazilian economist.[7] Because labor groups are weak and press reports are censored, such redistribution of income from wage earners to property holders has not aroused violent opposition. But American labor could not be expected to stand for indexing unless real income were stable or increasing. Furthermore, the Brazilian system depends on multiple "minidevaluations" to keep its rate of international exchange competitive and thereby prevent the flight of capital and harmful speculation. But the cruzeiro is not a standard in international markets, as the dollar is, and even with floating exchange rates, this poses a problem.

The real objection to indexing, however, is that by protecting the economy from the effects of inflation, the government has no incentive to institute the squeeze that can dampen rising prices. In Brazil the rate at which inflation decelerated slowed after 1967 when full indexing was introduced. And in the first quarter of 1974 Brazil's inflation stood at 28.5 percent, far above the 15 percent in the same quarter the year before.

2. Alvaro Brito Bezerra de Mello in Marvine Howe, "Test for Brazil's Inflation System," *New York Times*, April 4, 1974, sec. 3, p. 1.

3. Quoted in Lindley H. Clark, Jr., "Unmaking a Mess: Stopping the Inflation Is Easy in Theory, Painful in Practice," the *Wall Street Journal*, April 26, 1974, p. 27.

4. Quoted in Soma Golden, "Escalator Clauses Backed," *New York Times*, April 3, 1974, p. 59.

5. Ibid.

6. See R. W. Lougee, Jr., "Escalator Clause: A Dissent: 'Inflation Not All Bad Per Se . . . ,'" *Rochester Democrat and Chronicle*, April 21, 1974, sec. C, p. 1.

7. See Howe, *New York Times*, April 4, 1974.

Adoption of indexing by the government is unlikely. The Fed is skeptical because of the millions of contracts already in force that could not be changed to account for inflation. Instead Chairman Arthur Burns determined to keep a tight rein on the growth of the money supply. To combat the resulting unemployment, he suggested using public service employment. A Federal Reserve study of three alternative stimulants to employment—a tax cut, government spending, or public service employment—found that the largest and most rapid impact came from public employment programs. This alternative could create "two to three times the number of jobs generated by each of the other alternatives at the end of the year," according to another Federal Reserve member, Andrew F. Brimmer. Burns stressed also that public employment was temporary and "need not add permanently to governmental costs."[8]

But in a small town in New Hampshire people began their own experiment in indexing money in June 1972. Devised by Ralph Borsodi, an 88-year-old retired economist, the scheme was based on indexed money, known as constants, whose dollar value increased with the consumer price index. People deposited their dollars in a bank and were credited with constants; the dollars were then pooled and invested as backing for the constants. Constants could be redeemed for dollars using conversion tables widely distributed in town. Some of the people never withdrew their constants, using the account as a hedge against inflation, but others withdrew constants and spent them on everything from haircuts to parking tickets. The scheme raised an eyebrow or two at the Secret Service, but after they examined the system, it was decided everything was legal. The experiment was discontinued in January 1974, however, when the Securities and Exchange Commission paid a visit, and lawyers for the company involved advised not tangling with the issue of whether constants were a form of security that should be registered. Arbitrage International, the firm that has taken over Borsodi's ideas, is not giving up, however, and is working to perfect the indexing of constants using an international standard. "I think we demonstrated the feasibility and acceptability of an inflation-proof money," says Borsodi, "but I'm not likely to make governments very happy because my system can be run by banks and takes money creation completely out of the government's hands."[9]

8. Quoted in the *New York Times*, May 27, 1974, p. 24.

9. "Paying with Constants Instead of Dollars," *Business Week*, May 4, 1974, p. 29.

nition that a change is needed and the actual implementation of that change. Both can be shortened by appropriate forecasting and decision making.

Impact lags, which have created the most controversy among economists, refer to the time between the taking of a monetary action, such as buying and selling securities on the open market, and the observed effect of that action on the economy. The impact lag is a measure of the time it takes for a monetary-policy decision to work its way through the economy and produce the desired change. Whereas monetarists hold that the lags are so long and variable that it is impossible to use monetary policy as a countercyclical tool, Keynesians assert that lags last from three to six months after the policy decision has been made; accordingly, they maintain that monetary policy can be used in a countercyclical fashion so long as the time lags are taken into account.[7]

The monetarist view has been set forth by Milton Friedman, who believes that changes in the supply of money exert such powerful direct and indirect effects on the economy that it is impossible to predict when changes made six months ago have ceased to influence income and price levels. In his view, the fact that a change in the money supply has a particular effect upon the business cycle explains only part of the total change set into motion when the Fed buys or sells securities on the open market. For example, a monetary expansion may induce someone within two or three months to contemplate building a factory, within four or five months to draw up the plans, within six or seven months to get the construction started. The actual construction may take six months and much of the effect of the economy produced by the factory on the total income stream will be felt even later. Monetarists believe that increases in the money supply produce changes in income because they lead to increased spending on goods and services in the economy. Monetary policy cannot be used to counter short-term fluctuations in the economy because the short-term fluctuations of the business cycle represent adjustments to prior policy decisions to change the supply of money. In the above example, the construction of the factory took place one year after the original decision to expand the money supply. If the monetary authorities viewed the rise in interest rates which accompany capital investments as a signal that the economy was overheating, and hence followed a restrictive monetary policy, however, they would be defeating the original decision to follow an expansionary policy. Countercyclical policy, in this instance, would have a destabilizing effect on the economy, forcing interest rates for new construction to rise even higher.

Opponents of the monetarist position argue that the lags are not nearly so long and so variable as Friedman maintains. Part of the disagreement is

7. For an interesting discussion of the views held by a monetarist and a traditional economist on time lags in monetary policy, see John Culbertson, "Friedman on the Lag Effect of Monetary Policy," *Journal of Political Economy* 68 (December 1960): 617–621; and Milton Friedman and John Culbertson, "The Lag in Effect of Monetary Policy" and "Reply," *Journal of Political Economy* 69 (October 1961): 447–477. Friedman's essay is reprinted in *The Optimum Quantity of Money* (Chicago: Aldine, 1969).

based upon different interpretations of Friedman's data and questions relating to his statistical methods. A number of economists have concluded that the predominant effects of a countercyclical policy decision can be felt within three to six months, so that the decisions are not destabilizing so long as they are moderate and taken early in the business cycle.[8] These economists have also marshaled considerable statistical evidence.

Problems Concerning Policy Goals

Perhaps more serious than the lag effect in monetary policy are the difficulties which may result if the Federal Reserve takes the level of interest rates as a policy target from which to gauge monetary ease or tightness. We have seen the possible inflationary consequences which, in the view of monetarists, may arise. It is worthwhile to examine the actual conduct of monetary policy in connection with fiscal policy in the United States during the latter part of the 1960s in order to see how closely reality follows some of the theoretical concepts that have been suggested here.

First recall the simple quantity theory of equation (14.1):

$$\hat{M} + \hat{V} = \hat{P} + \hat{y}$$

Given $V = 0$, the simple quantity theory assumption, equation (14.1) may be written:

$$\hat{P} = \hat{M} - \hat{y} \tag{14.9}$$

Table 14.2 supplies actual figures for this equation.

As Table 14.2 shows, predictions based on equation (14.9) have been less than exact. For 1966, 1969, and 1973 the prediction about price behavior is particularly far from the mark. But over a five-year period, predicted price behavior is closer to actual behavior, and over a nine-year period, the results improve even more.

We saw in Chapter 13 that if interest rates rise (causing a reduction in the demand for money, represented by an increase in V) as the money stock is increasing, we would expect prices to rise faster than the money stock. That is, V is some function of the interest rate:

$$V = V(i)$$

where $\hat{V}/\hat{i} > 0$; as i rises, V rises, and as i falls, V falls. The relationship between the rate of change of the money stock and the rate of change of

---

8. Albert Ando, E. D. Brown, Robert Solow, John Karenken, "Lags in Fiscal and Monetary Policy," in Commission on Money and Credit, *Stabilization Policies*, pp. 1–163. See also Thomas Mayer, "The Lag in the Effect of Monetary Policy: Some Criticisms." *Western Economic Journal* 5 (September 1967): 324–342; Henry Simons, "Rules Versus Authorities in Monetary Policy," reprinted in American Economic Association, *Readings in Monetary Theory* (Homewood, Ill.: Irwin, 1951), for the idea of stabilizing the price level by increasing the stock of money at a rate indicated by changes in velocity, and Warren L. Smith, "A Neo-Keynesian View of Monetary Policy," in *Controlling Monetary Aggregates* (Boston: Boston Federal Reserve Bank, 1969).

Table 14.2 Explanation of Price Behavior in the United States by the Simple Quantity Theory 1966–1974 (first quarter)

Year	Percentage Annual Rate of Change of Money Stock (M)	Percentage Annual Rate of Change of Real Output (y)[a]	Percentage Annual Rate of Change of Consumer Prices (P)	
			ACTUAL[b]	PREDICTED
1966	1.3	2.3	3.7	−1.0
1967	7.1	3.4	3.5	3.7
1968	7.7	3.5	3.2	4.2
1969	2.1	1.3	6.3	0.8
1970	5.0	−1.0	5.6	6.0
Five-year average	4.6	1.9	4.5	2.7
1971	6.0	4.4	3.0	1.6
1972	8.5	7.8	2.6	0.7
1973	5.8	2.5	7.7	3.3
1974 (I)	12.4	−5.8	10.8	18.2
Four-year average	8.2	2.2	6.0	5.9
Nine-year average	6.4	2.0	5.3	4.3

SOURCE: St. Louis Federal Reserve Bank, *National Economic Trends,* 1971, 1974.
   a. Real growth in 1958 dollars.
   b. Implicit price deflator.

prices that we have described is modified by the behavior of the interest rate. Therefore, equation (14.9) becomes

$$\hat{P} = \hat{M} - \hat{y} + \hat{E}_{Vi}\, i \qquad\qquad (14.10)$$

where E_{Vi} is the elasticity of V with respect to the interest rate, or $\hat{V}/\hat{i}$.

In fact, typical money-market rates on four- to six-month loans to prime borrowers and on three-month Treasury bills or short-term bonds went from around 5 percent at the beginning of 1966 to around 8 percent at the beginning of 1970 and 11 percent at the beginning of 1974. If an increase in interest rates causes businesses and individuals to "economize" on money holdings, owing to a higher opportunity cost (in the form of interest earnings foregone) of holding money instead of bonds, we would expect prices to rise more rapidly than the rate of increase in the money stock. Changes in velocity due to changes in the interest rate may make the 4-percent rule less applicable at a given time. The question is whether by attempting to offset the impact of anticipated changes in velocity, the Federal Reserve acts to stabilize the behavior of the income stream (and prices) through time. We shall see that this depends to some extent upon exactly which goal the Fed focuses upon.

Policy considerations explain the other important reason why predictions of price behavior based on the growth of the money stock are not always reliable. Table 14.2 shows that on the average the prescription suggested by equation (14.9) and adjusted for changes in velocity is not a bad one. Monetary policy, like fiscal policy, is a means of stabilizing total demand in order to stabilize income, price, and interest-rate levels. Yet in the case of fiscal policy, not all government expenditure can be adjusted for stabilization goals and that, further, not all changes in government expenditure are actually aimed at stabilization goals. Thus the alteration of the money stock is often due to an effort to mitigate the impact of a destabilizing budget on the impact stream. Unfortunately, this has frequently tended to accentuate instability. Despite its legislated independence, the Federal Reserve is not entirely free of federal budget requirements; the use of monetary policy to pursue goals other than stable prices—such as low interest rates, full employment, growth, or balance of payments equilibrium—often implies changes in the money stock that are inconsistent with stable prices. Thus, if the actual rate of growth of the money stock differs from the rate of growth consistent with stable prices, we can conclude that the monetary authority (1) has a different target than the behavior of the money stock as an index of its policy; (2) does not wish to pursue a growth of the money stock consistent with stable prices as much as it wishes to (has to) pursue some other goal; or (3) is technically unable to make the money stock grow at some target rate, and therefore random or outside forces are causing its growth to diverge from a rate consistent with stable prices.

Suppose the Fed, consistent with possibility (1), identifies the level of interest rates as a proper goal for monetary policy. It is, in fact, sometimes suggested that the interest rate is the price of money—note that the interest rate is on the price axis of the liquidity preference demand for money. More accurately, the interest rate is the opportunity cost of holding money instead of bonds. At any rate, the level of interest rates undeniably has been a variable by which the tightness (high interest rates) or ease (low interest rates) of monetary policy has been judged. Suppose, then, that the Federal Reserve pursues a goal of low interest rates and that the federal government runs a large deficit—its expenditure greatly exceeds tax proceeds. The federal government can finance a deficit by either borrowing from the public or "borrowing" from the Federal Reserve, that is, selling a Treasury bond to the Federal Reserve. Because the second procedure results in a growth of the money supply, it is potentially inflationary; deficits are therefore more often financed by selling bonds to the public. In so doing, the government operates in the bond market like any other economic unit. The bond market is shown in Figure 14.1, in which the vertical axis $1/i$, represents an approximation of the "price" of a bond, where i is the interest rate on bonds. Notice that the bond supply rises as the interest rate falls—that is, as $1/i$ rises—and the demand for bonds rises as the interest rate rises.

The sale of a government bond will shift the bond supply schedule outward, causing B_S to move to B_S'. The resulting equilibrium interest rate at

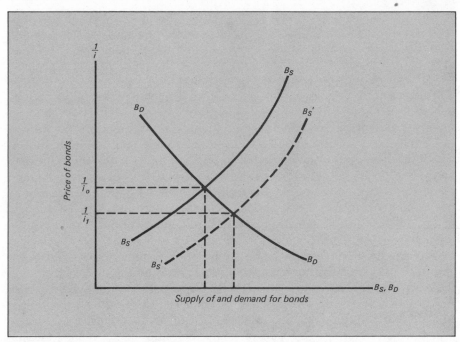

Figure 14.1 The bond market

$1/i_1$ has risen—from i_0 to i_1—because higher interest rates are necessary to induce lenders to part with more funds.

Suppose that the Federal Reserve wishes to keep interest rates at the relatively low levels represented by i_0. (Between the end of World War II and March 1951 the Fed tried to keep interest rates fixed at a low level in order to keep interest costs down on the national debt. An end of this inflexible policy, referred to as the "accord" between the Federal Reserve and the Treasury, came in March 1951, although the Fed still viewed interest-rate levels as a policy target.) One way to keep interest rates down in the presence of an increased demand for loans is to increase the available supply of loanable funds. The Federal Reserve can do this by way of an expansionary monetary policy that puts more money into the hands of the public through the commercial banking system. This will increase the demand for bonds at each rate of interest and put downward pressure on interest rates. The result of this procedure, where monetary policy is tied to the behavior of interest rates, may well be a growth of the money stock in excess of that dictated by a policy of stable prices. Thus, to the extent that the Treasury wishes to have its borrowing "eased" in order to avoid an unpopular increase in interest rates, the Federal Reserve may be under considerable political pressure to increase the money stock in the presence of heavy government borrowing to finance a deficit. An increase in the money stock at the same time the federal government is spending in excess of its receipts (creating excess demand) is likely to be inflationary and in addition will probably fail to keep interest rates down. Because increased demands on the credit market will push up interest rates, the Federal Reserve would be obliged to expand the money stock in order to get them down. Yet from 1966 to 1974 interest rates have been rising at the same time as the money stock has been increased at a fairly rapid rate.

The reason for this lies in the effect of prices on both interest rates and the demand for money. If the money stock is increased in an effort to lower interest rates, prices will rise, resulting over time in inflation. As we saw in Chapter 11 and 13, lenders will eventually anticipate inflation and increase the rate of interest, expressed in terms of money, that they charge to borrowers. Thus, if interest rates rise with heavy Treasury borrowing and the money supply is increased, the resulting upward pressure on prices may change more in money terms for loans, causing interest rates to rise further. If the Federal Reserve tries to bring them down by further expanding the money supply, the process begins again. This will result, over time, in a rapidly spiraling increase in the rate of inflation, leading to hyperinflation, and indicates the danger of choosing interest rates as a policy goal.

As we saw in Chapter 12, this is what happened in 1969, when a sharp reversal in fiscal policy resulted in a change from a $25 billion deficit in 1968 to a $3 billion surplus in 1969. This created a temporary stabilization in interest rates as a result of taking pressure off the money market. But rates climbed steeply during the fourth quarter of 1968 and during 1969, due to continued strong demand from private borrowers. Borrowers and lenders both were reacting to a sharp increase in the rate of inflation and the rapid increase in the money supply. The Federal Reserve, fearing that the sharp fiscal contraction would precipitate a downturn in the economy if it restricted the money supply, let it expand throughout late 1968. Thus moderate inflation (2.9 percent in 1965–1966) became rather high inflation (4.6 percent in 1967–1968) and finally serious inflation (6.1 percent in 1969–1970). Not only did the market of interest rate continue to rise in the face of expected inflation, so did the money rate (the cost of holding money), so that velocity also rose. Responding to the accelerating rate of inflation, the Fed then sharply cut the rate of growth of the money supply in 1969, so that the combination of expected inflation and tight money drove interest rates to record high levels in 1969.

MATHEMATICAL APPENDIX
A Model for the Determination of the Money Supply

We have seen that the U.S. money supply is created by the Federal Reserve, the U.S. Treasury, and the commercial banking system. Bills produced by the Fed and coins produced by the Treasury constitute currency; checking deposits are produced by the commercial banking system, based on fractional reserves of currency.

There are two important concepts connected with the money supply: the total money supply and the monetary base—the amount of currency held by individuals and firms and the amount held by commercial banks as reserves behind the demand deposits.

Writing these concepts in a shorthand form we get

$$M_S = C_p + D \tag{A14.1}$$

and

$$MB = C_p + R \tag{A14.2}$$

where M_S = total money supply

C_p = currency held by the public

D = demand deposits held by the public

MB = the monetary base, consisting of C_p (currency in the hands of the public) plus R—total currency reserves held by the commercial banks, consisting of required reserves plus any reserves above the required level that commercial banks may decide to hold.

Dividing equation (A14.1) by equation (A14.2) we obtain

$$\frac{M_S}{MB} = \frac{C_p + D}{C_p + R} \tag{A14.3}$$

Dividing the top and bottom of the right-hand side of equation (A14.3) by C_p gives

$$\frac{M_S}{MB} = \frac{1 + D/C_p}{1 + R/C_p} \tag{A14.4}$$

Multiplying the top and bottom of the right-hand side of equation (A14.4) by D/R gives

$$\frac{M_S}{MB} = \frac{D/R(1 + D/C_p)}{D/R + D/C_p} \tag{A14.5}$$

Multiplying both sides of equation (A14.5) by MB gives

$$M_S = MB\left(\frac{D/R(1 + D/C_p)}{D/R + D/C_p}\right) \tag{A14.6}$$

Equation (A14.6) is an expression for the level of money supply in terms of (1) the monetary base, MB; (2) the ratio of the demand deposits, D, to reserves of the commercial banks, R (if required reserves are .15 of D and banks hold contingency reserves over required reserves of .05 of D, then $D/R = 1/.20 = 5$); and (3) the ratio of demand deposits, D, held by the public to currency held by the public, C_p.

The actions of three groups—the Federal Reserve, the commercial banking system, and the public—are the primary determinants of the U.S. money supply. The Federal Reserve operates on $MB = C_p + R$ by printing money and affecting C_p and by open-market operations, which, as we have seen, affect commercial bank reserves, R. The Fed can also affect D/R by altering reserve requirements. The commercial banking system decides what level of reserves to hold above required reserves and can therefore affect D/R. The public decides whether to hold its money balances as currency or checks, thereby determining D/C_p.

From equation (14.6) it is not completely obvious what happens to the money supply if D/R or D/C_p rises or falls, because both are in both the numerator and denominator of the expression just to the right of MB. An increase in MB, with D/R and D/C_p fixed, will increase the money supply. Look at Figure A14.1, in which demand deposits are plotted on the horizontal axis and the monetary base on the vertical axis, both in millions of dollars. The solid line rising from left to right labeled C_p/D gives the ratio of currency to deposits as 1/4, or .25. As demand deposits rise, moving right along the horizontal axis, the part of the monetary base, MB, starting at 0, that is taken up by C_p rises as well. The solid line falling from left to right labeled R/D gives the ratio of reserves to deposits as 1/5, or .20. Starting at $MB = 100$ and moving right, the part of MB used up as reserves rises as demand deposits rise. When C_p/D and R/D cross, all of MB, taken here to be $100 million, is used up either as reserves or currency in the hands of

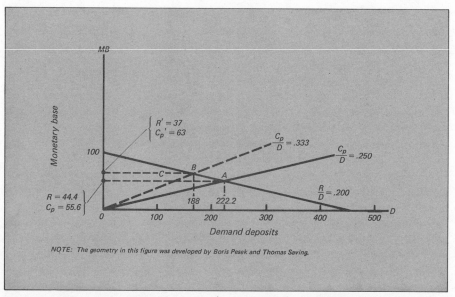

Figure A14.1 Money supply determination (hundreds of millions of dollars)

the public. The division of MB into these uses can be seen by running a line from point A to the MB axis. Also, the crossing at point A determines the level of D consistent with MB = 100, $C_p/D = .25$, and $R/D = .20$. That is, the crossing at point A tells what level of demand deposits MB = 100 will support, simultaneously, in the eyes of the public (C_p/D) and in the eyes of the commercial banks (R/D).

Suppose we know that MB = 100; $D/C_p = 4/1$, or $C_p/D = 1/4 = .25$; D/R = 5, or R/D = 1/5 = .20. Because these are all the values on the right-hand side of equation (A14.6) we have all of the information necessary to determine the money supply. From equations (A14.1) and (A14.2) we know that

$$MB = 100 = C_p + R$$

We know $C_p = .25D$ and R = .20D. Therefore MB = 100 = .25D + .20D

$$100 = .45D$$
$$\frac{100}{.45} = D$$
$$222.2 = D$$

The division of MB into C_p and R is given by

$$C_p = (.25)(222.2) = 55.6; \quad R = (.20)(222.2) = 44.4$$

The money supply equals C_p + D. Therefore $M_S = 55.6 + 222.2$

$$M_S = 277.8$$

Suppose the public decides to hold more currency and fewer checks, say in a period of lack of confidence in the commercial banks. People withdraw currency from their checking accounts, and C_p/D rises to $1/3 = .333$. This situation is shown by the dotted line above the original C_p/D line in Figure A14.1. We still have MB = 100 and R = .200D. But now $C_p = .333D$. So

$$B = 100 = .333D + .200D$$
$$100 = .533D$$
$$\frac{100}{.533} = D$$
$$188 = D$$

And

$$C_p = (.333)(188) = 63 \text{ approximately}$$

$$R = (.200)(188) = 37 \text{ approximately}$$

$$M_S = C_p + D = 63 + 188 = 251$$

The results are shown in Figure A14.1. Not surprisingly, the money supply falls as D/C_p falls (C_p/D rises). If depositors decide to withdraw cash from the commercial banks, the banks' reserves will fall. If D/R and B are held constant, there occurs for every dollar increase in C_p (equal to the decrease in R) a multiple deposit contraction.

In terms of the money supply, the reduction of D/C_p means

$$M_S = \uparrow C_p + \downarrow D$$

That is, currency in public hands rises as individuals withdraw funds from banks, and demand deposits fall as commercial banks adjust to lower reserves by lowering their liabilities, D. Actually, as Figure A14.1 illustrates, demand deposits fall more than C_p rises. The increase in C_p/D from .250 to .333 moves the intersection of C_p/D and R/D from point A to point B. The rise in C_p is given by BC, and the fall in D is given by CA. Because we know the slope of the line R/D is 1/5, we know BC = 1/5 CA, or CA = 5 BC. The fall in D is five times the rise in C_p (which is actually a fall in R because $MB = C_p + R$ and if MB is fixed, a rise in C_p must produce a fall in R). Our result arises from the multiple deposit contraction resulting from a fall in R.

Whereas we can predict that the money supply will fall as C_p/D rises, or D/C_p falls, it is difficult to predict by how much. But by looking at Figure A14.1 and the equations that accompany it, we can show that the money supply falls as R/D rises (the R/D line shifts downward as R/D rises). We can also calculate the relationship between changes in the monetary base and the changes in the money supply by letting MB change by, say, 20—to 120—and then calculating the new money supply for given values of C_p/D and R/D. Recall that with MB = 100, C_p/D = .25, and R/D = .20, the money supply was 277.8.

With MB = 120

$$120 = C_p + R$$

$$C_p = .25D$$

$$R = .20D$$

$$120 = .25D + .20D$$

$$120 = .45D$$

$$267 = D$$

$$C_p = (.25)(267) = 66.6$$

$$R = (.20)(267) = 53.4$$

$$M_S = 267 + 66.6 = 333.6$$

Given a change in MB of 20, from 100 to 120, we get a change in the money supply of 55.8, from 277.8 to 333.6. The complete money multiplier for changes in the monetary base is 2.79, or 55.8/20, for the values of R/D and C_p/D we have assumed. In the real world, however, changes such as these occur simultaneously. Thus, whereas it is usually possible to determine the direction of the impact on the money supply that a given change will cause, simultaneous changes usually render it impossible to calculate the exact amount.

Questions and Exercises

1. Assume that you unexpectedly inherit a substantial sum of money in the form of currency held in your great aunt's lock box at the bank. What actions would you be inclined to take and how would your decisions illustrate the trade-off between money, financial, and real assets?
2. Why do Keynesians believe that the velocity of money changes with the interest rate? What form of demand for money is affected primarily? Monetarists believe that interest elasticity is not particularly important. Why?
3. Assume you are on the staff of the Federal Reserve Board. Many members of the board are advocating the purchase of government securities because their price is falling. They feel that such an event is an indication that monetary policy must be eased. What would you say?
4. Suppose that the Federal Reserve engages in expansionary policy so that commercial banks find themselves with excess reserves and pressure to expand purchases of primary securities. What effects, if any, would you predict for interest rates? Would there tend to be any shifts from savings accounts? Why or why not? What would happen if savings and loan associations kept their accounts in commercial banks? What might be the net effect of the Federal Reserve action?
5. What might be the effect of long-term expected inflation on the demand and supply for long-term notes such as mortgages? Since older homes often have mortgages that the potential buyer can take over, might there be any shift in sales from the newly built home? Why or why not?
6. What adjustments, if any, would a commercial bank tend to undertake if the rediscount rate becomes higher than their prime rate? Some have argued that banks tend to use the Federal Reserve only as a lender of last resort regardless of the rate charged. What would be the implication for the effectiveness of the rediscount rate in monetary policy?
7. By the spring of 1974, housing starts had fallen to an alarmingly low level, apparently for two reasons: high interest rates and lack of funds for mortgages as well as increased costs of materials. What power does the Federal Reserve have to affect this situation?
8. By 1974, the cost of living was rising in excess of 10 percent, but the income obtainable from savings for most savers was below 10 percent. In this situation, what changes would you make if you had moderate savings? If others in the same boat responded as you did, what would be the consequences for V?
9. If there is unanticipated inflation, the tendency for wages to rise at a lower rate than prices could produce some dampening effect on inflation. In the long run, however, this is an unlikely effect. In fact, the effect could be quite the reverse as contracts come up for renegotiation. Why?
10. By 1973, there was a relatively high level of anticipated inflation and increased interest by many investors in the commodity markets. How would you explain this phenomenon?

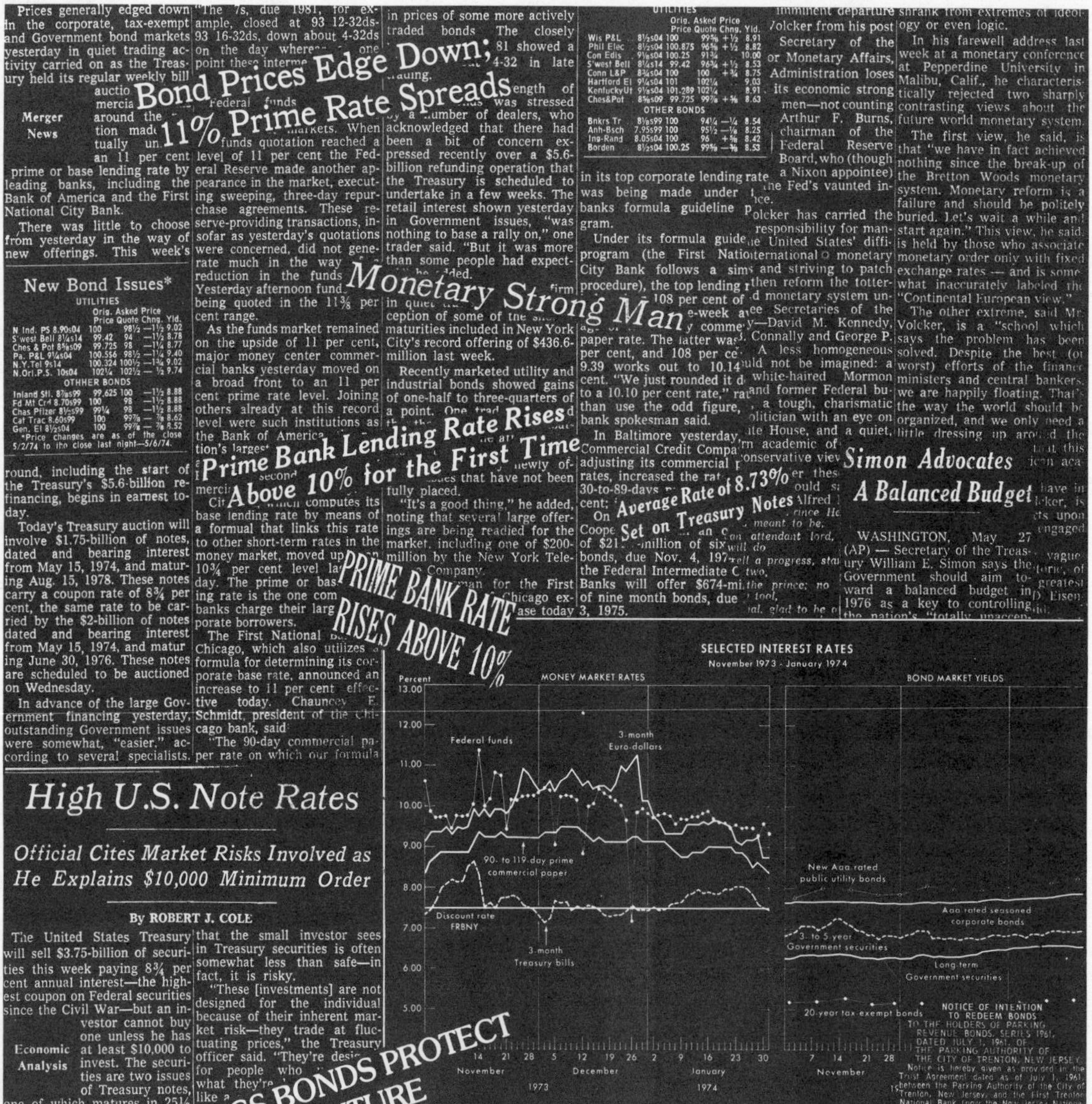

Prices generally edged down in the corporate, tax-exempt and Government bond markets yesterday in quiet trading activity carried on as the Treasury held its regular weekly bill auction.

Merger News

around the prime or base lending rate by leading banks, including the Bank of America and the First National City Bank.

There was little to choose from yesterday in the way of new offerings. This week's

New Bond Issues*

UTILITIES

	Orig. Asked Price		
	Price Quote Chng. Yld.		
N Ind. P5 8.90s04	100	98½—1½	9.02
S west Bell 8¼s14	99.42	94—1½	8.78
Ches & Pol 8⅞s09	99.725	98	—1½ 8.77
Pa. P&L 9¼s04	100.556	98½	—½ 9.40
N.Y. Tel 9s14	100.324	100½	—½ 9.02
N.Or.P.S. 10s04	102¼	102½	—½ 9.74

OTHER BONDS

Inland Stl. 8⅞s99	99.625	100	—1½ 8.88
Fd Mt Cr¶ 8.70s99	100	98	—1½ 8.88
Chas Pfizer 8½s99	99¼	99	—½ 8.88
Cat Trac 8.60s99	100	96	—¾ 8.42
Gen. El 8½s04	100	99⅞	—⅛ 8.52

*Price changes are as of the close 5/2/74 to the close last night—5/6/74.

round, including the start of the Treasury's $5.6-billion refinancing, begins in earnest today.

Today's Treasury auction will involve $1.75-billion of notes, dated and bearing interest from May 15, 1974, and maturing Aug. 15, 1978. These notes carry a coupon rate of 8¾ per cent, the same rate to be carried by the $2-billion of notes dated and bearing interest from May 15, 1974, and maturing June 30, 1976. These notes are scheduled to be auctioned on Wednesday.

In advance of the large Government financing yesterday, outstanding Government issues were somewhat "easier," according to several specialists.

High U.S. Note Rates

Official Cites Market Risks Involved as He Explains $10,000 Minimum Order

By ROBERT J. COLE

The United States Treasury will sell $3.75-billion of securities this week paying 8¾ per cent annual interest—the highest coupon on Federal securities since the Civil War—but an investor cannot buy one unless he has **Economic** at least $10,000 to **Analysis** invest. The securities are two issues of Treasury notes, one of which matures in 25½ months, the other in 4½ years. For these two issues ury has announced not acc minimu than $1

Howev of secur selling thi bonds mat

The 7s, due 1981, for example, closed at 93 12-32ds 93 16-32ds, down about 4-32ds on the day where point these interme

Federal funds merci around the tion made tually un an 11 per cent funds quotation reached a level of 11 per cent the Federal Reserve made another appearance in the market, executing sweeping, three-day repurchase agreements. These reserve-providing transactions, insofar as yesterday's quotations were concerned, did not generate much in the way reduction in the funds Yesterday afternoon fund being quoted in the 11⅜ per cent range.

As the funds market remained on the upside of 11 per cent, major money center commercial banks yesterday moved on a broad front to an 11 per cent prime rate level. Joining others already at this record level were such institutions as the Bank of America and the nation's largest

City computes its base lending rate by means of a formula that links this rate to other short-term rates in the money market, moved up 10¾ per cent level last day. The prime or base lending rate is the one commercial banks charge their large corporate borrowers.

The First National Bank of Chicago, which also utilizes a formula for determining its corporate base rate, announced an increase to 11 per cent effective today. Chauncey E. Schmidt, president of the Chicago bank, said

"The 90-day commercial paper rate on which our formula

in prices of some more actively traded bonds The closely 81 showed a 4-32 in late

ength of was stressed a number of dealers, who acknowledged that there had been a bit of concern expressed recently over a $5.6-billion refunding operation that the Treasury is scheduled to undertake in a few weeks. The retail interest shown yesterday in Government issues, "was nothing to base a rally on," one trader said. "But it was more than some people had expected."

ception of some of the maturities included in New York City's record offering of $436.6-million last week.

Recently marketed utility and industrial bonds showed gains of one-half to three-quarters of a point. One trad

"It's a good thing," he added, noting that several large offerings are being readied for the market, including one of $200-million by the New York Telephone Company.

man for the First Chicago exase today

UTILITIES

	Orig. Asked Price		
	Price Quote Chng. Yld.		
Wis P&L	8½s04 100	99¾ +½ 8.91
Phil Elec	8½s04 100.875	96⅝ +½ 8.82
Con Edis	9⅛s04 100.25	91¼ 10.00
S west Bell	8¼s14 99.42	94¼ +½ 8.53
Conn L&P	8¾s04 100	100 +⅛ 8.75
Hartford El	8½s04 101	99⅝ 9.03
KentuckyUt	9½s04 101.289	102½ — 8.91
Chas&Pot	8⅞s09 99.725	99⅞ +⅜ 8.63

OTHER BONDS

Bnkrs Tr	8⅝s99 100	96¾ —¼ 8.54
Anh-Bsch	7.95s99 100	95½ —⅛ 8.25
Ing-Rand	8.05s04 100	96 +⅝ 8.42
Borden	8½s04 100.25	99¾ —⅛ 8.53

in its top corporate lending rate was being made under banks formula guideline program.

Under its formula guide program (the First National City Bank follows a simi procedure), the top lending 108 per cent of e-week commercy paper rate. The latter war per cent, and 108 per ce 9.39 works out to 10.14 cent. "We just rounded it d to a 10.10 per cent rate," ra than use the odd figure, bank spokesman said.

In Baltimore yesterday, Commercial Credit Compa adjusting its commercial rates, increased the rat 30-to-89-days — of six bonds, due Nov. 4, 197 the Federal Intermediate C Banks will offer $674-million of nine month bonds, due 3, 1975.

imminent departure Volcker from his post

Secretary of the or Monetary Affairs, Administration loses its economic strong men—not counting Arthur F. Burns, chairman of the Federal Reserve Board, who (though a Nixon appointee) the Fed's vaunted in-

Polcker has carried the responsibility for man-United States' difftional monetary then reform the totter-d monetary system un-ee Secretaries of the —David M. Kennedy, Connally and George P. A less homogeneous uld not be imagined: a white-haired Mormon and former Federal bu-a tough, charismatic olitician with an eye on ite House, and a quiet, te academic of rn academic of onservative view er thes ould s rince H Alfred will do attendant lord, ell a progress, sta two, prince; no tood, al, glad to be h

shrank from extremes of ideology or even logic.

In his farewell address last week at a monetary conference at Pepperdine University in Malibu, Calif., he characteristically rejected two sharply contrasting views about the future world monetary system.

The first view, he said, is that "we have in fact achieved nothing since the break-up of the Bretton Woods monetary system. Monetary reform is a failure and should be politely buried. Let's wait a while and start again." This view, he said, is held by those who associate monetary order only with fixed exchange rates — and is some what inaccurately labeled the "Continental European view."

The other extreme, said Mr. Volcker, is a "school which says the problem has been solved. Despite the best (or worst) efforts of the finance ministers and central bankers we are happily floating. That's the way the world should be organized, and we only need a little dressing up around the

Simon Advocates
A Balanced Budget

WASHINGTON, May 27 (AP) — Secretary of the Treasury William E. Simon says the Government should aim toward a balanced budget in 1976 as a key to controlling the nation's "totally unacce

that the small investor sees in Treasury securities is often somewhat less than safe—in fact, it is risky.

"These [investments] are not designed for the individual because of their inherent market risk—they trade at fluctuating prices," the Treasury officer said. "They're desig for people who know what they're like a

If the investor wants to sell the notes before maturity, he runs the risk that the market

SELECTED INTEREST RATES
November 1973 - January 1974

available to small investors in amounts "as small as $1,000."

General-Equilibrium Monetary Theorists

15

The IS/LM model we developed in Part II describes a general-equilibrium system in which the IS line represents equilibrium in the commodity sector and the LM line represents equilibrium in the money sector. In Chapter 11 we looked at this model under conditions of full employment, concentrating on the effects of a shift in either the money supply (LM) or in autonomous spending (IS). An alternative system is suggested by a group of economists we shall call the general-equilibrium monetary theorists, who emphasize examination of the role of money within the general-equilibrium framework and in particular analyze the possible connection between changes in the money supply and changes in a real variable such as the interest rate. The legacy of this issue includes the classical economists, Keynes, Pigou, Patinkin, Metzler, and Mundell. The models of the general-equilibrium monetary theorists include a monetary sector; a "real," or commodity, sector; and in some cases a financial, or "bond," sector.

The Classical Dichotomy

The classical economists before Keynes were generally convinced that the average rate of exchange between money and goods—the price level—was determined in the monetary sector while real prices, or the rate of exchange between each pair of goods in the economy, were determined exclusively in the commodity sector. This view has come to be known as the **classical dichotomy.** The dichotomy between the real and monetary sectors means that a change in the money supply will affect the price level only; it will not affect relative or real prices of one good in terms of another.[1] More precisely, if a doubling of the quantity of money were to double the price level as well as all individual money prices of which the overall price level is an average, relative prices would be unaffected. This can be easily seen by taking the example of a two-good economy. Suppose output y takes two forms: y_1 and y_2. The price level, P, is given by an average of the prices of y_1 and y_2.

$$P = a_1 P_1 + a_2 P_2 \tag{15.1}$$

where $a_1 + a_2$, which sum to one, are taken to represent the shares of y_1 and y_2 in output. If 2M implies 2P because both P_1 and P_2 double (say $a_1 = a_2 = 0.5$):

$$P = .5P_1 + .5P_2$$
$$2P = .5 \times 2P_1 + .5 \times 2P_2$$

But the real price of y_1 in terms of y_2 is

$$\frac{P_1}{P_2} = \frac{2P_1}{2P_2} = \frac{P_1}{P_2} \tag{15.2}$$

which is unchanged by the doubling of the price level due to a doubling of all individual prices. Therefore the dichotomy is seen to hold under these conditions.

It is important to bear in mind that the classical dichotomy does not hold in the IS/LM model. We saw that a change in the money supply can affect the interest rate (in the absence of a liquidity trap) and that the interest rate determines the price of bonds or the relative price of future goods. However, in its simplest and most widely represented form, the IS/LM model does not account for the impact of real balance effects on commodity-market equilibrium.

---

1. It should be noted that real prices of goods are given by relative money prices. If a table costs 4 units of money while a chair costs 1 unit of money, then the cost of a table in terms of chairs is 4. The role of money as a convenient unit of account facilitates such calculation of real prices.

General-Equilibrium Monetary Analysis: Don Patinkin

Don Patinkin,[2] perhaps the most important general-equilibrium monetary theorist, has suggested that real balances *must* be present in the demand functions for commodities in order for the price level to be determinate. Patinkin's real-balance effect is analytically very close to the Pigou effect, stating that a change in real money balances, M/P, affects the demand for commodities. The major significance of the real-balance effect in the context of Patinkin's analysis is that it invalidates the classical dichotomy whereby changes in the money supply are taken to have no effect upon real variables like relative prices, affecting instead only the price level.

The "Invalid Dichotomy"

Patinkin showed the logical inconsistency of the classical dichotomy by means of a conceptual experiment. Suppose first that the classical dichotomy holds, so that equilibrium in the commodity sector depends only on relative money prices, and second, that the price level is determined in the monetary sector. Add to these propositions a basic general-equilibrium notion known as **Walras' Law,** which states simply that the sum of *excess* demands in each sector must be zero for a general equilibrium to hold. This gives us

$$E_C + E_M = 0 \qquad\qquad (15.3)$$

where E_C represents excess demand in the commodity market, and E_M represents excess demand in the money market. Notice that zero *excess* demand is merely a condition where demand equals supply. With each of the above conditions in mind, start with a condition of general equilibrium so that $E_C = E_M = 0$. Then suppose, arbitrarily, that the price *level* is doubled. According to the classical dichotomy, since a doubling of all money prices would not affect real prices, the equilibrium in the commodity sector would be undisturbed. But if this were the case, according to Walras' Law, expressed by the equation $E_C + E_M = 0$, equilibrium in the monetary sector would also be undisturbed. The logical inconsistency arises because the price *level* is supposed to be determined in the monetary sector. But our experiment, by allowing the classical dichotomy to hold, has doubled the money price without disturbing equilibrium in either the commodity or monetary sectors. The conclusion must be that the price level is indeterminate if the classical dichotomy holds. A theory that yields such a result is unacceptable, since it is inconsistent with readily observable facts. The price level does not wander about with no impact on the economy.

Patinkin's resolution to the "invalid dichotomy" of the classical economists is to include real money balances in the demand functions for com-

---

2. Don Patinkin, *Money, Interest, and Prices,* 2d ed. (New York: Harper, 1965).

modities. Under this condition a doubling of the price level does not leave the commodity sector undisturbed. Instead, a negative real-balance effect ensues, which lowers the demand for commodities, given the condition of a constant nominal money supply. The reduction in commodity demand results in excess supply in the commodity sector, which by Walras' Law reflects excess demand for money. This excess demand is satisfied, given a constant nominal money supply, by a determinate fall in the price level.

An understanding of the role of the real-balance effect as a logical necessity to invalidate the classical dichotomy enables us to compare Patinkin's general-equilibrium macro model to the IS/LM model. Patinkin's model begins with four sectors: labor, commodities, bonds, and money. Having shown, by use of a simpler model with only money and commodities, that the classical dichotomy is logically invalid, Patinkin was particularly interested in employing his model to see whether changes in the money supply will affect any real variables. The model concentrates on the real or relative price of "future goods" (bonds) represented by the inverse of the interest rate, $1/i$. As i rises, earnings from bonds rise, so the relative price of goods to be purchased in the future with proceeds from bond ownership is reduced in comparison with the current price of goods.

To achieve the desired focus, Patinkin first assumes that the labor sector is always in equilibrium, due to complete and instantaneous flexibility of money wages. This leaves commodity, bond, and money sectors. General equilibrium in these sectors is represented by Walras' Law as

$$E_C + E_M + E_B = 0 \qquad (15.4)$$

where E_B represents excess demand for bonds, and E_C and E_M are as defined in equation (15.3). Notice that in order to satisfy equation (15.4), which states that the sum of the three excess demands is identical to zero, if any two of the three excess demands on the left-hand side of equation (15.4) are equal to zero, the third must be also. Therefore, an analysis of *equilibrium* positions, or comparative statics, need only be concerned with two equations of a three-sector model, since by Walras' Law equilibrium in two sectors requires equilibrium in the third.

Patinkin's model is distinguished from the IS/LM analysis in three ways. First, whereas the IS/LM model uses this comparative-statics method to focus attention on the commodity and money sectors, Patinkin focuses attention on the commodity and bond sectors, leaving explicit treatment of the monetary sector out of his model. Second, whereas the IS/LM model takes the price level to be fixed and allows output to vary, Patinkin takes output to be fixed and allows the price level to vary. Finally, and most significantly, Patinkin allows real money balances to affect the demand for commodities and bonds, whereas the IS/LM model omits real-balance effects.

Patinkin's Model

Taken altogether, Patinkin's assumptions result in a two-equation general-

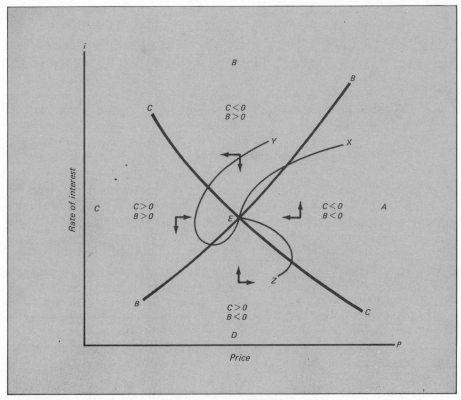

Figure 15.1 The Patinkin general-equilibrium model

equilibrium model of the commodity and bond sectors with two endogenous variables, the price level and the interest rate. As such, the model can be used to determine unique equilibrium values of i and P, just as the two-equation (commodities and money) IS/LM model can be used to determine unique equilibrium values of i and Y (given P fixed). Patinkin's model is represented in Figure 15.1, where i is measured along the vertical axis and P is measured along the horizontal axis; Figure 15.1 may be said to be drawn in i-P space.

First consider the CC line, which describes values of i and P that are consistent with equilibrium in the commodity market. The negative slope of this line says that the price level must rise as the interest rate falls in order to maintain equilibrium in the commodity market. The reason for such a slope arises from the fact that a rise in P and a fall in i have opposite effects upon the demand for commodities. As i falls, the demand for commodities is increased, due either to an increase in investment (leading to more pressure on current capacity in order to produce more capital goods) or to an increase in consumption. A higher price level, however, lowers real balances for a given money supply. The fall in real balances lowers the demand for commodities, in turn offsetting the increased commodity demand arising from a lower interest rate. The magnitude of each of these effects determines the steepness of the negative slope of CC.[3] Above and to the right of CC (quadrants A and B) either i is too high or P is too high for commodity market equilibrium. Since each of these changes lowers the demand for commodities, there exists an excess supply condition in the commodities market above and to the right of CC. This is indicated by $C < 0$, or "excess demand less than zero." Conversely, below and to the left of the CC line (quadrants C and D), there exists an excess demand for commodities denoted by $C > 0$.

The BB line describes values of i and P that are consistent with equilibrium in the bond market. Its positive slope reflects the fact that the demand for bonds rises relative to the supply of bonds as the interest rate rises and that a simultaneous increase in the price level is required to produce an excess supply of bonds to offset the excess demand occasioned by a higher interest rate. The fact that bond demanders are lenders while bond suppliers are borrowers makes it clear that an increase in the interest rate will produce an excess demand for bonds. As the interest rate rises, more funds become available for loans—bond demand rises—while at the same time the higher cost of borrowing deters borrowers from supplying bonds. In order to fully understand the effect of an increase in the price level on the excess supply of bonds, we must analyze factors influencing the supply and demand for bonds in somewhat greater detail.

It will be simplest to consider the impact of an increase in the price level first upon the demand for bonds and then upon the supply of bonds. The combination of these two effects will then represent the net impact of a price increase (or reduction) on the bond market. Turning first to the demand for bonds, an increase in the price level produces two effects, one which increases the demand for bonds and one which reduces the demand for bonds. If bond demanders (lenders) are concerned with maintaining the real value of their command over future goods as represented by their bond holdings, then the demand for bonds will be increased in proportion to a rise in the price level. However, if real money balances affect the demand for bonds, a rise in the price level will produce a negative real-balance effect, which will reduce the demand for bonds. Since it is unlikely that the real-balance

---

3. This can be seen by differentiating the equilibrium condition represented by CC. Writing C, the excess demand for commodities, as some function of i and P, we have

$$C = C(i, P)$$

Along CC, the change in C must be zero, and so differentiating the above equation gives

$$dC = 0 = (\partial C/\partial i)di + (\partial C/\partial P)dP$$

where $\partial C/\partial i < 0$ and $\partial C/\partial P < 0$.

The implied slope of CC where $dC = 0$ is derived from this last equation as

$$\frac{di}{dp}\bigg|_{CC} = -\frac{\partial C/\partial P}{\partial C/\partial i} < 0$$

effect will totally erase the initial increase in the demand for bonds in proportion to the increase in the price level, the net result of these two effects will be an increase in the demand for bonds that is proportionately less than the increase in the price level.

On the supply side, assume an initial increase in borrowing (bond supply) due to the reduction in the real value of liabilities of bond suppliers that is implicit in a higher price level. In addition, if borrowers have made plans for a given real value of loan proceeds, they may find it necessary to increase the supply of bonds further (borrow more) to finance higher money costs of the project for which they borrowed initially. These two factors combine to produce a greater-than-proportional increase in bond supply resulting from a price increase. This result, combined with the less-than-proportional increase in bond demand arising from a price increase, implies an excess supply of bonds as the result of a price increase.

Look again at Figure 15.1. As was the case with the CC line, the magnitude of the impact of interest-rate changes and price-level changes upon bond market equilibrium determines the steepness of the positive slope of BB.[4] In addition, below and to the right of BB in quadrants A and D, i is too low and P is too high for bond-market equilibrium. Since each of these changes lowers the demand for bonds relative to supply, an excess supply of bonds, B < 0, exists in these quadrants. Conversely, above and to the left of the BB line there exists an excess demand for bonds denoted by B > 0.

Having identified the excess demand or supply conditions in the bond or commodity market for each of the four quadrants of Figure 15.1, we can examine the dynamics of Patinkin's simple general-equilibrium model. Basically, the question of dynamics centers upon consideration of whether forces exist in each of the quadrants which will move i and P, the endogenous variables of the model, back toward the general-equilibrium position, E, where BB intersects CC. The dynamic forces in the vertical, or i, dimension are represented in each quadrant by vertical arrows. Below and to the right of BB an excess supply of bonds (or excess demand for loans) exists, meaning that in quadrants A and D the interest rate is too low for bond-market equilibrium. The excess demand for loans results in upward pressure on the interest rate in these quadrants (represented by the upward-pointing arrows). The reverse, an excess demand for bonds (supply of loans), holds

---

4. As with CC, write B, the excess demand for bonds as some function of i and P

$$B = B(i, P)$$

Since along BB the change in B must be zero, we differentiate to get

$$dB = 0 = (\partial B/\partial i)di + (\partial B/\partial P)dP$$

where $\partial B/\partial i > 0$ and $\partial B/\partial P < 0$.
The implied slope of BB is therefore

$$\left.\frac{di}{dP}\right|_{BB} = -\frac{\partial B/\partial P}{\partial B/\partial i} > 0$$

above and to the left of BB. The excess demand for bonds results in downward pressure on the interest rate in quadrants B and C (as represented by the downward-pointing arrows).

The horizontal arrows in Figure 15.1 represent the pressures on the price level resulting from a commodity market disequilibrium. An excess supply of commodities to the right of CC results in downward pressure on the price level as represented by the horizontal arrows in quadrants A and B. An excess demand for commodities to the left of CC results in upward pressure on the price level as represented by the horizontal arrows in quadrants C and D.[5]

With these dynamic forces in mind, it is possible to examine the disequilibrium behavior of the model represented in Figure 15.1. It is clear from the arrows in each quadrant that movement toward a general equilibrium at point E occurs in a generally counterclockwise direction. Notice that movement toward E from disequilibrium positions such as X, Y, or Z may occur virtually directly, as from X to E; in a spiraling or "oscillatory" manner, as from Y to E; or in a partially spiraling manner, as from Z to E. The fundamental point which emerges from Figure 15.1 regarding the dynamics of the Patinkin model is that it is stable. Disequilibria tend to approach the general equilibrium point E, from which there is no tendency to move.

At this point the significance of the parameters of the model can be seen clearly. Suppose that a rise in the price level resulted in an excess demand for commodities. In that case all of the horizontal arrows would be reversed in direction, and the dynamic forces in quadrants A and C would unambiguously point away from equilibrium. Market forces in these quadrants would move points like X, Y, or Z further and further from a general equilibrium at E. The model would be unstable.

However, the proposition $\partial C/\partial P < 0$, employed in the stable case of Figure 15.1, reflects the real-balance effect and is economically sound. Thus, the unstable case may be viewed as merely hypothetical, with little basis in economic theory. One other consideration exists, however, which may present more serious problems for the stability of the Patinkin model. It has so far been assumed that $C \neq 0$ affects only prices, while $B \neq 0$ affects only interest rates. To the extent that some substitutability exists between commodities and bonds (or future commodities), it must be recognized that $C \neq 0$ affects both P and I, as does $B \neq 0$. Analysis of dynamic stability in this case becomes more complex, requiring techniques beyond the scope of this book. Suffice it to say here that under this latter set of assumptions

5. Strictly speaking, the pressure on prices off the CC line results from the fact that real money balances are inconsistent with commodity-market equilibrium. If P is above CC, an excess supply of commodities results because the implied reduction in real money balances produces a negative real-balance effect. The price level falls as money holders cut expenditure in order to restore real money balances to their equilibrium level. Of course, the reverse result occurs to the left of CC, when P is too low for equilibrium in the commodity market.

dynamic stability of the Patinkin model remains likely but is not absolutely assured. At this point it is necessary to look carefully at the impact of a change in the money supply, as it is central to Patinkin's attempt to establish the neutrality of money (change in the money supply ultimately affects no real variables) in a general-equilibrium setting.

Impact of a Change in Money Supply: Patinkin and Friedman

In the Patinkin model we saw that real money balances affect both the demand for commodities and the demand for bonds. Since changes are assumed to occur in both bond and commodity markets along BB and CC as the price level changes, the nominal quantity of money is taken to be fixed for a given pair of these lines. A change in the nominal quantity of money will shift each of the lines.

In a strictly comparative-static analysis our only interest is with the final equilibrium condition, which emerges after all of the adjustments to a change, such as a doubling of the nominal quantity of money, have taken place. The result of such a doubling of the nominal quantity of money is shown in Figure 15.2. The broken lines (BB and CC) represent the original equilibrium position while the solid lines (B_1B_1 and C_1C_1) represent the final

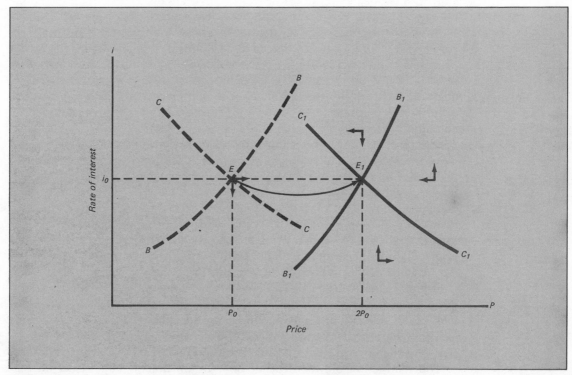

Figure 15.2 The impact of a doubling of the nominal quantity of money

equilibrium position. The long-run equilibrium result occurs when the real value of money balances is restored by a doubling of the price level from P_0 to $2P_0$. This represents a new equilibrium at the original interest rate, i, because with no real values changed, a restoration of equilibrium requires the real value of money balances to remain constant. This requires a doubling of the price level given a doubling of the nominal quantity of money.

The question which concerns us here is why the interest rate returns to its original level. This result is essential to Patinkin's attempt to establish the neutrality of money in a general-equilibrium setting. Patinkin's analysis of the neutrality of money depends heavily on the notion, discussed earlier, that an increase in the price level produces an excess supply of bonds. Examining the dynamic behavior between the comparative-static equilibrium at E and E_1 described by Patinkin's model, we find that the doubling of the money supply initially produces an excess demand for bonds which depresses the interest rate. The lower interest rate raises the demand for future goods and hence the demand for the means to produce future goods. In other words, a lower interest rate increases investment. Increased investment expenditure combines with an increase in the demand for commodities induced by an initial increase in the real money balances to put upward pressure on the price level. A rise in the price level produces an excess supply of bonds, which in turn results in a rise in the interest rate. The interest rate will continue to rise with price level increases until equilibrium is restored at the original interest rate. In effect, the initial downward pressure on the interest rate is reversed by the impact of a subsequent rise in the price level on the excess supply of bonds. The reversal ends at the original interest rate when prices have risen by enough to restore real money balances to their equilibrium level. At that point, with real balances and the interest rate unchanged, equilibrium is restored to both the bond and the commodity markets.

The most striking thing about this result is that it duplicates the single-equation, simple quantity theory result in a general-equilibrium setting. The parallel with Friedman's quantity theory is even more striking, since the long-run, comparative-static result and the dynamic result are similar. The conclusions from both Friedman's and Patinkin's analyses of the impact of changes in the nominal quantity of money are worth looking at again. In the long run, the price level rises at the same percentage rate as the nominal money supply, because money demanders, not money suppliers, determine the real quantity of money. Patinkin and Friedman thus conclude that the neutrality of money is a valid assumption even given the real-balance effect, but only in the long run. Both conclude that money matters a great deal, in fact, because of the impact of changes in the money supply which, in initially affecting real balances, affects the demand for bonds and commodities, and thereby results in a move from one equilibrium level to another.

The distinction between the demonstration that money affects no real variables in the long run and the implications of real-balance effects in the transition period between long-run equilibria emphasize the importance of dynamics over comparative statics in understanding the analyses of contemporary monetary theorists like Friedman and Patinkin. We might consider whether some of the difficulties of communications between Keynesians and monetarists have been due to the differences in the analytical techniques employed by the two groups. The Keynesians have tended to emphasize short-run impacts of changes in the money supply and changes in government expenditure under the assumption that either the price level or the wage level or both are taken to be fixed. The monetarists have tended to adopt the classical assumption that the labor market is cleared by wage flexibility and to emphasize both long-run and short-run implications of changes in the money supply. It is perhaps ironic that in terms of long-run, comparative-static equilibria, money does not matter to the monetarists in that changes in the money supply affect no real variables, while for the Keynesians, the assumption of downwardly rigid money wages means that changes in the money supply do indeed matter, because downward wage rigidity means that such changes can have long-run effects on real variables. In assessing the validity of the two approaches, as always it is the appropriateness of the assumptions which determines the outcome. Both approaches have achieved success insofar as each has apprehended significant aspects of economic reality.

As a final note on Patinkin's model, it should be pointed out that his analysis is not identical to Friedman's, particularly in terms of the transmission mechanism which conveys the impact of changes in the nominal money supply to the economy. The role of the impact of changes in the price level upon bond-market equilibrium is essential to Patinkin's analysis, but it does not play such a central role in Friedman's analysis of the transmission mechanism, as we saw in Chapter 13. Friedman's analysis is both more eclectic and less precise than Patinkin's formal, mechanical analysis, and thus, while intriguing, it is more difficult to test empirically than Patinkin's. Both emphasize that money matters a great deal in disequilibrium periods, but not at equilibrium, a conclusion which translates into a largely unqualified assertion that money matters, in view of the fact that an economy is seldom in equilibrium.

Monetary economists Lloyd Metzler and Robert Mundell have also examined the impact of changes in the money supply, with emphasis placed upon the significance of the manner in which the money supply is changed.

The Non-Neutrality of Money: Lloyd A. Metzler

In a highly influential article published in 1951,[6] Lloyd A. Metzler suggested that changes in the money supply effected by way of Federal Reserve open-

6. Lloyd A. Metzler, "Wealth, Saving and the Rate of Interest," *Journal of Political Economy* 59 (April 1951): 93–116.

Commentary: Empirical Analysis of the Real-Balance Effect

Because of the theoretical importance of the real-balance effect as an influence on aggregate demand, various econometric studies have been undertaken in an attempt to see whether the empirical evidence confirms the theory. These investigations have been summarized in a critique by economist Don Patinkin, which points out both the statistical difficulties involved in any attempts to quantify the relationship between changes in real-balance and consumption expenditures, and the definitional difficulties involved in deciding exactly which assets should be included in the determination of real balances.[1]

Patinkin examines a dozen different studies which present data relating to possible correlations between the consumption function and real balances. The studies covered a wide range of time periods, from the fifty-year span (1902–1952) used by Michio Morishima and Mitsuo Saito,[2] to the eight years (1942–1955) included in Arnold Zellner's investigations.[3] Ten of the twelve studies reported a "highly significant" correlation between real balances and the consumption function, where the coefficient linking changes in real balances and changes in consumption at least three times the standard error in almost every case.

Although ten of the twelve studies reported such statistically significant coefficients attached to real balances in the consumption equation, Patinkin was nevertheless concerned about the wide variation between the results; they varied by a factor of 5, which Patinkin considered puzzling. For example, those studies using quarterly figures reported much higher coefficients than those using annual figures. The author of one of these quarterly studies, Arnold Zellner, suggested that his results may indicate that the effects of a change in liquid assets may be exhausted during one year and therefore simply do not show up when annual data are used.

On a more fundamental basis, however, Patinkin questioned whether much of the empirical research efforts to date have indeed tested the real-balance effect theory adequately. Each of the studies he reviewed defined real balances in terms of either M_1 or M_2; that is, the assets used to determine real balances were restricted to liquid assets. Patinkin, on the other hand, suggests that it might be more realistic to use some measures of assets that approximated the "net financial assets of fixed money value" rather than the very narrow concept of assets included in either M_1 or M_2. Most definitions of M_2, for example, include only currency, demand deposits, time deposits, and U.S. government securities; net financial assets would add to this such additional assets as life insurance reserves; pension and retirement funds; mortgages; state, local, and private sector bonds; etc., or, in other words, any asset "whose real value is affected by an equiproportionate change in commodity prices."[4] In brief, Patinkin raises the question of whether empirical evidence regarding the correlations between consumption and real balances might be even more significant if the assets used to determine real-balance figures

1. Don Patinkin, *Money, Interest, and Prices*, 2d ed. (New York: Harper, 1965), pp. 651–664.
2. Michio Morishima and Mitsuo Saito, "A Dynamic Analysis of the American Economy, 1902–1952," *International Economic Review* 5 (May 1964): 129.
3. Arnold Zellner, "The Short-Run Consumption Function," *Econometrica* 25 (October 1957): 560.

4. Patinkin, *Money, Interest, and Prices*, p. 655.

included both monetary and nonmonetary wealth.

Patinkin offers some preliminary statistical evidence of his own indicating that his broader approach to the measurement of real balances might well indicate a higher degree of correlation. In addition he mentions some recent research efforts where the net worth of the household sector has been used as the wealth variable, a concept which is closer to his thesis than M_1 or M_2, the wealth variables used in the initial group of twelve studies he discussed earlier.[5] He concludes, however, by emphasizing the need for more analysis, particularly with recent data.

From a practical point of view, Patinkin's logic regarding the importance of expanding the measurement of those assets included in real balances appears obvious. For example, within the eleven years between 1963 and 1973, private noninsured pension funds increased from $46 billion to $124 billion,[6] putting many an American in a position where his equity in pension funds represented a larger part of his wealth than that presented by his purely monetary assets. Similarly, life insurance reserves, which are now more than $200 billion, and household ownership of other fixed assets such as municipal and corporate bonds are too substantial at this time to be ignored.[7]

Overall, the statistical evidence presented by Patinkin in his review of the field appears very impressive. It would be particularly interesting to see additional evidence reviewing the period beginning in late 1973. During this time, when double-digit inflation hit the United States, the real balances of most Americans were reduced substantially, and it is possible that the declines in retail sales and other measurements of consumption spending that occurred were at least in part a reflection of this reduction in real balances.

4. Patinkin, *Money, Interest, and Prices*, p. 655.

5. Albert Ando and Franco Modigliani, "The 'Life Cycle' Hypothesis of Saving," *American Economic Review* 53 (March 1963): 111–113; and John Arena, "The Wealth Effect and Consumption: A Statistical Inquiry," *Yale Economic Essays* 3 no. 2, (1963): 251–303.

6. Securities Exchange Commission, *Statistical Bulletin* 33 (April 3, 1974).

7. *Life Insurance Fact Book* (New York: Institute of Life Insurance, 1973).

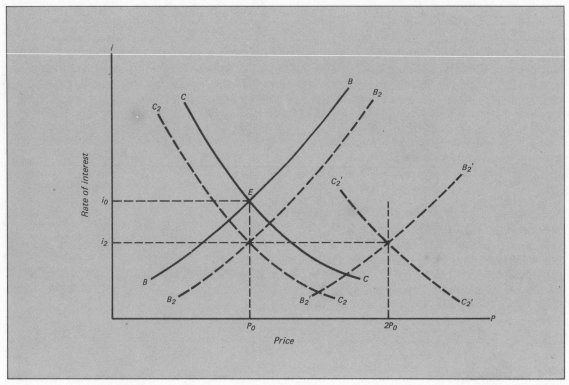

Figure 15.3 Metzler's analysis of the impact of a change in the money supply on the interest rate

market operations may lead to an equilibrium interest rate. This is equivalent to suggesting that money is non-neutral, because changes in the money supply can affect a real variable like the interest rate.

The impact of changes in the money supply effected by open-market operations is considered in Figure 15.3, which is identical to Figure 15.1 in terms of the initial equilibrium position, E.[7] Suppose the money supply is increased by means of an open-market purchase of bonds. The effect of lowering the quantity of bonds held by the public and replacing bond holdings with money is to reduce the wealth in the hands of the public *after the price level has doubled, resulting in what would have been a new comparative-static equilibrium in Patinkin's model.* The result of the lowered real wealth position of the public (due to the central bank's open-market purchase of

7. The actual diagram employed by Metzler places i on the vertical axis but measures M/P of M(1/P) along the horizontal axis while holding M fixed for each BB or CC schedule. The result of measuring 1/P instead of P along the horizontal axis is to impart a positive slope to CC and a negative slope to BB. Because this produces no change in results obtained with the model, the Patinkin formulation is retained here for purposes of continuity.

bonds) is to shift the CC schedule to C_2C_2, because more savings results at each price level (and consequently at each M/P). More savings requires more investment at each wealth (price) level for equilibrium to be restored in the commodity market, which is possible only with a lower interest rate at each price level. Therefore CC shifts down to C_2C_2. The BB schedule also shifts down to B_2B_2. Given a lower real supply of bonds at each price level, the bond market can only be cleared at each price level by lowering the demand for bonds. This requires a lower interest rate or, equivalently, a downward shift of BB to B_2B_2.

The result of the downward shifts of CC and BB at each price level is to produce a lower equilibrium interest rate at i_2 in Figure 15.3. The same effect could have been shown at $2P_0$ to reflect the impact of doubling the quantity of money, but since the effects on BB and CC occur at each price level, the price level at which the new equilibrium interest rate is established is immaterial. The result at $2P_0$ is shown in broken lines as a reminder of the path to the new equilibrium.

Essential to Metzler's results is the assumption that real savings depends upon both the interest rate and the real value of wealth in the hands of savers. This extends the classical assumption that both real savings and real investment depend only upon interest rate. Further, Metzler's analysis indicates that changes in the nominal quantity of money affect the equilibrium interest rate only when accompanied by changes in the value of privately held securities, as with open-market operations. Changes in the nominal quantity of money not accompanied by changes in the value of privately held securities will not affect the equilibrium interest rate and are therefore neutral. This point explains why some monetary theorists, such as Milton Friedman, at times allude to changes in the nominal quantity of money affected by dropping money out of helicopters. An equivalent change could be effected by a current account surplus in the balance of payments, provided that the capital account remained in equilibrium.

Modification of Metzler's Analysis: Robert A. Mundell

Robert Mundell has suggested some qualifications to Metzler's analysis based upon the possibility that an open-market operation may not, in fact, result in a perceived change in the value of privately held securities.[8] This eventually depends upon possible changes in government taxation arising from an open-market purchase, which effectively retires a government liability and thereby reduces the interest payments which must be made by the government to the owners of the bonds. In order to look at Mundell's hypothesis, suppose that the Federal Reserve increases the money supply by way of an open-market purchase, thereby lowering the quantity of outstanding gov-

8. Robert A. Mundell, "The Public Debt, Corporate Income Taxes, and the Rate of Interest," *Journal of Political Economy* 68 (December 1960): 622–626.

ernment bonds. If the government balances its budget, lower tax proceeds will be needed to meet the resulting reduction in required interest payments on the government's debt and thus taxes may be cut. The important thing in Mundell's analysis is the impact of such a tax cut upon the behavior of private wealth holders. If the tax cut results in a change in the value of private assets, which offsets the impact of an open-market purchase upon private wealth, the interest rate will be unaffected. This will likely occur if the government reduces corporate taxes. A reduction in corporate taxes causes the value of existing corporate bonds to rise by the present value of the reduction of taxes over time, since lower corporate taxes means higher dividends for owners of the corporation. In effect the value of the tax cut is capitalized. In the case of a balanced budget, the value of the tax cut will also equal the present value of the reduced interest payments on government debt, with the consequence that no net wealth change results from the open-market operation. Therefore, the equilibrium interest rate is unaffected, which is consistent with Metzler's analysis.

It is possible that an open-market purchase and accompanying tax cut will have even the opposite effect from that proposed by Metzler; that is, it may raise the equilibrium interest rate. This follows because if lower corporate taxes stimulate investment at each given level of interest rates

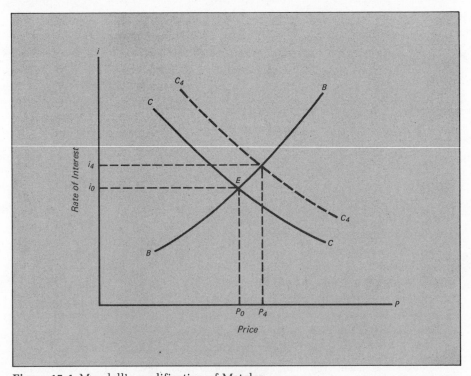

Figure 15.4 Mundell's modification of Metzler

and real balances (price level), then equilibrium in the commodity market requires a higher price level, P, at each interest rate, i, or, equivalently, a higher i at each P, both of which would increase savings. This change is represented by an upward shift of CC to C_4C_4 and a rise in the equilibrium interest rate to i_4 shown in Figure 15.4.

However, if instead of corporate taxes, the government chooses to cut personal taxes as a result of an open-market purchase, there would be nothing to offset the reduction in privately held wealth caused by the implied retirement of government debt. This is because the private sector does not hold securities which represent claims on the future of individual earnings. In short, the cut in personal taxes cannot be capitalized into the value of securities held by the public, because the capital markets do not effect sales of claims on services of individuals. Therefore, since no effect follows from lower personal taxes on private wealth, nothing removes the negative effect on private wealth of the open-market purchase. In this case, the Metzler result is preserved.

Concluding Note

The general-equilibrium monetary theorists are all concerned with analysis of the role of money in the economy within the context of a general equilibrium macro model, particularly with the possible connection between changes in the money supply and changes in a real variable such as the interest rate. The classics saw the interest rate as being independent of changes in the nominal money supply and therefore dichotomized the economy into monetary and real sectors, with the monetary sector determining only the absolute price level. In contrast, as we saw in the discussion of Keynesian monetary theory in Chapter 8, Keynes saw the rate of interest as being determined by the choice between money and other assets and perceived that a change in the quantity of money could affect the equilibrium interest rate. Pigou introduced the real-balance effect, which rescued the economic system from the possibility of the less-than-full-employment equilibrium suggested by Keynes. The Pigou effect, or real-balance effect, suggests that savings (or consumption) behavior is directly affected by the real value of money and thereby implies that an excess supply of money would affect the demand for commodities as well as bonds. In this case, the effects of changes in the quantity of money upon expenditure no longer relies exclusively upon the ability of changes in the money supply to affect the interest rate and thereby to affect investment expenditure. Rather, the "slips twixt the cup and the lip" suggested by Keynes in the form of a liquidity trap or unresponsiveness of investment spending to changes in the interest rate are bypassed by a direct link—the real-balance effect—between changes in the real quantity of money expenditure. In periods of slack demand for output, falling prices will, according to the real-balance effect, automatically increase real balances and in turn increase demand, thus eventually ending the condition of excess supply.

We have seen that Patinkin carefully examined the role of the real-balance effect; he attacked the "invalid dichotomy" of the classical economists with a demonstration that the price level would be indeterminate without the real-balance effect. Patinkin went on to show that under certain circumstances, however, even with the real-balance effect, the interest rate remains independent of changes in the nominal quantity of money. He reinstated neutrality of money (which had been removed by Keynes), incorporating the real-balance effect which he claimed had been improperly ignored by the classics as well as by Keynes. In retaining the effective, long-run independence between the monetary and real sectors of the economy Patinkin obtained the same long-run result in a general-equilibrium setting regarding the equality of percentage price-level changes and percentage nominal money-supply changes as was obtained with the modern quantity theory by Friedman in a partial equilibrium analysis.

In contrast to Patinkin, Metzler claimed that in salvaging one feature of classical economics, an automatic tendency toward full-employment equilibrium by way of the Pigou effect, the independence between the monetary and real sectors claimed by the classics had been lost. If a change in the money supply involves an exchange of one asset for another, as do open-market operations, the equilibrium interest rate is no longer independent of changes in the nominal money supply and the classical dichotomy no longer exists. Mundell extended Metzler's analysis with the suggestion that the form of tax change which accompanies a change in the quantity of interest-bearing debt outstanding for a budget-balancing government will determine whether or not the equilibrium interest rate is affected by a change in the nominal money supply. If the tax change is noncapitalizable, as with a change in personal taxes, the Metzler result follows; a capitalizable change in corporate taxes results either in a restoration of neutrality or in a change in the interest rate in the opposite direction to that hypothesized by Metzler.

The work of the general-equilibrium monetary theorists has advanced considerably the understanding of the role of monetary changes in affecting the economy. While the comparative-statics effects of monetary changes upon equilibrium real values such as the interest rate remain in dispute, the behavior of the economy between equilibria is generally agreed to be broadly affected by monetary changes. An increase in the quantity of money will lead to (1) an initial reduction in interest rates which will eventually be moderated or erased; (2) an increase in prices and real output which will be combined in a manner determined by the elasticity of the aggregate supply schedule; and (3) an eventual approximately equiproportional relationship between percentage changes in the money supply and percentage changes in the price level.

Questions and Exercises

1. Under what conditions does the classical dichotomy hold true? Why can't it be applied to the IS/LM model?
2. Explain the logical inconsistency of the classical dichotomy in terms of Patinkin's analysis. How does Patinkin resolve this inconsistency?
3. Why is the bond market central to Patinkin's general-equilibrium model? How does an increase in the price level affect bond supply and demand?
4. What is the significance of the positive slope of the BB line in Figure 15.1? What determines its steepness? What determines the steepness of the CC line?
5. What forces make the Patinkin model inherently stable? Trace the possible paths of movement from disequilibrium positions (e.g., X, Y, or Z) in Figure 15.1 to the general equilibrium point, E.
6. According to the comparative static analysis, the impact of a doubling of the money supply will be to double the price level, but in the long run, the interest rate returns to its original level. Trace this process, step by step.
7. In early 1974 the Fed allowed the money supply to rise at an annual rate of only 8 percent, while the prime rate jumped by about 40 percent in just two months. Does this invalidate the analysis you have outlined in the previous question?
8. How did Mundell modify Metzler's analysis? To what extent has it been relevant over the past decade?
9. What assumptions does Patinkin make enabling him to formulate his general-equilibrium model of the commodity and bond sectors?
10. Do you agree with the classics that the interest rate is independent of changes in the money supply or the Keynesian position that changes in the money supply could affect the equilibrium rate of interest? Is your thinking at all influenced by the rapid inflation of recent years?

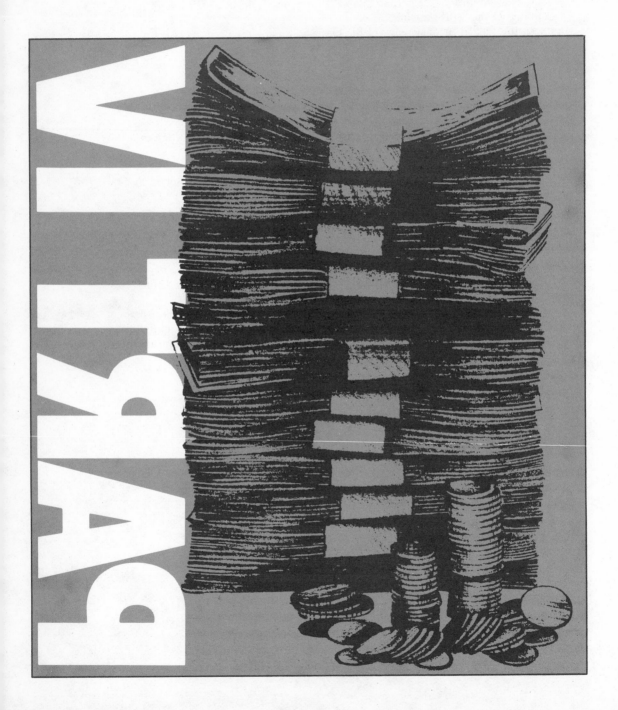

Problems of Macroeconomic Policy

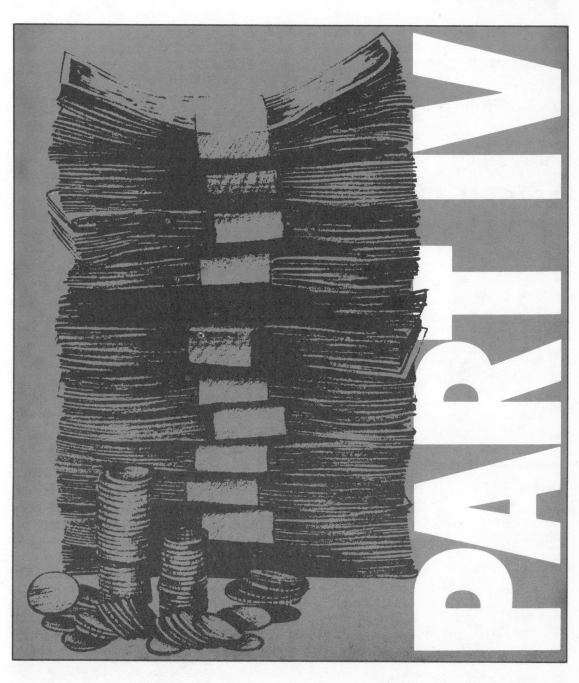

PART IV

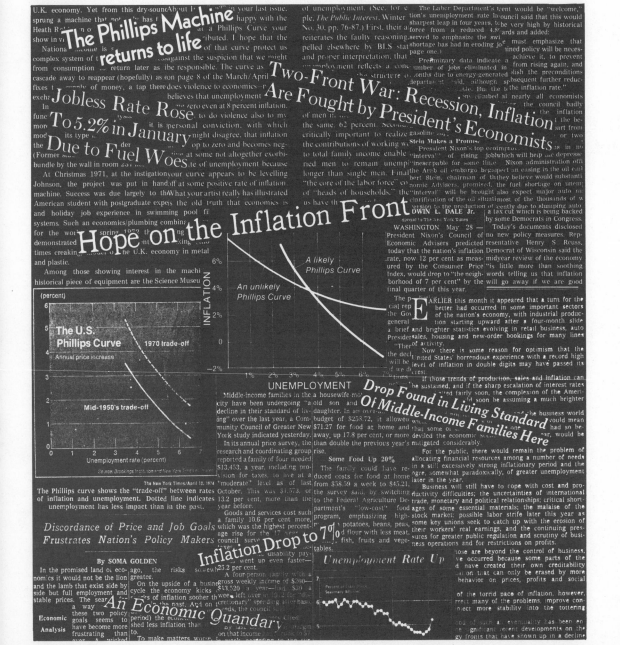

The Phillips Machine returns to life

Two-Front War: Recession, Inflation Are Fought by President's Economists

Jobless Rate Rose To 5.2% in January Due to Fuel Woes

Hope on the Inflation Front

An unlikely Phillips Curve

A likely Phillips Curve

The U.S. Phillips Curve — Annual price increase — 1970 trade-off — Mid-1950's trade-off

The New York Times/April 10, 1974
Source: Brookings Institution and New York Times estimate

The Phillips curve shows the "trade-off" between rates of inflation and unemployment. Dotted line indicates unemployment has less impact than in the past.

Drop Found in Living Standard Of Middle-Income Families Here

Discordance of Price and Job Goals Frustrates Nation's Policy Makers

By SOMA GOLDEN

Inflation Drop to 7%

Unemployment Rate Up

An Economic Quandary

Some Food Up 20%

UNEMPLOYMENT

The Phillips Curve: Inflation and Unemployment

16

It is clear by now that inflation is one of the most serious problems facing our economy. Unanticipated inflation reduces the purchasing power of individuals who live on fixed money incomes, while anticipated inflation leads to wasteful consumption of resources. Given that inflation is undesirable, the important question is how to control it. To answer this question, one must know the effects of counterinflationary monetary and fiscal policies on the level of aggregate demand in the economy. Recent research indicates that there is an inverse relationship between the rate of inflation and the level of unemployment. This finding suggests that to pursue a goal of stable prices the economy must put up with a higher rate of unemployment; conversely, to pursue a goal of low unemployment, usually the 4 percent rate considered to be full employment, the economy must suffer a higher level of inflation. Formulating a counterinflationary policy thus involves a trade-off between the goals of price stability and full employment. This relation-

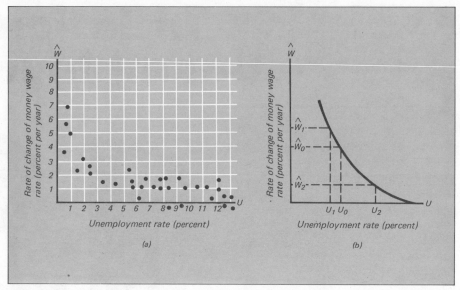

Figure 16.1 The Phillips curve

ship is represented by the Phillips curve, first identified by British economist A. W. Phillips.[1]

Using data about the British economy from 1861 to 1958, Phillips plotted changes in money-wage rates against changes in the level of unemployment for each year. The result was similar to the scatter diagram in Figure 16.1(a). Each point on the diagram represents the level of unemployment and the rate of money-wage changes for a given year. Using a simple statistical tool called regression analysis, Phillips fitted a curve to his observed data points, obtaining a curve like the one shown in Figure 16.1(b). From the data and the curve, Phillips explained the relationship which his curve specified with a simple hypothesis. When the demand for labor is high, fewer workers are unemployed. In order to expand production, employers must hire more workers and thereby bid up the price of labor so as to tempt the best-qualified workers to work for their firms. Thus wage rates rise very quickly when unemployment is low. In periods with a low demand for labor, unemployment is high, but workers are not willing to offer their services for much less than the prevailing wage rate. Hence, employers are not able to get workers to accept a lower wage rate as readily as they accept a higher wage rate. Thus the rate of change of money wages declines less rapidly than it rises. The result is the curve shown in Figure 16.1(b). At U_0 the rate of change of the wage rate is W_0. In order to expand production, thus obtaining a lower unemployment rate, U_1, employers bid up the rate of increase in the wage rate

1. A. W. Phillips, "The Relation between Unemployment and the Rate of Change of Money Wage Rates in the United Kingdom, 1861–1957," *Economica*, New Series 25 (November 1958): 283–299.

to W_1. If the demand for labor slackens, however, the unemployment level will fall to U_2, and the rate of increase in the wage rate will fall to W_2. From U_0 to U_1 the slope of the curve rises more rapidly than it does from U_0 to U_2, reflecting the fact that money-wage rates at given levels of unemployment rise more quickly than they fall.

Phillips' explanation for the shape of the curve is related to the Keynesian notion of money illusion, which we examined in Chapter 10. The so-called "naive" Keynesian view of the manner in which laborers form expectations regarding the future behavior of their wages is based upon money illusion in the labor market. This notion suggests that workers view their wages in money terms, ignoring the impact of inflation upon real wages. Under this view, real wages fall as inflation proceeds and fall more rapidly as inflation speeds up. Consequently, employers hire more labor at the resulting lower real-wage rates, thereby expanding output and lowering unemployment.

The Trade-Off: Inflation and Unemployment

Economists have transposed the Phillips relationship between unemployment and changes in money-wage rates into a generalized model showing the relationship between unemployment and inflation. Changes in wages are a basic component of changes in the price level. Thus, during a period of inflation, wages increase along with the price of raw materials. Not all wage increases, however, are inflationary; those which result from gains in productivity, for example, are not. The vertical axis of the original Phillips curve can be redrawn to separate changes in wages which result from increases in productivity from those which result from inflation. The vertical $\hat{\pi}$ range in Figure 16.2 indicates the percentage increase in labor productivity and hence in wage rates which can be generated without raising prices. Money-wage raises above productivity increases are inflationary. Therefore, the vertical axis may be labeled as the rate of increase of money prices above point Z where the distance OZ represents the rate of growth of labor productivity, $\hat{\pi}$.

The Phillips curve analysis, if accurate, is useful because it suggests the extent to which fiscal and monetary policy can be used to combat inflation without incurring unacceptably high levels of unemployment. In the United States the general consensus appears to be that an "acceptable" level of unemployment lies between 3.5 and 5.0 percent. The Phillips curve is useful to the extent that it tells the policymaker what rate of inflation has been historically compatible with a given level of unemployment. The exact location of the curve in relation to the horizontal and vertical axes is of critical importance. If the curve is close to the horizontal axis, this suggests that a lower level of inflation can be traded off for a given level of unemployment. On the other hand, the farther the curve from the vertical axis, the more difficult it is to achieve a low level of unemployment at a given rate of inflation.

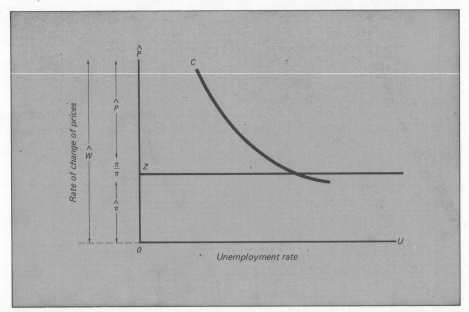

Figure 16.2 The Phillips curve transposed to a relationship between inflation and unemployment where $\hat{W} = \hat{P} + \hat{\pi}$

Since Phillips published his work in 1958, economists have attempted to specify Phillips curves for this country. An important study by Paul Samuelson and Robert Solow[2] suggests that an inflation rate of between 5 percent and 6 percent is necessary in order to hold wage increases in line with increases in productivity, given an unemployment level of between 4 percent and 5 percent. Moreover, to reduce unemployment to 3 percent, inflation might have to rise to 6 percent, a fairly significant increase. Today most economists who accept Phillips' trade-off agree that the terms of the trade-off have worsened in this country. Figure 16.3 shows Phillips curves drawn for the United States economy in the mid-1950s and 1970, from which we can see that the trade-off specified by the curve drawn for 1970 is worse than that for the curve drawn in the mid-1950s. For example, 4 percent unemployment required a 2½ percent price inflation in 1950 while 4 percent unemployment required a 4½ percent inflation rate in 1970.

The trade-off which the Phillips curve represents suggests several policy considerations. First of all, policymakers must decide whether the existing curve represents some combination of price stability and unemployment which is acceptable. If an acceptable level of price stability not accompanied by high unemployment appears feasible, then appropriate fiscal and monetary policy can be used to regulate the level of aggregate demand which will

2. See Paul A. Samuelson and Robert M. Solow, "Analytical Aspects of Anti-Inflation Policy," *American Economic Review* 50 (May 1960): 192.

produce the desired combination of price stability and unemployment. On the other hand, if an acceptable level of price stability appears incompatible with 4 percent unemployment, then policy must try to move the Phillips curve to the left. If, for example, policymakers decided that the trade-off shown in the 1970 curve in Figure 16.3 was unacceptable, their efforts should be directed toward moving the curve to the left, more in line with the 1950 trade-off. This could perhaps be accompanied by adopting policies which are designed to increase the mobility of labor and make workers more receptive to other forms of employment. On-job training, job information centers, and relocation loans are some of the kinds of policies which could accomplish these goals. A slight shift to the left might also be accomplished through efforts which make business more competitive, such as stricter enforcement of antitrust laws or more exposure to foreign competition through elimination of protective tariffs or quotas.

The Phillips curve trade-off presents policymakers with a dilemma since more inflation and more unemployment are both undesirable. The trade-off suggests a problem of choice under constraint. The Phillips curve and the

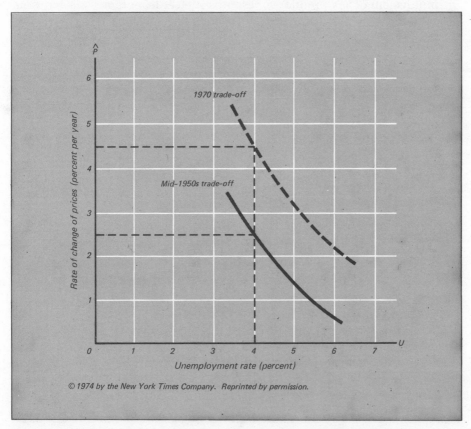

© 1974 by the New York Times Company. Reprinted by permission.

Figure 16.3 The Phillips curve in the United States, mid-1950s and 1970

nature of the constraint are shown in Figure 16.4, where the curve labeled C is the Phillips curve and curves I_1, I_2, and I_3 represent policymakers' indifference curves between unemployment and inflation. The curves are concave to the origin since the two alternatives are both bad ones, thereby representing negative utility. That is, curve I_1 represents a higher level of general welfare than curve I_2 since the curve contains lower levels of unemployment and inflation. Point Q represents the constrained optimum mix between inflation and unemployment. At that point the rate of trade-off between inflation and unemployment that is *possible* under the constraint specified by the Phillips curve is equal to the rate at which policymakers are *willing* to trade off between the equally undesirable inflation and unemployment, as specified along the policymaker's indifference curve, I_2.

Economists have found several conceptual difficulties in the policy trade-off represented by the Phillips curve, however. While decision-making behavior can be specified in a trade-off relationship between the goals of unemployment and inflation, it is not clear whether the trade-off adequately represents the wishes of the population at large. It is usually assumed that unemployment of any productive resource such as labor represents foregone output and that foregone output represents a real social cost. However, this

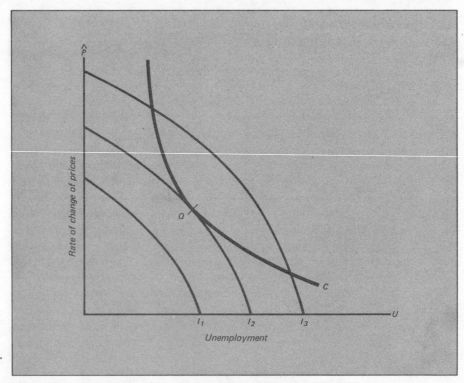

Figure 16.4 The Phillips curve and policy indifference curves

assignment of costs assumes that all unemployment is involuntary and fails to recognize the preference of some unemployed individuals for leisure.[3] In a mature economy such as the United States, preference for leisure among unemployed workers may be quite high. Hence, the social cost of unemployment may be lower than expected. If one assumes that unemployment is not involuntary, then the social costs of unemployment correlate more closely with output loss.

Problems also arise in connection with assigning a cost to inflation. Unanticipated inflation, as we have already seen, represents a transfer from holders of money-denominated assets to holders of money-denominated liabilities. For example, creditors lose during an unanticipated inflation and borrowers gain, since the real cost of repaying obligations has declined. There is no waste of resources, simply a transfer. In a strict accounting sense, the cost is zero. Anticipated inflation, as we have seen, represents certain costs. The tax on money implicit in an anticipated inflation causes the community to substitute other assets for money. Since money costs less to produce than the other assets, the community wastes resources in the production of money substitutes. The net loss may be reduced, however, if the government undertakes worthwhile projects from the proceeds of the inflationary tax. There may be also additional costs if the income redistributing effects produced by both anticipated and unanticipated inflation are viewed as undesirable. However, in order to accurately assess such costs, one must have in mind a clearly defined optimal distribution of income.

These problems associated with the measuring of the costs of the Phillips curve trade-off make the policy choices less clear. While a precise solution may be obtained in theory, it is not always possible to specify how much inflation can be traded off for how much unemployment and still meet the requirements of the community.

Critics of the Phillips Curve

Aside from the measurement problems examined here, there are other problems with the Phillips curve analysis. Economists question whether the curve is stable and whether the trade-off that it specifies actually exists. Implicit in this challenge to the Phillips curve is an alternate theory of how workers behave. We noted that the Phillips model is based on a notion of money illusion in the labor market; in effect, money illusion acts to fool workers into accepting a lower real wage. This notion is predicted on an assumption not that workers are irrational but rather that expectations are adjusted more slowly and that it takes a long period of time for employed individuals to recognize that their purchasing power has declined. Opponents of the money illusion theory argue that labor is much less gullible and,

3. See H. G. Johnson, *Macroeconomics and Monetary Theory* (Chicago: Aldine, 1972), pp. 156–160.

accordingly, that expectations about wages change more quickly. If expectations about real wages are revised quickly, there is likely to be little trade-off between inflation and unemployment.

If wage expectations do adjust rapidly when money wages increase, workers will recognize that their purchasing power has declined and hence demand higher wages in order to offset the rise in prices. Assume that the money wage rises by an amount just sufficient to restore the real wage to its previous higher level. Then the incentive which the employer had to expand production when the real wage was reduced by inflation no longer exists. Employment drops and unemployment returns to its previous level. The outcome is a higher rate of increase in prices and money wages but no change in the level of unemployment.

The Accelerationist Theory

Economists Milton Friedman and Edmund Phelps have mounted one of the theoretical attacks on the Phillips curve trade-off between inflation and unemployment.[4] Basically this view suggests that over time workers adjust their money wages in line with their real wages and, hence, that there is no long-run trade-off as specified by the Phillips curve. There is room in this theory, however, for short-run trade-offs similar to those specified by the Phillips curve. Figure 16.5 represents this "accelerationist" theory behind the Phillips curve.

The accelerationist argument admits that in the short run an unanticipated increase in the rate of inflation will lower real wages and reduce unemployment. Thus, unemployment in Figure 16.5 would move along the short-run Phillips curve, SRC_1 from point E_1 to point E_2. However, as soon as laborers (or their bargaining agents) realize that P_2 is a fact of life, they adjust money-wage demands upward to restore real wages to the level formerly held at E_1. The resultant increase in real wages over those prevailing at E_2 moves employment back to E_3 on SRC_2, which is the same level of unemployment which existed previously, except now the rate of increase in money wages and prices is higher than it was before. The long-run Phillips curve LRC is thus vertical at point N, taken to be the "natural" rate of unemployment, as determined by normal frictions in the labor market. A subsequent effort to reduce unemployment with further inflation may again be successful in the short run, causing the rate of unemployment to decline along SRC_2 to E_4 from E_3. If labor learns over time to adjust its expectations more rapidly, however, the unit impact of an increase in inflation on employment may fall so that even if the second increase in the rate of inflation equals the first—that is, the distance from E_5 to E_3 equals the distance from E_3 to E_1—the second reduction in employment for a given acceleration in the rate of inflation $(E_5 - E_3 = E_3 - E_1)$ will be reduced. Thus the distance from

4. This view is developed in Milton Friedman, "The Role of Monetary Policy," *The American Economic Review* 58 (March 1968): 1–17, and Edward Phelps, "Money-Wage Dynamics and Labor-Market Equilibrium." *Journal of Political Economy* 76 (July-August 1968): II, 678–711.

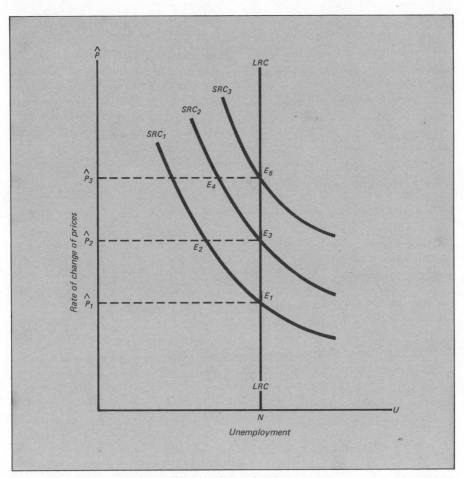

Figure 16.5 The accelerationist view of the Phillips curve

E_4 to E_5 will be less than the distance from E_2 to E_3. This behavior explains the term "accelerationist theory," since a greater increase in the rate of inflation is required for a given reduction in the level of unemployment, producing a required acceleration in the rate of inflation necessary to keep unemployment at a given level N in Figure 16.5. If prices are rising steadily over a long period of time, wage increases will stop lagging behind price increases as labor comes to fully anticipate the price increases and builds escalator clauses into contracts. To the extent that the discrepancies between expected and actual wages are reduced, the reduction in real wage which was caused by the rise in prices no longer occurs. Thus the reduction in real wages, which is the means by which the unemployment rate is reduced as production expands, no longer takes place. The trade-off between unemployment and inflation disappears in the long run. Unemployment will remain at the natural rate, N, as laborers learn to fully anticipate the reduction in real wages implied by inflation increases and to demand increases in money wages to maintain constant purchasing power at higher prices.

The "natural" rate of unemployment (line LRC in Figure 16.5) deserves more attention. When unemployment equals N it is claimed that there is no way that expansionary fiscal or monetary policy will be able to sustain a decrease in unemployment by increasing prices. Labor will ask for and get an increase in money wages to cover the increase in the price level. Point N is that rate of unemployment which corresponds to the real-wage rate which equates the supply and demand for labor. Below N excess demand pushes up the real-wage rate; above N excess supply reduces the real-wage rate. Professor Friedman maintains that the level of N is determined by the structural characteristics of the labor market itself—such as various kinds of skilled and unskilled workers, the cost of mobility, and seasonal and statistical variations.[5]

Friedman has argued that in recent years the level of natural unemployment for our economy has increased, pointing to the fact that automation and technological advances have reduced the demand for human labor. This factor, combined with the entry of large numbers of young people and previously unemployed women into the job market, has resulted in a large number of workers which the economy cannot absorb, even when the economy is at "full employment." The choices are therefore either to accept the fact of a "normal" unemployment rate over the long run in excess of 4 percent or to provide training programs and effect efforts to increase job mobility by improving the flow of information about job vacancies and available labor, as has been done in the Scandinavian countries. The result hopefully would be to shift the vertical line N farther to the left.

A Modified Phillips Curve

While Friedman's analysis is convincing, the fact remains that a substantial body of empirical evidence exists showing that something like the traditional Phillips curve obtains over long periods of time in industrialized countries. A theory of the Phillips curve has emerged recently which suggests a compromise between the traditional view and the accelerationist view. Figure 16.6 shows this modified curve, consisting of a positively sloped lower portion suggesting a trade-off between unemployment and inflation at relatively high levels of unemployment and a vertical line suggesting no trade-off at low levels of unemployment. This view was put forward by Professor James E. Tobin in 1972.[6] While it may appear as though Tobin is simply amalgamating the views of Phillips and Friedman, his theory is far more complex.

Tobin's model suggests that a Phillips trade-off exists within certain limits, but it becomes increasingly difficult to maintain the trade-off at low levels of unemployment. Tobin starts with the Keynesian view that there is

5. Ibid.
6. James Tobin, "Inflation and Unemployment," *American Economic Review* 62 (March 1972): 1–18.

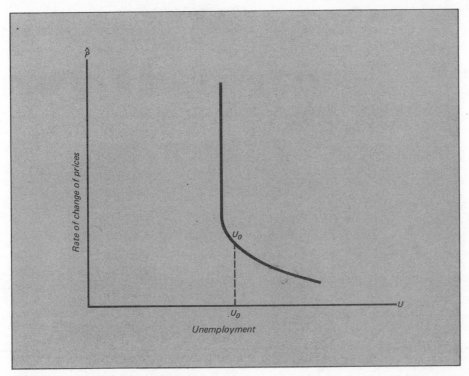

Figure 16.6 The modified Phillips curve

an asymmetry between the ability of the labor market to adjust to excess supply conditions and its ability to adjust to excess demand. In excess supply situations, as shown by U_0 in Figure 16.6, money wages are sticky downward, not because of money illusion, but because laborers resist a decline in their *relative* wages. That is, if wages were to fall, the process would have to begin somewhere, and no group of laborers wants to suffer the reduction in wages relative to their peers' wages that would arise if the process began with them. A general increase in prices due to an increase in aggregate demand remains as the only neutral, universal method to simultaneously reduce all real wages (with no change in relative wages) and thereby to reduce the excess supply condition in the labor market with a reduction in involuntary unemployment. In short, whatever unemployment can be removed by an increase in aggregate demand is viewed as involuntary. Of course the problems of sticky money wages does not arise in situations of excess demand for labor. Money wages move freely upward since workers welcome an increase in relative wages.

Professor Tobin further develops Keynes' asymmetry argument with regard to changes in money wages in situations of excess demand and excess supply. He suggests that a floor exists on wage changes in excess supply situations that is independent of the excess supply. The wage change is never negative, for example. In the range of relatively high unemployment, where many sectors of the labor market are in contact with the wage-change floor, increases in aggregate demand and resultant inflation will lower real wages to a point below the level possible with the wage-change floor and static prices, or with prices rising slower than or equal to money-wage rises. As overall demand and inflation increase, the frequency with which such wage-floor markets appear is diminished. When all sectors of the labor market are above the wage floor, the adjustment of money wages to price changes postulated by Friedman resumes, and the Phillips curve becomes vertical at what Tobin calls a "critically low rate of unemployment."

In effect, Tobin's analysis suggests that part of the Phillips curve is vertical whereas the rest is shaped like a "normal" Phillips curve. At high levels of unemployment, accelerating inflation will reduce involuntary unemployment. As unemployment falls, however, the trade-off disappears and changes in the rate of inflation become an ineffective means of affecting the level of unemployment. Tobin's discontinuous Phillips curve has the advantage that it does not imply the troublesome hypothesis that unemployment rates slightly above the natural, or critical, rate of unemployment will trigger an ever-accelerating deflation. Friedman's vertical Phillips curve does carry this implication.

Cast in terms of the Friedman model, the Tobin theory suggests a discontinuity in the manner in which labor adjusts its expectations regarding inflation. Changes in the rate of inflation at relatively low levels of existing unemployment can "fool" labor into accepting lower real wages for a time while similar changes at higher levels of inflation and lower levels of unemployment cannot. The discontinuity of the Phillips curve implied by Tobin's theory is perhaps its most troublesome aspect, violating as it does the dictum of the famous classical British economist Alfred Marshall that "nature seldom moves in jumps."

Under another possible interpretation, a discontinuous Phillips curve may do no more than describe the fact that when unemployment is high some workers are willing to accept employment at a cut in real wages. This notion may apply particularly to laborers with low productivity who are allegedly "protected" by minimum-wage legislation. If the minimum wage, set in dollars per hour, exceeds the value of the marginal product of some portion of the labor force, a higher rate of inflation may lower the real value of the minimum wage by enough to cause the value of the marginal product of many unskilled laborers to equal or exceed the minimum wage. As a result, hiring of these laborers is increased and unemployment falls. The effect lasts until the minimum wage is increased again to a level which exceeds the value of the marginal product of unskilled labor.

Considerable empirical research is necessary to establish which theory provides the best explanation of economic behavior. Economists have reached a consensus on several major issues, however. At a low level of unemployment, say 4 percent, most economists agree that expansionary monetary and fiscal policies cause the Phillips curve to "explode," that is, it becomes a vertical line and the trade-off between unemployment and inflation disappears. It is impossible to reduce unemployment below this level because there are more job vacancies than there are qualified applicants. Job seekers have the wrong skills or the jobs are in the wrong state or discrimination is strong, particularly against women and minorities.

In the past several years important structural changes have occurred in the labor market; a good example is the market for teenage labor. Teenagers relative to the entire labor force increased from 4.6 percent in 1962 to 6.3 percent in 1972. Their labor-force-participation rate increased from 47 percent to 52 percent in the same ten-year period. High costs of job information because of inexperience, institutional and legal constraints, and a lack of mobility keep teenage unemployment rates above those of other labor-force age groups. Even if he were to find employment in another town, a teenager might be unable to move. It is regrettably true that lower wages paid in this market would doubtless raise the availability of jobs. In 1973 the administration submitted a proposal to Congress which urged that lower minimum wages be accepted for teenage employment. Framers of the bill felt that the minimum-wage laws prevented employers from hiring teenagers for jobs which had a marginal productivity rate less than the minimum-wage rate. Similar programs for improving the structure of the labor markets for women and minorities have also been proposed.[7]

Price Expectations

Economists have recently begun to examine assumptions about price expectations and wage rates which form the basis of the Phillips curve analysis. Recall that both the Keynesian and accelerationist models focus on price expectations. In the Keynesian model, workers accept an increase in money wages when the general price level rises. In the acceleration model proposed by Friedman, workers accept an increase in money wages when the general price increases in the long run prevent the trade-off associated with the Phillips curve. Both models imply that expectations of the rate of change of prices are stable. Recent evidence shows that this might not be an accurate characterization of price expectations. In previous chapters we noted that consumer behavior can be explained by a weighted average of past levels of income; this same technique can be applied to workers' expectations about changes in the price level.[8] This view suggests that workers adjust their expectations of future changes in the price level to a weighted average of changes in the past. However, the weight attached to past observations constantly changes. Accordingly, it becomes very difficult for

7. See Robert E. Hall, "Prospects for Shifting the Phillips Curve through Manpower Policy," *Brookings Papers on Economic Activity*, vol. 3 (Washington, D.C.: Brookings Institute, 1971), p. 717.

8. Expected changes in the price level at time t can be shown by the following formula:

$$P_t = BP_{t-1} + B(1-B)P_{t-2} + B(1-B)^2 P_{t-3} + \ldots + B(1-B)^n P_{t-n}$$

where P_t is the rate of inflation at t, and B is the weight assigned to observations in the past.

Commentary: Structural Unemployment and the Expandable Labor Force

One of the aspects of persistent structural unemployment in this country is the growth of what is known as the secondary labor force. The secondary labor force consists of people who are not trained for the kinds of jobs which our highly technical economy generates in time of economic expansion, but who nevertheless seek to enter the labor force because of overall changes in the economy. People who do not look for work in normal times but begin to seek jobs when they think jobs will be easier to come by are also called the "hidden unemployed," a labor reserve not counted as unemployed until they actually try to enter the work force.

Statistical studies of labor force changes have detected "a clear tendency for the labor force to expand as the economy strengthens," due to the entrance of these workers. For example, an upturn in the economy will cause an increase in the number of women, teenagers, and old people seeking jobs because they feel that in a time of expansion opportunities are generally better for finding something, despite the fact that they do not possess the skills which the expanding economy requires. The hidden unemployed increase the level of measured unemployment in the economy, making it difficult to reduce unemployment without incurring increases in the level of inflation.

Economist Richard Perlman[1] has pointed out that the inflationary impact of the entrance of the hidden unemployed into the labor force is due to the fact that the vacancies which are created during an expansion of the economy can be filled only by individuals who, by and large, are already employed. With more vacancies than people qualified to fill them wage rates for skilled workers increase rapidly, accelerating existing inflationary trends. Moreover, the increase in unskilled workers retards efforts to reduce aggregate unemployment as the economy expands. Consequently, in order to reduce unemployment a greater increase in aggregate demand is necessary in this situation than would be needed if the labor force did not expand with rising employment. If demand increases to the extent that the hidden unemployed are able to find jobs, further inflationary trends are set in motion. The overall increase in demand produces further pressure on those labor market sectors in which the supply is already far short of the demand. Perlman explains the inflationary aspect of this process by reference to the fact that the wage-rise excess demand for labor relationship is nonlinear, a relationship originally identified by economist Richard Lipsey.[2] This means that the upward pressure on wages for labor in short supply increases at a very rapid rate.

Further, the greater the amount of structural unemployment in the economy, the stronger the inflationary trend. Professor Perlman explains the inflationary aspect of structural unemployment by reference to Lipsey's excess-demand inflation model, in which the labor force is broken down into sectors. Assume, for example, a two-sector labor force (skilled and unskilled, for simplicity), with unemployment rates of 2 percent and 8 percent respec-

1. Richard Perlman, *Labor Theory* (New York: Wiley, 1969), pp. 215–229.
2. Richard G. Lipsey, "The Relationship Between Unemployment and the Rate of Change of Money Wages in the United Kingdom, 1862–1957: A Further Analysis," *Economica* 27 (February 1960): 12–23.

tively. If policymakers decide to try to reduce the overall unemployment level to 4 percent, the rate would fall to 1½ percent in the first sector and 6½ percent in the second. The decrease in the first would be less than that in the second owing to the fact that the first sector is already at the frictional level, in this case, 2 percent. The frictional level represents the amount of unemployment necessarily present owing to the fact that workers switch from one job to another. Because a certain number of people will be out of work while seeking existing vacancies, it is impossible to reduce unemployment below this rate simply by creating more vacancies. Thus the result of increasing demand will be more job vacancies rather than less unemployment, which will increase wage pressure.

Now, if because of expansion of the economy the sector with 8 percent unemployment were to increase its labor supply by ½ percent, the same policy designed to produce 4 percent unemployment would result in a reduction to 7 percent in this sector and to 1½ percent in the other. Unless directed specifically to that sector with high unemployment, further increase in aggregate demand would simply increase pressure on wages in the first sector, where unemployment is below the frictional rate, and cause even greater inflation in the economy.

This situation poses a serious dilemma for policymakers seeking a tolerable level of unemployment which does not result in uncontrollable inflation. One study notes, moreover, that there is evidence that the elasticity of the secondary work force with respect to unemployment rates is increasing.[3] Thus, as more progress is made toward reducing the level of unemployment, it will become more difficult to make further progress since expansion of the economy will result in greater participation of the secondary work force in the labor markets.

These facts suggest a need for policies designed to increase the skills of the expandable secondary labor force so that when individuals seek jobs because of improved conditions in the economy, they will be able to obtain the kinds of jobs which the economy generates during an expansion. Educational programs designed to help married women obtain new skills or brush up on old ones in the event they decide to join the work force would be effective, as well as programs designed to increase the technical skills of young people. The majority of people under twenty years of age who decide to enter the work force do not have the skills needed to obtain the jobs which our economy creates. Efforts to increase the skills of the expandable labor force would do much to lessen the inflationary tendencies of this kind of structural unemployment.

3. Thomas Dernberg and Kenneth Strand, "Hidden Unemployment, 1953–1962," *American Economic Review* 56 (March 1966): 71–94.

policymakers to trade off inflation against unemployment, since workers are constantly readjusting their expectations and altering the weights derived from past experiences. When policymakers decide to increase inflation and thereby obtain a lower level of unemployment, they are actually attempting to get people to accept a lower real wage. New studies suggest that workers eventually learn to anticipate this kind of behavior.[9] Accordingly, labor will take this new knowledge into account and try to outsmart the policymakers in order to prevent a reduction in real wages. Thus workers' price expectations will be adjusted to reflect this new knowledge, and new policy moves will not be able to reduce unemployment, thus destroying the predictive value of the Phillips curve. This indicates that the variance of the rate of change of prices falls, resulting in a fall in the trade-off between unemployment and inflation. With no stability in expectations, it is nearly impossible to use the Phillips curve as a framework for analyzing policy choices.

Other studies have focused on the time horizon during which expectations about changes in the price level are made.[10] Most studies have assumed that expectations change over a long time horizon of one quarter to one year, whereas recent empirical evidence suggests that the time horizon may actually be two or three years. This discovery suggests that the Phillips curve may shift less rapidly than the accelerationist curve specified by Friedman and shown in Figure 16.4. These studies indicated that the short-run Phillips curve may therefore be worthwhile as a guide to policy.

The quality of the work done on the Phillips curve indicates that it has been a fruitful concept. The discussions have produced more light than heat, and some consensus can be identified. The naive suggestion of the Phillips curve that less unemployment can be traded for more inflation has been modified to suggest that the terms of trade between these goals may be so unstable as to lead policymakers to excessively inflationary actions. The manner in which the trade-off changes is widely agreed to depend upon the manner in which economic decision makers create expectations, particularly with regard to the rate of inflation. The introduction of the *variance* of the rate of inflation as a factor determining the stability of expectations is an important contribution to dynamic equilibrium analysis; an adequate theory of the manner in which expectations are formed would be equally useful.

It will be instructive to look again at the performance of the U.S. economy in the late 1960s and early 1970s to see how the actual figures recorded during that period compare with these concepts. But first we must return briefly to aggregate supply and demand.

9. R. E. Lucas, Jr., "Some International Evidence on Output-Inflation Tradeoffs," *The American Economic Review* 63 (June 1973): 326–334.

10. S. A. Ross and M. L. Wachter, "Wage Determination, Inflation and the Industrial Structure," *The American Economic Review* 63 (September 1973): 675–692.

Employment, Capacity, and the Cost-Push Theory of Inflation

A significant aspect of monetary and fiscal policies in recent years is their impact on the output of goods and services and consequently on the employment of capital and labor in producing those goods and services. Policymakers have focused particularly on the question of labor employment. This is a high priority goal because the immediate economic consequences of labor unemployment are highly visible, and they evoke emotional reactions. The economic loss when capital resources are unemployed may be just as great as the loss due to unemployed workers. But men and women, unlike machines, suffer hunger and feel the cold, and, as policymakers are aware, they also can vote to make the policymakers themselves unemployed.

An example of the relationship between monetary and fiscal policies and the general level of labor employment can be seen in the years 1967–1969. We noted in Chapter 14 that after the federal budget for fiscal 1969 shrank from an expansionary $25 billion deficit to a mildly contractionary $3 billion surplus, monetary policy was tightened in response to continually rising prices. When both monetary and fiscal policy are tightened, economic theory predicts that the demand for output will be reduced. Fewer goods will be sold, and therefore less labor will be required to produce the goods; unemployment will rise, perhaps with a slight lag. As Figure 16.7 shows, the predicted increase in unemployment was registered in 1970.

Although the pressure of excess demand was removed from the economy

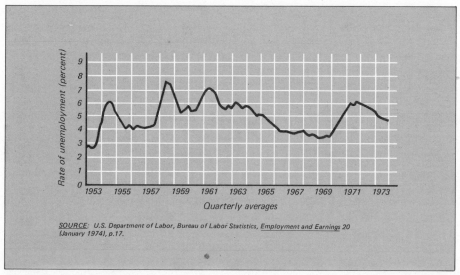

SOURCE: U.S. Department of Labor, Bureau of Labor Statistics, *Employment and Earnings 20* (January 1974), p.17.

Figure 16.7 Unemployment rate in the United States, 1953–1973 (percentages are annual rates of change for periods indicated)

by the federal government budget surplus in fiscal 1969 followed by a relatively tight monetary policy in 1969, prices continued to rise rapidly. Obviously, something other than demand increases was pushing prices up. Looking at the supply side of the markets and considering the likelihood of built-in inflationary expectations by 1969, we can explain the continued price rise by the cost-push phenomenon discussed in Chapter 10. The study of this inflationary pressure on the supply side also sheds some light on the behavior of real output and employment in the 1969–1970 period.

Figure 16.8 shows aggregate demand and aggregate supply in the years 1967 to 1969. Aggregate supply is shown to be increasing with prices, P, but the increase occurs at a diminishing rate per price increase as the level of the employment output, or capacity, is approached at Y_f. (The relationship of actual output to the capacity, or potential output, of the U.S. economy from 1954 to 1972 is illustrated in Figure 1.1.) The aggregate demand curve reflects the fact that lower prices produce a positive real balance effect—the real value of peoples' assets rise—so people demand more goods. There is no relative price effect, or substitution effect, because the aggregate demand curve is a conglomerate of all goods; the prices of all goods fall at the same time.

In fiscal 1968, the $25 billion federal government deficit and rapid monetary expansion produced a rightward shift of aggregate demand at each price level. Since the economy was close to capacity, prices rose rapidly along with output and employment (see Figure 16.7). Where the rate of inflation increases, workers include inflationary expectations in their wage demands; for the same quantity of work a higher price is demanded to enable workers to afford the increasing cost of living. Suppliers of raw materials, expecting price increases, also raise their prices. The result is a higher price for the same output, because money costs of production have risen. Aggregate supply shifts up, causing less of an increase in real output and more of an increase in prices. This is cost-push inflation at work.

In fiscal 1969, monetary and fiscal policy reduced aggregate demand nearly back to the 1967 level. But the expectation of inflation, which had been accelerating since 1966, produced a repetition of the cost-push phenomena on the supply side, manifested in yet another upward shift in the aggregate supply schedule. This brought on a period of even more rapid inflation and falling real output and hence a period of decreasing employment that continued through 1970.

It should be pointed out here that the initial cause of an inflationary sequence is inevitably excess demand pressure. Spending expands to a level that normal capacity to produce cannot satisfy at constant prices. Excess demand is therefore rationed by an increase in prices, resulting in a devaluation of peoples' money-denominated assets. If this demand-pull inflation continues, an expectation of rising prices is incorporated into the prices of suppliers of labor and raw materials, and cost-push inflation gets underway. In a prolonged period of inflation, a quick reduction of demand pressure will

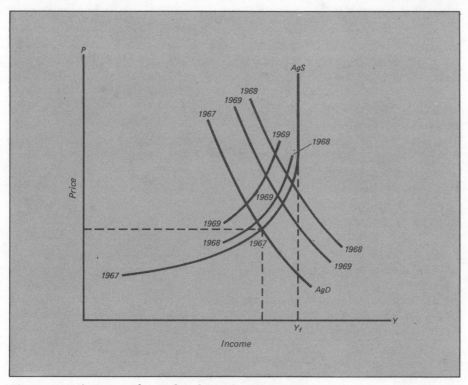

Figure 16.8 Aggregate demand and supply, 1967–1969

not lower prices; peoples' expectations, being formed largely from past experience, change slowly. Such a lagged adjustment of expectations about inflation suggests an explanation of the relationship, expressed in the Phillips curve, between the rate of unemployment and the rate of change of prices.

The Phillips curve suggests that as the rate of inflation is increased, the percent of the labor force unemployed is reduced. We can look at this relationship in the context of the period beginning with the $25 billion government deficit in July 1967. In mid-1967, inflation had leveled off, and unemployment stood at just below 4 percent. Over the 1968 fiscal year, the relationship suggested by the Phillips curve held up; the rate of unemployment fell to about 3.7 percent (see Figure 16.7). Fiscal 1969 saw inflation increase with little change in the unemployment rate; the Phillips curve was "crossed" during this period.

The value of the Phillips curve as a predictive tool deteriorates in the later phases of this inflationary period. The 1970 fiscal year saw a sharp increase in unemployment but no inflation abatement. This appears to be the result of the tight fiscal policy begun in mid-1968, followed by tight mone-

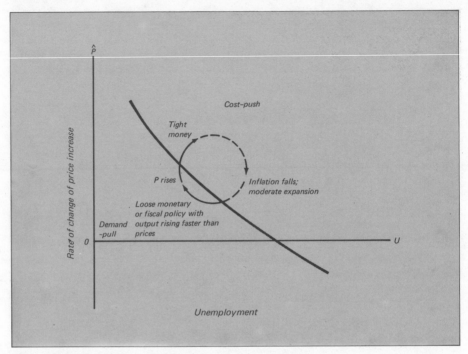

Figure 16.9 The Phillips curve orbit

tary policy through 1969. (The effects of tight fiscal and monetary policy will actually be felt with some variable lag after they are applied: it requires time for the policies to take effect.) The steady level of demand for output, together with a backward shift of aggregate supply at each level of money prices illustrated in Figure 16.8, produced a reduction in output and hence an increase in unemployment. By the end of fiscal 1971, there had appeared some abatement of inflation and unemployment, a move contrary to the Phillips curve.

The case we have examined suggests an "orbit" about the Phillips curve of the observed values of inflation and unemployment. This is shown in Figure 16.9. It has already been noted in some research that the level of the Phillips curve varies from economy to economy and from time to time. We have suggested that in the initial, or demand-pull, phase of an inflationary period, the negative relationship between the rate of inflation and the rate of unemployment suggested by the Phillips curve is maintained. Unemployment falls and prices rise only slightly as loose monetary or fiscal policy expands demand. If demand growth is excessive, however, price increases exceed the fall in unemployment, and the Phillips curve is crossed. A tightening of monetary or fiscal policy cuts aggregate demand, and although the inflation rate will no longer accelerate, expectations maintain inflation at the old rate through the cost-push phenomenon. Eventually control of excess demand and the fact of increasing supply bring prices down. A cautious return to an expansionary monetary and fiscal policy will then, barring other disturbances, increase output and lead to a fall in unemployment.

Questions and Exercises

1. The Phillips curve shown in Figure 16.1 reflects inflation and unemployment in England over the period 1861 to 1958. Redraw this curve based on post-World War II data for the United States. Why is this curve higher (farther from the origin)?
2. How do you explain the inverse relationship between unemployment and inflation? Is Phillips' hypothesis disproven by the recession on 1969–1970, when unemployment rose with no appreciable decline in the rate of inflation?
3. How is the Phillips explanation for the shape of the curve related to the Keynesian money illusion? How has the escalator clause that an increasing number of labor unions have had inserted in contracts detracted from the validity of the money illusion?
4. What are the policy implications of the Phillips curve? To what degree is the acceptability of the various combinations a political rather than a purely economic question?
5. What are the conceptual difficulties that economists have found with the Phillips curve? Are there any problems in assigning a cost to inflation?
6. How does Milton Friedman apply his concept of the natural unemployment rate to the experience of recent years? Does this disprove the existence of the Phillips curve?
7. Why does the Phillips curve become vertical at very low levels of unemployment, according to most economists? Why is it impossible to reduce unemployment below a certain level, say about 3 or 4 percent?
8. There have been several recent structural changes in the labor market such as automation and a sharp rise in the percentage of teenagers in the labor force. What are Milton Friedman's conclusions about such changes? Are there any ameliorative measures that you could suggest?
9. Was the inflation since 1966 basically of the cost-push variety? What role was played by monetary and fiscal policy in curbing this inflation? To what reasons do you attribute their lack of success?
10. Do you agree with the statement that the Phillips curve might be applicable to a demand-pull type of inflation but that in the latter stages of any inflation, it loses its applicability? Why or why not?

to the high level reached by such investment in 1973, according to a Conference Board report yesterday.

The report showed that in the first quarter of this year, foreign concerns announced plans for more than $340-million of investment in chemical, machinery, textile and other production facilities in all major regions of this country.

The first quarter report in part by David Bauer, international economist with the non-profit research organization. The study is believed to be the first to chart details of foreign manufacturing investment in this country according to industry, state, type of investment and country of origin.

Board Sets Plans

The Conference Board plans to continue the compilation on a quarterly basis. Comparable data on the lines of this study are not available for the first quarter last year.

An initial report in February this year, covering the first ten months of 1973, recorded WASHINGTON, April 26—The United States's balance of trade slipped into a deficit position in March for the first time in nine months, the Census Bureau reported today.

The major contributing factor the sharp of import

Census Bureau figures showed that the March deficit amounted to $171.3-million, using the regular Customs Bureau valuation of imports and excluding exports under military assistance programs.

If imports are valued to include insurance and freight, as well as their basic cost, the deficit was $702.7-million.

The value of imports, under the regular customs valuation system, was $7.85-billion, and exports were valued at $7.67-billion.

The March deficit surpluses of $21. February and $643. January to bring the which export earning payments for imports to months for the year under the regular valuation system. Including insurance and freight, there was a $834.3-million deficit for the quarter.

The regular monthly Census Bureau report on the trade figures cautioned, as always, that changes in the figures in a single month did not necessarily indicate a trend. The bureau prefers to look at the figures over four-month periods.

By JUAN de ONIS
Special to The New York Times

BEIRUT, May 30—The Government of Kuwait, after nationalizing 60 per cent of the foreign-owned Kuwait Oil Company, has come on the market with 1.25 million barrels a day of crude oil for direct sale to foreign customers.

The offering non-customers, supplied by The Oil Company because does not identify products that contribute to the changes in the balance.

However, a separate on trade from the Co Department's Bureau nomic Analysis said sharp jump in oil prices" accounted for cent of the rise in th value of imports in t three months of this ye

The bureau's analysis that the dollar value troleum imports increa 67 per cent in the qua face of a 20 per he physical vol ports.

World trade showed an sive growth of 36 per of 12 per cent er higher ial h orted today. ent ri de "real vo above the average growth in past years, port said. The boom the general prosperit strong economic growth industrial countries in 197

Total trade, measured dollar value of wor crossed the for reach for 1973 as a the fourth quarter. had reached an annual of $580-billion. The less-developed countries benefited about

has been 93 per cent of the posted price, which work out to about $10.74 a barrel.

The Kuwaiti offering, which is for deliveries from production during the second half of this year, indicates that Kuwait has broken off negotiations with the foreign partners in the Kuwait Oil Company—Gulf Oil the companies were reported to have offered $9.50 for the Government's share of production, but Kuwait had insisted on 93 per cent of the posted price.

TAIPEI, Taiwan — After more than a decade of spectacular economic growth, Taiwan is threatened with the loss of its all-important competitive advantage, which had been based on its cheap labor and ability to manufacture inexpensively for export.

According to in the 47-billion, or almost gross national billion. Co with import

Taiwan's exports, for example, last year totaled

thought that Mr Nixon's desire to chalk up another achievement on the foreign policy scoreboard, plus America's need for more exports, would give the Soviet Union a bargain. And many Americans believed—and still believe—that inside every Russian there is a rational western wanting to get out, and that trade can relea

It all started in March, 1972, when President Nixon visited Moscow, and a commission was set up to produce a commission was set up to promote trade between the superpowers. In July the famous grain deal was made; massive shipments began two months later, financed by the Commodity Credit Corporation on terms that were distinctly satisfactory for Russia. Then, in October, 1972, a comprehensive trade agreement was signed. This provided the framework for continued trade of all kinds and specified that each nation would accord most-favoured-nation (MFN) treatment to the other. In the same month, Mr Nixon made an official judgment that it was in America's national interest to trade with Russia; this had to be done to let the American Export-Import bank finance the down Pels.

If the oil is taken by customers in Japan and Western Europe—the traditional Kuwaiti customers—it will tend to stabilize prices at pres levels

ersian Gulf producers, is opposed to Saudi Arabia's declared intention of reducing oil prices from the region.

The Kuwaiti nation, for which the tw eign companies were than those factories in the United States must pay — plus rising labor costs have also affected South Korea, Hong Kong and Singapore, making it a major regional problem.

Economies Geared to Exports

The loss to Taiw these of national com particularly seri because their economies are largely geared to exports.

credits (whi to total mo in the fre

Accounting Schweiker

The recommendation was among the major provisions affecting sugar growers to the full consideration.

domestic and omputations, the committee decided on a minimum allocation of 6.69 million tons for the five categories of domestic suppliers. The re gas that the emaining 5.31 million tons would be earmarked for 32 foreign producers.

To allow for the possibility of increasing domestic production, the subcommittee agreed recommend an 8-million maximum quota for domestic areas. Subcommittee urces said the setting of a ceiling was in accordance with stipulation of the General prohibiting open-ended quotas.

The Russian accuse the sugar quotas would be follows: beet area, a 3.5 ion-ton minimum and 4-million-ton maximum; mainland 1.75 million and 2 million Texas, 125,000; and 200, Hawaii, 1.11 million and million, and Puerto Rico 0,000 and 300,000.

The subcommittee also ed to recommend ending half-cent excise tax on su June 30, 1975 while fix annual $9,400 per-farm subsidy payments.

American executive, who asked that his name not be used. "This used to be a great place to build your factory, get good, dependable, cheap labor, and turn out your product. Now it costs too much and we have to think about investing

'Real' Volume Was Up 12% in '73, I.M.F. Reports—U.S. Bill in Doubt

All consumer prices			Food prices			Wages		
Index 1970 =100	% change on previous 3 mths	% change on one year	Index 1970 =100	% change on previous 3 mths	% change on one year	Index 1970 =100	% change on previous 3 mths	% change on one year
								27.50
								105.00
								10.00
Germany								
124	+2½	+7½	121	+2½	+5½	139*	+½	+10
France								
127	+3	+10	133	+2½	+11½	na		na

The Open Economy: Problems of External Balance

17

An economic model is necessarily an oversimplification of the real world, based on assumptions that are incorrect if taken to represent literal fact. In our macroeconomic model we have so far relied on one very important assumption that we will now abandon, that of a closed economy. Although approximations of autarchic economies—those which rely entirely on internal production of goods and services for their own consumption—have existed in the past (Stalinist Russia in the 1920s and 1930s came close) and although during the worst of the "oil crisis" in 1974 the U.S. government directed the nation to rely totally on its own oil production by 1980, few economists consider such economic isolation a realistic or desirable goal. In the real world, national economies are to a greater or lesser extent interdependent. And in the Western industrial world the open economy is a reality.

An open economy both trades and carries on financial transactions with the outside world. Buyers import foreign goods, while domestic manufacturers export their products to foreign countries.[1] On the financial side, domestic borrowers sell securities (bonds) to foreigners, while domestic lenders buy foreign securities. From 1944 to August 15, 1971 (when the United States suspended the convertibility of the dollar into gold), this foreign intercourse (in both goods and securities) was carried on at generally fixed rates of exchange, that is, fixed ratios between the domestic currency and any foreign one. For most of this chapter we will assume that exchange rates remain fixed. Later this assumption will be dropped, and we will examine the theoretical and practical consequences of changes in the fixed rates and the alternative of freely floating exchange rates.

Taking the U.S. economy as an example of an open economy, we can assume initially that its foreign trade is carried out in dollars, an internationally accepted and convertible currency.[2] Importers and exporters, borrowers and lenders deal with foreigners (individuals, firms, banks, or governments) in dollars. But the totals of these incoming and outgoing dollar transactions do not necessarily balance. The U.S. balance of payments is equal to the sum of total trade and total capital transactions. Total trade consists of exports (which bring in dollars) and imports (which represent a leakage of dollars). Likewise, U.S. international borrowing (the sale of bonds to foreigners) brings in dollars, while U.S. international lending (the purchase of foreign securities) constitutes a dollar leakage on the capital market. If more dollars come in than go out, the United States is said to have a balance of payments surplus. If the opposite is true, a balance of payments deficit prevails. It should be remembered that each country's surplus is some other country's deficit. And, for reasons we will discuss more fully later, no surplus or deficit can continue on a large scale indefinitely without far-reaching consequences for the domestic economy.

Abandoning our assumption of a closed economy obliges us to modify our macroeconomic model, the core of which is the IS/LM analysis, in which simultaneous equilibrium in the commodities and money markets is represented in terms of the interest rate, i, and national income, Y.[3] We can see the effects of the foreign trade sector on the total economy by extending this framework; thus the conditions of balance of payments equilibrium can be plotted on the same axes, that is, within the same i-Y space.

The Import Function

First, however, we must understand how an economy's imports might vary with its level of income. There are certain goods that an economy is virtually forced to import, especially those it cannot produce itself, but other goods

1. In this discussion we include under "goods" such international services as shipping and insurance.

2. In fact, U.S. trade is carried out either in dollars or foreign currencies with exact, if temporary, dollar equivalents.

3. In the discussion of the open economy with fixed exchange rates, the price level is taken to be fixed.

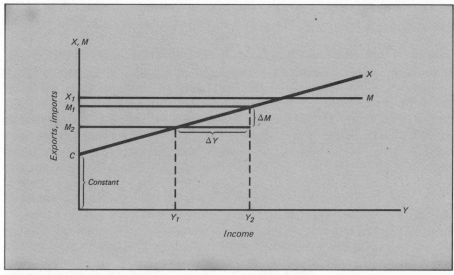

Figure 17.1 The import function

are imported in increasing amounts as the economy's level of income increases and it becomes more prosperous. Therefore, the **import function** consists of a constant term plus the nation's **marginal propensity to import** (MPI), which varies positively as level of income varies. This is shown in Figure 17.1.

The import function is written as

$$M = e + gY \tag{17.1}$$

where M denotes imports; e represents the constant term, or the portion of imports not related to income; and g represents the marginal propensity to import, or

$$g = MPI = \frac{\Delta M}{\Delta Y} \tag{17.2}$$

In Figure 17.1, as the level of income rises from Y_1 to Y_2, imports rise from M_1 to M_2.

As we can see from Figure 17.1, the country's imports gradually increase as its level of income increases. The import function represented in Figure 17.1 is directly analogous to the savings or consumption function in that imports are determined by some constant plus a "marginal propensity to spend" (on imports) times income. The **average propensity to import** (API) is likewise analogous to that for the savings or consumption function, defining the ratio of imports to income, or

$$API = \frac{M}{Y} = \frac{e}{Y} + g \tag{17.3}$$

Of course not all countries have similar import functions; the API is generally taken as an index of the degree of dependence upon foreign trade or "openness" of an economy. The United States, which among industrial nations is relatively independent of foreign trade, had an API of 6.3 percent in 1972 as compared with 22.1 percent for the United Kingdom and 44.2 percent for the Netherlands. Interestingly enough, there is some evidence that MPI for the United States is higher than it is for many European countries. Therefore, from equations (17.2) and (17.3), it can be seen that while g, or MPI, may be particularly high for the United States, e, or the autonomous portion of imports not related to income (and essential where a resource is not produced domestically, such as petroleum for Japan), is relatively low for the United States.

Imports are thus seen to be endogenous to the model, systematically related to variables *within* the domestic economy such as the level of income once e is given. Exports, on the other hand, are not considered to be determined by conditions within the domestic economy. Instead, exports, which are really another country's imports, depend on the level of income enjoyed by foreign economies. If a foreign country prospers, it is more likely to increase its demand for U.S. goods, and the United States will be able to increase its own exports. Thus exports are considered *exogenous* to the model, just as government expenditure and investment were taken to be exogenous in the income determination model in Chapter 4.[4] In Figure 17.1, the export function, X, is therefore drawn in as a horizontal line at X_1. Regardless of domestic income this will not change. It may in fact shift upward or downward, and such shifts will be important, but the shift will not be directly related to changes in the level of domestic income. According to Figure 17.1, even after the economy's income level increases from Y_1 to Y_2 exports exceed imports (X_1 is greater than M_2), so the economy has a trade balance surplus.[5]

If exports are unrelated to the level of income, while imports increase as income increases, the balance of trade surplus, T, which equals the trade balance, or the difference between exports and imports ($T = X - M$), is inversely related to the level of income. For the open-economy model we must modify the IS schedule to take account of foreign trade leakages from (or injections to) aggregate demand, since the trade account may be positive or negative. Imports represent a leakage from domestic income, so they are analogous to savings and taxes. Exports are an injection of demand for the

4. In fact, exports depend to some extent upon the import function. If our national income rises, for example, we can see from the import function that this means we import more goods. More of our imports is equivalent to more foreign exports, and as foreign exports increase, foreign income rises, which increases our exports. However, these effects are generally slow to operate and difficult to trace.

5. Note that Figure 17.1 shows only the trade account. If the same country simultaneously lends (buys foreign securities) far more than it borrows abroad, it could still have a net balance of payments deficit because of the large deficit on the capital account. Through most of the 1960s the United States had just such a trade surplus and balance of payments deficit.

domestic economy, analogous to investment and government expenditures. Thus, we can define the conditions for the modified IS line in the open-economy model.

Starting with the simplest income-expenditure equilibrium condition, $I = S$, and adding a government sector in Chapter 5 gave

$$I + G = S + T$$

Now, adding a foreign sector, we have

$$I + G + X = S + T + M$$

or, in functional form,

$$I(i) + G + X = S(Y) + T(Y) + M(Y) \qquad (17.4)$$

Equation (17.4) states that along the IS line as modified for an open economy, values of i and Y must be such that the total of investment plus exports plus government expenditure is equal to the total of savings plus taxes plus imports. The modified IS line retains its negative slope since as Y rises, savings, taxes, and imports each rise, so i must fall in order to increase investment and maintain the equilibrium condition given by equation (17.4). In fact, the open-economy IS line is steeper than the closed-economy IS line, since as Y rises, imports represent an additional leakage out of expenditure which must be overcome to maintain equilibrium as represented by equation (17.4). As we noted in Chapter 5, the government expenditure multiplier falls as leakages rise; since imports represent an additional leakage out of expenditure on domestically produced goods, the multiplier falls once the economy is opened up.

Whereas imports and exports are unlikely to vary significantly with changes in the interest rate, borrowing from and lending to foreigners does vary considerably. Borrowing from foreigners (the sale of bonds to foreigners) will increase as domestic interest rates rise, since foreign loans will become relatively cheaper than before and foreigners will be more likely to want to lend at higher interest rates. Lending to foreigners (the purchase of bonds from foreigners) will tend to drop off as domestic interest rates rise, since few foreigners will want loans at the new, relatively higher interest rates and domestic lenders will prefer to lend more at home. Since borrowing brings in dollars, as domestic interest rates increase the capital account balance (borrowing minus lending) becomes more positive (or less negative).

Balance of Payments Equilibrium

The total balance of payments consists of the surplus (or deficit) on the trade account—net sales (or purchases) of goods and services to foreigners—plus the surplus (or deficit) on the capital account—net sales (or purchases) of securities to foreigners. The trade balance, as we have seen, is a negative function of income. The capital balance is a positive function of the interest rate. The total balance of payments, therefore, can be represented by

$$B = (X - M) + (b^f - l^f) \tag{17.5}$$

where B represents balance of payments, b^f represents borrowing from foreigners (sales of bonds to foreigners), and l^f represents lending to foreigners (purchase of bonds from foreigners). Since $X - M$ is the trade balance, which varies negatively with Y, and since $b^f - l^f$ is the capital balance, which varies positively with i, the conditions for balance of payments equilibrium in terms of the domestic economic variables affecting it can be written as

$$B = T(Y) + K(i) \tag{17.6}$$

where T represents trade balance (exports minus imports), which falls as Y rises, $\Delta T/\Delta Y < 0$, and K represents capital balance (net capital inflows), which rises with i, $\Delta K/\Delta i = 0$.

We now have the conditions of balance of payments equilibrium expressed in terms of i and Y, thus enabling us to represent the balance of payments schedule, BB, in the same i-Y space as the IS/LM model. The slope of the BB line will depend on the relative magnitudes of the two variables—trade balance, T, and capital balance, K—that constitute the balance of payments. These magnitudes depend in turn on the responsiveness of imports to changes in domestic income, and of borrowing and lending to changes in the domestic interest rate. Figure 17.2 shows the IS/LM model with two BB lines, each one representing different assumptions about the strength of the terms T and K. Since

$$B = T(Y) + K(i)$$

when the balance of payments is in equilibrium

$$B = 0$$

The BB line represents a map of i and Y values for which this equilibrium condition holds, where total sales of goods and securities to foreigners are equal to total purchases of goods and securities from foreigners. Therefore, along the BB line, the effects of changes in Y and i upon B must balance each other, or else changes in Y or i would lead to a net change in B. Therefore, along BB

$$0 = \Delta B = T_Y(\Delta Y) + K_i(\Delta i) \tag{17.7}$$

or, solving for $\Delta i/\Delta Y$;

$$\frac{\Delta i}{\Delta Y} = \frac{-T_Y}{K_i} = \text{slope of the BB line} \tag{17.8}$$

where T_Y is the negative impact of income on the trade balance, holding all else constant, and K_i is the positive impact of the interest rate on net capital inflows, holding all else constant. Since exports are not affected by income,

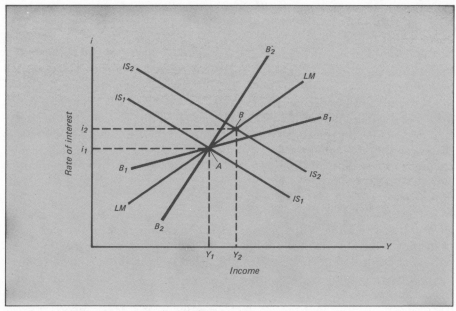

Figure 17.2 The IS/LM model with balance of payments

given $T = X - M$, T_Y is really the negative of the MPI. Since T_Y is negative and K_i is positive, the slope of the BB line is positive; it reflects the relative strengths of the marginal propensity to import and the responsiveness of net borrowing from foreigners to the domestic interest rate.

It should be pointed out that the BB line may be steeper or flatter than the LM line. If the marginal propensity to import is high, $T(Y)$ is relatively large, and the BB line is relatively steep, as indicated by the B_2 line in Figure 17.2. If the sale and purchase of securities to and from foreigners is highly sensitive to the domestic interest rate, $K(i)$ is relatively large, and the BB line is relatively flat, as indicated by line B_1. This is because if a small rise in i attracts a large capital inflow producing a balance of payments surplus, Y must rise considerably in order to raise imports and produce an overall zero net effect on the balance of payments from changes in i and Y. In either case there could be, but need not be, simultaneous equilibrium in the commodity, money, and balance of payments sectors. Such an equilibrium initially obtains in Figure 17.2 at income level Y_1 and interest rate i_1. But the slope of the BB line is important if there should be a shift away from such an equilibrium position.

Shifting the BB Line

In our previous discussion of the IS/LM diagram, we used the example of changes in government expenditure, G, as a policy tool when we wanted to shift the IS line, and changes in the money supply, M_S, when we wanted to shift the LM line. Now we will consider what effect changes in G and M_S have on the economy's balance of payments. The first observation we can make is that the results of changes in G are ambiguous. That is, the impact on the balance of payments will depend on the slope of the BB line relative to the LM line. This is because when G is increased, Y and i increase as well (assuming that the money supply is held constant). But a higher value for Y tends to increase imports, which has a deficit effect, whereas a higher value for i increases the net inflow of foreign capital, which has a surplus effect. Which effect is stronger depends on the slope of the BB line. Changes in the money supply, by contrast, have an unambiguous impact on the balance of payments. Regardless of the slope of the BB line, an increase in the money supply will raise Y and lower i. Both will produce a deficit in the balance of payments.

We can trace the impact of an increase in G in Figure 17.2. An increase in government spending will shift the IS schedule upward and to the right, from IS_1 to IS_2. Starting from point A, the new equilibrium IS/LM position will be at point B, representing Y_2 and i_2. That is, both the income level and the interest rate increase. If the BB line is steep, as is the case for line B_2, the impact on the trade balance is greater than on the capital balance. This is because a steep BB line is the result of a relatively large MPI, and an increase in income will cause a relatively large increase in imports. This results in a balance of payments deficit. In terms of Figure 17.2, therefore, if the IS line intersects the LM line at a point below the BB line, a balance of payments deficit prevails, because Y is too high or i too low for a balance of payments equilibrium. By the same reasoning, if the BB line is relatively flat, as is the case with line B_1, the intersection of LM and IS_2 is above the BB line and a balance of payments surplus prevails. This is because the impact of the IS line shift is greater on the capital balance than on the trade balance. More dollars flow in to take advantage of the relatively higher domestic interest rates than flow out due to increased imports.

Figure 17.3 shows the impact of an increase in the money supply on the balance of payments. As we saw in our IS/LM analysis, an increase in the money supply will shift the LM schedule down and to the right, from LM_1 to LM_2. The new intersection of the IS and LM schedules is at point C, which represents a higher income and lower level of interest rates than the initial position at point A. Both higher income and lower interest rates have deficit effects on the balance of payments, since imports will increase and capital will flow out to foreign economies. Regardless of the slope of the BB line, the economy will have a balance of payments deficit, since point C is below both B_1 and B_2. This leads us to an important practical policy conclusion: if a country has a balance of payments deficit, it can eliminate (or at least reduce) this deficit by cutting the money supply (pursuing a tight money policy at home). Of course, this will have the additional consequence of reducing the level of national income, and that may be considered unacceptable. For example, if point C represents a full-employment level of national income,

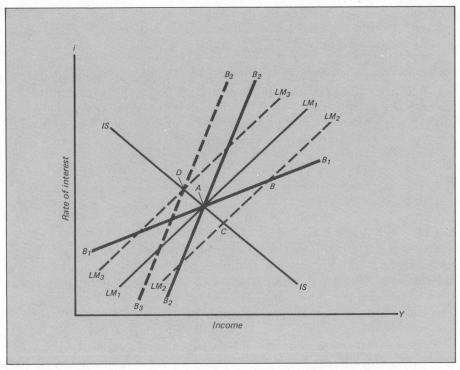

Figure 17.3 The impact of an increase in the money supply on the balance of payments

the country's political leaders may prefer to continue running a balance of payments deficit rather than cut the income level back to point A and suffer rising unemployment. We will return to this dilemma below.

Although the IS/LM model is now significantly modified in the direction of real-world approximation, we should keep in mind that the BB line assumes that all of the following are fixed: the domestic price level, foreign interest rates, exchange rates and expected changes in these rates, foreign incomes, and foreign price levels. As we shall see, some or all of these factors may change in ways that affect the shape and location of the BB line and enhance or frustrate the efforts of domestic policymakers to achieve full-employment equilibrium with a minimum of inflation and a satisfactory balance of payments situation.

Fixed Exchange Rates

Between 1944 and August 1971, the Western industrial countries all conducted their foreign currency and financial dealings in accordance with the so-called Bretton Woods system. The main characteristic of the Bretton

Woods system was that exchange rates between currencies were set, or pegged, by the governments at a fixed price in terms of the U.S. dollar, which in turn was pegged to gold at $35 per ounce. With all currencies pegged to the U.S. dollar, their prices in terms of each other were also fixed: hence the fixed exchange rate system. The central bank of each country was pledged to buy and sell foreign currency in order to keep the market exchange rate for its currency within 1 percent of these parity rates. If the central bank was unable to maintain a particular exchange rate indefinitely, it was forced to devalue or revalue its currency relative to the others and declare its intention to maintain the new rate. A devaluation means an increase in the domestic money price of foreign money, or a reduction in the foreign money price of domestic money. Its purpose is to help remove a balance of payments deficit by reducing purchases of foreign goods and increasing foreign purchases of domestic goods. An up-valuation, or revaluation as it is more frequently called, is simply the reverse of a devaluation.

On August 15, 1971, the United States announced it would abandon the gold standard. Subsequent international negotiations concerning a new international monetary system have been inconclusive.[6] Later in the chapter we will consider the implications of some of the more recent developments, especially freely floating exchange rates, but first it will be instructive to examine the system of fixed exchange rates more closely.

Exchange rates were fixed initially because they were thought to encourage trade by making prices for items involved in foreign trade more predictable and removing fears that holding large amounts of foreign currency might lead to losses if a currency's value dropped. If the value could not fluctuate more than 1 percent, holding foreign currency presented minimal risks unless the currency was officially devalued—an infrequent occurrence. In the absence of such agreements and practices, exchange rates would float up or down in response to market conditions.

The market conditions for foreign exchange reflect supply and demand for various foreign currencies. There is a private international market for foreign currency because in order to conduct foreign trade currencies must be bought and sold. A U.S. importer of German cars is most likely to pay for them in Germany in that country's legal tender, the deutsche mark. The importer buys marks in exchange for dollars through his bank at the prevailing exchange rate and pays for the goods in marks. German and U.S. banks are constantly buying and selling marks and dollars to expedite international deals by their customers, and through this dealing a market exchange rate emerges within the 1 percent range of the parity rate. If the rate were not pegged by central bank intervention, it would fluctuate entirely according to supply and demand conditions prevailing in the private market. If there were a large net demand for marks in excess of dollars over an ex-

6. For a discussion of conditions leading up to and following U.S. abandonment of the gold standard, see John H. Makin, "Capital Flows and Exchange-Rate Flexibility in the Post Bretton Woods Era," Princeton University, *Essays in International Finance*, no. 103 (February 1974).

tended period, eventually the German central bank (which holds reserves of marks, gold, dollars, and other foreign currencies) would collect too many dollars, since it would be selling marks at an artificially low price.

The resulting rapid accumulation of dollars (and other foreign exchange) at the German central bank, or, equivalently, a chronic German balance of payments surplus mirrored by a chronic U.S. balance of payments deficit, would tend to generate expectations that either the dollar would be devalued or the deutsche mark would be revalued. The expected appreciation of deutsche marks in terms of dollars (depreciation of dollars in terms of deutsche marks) would lower the international demand for dollars and increase the demand for deutsche marks. As a result, the U.S. deficit would increase further while the German surplus increased further, increasing the likelihood either of a dollar devaluation or a deutsche mark revaluation.

Maintaining a fixed exchange rate under such circumstances requires a very high level of central bank intervention in the foreign exchange market. We have said that under the Bretton Woods system central banks were committed to keeping their currencies within a narrow range of parity exchange rates. To keep the exchange rate from fluctuating far from parity, the central bank intervenes in the private exchange markets and buys and sells its own foreign currencies. Since a deficit country confronts excess demand for foreign exchange, the central bank must sell (and thereby diminish) part of its own reserves of foreign currencies. With the central bank of a deficit country losing reserves of foreign exchange (while the central bank of a surplus country gains reserves of foreign exchange) the deficit country is in a far weaker position to resist an exchange rate change in view of the fact that it is running short of reserves rather than accumulating them. Therefore, the likelihood is higher that chronic balance of payments disequilibria will be resolved by devaluations than by revaluations.

Since devaluations raise the prices of imported goods and their substitutes, they tend to be inflationary. Therefore, the devaluation-bias of a fixed exchange rate system imparts an inflationary-bias to the economies of the world, particularly when the incidence of chronic balance of payments disequilibria is as high as it has been since the late 1960s. Some economists have claimed that devaluation-bias is responsible in some part for the high rate of inflation that grew up in many countries during 1973 and 1974.[7]

Eventually, if the central bank of the deficit country is passive, the deficit will be self-correcting due to higher domestic interest rates and a lower level of income induced by the monetary contraction implicit in a deficit. This is the equivalent of shifting the LM schedule to the left in Figure 17.3. Thus, a continuous loss of reserves by the central bank mirrors a reduction in the domestic money supply and is ultimately deflationary. Another way of

7. R. A. Mundell and A. B. Laffer have argued that in addition to being inflationary, exchange rate changes are of little real help in dealing with balance of payments disequilibria. For a summary of the Mundell-Laffer argument, see Jude Wanniski, "The Case for Fixed Exchange Rates," *Wall Street Journal*, June 14, 1974.

looking at this is to say that increased purchases of foreign goods and securities may lead to increased leakages from the stock of money balances within the home country. Therefore, a balance of payments deficit is a difficult problem for any country and its monetary authorities, particularly when the goals for income levels or interest rates are inconsistent with the levels of these variables implied by a falling money supply in the face of a chronic balance of payments deficit. The situation faced by a chronic surplus country may be less troublesome in the short run. In such a case, the central bank gains reserves (of foreign exchange or gold) when the supply of foreign exchange exceeds its own residents' demand for foreign exchange. This leads to an increase in the domestic money supply, raises income, and lowers interest rates (and may be inflationary if the surplus country is close to full employment).

Sterilization

Thus far we have discussed only the automatic responses of the money supply to balance of payments disequilibrium. But monetary authorities usually do not remain passive in the face of a balance of payments disequilibrium that threatens the economy's prosperity or the attainment of its primary goals. Suppose, for example, that country 1 has achieved a full-employment level of national income, along with stable prices and equilibrium in its balance of payments. If another country, country 2, with which country 1 has a high level of trade and financial dealings, decides to pursue a tight money policy, this will have an impact on country 1. In country 2 interest rates will rise, while incomes will drop. Capital will flow from country 1 to country 2, and residents of country 2 (with lower income) will now import less from country 1. This is reflected in Figure 17.3 by a shift from B_2 to B_3 for country 1; it will cause a deficit at point A for country 1, which formerly enjoyed a balance of payments equilibrium. The monetary authorities there may remain passive, within the rules of the international agreements that fix the exchange rate. This would mean allowing the domestic money supply to fall, thereby increasing domestic interest rates and lowering income below the full-employment level. Such a passive policy— the equivalent of allowing the LM schedule to shift from LM_1 to LM_3 in Figure 17.3—would eliminate the deficit, but at the cost of abandoning another primary goal, full employment (which we take to occur at point A).

If the monetary authority considers this change unacceptable, it can pursue what is known as a "sterilization" policy in an effort to minimize the impact of balance of payments disequilibria on the domestic economy by nullifying, or sterilizing, its impact on the domestic money supply. In the example above, the monetary authority could sterilize, or offset, the deficit by means of an expansionary monetary policy at home. If, for example, the central bank buys government bonds on the open market, it could counteract the deficit's tendency to reduce the domestic money supply. Instead of a contraction, the expansionary policy would keep interest rates low and the level of income at full employment. Referring again to Figure 17.3, this would mean keeping the LM schedule at LM_1 (point A), rather than passively permitting it to shift back to LM_3 (point D). Of course, this does not eliminate the deficit, and this type of policy cannot be continued indefinitely in the face of large deficits. The country may run out of reserves. But if the country has large enough reserves to keep paying out for a while, other factors (such as expansion of demand in a third major country) may help eliminate the deficit. Meanwhile, the monetary authority will have protected the domestic economy against exogenous shocks. Sterilization policy thus enables the monetary authority to regain some short-run control over the domestic economy that the open economy removes. Unfortunately, experience under the Bretton Woods system has demonstrated the inability of most monetary authorities to distinguish between short-run disequilibria, which may legitimately be sterilized, and chronic or long-run disequilibria, for which sterilization attempts will lead only to a requisite exchange rate change in a crisis atmosphere.

If factors beyond the country's control should create a balance of payments surplus, an opposite policy may be required to sterilize the effects. But why should a country object to a balance of payments surplus? Assume that a country is at point D in Figure 17.3, where the LM_3 schedule intersects the IS schedule. If the BB line intersects the IS line at point A, the country will have a surplus. But suppose that we now assume that point D represents a full-employment level of income. Then to permit the automatic adjustment to take place (shifting LM to LM_1) would also mean expanding the money supply and pushing income beyond full employment, which would simply lead to inflation.

To avoid this inflation, the monetary authorities may choose to sterilize and remain at point D. This would require a contractionary monetary policy. As a result, the surplus would continue since point D represents levels of i and Y that are inconsistent with balance of payments equilibrium. Reserves of foreign currency would build up. This may be all right for a while, especially if the country is low in reserves, but, in effect, it represents exchanging exports for financial claims on foreign countries (foreign exchange reserves). Such a mercantilist policy will result in a shortage of goods and financial capital in the surplus country since the surplus mirrors the excess of sales of goods and securities to foreigners over purchases from foreigners.

Eventually, when a country has accumulated enough reserves, the monetary authority may decide to revalue the currency, thereby eliminating the surplus. This will permit that country's residents to enjoy lower prices on imported goods, thereby increasing real income with no extra work effort or claims against resources. It will also help to protect the country's trade markets, since continuous surpluses are always someone else's deficits and thus may engender retaliation in the form of tariffs or quotas imposed on the exports of a chronic surplus country. It should be clear, however, that a deficit is generally a more pressing problem for a country than a surplus. In the deficit case the central bank must pay out of its finite reserves to finance its sterilization policy. In the surplus case the central bank can collect reserves as long as the artificially low standard of living that results is acceptable to its residents or political leaders. For example, in the early 1970s Japan had a large balance of payments surplus. With an undervalued currency, it exported far more than it imported. A domestic consumer protest movement arose, however, which objected to the surplus, arguing that Japan had a scarcity of certain domestic products, the bulk of which were being exported. This consumer movement recognized the reality behind such a surplus, namely that goods were being transferred from abroad to the detriment of the domestic standard of living. Of course, another effect of such a surplus is the accumulation of huge reserves. These are not without value for a country's economy. They can be depleted later when the economy has a "rainy day," and therefore constitute a form of forced saving.

The fundamental point of the discussion of an open economy with fixed exchange rates is that, over the long run, the central bank cannot control its own money supply in real terms. In the face of chronic balance of payments disequilibria it may try to do so by sterilizing the impact upon the nominal money supply, but the eventual result will only be an exchange rate change. The change will restore, through induced price-level changes, the real quantity of money to a level consistent with balance of payments equilibrium. For example, a deficit country which through sterilization maintains an artificially large nominal money supply will eventually have to reduce the real money supply by means of an inflationary devaluation. In short, balance of payments equilibrium can be maintained in the face of disequilibrating forces either by permitting a free adjustment in the relative quantity of money among countries by avoiding sterilization or by effecting changes in the relative prices of national monies through devaluation or revaluation.

Adjustable Exchange Rates

The role of exchange rate adjustments as an equilibrating mechanism can be considered within the context of the IS/LM model. Suppose the economy is at point C in Figure 17.3. The monetary authority will not want to allow the money supply to contract automatically and return to point A if point C represents the full-employment level of income. Instead, it may choose to sterilize by expanding the money supply and allowing the deficit to continue. But if the deficit continues too long and the country's foreign exchange reserves are depleted too far, the country may have little choice but to devalue its currency.

Devaluation, as we have seen, means increasing the domestic money price of foreign money: after devaluation all imported goods cost more in terms of

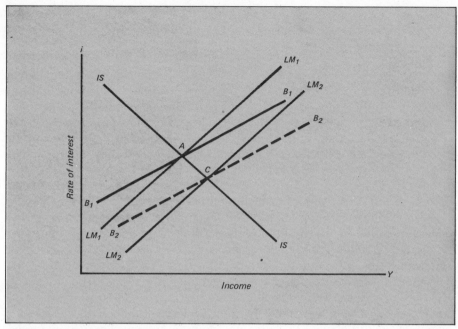

Figure 17.4 Devaluation

the domestic currency. For example, if one dollar bought four West German deutsche marks before a dollar devaluation, after a 33⅓ percent devaluation the same dollar would buy only three marks. That is, whereas the dollar price of each mark was formerly $0.25, after the devaluation it would have increased to $0.33. The effect of such a devaluation is to shift the BB line from B_1 to B_2, as shown in Figure 17.4.

At the original exchange rate the economy was at point C, determined by the intersection of the IS and LM schedules, while the values of i and Y consistent with balance of payments equilibrium at the original exchange rate were shown by line B_1. Devaluation shifts B_1 to B_2, because at a higher domestic money price for foreign money imported goods will cost more, so people will buy fewer imported goods. Likewise, exporters will be able to sell more goods to foreigners, since the devaluation makes a country's export goods more attractive (cheaper) to foreigners. This shift in the exchange rate permits balance of payments equilibrium for any given level of income (such as the full-employment level at point C) at a lower level of interest, and hence the shift of B_1 to B_2. At point C there is no longer a balance of payments deficit, and full employment has been retained. There will be no tendency to shift back to point A and no need to sterilize. Devaluation seems to have worked wonders.

Devaluation, however, presents problems of its own. The first, which occurs even before a country devalues, is the decision of how much to devalue. If the monetary authority devalues too much, it will wind up with a balance of payments surplus. This may not be undesired, if it had been running a large deficit and needs reserves. But, since each country's surplus is another country's deficit, a large surplus is always an invitation to other countries to retaliate by devaluing their own currencies. If they do retaliate, their devaluation may shift the first country's BB line back to B_1 and nullify the gain. On the other hand, if the devaluation is too small and the deficit continues, holders of the devalued currency may suspect that a further devaluation is to come, and they will not want to be caught holding much of that currency. A speculative run against currency will probably result, which in itself may shift the BB line back to B_1—or even further. Such speculation in turn increases the pressure on the monetary authority to devalue further, so it is in the nature of a self-fulfilling prophecy.

Besides encouraging retaliation or speculation, a devaluation results in domestic inflation, since all imports become more costly and the greater demand by foreigners for the new, cheaper export products puts pressure on domestic prices. Residents of the country find that after devaluation they pay more for foreign goods and have to compete more with foreigners for their own products. While the effects of inflation will be considered further below, we can see now that devaluation-induced inflation will cause the LM schedule to shift above LM_2 unless the nominal money supply is increased. This in turn induces a surplus which, while it may be desirable for a country that has run down its reserves due to prolonged deficits, will tend to complicate relations with trading partners. Finally, if the effect of real balances are included so that a different IS schedule results from every price level change, a shift to the left results, with higher prices adding to a potential surplus, and analysis of the full effects of devaluation becomes complex.

An opposite series of events occurs in the case of a revaluation. If a country revalues too much, it may create its own deficit. If it revalues too little, speculators may expect further revaluation, so there will be a speculative flow toward that country, which merely increases an already objectionable surplus. Revaluation may also have a deflationary effect, although it does not usually lead to retaliation.

If changing the exchange rate, especially in the case of devaluation, is fraught with such problems, is there any alternative? Unfortunately, the main alternative practiced by many countries is a sophisticated form of wishful thinking. Essentially, this consists of a policy of sterilization at home while hoping that something will change abroad to eliminate the deficit. Britain, for example, had a severe balance of payments deficit between 1964 and 1967. The British government was unwilling to abandon the fixed exchange rate of $2.80 to the pound sterling that had prevailed through the postwar period, even though most of Britain's major trading partners had gained in productivity relative to Britain during that period. British products were no longer competitive at the fixed exchange rate, but too much prestige was seen to rest on maintaining the fixed rate. Instead of devaluing, the government supported the pound, watched its reserves drain away, and hoped the drain would diminish either because of greater foreign inflation (which would make British goods relatively more competitive) or because of lower interest rates abroad (which would lead to a capital flow toward Britain). This is not to say that they did not try to lessen the deficit: the British government sponsored a program of export promotion, which meant tacitly subsidizing British industries that brought in foreign currency and favoring them over domestic industries. Further, it reduced its still sizable overseas military presence, especially in the area "East of Suez." None of this was sufficient to stem the deficit, however, and in 1967 Britain devalued by about 14 percent—from $2.80 to $2.40.

A similar long-term deficit plagued the United States during the 1960s and into the 1970s, attended by many of the same forms of wishful thinking. The U.S. government added an additional form of its own—putting pressure on countries with surpluses to revalue and relieve pressure on the U.S. balance of payments. This was rationalized because it was believed that the main "culprits" were our allies, Japan and West Germany, with whom we had military-security pacts and on whose soil we had troops stationed. Moreover, since the U.S. dollar is the main reserve currency for international trade and finance, our chronic deficit, by threatening the stability of the dollar, also threatened the very international trade system on which Japanese and German prosperity depended. In this case too, however, wishful thinking failed, and in August 1971 the United States effectively devalued the dollar (by allowing its value to float downward), abandoned gold convertibility, and imposed a temporary import "surcharge" (tariff) to discourage U.S. residents from importing foreign goods.

The problem with remedies that rely on wishful thinking is that they tend to create expectations which make matters worse than they were to begin with. For example, the obvious determination of Britain to retain its fixed rate made its countermeasures appear desperate and feeble. Meanwhile, for years reserves dwindled, as the Labour government was determined not to preside over another devaluation of the pound (the previous one occurred in 1949), and spectators began expecting one. Once a devaluation was firmly anticipated, those (including private citizens with wealth, Arab oil sheiks, multinational corporations, etc.—all potential speculators) who could choose whether to hold their assets in British pounds or in other currencies abandoned the pound, thereby increasing downward pressure on the pound and making an eventual devaluation inevitable.

Let us look at this process in terms of the IS/LM model and the BB line, as shown in Figure 17.4. Suppose the British economy (1964–1967) is at point C, with the BB line at B_1. It is at full employment and has a considerable rate of inflation, but it also has a balance of payments deficit. The government chooses to sterilize the deficit, preferring a drain on reserves to an extreme austerity policy and high unemployment. It hopes for positive developments abroad, which might shift B_1 to the right with no real sacrifice in Britain, engages in weak efforts to cure the deficit (export promotion, cutting overseas military spending, etc.), and by retaining the fixed exchange rate assures itself of a continuous loss of reserves. All of these acts are aimed at shifting the BB line to or toward B_2 through the creation of positive expectations of its economic health and an inflow of foreign capital. Instead, observers watch the continuous loss of reserves and become nervous about investing in Britain or holding British securities. This is because if Britain *is* eventually forced to devalue, the securities will be worth less (in terms of foreign currencies) when they mature than they were expected to be worth when originally purchased. Capital moves away from Britain, and this shifts the BB line further to the left, not to the right, so the deficit at point C becomes even worse.

The tendency of the BB line to shift further to the left becomes greater as time passes, because a larger loss of reserves makes it likely that any eventual devaluation will have to be larger than first expected. Speculators in foreign currency markets sell pounds in large amounts as soon as the crisis atmosphere develops, and this intensifies the crisis. The central bank may respond with pious promises to continue supporting the pound at the fixed rate, but if the rate of speculation is so great that it has to lose reserves at a rate of several billion dollars in a single week (as has happened), these warnings fall on deaf ears.

Speculation and a long-term loss of confidence in the pound led to the British devaluation of November 1967. Because it had been resisted so long, it was a larger devaluation (14.3 percent against the dollar) than many had originally thought necessary, yet it was not enough to restore confidence or produce a lasting balance of payments surplus. By contrast, in 1968 the French franc was devalued after a much shorter-lasting loss of reserves and buildup of speculation against it. This was more successful because it appeared to be merely a short-term adjustment, rather than reflecting a long-term crisis. We have seen that expectations may shift the BB line in either direction. Wishful thinking and delay in adjusting to balance of payments realities usually serve to foster negative expectations. This is the danger involved in sterilizing a deficit and trying to live with a loss of reserves for an extended period. It usually fails, and then the ultimate devaluation must be larger, and its success in stemming the deficit is far less certain.

Effect of Balance of Payments Disequilibrium on Prices

The long-term or underlying cause of balance of payments difficulties for a country is normally a loss of productivity or competitive advantage relative to its major trading partners. In the 1960s and into the 1970s the United States and Britain became relatively less efficient in their production of goods and services than Japan and West Germany; they thus faced growing balance of payments problems and eventually were forced to devalue. Because one short-term cause of balance of payments problems is often a high rate of inflation, we will abandon our assumption of fixed prices, i.e., a zero

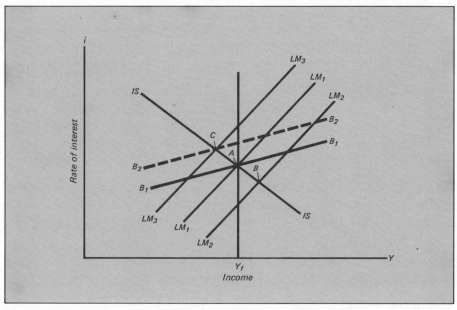

Figure 17.5 The effect of a shift in the LM schedule on the balance of payments where the price level is flexible

rate of inflation, in order to examine what happens if prices are permitted to fluctuate.[8]

Assume that there is a shift in the LM schedule that affects the price level by raising income beyond the full-employment level, as shown by the shift from LM_1 to LM_2 in Figure 17.5. Initially the economy is at point A at a full-employment level of Y, with the B_1 line indicating a balance of payments equilibrium. When the LM line shifts from LM_1 to LM_2 the intersection with IS is at point B, which is beyond Y_f, the full-employment level of income. This will lead to inflation, and as the price level rises, the real money supply will be reduced, which will tend to return to point A. Point B also represents a balance of payments deficit, which also would lead to a reduction in the domestic money supply if there is not a policy of sterilization. So far, then, it looks as though a change in the price level merely helps to expedite the adjustment process in response to a disequilibrium. But after the initial shift in the LM schedule, as the price level rises the economy's competitive position abroad is harmed. Its products become relatively more expensive (unless other countries have an equally high inflation rate), so the BB line shifts from B_1 to B_2, thereby increasing the deficit. Now, in order to correct

8. Here we shall leave aside the impact of real balances on expenditure, which as noted earlier would produce a different IS line for every price level. This avoids complicating our analysis without sacrificing the points regarding an open economy that are of primary concern to us here.

the deficit, the LM line will have to shift further than in the closed economy case. It will have to shift back to point C (LM$_3$), where Y is below and i is above point A. That is, equilibrium will have to occur at less than full employment. Thus, inflation has led to a need for overcompensation to correct the deficit.

Faced with this situation, the country may try to avoid the worst by devaluing. This could restore the BB line to B$_1$ and make equilibrium possible at point A, where there would be full employment. But devaluation itself will lead to a new rise in the domestic price level, since it leads to higher import prices and is, therefore, inflationary. The economy is caught in a vicious circle of inflation, and this is aggravated by the open economy situation. The moral of the story is to prevent the inflation from getting started, i.e., to avoid increases in the money supply that permit the LM schedule to shift to LM$_2$ in the first place. Here we again see the importance of a finely tuned monetary policy.

Freely Floating Exchange Rates

If we look at the problems caused for our model by the open economy, it is tempting to view the economic problems introduced by the foreign trade sector as resulting mainly from one institutional condition: fixed exchange rates. With a fixed exchange rate it is a great coincidence if the BB line meets the intersection of IS and LM at full employment. If the monetary authority is passive, balance of payments equilibrium is assured, given fixed exchange rates, by changes in the money supply induced by foreign exchange market disequilibria. But since most countries are unwilling to accept the consequences of such an automatic equilibrium in terms of the level of income and the domestic rate of interest, the money supply is controlled by sterilization policies. Allowing exchange rates to float freely, however, means that the central banks of countries decide not to intervene in the private international market for foreign currency. Exchange rates are, therefore, flexible and free to shift rapidly to adjust to changes in the level of supply and demand. This leads to automatic adjustment of the BB line to coincide with the equilibrium level of income and interest rate determined by the intersection of the IS and LM schedules. If a certain prevailing exchange rate tends to cause a deficit, the excess demand for foreign currency bids up the price of foreign currency, and this results in an automatic de facto devaluation of the domestic currency of just the right amount to (temporarily) eliminate the deficit. That is, the BB schedule will shift automatically to the point where the IS and LM schedules cross. The reverse occurs given an excess supply of foreign exchange at the initially prevailing exchange rate.

Freely floating exchange rates do not provide all the solutions, however. After all, with flexible exchange rates the BB line adjusts automatically to assure balance of payments equilibrium at the intersection of the IS and LM schedules, whereas with fixed exchange rates and no sterilization the LM-schedule shifts automatically to accomplish the same thing. In either case, a country may end up with an equilibrium position consistent with balance of payments equilibrium that it does not like—with high unemployment or high inflation if a long series of increases in the price of foreign exchange are required for balance of payments equilibrium. Neither fixed nor flexible exchange rates eliminates the necessity faced by open economies to adjust to balance of payments disequilibria, but flexible rates permit economies to make smaller, piecemeal adjustments to changes in international supply and demand than those required under fixed exchange rates and seemingly inevitable sterilization. Flexible rates eliminate the need to make occasional major adjustments in a crisis atmosphere, and they prevent large disequilibria from arising. The day of reckoning still comes, but it comes as less of a shock to the domestic economy. Adjustment is automatic and steady, rather than erratic and subject to speculation, manipulation, and politically motivated delay.

The eventual consequences for the domestic economy are the same in either case. If there is a tendency toward a deficit, the country must "spend less." In the case of fixed exchange rates this means it must make an effort to stem the outflow of reserves by reducing imports and coaxing its investors to purchase fewer foreign securities. If exchange rates are flexible, the automatic adjustment of rates will also reduce the amount spent abroad. At the same time, a country with a deficit must "sell more" abroad. As in the British case mentioned, if there are fixed exchange rates the country may, for example, subsidize its own export industries or encourage foreigners (through advertising) to fly its national airline. If there are flexible rates, the country will automatically "sell more" at the devalued rate. In either case, the deficit country is forced to reduce its own current consumption. Thus, the debate over fixed versus flexible rates is really a debate over the best way for an economy to adjust to the structures imposed by the balance of payments constraint.

One final advantage of flexible rates over fixed rates is worth mentioning, however. It is very difficult to predict how much of a devaluation is needed, even when devaluation is seen as unavoidable. Too small a devaluation encourages speculative pressures that may lead to a large further devaluation. And yet countries are very reluctant to devalue too far, since devaluation leads to an increase in import prices, which is inflationary. In addition, excessive devaluation invites retaliation from other countries that see the devaluing country pursuing a "beggar-thy-neighbor" policy, i.e., attempting to gain a trade advantage. Thus, it is important, under fixed exchange rate conditions, to choose very carefully the amount to devalue.

This task is always difficult, and it is even more difficult if the home country's balance of payments position has evolved differently relative to different trading partners. Such was the case for the United States when facing possible devaluation in August 1971. Japan and Germany, in partic-

Commentary: Recycling Petrodollars

In October 1973 the Middle East oil-producing nations introduced the first of a series of oil price increases which were to quadruple the price of oil within the next few months; this confronted the international financial markets with their most serious problem since the end of World War II. Because the demand for oil has proven to be fairly inelastic, at least temporarily, the effect of the sharp increase in price has been a tremendous inflow of funds to the oil-producing nations, and an equal outflow from the oil-importing countries. Moreover, owing to both the suddenness and the magnitude of the inflow of funds to the relatively small oil-producing nations, there was no opportunity for these monies to be recycled through the normal channels of world trade (at least in the short term) in the form of increased imports. Instead, the net result for 1974 will probably be something in the neighborhood of a $50 billion balance of payments surplus for Saudi Arabia, Kuwait, and the other Persian Gulf sheikdoms alone, which will be matched by a $50 billion trade deficit for Western Europe and Japan.[1]

The problem now facing international financial markets is to find an acceptable means through which the balance of payments deficits of the oil importers can be financed. It is clear that the reserves of the oil-importing countries are inadequate to handle the problem: one estimate shows that the total foreign currency and gold reserves of Western Europe and Japan would be completely eliminated in less than three years if they were used to meet deficits that continued to run at 1974 levels.

The only short-term alternative for the oil importers is to borrow the money to pay for their oil needs, and the most logical source of funds for loans seems to be these same surpluses which are now being accumulated by the oil-producing countries.

Many experts consider the Eurobanks, a group of European-based branches of American and foreign banks, to be the most effective means through which the surplus monies of the exporting nations can be channeled into the hands of those nations with payments deficits. In theory, these financial intermediaries are ideally situated to accept the deposits of the oil producers and then lend these monies to the oil-importing nations in order to finance their oil imports. The situation is complicated, however, by the fact that the oil producers have been reluctant to tie up their funds for any significant period, preferring instead to place them in the banks in the form of short-term deposits, often no longer than thirty to ninety days. The potential borrowers, on the other hand, recognize that it will take several years before they can readjust their domestic economies so that they can regularly earn enough foreign exchange to pay for the higher cost of the oil—and they are therefore desirous of long-term loans. This confronts the banks with what one commentator has described as "the classic formula for trouble":[2] the squeeze that can occur when a bank borrows short and lends long. The "trouble" can arise if a bank finds itself with long-term assets (its claims on borrowers) when its short-term depositors, the oil producers, decide to withdraw their funds. Such withdrawals require available cash which could in theory be raised by selling long-term assets to other investors. But where a very large quantity of withdrawals is involved, too many sellers of long-term assets appear at once; the prices of such assets

---

1. William Cates, "Arab Oil and the Currency Crisis," *Wall Street Journal*, February 11, 1974.

2. Charles N. Stabler, "Jitters on the Euromarket," *Wall Street Journal*, June 28, 1974, p. 14.

are thereby depressed. The resulting capital losses on banks' assets can lead to serious difficulties regarding their liquidity and solvency. Compounding the problem is the question of the credit worthiness of some of the lenders. In mid-1974, for example, Italy appeared on the verge of bankruptcy (the city of Rome was actually unable to pay the interest on its municipal debt), and nervous bankers were becoming increasingly reluctant to lend new sums to other nations with political problems and/or growing deficits, such as Bangladesh, India, and Denmark.[3]

Fortunately, the foreign-based Eurobanks, although theoretically without a "lender of last resort" comparable to the central banks that can rescue an overextended domestic bank, do in fact have resources that they can fall back upon should difficulties develop because their depositors withdraw funds and/or their borrowers become unable to repay. Each of the banks, if pressed for funds, could call upon its home office for additional monies: a Chase branch in Zurich, for example, could request monies from Chase in New York. If the amount were not excessive, the home office could probably borrow it in the open market from its own sources; if not, it could always call on *its* lender of last resort (in this case, the Federal Reserve) for additional borrowings.

In the past, the Eurobanks have been able to manage similar recycling problems with ease and efficiency, and there were perhaps $105 billion net in such Eurobank deposits by the end of 1972. But this increased to $150 billion at the end of 1973 and was increasing more rapidly in the first quarter of 1974; following the jump in prices, the sheer size of the petrodollar total that must be handled during the next few years raises some questions about the ability of the banks to manage on their own at this point. There are signs, for example, that some of the recycling may be bypassing the Eurobanks completely: in mid-1974 there were reports of talks between Saudi Arabia and the U.S. Treasury designed to encourage direct purchase by Saudi Arabia of U.S. Treasury bonds.[4] Furthermore, the oil exporters have shown some indications of increased willingness to lend to official international lending institutions, which could in turn supply funds to those countries experiencing oil-related balance of payments deficits: in 1973–1974 Iran loaned the World Bank $200 million, Saudi Arabia loaned $140.8 million, and Kuwait loaned $42.2 million.[5]

The challenge of recycling petrodollars represents a major test of the resiliency of the international financial markets. Whether this is accomplished through the vehicle of the Eurobanks, through direct government-to-government loans, or through international institutions like the World Bank is of secondary importance. The crucial question is whether or not such recycling will occur, because the alternatives—worldwide reduced imports, competitive currency devaluations, high unemployment, and economic slowdown—are ominous indeed.

4. *Wall Street Journal,* July 5, 1974, p. 13.
5. Stabler, *Wall Street Journal,* June 28, 1974.

3. Ibid.

ular, had gained such a large trade advantage over the United States at existing exchange rates that a large devaluation (well over 10 percent) would be needed to correct it, but other countries, notably Britain and Italy, had less of an advantage, or none at all. A large devaluation might be insufficient to even out trade with Japan and Germany, while hurting Britain and Italy severely. Unable to estimate a single percentage to devalue the dollar, the administration chose to allow the dollar to float (downward) between August and December 1971. The effective devaluation which resulted was about 17 percent relative to the Japanese yen and about 14 percent relative to the German mark. Then, in the Smithsonian agreement of December 1971 a new set of parity rates was set, with wider bands within which central banks were committed to holding their currencies' values (2¼ percent in each direction, rather than 1 percent). Even this method was insufficient to eliminate the pressures on the dollar. Fourteen months later, in February 1973, the dollar had to be devalued again as record capital outflows amounting to $9 billion in three weeks (January–February 1973) left the United States and were accumulated by the German, Japanese, and other central banks.

Given the difficulty of estimating a correct amount to devalue, freely floating exchange rates have now been adopted by default. The fixed-rate Bretton Woods system had the advantage of fostering a high level of international liquidity and trade at the expense of adjustment difficulties. That is, money was able to move across borders relatively freely, without much fear of short-term losses, which encouraged a high level of international trade. The cost in terms of adjustment problems was high, however, as shown in recent international monetary crises. The floating exchange rate system now prevailing favors ease of rate adjustment over liquidity. With volatile conditions in the foreign exchange markets, importers and exporters may face possible losses or gains due to rapid exchange rate fluctuations, which add an element of uncertainty to foreign trade and investment decisions. But this disadvantage now appears to be less onerous than the dangers of crisis and breakdown (along with huge readjustments) which plagued the fixed-rate system.

Questions and Exercises

1. What is meant by the term "open economy"? To what degree would you classify ours as an open economy?
2. How are imports analogous to savings and taxes? How are exports analogous to investment and government expenditures?
3. Why is the trade balance a negative function of income and the capital balance a positive function of the interest rate?
4. Explain in terms of the graph in Figure 17.2 why the results of changes in government expenditures, G, are ambiguous. Why might a rise in G sometimes move

our balance of payments toward a deficit position and other times move it toward a surplus position?

5. Did chronic U.S. balance of payments deficits contribute to the demise of the Bretton Woods system? How have we deviated from that system since 1971?

6. Demonstrate by means of the graph in Figure 17.3 that a balance of payments deficit can be reduced, if not eliminated, by cutting the money supply. Why haven't we followed this policy in recent years?

7. What are the ultimate checks to a country's balance of payments deficits? Why are these checks usually politically unacceptable?

8. How would the monetary authorities of a country conduct a sterilization policy to minimize the impact of balance of payments disequilibria? Why is it essential that the monetary authorities distinguish between short-run and long-run disequilibria?

9. When would a nation revalue its currency, and what effects would that have domestically and internationally?

10. Assume a country has an open economy with fixed exchange rates. In the long run, why would it be impossible for the central bank to control its own money supply in real terms?

300
250
200
150

R O

1973 1975 1976
—estimates—

*with full employment current rates of taxes would yield more of our...

+
0
5
10
15
20
25

DEFICIT

1969 70 71 72 73 74 75 76
—estimates—

HUMAN RESOURCES* 87·7

40
30
20
10
0

PHYSICAL RESOURCES 29·1
INTEREST 24·9
INTERNATIONAL AFFAIRS 4·1

1960 1965 1970 73 74 75
est

*Education, health, social security, ex-servicemen
†Agriculture, environment, transport, housing etc

ork Times

This lack of public understanding seriously threatens the continuation of our competitive private enterprise system.

I idea, public understanding is fur... still have the ult... not on Ca... tion—except anyw... America the people, imperfect, however capit... cratic system may seem. In the last applysis, the people determine what that ctions will govern our economy of Ark... onduct of our business, as the opportun... we used to say, sought to reduce cap...en can't be taxes by changing the... system of taxing these gains.

Sliding Tax

The idea that Cha... has long advocated... one that stems certain to have... the backing of the Nixon Administration—is a sliding scale of taxes on the gain that an individual realizes from the sale of stocks, real estate or other property that has risen in value since he acquired it. At present, such gains are...

can be wrong on balance if a growing number of them believe, as they seem to, that profits are too high, that more regulation is needed, and that big business is getting too big.

The opinion polls present a grim arithmetic. According to a recent survey, only 3 per cent of the American people think business as a whole is not the... t making enough profit, while 35... re than ten times as... ss is making too mu... st public estimate the... rage manufacturer's after... s on the dollar, rns in the neighborhood of a...

For the first ti... II, a majority of... thinks that comp... lowed to make all... The trend instea... all but the very...

While it would be... slid... cale of... capital gains... total amount of tax uncha... it is clear that a net reducna... in over-all capital gains... is what Mr. Mills wants to...

Passage Is Uncertain

Whether Mr. Mills can... this or any other aspect...

SCHEDULE D
(Form 1040)
Department of the Treasury
Internal Revenue Service

Sales or Exchanges of Prop
▶ See instructions on D–1 and D–2.
▶ If you use this schedule, attach it to Form 1040.

Name as shown on Form 1040

public support for a government ceiling on profits. And it may be significant that this study was taken before the energy situation was brought to the forefront of public attention... oil embarg...

The put... wrong, bec... is not the... accessible g... it to be. On... contrary, it is one of the most flexible and responsive of man's creations. It takes on the character of its times.

We in General Motors know there is no conflict between corporate prof... WASHINGTON, May 31—Kenneth Rush, the new coun... selor to the President, said today that he would be Mr. Nixon's "primary adviser" on economic policy and would have "more access" to the President than other top officials.

Mr. Rush told a breakfast meeting with reporters that he would be chairman of the informal daily meetings of top officials on economic policy and would also be chairman of h official bodies as the Cost of Living Council and the ational Economic Policy.

economic "czar" said he wou... cials as William E. Simon, the Secreta... Roy L. Ash, Director of the Office of Management a... Budget.

But he said he would be the "first spokesman" of the Administration on economic policy and would be "more than a traffic cop" in channeling issues to the President.

Among other things, he said, he would coordinate Presidential speeches and news releases as well...

¶Full endorsement of the current somewhat restrictive monetary policy of the Federal Reserve Board.

¶Belief that the government should aim for a balanced budget next year and to reduce the scheduled deficit of $11-billion in the budget for the fiscal year beginning July 1.

¶Opposition to price or profit ontrols.

Mr. Rush described himself as an "economic conservative."

Asked in an interview in the ent issue of Business Week azine about his qualifica-

be. The President and the Secretary of the Treasury, Mr Shultz, call it a budget of "moderate restraint" on the economy, implying that the main target is still inflation. Mr Stein, the chairman of the President's Council of Economic Advisers, says himself that it will be "supportive" of expansion in the economy, but the council's Economic Report calls it "fairly neutral", and that is probably what it is.

In any case, the United States can certainly not be accused of the presumed sin of a sharply restrictive policy in an old-fashioned response to the near-next fellow. ord rate of inflation last year and to the dead prospect, because of the huge jump rational Gov oil... se back into deficit... ount of the balance of onal payments. The budget per... ns, I kno its larger increase in total spending can people w n had been foreseen only two months will all get un it has a sizeable estimated deficit of is gained of ti billion and there is a readiness to Somehow, we ease spending further if necessary more people heck a slump. "The President is very that a corpor heck a slump. "The President is very that matte" said Mr Malek, the deputy director

Q. When you were Chairman of the Cou of Economic Advisers, you had two well-kn pupils. The first was John F. Kennedy and second was Lyndon Baines Johnson. Did they h any aptitude for economics?

A. I've said on occasion that Kennedy was the economics student I ever had and it's only fai LBJ to say that he was a close second. In ot words, both these men were—and I suppose the bound to be an element of ego in this—both m men were highly responsive to their economic ook a while for Mr. Kennedy to ength, and when I "our" I'm rmit Gordon and Tobin and later on Gardner Ackley. But he cau on fast and knew the right questions to ask. was an absolute joy to work with. One of his m remarkable displays of economic understand took place while h a meeting in ation ortly before guided the discussion of ct wit esse but actually caught a world-renowned mo nconsistency on a highly te cal point.

Lyndon Johnson also responded extremely v to economic education and information. As a n ter of fact, he insisted on memos three times a w

President's Watchword Is to Act 'With Caution' in Uncertain Times

There were mutterings on Capitol Hill about a constitutional crisis between the executive and the legislative branches.

This year, the President has not changed his tune, but he is playing it pianissimo. Today's budget message did not renew the demand for a spending ceiling. The President merely noted that

He set forth 1972 State of series of 15 ra casts made campaign, and Garnett D. Ho Star-News just

He told Mr. Administration form—"more any Administ Roosevelt's in different direct

The directic toward "using ly," letting pe selves," and

Big spender keeps on spending

Top Economic Role Is Claimed by Rush

The Profit System and America's Growth

Let's Tailor the Policies to Fit the Problems

Part I—CAPITAL ASSETS—Short-term capital gains and losses—assets held

a. Kind of property. Indicate security, real estate, or other (Specify)	b. Description (Examples: 100 sh. of "Z" Co., 2 story brick, etc.)	c. How acquired. Enter letter symbol (See instr.)	d. Date acquired (mo., day, yr.)	e. Date sold (mo., day, yr.)	f. Gross price	allow allowa acq
1						
2						
3						
4						
5						

Major Restructuring of U.S. Tax Laws Sought by Several Groups in Congress

2 Enter... term gain (or loss) from partnerships and fiduciaries
3 E... ed short-ter... rryove... from preceding taxable years (attach statemen
4 Net... oss) from...
Long-term gain... assets (12 months or m
5 Enter gain from Part II, line 3

The Theory of Economic Policy

18

The theory of economic policy examines the feasibility of achieving a combination of goals such as full employment, price stability, balance of payments equilibrium, and growth with policy instruments such as changes in the level of government expenditure, changes in tax rates, changes in the supply of money, or changes in the rate of exchange of the dollar.

Hardly anyone would disagree with the desirability of achieving these most frequently stated macro-policy goals. The order in which they are listed presumably represents the priorities of those who make our macro policy, judging from the policy mix since the federal government first explicitly assumed responsibility for management of the economy. (Presumably this ordering in turn reflects the priorities of those governed.) The initial formulation of economic policy goals for the United States was the Employment Act of 1946, which states:

The Congress hereby declares that it is the continuing policy and responsibility of the Federal Government to use all practicable means consistent with its needs and obligations and other essential considerations of national policy, with the assistance and cooperation of industry, agriculture, labor and State and local governments, to coordinate and utilize all its plans, functions, and resources for the purpose of creating and maintaining, in a manner calculated to foster and promote free competitive enterprise and the general welfare, conditions under which there will be afforded useful employment opportunities, including self-employment, for those able, willing, and seeking to work, and to promote maximum employment, production, and purchasing power.[1]

In order to understand the intentions of this act it is important to remember that it is dealing with *macroeconomic* policy goals, as has our discussion. Macroeconomics is concerned with the *general* level of employment of the labor force, for example, not with the employment (or unemployment) problems of any particular segment of the labor force. Price stability is almost automatically not a sectoral problem in terms of particular groups of individuals, but it is often a problem in terms of a particular group of goods and services. Again, macroeconomic policy is concerned with the behavior of a general price index taken to represent the price of a typical "market basket" of goods and services purchased by a typical consumer. The same general approach characterizes balance of payments policy. In developing a theory of economic policy, therefore, we must focus on the average or broad picture. Of course, attention to the whole implies some attention to each of the parts, but looking at goals for particular subgroups only complicates the picture. We will not consider one sector by itself, therefore, but will examine the manner in which some instrument affects some aggregate policy goal.

The major thing to realize about policy goals is that the difficulty of achieving them simultaneously increases with their numbers. In theory, each policy goal ought to have a policy instrument. Because, generally speaking, we have only two policy instruments, monetary and fiscal, and we have already listed four specific policy goals—full employment, price stability, high growth rates, and balance of payments equilibrium—a frequent problem is that of conflicting goals. It is far easier to produce a list of desirable goals than it is to evolve policies sufficient for their simultaneous or even singular attainment. Policymakers must *choose* among stated goals and establish priorities. In order to consider possible conflicts and possible chances for coordination among policy goals, let us review what each of these goals means for an economy.

In the strictest sense, full employment means that all labor and capital in the economy, all of our productive resources, are being utilized to the fullest extent. What the economy *could* produce if this condition were being fulfilled is referred to as the *capacity* of the economy to produce, as we noted

1. 60 Stat. 23. Public Law 304, 79th Congress.

in Chapter 1 and again in Chapters 11 and 12. The comparison of actual and potential GNP, as estimated by the Department of Commerce and the Council of Economic Advisors, respectively, since 1954 (and projected to the end of 1973), is charted graphically in Figure 1.1. Notice that from 1965 to 1968 the actual output of the economy exceeded its estimated potential. This implies a heavy utilization of capacity—in fact, overutilization. When normal supply capacity of the economy is being exceeded, we can expect high employment of resources accompanied by rising prices. This, as we saw in Chapter 16, suggests a policy conflict between full employment and stable prices.

While the best way to ensure high employment of the labor force is to keep demand for the output at a high level, the resulting high inflation rates may make our goods less attractive to foreigners, and thus the balance of trade segment of our balance of payments tends to suffer. (The balance of trade depends also on the rate of inflation elsewhere *relative* to our own.) High employment and growth of output are consistent goals, although there may be some conflict between rapid growth and the balance of trade. There is some evidence that the overall impact of rapid growth rates on the balance of payments is favorable. If growth is pushed too hard—that is, if demand is expanded too rapidly relative to the capacity of the economy to produce as well as relative to its *addition* to its capacity to produce—inflation may be the result. The nature of goal interrelationships is summarized in Table 18.1. All of the relationships between goals can be perceived by looking at either side of the diagonal row of Xs (blank spaces): the relationship between full employment and price stability in row 2, column (1), is the same as that between price stability and full employment in row 1, column (2).

In order to understand the necessity for identifying conflicting goals and establishing priorities we shall look first at a hypothetical policy problem in the simplest single-goal, single-instrument framework before considering approaches to multiple goal-instrument problems.

Table 18.1   Interrelationships Between Policy Goals

Goals	(1) Full Employment	(2) Price Stability	(3) Balance of Payments Equilibrium	(4) Growth
Full employment	X	—	—?	+
Price stability	—	X	+	—?
Balance of payments equilibrium	—?	+	X	?
Growth	+	—?	?	X

+ represents generally consistent goals
— represents generally inconsistent goals
? represents uncertainty due to disagreement among policy analysts and conflicting evidence
—? represents general inconsistency, but with some doubt

The Single-Goal, Single-Instrument Case: Fiscal Policy

In the simple, Keynesian, income-expenditure model, outlined in Chapters 4 and 5, in which the price level is taken to be fixed, income, Y, may be written in terms of the multiplier and non-income-induced expenditure as

$$Y = kA \qquad (18.1)$$

where A represents total autonomous expenditure and k is the multiplier.[2] Given this equation, if we know A and if k is fixed based upon a given marginal propensity to consume, b, and a given tax rate, t, then Y will be determined in this simplified setting. In other words, if A can be stabilized over time, Y can also be stabilized at some target level that is coincident, say, with full employment.

Chapter 5 described a policy system in which, if private investment falls, government expenditure is increased by an equal amount in order to keep non-income-induced expenditure constant. Similarly, if autonomous consumption expenditure, a, were to fall, it too could be offset by an increase in government expenditure.

The problem is that accurate measurement of the change in investment is next to impossible *while it is occurring*. Some time after it has occurred, we may observe a fall in income if the government, not realizing I has fallen, has held G fixed. If *then* a decision is made to increase government expenditure, the fall in investment still may not be measured accurately and the government may decide on too much or too little increase in expenditure. Moreover, as we have seen, deciding to change government expenditure and effecting an actual change in the expenditure may be very different things— complicated hearings and legislative roadblocks frequently prohibit a quick change. In addition, the change in expenditure prescribed by stabilization policy may be inconsistent with (1) the amount of expenditure to short-run variation and (2) other expenditure requirements.

Another problem that fiscal policy practitioners encounter is the difficulty of *projecting* a balanced budget. Suppose it is desired to balance the federal budget with G set equal to T. We have already seen that government expenditures must be planned over the period of a fiscal year in advance of actual tax collection. We have also represented tax proceeds as a function of income with the proportional tax expression $T = tY$. In order to balance the budget perfectly, the economic planners must project national income, Y, exactly, so that given $G = G_0$,

$$G_0 = T_0 = tY_0$$

The zero subscripts indicate that government expenditures and taxes are measured in the same year, a difficult feat, as evidenced by the recent

2. It would be possible to employ the simple quantity framework outlined in Chapter 13, $Y = VM$, to replace the present discussion of G as a policy instrument to obtain a target Y with a discussion of M as a policy instrument to obtain a target Y.

discrepancies between actual and projected deficits in the United States.

Statements about the posture of the federal government's fiscal policy combine figures for the past actual and current projected (over the next fiscal year) full-employment budget along with the past actual and current projected actual budget. From a policy standpoint, the past budget items must be viewed as water over the dam. Future budget items, however, rely upon the accuracy of projections about the behavior of major items of private expenditure and their impact upon income. It is necessary to predict (1) the timing and extent of changes in private expenditure and (2) the impact of such changes on incomes and prices and in turn upon employment of the economy's resources. We have seen already that item (1) is very difficult to achieve. Furthermore, *if* we are to be successful, we must rely heavily on the accuracy of equation (18.1) to predict the response of income to changes in G that themselves are a response to changes in A. Thus, the simple income-expenditure model is inadequate to express a multiplier relationship in a money economy. Where monetary and fiscal policy are to be simultaneously employed to achieve multiple goals, an expanded model as well as an expanded policy framework are required.

Multiple Goals and Instruments

The theory of economic policy has grown up largely around the problem of maintaining simultaneous balance in the domestic economy with balance of payments equilibrium. Chapter 17 indicated some of the problems for an open economy; it is therefore not surprising that economists from a small open economy like the Netherlands have been the pioneers in the field. While the theory can be employed in any multiple goal-instrument problem, we shall develop our analysis in the open economy setting.

An important pioneer of the theory of economic policy in a multiple goal-instrument setting has been Jan Tinbergen.[3] The **Tinbergen principle** states that in cases where policymakers have fixed target values for their policy goals, the number of policy instruments must be equal to the number of goals if all goals are to be obtained. For example, if policymakers boldly announce that they will achieve full employment, stable prices, balance of payments equilibrium, and growth, they will require four separate and effective policy instruments to achieve fixed-target values for each goal. Failure to fully recognize this requirement has been an underlying cause for the frustration of many ambitious sets of economic policies.

Further work on the theory of economic policy has shown that if fixed targets are replaced by some objective function, akin to an individual's utility function, expressed in terms of goals, and if policymakers are willing to trade off among goals, then it is possible to obtain a set of highest possible values for each so long as the number of instruments is less than or equal to

3. Jan Tinbergen, *On the Theory of Economic Policy* (Amsterdam: North Holland, 1951). See also James E. Meade, *The Theory of International Economic Policy*, Vol. 1, *The Balance of Payments* (London: Oxford, 1951).

the number of goals. This is called the variable-targets approach, first developed by Tinbergen[4] and extended by Henry Theil.[5]

In order to see this approach more clearly, suppose, for example, that a policymaker has an objective function which is expressed in terms of the goals of full employment, price stability, balance of payments equilibrium, and growth. This is comparable to an individual's utility function expressed in terms of the quantities of goods available to the individual. Basically, policymakers are happier the closer they come to reaching the target level for each goal variable; thus they set their instruments accordingly, consistent with the constraints imposed by the economic parameters of the model. In other words, if they elect to use monetary policy to obtain balance of payments equilibrium, they must consistently adjust the quantity of money with the ability of changes in the quantity of money to affect the balance of payments. The same is done for each instrument. In the variable-targets approach, however, policymakers might give up some unemployment for more price stability or some balance of payments disequilibrium for fuller employment. The ability to make such trade-offs places less constraints upon policymakers than the fixed-targets approach and consequently permits achievement of less rigidly defined goals under less stringent conditions.

The Fixed-Targets Approach

Whereas the variable-targets approach is therefore most appropriate in a wide variety of circumstances, more attention has been given to the fixed-targets approach in extending the theory of economic policy to applications to actual policy problems. This may be due to the fact that the variable-targets approach was not fully developed until the last ten years or to the uneasiness which some theorists feel in assigning an objective function to such a disembodied entity as a "policymaker." Fortunately, the essentials of the theory of economic policy and its applications can be understood by employing the technically easier fixed-targets approach, and so we shall employ that framework.

The major development in the application of Tinbergen's fixed-targets approach is R. A. Mundell's **principle of effective market classification,** which states that policy instruments should be aimed at the goals upon which they have the most influence.[6] In effect, this analysis amounts to a division of labor between policy instruments based on a law of comparative advantage.[7] While this proposition seems reasonable enough, it is not im-

4. Jan Tinbergen, *Centralization and Decentralization in Economic Policy* (Amsterdam: North Holland, 1954).

5. Henry Theil, *Optimal Decision Rules for Government and Industry* (Amsterdam: North Holland, 1964).

6. See R. A. Mundell, "The Appropriate Use of Monetary and Fiscal Policy for Internal and External Stability," International Monetary Fund, *Staff Papers*, March 1962, pp. 70-77.

7. This observation was made by Jurg Niehans in "Monetary and Fiscal Policies in Open Economies under Fixed Exchange Rates: An Optimizing Approach," *Journal of Political Economy* 76 (July-August 1968): II, 894.

mediately obvious that its violation can lead to rather disastrous results. Mundell clearly demonstrated some of these in connection with the employment of monetary or fiscal policy for internal (full-employment) and external (balance of payments equilibrium) balance.

Suppose that we identify a target level of full employment income as Y^* and an equilibrium target for the balance of payments as B^*. We noted in Chapter 17 that in theory these values can be obtained with some combination of monetary- and fiscal-policy instruments defined as the quantity of money, M, and the level of government expenditure, G. Therefore each of the two goals can be expressed in terms of the two policy instruments as

$$Y^* = Y(G, M) \tag{18.2}$$

$$B^* = B(G, M) \tag{18.3}$$

This is consistent with the requirements of the fixed-targets approach since there are two goals, Y^* and B^*, and two instruments, G and M.

First we must investigate qualitatively what relationship between changes in G and M will maintain $Y = Y^*$, which is equivalent to full employment or what we shall call internal balance. The same question must be answered for maintaining $B = B^*$, or external balance, where the balance of payments is in equilibrium. In order to do this we look at expressions for the change in equations (18.2) and (18.3)

$$\Delta Y^* = 0 = Y_G \, \Delta G + Y_M \, \Delta M \tag{18.4}$$

$$\Delta B^* = 0 = B_G \, \Delta G + B_M \, \Delta M \tag{18.5}$$

Equation (18.4) states that the change in the target value of Y, ΔY^*, which is zero in the fixed-target case, equals the impact of a change in G on Y holding all else constant, Y_G, times the change in G, ΔG, plus the impact of a change in M on Y holding all else constant, Y_M, times the change in M, ΔM. In effect, Y_G and Y_M are the government expenditure multiplier and money multiplier respectively. Equation (18.5) simply replaces the change in Y with a change in B and is otherwise identical to equation (18.4). We noted in Chapter 17 that the impact of a change in G on the balance of payments, B_G, may be positive or negative, while the impact of a change in M on the balance of payments, B_M, is negative.

The qualitative relationship between ΔG and ΔM required to keep $Y = Y^*$ is given by solving equation (18.4) for

$$\left.\frac{\Delta G}{\Delta M}\right|_{Y=Y^*} = -\frac{Y_M}{Y_G} < 0 \tag{18.6}$$

since, beginning with equation (18.2), where target Y, Y^*, equals actual Y, expressed in terms of policy instruments G and M, as Y(G, M), given that $\Delta Y^* = 0$, equality of Y with Y^* requires that $\Delta Y = 0$ as expressed by equation (18.4). Equation (18.6) states that as G rises, M must fall in order to keep $Y = Y^*$. This is clearly consistent with the fact that if increases in G and

Commentary: Open-Economy Macro Policy

The British student of economics lives in an economy more vulnerable to external events than the U.S. economy. Although no longer the "workshop of the world," Britain's economy is still uncomfortably open, through both necessity and deliberate policy. One of the most densely populated nations on earth, its generally efficient agricultural sector is able to supply the nation with only a little more than half its food (53.6 percent in 1972); the rest must be imported. Britain must also import nearly all the raw materials and most of the sources of energy needed to sustain its domestic economy and to manufacture the exports required to pay for its imports.[1]

With the formation of the British Commonwealth, Britain gave trade preferences to many developed and underdeveloped nations (former members of the British Empire); traditionally this trade network had involved British imports of raw materials and food and corresponding exports of manufactured goods and services (shipping, insurance, etc.). This pattern has changed to some extent with industrialization in these nations and their increasing ability to compete in world and domestic markets with traditional British exports, such as textiles. Joining the Common Market obliged Britain to open its economy even further to the relatively efficient manufacturing centers of continental Europe.

As a result of these policies and necessities, Britain ran a trade deficit of £1.80 billion on total exports of goods and services of £16.46 billion in 1973, which constituted 26.2 percent of GNP. This deficit was only the latest in a string of trade and current account deficits which have periodically plagued the British economy since World War II.

As in the case with double-digit inflation in the United States, persistent deficits indicate living beyond one's means; both are generally perceived to represent an imminent threat to national living standards and other domestic policy goals. Depending to some extent on the party in power, Britain's economic goals have included full employment, domestic economic growth, low rates of inflation, "cheap" food, improved social welfare, some foreign military commitments and aid to poor nations, and maintenance of the value of the pound and of London as a center of international finance.

The instruments to which various British governments have resorted in efforts to maintain external balance have included monetary policy (manipulation of the bank rate and devaluation), fiscal policy, "jaw-boning," or persuasion, direct controls on merchandise imports and capital exports, export incentives, and the reduction of overseas commitments, both military and civilian. In some instances, the trade deficits themselves (and the methods required to finance them) have made certain goals more difficult to achieve; in most cases, however, with the number of goals exceeding the number of available instruments, the high priority accorded to the maintenance of external balance has resulted in policies involving the temporary abandonment of some goals and/or a reduction in the target levels of others.

In 1963–1964, for example, a Conservative government tried to continue a policy aimed at achieving high rates of domestic growth in the face of increasing external imbalance. It was argued that if the deficit could be financed through borrowing from international organizations, running down reserves, and so on, exports would begin to rise more rapidly than imports as export competitiveness and productivity increased. In fact, the Conservative government had argued that much of the increase in imports during this period was due to increases in inventories; this turned out not

---

1. North Sea oil fields come into full production around 1980. At present, Britain obtains nearly 70 percent of its electrical power from coal.

to be the case, and a large proportion of the increase in imports in 1964 was made up of manufactured goods for final consumption. At the same time, resources were diverted from export markets by the pressure of domestic demand, a recurring problem in Britain when policymakers attempt to achieve external balance together with relatively rapid domestic growth. Consequently, a large external imbalance and serious pressure on reserves forced policymakers to abandon the policy of rapid growth in favor of one involving restoration of external balance. This involved a 15 percent surcharge on manufactured imports, a 2 percent export rebate, and the establishment of an "incomes policy" by the Labour government which took office in October 1964. By November the new government was forced to invoke fiscal policy, including an increase in gasoline taxes, income taxes, corporation taxes, and in National Insurance benefits and contributions.[2] This balance of payments crisis was dealt with, only to be followed by another in 1967; this time the government reluctantly devalued the pound.

In more general terms, the causes of the recurring external imbalance and the policies required to deal most effectively with it are a continuing subject of controversy. The record deficit of 1973, for example, has been blamed on world prices for raw materials (by the Conservative Party), on the Conservative Party's creation of excessive domestic demand (by the Labour Party), and on excessive government spending (by Messrs. Cripps and Godley[3]). The Conservative Party argument rests on the fact that the terms of trade (export prices/import prices), which have been rising during most of the period between 1950 and 1972, plunged down in 1973, largely due to increases in the price of raw materials and oil. The Conservative government estimated that this caused about 80 percent of the deficit.[4]

2. See C. D. Cohen, *British Economic Policy, 1960–1969* (London: Butterworths, 1971).

3. See reference to "Messrs. Cripps and Godley," *The London and Cambridge Economic Bulletin,* in the *Economist,* February 9, 1974, p. 58.

4. The *Economist,* February 9, 1974.

In contrast, the Cripps and Godley argument holds that the public sector's deficit (£3–£4 billion in 1973) "fully determines" the current-account deficit. At the same time, they argue that the rise in the prices of imports cut real domestic income, thus reducing total demand and therefore imports below what they would have been otherwise; this explains why imports rose only 1 percent faster than exports in 1973. In other words, they argue that the worsening of the terms of trade in 1973 did not affect the size of the current deficit.

The policy implications of accepting one of these explanations rather than another are considerable. Given the continuing rise in import prices, "slamming on the brakes" to reduce domestic demand enough to put the economy into external balance might lead to a serious recession. If the recession led to reductions in investment, it might reduce Britain's already shaky ability to compete in world markets with her industrial exports. It might also lead to the type of high-unemployment inflation which characterizes economies in transition from high rates of demand-induced inflation to tight-demand policies which fail to stem inflationary expectations.

Although it may be tempting to deal with large deficits by means of devaluation, such action means that prices of imports are increased almost immediately, on top of the continuing world price increases, whereas reduced prices of British exports occur only after a lag. Internal inflation in the meantime could cancel out the gains from devaluation as labor and raw materials costs rise even more rapidly. This prognosis is affected by relative rates of inflation in countries which compete for trade with Britain; if their rates are significantly higher, while they face the same world commodity price increases, British prices may become relatively more competitive. Another factor is the pressure of demand in those nations, and thus their demand for imports: stagnation or recession in Britain's major trading partners could have devastating effects upon the demand for British exports.

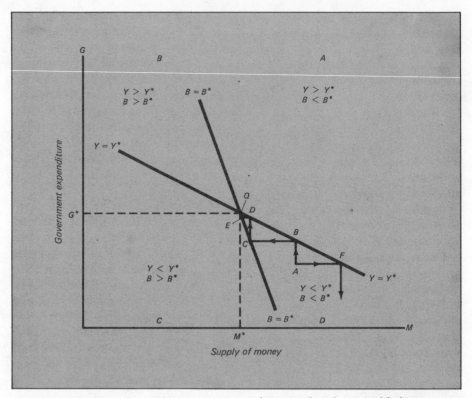

Figure 18.1 Values of G and M consistent with internal and external balance

M both raise Y, then the instruments must be changed simultaneously but in opposite directions to keep Y = Y*.

Based upon the same reasoning, the qualitative relationship between ΔG and ΔM required to keep B = B* is given by solving equation (18.5) for

$$\left.\frac{\Delta G}{\Delta M}\right|_{B=B^*} = -\frac{B_M}{B_G} \gtrless 0 \qquad (18.7)$$

The sign of equation (18.7) is uncertain because of the possibility of $B_G \gtrless 0$. For our purposes we shall assume that $B_G < 0$ so that $-(B_M/B_G) < 0$. This will allow a more effective demonstration of the principle of effective market classification, because taking $B_G < 0$ assumes that the income effects arising from ΔG upon the trade balance dominate the interest-rate effects arising from ΔG upon the capital accounts, as we saw in Chapter 17.

The values of G and M which satisfy internal and external balance based upon equations (18.6) and (18.7) are represented in Figure 18.1. Notice that the figure drawn is consistent with a comparative advantage for G in affecting Y and for M in affecting B. This can be seen from equation (18.6): note that $(\Delta G/\Delta M)_{Y=Y^*}$ will be relatively flat if Y_G is greater than Y_M. Recalling the discussion in Chapter 9, the relatively large government expenditure multiplier and a low money multiplier are both consistent with a high elasticity of demand for money, which we shall assume to hold here.

Turning to external balance, it can be seen from equation (18.7) that $(\Delta G/\Delta M)_{B=B^*}$ will be relatively steep if B_M is greater in absolute value[8] than B_G. And in Chapter 17 we noted that the impact of changes in the money supply on both income and the interest rate operate in the same direction so that the assumption that $B_M < 0$ always holds, whereas B_G is uncertain. For the assumption that $B_G < 0$ to hold, the income effect arising from ΔG on the trade balance must outweigh the interest effect arising from ΔG on the capital account.

This discussion enables us to apply the analysis contained in Mundell's principle of effective market classification. Its significance can best be seen by investigating the consequences of violating the assumptions illustrated in Figure 18.1, that is, that fiscal policy has the greatest influence on Y while monetary policy has the greatest influence on B.

Figure 18.1 is divided into four quadrants, each of which is distinguished by some combination of $Y \gtreqless Y^*$ and $B \gtreqless B^*$. The relationship of Y to Y^* must be read with reference to the $Y = Y^*$ line. In quadrant A, note that $Y > Y^*$ and $B < B^*$. Here and in quadrant B both G and M are above levels consistent with $Y = Y^*$. Since both $Y_G > 0$ and $Y_M > 0$, the result is $Y > Y^*$. Below $Y = Y^*$ the reverse holds. Similarly the relationship of B to B^* must be read with reference to the $B = B^*$ line. In quadrants A and D both G and M are above levels consistent with $B = B^*$ and since both $B_G < 0$ and $B_M < 0$, the result is $B < B^*$. Thus each of the four quadrants represents a policy problem. If a policymaker adjusts G and M to G^* and M^* properly, according to the Tinbergen principle, it is possible to achieve both internal and external balance simultaneously; two instruments, G and M, permit attainment of two goals, $Y = Y^*$ and $B = B^*$. However, Mundell's analysis implies that while this is possible, it will not necessarily be achieved, unless the principle of effective market classification is obeyed.

Suppose, for example, that the policymaker confronts a situation such as point A in quadrant D, combining unemployment $(Y < Y^*)$ with a balance of payments deficit $(B < B^*)$. Such a combination is sometimes called a "policy dilemma" since the internal imbalance $(Y < Y^*)$ calls for expansionary policies while the external imbalance $(B < B^*)$ calls for contractionary policies. Under the Tinbergen principle the dilemma can be resolved by expansionary fiscal policy and a tight monetary policy, a combination of instruments and goals that is consistent with Mundell's principle. The actual policy sequence could be as follows: expansionary fiscal policy from A to B; tight monetary policy from B to C; expansionary fiscal policy from C to D; tight money from D to E, and so on until point Q is reached where $Y = Y^*$

---

8. Absolute value merely abstracts from the sign since both B_M and B_G are taken here to be negative. In effect, we are saying that a number like -2 is greater than -1.

and $B = B^*$. But suppose that starting at point A, the principle of effective market classification is violated by pairing fiscal policy with external balance and monetary policy with internal balance. Given unemployment and $Y_M > 0$, a policy of loose money would move the economy from point A to point F. Given a deficit and $B_G < 0$, tight fiscal policy would move the economy from point F toward the M axis. Clearly, violating the Mundell principle would result in policy actions that move the economy further and further from equilibrium.

It should be remembered that it is the *relative* slopes of the internal and external balance lines, $Y = Y^*$ and $B = B^*$, which represent the comparative advantage of each of the instruments and therefore dictate the pairing of instruments and goals consistent with the principle of effective market classification. In a situation where monetary policy has a comparative advantage in affecting Y while fiscal policy has a comparative advantage in affecting B, the relative slopes of the internal and external balance lines would be reversed and the stable pairing would be given by tying monetary policy to internal balance and fiscal policy to external balance. A third situation is possible in which $B_G > 0$, and a positively sloped external balance line obtains; a policy pairing consistent with the principle of effective market classification could be found here too.

More generally, it is to be remembered that any two-goal, two-instrument case can be investigated with an apparatus like Figure 18.1 and the accompanying equations. The Tinbergen principle will be satisfied when both policy goals will be satisfied by some effective use of each instrument, analogous to point Q representing G^*, M^* in Figure 18.1. Because this geometric approach is constrained to the two dimensions of a page, a more mathematical approach is necessary where more than two goals or instruments are involved. However, the same fundamentals demonstrated here for the two-dimensional case can be seen to hold for more elaborate models.

Theory of Economic Policy Applications

The theory of economic policy actually represents the application of microeconomic theory of the firm and of consumer theory to the problem of most effectively employing limited policy resources in order to achieve a multitude of goals. In the fixed-targets approach the policymaker may be viewed as the manager of a firm with a number of factors of production at his or her disposal. The constraints on the policymaker are in a way even more severe than those on the firm manager, since the latter has only one objective, to maximize profits, while the policymaker has as many objectives as there are explicitly identified policy goals. Further, with fixed target values of goal variables, the macroeconomic policymaker must be certain (1) that the number of instruments matches the number of goals, and (2) that the comparative advantage of each instrument in affecting goal variables is known and applied according to the principle of comparative market classification. This knowledge in turn requires that each of the economic parameters which determines the actual impact of instruments upon goals is known with some accuracy, both qualitatively and quantitatively.

The stringency of these requirements may account for some failures to apply the theory of economic policy in practice. Nevertheless, the theory for the proper alignment of fiscal and monetary policy for achievement of internal and external balance based upon the principle of effective market classification has had a widespread influence on the thinking of policymakers. The far-reaching implications of the relatively simple model represented by Figure 18.1 suggest the power of highly abstract yet artfully applied theory. Failure to apply the principle of effective market classification can result in destabilization due to seemingly stabilizing actions. The power of the theoretical approach to the design of economic policy lies precisely in the revelation of such counterintuitive truths.

Questions and Exercises

1. What are some of the basic conflicts between the various policy goals? Can you recall any time in our recent history when we attained full employment and relative price stability simultaneously?

2. Assume that private investment has fallen, and G is to be raised by the same amount. Why are the questions "how much" and "when" rather difficult ones to answer?

3. Why is it difficult to project a balanced budget? Why will tax receipts depend partially on government expenditures?

4. Why is the simple income-expenditure model inadequate to express a multiplier relationship in a money economy?

5. Outline the variable-targets approach. How is it analogous to an individual's utility function?

6. In the fixed-targets approach, the number of policy instruments must equal the number of goals if all goals are to be obtained. How do you explain this condition? Can you demonstrate how fiscal policymakers would be frustrated if they relied solely on that instrument to attain full employment and relative price stability?

7. Demonstrate, by means of the graph in Figure 18.1, that fiscal policy has the most influence on Y, while monetary policy has the most influence on B. Why does point A in quadrant D of Figure 18.1 represent a policy dilemma?

8. What is the Tinbergen principle and under what conditions can it be satisfied? What is meant by the principle of effective market classification and what are the consequences of violating this principle?

9. Is it possible to attain external and internal balance simultaneously? How can this be attempted by means of monetary and fiscal policy? Why is it necessary to use two separate policy instruments?

10. Do you think it is realistic to pursue several policy goals simultaneously or should one set priorities and possibly compromise by accepting partial goals?

Gross private domestic investment	40.4	27.4	16.8	4.7	5.3	9.4	18.0
Fixed investment	36.9	28.0	19.2	10.9	9.7	12.1	15.6
Nonresidential	26.5	21.7	14.1	8.2	7.6	9.2	11.5
Structures	13.9	11.8	7.5	4.4	3.3	3.6	4.0
Producers' durable equipment	12.6	9.9	6.6	3.8	4.3	5.6	7.5
Residential structures	10.4	6.3	5.1	2.7	2.1	2.9	4.0
Nonfarm	9.9	6.0	4.9	2.5	1.9	2.7	3.8
Farm	.4	.3	.2	.1	.2	.2	.3
Change in business inventories	3.5	-.6	-2.4	-6.2	-4.2	-2.7	2.4
Nonfarm	3.6	-.3	-3.9	-7.0	-3.8	3.1	1.0
Farm	—	—	—	—	—	—	—

MEXICO CITY, May 26—In a policy reversal that was embarked upon gradually, the Mexican Government is trying to slow the country's explosive birth with a nationwide campaign has also been prepared to fight opposition to birth control. The Roman Catholic Church, which is weak politically, though still influential among the people, reacted cautiously to the change Government policy, merely reiterating its support for "responsible

Mexico Offers Family-Planning Help

parenthood" ... But the pro-Catholic ning."

But it avoids the terms "birth control" or "population control."

"There will be no birth control or coercion," Health Minister Jorge Jiménez Cantú said at a news conference last month, apparently seeking to dispel some fears of compulsory sterilization. "We just have a program that will enable couples to determine the number of children they want."

Education Campaign On

Thousands of Government clinics and hospitals are offering, free of charge, all family-planning methods except sterilization. The pill, the intra uterine device and the diaphragm are distributed, and Government doctors are seeking out women who have just given

Heilbroner's premonition of a new Dark Age [VYR, January 24] is credible in the sense of a disintegration of traditional values, institutions, and ways of life. But there is at least the possibility, and I believe the probability (barring a nuclear holocaust), that the coming Dark Age, like the medieval original, will be a time of regeneration as well as disintegration. Historians now are generally agreed that the centuries following the collapse of the

An Exchange on The Human Prospect

ordinary crust ... of modern ... time of disappear ... and crumbling of roads and aqueducts and palaces. But it was also a time of fateful social mutation of evolving new relationships between man and man and between man and nature. "All in all," concludes the historian Robert Lopez, "the [barbarian] invasions gave the coup de grâce to a culture which had come to a standstill after reaching its apogee and seemed doomed to wither away. We are reminded of the cruel bombings in our own day which destroyed ramshackle old buildings and so made possible the reconstruction of towns on more modern lines." The analogy is relevant for our age, which is undergoing a disintegration-reintegration experience similar to that precipitated by the barbarian invasions and the World War II bombings.

My quarrel with Heilbroner is that in this appraisal, in contrast to his earlier writings, he has focused on the current

A Change in 1972

In a land whose population rose from 26 million in 1950 to 58 million today, and appears headed for 71 million in 1980 and 151 million in 2000, official policy had long been that Mexico was large enough for even 200 million.

As late as 1970, President Luis Echeverría Alvarez, himself a father of eight, declared during his election campaign that "to govern is to populate."

The change in policy, first noted in 1972, was said to have resulted ... been tackled with significant and equally significant results. Malnutrition has been eliminated, the population explosion has been effectively curbed, the traditional dichotomy between urban center and rural countryside is being reduced, is also the dichotomy between manual and mental work, and the nation's organizational structure is being transformed into a vast federation of self-sufficient communities with ... nt positive repercussions ...

growing population w ... cient food, housing ... employment and educ ...

According to Dr ... Chavez of the Natio ... tion Institute, 15 pe ... the children born in t ... of malnutrition, and ... per cent suffer menta ... cal retardation as a ... deficient feeding. ... ng a visit to M ... wife remarked th ... dramatic problem in ... try is the malnutrition ... sands upon thousand ... dren."

According to offi ... rates, 25 million ... or nearly half the p ... have no access to med ... ices. Only 5 per ... country's youth ... have access to h ... tion.

With 46 per cent of ... lation under the age ... demand for education ... eral is overwhelming ...

At present, of som ... lion Mexican women ... bearing age, the Socia ... Institute is providin ... directly by the Chin ... institutional innovati ...

WASHINGTON—The economy spell of "stagflation" in the fo economic growth slowed to a 1.3% annual rate and inflation accelera 7.9% annual rate, the worst in the government reported.

The economy probably wil more poorly this quarter ... tration economist indicate expected to continue at a high rate, omy probably won't show any real growth a may show an outright decline in the January-March period, Sidney Jones, assistant Secretary of Commerce, told newsmen. He said a "rather pervasive slowdown," influenced but not "dominated" by the energy crisis, is under way.

The Commerce Department's report on fourth quarter gross national product, which measures the value of the economy's total output of goods and services, showed the lowest ... since the final period of 1970, ... ctually dropped 4.8%, primarily due to a General Motors Corp. strike. The 1.3% annual rate of growth in the fourth quarter's "real" GNP, which is adjusted for price in-creases, was about in line with ear mates by government eco pared with a 3.4% rate the third per ...

Birth, Fertility Rates At a New Low in U.S.

... the first ... e in the first ... the Korean war price ... ued the 7% inflation rate of the ... quarter and was more than double the 3.3% pace of price increase in the year-earlier period.

GNP Rose $29.5 Billion

The Commerce Department said the fourth quarter's GNP increased $29.5 billion, or at a 9.4% annual rate, to a seasonally adjusted $1.334 trillion yearly pace. The rise fell short of the $32.5 billion increase, equal to a 10.6% annual ...

Debate on the growth-antigrowth theme has become a fashionable pastime over the past five years.

And since its continued enjoyment must depend to a large extent on its inconclusiveness, it would be boorish as well as presumptuous to propose that we try to reach a settled conclusion.

But the present enjoyment in the continual conflicts of opinion may become marred by a growing sense of frustration from repeated failure to orga ... rights and to acquire perspective on ... re to steer the debate

Growth and Antigrowth: What Are the Issues?

away from ... ct confrontation—less ba ... I propose, therefore, that we d ... dow ... round rules ... these green shoots an ... other, ... orms: the awakening of hitherto nationalities, the protest of against their traditional sub-the unrest of workers seeking trol of shops and offices, the f youth against war and injustice, iveness of hitherto quiescent or subcultures such as those of als, gypsies, priests and nuns, and nd of frustrated citizens that the epresentative democracy be trans-nto participatory democracy and from the political to the eco-d social aspects of life.

ople's Republic of China is p ... st ... he refers ... 'cesspool of ...

odd jobs await billion-bubble foams?

... out to be almost limitless; the ... ooth performance, literally flabbergasting. slum ... Foam — it appears — might solve doz-for ... unlicked problems in fields Mr ... ar as agriculture, stock ... ing housing, national defense, Horod ... ackaging, dust control and ... vices. With some innovative econo ...inking, foam technology can under-a shorn some brand new products and "Weak vice businesses!

Mr ... form ### High Expansion Aqueous Foams slow "surprise declined ew technologists who wet their tion tha ...s in the collar on a cold beer or though ... irt an extinguisher on a lab bench be a r ... growth ... aze give more than a passing thought

Into the foam. But Monsanto research-ceded ... s were handed a contract research 9% to ... oblem. The culprit was coal dust. ... e client wanted it trapped and con-d — as it billowed from the cut-oits of continuous miners that chewed tons-per-minute bites from a wea ... coal seam. An atomized water spray yea ... trill didn't trap enough; too much danger-out ... dous micronized coal dust escaped. A when ... ar better way was needed to suppress was th ... 5 micron and smaller particles. in 1951 ...

But Monsanto researchers opted for crease .m. Their objective: develop high price ... pansion foam materials, simulate with ... pplication, and evaluate effectiveness. year ... This started a program that created a rate ... eguiling variety of aqueous ... ie of them, a polymer-water-base foam, did the

By THEODORE SHABAD

The Soviet Union has announced the start-up of its first one-million-kilowatt nuclear reactor in a rapidly expanding atomic energy program.

The big electric power unit situated in the area of Leningrad, the country's second largest city, became operational last December, but this was disclosed only this ... at by the ... ncy Tass. ... printed in ... Communist party newspaper Pravada or May ... 8, reported that the ... rad reactor had generated its first billion kilowatt-hours of electricity This was the first news that the unit was in operation.

In a growing effort to develop its atomic power industry, the Soviet Union has thus joined the United States in progressing to nuclear generating units of increasingly larger capacity. The first three one-million-kilowatt units in American nuclear stations became operational last year.

The Leni ... station city of ... is the first of a series of Soviet ... ped with ... hers tha

Even West such as Jo feller's, have the full be communal possible to "the treme is best in what mak another an to one ano

Such ...

Economic Growth Slowed to 1.3% Annually, ... Rate in 4th Quarter

Children Per Family in the U.S.
(Total Fertility Rate)

1945 1950 1955 1960 1965 1970 1973

4.0

3.5

3.0

2.5

2.0

Replacement level: 2.1

Economic Growth

19

Although growth has been a major concern of the human race since people discovered that their own lives did not necessarily have to be lived at the same level of consumption as those of their parents or grandparents, economic theory has only recently begun to explain the causes and mechanisms of growth. In part this is because comparative statics analysis (which we have been using for most of this book) is inadequate when dealing with the time dimension inherent in economic growth and development.

In 1940, however, economist Sir Roy Harrod began to use dynamic analysis in order to deal with long-term growth and, to a certain extent, with departures from equilibrium growth paths. The purpose of this chapter and its appendix is to consider the sources of economic growth, past patterns of growth, particularly in the United States, theories of short- and long-term growth, and policy for keeping short-term growth on an equilibrium path and for dealing with the problems created by long-term growth.

The term "economic growth" has many meanings to both economists and laymen. For the purposes of this chapter, we shall define economic growth as the increase in an economy's potential output, or productivity capacity, which is the level of output realized when all factors of production are fully utilized. For lack of a better measure, the rate of economic growth during a particular period of time, say twenty years, is measured by the change in GNP, at constant prices, between year one and year twenty. This measurement is valid only if the economy is functioning at its productive capacity during both year one and year twenty; when the economy functions at a level significantly below its productive capacity, it may increase its GNP by simply increasing the rate of utilization of its labor force and capital stock, without increasing its productive capacity at all. Such an increase in GNP does not represent economic growth.[1]

As we saw in Chapter 1, the concept of potential GNP was developed by President Kennedy's Council of Economic Advisers in 1961, when the economy was in a slump. The base period for the calculation of the growth of potential output was mid-1955, when unemployment was 4 percent ("full employment") and it was felt that actual and potential output were approximately equal. The rate of growth of GNP (in constant dollars) during this period was 3.5 percent, and this rate was projected as the trend rate of growth of potential output through 1962, when the rate was increased to 3.75 percent. The rate was raised to 4 percent for 1965 through 1968, during most of which time actual GNP was higher than potential GNP (unemployment was below 4 percent). Although President Nixon's Council of Economic Advisors abandoned the concept in 1970, it is a useful one for looking at the problems of measuring, understanding, and influencing economic growth in the real world.

If economists could devise a statistic called "productive capacity," which would measure the final value of the goods and services the economy is *capable* of producing during a given year, the rate of change of this measure would provide the rate of economic growth. (The concept of potential GNP is somewhat primitive—actual GNP exceeding potential GNP is a logical contradiction in terms.) But the problems are considerable, for theoretical as well as practical reasons. For example, the Council (and other economists) have defined "full employment" as a 4 percent un-

---

1. The difference that choice of base years makes to the calculation of long-term growth rates may be easily seen by noting that the average annual growth rate of the American economy between 1929 and 1949 was 2.4 percent, while the rate of growth between 1933 and 1949 was 5.4 percent. The difference is accounted for by the fact that in 1929 the economy was functioning at close to its productive capacity, while in 1933 it was in a deep depression. Thus, the apparent rate of 5.4 percent actually includes a great deal of "catching up," in which the economy was taking up the capacity in labor and capital which had been idle in 1933, and is thus much higher than the actual rate of growth of productive capacity between 1933 and 1949. These figures, which are based on estimates of real Gross National Product expressed in 1954 dollars, are taken from Edward F. Denison, *The Sources of Economic Growth in the United States and the Alternatives Before Us,* Supplementary Paper No. 13 (Washington, D.C.: Committee for Economic Development, 1962), p. 17.

employment rate, arguing that a lower rate involves "overutilization" and is thus unsustainable over any significant length of time. But the experience of other industrialized nations whose labor-force participation rates are higher and unemployment rates consistently lower than those of the United States casts doubt on this argument.[2] We saw in Chapter 3 that a measure of changes in economic well-being might demand a different definition of growth from the one used here, but most economists agree that economic growth makes increased well-being possible by easing the constraints imposed upon a society by a scarcity of resources.

We must also distinguish between economic growth and economic development. Economic development typically involves the transformation of a rural and agricultural society into a "modern" economy in which only a relatively small proportion of the labor force is required to produce food and other raw materials necessary for subsistence. Most of the labor force is involved in the production of manufactured goods, services, and, possibly, agricultural products and raw materials for export. (Thus the emphasis on increasing efficiency in the agricultural sector is normally a prerequisite for economic development, and the existence of a large agricultural population does not necessarily imply that an economy is underdeveloped.) Although it is not always clear at what point in this transformation a given economy is at a given point in time, it is normally possible to decide whether an economy is "developed," "developing," or stagnating in a state of underdevelopment.

Sources of Economic Growth

Economic growth as we have defined it occurs through increases in the amount and/or quality of the economy's factors of production (capital, labor, land, natural resources, and technical expertise). The major sources of economic growth therefore include (1) capital accumulation; (2) technological change (increase in the "quality" of capital); (3) growth in the size and "quality" of the labor force; and (4) an increase in the amount and/or quality of land and/or other natural resources available to the economy. The factor described as technical expertise is considered here to be incorporated in capital and labor.

Capital Accumulation
Capital accumulation refers to an increase in the stock of manufactured physical goods used to produce final goods and services; such capital includes everything from a farmer's barbed wire to the telephone company's switching networks, from barbers' shears to cold roll presses that produce

2. Some enlightening comparisons of labor input to GNP in various industrialized nations can be found in Edward F. Denison, *Why Growth Rates Differ* (Washington, D.C.: The Brookings Institution, 1967), Ch. 5.

sheet metal. Capital accumulation is identical to net investment.[3] Although the importance of capital accumulation to economic growth has been recognized by nearly all economists, the *ways* in which capital accumulation leads to growth are the subject of much debate and analysis. This is in part due to the difficulty of separating capital accumulation from technological change: new capital often incorporates changes which increase the efficiency (output per unit of input) of all factors of production, not only capital.

Technological Change

Technological change might be thought of as one side of a coin whose other side is increasing productivity; the entire coin contributes to economic growth and is in turn increased by economic growth. An increase in productivity is most easily defined as an increase in output per unit of factor input—capital, labor, or natural resources. Technological change usually refers to changes in the nature of the capital stock and the effectiveness with which it is utilized, along with other factors of production to increase output. The effect of technological change may be demonstrated by employing an isoquant map closely related to the one used in Chapter 10. Figure 19.1 represents a "unit isoquant," y_1, which describes the combinations of capital, UK, and labor, UN, which can be employed to produce a *single unit of output*.[4] Point A presents the initial situation, where the unit isoquant y_1 is tangent to the line DF. Line DF represents the ratio of the price of labor to the price of capital, P_N/P_K. At point A, a quantity, OC, of capital and a quantity, OB, of labor are required to produce a unit of output. The rate of profit is given by 1/OD. Since the slope of line DF represents P_N/P_K,

$$\frac{P_N}{P_K} = \frac{DC}{CA} = \frac{UK}{UN}$$

since CA = OB. Therefore,

$$DC = \frac{P_N UN}{P_K}$$

With OC = UK,

$$OD = DC + OC = \frac{1}{P_K} [P_N UN + P_K UK]$$

3. In the national income accounts, gross private domestic investment includes the sum of net capital accumulation and the capital required to replace worn-out capital (depreciation). Since economic growth takes place only through the *net* increase in the stock of capital (leaving aside technological change incorporated in the replacement capital), capital consumption allowances must be deducted from estimates of GPDI to arrive at estimates of net capital accumulation.

4. This approach to analysis of technological change is derived from Ronald W. Jones, "'Neutral' Technological Change and the Isoquant Map," *American Economic Review* 55 (September 1965): 848–855. Here it is assumed that the production function which relates units of capital and labor inputs to output is linear homogeneous. This means that if inputs of capital and labor are both doubled (or increased by n times the original level) then output will double (increase by n times the original level).

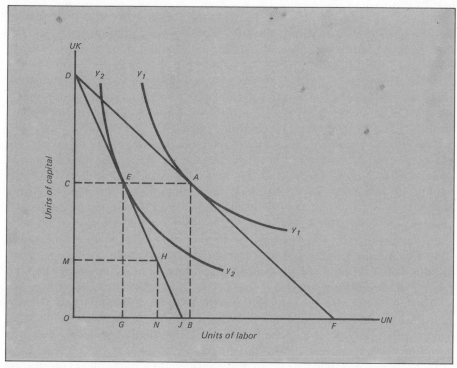

Figure 19.1 The effect of technological change upon the unit isoquant

In a competitive model, the price of output is given by the unit cost of output expressed in brackets. The rate of profit is given by

$$\frac{P_K}{(P_N UN + P_K UK)} = \frac{1}{OD}$$

or the portion of total unit cost going to a unit of capital owned by the recipient of profits. Notice that the capital-output ratio, K/y, or the quantity of capital per unit of output, is given in Figure 19.1 by the distance OC. The labor-output ratio is measured by distances OB or AC.

With these concepts we can grasp the impact of technological change in an economy. Technological change shifts the unit isoquant y_1 inward to y_2 in Figure 19.1. After such a shift, a unit of output could be produced with OC of capital and OG = CE of labor. The technological progress represented here is "Harrod neutral,"[5] since at a constant rate of profit, OD, the capital-output ratio remains constant. The quantity of labor required to produce a unit of output falls from CA to CE for a percentage improvement in labor productivity of AE/CA.

If isoquant y_2 were tangent to the budget line DJ at a point like H, the

5. So called because growth theorist Roy Harrod introduced the criteria for neutrality, namely, that technological change is neither labor-saving nor capital-saving.

technological change would be "Harrod capital-saving," since, at a constant rate of profit, the capital-output ratio would have fallen from OC to OM; equivalently, output per unit of capital would rise from (1/OC) to (1/OM). Moreover, output per unit of labor would rise by 1/ON, less than in the Harrod neutral case, 1/OG. If y_2 were tangent to DJ at some point above E, the technological change would be "Harrod labor-saving," since productivity per unit of labor would rise above 1/OG, whereas productivity per unit of capital would fall below its original level at 1/OC.

Clearly, the fundamental feature of technological change is that it enables more output per unit of input. The technological change may be biased toward increasing labor productivity more than capital productivity (labor-saving) or toward a relatively large improvement in capital productivity (capital-saving). The concepts of capital- or labor-saving technological change can be defined rigorously only given some criterion such as a constant profit rate at which factor productivity is compared before and after the technological change. Although criteria other than Harrod's exist, the fundamental notion conveyed by the terms "labor-saving" or "capital-saving" is similar in all of them.

Technological change may also be illustrated by example. Leo Tolstoy, a careful observer of Russian farming methods in the 1870s, noted in *Anna Karenina* that it took forty-two peasants all day to mow one large meadow on Levin's estate. Although Tolstoy does not tell us how large it was, we can be fairly certain that this task could have been accomplished by a modern American farmer with a heavy-duty tractor in, at most, one long working day. Thus, output per unit of labor input (work-hours) is greatly increased by the invention of the tractor: if we assume, for example, that the meadow contained 168 acres and that each peasant and the American farmer worked eight hours, output per work-hour is increased from .5 acres per hour to 21 acres per hour.

Increasing productivity (and increased productive capacity) is related to two other economic aspects of technological change: the increasing returns to scale and specialization of labor functions. Increasing returns to scale occurs when output per unit of factor input is increased purely through an increase in the scale of production. For example, output per unit of input is generally higher on farms with large fields than on farms with small fields. Small-field farms have a higher proportion of uncultivable land (fence rows, etc.), and farmers not only waste more time when cultivating crops, but also may be forced to use less productive equipment, thus reducing their overall productivity.

The classical example of the gains derived from specialization of labor functions is the assembly line; Adam Smith first described its merits in the manufacture of pins:

> One man draws out the wire, another straights it, a third cuts it, a fourth points it, a fifth grinds it at the top for receiving the head; to make the head requires two or three distinct operations; to put it on, is a peculiar business, to whiten the pins

is another; it is even a trade by itself to put them into the paper; and the important business of making a pin is, in this manner, divided into about eighteen distinct operations, which, in some manufactories, are all performed by distinct hands. . . . I have seen a small manufactory of this kind where the men . . . could . . . make among them about twelve pounds . . . (or) forty-eight thousand pins in a day. Each person, therefore making a tenth part of forty-eight thousand pins, might be considered as making four-thousand eight-hundred pins in a day. But if they had all wrought separately and independently . . . they certain could not each of them have made twenty, perhaps not one pin in a day.[6]

From this he concluded that the division of labor results in increased productivity, the truth of which has been amply demonstrated ever since.

Growth in the Size and Quality of the Labor Force

The labor force is defined as persons working for money wages or seeking work. Thus, in the short term the labor force (and the economy's productive capacity) can grow through a reduction in unemployment and/or an increase in the proportion of the adult population choosing and allowed to work. During wartime, for example, the work force can be increased rapidly by bringing back retired persons, encouraging women to work outside the home, and reducing unemployment to a minimum. In the longer run, the labor force grows through increases in the population of working age, and by changes in law, custom, or economic health which encourage a greater proportion of this population to enter the labor force.

As we can see in Table 19.1, column (6), the proportion of the working-age population (aged 15–64 years) in the labor force varies greatly among industrialized countries—from nearly 75 percent in Denmark to less than 60 percent in the Netherlands (in 1960). The figure for the United States is midway between the two (67.8 percent). The working-age population is increased through net immigration of adults and through population growth in which the number of persons reaching working age is larger than those reaching retiring age (aged 60–65 years). During the period from 1950 to 1962, the U.S. rate of population growth was greater than that of most European countries; those countries in Europe which had a relatively large increase in employment generally imported large numbers of foreign laborers. This (together with a decline in unemployment) accounted for most of the 27 percent increase in employment in Germany between 1950 and 1962, shown in columns (8) and (9).

The contribution of the labor force to the productive capacity of an economy involves not only an increase in size, but also an increase in quality; the value of its contribution varies greatly with the educational attainment, skills, and attitudes of its members. Increases in the quality of the labor force increase output per unit of labor input and therefore constitute a form of technological change. Such an increase in labor productivity in fact could be the explanation for the technological change which shifts y_1 to y_2 in

---

6. Adam Smith, *The Wealth of Nations* (New York: Modern Library, 1937), pp. 4–5.

Table 19-1 Population, Employment, and Selected Labor-Force Ratios, 1960, and Employment Indices, 1950 and 1962 for the United States and Selected Western European Countries

Area	(1) Population (millions) 1960	(2) Labor Force (millions) 1960	(3) Employment (millions) 1960	(4) Labor Force as percent of Population 1960 (percent)	(5) Employment as percent of Population 1960 (percent)	(6) Labor Force as percent of Population Aged 15–64 1960 (percent)	(7) Labor Force as percent of Female Population (15–64) 1960 (percent)	(8) Indices of Employment 1950	(9) Indices of Employment 1962
United States	180.68	73.13	69.20	40.5	38.3	67.8	43.2	100.0	114.6
Northwest Europe[a]	182.46	82.77	81.70	45.4	44.8	70.2	46.5	100.0	111.6
Denmark	4.58	2.20	2.15	48.0	46.9	74.8	51.5	100.0	111.7
France	45.68	19.72	19.48	43.2	42.6	69.6	47.0	100.0	101.3
Germany	55.43	26.52	26.25	47.8	47.3	71.2	49.8	100.0	126.9
Netherlands	11.49	4.19	4.14	36.5	36.1	59.8	27.2	100.0	113.3
United Kingdom	52.54	25.03	24.70	47.6	47.0	73.2	48.0	100.0	108.1
Italy	49.64	21.21	20.37	42.7	41.0	62.9	36.1	100.0	104.9

SOURCE: Edward F. Denison, *Why Growth Rates Differ: Postwar Experience in Nine Western Countries* (Washington, D.C.: The Brookings Institution, 1967), Tables 5–2 and 5–3.

a. Includes Belgium, Denmark, France, Germany, Netherlands, Norway, and the United Kingdom.

Figure 19.1. The result is an increase in labor productivity (in the Harrod neutral case) from 1/OB to 1/OG.[7]

Measured by educational attainment, the increase in the quality of the American labor force was enormous between 1910 and 1960. The average worker in 1930 had spent 2.5 times as many days in school as his counterpart in 1910, while the worker of 1960 had spent 80 percent more days in school than the worker of 1930.[8] Economist Edward F. Denison concluded that the increasing quality of the labor force was one of the most important contributors to economic growth in the United States in the first sixty years of the twentieth century.

Increase in Amount and Quality of Land or other Natural Resources

Although the total quantity of land and nonrenewable resources available to the world economy is a constant, its contribution to the economy's productive capacity varies greatly according to location, ease of access, and in the case of land, innate suitability as farm or forest land. The quantity of renewable resources (forests, fisheries, etc.) depends not only on the amount of land and ocean available to support these resources, but also on the methods used to husband and develop them.

The contribution of both renewable and nonrenewable natural resources to the productive capacity of a particular economy depends on their relative availability (in terms of price, transportation costs, and political constraints), their innate "quality," and the efficiency with which they can be combined with other inputs to produce outputs. A technological advance which increases output per physical unit of input of a natural resource would contribute to an increase in productive capacity (assuming all factors are used to capacity) only if the resource were available and cheap enough to make any required changes in capital worthwhile. Examples of this interaction abound: new coal-burning electric power plants greatly increase the efficiency with which the fuel is used, but this increase is due to technological progress and economies of scale combined, not to any change in the coal. The coal, however, must be available and be relatively cheap to make the new plants competitive with older plants because of new capital costs.

Denison has attempted to determine the relative contributions of each of these sources to economic growth in the United States and certain European countries for various periods during the twentieth century. He divided the sources of economic growth into two categories: (1) changes in the quantity of inputs, or factors of production, and (2) increases in output per unit of input, or productivity changes. For the years 1929 to 1957 in the United States, Denison estimated that growth of real national income

---

7. The "quality" of the labor force must be distinguished from the quantity of knowledge available to the society. The latter governs the productive mix of given inputs which produce an increased output and is thus closely related to technological change (the development of computers, for example); the former refers to the increase in output from a given set of physical inputs and a given amount of knowledge (the increase in skills among the population to enable them to make use of computers to increase productivity, for example).

8. Denison, *Sources of Economic Growth in the United States*, p. 73.

Table 19.2 Sources of Growth of Total National Income and National Income per Person Employed in the United States, 1950–1962

(1) SOURCE OF GROWTH	Total National Income		National Income per Person Employed	
	(2) CONTRIBUTION TO GROWTH RATE IN PERCENTAGE POINTS	(3) PERCENTAGE DISTRIBUTION	(4) CONTRIBUTION TO GROWTH RATE IN PERCENTAGE TERMS	(5) PERCENTAGE DISTRIBUTION
Total factor input	1.95	58%	.79	36%
Labor	1.12	33	.22	10
Employment	.90	27	—	—
Hours of work	−.17	− 5	−.17	− 8
Age-sex composition	−.10	− 3	−.10	− 5
Education	.49	15	.49	17
Capital	.83	25	.60	27
Dwellings	.25	7	.21	10
International assets	.05	1	.04	2
Nonresidential structures and equipment	.43	13	.29	13
Inventories	.10	3	.06	3
Land	0.00	0	−.03	− 1
Adjusted output per unit of input	1.41	42%	1.40	62%
Advances of knowledge	.76	23	.75	34
Improved allocation of resources	.29	9	.29	13
Contraction of agricultural inputs	.25	7	.25	11
Contraction of nonagricultural employment	.04	1	.04	2
Reduction of international trade barriers	.00	0	.00	0
Economies of scale	.36	11	.36	16
Adjusted national income	3.36	100%	2.19	100%

SOURCE: Denison, *Why Growth Rates Differ*, Tables 21–1 and 21–2.
NOTE: Details in columns 3 and 5 may not add to totals because of rounding.

averaged 2.93 percent per year, 68 percent of which was due to increases in total inputs and 32 percent to increases in output per unit of input.[9]

Table 19.2 shows Denison's more recent estimates for the period 1950–1962; these indicate that real "adjusted" national income grew by an average of 3.36 percent per year during this period.[10] Of this increase, 58 percent was accounted for by increases in total factor inputs and 42 percent by increases in output per unit of input. Within the total factor input increases, 42 percent was due to increases in capital, and the rest to increases in the quantity and quality of labor. By Denison's definition, land does not account for any increase in factor inputs. Columns (4) and (5) of the table show the rate of growth of national income per person employed—in other words, when the effect of increases in employment is removed. Whether measured in per capita or total terms, the increase in the stock of knowledge available to the society accounted for more than half of the increase in output per unit of input. Economies of scale and improved allocation of resources accounted for the rest.

The calculations upon which these estimates are based are complex, subject to large measurement errors, and, in some instances, arbitrary. One economist has written that "it goes without saying that, at the present moment, these estimates are far more art than science."[11] But they are a beginning, and when they become more reliable, such estimates can guide policymakers who wish to increase their economy's growth rate in the most efficient manner possible.

Patterns of Economic Growth

Historically, economic growth generally has occurred in cycles based on population growth and decline due to war, pestilence, and famine. Since output per worker grew only slowly, if at all, before the Industrial Revolution, output at the peak of one cycle would probably be only little greater than at the peak of the previous cycle. Thomas Malthus, an English minister, predicated his famous and pessimistic theory upon this cycle, created by a geometric rate of growth of population combined with an arithmetic rate of growth of agricultural output: the end result would be famine, a population reduction, and the beginning of a new cycle as surplus agricultural land becomes available to support a newly growing population.[12]

9. Ibid., Table 32, p. 266.

10. Denison actually produces two estimates of national income and output per unit of input; the "adjusted" figure excludes a complex component called "irregularities in pressure of demand." See *Why Growth Rates Differ: Postwar Experience in Nine Western Countries* (Washington D.C.: The Brookings Institution, 1967), pp. 273–278, 298.

11. Richard T. Gill, *Economic Development: Past and Present* (Englewood Cliffs, N.J.: Prentice-Hall, 1964), p. 75.

12. A geometric rate of growth is one in which the quantity involved grows at a constant *rate* over equal intervals of time (Malthus postulated that a population unchecked by famine would double every twenty-five years), while an arithmetic rate is one where the quantity involved grows by a constant *amount* over equal intervals of time (Malthus assumed that food production could grow by a constant amount every twenty-five years). See Thomas Malthus, *Essay on the Principle of Population as it Affects the Future Improvement of Society* (1798; reprint ed., *First Essay on Population, 1798*, New York: Augustus M. Kelley, 1965).

Economic development may thus be viewed as the complex process by which an economy breaks out of this pattern and creates a new one characterized by long-term increases in productive capacity in agriculture, the development of banking, industries, trade and internal and/or foreign markets for the products of those industries. In medieval Europe, the process started slowly with technological changes which increased agricultural output and the gradual development of new and expanded markets—the growth in the "extent of the market," which was viewed by Adam Smith as a fundamental prerequisite to economic growth and industrial development.[13] As towns and cities grew, their inhabitants began to acquire new ideas about the individual's place in the world and his ability to understand and ultimately control nature. The rise of nation-states increased the size and stability of markets and helped create a climate in which banking and later, the beginnings of industry could develop. It has been argued that Protestantism brought with it new attitudes toward the moral desirability of the accumulation of worldly goods and productive capital and was thus an important factor in the development of the set of attitudes which preceded the Industrial Revolution in England.[14]

The discovery and exploitation of the resources of the New World were made possible by these changes. They in turn created further change in sixteenth- and seventeenth-century Europe, particularly in England and to some extent in Spain. The precious metals brought from South America inflated existing currencies, further undercutting traditional ways and opening economic opportunity to newly rising merchant classes. The colonies provided new markets for finished goods, especially textiles, and raw materials for the growing European manufacturers as well as agricultural products for the continent's growing population.

When George II died in 1760, England was on the brink of the Industrial Revolution.[15] The development of the British economy which followed over the next fifty years can be viewed in terms of the causes of economic growth we have just identified. Capital accumulation in the form of factories and equipment rose rapidly and combined with technological change to totally change ways of manufacturing many goods and increase many

13. Smith, *The Wealth of Nations*, Ch. 3.

14. This theory's most famous protagonists were Max Weber and R. H. Tawney. See Weber's *The Protestant Ethic and the Spirit of Capitalism* (1904; new ed., New York: Scribners, 1958), and Tawney's *Religion and the Rise of Capitalism* (1922; reprint ed., Middlesex: Penguin Books, 1938). More recent investigations into the roles of Italian Catholic bankers before and during the Renaissance and of Jewish merchants throughout Medieval Europe (not to speak of nineteenth-century Japanese) have tended to suggest the Protestant religion is not a necessary prerequisite to the development of the "Protestant ethic." See, for example, Richard W. Kaeuper, *Bankers and the Crown: The Riccardi of Lucca and Edward I* (Princeton, N.J.: Princeton University Press, 1973); and Herbert I. Bloom, *The Economic Activities of the Jews of Amsterdam in the Seventeenth and Eighteenth Centuries* (New York: Kennikat Press, 1969).

15. Some economic histories have argued that the term "revolution" is a misnomer, the process being a continuum from the fifteenth century, if not earlier. See Christopher Hill, *Reformation to Industrial Revolution* (Middlesex: Penguin Books, 1969), vol. 2, for a discussion of economic life in Britain during the two centuries preceding the Industrial Revolution.

times the amounts produced. The classic example is the textile industry, often considered the dynamo of the Industrial Revolution. Production figures for this industry are lacking, but after a series of technological changes beginning with the flying shuttle in 1733, British imports of raw cotton grew from around 3 million pounds in weight in 1750 to 5.3 million pounds in 1802.[16] In fact, one could argue that the essential characteristic of this first Industrial Revolution was the tremendous increase in energy available per worker as technological change (methods of harnessing steam created by the burning of coal) combined with available nonrenewable natural resources (coal) to supersede output produced by human, animal, and to some extent, water power, the source of all previous production.[17]

The industrial working force also grew rapidly during this period, in part through the development of "enclosures," which forced tenants off farms and into the growing factory towns and cities.[18] The quality of the labor force can be said to have improved only in its discipline to the rigors of the factory system; in almost all other ways—level of education, nutrition, life expectancy—the newly forming English working class was no better off, and in many ways worse off, than it had been when its members had been primarily agricultural laborers.[19]

The American colonies were profoundly affected by the English Industrial Revolution, but economic development in the United States proceeded along somewhat different lines from that of the mother country. In 1770 the colonies were largely agricultural, exporting timbers, furs, and foodstuffs to England and receiving manufactured goods in return. The critical period of American economic development, which lasted from 1790 to 1860,[20] can also be considered in terms of the previously discussed causes of economic growth. Capital accumulation on an immense scale combined with rapid technological progress, some of it borrowed from England and adapted to the North American continent, were characteristic of the American economy during the entire nineteenth century. Thus, Simon Kuznets

16. Paul Mantoux, *The Industrial Revolution in the Eighteenth Century* (1927; reprint ed., London: University Paperbacks, 1961), p. 252.

17. Ibid. See also T. S. Ashton, *The Industrial Revolution* (London: Home University Library, 1948).

18. See Hill, *Reformation to Industrial Revolution*, pp. 268–273; Mantoux, *The Industrial Revolution*, pp. 136–183; and E. Kerridge, *The Agricultural Revolution* (London: Allen and Unwin, 1967) for discussions of the enclosures. Some indications of the massive scale of population movements can be seen by noting that the population of agricultural countries in England barely changed between 1700 and 1800, while the population of Lancashire, the core of the revolution, nearly tripled. Manchester had perhaps 10,000 inhabitants in 1700; in 1801 it had 95,000 (Mantoux, *The Industrial Revolution*, pp. 354–360).

19. See G. D. H. Cole and Raymond W. Postgate, *The Common People, 1746–1938* (London: Methuen, 1938); for an account of the effects of the Industrial Revolution on the nineteenth-century working class, see E. P. Thompson, *The Making of the English Working Class* (New York: Vintage Books, 1966).

20. See Douglass C. North, *The Economic Growth of the United States, 1790–1860* (Englewood Cliffs, N.J.: Prentice-Hall, 1961). Before North's work, economic historians considered the critical period to be 1865–1895.

has estimated that reproducible capital per member of the labor force increased by more than 200 percent, while total capital, including land and subsoil resources per worker, increased by nearly 175 percent during the period 1879 through 1944.[21] The United States also supported a vast increase in population, a great part of it due to adult immigrants whose skills were added almost immediately to the labor force. The construction of the railroads and an American shipping industry created a continent-wide and then a worldwide market for this country's manufactured goods, agricultural products, and other raw materials. According to one estimate, the rate of growth of "reproducible tangible wealth" per head between 1805 and 1950 averaged 2 percent per year. Since the rate of growth of population during this period averaged 2.2 percent per year, the rate of growth for total civilian reproducible tangible wealth was 4.21 percent per year.[22]

Short-Term Economic Growth Theories

Short-term growth theories are concerned with determining the mathematical relationships between a given rate of growth and the factors we have discussed, particularly changes in the stock of capital and in the labor force. Although some growth theories attempt to deal with technological change and with natural resources, few try to deal with the increasing quality of the labor force and "advance of knowledge," to use Denison's term for one of the most important factors in American economic growth.

One of the simplest models of short-term growth is the Harrod-Domar model, named for the economists whose ideas it embodies. Its extreme simplicity is manifest by the assumptions involved in its specification. The first assumption is that of a single, homogenous output, which is used both for consumption and as a capital input for the production of more output. The labor force is assumed to grow at a constant rate. The model defines an equilibrium or **warranted rate of growth** where the equilibrium capital stock is fully employed and the simple Keynesian flow equilibrium condition in the product market is satisfied where savings is equal to investment. These conditions are discussed with more precision in the appendix to this chapter.

However, numerous inconsistencies intrude between the Harrod-Domar model and the real world. Empirical facts are not consistent with certain of the fundamental assumptions of the model, particularly the assumption

21. Figures are for reproducible and total capital adjusted for standard hours. Simon Kuznets, "Long-Term Changes in the National Income of the United States Since 1870," in *Income and Wealth of the United States*, Income and Wealth Series II (Baltimore: Johns Hopkins University Press, 1952), p. 78.

22. Raymond W. Goldsmith, "The Growth of Reproducible Wealth of the United States of America from 1805 to 1950," ibid., p. 267. (These data are calculated on the basis of "all available benchmark values" between 1805 and 1950.)

that the MPS and the capital-output ratio are constants.[23] Indeed, one of the most important results of an acceptable growth theory would be some explanation for observed fluctuations in these two variables. The assumptions about the reactions of corporations to short-term changes in demand are also open to question, particularly in those industries (public utilities, petroleum, etc.) in which the time span between decisions concerning new investment and production resulting from that investment is relatively long.[24] In such cases, the capital-output ratio may be permitted to fall to some critical level before the capital stock is increased.

Based on different assumptions, a group of theories which we shall call neoclassical permit a change in the capital-output ratio. As we shall see in the appendix to this chapter, these suggest that there may be an infinite number of capital-output ratios, which may vary over time as proportions of the various factors of production in the total growth mix change. Using assumptions of perfect competition and a full-employment equilibrium, they conclude that the rate of economic growth is determined by the rates of growth of the various factors of production.

The neoclassicists have often utilized the Cobb-Douglas production function, examined in the appendix. This states that output is a function of technological progress, capital, and labor, while growth in output (productive capacity) is a function of the sum of the changes in these three variables. This model treats technological progress as "disembodied"— growing at a constant rate and unaffected by investment—and assumes constant substitutability of labor for capital.[25]

Short-Term Economic Growth Policy

Growth policy designed to increase the economy's productive capacity must be distinguished from stabilization policy aimed at inducing the economy to take up slack (unemployed capital and/or labor) during times of recession. The short-term effect may be the same statistically—an increase in GNP—but the policies and the theory behind them are very different. In practice, however, it is hard to disentangle the two types of policies,

23. A rough indication of the problem with this assumption can be gained from Denison's data comparing rate of growth of capital to that of real national income over various periods of time; this ratio varied from 1.23 for the period 1909–1927 to an estimated .75 for the period 1960–1980. (Denison, *Sources of Economic Growth in the United States*, p. 165.)

24. See John Kenneth Galbraith, *Economics and the Public Purpose* (Boston: Houghton Mifflin, 1973) for a discussion of the implications of this lag for business behavior.

25. These assumptions are open to question, particularly in light of Denison's data. Robert M. Solow tried to deal with the problem of technological change by viewing it as "embodied" in the capital stock. Capital is divided into "vintages" which correspond to the year of production. The older the machine, the less productive. Thus Solow argues that an increase in the savings rate may lead to a reduction in the average age of capital and thus increase output by increasing the "average quality" of the total capital stock. See Robert M. Solow, "Investment and Technical Progress," in Kenneth Arrow, et al., eds., *Mathematical Methods in the Social Sciences 1959* (Stanford, Cal.: Stanford University Press, 1960).

partly because policies designed to increase productive capacity are often undertaken in periods of recession.[26]

We have seen that policies designed to increase the rate of capital accumulation, or investment, may include tax credits for certain types of investment, artificially increased rates of depreciation, and, more indirectly, corporation tax cuts and efforts to keep interest rates low in order to facilitate borrowing to increase corporate capital stock. Policies designed to increase the rate of technological change may include government sponsorship of research, the development of prototypes, and patent and copyright laws according to which the results of technological change can be disseminated in an orderly manner. One of the most important examples of government-financed research and development is in agriculture, which has been "revolutionized" by new methods, equipment, seeds, and breeding stock, most of which were developed directly by the Department of Agriculture, or indirectly, by research departments of the land-grant colleges.[27]

An increased labor force may be encouraged by policies favoring large families or high net rates of immigration. The provision of day-care centers and tax deductions for child care would certainly encourage more women to join the labor force; similarly, efforts to reduce discrimination against teenagers, older persons, blacks, and other ethnic minorities may encourage "discouraged" workers in these groups to rejoin the labor force as well. Policies designed primarily to increase labor-force quality may indirectly encourage unskilled, discouraged workers to rejoin the labor force. Encouraging growth of the labor force requires, however, that demand for a growing labor force be assured.

Policies designed to improve the quality of the labor force have a long history in the United States, not only in the provision of primary and secondary education, but in higher education as well, as the land-grant colleges illustrate. It is clear that the great increase in formal education among workers which occurred between 1900 and 1970 contributed a good deal to the growth of output during that period (See Table 19.2).

Policies of purchase and expansion in the United States since the eighteenth century have tended to increase the amount of land and natural resources available for increasing the productive capacity of the economy. The use of the land was encouraged by the Homestead Act of 1862 and other laws designed to encourage settlement by Europeans. The building of the railroads, which was encouraged by vast land grants, opened land for agriculture and the extraction of renewable and nonrenewable resources. Land conservation is presently encouraged by numerous federal and state incentives and regulations and exploitation of nonrenewable resources is fostered through leases of federally-owned lands and tax incentives.

26. Thus the corporate tax cut passed by the Congress in January 1964 was designed to move the sluggish economy closer to full-employment output partially through a rise in investment spending which would lead to increased GNP as well as increased productive capacity.

27. Land-grant colleges were established under the Morrill Act of 1862, which set aside 30,000 acres of federal land for each member of Congress from a given state. The land was to be

Long-Term Economic Growth Theories

After a flurry of interest in the nineteenth century, economists generally abandoned the study of long-term growth for detailed analyses of the price system of a hypothetical economy functioning under the dictates of pure competition, and later on, for comparative statics analysis of economic aggregates and the role of monetary- and fiscal-policy actions in affecting such aggregates. Projections of future growth, even over short time spans, were rare (Denison being the exception). Recently, however, spurred by biologists, demographers, and physicists, economists have once again become concerned with understanding the dynamics of long-term economic growth in the United States and other industrialized countries as well as in the underdeveloped nations.

Three basic schools of thought about future long-term growth in the industrialized nations are illustrated in Figure 19.2. Deliberately, neither axis (time and rate of growth) is qualified, but time is measured in decades rather than years, and the maximum rate of growth foreseen by any school is no higher than the maximum rate experienced by any industrialized nation in any given year—say around 15 percent. The three schools include (1) the stagnationists, who foresee the rate of growth gradually declining to zero; (2) the "steady statists," who foresee long-term growth continuing pretty much as it has since 1950 with fluctuations according to business cycles and perhaps a gradual increase in the rate of growth; and (3) the prophets of "explosion and collapse," who foresee rapidly, even exponentially, increasing rates of growth leading to collapse and ultimately negative growth rates.

Classical economic thought tended toward stagnationism; it included theories in which equilibrium consisted of a stationary state without growth. In the twentieth century, stagnation theory is associated with American economist Alvin Hansen. Promulgated at the end of the Depression, Hansen's theory held that declining populations, growth in savings, the end·to territorial expansion, and shifts from capital-absorbing to capital-saving innovations would lead to stagnation. Hansen's theory is examined in more detail in the appendix, along with those of the more important classical economists who prophesied stagnation—Smith, Ricardo, and Mill. Malthus is sometimes regarded as a stagnationist, but his theory is much more closely related to that of the prophets of explosion and collapse than it is to modern or even classical stagnation theory.

The argument of the steady statists is, essentially, that the future will be like the past and that both the premises and conclusions of the stagnationists and the prophets of doom are incorrect. For example, Robert M. Solow has attempted to develop a "model of long-run growth which

sold to provide an endowment for at least one college "where the leading object shall be . . . to teach such branches of learning as are related to agriculture and the mechanic arts." In 1887 the Hatch Act was passed; it provided federal aid to agricultural experiment stations established at land-grant colleges.

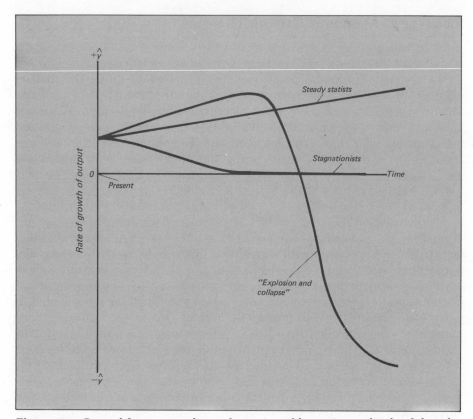

Figure 19.2 General future growth trends as viewed by various schools of thought

accepts all the Harrod-Domar assumptions except that of fixed proportions."[28] In Solow's model, discussed in the appendix, the "razor's edge"
problem disappears because of an ability to substitute labor for capital in
the production of output. Elsewhere, Solow describes such an economy
as eventually settling down to "growth at its natural rate. The natural rate
of growth in the simplest case—where there is a steady state—is the sum
of the rate of growth of the labor supply and the rate of purely labor-augmenting technical progress."[29] This last condition is related to the Harrod labor-
saving technological change discussed earlier. Obviously, then, growth
can be expected to continue as long as the labor supply grows and some
technological progress takes place.

Events have borne out steady-statist refutations of the stagnationists,
and their arguments with the prophets of doom will be discussed in more
detail after we have considered the "explosion and collapse" theory.

There are really three variants of the explosion and collapse school

28. Robert M. Solow, "A Contribution to the Theory of Economic Growth," *Quarterly Journal of Economics* 70 (February 1956): 65–94.

29. Robert M. Solow, *Growth Theory: An Exposition* (New York: Oxford University Press,
1970), p. 77.

of thought. It is possible, if unorthodox, to consider Marxian economic theory as the first of these, because of its emphasis on the collapse of capitalism due to "internal contradictions."[30] The usefulness of Marxian theory to the development of a valid theory of long-term economic growth in industrialized nations is limited because of its inability to deal with the actual and potential effects of capital accumulation.

The second variant is that promulgated by the intellectual descendants of Malthus; they consider Malthus not incorrect, but incomplete.[31] They have been attempting to complete the Malthusian analysis by the analysis of constraints in addition to food production and exponentially growing variables in addition to population. In the best-known and most controversial analysis of this school, *The Limits to Growth*, the constraints include "the *physical* necessities that support all physiological and industrial activity—food, raw materials, fossil and nuclear fuels, and the ecological systems of the planet which absorb wastes and recycle important basic chemical substances."[32] The exponentially growing variables include those components of economic growth characterized by increasing industrial production and the mechanization of agriculture: namely, the demand for both renewable and nonrenewable resources, fossil and nuclear fuels, and the byproducts summarily labeled "pollutants," including heat, poisonous chemicals, putrification agents, and other disrupters of the planetary ecology.

Beginning with these variables and constraints and certain assumptions about their future behavior and the relationship among them, a model of the world economy was constructed and used to simulate the course of change in population, economic growth and certain other variables over the next 130 years.[33] One example, reproduced as Figure 19.3 and called "World Model Standard Run" is based on the assumption "of no major changes in the physical, economic or social relationships that have historically governed the development of the world system."[34]

30. Marxist theory is beyond the scope of this book, but Marx shares with Ricardo the idea that capital accumulation would be checked by falling profits, as well as the stagnationist thesis that excess capacity, high unemployment, and ever-deepening depressions would create a growing gap between potential and actual GNP. See Karl Marx, *Capital* (New York: International Publishers, 1967), Vol. II, Ch. 25.

31. See Jay W. Forrester, *World Dynamics* (Cambridge, Mass.: Wright-Allen, 1971), p. 2.

32. Donella H. Meadows, et al., *The Limits to Growth: A Report for the Club of Rome's Project on the Predicament of Mankind* (New York: New American Library, 1972), p. 55. The methodology in this study is adapted from the above-mentioned work by Jay Forrester. These and other related papers are collected in *Toward Global Equilibrium*: Collected Papers for *The Limits of Growth* (Cambridge, Mass.: Wright-Allen, 1973).

33. A summary of the model used in the computer simulations, an example of which is shown in Figure 19.3, is shown in *The Limits to Growth*, pp. 110–111. The equations of the original model upon which this model is based are contained in Forrester, *World Dynamics*, pp. 132–134.

34. In this model, "food, industrial output, and population grow exponentially until the rapidly diminishing resource base forces a slowdown in industrial growth. Because of natural delays in the system, both population and pollution continue to increase for some time after the peak of industrialization. Population growth is finally halted by a rise in the death rate due to decreased food and medical services" (*The Limits to Growth*, p. 129).

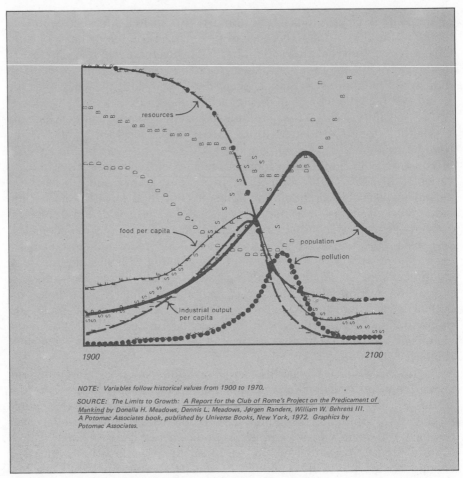

NOTE: Variables follow historical values from 1900 to 1970.

SOURCE: The Limits to Growth: A Report for the Club of Rome's Project on the Predicament of Mankind by Donella H. Meadows, Dennis L. Meadows, Jørgen Randers, William W. Behrens III. A Potomac Associates book, published by Universe Books, New York, 1972. Graphics by Potomac Associates.

Figure 19.3 "The world model standard run"

When certain assumptions about the variables and the constraints are changed, the patterns of growth and the causes of the collapse change as well. For example, when resources are assumed to be "unlimited" (due to nuclear power which will increase the resources that can be exploited and allow for extensive recycling and substitution) growth is eventually stopped by pollution, leading to a sharp fall in industrial production, available food, and thus population.[35] In all cases, the result is the same—explosive growth for a time followed by collapse.

The controversy aroused by this analysis has been immense and may be summarized by an exchange of views at a conference on world priorities as reported by the *New York Times*.[36] Nobel-prize-winning econometrician Jan Tinbergen was quoted as saying, in regard to "upheavals" early in the

35. Ibid., pp. 132–133.
36. *New York Times*, May 7, 1974, p. 48.

twenty-first century, "my own down-to-earth forecast is that we probably won't make it and very bad things will happen." He was "influenced" by the Club of Rome study, although "various aspects of it were open to criticism," and he felt that the crisis would come from mass hunger, rather than pollution.

On the other side, Dr. Martin Shubik, a professor of the Economics of Organization at Yale, was reported as describing "such 'doomsday' projects as naive" and "of little practical value." The study had " 'grossly underestimated' the number of alternatives" available to the world's future. In more general terms, those who quarrel with the doomsday analysis do so on any of several grounds: (1) exponential growth will not continue because of technological change, which will increase efficiency with which resources are utilized, enable populations to be stabilized, and reduce the rate of growth of pollution; (2) the constraints are not really constraints, because additional resources are available, particularly if massive amounts of energy can be obtained from fission and fusion power to extract them; (3) the interrelationships within the "world model" are inaccurate and too simplistic, while the conclusions derived from the model do not take into account political and social variables which will change mankind's behavior long before doomsday arrives.

It is, of course, extremely difficult to evaluate these arguments, particularly those suggesting that increased efficiency will obviate problems of insufficient nonrenewable resources. The third variant of the prophets of doom theory deals with the second of these arguments—namely, the possibility of staving off disaster through massive applications of energy to agriculture, resource extraction, and pollution control. This argument, developed by physicists, is neatly summarized by economist Robert Heilbroner, in which he refers to it as an "ultimatum from nature."[37]

The argument begins with two physical facts: first, the second law of thermodynamics tells us that all energy used ultimately ends up as heat, regardless of its source, how it is used, or the kind of work it does. Second, there are three sources of energy available to the earth: (1) energy stored in matter when the universe began; (2) energy radiated by the sun in the past, stored by the action of plants and/or animals, and turned into fossil fuels (coal, oil, and natural gas) or combustible organic matter (wood, dung, hay); and (3) energy currently radiating onto the earth from the sun (the solar flux).

The argument arises because, although the earth radiates some energy back into space, whenever stored energy of any type is utilized, some of the heat produced is retained by the earth—in the atmosphere, the land, or the seas. The amount of heat which the earth can absorb while maintaining plant and animal life as we know it is fixed, while the emission of heat from stored energy is growing at an exponential rate. Thus, the earth is faced with its "ultimatum" from nature, to be delivered in about 250

37. Robert Heilbroner, *An Inquiry into the Human Prospect* (New York: Norton, 1974), p. 50.

years, according to the calculations of physicists Robert Ayres and Allen Kneese. "Present emission of energy [heat] is about 1/15,000 of the absorbed solar flux. But if the present rate of growth continued for 250 years emissions would reach one-hundred percent of the absorbed solar flux. The resulting increase in the earth's temperature would be about 50°C. [90°F.]— a condition totally unsuitable for human habitation.[38]

Two-hundred and fifty years may seem a long time to deal with this problem, but as Heilbroner points out, the peculiar nature of exponential growth conceals the gravity of the problem. At a 4 percent rate of growth, 150 years would elapse before the atmosphere began to warm up appreciably, but then further exponential growth would create enormous multiple effects, and "extinction [would] beckon if exponential growth continues for only another generation or two."[39]

The argument made against this is that exponential rates of growth in the utilization of stored energy will not continue, either because of a switch-over to solar energy (which adds nothing to the solar flux) or increased efficiency in resource utilization or a reduction in economic growth. But there is little evidence that any of these solutions will be attempted in the near future; the effort, rather, appears to be one of *increasing* non-solar-derived energy use through the development of fastbreeder reactors (self-perpetuating manufacturers of nuclear fuel) and fission reactors.

Long-Term Economic Growth Policy

The formulation of long-term growth policy obviously depends on acceptance of one of the long-term growth theories. We can ignore long-term policy aimed at dealing with structural stagnation (as opposed to recessions), however, since the problem has not arisen in any industrialized nation. The steady statists would presumably advocate long-term policy as an extension of short-term policy, designed mainly to deal with business cycles and otherwise keep growth on an even keel.

Dealing with the problems of explosive growth followed by collapse is another matter, given the acceptance of any variant of the theory. It must begin with a recognition that the problems and the solutions are shared by all the world's nations, the richest and the poorest, and that many of the "solutions" which might be feasible for the rich nations would be absolutely devastating to the poorest ones. One aspect of the solution is population control, but for various reasons, economic and social, the prospects for this appear exceedingly dim at this point in time.[40] The problems

38. In other words, if the mean annual temperature of an area were 45°F., an increase of 50°C. would lead to a mean annual temperature of 135°F., far above that in which human beings can exist for any more than a few minutes. Robert U. Ayres and Allen V. Kneese, "Economic and Ecological Effects of a Stationary State," *Resources for the Future*, Reprint No. 99, December 1972, p. 16, as quoted in Heilbroner, *An Inquiry into the Human Prospect*, p. 51.

39. Heilbroner, *An Inquiry into the Human Prospect*, p. 52.

40. Projections of population trends in developed and underdeveloped nations can be found in Department of Economic and Social Affairs of the United Nations, *Growth of the World's*

involved in a reduction of the rate of economic growth are also immense, particularly for the underdeveloped nations: a shift of output to services and other activities utilizing lower amounts of nonrenewable resources and energy per unit of GNP may hold some hope for the industrialized nations, but this should not be overemphasized as a cure-all.

The chief problem for both rich and poor nations is agriculture. First, it must be remembered that the amount of food (in calories) which can be produced on the earth's surface is fixed, limited by the amount of sunlight falling on the earth and maximum biological limits to the efficiency with which the photosynthetic systems of plants can convert the sun's energy into calories of food. The actual amount of land devoted to food is limited by the need for other crops (fibers, woodstuffs), the nature of the land, climatic conditions, and land needed for human settlement and the production of solar energy. In addition, the mechanized agriculture of the industrialized nations and the new methods commonly referred to as the "green revolution," in addition to creating unanticipated social problems, also require enormous amounts of stored energy. One recent study has estimated that if all of the world's agriculture utilized energy at the rate it is consumed by the "American food system," 80 percent of the world's current consumption of energy would be required to produce and market its current agricultural output.[41]

If one accepts that nature has in fact delivered an ultimatum and that humankind must live within the constraints imposed by the sword above its collective head, some fundamental changes may be required in the way that economists think about and deal with economic activity. It also suggests that economists have an immense amount to contribute to the analysis of these problems—and, hopefully, to devising long-term solutions. For example, it seems to be clear that a larger and larger proportion of all energy must be obtained from the solar flux. But this involves additional priorities as energy from the solar flux must also be used to produce food.

For another example, we can return to Tolstoy's estate and our modern American farmer. We noted that the transformation from one method to the other greatly increases output per unit of labor and output per unit of land (although this is not directly illustrated by our example, other empirical studies leave no doubt of its general truth). The amount of capital available to the American farmer is enormously larger than that available to the Russian peasant. On the other hand, output per physical unit of nonrenewable resources (oil, iron, copper) used has clearly fallen greatly.

Traditionally, total output per unit of combined factor input would be calculated in terms of the price of the output (a bushel of wheat, for example) and the prices of the total inputs—labor (wages), capital, and

Urban and Rural Population, 1920–2000, no. 44 (New York, 1969), pp. 58–63. The possibilities for and possible consequences of population control in poor countries are explored in Goran Ohlin. *Population Control and Economic Development* (Paris: Development Centre of the Organisation for Economic Co-operation and Development, 1967).

41. J. S. and C. E. Steinhart, "Energy Use in the U.S. Food System," *Science* 184, no. 4134 (April 19, 1974): 312.

Commentary: Too Many People?

The conviction that there are too many people in the world is a fundamental and self-evident truth to most environmentalists. In developed nations such as the United States, the "population problem" is seen by such groups as a central reason for the gradual deterioration of the quality of life. Our highways are jammed with cars and strewn with litter; our outdoor recreational facilities are too mobbed to be enjoyed; we are packed into subway cars and pushed by crowds wherever we go in the urban centers. The wide open spaces seem further away and smaller all the time.

Although industrialized nations include only one-third of the world's population, they use disproportionate amounts of the world's resources to maintain what is felt to be an adequate standard of living. According to Paul Ehrlich, probably the best-known advocate of population control, the consumption patterns of the affluent "are wasting the resources of our planet and destroying its environment."[1] Most people in the developed nations have enough to eat, but this is not because these countries can produce enough food to feed their populations; it is rather because they have the resources available to produce enough other goods to exchange for the food they need.

In the underdeveloped countries, where two-thirds of the world's population lives, too many people create a much more graphic dilemma: each year more people are starving. Because these countries do not produce and cannot buy enough food to nourish their existing populations, many children born in these countries are almost sure to go hungry. This problem has become more acute since World War II because the improvement of medical services in these countries has produced significant declines in the death rate with no parallel drop in the birth rate. The average death rate in the world in 1969 was estimated to be 15 per thousand, compared with 35 to 45 per thousand in previous years.[2] Birth rates in developing countries for the same period have been estimated at from 35 to 50 per thousand.

Increasing populations double themselves faster and faster as they grow. The period required for a doubling of the world's population has decreased from 200 years between 1650 and 1850 to approximately 35 years today. In underdeveloped countries the number of years is even lower, and the problems created by such a fast rate of growth are immeasurably complicated by the inability of these countries to provide essential services to their existing populations.

The environmentalist's answer to too much pollution and too many hungry is to reduce the growth of the world's population so that the economies of the various countries can sustain a high standard of living for all of their inhabitants. In this view the problem is too many people and the solution is worldwide birth control. One influential group advocates what it calls "zero population growth" as the goal: every couple is to produce no more than two children so that the population of the world is gradually stabilized at the point where the birth rate and the death rate are the same. Among the policies supported by these activists are legalized abortion on demand and universal availability of sterilization and contraceptive devices.

---

1. Paul R. Ehrlich and Richard L. Harriman, *How To Be a Survivor* (New York: Ballantine Books, 1971), p. 22.

2. Death rates and birth rates are calculated by dividing the total number of deaths or births in a year by the total population at the midpoint of the year and multiplying that figure by 1,000.

The birth-control movement has encouraged the development of many programs around the world that are supported both by voluntary organizations and by governments. None of these programs has been dramatically successful in reducing the birth rate, however.[3] In countries such as Taiwan where large-scale birth-control programs have been instituted, the fall in the birth rate, where it has occurred, has been linked to rises in the standard of living and to education rather than to the programs themselves. A central reason for the failure of these efforts to reduce the population may be that most birth-control planners assume that families are poor *because* they are large and that poor families will accept contraception devices and use them if they are made available. At least one detailed study indicates just the opposite: families are not poor because they are large; they are large because they are poor.

The study involved a village in India called Manupur, which was selected for a long-term population field study because it was in a district whose population density was 75 percent higher than that of India as a whole.[4] Birth-control information and devices were made available to the villagers, but at the end of the study no appreciable change had occurred in the village birth rate. The planners did not realize that large families were essential in this economy. Almost everyone in Manupur is a farmer, and each family needs many strong sons to work the land. If a family is land poor, their only hope is to send an educated son away from the village to earn money so that more land can be purchased. Children are the only source of support for the aged in Manupur. Even the protection system in the village requires a family with many sons who can defend the household from other families. In short, the poverty of these villagers means that they have to have large families if they are to survive at all.

This relationship between poverty and the need for a large family is supported by demographic trends in the industrialized nations. Population growth in these countries has declined as a result of what is called the demographic transition. As industrialization progresses, children become less important as a labor force; at the same time, a longer and more expensive education process is required to develop the skills needed for industrial production. Medical services improve, and fewer children die before they reach adulthood. For all of these reasons, people in industrialized nations want fewer children and so the population growth in these nations declines. It seems that the real answer to reducing population growth lies in improving people's economic lives so that they no longer need large families in order to survive.

Beyond this, there are some planners who believe that population growth is not the problem at all. They feel that the current dilemma is not one of too few resources or too little food but one of poor management of our resources and underutilization of the technology now available to feed the world. According to these thinkers, the best-known of whom is R. Buckminster Fuller,[5] methods can be devised to improve upon the current state of food production and distribution. It is therefore essential to rearrange our global priorities so that we use the earth's resources to produce and distribute the food that the people of the world need.

5. See R. Buckminster Fuller, *Utopia or Oblivion: The Prospects for Humanity* (New York: Bantam, 1969).

3. American Friends Service Committee, *Who Shall Live?* (New York, Hill and Wang, 1970), p. 11.
4. Mahmood Mamdani, *The Myth of Population Control* (New York: Monthly Review Press), 1972.

land (rent)—required to produce that output. Until recently, the nonrenewable resources used up in production were considered simply as components of the capital cost, based on their current prices in the marketplace. However, it seems clear that this is no longer an acceptable method of making long-term comparisons of various methods of production involving different ratios of factor inputs. (Such comparisons are necessary to devise methods to increase the efficiency with which inputs are utilized to increase the productive capacity of the economy, as well as for cost-benefit analyses.) Rather, it may be necessary to devise hypothetical prices for nonrenewable resources and for energy which somehow discount for their future reduction in availability as well as their external costs (increased pollution, increased amount of heat), thus increasing their present prices. Under this method, even assuming that the Russian peasants and the American farmer received the same real wages, it is entirely possible that the American wheat costs far more to produce than the Russian wheat.

Continued research along these lines is clearly urgently needed; further simulation studies along the lines of those reported in *The Limits to Growth*, as well as the development of more realistic long-term growth models, are areas which must be explored if we are to grasp the full implications of growth in a modern world.

Questions and Exercises

1. How would you distinguish economic growth from economic development?
2. What are the major sources of economic growth? According to Denison, which is the *least* important of these sources?
3. Why is it sometimes difficult to separate capital accumulation from technological change? Show, by means of Figure 19.1, how a shift in the production function can lead to increased productivity. Why is this productivity increase due to technological change rather than capital accumulation?
4. Assume that ten people using two machines could do a particular job but that it is now done by one person using one machine (assume that each machine costs the same amount). By how much have labor and capital productivity risen?
5. Explain why increasing returns to scale do not represent an increase in productivity, while specialization of labor function does.
6. Assume we are at full employment, as it is defined by the President's Council of Economic Advisers. How is it possible to increase employment in the short run? In the long run?
7. What is meant by labor force quality? Why does Denison consider the increasing quality of the labor force to have been so important to U.S. economic growth?
8. Explain briefly Domar's theory of short-term growth. How did Harrod extend this theory, and what did he predict would happen if the economy deviated from its equilibrium growth rate?
9. How did the neoclassical theorists approach the question of growth? Why does the Cobb-Douglas function exemplify this approach?
10. How does technological change tend to mitigate the danger of our running out of natural resources?

Appendix: Economic Growth Theories

As we noted in the text of this chapter, theories of economic growth can be divided into short-term and long-term theories. Short-term theories are concerned with determining the relationship between an economy's rate of growth (an increase in productive capacity) and the sources of economic growth: capital accumulation, growth in the size and quality of the labor force, technological change, and an increase in the amount and/or quality of natural resources, including land. Long-term theories, as we noted, are concerned with forecasting future rates of growth—perceived as static, declining, or accelerating greatly and then declining.

The short-term growth theories we shall examine are concerned with the relationship between growth and the first two of the sources mentioned: that is, the capital stock and/or the size of the labor force. They include: (1) the Harrod-Domar model, (2) neoclassical growth models, and (3) the Cobb-Douglas production function.

The long-term growth models which we shall consider briefly are (1) the stagnationist model, associated with Alvin Hansen, (2) the long-term neoclassical model developed by Robert M. Solow (the "steady-state" model with variable factor proportions), and (3) the neoclassical model with money.

The Harrod-Domar Model

The Harrod-Domar growth model[1] defines an equilibrium rate of growth called the **warranted rate of growth.** A rigid capital-output ratio determines the level of output at which the capital stock is fully utilized. This condition, along with the change in the capital stock or investment equal to savings, must be satisfied in order to determine the warranted rate of growth. These two conditions are specified below in equations (A19.1) and (A19.2); a further condition, the **natural rate of growth** of the labor supplied, is specified in equation (A19.3).[2]

At full capacity, represented by point A in Figure 19.1, the capital-output ratio is given by v, or the distance OC in Figure 19.1. Therefore, we have

$$K = vy \qquad \text{(A19.1)}$$

Recalling $I = \Delta K$, the saving equals investment condition is given by

$$\Delta K = sy \qquad \text{(A19.2)}$$

where s is the marginal propensity to save, taking a, the autonomous portion of consumption, to be zero. Finally, the full-employment condition for the labor force is given by

$$N = uy \qquad \text{(A19.3)}$$

Although equation (A19.3) is not essential for the solution of the Harrod-Domar model, it is included here as a reminder that the labor-output ratio is taken here to be constant. Taking v as a constant, we may differentiate equation (A19.1) to obtain

$$\Delta K = v\Delta y \qquad \text{(A19.4)}$$

Substituting from equation (A19.4) for ΔK into equation (A19.2) gives

$$v\Delta y = sy$$

or

$$\frac{\Delta y}{y} = \frac{s}{v}$$

which may be rewritten using the percentage rate of change notation employed in Chapter 13 as

$$\hat{y} = \frac{s}{v} \qquad \text{(A19.5)}$$

Equation (A19.5) represents the Harrod-Domar warranted rate of growth.

1. See Evsey S. Domar, "Capital Expansion, Rate of Growth and Employment," *Econometrica* 14 (April 1946): 137–147, and Roy F. Harrod, "An Essay in Dynamic Theory," *The Economic Journal* 44 (March 1939): 14–53.

2. Another version of the Harrod-Domar model exists, but the solution for the warranted rate of growth is identical to the solution obtained here. This may be seen along with further discussion of the nature of technological change and more elaborate two-sector growth models in R. G. D. Allen, *Macro-Economic Theory, A Mathematical Treatment* (New York: St. Martin's Press, 1967), Chs. 11–16.

Notice also that based on equations (A19.1) and (A19.2),

$$y = \frac{K}{v} \ , \ \ y = \frac{\Delta K}{s}, \ \frac{K}{v} = \frac{\Delta K}{s}$$

or

$$\frac{\Delta K}{K} = \hat{K} = \frac{s}{v} \tag{A19.6}$$

When equations (A19.1) and (A19.2) are satisfied, so that capital is being used to full capacity and savings equals investment, both output and the capital stock are rising at the warranted rate of growth. That is,

$$\hat{y} = \hat{K} = \frac{s}{v} \tag{A19.7}$$

The natural rate of growth is defined by the rate of growth of the labor force, $\hat{N}$. The full-equilibrium growth path occurs where the rate of growth of output is equal to the rate of growth of capital, so that capital stock and flow equilibrium conditions are met. The rate of growth of the labor supply is in turn equal to the (equal) rates of growth of capital and output.

$$\hat{N} = \frac{s}{v} = \hat{K} \tag{A19.8}$$

Therefore, growth occurs under conditions of product-market equilibrium, capacity output, and a steady capital-labor ratio, since when $\hat{K} = \hat{N}$,

$$\left(\frac{\hat{K}}{N}\right) = \hat{K} - \hat{N} = 0$$

Neoclassical Growth Models

Neoclassical growth models represent, in part, a return to certain themes considered by the classical economists, particularly Mill and Ricardo; these include the relationship between capital accumulation and changing productivity. Neoclassical models also extend the Harrod-Domar model by eliminating certain empirically untenable assumptions, particularly the assumption that v is a constant. Neoclassical theory is associated mainly with Robert M. Solow and James Tobin, as well as T. W. Swan.[3]

The neoclassical theorists have generally dropped the assumption of fixed factor proportions and thus a constant capital-output ratio, v. That is, if output can rise with no corresponding increase in capital, due to an increase in the proportion of labor used in the production process, v has

3. See Robert M. Solow, "A Contribution to the Theory of Economic Growth," *Quarterly Journal of Economics* 70 (February 1956): 65–94; *Growth Theory: An Exposition* (New York: Oxford University Press, 1970); R. M. Solow, J. Tobin, M. E. Yaari, and C. von Weizacker, "Neoclassical Growth with Fixed Factor Proportions," *Review of Economic Studies* 33 (April 1966): 79–116. See also T. W. Swan, "Economic Growth and Capital Accumulation," *The Economic Record* 32 (November 1956). For an excellent survey of neoclassical growth theory and of growth theory in general, see F. H. Hahn and R. C. O. Matthews, "The Theory of Economic Growth: A Survey," *Economic Journal* 74 (December 1964), reprinted in *Surveys of Economic Theory*, Vol. II (New York: Macmillan, 1965), pp. 1–124.

obviously fallen. The key assumption of the neoclassicists is the classical assumption of perfect competition wherein all factors of production will be fully employed due to flexibility in factor payments and output prices. This full-employment equilibrium also implies that S = I; the equilibrating mechanism is generally held to be the interest rate.

The neoclassical production function expresses output, y, as some function of the quantity of capital and labor. Thus we may write

$$y = y(K,N) \tag{A19.9}$$

Differentiating equation (A19.9) gives

$$y = \frac{\partial y}{\partial K} \cdot \Delta K + \frac{\partial y}{\partial N} \cdot \Delta N \tag{A19.10}$$

or, equivalently

$$y = MPP_K \cdot \Delta K + MPP_N \cdot \Delta N \tag{A19.11}$$

Equation (A19.11) states that the change in output is equal to the marginal physical product of capital times the change in the capital stock plus the marginal physical product of labor times the change in the quantity of labor. The rate of growth of output, $\Delta y/y$, can be found by dividing through by y:

$$\frac{\Delta y}{y} = \frac{MPP_N \cdot \Delta N}{y} + \frac{MPP_K \cdot \Delta K}{y} \tag{A19.12}$$

We saw in Chapter 10 that under the assumption of perfect competition the return to each of the two factors of production—capital and labor—is equal to its marginal physical product multiplied by the price of the product produced, a quantity known as the **marginal revenue product.** Thus, total returns to labor are $MPP_N \cdot N$, whereas total returns to capital are $MPP_K \cdot K$. Since labor and capital are the only factors of production, total returns to the two factors will equal total output:

$$MPP_N \cdot N + MPP_K \cdot K = y \tag{A19.13}$$

From here we can define the proportionate shares of total production by labor and capital as

$$a = \frac{MPP_N \cdot N}{y} \tag{A19.14}$$

$$b = \frac{MPP_K \cdot K}{y} \tag{A19.15}$$

where

$$a + b = 1 \tag{A19.16}$$

if returns to capital and labor exhaust total output.

Thus, a and b may be thought of as the respective contributions of labor and capital to output, or their respective shares of production under the marginal productivity theory of distribution.

We can now use equations (A19,12) and (A19.16) to derive $\Delta y/y$ in terms of a and b. Multiplying through as follows we have:

$$\frac{\Delta y}{y} = \left(\frac{MPP_N \cdot \Delta N}{y}\right) \cdot \left(\frac{N}{N}\right) + \left(\frac{MPP_K \cdot \Delta K}{y}\right) \cdot \left(\frac{K}{K}\right) \qquad \text{(A19.17)}$$

$$\frac{\Delta y}{y} = \left(\frac{MPP_N \cdot N}{y}\right) \cdot \left(\frac{\Delta N}{N}\right) + \left(\frac{MPP_K \cdot K}{y}\right) \cdot \left(\frac{\Delta K}{K}\right) \qquad \text{(A19.18)}$$

or

$$\hat{y} = a\hat{N} + b\hat{K} \qquad \text{(A19.19)}$$

In other words, the rate of change of output ($\Delta y/y$) is equal to the proportionate contribution of labor to production times the rate of growth of the labor force ($\Delta N/N$) plus the proportionate contribution of capital to production times the rate of growth of the capital stock, $\Delta K/K$.

The Cobb-Douglas Production Function

The Cobb-Douglas production function is a specific form of the neoclassical model that has been widely employed as a means to measure actual sources of growth in the economy. It is written, where technological progress is present, as

$$y = AK^a N^b \qquad \text{(A19.20)}$$

This production function embodies the neoclassical conditions of constant returns to scale, constant substitutability of labor for capital, and diminishing returns. At the same time, the Cobb-Douglas production function does allow for technological change, but only as a constant; it does not deal with the problem of "embodied" technological progress mentioned in the text. The fact is that "machines unalterably embody the technology of their date of construction. Machines built at different dates . . . are therefore qualitatively dissimilar, and cannot in the general case be aggregated into a single measure of capital."[4] However, in the Cobb-Douglas production function, technological change is considered to be "disembodied," that is, it is assumed to advance at a uniform speed, unaffected by actual investment. The production function also assumes that all productive capacity and all workers benefit uniformly from technological progress. Given the Cobb-Douglas production function, the rate of growth of output[5] may be written

$$\hat{y} = \hat{A} + a\hat{K} + b\hat{N} \qquad \text{(A19.21)}$$

4. Hahn and Matthews, "Theory of Economic Growth," p. 59.
5. This can be shown by writing equation (A19.20) in log form as

$$\log y = \log A + a \log K + b \log N$$

Differentiating with respect to time gives

$$\frac{d \log y}{dt} = \frac{d \log A}{dt} + a \frac{d \log K}{dt} + b \frac{d \log N}{dt}$$

which is equivalent to equation (A19.21).

Equation (A19.21) is perhaps the most straightforward representation of growth theory. This says that the rate of growth of output depends upon the rates of growth of capital and labor inputs and the rate of technological change, $\hat{A}$. The parameter a here represents the elasticity of output with respect to capital or $\hat{y}/\hat{K}$, while b represents the elasticity of output with respect to labor or $\hat{y}/\hat{N}$. If the production function exhibits constant returns to scale, then $a + b = 1$. Under this condition, with no technological change ($\hat{A} = 0$) the rate of growth of output will be equal to a weighted sum of the rate of growth in inputs. If $\hat{K} = \hat{N}$ then, given $a + b = 1$, $\hat{y} = \hat{K} = \hat{N}$. For example, given constant returns to scale, doubling K and doubling N ($\hat{K} = \hat{N} = 100\%$) will double output. More formally, this condition is referred to as **linear homogeneity.** If $a + b$ exceeds 1, increasing returns to scale exist; if $a + b$ is less than one, diminishing returns to scale are present.

Most efforts at measurement have shown $a + b$ to be less than one. In addition, $\hat{A}$, or technological change, has been shown to have been a large contributor to the growth of output in countries like the United States. The problem with such a discovery is that $\hat{A}$ really only captures all of $\hat{y}$ which is *not* due to $\hat{K}$ or $\hat{N}$. As such, it represents a residual or catch-all category with little specific content. Efforts to identify the residual more concretely, such as that of Denison noted in the text of this chapter, have found that improvement in the quality of the labor force through education has been a large contributor to the growth of output in the United States.

The Stagnationist Model

The stagnationist model promulgated by Alvin Hansen was a product of the Depression of the 1930s; the economic situation at that time was simply projected into the long-term future.[6] Hansen considered that the four factors underlying the expansion of investment—the rate of population growth, territorial expansion, growth of business and personal savings, and the shift from capital-absorbing to capital-saving innovations—had been played out. During the Depression the growth in these factors was negligible: fertility rates were very low so that a stable population for the United States was predicted within a generation or two; the continental United States had reached its limits; dissavings actually existed during some periods of the Depression; and little investment and thus little technological change, as embodied in new capital stock, occurred.

The stagnationist theory is a classical thesis, right in the tradition of Mill and Ricardo.[7] Like these classical theorists, Hansen regarded economic

6. See Alvin Hansen, "Economic Progress and Declining Population Growth," *American Economic Review* 29 (March 1939).

7. Smith's stationary state had a high unemployment rate. See Adam Smith, *The Wealth of Nations* (New York: Modern Library, 1937), Book I, Ch. 8, pp. 64–86. Ricardo foresaw a fall in the rate of profit and a consequent choking off of capital accumulation. See Ricardo, *Principles of Political Economy and Taxation*, Chs. 6 and 21. John Stuart Mill's view of the immediate future was equally pessimistic. See W. J. Ashley, ed., *Principles of Political Economy*, 2 vols. (London, 1909).

growth as the outcome of a race between diminishing returns and technological progress; growth would eventually decline toward zero.

Solow's Long-Term Neoclassical Model

The Solow model begins with certain of the same assumptions as Hansen, but goes on to quite a different set of conclusions: namely, that under certain circumstances, a *stable* long-term ("steady state") path of economic growth can be achieved.[8] Closely related to the short-term neoclassical models, this is a one-commodity model with a rate of production of output equal to y(t). The rate of savings is sy(t), where s is a constant. The economy's stock of capital, K(t), is simply the accumulation of the one composite commodity, so that net investment is dK/dt. Thus we have,

$$\frac{dK}{dt} = sy \qquad (A19.22)$$

Output is produced by two factors of production, capital and labor. The production function is thus neoclassical:

$$y = y(K, N) \qquad (A19.23)$$

Combining equations (A19.22) and (A19.23) we have

$$\frac{dK}{dt} = sy(K, N) \qquad (A19.24)$$

Since capital and labor are both unknown in this equation, Solow uses the exogenous variable, n, the growth in the labor force, which is simply

$$\frac{\frac{dN}{dt}}{N} = \hat{N}$$

When there is no increase in labor productivity, n is Harrod's natural rate of growth. Thus:

$$N(t) = N_0 e^{nt} \,^9 \qquad (A19.25)$$

Inserting equation (A19.25) into equation (A19.24) we have one equation with one endogenous variable, K:

$$\frac{dK}{dt} = sy(K, N_0 e^{nt}) \qquad (A19.26)$$

Equation (A19.26) determines the time path of capital accumulation that must be followed in order to employ all available labor. This time path will, in turn, provide the time path of y.

Because a quantitative solution of this equation is impossible without

8. Solow, "A Contribution to the Theory of Economic Growth." See also "Technical Change and the Aggregate Production Function," *Review of Economics and Statistics* 39 (August 1957): 312–320.

9. Since $\frac{d \log N}{dt} = n = \hat{N}$

specifying exactly the shape of the production function, $y = y(K, N)$, Solow introduces a new variable, $k = K/N$. Given equation (A19.25), we have,

$$K = kN_0e^{nt} \tag{A19.27}$$

Differentiating with respect to time,

$$\frac{dK}{dt} = N_0e^{nt}\frac{dk}{dt} + nkN_0e^{nt} = N_0e^{nt}\left(\frac{dk}{dt} + nk\right) \tag{A19.28}$$

Substituting this in equation (A19.26),

$$\left(\frac{dk}{dt} + nk\right)N_0e^{nt} = sy(K, N_0e^{nt}) \tag{A19.29}$$

Because of constant returns to scale, or linear homogeneity. Solow is able to divide both the variables in the function y by N, provided he multiplies y by the same factor. Given equation (A19.25),

$$\left(\frac{dk}{dt} + nk\right)N_0e^{nt} = sNy\left(\frac{K}{N}, \frac{N}{N}\right) \tag{A19.30}$$

Dividing both sides by $N = N_0e^{nt}$ and rearranging terms gives:

$$\frac{dk}{dt} = sy(k, 1) - nk \tag{A19.31}$$

Solow interprets the production function $y(k, 1)$ as the total product curve when varying amounts of capital are employed with one unit of labor. (Remember, $k = K/N$, so that if $N = 1$, $k = K$.) When $dk/dt = 0$ (k is constant),

$$sy(k, 1) = nk \tag{A19.32}$$

Notice that this is identical to the general neoclassical result in Figure 19.1. Consistent with Figure 19.1, Solow defines k^* as the value of k where $dk/dt = 0$ and argues that if it is once reached, it will be maintained, and the constant proportionate growth of capital and labor will continue. He then argues that this is a stable equilibrium; that is, if k is somehow jarred away from k^* it will tend to return to the value k^*. This will occur when the shape of the function is such as to provide for diminishing marginal productivity, as in Figure 19.1, and values of s and n are such that a point of intersection, k^*, exists, as at point Z in Figure 19.1.

The Neoclassical Growth Model with Money

The extension of the neoclassical growth model to include a store of value in addition to real capital, "money," is associated primarily with James Tobin and H. G. Johnson.[10] These analyses essentially begin with the Solow

10. James Tobin, "A Dynamic Aggregative Model," *Journal of Political Economy* 63 (April 1955): 103–115; "Money and Economic Growth," *Econometrica* 33 (October 1965): 671–684; H. G. Johnson, "Money in a Neo-Classical One-Sector Growth Model," in *Essays in Monetary Economics* (London: Allen and Unwin, 1967), pp. 143–178. See also Solow, *Growth Theory: An Exposition*, Ch. 4.

model. Tobin begins by arguing that the neoclassical model has only one type of asset which can serve as a store of wealth—real capital. Tobin is concerned with determining the equilibrium value of capital intensity, k (or $k*$ in Solow's terminology[11]), and the yield on capital in a situation in which there is a "competitive" asset like money.

Tobin assumes that the neoclassical model has a single monetary asset which is issued by the government (thus representing neither a commodity nor a private debt) and is the medium of exchange, while its yield ("the amount of the asset that is earned by holding a unit of the asset a given period of time") is fixed. He also assumes that the value of the asset in terms of the goods is initially fixed. Thus, the economy has two types of wealth: real goods obtained through past investment and paper goods manufactured by the government. Tobin argues that if people hold real capital and money assets in amounts proportionate to their respective yields, monetary policy will be able to influence the return to holding money and thereby influence investment behavior. If the government increases the rate of growth of the money supply to a point where inflation results, for example, thus reducing the marginal yield from holding money, wealth holders will equilibrate the returns from assets at the margin by purchasing more physical capital. This will raise the capital-labor ratio, thus lowering the marginal product of capital to a level equal to the lower marginal yield on money balances which are depreciating in terms of goods at the rate of inflation. As we saw in the discussion of the neoclassical model, the higher capital-labor ratio will raise output per capita, thereby making wealth holders better off.

H. G. Johnson qualifies Tobin's assertion of the unambiguously beneficial effects of inducing "capital-deepening" (affecting the equilibrium capital-labor ratio) by the use of monetary policy. Johnson points out that the assumption of a demand for real money balances in the first place assumes that such balances yield a stream of "convenience services" which ought to be included in the definition of income. Therefore, the impact upon real income per capita of the "capital-deepening" process must include the negative effect induced by a lower equilibrium stock of real money balances yielding, in turn, a smaller stream of convenience services due to inflation.

Whatever the net outcome, both analyses develop the notion that monetary policy can influence a real magnitude such as the equilibrium growth path of the economy. This supports the thesis of the non-neutrality of money developed in Chapter 15; here, however, we are looking at the role of money in a dynamic context instead of a comparative statics framework.

11. Tobin's k is defined as the "quantity of capital (measured in physical units of output) per effective manhour of labor. . . . the term 'effective' is to allow for improvements in the quality of labor inputs due to 'labor-augmenting' technological progress. Thus if a 1964 manhour is equivalent in the production function to two manhours in the base period, say 1930, k measures the amount of capital per man half-hour 1964 or per manhour 1930." (Tobin, "Money and Economic Growth," p. 294.)

ANOTHER classic confrontation may be erupting between the Congress and an incumbent Administration over national economic policies in this era of high inflation and increasing employment—or it may all turn out to be no more than political maneuvering keyed to next November's elections.

The potential clash, which has been simmering for some months with the growth of public furore over the intolerable level of prices, burst into the open last week when a large number of Senate Democrats indicated they favored a last-minute reprieve for the economic-control program...

Both proposals seem highly inadvisable in the present atmosphere and probably are doomed to defeat, though anything can happen when tensions run so high as they are now over the unrelenting upward march of prices and services.

For various reasons, wage-price controls have not been working, especially since the shift to Phase 3 in January, 1973, and ought to be scuttled so that the free market can operate again without the restrictive harness that has exacerbated supply problems—one of the roots of the present horrendous double-digit inflation trend.

The proposal for a tax cut should also be consigned quickly to the inactive file because it is precisely the wrong medicine for an inflation-ridden economy at this time. It would only serve to intensify the inflation problem without according any real benefits for the hard-pressed American public.

While a tax cut may seem enticing on its face to provide financial relief, chiefly for one group, it would really be a cruel illusion. It would tend to create bigger deficits in the Federal budget than now envisioned and reinforce the inflationary pressures in the economy that take so much out of everyone's pocketbook.

Even if a tax reduction were appropriate, it probably would be some time before it could wend its way through the legislative mill and would arrive on the scene when, hopefully, the economy is on an upward path again and

the rate down to any meaningful, table level by 1976 or 1977. Unlike other countries, we have our important thrift institutions with over $300-billion in mortgages that are highly vulnerable to the impact of inflation and are already subject to disintermediation."

He was referring, of course, to the outflow of funds from the savings banks, savings and loan associations and insurance companies as short-term interest rates are so high...

...home buying, where...have been counted upon this year as one of the major props for an economic rebound.

What is clearly needed now is a firm rein on monetary growth by the Federal Reserve and on spending by the Government. This is apparently the only real solution—the classical one—that has been stressed in many...to be applied...to work.

Controls Program Has Cost U.S. Around $200 Million

By a WALL STREET JOURNAL Staff Reporter

WASHINGTON—The Nixon administration said that more than 2½ years of wage-price controls have cost the government nearly $200 million and industry $721 million to $2 billion.

John T. Dunlop, Cost of Living Council director, told Congress that the Phase 4 program, which started last June 13, will have cost $79.7 million in salaries and...federal expenses by April 30, when...Previous phases and...

Various private studies of businessmen have spent $721 million...than $2 billion in complying with the controls regulations, Mr. Dunlop said.

If Congress accepts administration recommendations for the future of controls, the costs should drop. The staff of the controls program would be pared back substantially...also would...details of the...

Long Lines at Gas Stations Are Gone
But Inquiries and Litigation Linger

By FRED FERRETTI

For most of the metropolitan area, the recent energy shortage is a faint, irksome memory. For the region's politicians, prosecutors, investigators, judges and grand juries, it is the subject of continuing scrutiny.

Visible reminders of the energy crisis, which frightened and inconvenienced most people last winter, are the 50 per cent increases in fuel costs that are paying. The...shortages...the new bureaucracies created in haste—are still developing and can be expected to surface sporadically in the months to come.

In the tristate metropolitan area, the hardest-hit pocket the hardest-hit region of country during those months many charges of collusive price ing and marketing practices were leveled at major oil companies and several investments remain active and are in various stages of prosecution.

In New York, State Attorney

witz charged in a Feb. 11 complaint that four oil companies —all members of the Royal Dutch Shell Petroleum Group— had diverted a million gallons of heating oil and sold it at "exorbitant" prices during the fuel shortage after the Arab oil embargo.

The oil companies, Shell, Asiatic Petroleum, Compania Shell de Venezuela, and Shell Curacao, N.V., denied the allegations. They went to court to argue against Lefkowitz' application for an injunction.

Justice Hyman charged...the injunction, suggested an immediate trial and...

WASHINGTON—The Senate Banking Committee voted last week to let all price and wage controls expire as scheduled at midnight April 30.

The Cost of Living Council, in exchange for price-restraint commitments from key companies, lifted wage and price controls on three major industries—coal, aluminum and aircraft-aerospace.

These decisions may prove to be the last significant happening...

Some Hold Machinery Should Be Retained

and measures to stimulate the economy.

Ninety days later, Phase 2 of controls began. As 1972 unfolded, the rate of wage and price climb

Few Mourn for Controls

Child of Uncertain Lineage, He Fought Inflation, Before the Final Countdown

By LEONARD SILK

Price W. Controls, a child of the Nixon Administration—renowned as an anti-inflation fighter in his youth but failing in health for more than a year—expired in Washington last night at the age of 2 years 8 months. Conservative doctors gave old age as the cause of death, but an autopsy is to be held to determine whether there was foul play.

Controls was born at Laurel Lodge, Camp David, Md., on Aug. 15, 1971, after a labor that began on Aug. 13. The baby was delivered by John B. Connally of Texas, then Secretary of the Treasury.

John Ehrlichman, then President Nixon's chief assistant for domestic affairs, later said that Mr. Connally saw a great political future for Controls, "but he wasn't the only one by any means." There were also some old Nixon hands who also measured the political realities...".

Shultz Disliked the Youth

George P. Shultz, then director of the Office of Management and Budget, who was to succeed Mr. Connally as Secretary of the Treasury, was regarded by some as an evil spirit at the birth of Controls.

The former University of Chicago Business School dean often expressed his antipathy to Controls. Yet friends of Mr. Shultz insist he did a loyal job of standing in loco parentis, despite his prejudices.

...former controllers...considered

Indeed its...her is unknown, Dr. Arthur F. Burns, chairman of the Federal Reserve Board, is generally...only the god-father...before he was born.

Nixon Disdained Child

President Nixon never claimed...for Controls. He appeared to dislike the child as much as Mr. Shultz. The President rarely played with Controls or even consulted with his guardians. So of his wards...or get to...plained of...like an orphan.

Some of his detractors in the Administration accused the news media of being his true father.

Mr. Nixon had been distantly connected with Controls's grandfather, John. The meaning...and other interest rates have...will the Fed tolerate rising rates so much turmoil in the financial industry in general?

The Fed's role must be...

The New York Times

BUSINESS AND FINANCE

Capitol Hill and Prodlop's notion that a stabilization...soon begram should try...Task Force...actions that would help boost capacity. But there is Congressional distrust of the Administration's ability to do something...to convince voters that they are at least trying to do something about rising prices. "I don't think we can abdicate our role," says Representative Henry Reuss (D-Wis.). "If we do nothing, then part of the reason for continued inflation could, and quite too, properly so, be blamed on Congress."

Rival proposals. A variety of Congressional remedies is emerging as both the House and Senate Banking committees draw up legislation. Representative Wright Patman (D-Tex.) would extend current authority for...Reuss would continue to...and help solve long-term...problems, while also allowing the CLC to pursue similar supply actions.

Monitoring plan. A proposal by Senator William Proxmire (D-Wis.)...J. Bennett Johnston, Jr. (D-La.), head...of the Senate stabilization subcommittee...

Congress seeks a price ombudsman and approval over wage-price changes

apply to pacesetter industries. Business is opposed to an ombudsman-type approach. For example, Hatfield, chairman of Co., testified: "Controls...

Wage and Price Controls

Reconciling the goals of price stability, full employment, and balance of payments equilibrium has become the crucial macroeconomic policy issue of the 1970s. Discretionary fiscal policy during the recession year 1970 was fairly unaggressive, probably because the administration was preoccupied with the continuing high level of inflation, as reflected in the 6.2 point increase in the CPI during 1970. Nevertheless, largely because of the operation of automatic stabilizers, the budget was nearly $12 billion in deficit for the year. Monetary policy, however, showed a significant turnaround: switching from the no-growth money supply policy of late 1969, the Fed permitted the money supply to grow by more than 5 percent during 1970 and cut the discount rate several times. According to the National Bureau of Economic Research, the recession ended late in 1970; by early 1971, real GNP was moving up modestly, as was capacity utilization. Unemployment, however, remained a problem at around 6 percent, while the inflation rate continued at what was then considered to be an unacceptably high rate of more than 5 percent. By mid-year the sluggish nature of the recovery was obvious to everyone. Confronting an election at a time when the economy was stricken with alarming stagflation and a steadily deteriorating balance of payments position, President Nixon rejected traditional fiscal and monetary policy altogether: on August 15, 1971, he announced his New Economic Policy, a ninety-day freeze on all wage and price increases, followed by guidelines limiting these increases, a schedule of tax cuts, and the suspension of gold convertibility for the dollar.

Hailed by business and labor alike at the time of their inception—"at last the government has done *something*"—controls had failed to satisfy either by the end of Phases I, II, and III. When they were lifted in early 1974, however, inflation rates again began to rise dramatically, reaching "double-digit" levels for the first time in this country's history.

Although few would argue that the controls were a success, few agree on the reasons for their failure. Economists, historians, and social critics are heard to argue: Are controls always useless or only these controls (or controllers)? What should they be expected to achieve? Are economic goals the sole criterion for success, or are there political and egalitarian criteria as well? Similarly, few people agree on preferable alternatives. The issue is an emotional one, and we have decided to preserve its drama: instead of providing a dispassionate summary of opposing views, therefore, we invited three individuals to debate the issue. Mr. Makin will be recognized as the economist; Mr. Dickinson and Ms. Arnow, both formally identified in the acknowledgments, are more difficult to categorize. At this point we can consider all three to be observers of the wage-price control experiment; their positions should become clear by the end of this debate.

MODERATOR: Perhaps we can begin by specifying the types of wage and price controls we will be discussing.

MAKIN: Most generally, wage and price controls refer to government intervention in markets to set prices different from those which would appear if market forces were permitted to operate unhampered. To quote Galbraith in his little book, *A Theory of Price Control,* which appeared in 1952, "Price-fixing by authority . . . is clearly a case of government without the consent of the governed." More specifically, controls on either wages or prices may take the form of absolute ceilings or permitted annual rates of change. Perhaps most typical is the case of 1971 and 1972—an imposition of price ceilings above which prices were not permitted to rise (unless a successful appeal could be made for exception), along with "productivity guidelines" whereby wages were only permitted to rise at a certain rate, presumably determined by the rate of increase in labor productivity. This situation must be distinguished from the initial ninety-day wage and price "freeze" from August 1971 to November 1971, during which wages and prices were simply fixed at August 15, 1971, levels by government edict.

ARNOW: Certainly there are some sectors of the economy in which market forces operate to equalize supply and demand through the price mechanism. But in many important areas prices are set through edict, whether the edict of the government or of the Board of Directors of an oligopoly or monopoly. In these sectors, price and wage controls as defined here simply involve a difference in the bureaucracy which sets the price—and a difference in the philosophy involved, of course. Rather than maximizing windfall (monopoly) profits, the object of the pricing structure would be to reduce the rate of inflation and decrease the inequity which arises through inflation.

MAKIN: I think it needs to be shown, first, that highly concentrated industries earn consistently higher profits than others, and, second, that the actual impact of wage and price controls is to reduce inequities arising from inflation. I know of no systematic evidence on either point. In fact, preservation of monopoly profits requires collusion between government and industry, such as exists in some sectors of the transportation, banking, and medical-care industries to restrict entry and in the steel, chemical, petroleum, and auto industries to insulate domestic producers from foreign competition.

DICKINSON: I think wage and price "controls" in the 1971–1974 episode must be distinguished from wage and price "administration," a term used to refer to the same activity in the United States during World War II and the Korean war. The word "controls" suggests the government stepping in to take charge of a private-sector situation that is literally "out of control," while "administration" refers to government price fixing by authority. In the second case a need for rationing goods is delegated to sellers with private-sector excess demand siphoned off into liquid assets so that the government can command more of the economy's resources. For a war effort, for example.

MAKIN: One might say that wage and price *controls* of the early seventies were aimed at checking already extant inflation whereas wage and price *administration* is aimed at avoiding incipient inflation as the government anticipates taking command of more of the resources of an economy.

DICKINSON: There is also the case of government interventions into specific markets whereby price ceilings or floors may be set for a single commodity. To be successful over a long time these specific actions require government to play the role of residual demander where price floors, such as those which exist for some agricultural products in the United States, are in effect. The result, of course, is government stockpiling of such commodities.

The Federal Trade Commission takes off after price cutters as often as it does after price raisers. When you have a vested interest in maintaining inefficiency at one end of the economic scale, you are unlikely to admit that you can't do anything about the relative price adjustments which are the cost of efficiency at the other.

MODERATOR; You are suggesting that wage-price controls are nothing new?

DICKINSON: Precisely. For two thousand years price controls have had the most depressing experience. The most famous example is Emperor Diocletian's *De Maximus Pretiis*, in 301 A.D., which fixed wages and set maximum prices. It was very Roman: exact and brutal. About a thousand items, down to pocket handkerchiefs, were regulated; buyers as well as sellers who broke the law were to be executed. But the edict, designed to prevent excessive profits and inflation, was unenforceable and faded decently away. More interesting is the experience of the Islamic countries; for centuries, over a thousand years in some places, there have been systematic endeavors to regulate prices, and all of them have failed.

ARNOW: What do you mean by failure?

DICKINSON: There is a fascinating memorandum by a sixteenth-century Ottoman vizier, for example, in which he says how utterly important it is to control prices in the interest of the poor. He says it is of great importance to prohibit the government ministers' trading, which apparently was very common because they were the people who could get around the price regulations. In fact, price regulation appears to have been merely a means of making it profitable for the really powerful to get into business. And there is an enormous corpus of Islamic law called *Hiyal* which deals with how to get around the commandments of the Prophet. The classic one is that the Prophet says that you can't charge interest. But he has said nothing about discount. So most long-term loans in the Arab world are heavily discounted at the outset.

MODERATOR: Then wage-price controls will always be circumvented?

DICKINSON: Yes.

ARNOW: It depends on who is getting hurt, and whether they have the political power to get round the controls. Sometimes they fall apart because they are applied stupidly, and sometimes political leaders haven't got the courage of their convictions.

MODERATOR: Apart from faint-heartedness on the part of the administrators, what have the mechanisms been for destroying the effectiveness of wage-price controls?

DICKINSON: Sometimes it is the mechanism of inflation, such as the enormous price rise of the sixteenth century, as the Spanish ships brought the gold and silver from the Americas to Europe. Economic arrangements were fixed in money terms, and the money terms just became unrealistic; the institutions built around them—such as guilds, for example—just disintegrated because the government did not move fast enough to adjust for inflation. Sometimes, as in the Persian Empire from the fourth to the sixth century B.C., taxes remained at the same level for a couple of hundred very stable years while government expenditures came to a halt. As money poured into the King's treasury, the economy's money supply dwindled and the price of money went way up. Peasants couldn't get money to pay their taxes, so the various provinces simply became estates of their governors, who were sort of reverse sharecroppers, lending their tax money out to the peasants, then retaxing them and accumulating all the property. As a result, the free peasant population was virtually eliminated. The independent farmers had formed the backbone of the Persian army, so with the first impact of a powerful military outsider, Alexander, the Persian system collapsed. This released a fabulous amount of monetary treasure to the conquering Greeks, and then we have the first really well-documented inflation in which prices are rising and the most absurd goods are being bought in the market. People hunted birds with twelve miles of net. It was a grave misallocation of resources.

MODERATOR: But is it fair to say that wage-price controls have been more the norm throughout history than the exception?

DICKINSON: Absolutely. The operation of a more-or-less free market is the anomaly of human history, not the reverse. Furthermore, the notion of a national market is a product of advances in transportation brought on by canals and railways and probably most of all by the advent of the internal combustion engine. Until the creation of a Federal Reserve Board, there wasn't even a fully integrated national money market. You know that $50 checks in New York could fetch $53 in St. Louis because there was a 6 percent premium on New York money in the Middle West. The notion that merchants and industrialists and so on set prices according to a nationwide cost level is just ahistoric.

ARNOW: As is the laissez-faire ideal of government leaving the price sector alone to set those prices.

MODERATOR: Why this obsession by government with controls over prices?

DICKINSON: Government is perpetually of two minds as to whether it dislikes the uncertainties of the market more than it dislikes the uncertainties of monopoly, and it usually likes to have a fairly inelastic, fairly viscous economic flow in which it can keep an eye on everyone. As a result, oligopoly seems the state of mind which government is happiest with. Fifty years ago, Pirenne, a very great historian, wrote a fascinating essay in *The American Historical Review* in which he argues that capitalism oscillates between wide-open, highly competitive situations and epochs in which government cartelization, intervention—which is sometimes indistinguishable from government partnership—and so on take over. Now, when business feels unsafe it nearly always finds a very sympathetic partner in government, which under the appearance of policing business is actually offering the existing business arrangements of the epoch extensive protection. You see that in the co-optation of government regulatory agencies.

MAKIN: Not to mention the restriction of foreign competition, as in the case of the oil industry where oil import quotas were in effect until May 1973.

DICKINSON: There is a permanent willingness on the part of 90 percent of businessmen and 95 percent of government officials to create the loathsome partnership of business and government.

ARNOW: If the "loathsome" partnership already exists, then this implies to me controls may become more, rather than less, necessary.

MAKIN: On the contrary, breaking up such a partnership requires less, not more, government control of the private sector. If we agree that monopoly power is enhanced by cooperation between business and government "regulatory" agencies, then it seems absurd to argue that further government intervention will reduce monopoly power which is alleged to be pushing up prices. With no barriers to entry, competition will prevent the exercise of monopoly power as a means to raise the prices above levels consistent with rates of return in competitive industries.

MODERATOR: What would you say characterized wartime controls, partnership, or active circumvention, or both?

DICKINSON: Well, in World War I there was no really serious program of controls. There were individual management efforts, rationing, labor agreements; there were government corporations, but it did not add up to a program of controlled wages and prices. The various governments were much more obsessed with financing their wars, and of course managing the consequences. In fact, the last truly classic postwar depression took place in 1919–1921 because in effect the government said, "O.K. boys, war over, back to the real world," and wandered off leaving economies caving in all over the place.

MAKIN: In World War I and in the Civil War in the United States there was considerable inflation because in many cases governments simply increased the money supply in order to pay for war goods in quantities over and above the amounts they could borrow. The National Banking System in the United States was created during the period from 1863–1865 to finance the Civil War. The resulting inflationary issue of "greenbacks" circulated in the United States until about 1870, when the U.S. government ceased to put a ceiling on the free market price of silver. In effect, money creation to finance wartime deficits amounted to imposition of an inflationary tax on money holders. As in the case of the Vietnam war, this is likely to happen when a government can't impose direct taxes to pay for a war effort due either to administrative shortcomings or the unpopularity of the war. The inflation underway in 1971 was largely related to inflationary deficits resulting from Vietnam. Wage and price controls represented a cynical attempt by the government to project the blame for inflation onto the private sector.

DICKINSON: Here of course we have the interesting question of the distribution of wealth. In World War I much more money flowed to the rentier classes who patriotically turned it into public funds at very high rates of interest financed by taxes on the income of all classes. So you had counter-inflationary forces operating as a function of what we would all regard as a less just society.

MAKIN: You could siphon off a great deal of liquidity from highly concentrated sources willing and able to effect transfer of current claims on resources to the government with little impact on their own high level of expenditure. In effect, with a highly concentrated ruling class, government loans in wartime could be seen as prudent investment.

DICKINSON: Also, the United States had not been operating at full capacity in 1914, so the Allied need for supplies took up an enormous amount of the slack industrial capacity before inflation could set in. There was inflation, but it was not the inflation of the spectacularly dynamic economies of World War II.

MODERATOR: How was the World War II situation different?

MAKIN: Well, leading up to the war in the United States we had a period of depression as you recall it, people in a very illiquid position, to say the least. People accustomed to doing without certain consumer goods.

DICKINSON: And a badly chastened business class, which is nothing that should be underestimated. And a labor movement not only highly patriotic but also highly committed to the party in power.

MODERATOR: When plans were made for the imposition of wage-price controls, had the governments involved studied the experience, such as it was, of World War I?

DICKINSON: Oh yes. By World War II the governing elites had had time to do a lot of thinking on the lessons of World War I. The British, French, Americans, and Germans all prepared enormous histories of their various ministries, some of which were only declassified in the 1940s and 1950s.

MAKIN: Galbraith suggests in *A Theory of Price Control* that most people prior to World War II felt that comprehensive wage and price controls of the sort envisioned by World War II planners on a scope sufficient to effect both economic stabilization and wartime resource mobilization were both unwise and unworkable.

DICKINSON: Yes. No one believed that they would work. Partly it was the administrative problem that in wartime your best civil servants and outside administrators are engaged in the supervising of the manufacture of armaments and the moving of troops. There was a question of scarcity: Did you have competent people? Secondly, descriptive knowledge of the economy had been really rather trivial in 1914, and people just hadn't known what to do in large part. It had been immensely ad hoc.

MODERATOR: Did governments have no other examples in 1939–1940?

DICKINSON: In 1936 very elaborate price controls were slammed on in Germany. The task was considerable; but it was accomplished by outrageous currency manipulation: in 1936–1937 there were 237 simultaneous prices for the mark in terms of foreign currency.

ARNOW: Surely a case where controls worked very well. Indeed they stayed in effect after the war.

DICKINSON: Germany is perhaps a special case. The German people have reason to be terrified by inflation. They have been through the second or third worst inflation of all time in the middle twenties and in 1945–1946— well, we know that in 1949 when the reichsmarks were called in and the new bundesmarks distributed, there was a 93 percent depreciation of currency; you got seven bundesmarks for every hundred reichsmarks. Everyone knew they were living in an unreal world. And the German industrialists of that generation were natural cartelizers. The price leaders administered their prices down rather than up.

MODERATOR: When were price controls established in this country?

MAKIN: In 1942. In fact, the problem of effective implementation of comprehensive wage and price controls was probably far better perceived when the Emergency Price Control Act set up the Office of Price Administration (OPA) in the winter of 1942 than in August 1971 when the New Economic Program (NEP) went into effect. Even though no one had much experience with such programs in 1942, it was clearly recognized that the program amounted to a comprehensive effort at economic stabilization in the face of a very high but incipient level of resource mobilization for war. It was seen as an alternative to taxes or other fiscal measures to balance aggregate demand and supply. Like NEP it represented a transfer of Congressional responsibility to the Executive for price stability action. Unlike NEP, it recognized that excess demand was the essential cause of sustained inflation. NEP was effected only after a period of persistent war-related deficits in the federal budget in the belief that a freeze could "break the back" of inflation.

MODERATOR: How then did the OPA program work?

MAKIN: It is easier to control prices in concentrated industries with relatively few sellers, and in those cases the resources of the OPA were very effective in putting the price controls into effect. However, they had two-thirds of their resources dealing with the more competitive sector, where there was a larger numbers of buyers and sellers, and there they were less successful.

There they had a higher likelihood that there would be, as Galbraith puts it, the collusion between buyer and seller.

ARNOW: True, but the perceived political success of wage and price controls was considerable in World War II in the United States, and it was a very important component of the war effort. Collusion is a problem when it tends to increase perceived inequities—and if it results in pumping increased income into the economy and/or increases supply dislocations. Mr. Dickinson told me about an incident recounted in Evans' and Novak's *Life of Lyndon Johnson*. It seems that Paul Porter, who ran the OPA for a time during the war, was having dinner at the LBJ ranch sometime in the fifties, and at one point was talking about how he had been demanding gas rationing. One of the guests nodded to Lyndon across the table and said, "Well, we didn't have gas rationing in Texas, in this part of the world, Mr. Porter."

This is a very real problem in administration of controls, but again, it's not an argument against controls per se, only an argument that their administration is difficult.

DICKINSON: I think this is a more general problem. There was an enormous trade-off of efficient control against acquiescence. For all the talk of individualist businessmen who hated Roosevelt, there were remarkable numbers of businessmen who were already happily prepared to live with the government guarantee that they could sell almost anything at a given price. So introducing the notion that the government was going to legislate such a thing didn't induce the kind of panic that it would induce today.

MAKIN: I think conditions in the United States were uniquely favorable in 1941–1942. The thirties were characterized by general deflation and generally slack demand. This induced deflationary expectations which made already patriotically disposed citizens willing to accumulate financial assets. There were widespread expectations, based on the fairly sparse evidence of post–Civil War and post–World War I episodes, that the war would be followed by a sharp contraction and lower prices. Lending to the government during the war seemed an attractive prospect given the expectation of lower prices: dollars put away during the war would be worth more in the deflationary period after it was over. Such deflationary expectations were replaced by inflationary expectations in the 1971 situation, so the likelihood of being able to induce higher savings to lower demand was less.

MODERATOR: Did controls work the same way in other countries as the war went on? What happened in Germany?

MAKIN: In Germany as the war went on everyone presumably began to suspect that indeed there was not going to be a large postwar bonus in the form of lower prices. The marks that they were accumulating were not going to exchange on favorable terms for goods. Indeed, doubts probably arose as to whether any goods would be available at all after the war. This would produce a great desire to spend now and thus generate inflationary pressure.

DICKINSON: There was considerable inflationary pressure. First, Germany in effect ceased to mobilize in 1941, after the victory in France. By 1942, Britain and several Allied countries passed Germany in degree of mobilization, and the civilian sector went on just supplying nonessential goods. Consumer goods were widely available in Germany. One of the really startling things is that the large-scale Allied bombing raids of 1944 actually stimulated Germany's war mobilization because they were aimed at the densest areas of the German cities where the peace-oriented industries happened to be. They were knocked out, and thousands of laborers were put involuntarily on the market; government and war production soaked them up. German defense management was at a very low level in 1943–1944, so you had considerable absorption of capacity and steadily increasing prices.

MODERATOR: What can we learn from the experiences of various nations in World War II?

MAKIN: The lesson is that where you have inadequate demand the introduction of price ceilings won't produce the kind of panic that it would produce now or that it produced in 1971.

ARNOW: It didn't induce panic in 1971 unless you had your life savings in commodities. It produced dancing for joy on the floor of the New York Stock Exchange.

MAKIN: In 1971 economists and businessmen knew that excess demand was responsible for a good part of the persistent inflation and that that source of pressure wasn't just going to disappear. Therefore you saw panic buying in anticipation of shortages which were expected to, and did, materialize in many markets where price ceilings were imposed. Moreover, widespread segments of the business and labor community called for an end to wage and price controls well before they were terminated for the very reason the serious shortages were appearing in many markets. Businessmen couldn't earn their allegedly monopolistic profits if they couldn't even obtain the raw materials with which to produce their output.

DICKINSON: Again, the contrast between 1942 and 1971 is important. There is an enormous difference between a deflated economy being administratively controlled as demand pressure builds in a fully mobilized wartime setting and export regulation of an economy already characterized by widespread excess demand.

ARNOW: Agreed. But the difference isn't necessarily an argument against controls being placed on a hyperactive economy. I would argue that controls have at least two components. First, there is the political component I mentioned—perceived success or failure of the controls, as viewed by the populace living under them. This has to do with the difference between the way things were before and the way they were afterward, and I am inclined to think that slamming on the brakes of a hyperactive economy in which many people have become very frightened may produce more perceived success than controls in an economy gearing up. In fact, perceived success or failure may be more important than economic success—in terms of changes in the CPI, and so on—because controls in their most extreme cases may be needed to keep an economy from flying apart through perceived inequity and runaway inflation.

The economic component has to do with what price and wage controls do to wage and price indicators, to the distribution of income and to supply schedules—that is, any dislocations of supply which may arise from the controls and which would not arise otherwise.

MAKIN: The economic damage arising from controls has been highly visible. Some of the costs of the freeze and subsequent controls are manifest in current high rates of inflation and unemployment. Capital formation was curtailed during the period of controls because investors were simply not about to invest in capital equipment formation where price ceilings were set at levels inconsistent with profitable use of the capital. The result has been a failure of capacity growth to keep pace with demand and resultant intensification of inflationary pressures. Further, a slower growth in productive capacity lowers growth in the demand for labor. Other costs involved the need to resort to barter that was implicit in price controls. This became widespread enough by 1973 to be reported in the *Wall Street Journal*. Such arrangements were necessary to avoid money price ceilings in many cases. The imposition of controls, therefore, produced distortions serious enough to jeopardize the extremely important role of money as a unit of account and as a medium of exchange.

ARNOW: In World War II the political effect of controls may have been more important than the purely economic effects. It would have been more difficult to wage the war with runaway domestic inflation, but not impossible.

MAKIN: In the mobilized wartime economy coming out of a period of slack demand, price controls are simply going to introduce some other decisions in allocating resources. As Galbraith puts it, controls delegate the job of rationing to sellers on whose goods you put price ceilings. Although it is interesting to note that by late 1942 the Under-Secretaries of the Navy and of War requested that the price ceilings on war-related goods be removed. In other words, prices of war-related goods became market determined, and the main thrust of the effort was to keep the price of war-related goods fixed in order to prevent a wage-price spiral. To me this is a piece of evidence that when you really have a difficult market situation and you really want to ration things in the most efficient way with no time to fool around, you rely on the price mechanism.

DICKINSON: No, you need more than that. I think inflation is a social solvent, it breaks down the social bond. If people believe the government is doing nothing, they suffer. As someone said the other day, inflation in society is like the rush to get off the *Titanic*—decent priorities are lost. The importance of wage-price controls is (a) to show that someone cares and (b) to prevent the feeling, which is especially dangerous, that the strong unions and big corporations are getting away with something that the weak cannot do. Inflation is an encourager of every kind of dangerous movement from Putschism on the right to what have you on the left. But while the state has to show it is a match for these powers, I believe that good old antitrust is the way to break up concentrations of economic power. Particularly private antitrust action.

MAKIN: I suppose my predilection is to rely more on international competition than on antitrust.

ARNOW: Since government refuses to enforce antitrust legislation and is unable to force multinational corporations to engage in competition, it hardly matters—neither is effective.

MAKIN: Government enforcement of antitrust would be far less necessary in the absence of barriers to free international flows of goods. Multinational corporations are in fact engaging in competition; most government directives regarding multinationals reduce this competition by shielding less efficient domestic firms from direct competition with multinationals.

The viability of foreign competition as a means to check monopoly power is enhanced by the link between locally monopolistic industries and economies of scale. Industries which contain few firms due to economies of scale as a powerful barrier to entry are the very ones in which access to foreign markets will be sought, especially by firms with relatively small home markets, in order to realize economies of scale. Competition in the auto industry from Germany and Japan and in the steel industry from Belgium are perfect examples of this phenomenon. Tendency toward monopoly in domestic industries (due to large-scale production) is thus offset by competition from foreign producers with small national markets.

MODERATOR: Let's talk a little more about the difference between World War II and the period leading up to the New Economic Policy in August 1971.

MAKIN: To amplify what I said earlier, I think the key difference is in price expectations. In 1942 you had the combination of a recent history in the 1930s of falling prices and a generally anticipated decline after the war. People are much more willing to forego current consumption under those circumstances than in a situation where inflation is accelerating as it was in 1971. It seems to me also that it is hard to get away from the fact that even though you're going to be generating high incomes during the war, a normal array of consumer goods is probably not going to be available.

DICKINSON: The striking difference is in economic psychology in 1943 and 1971. The most incredible period of economic expansion took place from 1963 to, say, 1970. Moreover, federal budget deficits were fundamentally beneficial to consumers while they had not reached a point where they had major additional consequences. Then in 1970 and in 1971 in an economy that has been running as close to full blast as I think any economy has run in history, you were running fairly large deficits which were unanticipated in the late sixties. The late sixties' fiscal years were times when you had planned to have the Vietnam war out of the way, but it was not out of the way. In anticipation of that, however, absolutely disgraceful fiscal arrangements had been made in 1966 and 1967. Even if the war in Vietnam had ended in 1967, there was a very considerable overhang of unabsorbed debt that was going to have led to an inflationary push in 1968 or 1969. In fact, a much larger debt than the government was willing to acknowledge.

MAKIN: Actually, federal budgeting policy was quite uneven in the late 1960s. We had a $25 billion deficit in the 1968 fiscal year and a $3 billion surplus in the 1969 fiscal year. Together with uneven monetary policy this set in motion the disturbances in international capital markets which were to lead to the breakdown of the fixed exchange rate system in 1971, and moved us into a period of accelerating inflation.

ARNOW: It's probably worth noting also that the 1940s did not see the credit creation against common stock holding which was massive in the late 1960s since the stock market had been through such hard times. With less ability to borrow and thereby to enhance current demand, you had far less imminent inflationary pressure in 1942 than in 1971.

DICKINSON: There is another question here too. And that is the ease with which you can translate the extreme complexities of modern industry into a series of elementary relationships. You know, in 1942, a wage-price controller could probably master the section of industry that he was controlling quite fast. The bright young men like Richard Milhous Nixon at OPA were felt to be able to grasp the fundamentals of car production or whatever. But I remain much more skeptical of the ability of these intelligent generalists to learn in quantity terms the fundamentals of a given industry today. Suppose that you chose to cooperate with the government by laying every single specification for the F-111 on some wretched little fellow out of Harvard Law School whose mathematics stopped at elementary calculus and expect him to make sense of it. There is such a thing as killing a cat with cream, and in such cases I think you can do that very easily. Also, in 1942 most of the American business class just wanted to get on with the war. This led them to cooperate and simplify things as much as possible for the controller's benefit. Now there is an enormous potential for bottlenecking just in the matter of administration.

ARNOW: I'm not sure that is a valid argument *against* reimposing them in a situation in which industry feels less cooperative because you're cutting down their windfall profits. I mentioned earlier that there is a large political element in introducing controls during wartime—to keep at least a semblance of equity in the sacrifices made by the population. . . .

MAKIN: I suppose there is a political element in that wage and price controls in 1942 were fundamentally subordinated to getting on with the war.

DICKINSON: It was a reallocation of resources, with endeavors to reallocate humanely, whereas in 1971 the efforts were directed at stemming an already fairly serious inflation. In 1942 the 1937 recession was not altogether over for some parts of the economy.

MODERATOR: Are you saying that apart from confidence in government, price controls can work to reallocate resources but are unlikely to work in curtailing inflation?

MAKIN: Yes, price controls in the midst of an inflationary period probably have three things going against them. First, incipient inflationary expectations are going to work against the liquidity absorbing programs instituted to drain purchasing power out of the economy. It is very hard to drain purchasing power out of the economy when people want to buy now before the price goes up even further. Second, you have the problem of anticipated shortages. People realize that with inflationary pressure price ceilings may mean that the recorded price may not go up but in such a case the goods disappear into hoards or move through black markets. Third, there is disruption due to avoidance of controls. During the freeze a great many new positions were created in order to grant raises. In many cases goods were simply sold abroad to avoid domestic controls. Raisins virtually disappeared from the U.S. market in 1973 because they were sold abroad at higher prices than were permitted in the United States.

ARNOW: I feel if wage and price controls are put on in time, inflationary expectations can be curtailed.

DICKINSON: I disagree. They simply accumulate through the economy.

ARNOW: Not if the controls are viewed as a tool to get rid of the inflationary psychology. It's like putting a wet blanket on a bonfire. If you know it's going to be left on long enough to put the fire out, you will act accordingly. Obviously, if you think some controller will take the blanket off too soon, because he doesn't understand bonfires or he is subject to other pressures, you'll stick around waiting for the fire to flare up again.

We should distinguish between inflationary expectations and accumulated purchasing power arising because of enforced (or voluntary) savings and shortages. The latter, if not managed correctly, can lead to a new fire—it can also lead to a wave of controlled expansion, as occurred after World War II. Proper management of the money supply can prevent the starting of a new fire once inflationary expectations have been assuaged.

When the government finally instituted controls in 1971 the CPI virtually stopped rising. By late 1972 the rate of inflation had fallen to almost 3 percent. Then the government pulled off the blanket and the fire raged all over again—probably inflation was even worse because of Phase III than it would have been had there been no controls at all.

MAKIN: But if you keep the wet blanket of controls on it long enough, you will kill the economy with accumulated shortages. This is exactly why controls were lifted. During the period from January 1973 to March 1974, inflation accelerated from about 4 percent to over 10 percent while real output went from an annual growth rate of 8.5 percent to a 6.3 percent annual rate of decline by the first quarter of 1974. There is such a thing as throwing out the baby with the bathwater. Surely you agree that wage and price controls are a temporary expedient which means that you are going to put them on and then you're going to take them off. Now when you take them off, if you have been successful in controlling demand, in the sense that people have accumulated assets instead of spending, as they did in World War II, then you have the problem of do you take them off presto or do you take them off gradually? Obviously if you don't want inflationary bulge you take them off gradually. But the problem that always comes up is when are you going to take them off when they are not going to lead to inflationary pressure? Galbraith's answer to this is that the longer people hold an asset, the longer they have that savings account, the less likely they are to spend it. But there is little evidence to support this.

MODERATOR: Do you see any other alternatives?

DICKINSON: I cannot imagine the public agreeing to permanent controls. Certainly an improvement over their present arbitrary nature, however, would be to say they will go into effect automatically when inflation reaches a certain level. Say 5 percent. The trouble is, of course, how to determine a point where inflation has evened out sufficiently to trigger their removal.

ARNOW: But permanent non-market-determined controls exist in many, if not most, sectors of the economy, which prevent wages and prices from falling. A great example was the recently passed bill to support the prices of meat and poultry; the meat producers miscalculated the demand and overproduced, so they got the government to buy the stuff. Whatever happened to the free-market axiom that the least efficient producers should go out of business? Gone with the family farm, I guess. The point about the existing system of public and private controls is that its haphazard in its administration and that it responds most successfully to the politically (or financially) strongest segements of the economy.

An automatic trigger would be useful because it would help dampen inflationary expectations by its presence on the books. It reduces the kind of fear on a small scale that causes somebody to go into hock to buy a stereo because it may cost twice as much next year; this reduces pressure on demand for credit when borrowers expect a windfall due to inflation.

MAKIN: The meat case simply confirms my assertion that *collusion* between government and industry persistently frustrates market forces and that what's needed for more competition and lower prices for consumers is less government intervention, not more. Business needs government to preserve its monopoly power; otherwise, why spend all that money on lobbies?

MODERATOR: Mr. Dickinson would advocate antitrust action instead, yes?

DICKINSON: I regard the choice between antitrust and wage and price controls as a marginal one because I regard the inflationary phenomenon as something which maybe is exacerbated by trustification but is certainly not going to be ended by antitrust. At the heart of inflation lies the monetary question. One can't get around it.

MAKIN: I think this comes back to the point that antitrust is a way to remove distortions in relative prices, whereas wage and price controls exacerbate them. In other words, if the goods produced by highly concentrated industries are out of line in relative price, meaning that the industries have too much market power on the supply side, then antitrust is a possible approach to take if foreign competition is deemed too slow. Where we are talking about the aggregate phenomenon of general inflation, the argument against wage and price control is that either you have too persistent a government deficit, which means the government is pumping too much spending power into the economy, and/or you have the intimately related phenomenon of a high rate of growth of the money supply to prevent (in the short run) higher interest rates arising from having government borrowing to finance a deficit. More fundamentally you have the well-documented relationship between inflation and growth of the money supply in excess of the rate of growth of output.

MODERATOR: If the growth of the money supply is responsible for inflation, are wage and price controls useless? Or do wage and price controls have an influence on the growth of the money?

MAKIN: There is not an economic link. You could have a correspondence for a number of reasons, but there is no necessary economic principle that links them together. But you may have and what we did have in 1971 was a period of fairly rapid monetary expansion during which the central bank was probably aiming at relatively low interest rates rather than a particular rate of growth of the money supply. At the same time the Fed may have hoped for reduction in inflationary pressure from the controls and used this as an excuse to resist pressure to reduce the rate of growth of money supply in view of the hardship that such action would put on industries like housing.

DICKINSON: In 1972, under the shield of wage-price controls, the Federal Reserve Board was—I don't think it's too harsh to say—promoting the reelection of Richard Nixon by having absurdly loose monetary policy by any standard if you had any hope of controlling inflation in the future.

MAKIN: I think it a serious charge to suggest that the central bank of the United States was a political instrument. I think that their policy in 1972 was extremely ill-advised, but reducing unemployment was a target after all.

DICKINSON: Let us say they were afraid of upsetting confidence. Profoundly as I desire full employment, I just believe they behaved in a manner to make the economy squishy for a long time and that all the reasons were bad reasons.

MAKIN: I think that a very wide range of opinion would hold the Federal Reserve Board culpable, in the sense of rapid growth of the money supply for whatever reason in 1972, particularly. Doubly culpable, because we had administered ceilings on wages and prices at the same time the Fed was pumping up the money supply at a rapid rate and increasing demand pressure on ceilings. And where there is demand pressure on current output of goods and therefore on price ceilings, you are going to have shortages and tremendous rationing problems. Responsibility for bringing demand into line with output was passed from the Federal Reserve to the wage and price controls to the supplier of the commodities that were in short supply. They ended up doing the rationing. Business began bartering for rolled steel because no one would sell rolled steel at the administration price ceiling and if you desperately needed it, you could perhaps trade chemicals for it that no one could get at their price ceilings. Two forces operated to erode the viability of a money economy. First, a rapid rate of inflation eroding the purchasing power of money. If you push it too far, you will completely do away with the store-of-value role of money which is a necessary condition for the medium of exchange and in it of account roles. Second, bypassing money transactions by bartering, which was like giving up the use of modern transportation facilities and suggesting that people use covered wagons.

DICKINSON: In short, by setting wage-price controls you have not beaten the market but created another market signalized by a definition of prices in terms other than monetary.

MAKIN: Precisely.

DICKINSON: In addition you create dislocations in a broad spectrum of financial markets where prices (interest rates) are set and regulated in money terms. Inflationary expectations get added on to interest rates charged by unregulated lenders and paid by unregulated borrowers. Therefore, financial intermediaries like banks and saving and loan institutions face severe disintermediation problems because there are "legal maxima" on rates they can pay. That is to say, people take their money out of these institutions and buy bonds directly. As a result, little money is available at level ceilings for home mortgages. I think now, it is now an upper-middle-class undertaking to buy a house, lower-middle-class and middle-middle-class people tend not to and that is about the one commodity which is regarded as a safe bet. So people frozen out of housing in this way are just cursing and hanging onto their money.

MODERATOR: Surely President Nixon has never been an advocate of deficit budgets. Why did the administration not reduce government spending to control inflation?

DICKINSON: Congress was daring Nixon to address himself to the problem of wages and prices by facing up to business and labor with an instrument that they drafted but he had to put into effect. He put it into effect, but when he put it into effect he appeared to have done so less at the urging of Arthur Burns, who'd been running around in small circles talking about the trade cycle, but at the urging of Connally, who was seriously concerned to adjust the United States position vis-à-vis the rest of the world.

ARNOW: Of course, here is another confusing aspect of the 1971 situation. Although we have been evaluating the effect of controls in terms of reducing inflation, and I think this is fair because that is what they were designed by Congress to do; they were not in fact *put into effect* for that reason. They were put into effect because of our rapidly deteriorating balance of payments position.

DICKINSON: Precisely, a situation where if the government had been prepared to let business face up to foreign competition, by removing trade barriers, we might have been better off.

MAKIN: I think the problem went beyond this. Our passive balance of payments stance during the sixties in the face of aggressive development of export markets by countries like Germany and Japan had led to a fairly serious overevaluation of the U.S. dollar. Our goods were too expensive in foreign markets, and foreign goods were too cheap in our markets. Domestic producers of exports and goods competing with imports like autos and steel were demanding some action to put them on a competitive basis with foreign goods. What we got was a policy designed to improve our trade balance as a means to right our overall balance of payments disequilibrium. In order to convince our trading partners that we were serious in this policy, we needed to take decisive action to stem domestic inflation. Wage and price controls were the most visible action, far more visible in the short run than an appropriately restrictive monetary policy. I agree with Ms. Arnow that we were perhaps not equally serious about implementing this program, as indicated by its power staffing and planning.

ARNOW: The reason was political, I think, not economic. President Nixon was up for reelection: he wanted to avoid international embarrassment as much as skyrocketing inflation. But since he was up for reelection, he couldn't just slam on the brakes and head the country into a recession, by either fiscal or monetary policy. Nixon has always maintained he lost the 1960 election because of the sluggishness of the economy in 1959–1960, and he wasn't about to repeat history.

MODERATOR: Would you have advocated tight money instead?

ARNOW: I think I might have advocated a mixed policy: firm controls, together with a more restrictive monetary policy and some cuts in government expenditures, particularly in those areas which contributed to the balance of payments problems—Vietnam was costing a lot of money in 1971.

MAKIN: Tight money has the advantage that it doesn't distort relative prices. It has the disadvantage that it would probably take hold more slowly than wage and price controls and may give the appearance that the government is passively acquiescing to a period of rapid inflation.

ARNOW: Also, monetary policy is hard to carry out, because of the lead times involved.

MAKIN: Precisely. The Federal Reserve could say we are going to follow a policy of 6 percent annual growth in the money supply and we anticipate transitional unemployment. There would be two further difficulties: one, how close can the Fed hit a 6 percent annual growth rate of the money supply, and, two, how close will we be in terms of timing and sequence? But in terms of alternatives to wage and price controls I think that it honestly has to be admitted that it is a far more political act to say that we are moving decisively to control wages and prices than to say that with an admittedly imperfect art we are going to alter the rate of growth of the money supply and hope to see the same roughly described effects follow in a year and a half. Wage and price controls, on the other hand, are appealingly precise.

ARNOW: But monetary policy avoids large bureaucracies and endless opportunities for logrolling. The obvious alternative is to raise taxes, but the government is determined to avoid finding out exactly what the public wants to pay for. For instance, support of a composite majority of the electorate for price supports on agriculture or giving the admirals and the generals whatever they want becomes much more chilly when they have to pay for it by giving up, say, education and health programs.

MODERATOR: Can you ever raise taxes and have it be even accepted as a necessary evil by the public?

DICKINSON: Friedman makes the point that soon the public is going to become so frightened by inflation that it will acquiesce to something drastic to end it and will then find itself in a substantial recession. I think by the same token when inflation becomes really scary, if the matter is laid before them the public will acquiesce less in taxes than in the cutting of expenditures. For my money, there is a lot of room for cutting expenditures.

ARNOW: I agree, if we could just get the cuts made in the right places. The problem is that the most wasteful expenditures are made for the benefit of the most powerful, and the least wasteful for the relatively powerless, and it's the latter which get cut first.

MAKIN: What do you mean by wasteful?

ARNOW: Expenditures which do not contribute to the social and political goals established by Congress, and this includes excessive defense spending—where the rivalry between the services prompts them to produce two or sometimes three of everything; some farm supports, although the excessives here have been reduced; support for the American merchant marine establishment, which is an economic disaster for everybody except the American sailors and the shipping industry—I could go on. The highway lobby, for example.

MODERATOR: Does it look as if the federal government is going to be willing to tolerate higher unemployment if it is required to lower inflation?

MAKIN: The tenor of government pronouncements in the first half of 1974 certainly suggests that that is the message on the wind. We see Simon, we see Rush, we see Herb Stein all saying that we are going to have to tolerate a little unemployment to get this inflation under control, or I've always been for high rates of employment but when inflation reaches double digits we have got to make this compromise. We have got to do something drastic.

MODERATOR: What effects of fiscal "belt-tightening" do you anticipate?

ARNOW: That's a good question. Judging purely by GNP, we're in a recession right now, but inflation is not moderating. It's a world-wide inflation whose basic causes are beyond our control—excess world-wide demand for almost everything coupled with world-wide shortages of supplies. In addition, we have high interest rates, rates so high as to be inflationary in themselves, along with sluggish consumer demand and an enormous "tax," in the words of Leonard Silk, being extracted from most developed nations by the oil-producing nations.

Predicting the effects of serious efforts at fiscal belt-tightening is difficult. Take the President's July 25 speech, in which he urged the people to reduce their expenditures 1.5 percent of income. The next day one of his advisers suggested that he didn't want a "consumer boycott" and that one really could disregard this suggestion. Somebody had pointed out to him that such a reduction would involve the removal of $12 billion in purchasing power from the U.S. economy, with consumer demand already sluggish.

The inflation will certainly lead to a continuing redistribution of income, and we should see a lot of pressure in the housing market, as supplies dry up and landlords try to remain solvent or keep their previous levels of profits. Consumer demand is sluggish, and obviously will become more so, and you'll get a lot of bankruptcies. One of the biggest problems will be maintaining external balance—we just have to hope that other nations' inflations are worse than ours and that our farmers produce enough food for export to keep the books from getting hopelessly out of balance. But the problem comes when the poor nations run out of money to buy food.

MAKIN: Of course, there will be the transitional period that we have been in, particularly the first quarter of 1974, where we have the worst of both worlds. But inflation has fallen from an annual rate of about 12 percent in the first quarter of this year to an annual rate of 8 percent in the second. Stagflation comes about because of a gigantic problem in the markets. You get supply shifting backward with expectations of rising prices, while demand shifts down for the same reason. As a result, prices are still rising with real output going down; in effect, an inflationary recession.

ARNOW: Just the sort of thing wage-price controls are designed to avoid.

MAKIN: Controls have simply created shortages. You still have dislocations, and if you haven't totally crushed the economy before they are removed, you get a resumption of inflationary pressure upon removal accompanied by the sort of aggregate supply and demand shifts I have already described.

MODERATOR: Couldn't indexing avoid this?

MAKIN: Well, simply adjusting prices all the time can itself absorb real resources—someone has to change the labels. There is also the problem of money balances, which would be unlikely to be handled by indexing. As long as you hold claims on the government and the government does not pay interest on those claims, then they are depreciating whatever rate of inflation is underway, you are forced to economize on holding those claims, and some people are forced to forego the liquidity services of money.

MODERATOR: Can wage and price controls reduce the social inequities that come up in an inflationary period?

ARNOW: Of course they can help, simply by stopping the reduction in the real incomes of the elderly, the nonunionized wage-earners, and others with relatively little bargaining power. They also reduce the redistribution of income from lenders to borrowers which occurs in a rapid inflation and put something of a check on the predatory behavior of the monopolistic and oligopolistic sectors.

DICKINSON: Whereas controls are meant to ensure the powerful are not going to get away with it, from my point of view this actually is the best chance for them to do so. They merely make inequities less visible. Moreover, the resulting shortages create inequities. If you regulate the price of fuel oils in a country like, say, Chile, where the fuel oil price is a very important part of the price of food because everything has to be trucked over X miles, the scarcities that you are going to create are going to have an effect upon the very poor, because of the inelasticity of food demands. In other socieites, in other goods, scarcity may be what we might call rugged egalitarianism as opposed to sophisticated egalitarianism. The fact is that most of the inconveniences caused to the rich by wage and price controls are part of the general pattern of opportunity costs. Wage and price controls have a very high component of opportunity costs. And the rich have a larger range of options, and so are less likely to suffer these costs than the poor. In terms of actual redistribution of comfort, opportunity, and so on, there is likely to be a relative redistribution upward to the well-off.

MAKIN: Moreover, by imposing ceilings, you remove the likelihood that people will adapt. If you put a ceiling price on gasoline, say, then all the incentives would be wrong. When people's automobiles wore out, they wouldn't be as likely to buy a car that consumed less gasoline if the price of gas were nominally at 40 cents a gallon than they would if the price had gone up. Although you could argue that if because of price ceilings, say rationing, they might buy a more economical car because it would go further on the gas you get, but again, there is a problem of equality of information. The price message is clearer than the fact that the gasoline may or may not be available at the rationed price. If the price doubles to 80 cents there is no doubt about that, you know it is very clear that in order to get X miles, you want to get a car that gets better mileage.

MODERATOR: What about monetary policy and social equity?

DICKINSON: I think monetary contraction probably shows up more in underemployment than it does in unemployment. That is my intuition on the subject. Firms don't like firing people, and there is less overtime. In a wage-price control situation you may get the resources being used, but wasted.

MAKIN: More generally, with bad relative price messages you get wasted resources with the result that what is available to buy is reduced.

ARNOW: Hardly an issue for the unemployed.

DICKINSON: But the people who do have money accumulated play a very important part in the economy. Secondly, reduced capital formation reduces the demand for labor.

MODERATOR: Very briefly, what position do you take on wage and price controls in view of the recent experience?

ARNOW: They must be applied longer and with more skill than they were in 1971–1974.

MAKIN: They simply transposed inflationary pressure forward in time and imposed heavy resource misallocation costs on the economy in the process.

DICKINSON: Perhaps we should let Keynes have the last word on the subject. In remarks to the members of the Economic Advisory Council in July 1930, he said: "Accordingly I favor an electric programme, making use of suggestions from all quarters, not expecting too much from the application of any one of them, but hoping that they may do something in the aggregate."

Index

Note: numbers in italics indicate pages on which graphic illustrations appear.